Poetical Works

OF

LORD BYRON.

Walker & Boutall, ph. sc

Lord Byron

from a portrait by W. E. West in the possession of Mr. Percy Kent.

The Works

V. 5,

OF

LORD BYRON.

A NEW, REVISED AND ENLARGED EDITION, WITH ILLUSTRATIONS.

Poetry. Vol. V.

EDITED BY

ERNEST HARTLEY COLERIDGE, M.A.,

HON. F.R.S.L.

1966

OCTAGON BOOKS, INC.

New York

Originally published 1898-1904 by John Murray (Publishers) Ltd.

Reprinted 1966
by special arrangement with John Murray (Publishers) Ltd.

OCTAGON BOOKS, INC.
175 FIFTH AVENUE
NEW YORK, N.Y. 10010

LIBRARY OF CONGRESS CATALOG CARD NUMBER: 66-29122

Printed in U.S.A. by
NOBLE OFFSET PRINTERS, INC.
NEW YORK 3, N. Y.

PREFACE TO
THE FIFTH VOLUME.

—◦◦—

THE plays and poems contained in this volume were
written within the space of two years—the last two years
of Byron's career as a poet. But that was not all.
Cantos VI.—XV. of *Don Juan*, *The Vision of Judgment*,
The Blues, *The Irish Avatar*, and other minor poems,
belong to the same period. The end was near, and, as
though he had received a warning, he hastened to make
the roll complete.

Proof is impossible, but the impression remains that
the greater part of this volume has been passed over and
left unread by at least two generations of readers. Old
play-goers recall Macready as " Werner," and many persons have read *Cain ;* but apart from students of literature,
readers of *Sardanapalus* and of *The Two Foscari* are
rare ; of *The Age of Bronze* and *The Island* rarer still.
A few of Byron's later poems have shared the fate of
Southey's epics ; and, yet, with something of Southey's
persistence, Byron believed that posterity would weigh
his " regular dramas " in a fresh balance, and that his

heedless critics would kick the beam. But "can these bones live"? Can dramas which excited the wondering admiration of Goethe and Lamartine and Sir Walter Scott touch or lay hold of the more adventurous reader of the present day? It is certain that even the half-forgotten works of a great and still popular poet, which have left their mark on the creative imagination of the poets and playwrights of three quarters of a century, will always be studied by the few from motives of curiosity, or for purposes of reference; but it is improbable, though not impossible, that in the revolution of taste and sentiment, moribund or extinct poetry will be born again into the land of the living. Poetry which has never had its day, such as Blake's *Songs of Innocence*, the *Lyrical Ballads*, or Fitzgerald's *Omar Khayyám*, may come, in due time, to be recognized at its full worth; but it is a harder matter for a poem which has lost its vogue to recapture the interest and enthusiasm of the many.

Byron is only an instance in point. Bygone poetry has little or no attraction for modern readers. This poem or that drama may be referred to, and occasionally examined in the interests of general culture, or in support of a particular belief or line of conduct, as a classical or quasi-scriptural authority; but, with the rarest exceptions, plays and narrative poems are not read spontaneously or with any genuine satisfaction or delight. An old-world poem which will not yield up its secret to the idle *reader* "of an empty day" is more or less "rudely dismissed," without even a show of favour or hospitality.

And yet these forgotten works of the imagination are full of hidden treasures! There is not one of Byron's "impressionist studies" of striking episodes of history or historical legend, flung, as it were, with a "Take it or leave it" in the face of friend or foe, which does not transform names and shadows into persons and substance, which does not contain lines and passages of unquestionable beauty and distinction.

But some would have it that Byron's plays, as a whole, are dull and uninspiring, monotonous harpings on worn-out themes, which every one has mastered or wishes to forget. A close study of the text, together with some knowledge of the subject as it presented itself to the author and arrested *his* attention, may compel these impatient critics to a different conclusion. Byron did not scruple to refer the reader to his "sources," and was at pains to publish, in the notes and appendices to his dramas and poems, long extracts from old chronicles, from Plutarch's *Lives*, from French and Italian histories, which he had read himself, and, as he fondly believed, would be read by others, who were willing to submit themselves to his guidance. He expected his readers to take some trouble and to display some intelligence.

Poetry is successful only so far as it is intelligible. To a clear cry an answer comes, but not to a muffled call. The reader who comes within speaking distance of his author can hear him, and to bring the living within speaking distance of the dead, the living must know the facts, and understand the ideas which informed and inspired the dead. Thought and attention are scarcely to be reckoned among necromantic arts, but thought and knowledge " can make these bones live," and stand upon their feet, if they do not leap and sing.

I desire to renew my acknowledgments of the generous assistance of the officials of the British Museum, and, more especially, of Mr. Ernest Wallis Budge, Litt.D., M.A., *Keeper of Egyptian and Assyrian Antiquities;* of Mr. Leonard W. King, M.A., of the same department ; and of Mr. George F. Barwick, *Superintendent of the Reading Room.*

To Dr. Garnett, C.B., I am greatly indebted for invaluable hints and suggestions with regard to the interpretation of some obscure passages in *The Age of Bronze* and other parts of the volume, and for reading the proofs of the " Introduction " and " Note to the Introduction to *Werner.*"

I have also to acknowledge the assistance and advice of Mr. W. Hale White, and of my friend Mr. Frank E. Taylor, of Chertsey.

For assistance during the preparation of the volume, and more especially in the revision of proofs, I desire to express my cordial thanks to Mr. John Murray.

ERNEST HARTLEY COLERIDGE.

December 3, 1901.

CONTENTS OF VOL. V.

—·◦·—

LIST OF ILLUSTRATIONS.

——◆◆◆——

SARDANAPALUS:

A TRAGEDY.

[*Sardanapale, Tragédie Imitée de Lord Byron*, par L. Alvin, was performed at the Théatre Royal at Brussels, January 13, 16, 1834.

Sardanapalus, a Tragedy, was played for the first time at Drury Lane Theatre, April 10, 1834, and (for the twenty-second time) June 5, 1834. Macready appeared as " Sardanapalus," Miss Phillips as " Zarina," and Miss Ellen Tree as " Myrrha." [In his diary for April 11, 1834 (see *Reminiscences*, 1875, i. 414, 415) Macready wrote, " On arriving at my chambers . . . I found a letter without a signature ; the seal was the head of Byron, and in the envelope was a folded sheet with merely the words, 'Werner, Nov., 1830. Byron, Ravenna, 1821,' and ' Sardanapalus, April 10th, 1834.' Encircling the name of Byron, etc., was a lock of grey hair fastened by a gold thread, which I am sure was Byron's, . . . it surprised and pleased me."]

Sardanapalus, King of Assyria, was produced at the Princess's Theatre, June 13, 1853, and played till September 2, 1853. Charles Kean appeared as " Sardanapalus," Miss Heath as " Zarina," and Mrs. Charles Kean as " Myrrha."

Sardanapale, Opéra en Trois Actes, par M. Henry Becque, Musique de M. Victorin Joncières, was performed for the first time at the Théatre Impérial-Lyrique, February 8, 1867.

Lord Byron's Tragedy of Sardanapalus, in four acts, was performed at the Theatre Royal, Manchester, March 31—April 28, 1877. Charles Calvert (the adapter) played " Sardanapalus," Miss Hathaway " Zarina," and Miss Fanny Ensor " Myrrha ; " and June 26—July 27, 1877, at the Royal Alexandra Theatre, Liverpool. Calvert's adaptation was also performed at Booth's Theatre, New York.]

INTRODUCTION TO *SARDANAPALUS.*

BYRON'S passion or infatuation for the regular drama lasted a little over a year. *Marino Faliero, Sardanapalus,* and the *Two Foscari,* were the fruits of his " self-denying ordinance to dramatize, like the Greeks . . . striking passages of history " (letter to Murray, July 14, 1821, *Letters,* 1901, v. 323). The mood was destined to pass, but for a while the neophyte was spell-bound.

Sardanapalus, a Tragedy, the second and, perhaps, the most successful of these studies in the poetry of history, was begun at Ravenna, January 13, 1821, " with all deliberate speed ; " but, for a time, from laziness or depression of spirits, or, perhaps, from the counter-excitement of "the poetry of politics " (*Letters,* 1901, v. 205), that is, the revolutionary drama which had begun to run its course, a month went by before he had finished the first act (February 15). Three months later (May 28) he announces the completion of the drama, the last act having been "dashed off" in two or three days (*Letters,* 1901, v. 300).

For the story of Sardanapalus, which had excited his interest as a schoolboy, Byron consulted the pages of Diodorus Siculus (*Bibliothecæ Historicæ,* lib. ii. pp. 78, *sq.,* ed. 1604), and, possibly to ward off and neutralize the distracting influence of Shakespeare and other barbarian dramatists, he "turned over" the tragedies of Seneca (*Letters,* 1901, v. 173). It is hardly necessary to remind the modern reader that the Sardanapalus of history is an unverified if not an unverifiable personage. Diodorus the Sicilian, who was contemporary with Cicero, derived his knowledge of Assyrian history from the *Persica* of Ctesias of Cnidos, who was private physician at the court of Artaxerxes Mnemon (B.C. 405–359), and is said to have had access to, and to have consulted, the " Persian authorities " (διφθέραι βασιλικαί).

The character which Ctesias depicted or invented, an

effeminate debauchee, sunk in luxury and sloth, who at the
last was driven to take up arms, and, after a prolonged but
ineffectual resistance, avoided capture by suicide, cannot be
identified. Asurbanipal (Ašur-bāni-apli), the son of Esar-
haddon and grandson of Sennacherib, who ascended the
throne B.C. 668, and reigned for about forty years, was, as
the cuneiform records and the friezes of his palace testify,
a bold hunter and a mighty warrior. He vanquished Tarķū
(Tirhakah) of Ethiopia, and his successor, Urdamanē.
Ba'al King of Tyre, Yakinlū King of the island-city of Arvad,
Sandāsarmū of Cilicia, Teumman of Elam, and other potentates, suffered defeat at his hands. "The land of Elam,"
writes the king or his "Historiographer Royal," "through
its extent I covered as when a mighty storm approaches ;
I cut off the head of Teumman, their king . . . Beyond
number I slew his warriors ; alive in my hands I took his
fighting men ; with their corpses, as with thorns and thistles,
I filled the vicinity of Susa ; their blood I caused to flow in
the Eulæus, and I stained its waters like wool." Clearly
the Sardanapalus who painted his face and carded purple
wool in the *penetralia* of his seraglio does not bear even
a traditional resemblance to Ašur-bāni-apli the Conqueror.

All that can be affirmed with any certainty is that within
twenty years of the death of Asurbanipal, the Assyrian
Empire passed into the hands of the Medes ;[1] but there is
nothing to show whether the period of decay had already set
in before the close of his reign, or under which of his two
successors, Āsur-etil-ilāni or Sin-šar-iškun, the final catastrophe (B.C. 606) took place (*Encyclopedia Biblica*, art.
"Assyria," art. "Asur-bani-pal," by Leonard W. King).

" I have made," writes Byron (May 25, 1821), "Sardanapalus brave though voluptuous (as history represents him),
and as amiable as my poor pen could make him." Diodorus,
or rather Ctesias, who may have drawn upon personal
reminiscences of his patron, Artaxerxes Mnemon (see Plutarch's *Artaxerxes, passim*), does not enlarge upon his
amiability, and credits him only with the courage of despair.
Byron's Sardanapalus, with his sudden transition from

---

1. [For a description of the fall of Nineveh, see *Nahum* ii. 1, *sqq.*—
" He that dasheth in pieces is come up before thy face. . . . The
shield of his mighty men is made red, the valiant men are in scarlet.
. . . The chariots shall rage in the streets, they shall justle one against
another in the broad ways : they shall seem like torches, they shall run
like the lightnings. He shall recount his worthies : they shall stumble
in their walk ; they shall make haste to the wall thereof, and the defence shall be prepared. The gates of the rivers shall be opened, and
the palace shall be dissolved," etc.]

voluptuous abandonment to heroic chivalry, his remorseful recognition of the sanctities of wedlock, his general good nature, his "sly, insinuating sarcasms" (Moore's Diary, September 30, 1821, *Memoirs*, iii. 282), "all made out of the carver's brain," resembles *history* as little as *history* resembles the Assyrian record. Fortunately, the genius of the poet escaped from the meshes which he had woven round himself, and, in spite of himself, he was constrained to "beat his music out," regardless of his authorities.

The character of Myrrha, which bears some resemblance to Aspasia, "a native of Phocea in Ionia—the favourite mistress of Cyrus" (see Plutarch's *Artaxerxes*, Langhorne's Translation, 1838, p. 699), was introduced partly to pacify the Countess Guiccioli, who had quarrelled with him for maintaining that "love was not the loftiest theme for true tragedy," and, in part, to prove that he was not a slave to his own ideals, and could imagine and delineate a woman who was both passionate and high-minded. Diodorus (*Bibl. Hist.*, lib. iii. p. 130) records the exploits of Myrina, Queen of the Amazons, but it is probable that Byron named his Ionian slave after Mirra, who gives her name to Alfieri's tragedy, which brought on a convulsive fit of tears and shuddering when he first saw it played at Bologna in August, 1819 (*Letters*, 1900, iv. 339).

Sardanapalus, a Tragedy, was published together with *The Two Foscari, a Tragedy*, and *Cain, a Mystery*, December 19, 1821.

The three plays were reviewed by Heber in the *Quarterly Review*, July, 1822, vol. xxvii. pp. 476–524; by Jeffrey in the *Edinburgh Review*, February, 1822, vol. 36, pp. 413–452; in *Blackwood's Edinburgh Magazine*, February, 1822, vol. xi. pp. 212–217; and in the *Portfolio* (Philadelphia), December, 1822, vol. xiv. pp. 487–492.

THE ILLUSTRIOUS GOETHE

A STRANGER

PRESUMES TO OFFER THE HOMAGE

OF A LITERARY VASSAL TO HIS LIEGE LORD,

THE FIRST OF EXISTING WRITERS,

WHO HAS CREATED

THE LITERATURE OF HIS OWN COUNTRY,

AND ILLUSTRATED THAT OF EUROPE.

THE UNWORTHY PRODUCTION

WHICH THE AUTHOR VENTURES TO INSCRIBE TO HIM

IS ENTITLED

SARDANAPALUS.[1]

1. ["A manuscript dedication of *Sardanapalus* . . . was forwarded to him, with an obliging inquiry whether it might be prefixed to the tragedy. The German, who, at his advanced age, was conscious of his own powers, and of their effects, could only gratefully and modestly consider this Dedication as the expression of an inexhaustible intellect, deeply feeling and creating its own object. He was by no means dissatisfied when, after long delay, *Sardanapalus* appeared without the Dedication ; and was made happy by the possession of a facsimile of it, engraved on stone, which he considered a precious memorial."— *Lebensverhältnik zu Byron, Werke*, 1833, xlvi. 221-225. (See, too, for translation, *Life*, p. 593.)]

PREFACE.

In publishing the following Tragedies[1] I have only to repeat, that they were not composed with the most remote view to the stage. On the attempt made by the managers in a former instance, the public opinion has been already expressed. With regard to my own private feelings, as it seems that they are to stand for nothing, I shall say nothing.

For the historical foundation of the following compositions the reader is referred to the Notes.

The Author has in one instance attempted to preserve, and in the other to approach, the "unities;" conceiving that with any very distant departure from them, there may be poetry, but can be no drama. He is aware of the unpopularity of this notion in present English literature; but it is not a system of his own, being merely an opinion, which, not very long ago, was the law of literature throughout the world, and is still so in the more civilised parts of it. But "nous avons changé tout cela," and are reaping the advantages of the change. The writer is far from conceiving that any thing he can adduce by personal precept or example can at all approach his regular, or even irregular predecessors: he is merely giving a reason why he preferred the more regular formation of a structure, however feeble, to an entire abandonment of all rules whatsoever. Where he has failed, the failure is in the architect,—and not in the art.

1. [*Sardanapalus* originally appeared in the same volume with *The Two Foscari* and *Cain*. The date of publication was December 19, 1821.]

In this tragedy it has been my intention to follow the account of Diodorus Siculus;[1] reducing it, however, to such dramatic regularity as I best could, and trying to approach the unities. I therefore suppose the rebellion to explode and succeed in one day by a sudden conspiracy, instead of the long war of the history.

1. ["Sardanapalus, the Thirtieth from Ninus, and the last King of the Assyrians, exceeded all his Predecessors in Sloth and Luxury; for besides that he was seen of none out of his family, he led a most effeminate life: for wallowing in Pleasure and wanton Dalliances, he cloathed himself in Womens' attire, and spun fine Wool and Purple amongst the throngs of his Whores and Concubines. He painted likewise his Face, and decked his whole Body with other Allurements. . . . He imitated likewise a Woman's voice . . .; and proceeded to such a degree of voluptuousness that he composed verses for his Epitaph . . . which were thus translated by a Grecian out of the Barbarian language—

Ταῦτ᾽ ἔχω ὅσ᾽ ἔφαγον καὶ ἐφύβρισα, καὶ μετ᾽ ἔρωτος
Τέρπν᾽ ἔπαθον᾽ τὰ δὲ πολλὰ καὶ ὄλβια κεῖνα λέλειπται.

"What once I gorged I now enjoy,
And wanton Lusts me still employ;
All other things by Mortals prized
Are left as dirt by me despised."

—*The Historical Library of Diodorus the Sicilian*, made English by G. Booth, of the City of Chester, Esquire, 1700, p. 65.
"Another king of the sort was Sardanapalus. . . . And so, when Arbaces, who was one of the generals under him, a Mede by birth, endeavoured to manage by the assistance of one of the eunuchs, whose name was Sparamizus, to see Sardanapalus: and when . . . he saw him painted with vermilion, and adorned like a woman, sitting among his concubines, carding purple wool, and sitting among them with his feet up, wearing a woman's robe, and with his beard carefully scraped, and his face smoothed with pumice stone (for he was whiter than milk, and pencilled under his eyes and eyebrows; and when he saw Arbaces he was putting a little more white under his eyes). Most historians, of whom Duris is one, relate that Arbaces, being indignant at his countrymen being ruled over by such a monarch as that, stabbed him and slew him. But Ctesias says that he went to war with him, and collected a great army, and then that Sardanapalus, being dethroned by Arbaces, died, burning himself alive in his palace, having heaped up a funeral pile four plethra in extent, on which he placed 150 golden couches."
—*The Deipnosophistæ* . . . of Athenæus, bk. xii. c. 38, translated by C. D. Yonge, 1854, iii. 847.]

DRAMATIS PERSONÆ.

———◆◇◆———

MEN.

SARDANAPALUS, *King of Nineveh and Assyria, etc.*

ARBACES, *the Mede who aspired to the Throne.*

BELESES, *a Chaldean and Soothsayer.*

SALEMENES, *the King's Brother-in-Law.*

ALTADA, *an Assyrian Officer of the Palace.*

PANIA.

ZAMES.

SFERO.

BALEA.

WOMEN.

ZARINA, *the Queen.*

MYRRHA, *an Ionian female Slave, and the Favourite Mistress of* SARDANAPALUS.

Women composing the Harem of SARDANAPALUS, *Guards, Attendants, Chaldean Priests, Medes, etc., etc.*

SCENE.—A Hall in the Royal Palace of Nineveh.

Walker & Cockerell, ph. sc.

Assur-Bani-Pal.

from a slab in the British Museum.

SARDANAPALUS.[1]

ACT I.

Scene I.—*A Hall in the Palace.*

Salemenes (solus). HE hath wronged his queen, but
 still he is her lord ;
He hath wronged my sister—still he is my brother ;

1. [This prince surpassed all his predecessors in effeminacy, luxury,
and cowardice. He never went out of his palace, but spent all his
time among a company of women, dressed and painted like them, and
employed like them at the distaff. He placed all his happiness and
glory in the possession of immense treasures, in feasting and rioting,
and indulging himself in all the most infamous and criminal pleasures.
He ordered two verses to be put upon his tomb, signifying that he
carried away with him all he had eaten, and all the pleasures he had
enjoyed, but left everything else behind him,—*an epitaph,* says Aristotle,
fit for a hog. Arbaces, governor of Media, having found means to get
into the palace, and having with his own eyes seen Sardanapalus in the
midst of his infamous seraglio, enraged at such a spectacle, and not
able to endure that so many brave men should be subjected to a prince
more soft and effeminate than the women themselves, immediately
formed a conspiracy against him. Beleses, governor of Babylon, and
several others, entered into it. On the first rumour of this revolt the
king hid himself in the inmost part of his palace. Being afterwards
obliged to take the field with some forces which he had assembled, he at
first gained three successive victories over the enemy, but was afterwards
overcome, and pursued to the gates of Nineveh ; wherein he shut himself, in hopes the rebels would never be able to take a city so well
fortified, and stored with provisions for a considerable time. The siege
proved indeed of very great length. It had been declared by an ancient
oracle that Nineveh could never be taken unless the river became an
enemy to the city. These words buoyed up Sardanapalus, because he
looked upon the thing as impossible. But when he saw that the Tigris,
by a violent inundation, had thrown down twenty stadia (two miles
and a half) of the city wall, and by that means opened a passage to the
enemy, he understood the meaning of the oracle, and thought himself
lost. He resolved, however, to die in such a manner as, according to

He hath wronged his people—still he is their sovereign—
And I must be his friend as well as subject :
He must not perish thus.   I will not see
The blood of Nimrod and Semiramis
Sink in the earth, and thirteen hundred years
Of Empire ending like a shepherd's tale ;
He must be roused.   In his effeminate heart
There is a careless courage which Corruption   10
Has not all quenched, and latent energies,
Repressed by circumstance, but not destroyed—
Steeped, but not drowned, in deep voluptuousness.
If born a peasant, he had been a man
To have reached an empire : to an empire born,
He will bequeath none ; nothing but a name,
Which his sons will not prize in heritage :—
Yet—not all lost—even yet—he may redeem
His sloth and shame, by only being that
Which he should be, as easily as the thing   20
He should not be and is.   Were it less toil
To sway his nations than consume his life?
To head an army than to rule a harem ?
He sweats in palling pleasures, dulls his soul,[i.]
And saps his goodly strength, in toils which yield not
Health like the chase, nor glory like the war—
He must be roused.   Alas ! there is no sound
                    [*Sound of soft music heard from within.*
To rouse him short of thunder.   Hark ! the lute—
The lyre—the timbrel ; the lascivious tinklings
Of lulling instruments, the softening voices   30
Of women, and of beings less than women,
Must chime in to the echo of his revel,
While the great King of all we know of earth
Lolls crowned with roses, and his diadem
Lies negligently by to be caught up
By the first manly hand which dares to snatch it.
Lo, where they come ! already I perceive

i. *He sweats in dreary, dulled effeminacy.*—[*MS. M. erased.*]

his opinion, should cover the infamy of his scandalous and effeminate
life.   He ordered a pile of wood to be made in his palace, and, setting
fire to it, burnt himself, his eunuchs, his women, and his treasures.—
Diod. Sic., *Bibl. Hist.*, lib. ii. pag. 78, *sqq.*, ed. 1604, p. 109.]

The reeking odours of the perfumed trains,
And see the bright gems of the glittering girls,[L]
At once his Chorus and his Council, flash   40
Along the gallery, and amidst the damsels,
As femininely garbed, and scarce less female,
The grandson of Semiramis, the Man-Queen.—
He comes! Shall I await him? yes, and front him,
And tell him what all good men tell each other,
Speaking of him and his.   They come, the slaves
Led by the monarch subject to his slaves.

Scene II.

Enter SARDANAPALUS *effeminately dressed, his Head
crowned with Flowers, and his- Robe negligently
flowing, attended by a Train of Women and young
Slaves.*

   Sar. (*speaking to some of his attendants*). Let the
      pavilion [1] over the Euphrates
Be garlanded, and lit, and furnished forth
For an especial banquet; at the hour
Of midnight we will sup there: see nought wanting,
And bid the galley be prepared.   There is
A cooling breeze which crisps the broad clear river:
We will embark anon.   Fair Nymphs, who deign

----

   i. *And see the gewgaws of the glittering girls.—*[*MS. M. erased.*]

   1. ["The words *Queen* (*vide infra*, line 83) and *pavilion* occur, but it
is not an allusion to his Britannic Majesty, as you may tremulously (for
the admiralty custom) imagine.   This you will one day see (if I finish
it), as I have made Sardanapalus *brave* (though voluptuous, as history
represents him), and also as *amiable* as my poor powers could render
him.   So that it could neither be truth nor satire on any living
monarch."—Letter to Murray, May 25, 1821, *Letters*, 1901, v. 299.
   Byron pretended, or, perhaps, really thought, that such a phrase as
the "Queen's wrongs" would be supposed to contain an allusion to the
trial of Queen Caroline (August—November, 1820), and to the exclusion of her name from the State prayers, etc.   Unquestionably if
the play had been put on the stage at this time, the pit and gallery
would have applauded the sentiment to the echo.   There was, too,
but one "pavilion" in 1821, and that was not on the banks of the
Euphrates, but at Brighton.   *Qui s'excuse s'accuse.*   Byron was not
above "paltering" with his readers "in a double sense."

To share the soft hours of Sardanapalus,
We'll meet again in that the sweetest hour,
When we shall gather like the stars above us,   10
And you will form a heaven as bright as theirs ;
Till then, let each be mistress of her time,
And thou, my own Ionian Myrrha,[1] choose ;
Wilt thou along with them or me ?
    Myr.   My Lord——
    Sar. My Lord !—my Life ! why answerest thou so
        coldly ?
It is the curse of kings to be so answered.
Rule thy own hours, thou rulest mine—say, wouldst thou
Accompany our guests, or charm away
The moments from me ?
    Myr.   The King's choice is mine.
    Sar. I pray thee say not so : my chiefest joy   20
Is to contribute to thine every wish.
I do not dare to breathe my own desire,
Lest it should clash with thine ; for thou art still
Too prompt to sacrifice thy thoughts for others.
    Myr. I would remain : I have no happiness
Save in beholding thine ; yet——
    Sar.   Yet ! what YET ?
Thy own sweet will shall be the only barrier
Which ever rises betwixt thee and me.
    Myr. I think the present is the wonted hour
Of council ; it were better I retire.   30
    Sal. (*comes forward and says*) The Ionian slave says
        well : let her retire.
    Sar. Who answers ? How now, brother ?
    Sal.   The *Queen's* brother,
And your most faithful vassal, royal Lord.
    Sar. (*addressing his train*). As I have said, let all
        dispose their hours
Till midnight, when again we pray your presence.
                [*The court retiring.*

---

    1. " The Ionian name had been still more comprehensive ; having
included the Achaians and the Bœotians, who, together with those to
whom it was afterwards confined, would make nearly the whole of the
Greek nation ; and among the Orientals it was always the general name
for the Greeks."—MITFORD'S *Greece*, 1818, i. 199.

(*To* MYRRHA,[i] *who is going.*) Myrrha! I thought *thou*
  wouldst remain.

  Myr.   Great King,
Thou didst not say so.

  Sar.   But *thou* looked'st it:
I know each glance of those Ionic eyes,[ii]
Which said thou wouldst not leave me.

  Myr.   Sire! your brother——

  Sal. His *Consort's* brother, minion of Ionia!   40
How darest *thou* name *me* and not blush?

  Sar.   Not blush!
Thou hast no more eyes than heart to make her crimson
Like to the dying day on Caucasus,
Where sunset tints the snow with rosy shadows,
And then reproach her with thine own cold blindness,
Which will not see it. What! in tears, my Myrrha?

  Sal. Let them flow on; she weeps for more than one,
And is herself the cause of bitterer tears.

  Sar. Curséd be he who caused those tears to flow!

  Sal. Curse not thyself—millions do that already. 50

  Sar. Thou dost forget thee: make me not remember
I am a monarch.

  Sal.   Would thou couldst!

  Myr.   My sovereign,
I pray, and thou, too, Prince, permit my absence.

  Sar. Since it must be so, and this churl has checked
Thy gentle spirit, go; but recollect
That we must forthwith meet: I had rather lose
An empire than thy presence.   [*Exit* MYRRHA.

  Sal.   It may be,
Thou wilt lose both—and both for ever!

  Sar.   Brother!
I can at least command myself, who listen
To language such as this: yet urge me not   60
Beyond my easy nature.

  Sal.   'Tis beyond
That easy—far too easy—idle nature,
Which I would urge thee. O that I could rouse thee!

---

i. *To Byblis* ——.—[*MS. M.*]
ii. *I know each glance of those deep Greek-souled eyes.*—[*MS. M. erased.*]

Though 'twere against myself.

Sar.   By the god Baal!
The man would make me tyrant.

Sal.   So thou art.
Think'st thou there is no tyranny but that
Of blood and chains? The despotism of vice,
The weakness and the wickedness of luxury,
The negligence, the apathy, the evils
Of sensual sloth—produce ten thousand tyrants,   70
Whose delegated cruelty surpasses
The worst acts of one energetic master,
However harsh and hard in his own bearing.
The false and fond examples of thy lusts
Corrupt no less than they oppress, and sap
In the same moment all thy pageant power
And those who should sustain it; so that whether
A foreign foe invade, or civil broil
Distract within, both will alike prove fatal:
The first thy subjects have no heart to conquer;   80
The last they rather would assist than vanquish.

    Sar. Why, what makes thee the mouth-piece of the
      people?

    Sal. Forgiveness of the Queen, my sister wrongs;
A natural love unto my infant nephews;
Faith to the King, a faith he may need shortly,
In more than words; respect for Nimrod's line;
Also, another thing thou knowest not.

    Sar. What's that?

    Sal.   To thee an unknown word.

    Sar.   Yet speak it;
I love to learn.

    Sal.   Virtue.

    Sar.   Not know the word!
Never was word yet rung so in my ears—   90
Worse than the rabble's shout, or splitting trumpet:
I've heard thy sister talk of nothing else.

    Sal. To change the irksome theme, then, hear of vice.

    Sar. From whom?

    Sal.   Even from the winds, if thou couldst listen
Unto the echoes of the Nation's voice.

    Sar. Come, I'm indulgent, as thou knowest, patient,

As thou hast often proved—speak out, what moves thee?
 Sal. Thy peril.
 Sar.   Say on.
 Sal.   Thus, then: all the nations,
For they are many, whom thy father left
In heritage, are loud in wrath against thee.   100
 Sar. 'Gainst *me! /* What would the slaves?
 Sal.   A king.
 Sar.   And what
Am I then?
 Sal.   In their eyes a nothing; but
In mine a man who might be something still.
 Sar. The railing drunkards! why, what would they
   have?
Have they not peace and plenty?
 Sal.   Of the first
More than is glorious; of the last, far less
Than the King recks of.
 Sar.   Whose then is the crime,
But the false satraps, who provide no better?
 Sal. And somewhat in the Monarch who ne'er looks
Beyond his palace walls, or if he stirs   110
Beyond them, 'tis but to some mountain palace,
Till summer heats wear down. O glorious Baal!
Who built up this vast empire, and wert made
A God, or at the least shinest like a God
Through the long centuries of thy renown,
This, thy presumed descendant, ne'er beheld
As king the kingdoms thou didst leave as hero,
Won with thy blood, and toil, and time, and peril!
For what? to furnish imposts for a revel,
Or multiplied extortions for a minion.   120
 Sar. I understand thee—thou wouldst have me go
Forth as a conqueror. By all the stars
Which the Chaldeans read—the restless slaves [i.]
Deserve that I should curse them with their wishes,
And lead them forth to glory.
 Sal.   Wherefore not?
Semiramis—a woman only—led

i.   —— *I have a mind*
 To curse the restless slaves with their own wishes.—[MS. M. *erased.*]

These our Assyrians to the solar shores
Of Ganges.

    Sar.   'Tis most true.   And *how* returned ?

    Sal. Why, like a *man*—a hero ; baffled, but
Not vanquished.   With but twenty guards, she made
Good her retreat to Bactria.

    Sar.   And how many   131
Left she behind in India to the vultures ?

    Sal. Our annals say not.

    Sar.   Then I will say for them—
That she had better woven within her palace
Some twenty garments, than with twenty guards
Have fled to Bactria, leaving to the ravens,
And wolves, and men—the fiercer of the three,
Her myriads of fond subjects.   Is *this* Glory?
Then let me live in ignominy ever.

    Sal. All warlike spirits have not the same fate.   140
Semiramis, the glorious parent of
A hundred kings, although she failed in India,
Brought Persia—Media—Bactria—to the realm
Which she once swayed—and thou *mightst* sway.

    Sar.   *I sway* them—
She but subdued them.

    Sal.   It may be ere long
That they will need her sword more than your sceptre

    Sar. There was a certain Bacchus, was there not ?
I've heard my Greek girls speak of such—they say
He was a God, that is, a Grecian god,
An idol foreign to Assyria's worship,   150
Who conquered this same golden realm of Ind
Thou prat'st of, where Semiramis was vanquished.

    Sal. I have heard of such a man ; and thou perceiv'st
That he is deemed a God for what he did.

    Sar. And in his godship I will honour him—
Not much as man.   What, ho ! my cupbearer !

    Sal. What means the King?

    Sar.   To worship your new God
And ancient conqueror.   Some wine, I say.

Enter Cupbearer.

Sar. (*addressing the Cupbearer*). Bring me the golden
    goblet thick with gems,
Which bears the name of Nimrod's chalice. Hence, 160
Fill full, and bear it quickly.   [*Exit Cupbearer.*
    Sal.   Is this moment
A fitting one for the resumption of
Thy yet unslept-off revels?

Re-enter Cupbearer, with wine.

    Sar. (*taking the cup from him*). Noble kinsman,
If these barbarian Greeks of the far shores
And skirts of these our realms lie not, this Bacchus
Conquered the whole of India,[1] did he not?
    Sal. He did, and thence was deemed a Deity.[i.]
    Sar. Not so :—of all his conquests a few columns.[2]
Which may be his, and might be mine, if I
Thought them worth purchase and conveyance, are 170
The landmarks of the seas of gore he shed,
The realms he wasted, and the hearts he broke.
But here—here in this goblet is his title
To immortality—the immortal grape
From which he first expressed the soul, and gave
To gladden that of man, as some atonement
For the victorious mischiefs he had done.
Had it not been for this, he would have been
A mortal still in name as in his grave ;
And, like my ancestor Semiramis,   180
A sort of semi-glorious human monster.
Here's that which deified him—let it now
Humanise thee ; my surly, chiding brother,

---

i. *He did, and thence was deemed a God in story.*—[*MS. M. erased.*]

    1. [For the occupation of India by Dionysus, see Diod. Siculi *Bib. Hist.*, lib. ii. pag. 87, c.]
    2. [Strabo (*Rerum Geog.*, lib. iii. 1807, p. 235) throws some doubt on the existence of these columns, which he suggests were islands or "pillar" rocks. According to Plutarch (Langhorne's Translation, 1838, p. 490), Alexander built great altars on the banks of the Ganges, on which the native kings were wont to "offer sacrifices in the Grecian manner." Hence, perhaps, the legend of the columns erected by Dionysus.]

Pledge me to the Greek God !
   Sal.   For all thy realms
I would not so blaspheme our country's creed.
   Sar. That is to say, thou thinkest him a hero,
That he shed blood by oceans ; and no God,
Because he turned a fruit to an enchantment,
Which cheers the sad, revives the old, inspires
The young, makes Weariness forget his toil,   190
And Fear her danger; opens a new world
When this, the present, palls.   Well, then *I* pledge thee
And *him* as a true man, who did his utmost
In good or evil to surprise mankind.   [*Drinks.*
   Sal. Wilt thou resume a revel at this hour?
   Sar. And if I did, 'twere better than a trophy,
Being bought without a tear.   But that is not
My present purpose : since thou wilt not pledge me,
Continue what thou pleasest.
(*To the Cupbearer.*)   Boy, retire.
                      [*Exit Cupbearer.*
   Sal. I would but have recalled thee from thy dream ;
Better by me awakened than rebellion.   201
   Sar. Who should rebel ? or why ? what cause? pretext?
I am the lawful King, descended from
A race of Kings who knew no predecessors.
What have I done to thee, or to the people,
That thou shouldst rail, or they rise up against me ?
   Sal. Of what thou hast done to me, I speak not.
   Sar.   But
Thou think'st that I have wronged the Queen : is't not so ?
   Sal. Think / Thou hast wronged her !
   Sar.   Patience, Prince, and hear me.
She has all power and splendour of her station,   210
Respect, the tutelage of Assyria's heirs,
The homage and the appanage of sovereignty.
I married her as monarchs wed—for state,
And loved her as most husbands love their wives.
If she or thou supposedst I could link me
Like a Chaldean peasant to his mate,
Ye knew nor me—nor monarchs—nor mankind.
   Sal. I pray thee, change the theme : my blood disdains
Complaint, and Salemenes' sister seeks not

Reluctant love even from Assyria's lord !   220
Nor would she deign to accept divided passion
With foreign strumpets and Ionian slaves.
The Queen is silent.
  Sar.   And why not her brother ?
  Sal. I only echo thee the voice of empires,
Which he who long neglects not long will govern.
  Sar. The ungrateful and ungracious slaves ! they
    murmur
Because I have not shed their blood, nor led them
To dry into the desert's dust by myriads,
Or whiten with their bones the banks of Ganges ;
Nor decimated them with savage laws,   230
Nor sweated them to build up Pyramids,
Or Babylonian walls.
  Sal.   Yet these are trophies
More worthy of a people and their prince
Than songs, and lutes, and feasts, and concubines,
And lavished treasures, and contemnéd virtues.
  Sar. Or for my trophies I have founded cities :
There's Tarsus and Anchialus, both built
In one day—what could that blood-loving beldame,
My martial grandam, chaste Semiramis,
Do more, except destroy them ?
  Sal.   'Tis most true ;   240
I own thy merit in those founded cities,
Built for a whim, recorded with a verse
Which shames both them and thee to coming ages.
  Sar. Shame me ! By Baal, the cities, though well built,
Are not more goodly than the verse ! Say what
Thou wilt 'gainst me, my mode of life or rule,
But nothing 'gainst the truth of that brief record.
Why, those few lines contain the history
Of all things human : hear—" Sardanapalus,
The king, and son of Anacyndaraxes,   250
In one day built Anchialus and Tarsus.
Eat, drink, and love ; the rest's not worth a fillip." [1]

---

1. " For this expedition he took only a small chosen body of the
phalanx, but all his light troops. In the first day's march he reached
Anchialus, a town said to have been founded by the king of Assyria,
Sardanapalus. The fortifications, in their magnitude and extent, still

Sal. A worthy moral, and a wise inscription,
For a king to put up before his subjects !

in Arrian's time, bore the character of greatness, which the Assyrians
appear singularly to have affected in works of the kind. A monument
representing Sardanapalus was found there, warranted by an inscription in Assyrian characters, of course in the old Assyrian language,
which the Greeks, whether well or ill, interpreted thus : ' Sardanapalus,
son of Anacynaraxes, in one day founded Anchialus and Tarsus.
Eat, drink, play ; all other human joys are not worth a fillip.' Supposing this version nearly exact (for Arrian says it was not quite so),
whether the purpose has not been to invite to civil order a people
disposed to turbulence, rather than to recommend immoderate luxury,
may perhaps reasonably be questioned. What, indeed, could be the
object of a king of Assyria in founding such towns in a country so
distant from his capital, and so divided from it by an immense extent
of sandy deserts and lofty mountains, and, still more, how the inhabitants could be at once in circumstances to abandon themselves to
the intemperate joys which their prince has been supposed to have
recommended, is not obvious. But it may deserve observation that, in
that line of coast, the southern of Lesser Asia, ruins of cities, evidently
of an age after Alexander, yet barely named in history, at this day
astonish the adventurous traveller by their magnificence and elegance
amid the desolation which, under a singularly barbarian government,
has for so many centuries been daily spreading in the finest countries
of the globe. Whether more from soil and climate, or from opportunities
for commerce, extraordinary means must have been found for com-
munities to flourish there ; whence it may seem that the measures of
Sardanapalus were directed by juster views than have been commonly
ascribed to him. But that monarch having been the last of a dynasty
ended by a revolution, obloquy on his memory would follow of course
from the policy of his successors and their partisans. The incon-
sistency of traditions concerning Sardanapalus is striking in Diodorus's
account of him."—MITFORD'S *Greece*, 1820, ix. 311-313, and *note* I.
[The story of the sepulchral monument with its cynical inscription
rests on the authority of Aristobulus, who served under Alexander, and
wrote his history. The passage is quoted by Strabo (lib. xiv. ed. 1808,
p. 958), and as follows by Athenæus (lib. xii. cap. 40) in the *Deipnosophistæ*: "And Aristobulus says, ' In Anchiale, which was built by
Sardanapalus, did Alexander, when he was on his expedition against
the Persians, pitch his camp. And at no great distance was the
monument of Sardanapalus, on which there is a marble figure putting
together the fingers of its right hand, as if it were giving a fillip. And
there was on it the following inscription in Assyrian characters :—

' Sardanapalus
The king, and son of Anacyndaraxes,
In one day built Anchiale and Tarsus :
Eat, drink, and love, the rest's not worth e'en this.

By ' *this* ' meaning the fillip he was giving with his fingers."
"We may conjecture," says Canon Rawlinson, "that the monument
was in reality a stele containing the king [Sennacherib] in an arched
frame, with the right hand raised above the left, which is the ordinary
attitude, and an inscription commemorating the occasion of its
erection" [the conquest of Cilicia and settlement of Tarsus].—*The
Five Great Monarchies, etc.*, 1871, ii. 216.]

Sar. Oh, thou wouldst have me doubtless set up
      edicts—
" Obey the king—contribute to his treasure—
Recruit his phalanx—spill your blood at bidding—
Fall down and worship, or get up and toil."
Or thus—" Sardanapalus on this spot
Slew fifty thousand of his enemies.   260
These are their sepulchres, and this his trophy."
I leave such things to conquerors ; enough
For me, if I can make my subjects feel
The weight of human misery less, and glide
Ungroaning to the tomb : I take no license
Which I deny to them.   We all are men.
    Sal. Thy Sires have been revered as Gods—
    Sar.   In dust
And death, where they are neither Gods nor men.
Talk not of such to me ! the worms are Gods ; [1]
At least they banqueted upon your Gods,   270
And died for lack of farther nutriment.
Those Gods were merely men ; look to their issue—
I feel a thousand mortal things about me,
But nothing godlike,—unless it may be
The thing which you condemn, a disposition
To love and to be merciful, to pardon
The follies of my species, and (that's human)
To be indulgent to my own.
    Sal.   Alas !
The doom of Nineveh is sealed.—Woe—woe
To the unrivalled city !
    Sar.   What dost dread ?   280
    Sal. Thou art guarded by thy foes : in a few hours
The tempest may break out which overwhelms thee,
And thine and mine ; and in another day
What *is* shall be the past of Belus' race.
    Sar. What must we dread ?
    Sal.   Ambitious treachery,
Which has environed thee with snares ; but yet
There is resource : empower me with thy signet

---

1. [Compare " Your worm is your only emperor for diet : we fat all
creatures else to fat us ; and we fat ourselves for maggots."—*Hamlet*,
act iv. sc. 3, lines 21-23.]

To quell the machinations, and I lay
The heads of thy chief foes before thy feet.
   Sar. The heads—how many ?
   Sal.   Must I stay to number
When even thine own's in peril ? Let me go ;   291
Give me thy signet—trust me with the rest.
   Sar. I will trust no man with unlimited lives.
When we take those from others, we nor know
What we have taken, nor the thing we give.
   Sal. Wouldst thou not take their lives who seek for
      thine ?
   Sar. That's a hard question—But I answer, Yes.
Cannot the thing be done without ? Who are they
Whom thou suspectest ?—Let them be arrested.
   Sal. I would thou wouldst not ask me ; the next
      moment   300
Will send my answer through thy babbling troop
Of paramours, and thence fly o'er the palace,
Even to the city, and so baffle all.—
Trust me.
   Sar.   Thou knowest I have done so ever ;
Take thou the signet.   [*Gives the signet.*
   Sal.   I have one more request.
   Sar. Name it.
   Sal.   That thou this night forbear the banquet
In the pavilion over the Euphrates.
   Sar. Forbear the banquet ! Not for all the plotters
That ever shook a kingdom ! Let them come,
And do their worst : I shall not blench for them ; 310
Nor rise the sooner ; nor forbear the goblet ;
Nor crown me with a single rose the less ;
Nor lose one joyous hour.—I fear them not.
   Sal. But thou wouldst arm thee, wouldst thou not, if
      needful ?
   Sar. Perhaps. I have the goodliest armour, and
A sword of such a temper, and a bow,
And javelin, which might furnish Nimrod forth :
A little heavy, but yet not unwieldy.
And now I think on't, 'tis long since I've used them,
Even in the chase. Hast ever seen them, brother ? 320
   Sal. Is this a time for such fantastic trifling ?—

If need be, wilt thou wear them?
  Sar.   Will I not?
Oh! if it must be so, and these rash slaves
Will not be ruled with less, I'll use the sword
Till they shall wish it turned into a distaff.
  Sal. They say thy Sceptre's turned to that already.
  Sar. That's false! but let them say so: the old Greeks,
Of whom our captives often sing, related
The same of their chief hero, Hercules,
Because he loved a Lydian queen: thou seest   330
The populace of all the nations seize
Each calumny they can to sink their sovereigns.
  Sal. They did not speak thus of thy fathers.
  Sar.   No;
They dared not. They were kept to toil and combat;
And never changed their chains but for their armour:
Now they have peace and pastime, and the license
To revel and to rail; it irks me not.
I would not give the smile of one fair girl
For all the popular breath [1] that e'er divided
A name from nothing. What are the rank tongues [2] 340
Of this vile herd, grown insolent with feeding,
That I should prize their noisy praise, or dread
Their noisome clamour?
  Sal.   You have said they are men;
As such their hearts are something.
  Sar.   So my dogs' are;
And better, as more faithful:—but, proceed;
Thou hast my signet:—since they are tumultuous,
Let them be tempered, yet not roughly, till
Necessity enforce it. I hate all pain,
Given or received; we have enough within us,
The meanest vassal as the loftiest monarch,   350
Not to add to each other's natural burthen

1. [Compare—
        " The fickle reek of popular breath."
           Childe Harold, Canto IV. stanza clxxi. line 2.]
2. [Compare—
        " I have not flattered its rank breath."
           Childe Harold, Canto III. stanza cxiii. line 2.
Compare, too, Shakespeare, *Coriolanus*, act iii. sc. 1, lines 66, 67.]

Of mortal misery, but rather lessen,
By mild reciprocal alleviation,
The fatal penalties imposed on life :
But this they know not, or they will not know.
I have, by Baal ! done all I could to soothe them :
I made no wars, I added no new imposts,
I interfered not with their civic lives,
I let them pass their days as best might suit them,
Passing my own as suited me.
    Sal.   Thou stopp'st   360
Short of the duties of a king ; and therefore
They say thou art unfit to be a monarch.
    Sar. They lie.—Unhappily, I am unfit
To be aught save a monarch ; else for me
The meanest Mede might be the king instead.
    Sal. There is one Mede, at least, who seeks to be so.
    Sar. What mean'st thou !—'tis thy secret ; thou
        desirest
Few questions, and I'm not of curious nature.
Take the fit steps ; and, since necessity
Requires, I sanction and support thee. Ne'er   370
Was man who more desired to rule in peace
The peaceful only : if they rouse me, better
They had conjured up stern Nimrod from his ashes,
" The Mighty Hunter ! " I will turn these realms
To one wide desert chase of brutes, who *were*,
But *would* no more, by their own choice, be human.
What they have found me, they belie ; *that which*
They yet may find me—shall defy their wish
To speak it worse ; and let them thank themselves.
    Sal. Then thou at last canst feel ?
    Sar.   Feel ! who feels not
Ingratitude ?[1]
    Sal.   I will not pause to answer   381
With words, but deeds.   Keep thou awake that energy
Which sleeps at times, but is not dead within thee,

---

1. [" Rode. Winter's wind somewhat more unkind than ingratitude
itself, though Shakespeare says otherwise. At least, I am so much
more accustomed to meet with ingratitude than the north wind, that I
thought the latter the sharper of the two. I had met with both in the
course of the twenty-four hours, so could judge."—*Extracts from a
Diary*, January 19, 1821, *Letters*, 1901, v. 177.]

And thou may'st yet be glorious in thy reign,
As powerful in thy realm.　Farewell !　[*Exit* SALEMENES.
　Sar. (*solus*).　　　　　　　　　　Farewell !
He's gone ; and on his finger bears my signet,
Which is to him a sceptre.　He is stern
As I am heedless ; and the slaves deserve
To feel a master.　What may be the danger,
I know not : he hath found it, let him quell it.　390
Must I consume my life—this little life—
In guarding against all may make it less ?
It is not worth so much !　It were to die
Before my hour, to live in dread of death,
Tracing revolt ; suspecting all about me,
Because they are near ; and all who are remote,
Because they are far.　But if it should be so—
If they should sweep me off from Earth and Empire,
Why, what is Earth or Empire of the Earth ?
I have loved, and lived, and multiplied my image ;　400
To die is no less natural than those
Acts of this clay !　'Tis true I have not shed
Blood as I might have done, in oceans, till
My name became the synonyme of Death—
A terror and a trophy.　But for this
I feel no penitence ; my life is love :
If I must shed blood, it shall be by force.
Till now, no drop from an Assyrian vein
Hath flowed for me, nor hath the smallest coin
Of Nineveh's vast treasures e'er been lavished　410
On objects which could cost her sons a tear :
If then they hate me, 'tis because I hate not :
If they rebel, 'tis because I oppress not.
Oh, men ! ye must be ruled with scythes, not sceptres,
And mowed down like the grass, else all we reap
Is rank abundance, and a rotten harvest
Of discontents infecting the fair soil,
Making a desert of fertility.—
I'll think no more.——Within there, ho !

　　　　　Enter an ATTENDANT.
　Sar.　　　　　　　　　　　　　　Slave, tell
The Ionian Myrrha we would crave her presence.　420
　Attend.　King, she is here.

MYRRHA *enters.*

Sar. (apart to Attendant).   Away !
(*Addressing* MYRRHA.)   Beautiful being !
Thou dost almost anticipate my heart ;
It throbbed for thee, and here thou comest : let me
Deem that some unknown influence, some sweet oracle,
Communicates between us, though unseen,
In absence, and attracts us to each other.
    Myr. There doth.
    Sar.   I know there doth, but not its name :
What is it ?
    Myr.   In my native land a God,
And in my heart a feeling like a God's,
Exalted ; yet I own 'tis only mortal ;   430
For what I feel is humble, and yet happy—
That is, it would be happy ; but——   [MYRRHA *pauses.*
    Sar.   There comes
For ever something between us and what
We deem our happiness : let me remove
The barrier which that hesitating accent
Proclaims to thine, and mine is sealed.
    Myr.   My Lord !—
    Sar. My Lord—my King—Sire—Sovereign ; thus it
is—
For ever thus, addressed with awe. I ne'er
Can see a smile, unless in some broad banquet's
Intoxicating glare, when the buffoons   440
Have gorged themselves up to equality,
Or I have quaffed me down to their abasement.
Myrrha, I can hear all these things, these names,
Lord—King—Sire—Monarch—nay, time was I prized
        them ;
That is, I suffered them—from slaves and nobles ;
But when they falter from the lips I love,
The lips which have been pressed to mine, a chill
Comes o'er my heart, a cold sense of the falsehood
Of this my station, which represses feeling
In those for whom I have felt most, and makes me   450
Wish that I could lay down the dull tiara,
And share a cottage on the Caucasus

With thee—and wear no crowns but those of flowers.
  Myr. Would that we could !
  Sar.   And dost *thou* feel this ?—Why ?
  Myr. Then thou wouldst know what thou canst never
    know.
  Sar. And that is——
  Myr.   The true value of a heart ;
At least, a woman's.
  Sar.   I have proved a thousand—
A thousand, and a thousand.
  Myr.   Hearts ?
  Sar.   I think so.
  Myr. Not one ! the time may come thou may'st.
  Sar.   It will.
Hear, Myrrha ; Salemenes has declared—   460
Or why or how he hath divined it, Belus,
Who founded our great realm, knows more than I—
But Salemenes hath declared my throne
In peril.
  Myr.   He did well.
  Sar.   And say'st *thou* so ?
Thou whom he spurned so harshly, and now dared [i.]
Drive from our presence with his savage jeers,
And made thee weep and blush ?
  Myr.   I should do both
More frequently, and he did well to call me
Back to my duty. But thou spakest of peril
Peril to thee——
  Sar.   Aye, from dark plots and snares 470
From Medes—and discontented troops and nations.
I know not what—a labyrinth of things—
A maze of muttered threats and mysteries :
Thou know'st the man—it is his usual custom.
But he is honest. Come, we'll think no more on't—
But of the midnight festival.
  Myr.   'Tis time
To think of aught save festivals. Thou hast not
Spurned his sage cautions ?
  Sar.   What ?—and dost thou fear ?

i.   —— *and even dared*
    Profane our presence with his savage jeers.—[*MS. M.*]

Myr. Fear !—I'm a Greek, and how should I fear
    death ?
A slave, and wherefore should I dread my freedom ? 480
    Sar. Then wherefore dost thou turn so pale ?
    Myr.   I love.
    Sar. And do not I ?   I love thee far—far more
Than either the brief life or the wide realm,
Which, it may be, are menaced ;—yet I blench not.
    Myr. That means thou lovest nor thyself nor me ;
For he who loves another loves himself,
Even for that other's sake.   This is too rash :
Kingdoms and lives are not to be so lost.
    Sar. Lost !—why, who is the aspiring chief who dared
Assume to win them ?
    Myr.   Who is he should dread   490
To try so much ?   When he who is their ruler
Forgets himself—will they remember him ?
    Sar. Myrrha !
    Myr.   Frown not upon me : you have smiled
Too often on me not to make those frowns
Bitterer to bear than any punishment
Which they may augur.—King, I am your subject !
Master, I am your slave !   Man, I have loved you !—
Loved you, I know not by what fatal weakness,
Although a Greek, and born a foe to monarchs—
A slave, and hating fetters—an Ionian,   500
And, therefore, when I love a stranger, more
Degraded by that passion than by chains !
Still I have loved you.   If that love were strong
Enough to overcome all former nature,
Shall it not claim the privilege to save you ?
    Sar. *Save* me, my beauty !   Thou art very fair,
And what I seek of thee is love—not safety.
    Myr. And without love where dwells security ?
    Sar. I speak of woman's love.
    Myr.   The very first
Of human life must spring from woman's breast,   510
Your first small words are taught you from her lips,
Your first tears quenched by her, and your last sighs
Too often breathed out in a woman's hearing,
When men have shrunk from the ignoble care

Of watching the last hour of him who led them.

Sar. My eloquent Ionian ! thou speak'st music :
The very chorus of the tragic song
I have heard thee talk of as the favourite pastime
Of thy far father-land.   Nay, weep not—calm thee.

Myr. I weep not.—But I pray thee, do not speak   520
About my fathers or their land.

Sar.   Yet oft
Thou speakest of them.

Myr.   True—true : constant thought
Will overflow in words unconsciously ;
But when another speaks of Greeks, it wounds me.

Sar. Well, then, how wouldst thou *save* me, as thou
          saidst ?

Myr. By teaching thee to save thyself, and not
Thyself alone, but these vast realms, from all
The rage of the worst war—the war of brethren.

Sar. Why, child, I loathe all war, and warriors ;
I live in peace and pleasure : what can man   530
Do more ?

Myr.   Alas ! my Lord, with common men
There needs too oft the show of war to keep
The substance of sweet peace ; and, for a king,
'Tis sometimes better to be feared than loved.

Sar. And I have never sought but for the last.

Myr. And now art neither.

Sar.   Dost *thou* say so, Myrrha ?

Myr. I speak of civic popular love, *self*-love,
Which means that men are kept in awe and law,
Yet not oppressed—at least they must not think so,
Or, if they think so, deem it necessary,   540
To ward off worse oppression, their own passions.
A King of feasts, and flowers, and wine, and revel,
And love, and mirth, was never King of Glory.

Sar. Glory ! what's that ?

Myr.   Ask of the Gods thy fathers.

Sar. They cannot answer ; when the priests speak for
          them,
'Tis for some small addition to the temple.

Myr. Look to the annals of thine Empire's founders.

Sar. They are so blotted o'er with blood, I cannot.

But what wouldst have? the Empire *has been* founded.
I cannot go on multiplying empires.   550
    Myr. Preserve thine own.
    Sar.   At least, I will enjoy it.
Come, Myrrha, let us go on to the Euphrates:
The hour invites, the galley is prepared,
And the pavilion, decked for our return,
In fit adornment for the evening banquet,
Shall blaze with beauty and with light, until
It seems unto the stars which are above us
Itself an opposite star; and we will sit
Crowned with fresh flowers like——
    Myr.   Victims.
    Sar.   No, like sovereigns,
The Shepherd Kings of patriarchal times,   560
Who knew no brighter gems than summer wreaths,[i.]
And none but tearless triumphs. Let us on.

Enter PANIA.

    Pan. May the King live for ever!
    Sar.   Not an hour
Longer than he can love. How my soul hates
This language, which makes life itself a lie,
Flattering dust with eternity.[ii.] Well, Pania!
Be brief.
    Pan.   I am charged by Salemenes to
Reiterate his prayer unto the King,
That for this day, at least, he will not quit
The palace: when the General returns,   570
He will adduce such reasons as will warrant
His daring, and perhaps obtain the pardon
Of his presumption.
    Sar.   What! am I then cooped?
Already captive? can I not even breathe
The breath of heaven? Tell prince Salemenes,
Were all Assyria raging round the walls
In mutinous myriads, I would still go forth.
    Pan. I must obey, and yet——

---

    i. *Who loved no gems so well as those of nature.*—[MS. M.]
    ii. *Wishing eternity to dust* ——.—[MS. M.]

Myr.   Oh, Monarch, listen.—
How many a day and moon thou hast reclined
Within these palace walls in silken dalliance,   580
And never shown thee to thy people's longing;
Leaving thy subjects' eyes ungratified,
The satraps uncontrolled, the Gods unworshipped,
And all things in the anarchy of sloth,
Till all, save evil, slumbered through the realm !
And wilt thou not now tarry for a day,—
A day which may redeem thee?   Wilt thou not
Yield to the few still faithful a few hours,
For them, for thee, for thy past fathers' race,
And for thy sons' inheritance ?
    Pan.   'Tis true !   590
From the deep urgency with which the Prince
Despatched me to your sacred presence, I
Must dare to add my feeble voice to that
Which now has spoken.
    Sar.   No, it must not be.
    Myr. For the sake of thy realm !
    Sar.   Away !
    Pan.   For that
Of all thy faithful subjects, who will rally
Round thee and thine.
    Sar.   These are mere fantasies :
There is no peril :—'tis a sullen scheme
Of Salemenes, to approve his zeal,
And show himself more necessary to us.   600
    Myr. By all that's good and glorious take this counsel.
    Sar. Business to-morrow.
    Myr.   Aye—or death to-night.
    Sar. Why let it come then unexpectedly,
'Midst joy and gentleness, and mirth and love ;
So let me fall like the plucked rose !—far better
Thus than be withered.
    Myr.   Then thou wilt not yield,
Even for the sake of all that ever stirred
A monarch into action, to forego
A trifling revel.
    Sar.   No.
    Myr.   Then yield for *mine ;*

For my sake!

 Sar.   Thine, my Myrrha!

 Myr.   'Tis the first 610
Boon which I ever asked Assyria's king.

 Sar. That's true, and, wer't my kingdom, must be
  granted.
Well, for thy sake, I yield me. Pania, hence!
Thou hear'st me.

 Pan.   And obey.   [*Exit* PANIA.

 Sar.   I marvel at thee.
What is thy motive, Myrrha, thus to urge me?

 Myr. Thy safety; and the certainty that nought
Could urge the Prince thy kinsman to require
Thus much from thee, but some impending danger.

 Sar. And if I do not dread it, why shouldst thou?

 Myr. Because *thou* dost not fear, I fear for *thee*. 620

 Sar. To-morrow thou wilt smile at these vain fancies.

 Myr. If the worst come, I shall be where none weep,
And that is better than the power to smile.
And thou?

 Sar.   I shall be King, as heretofore.

 Myr. Where?

 Sar.   With Baal, Nimrod, and Semiramis,
Sole in Assyria, or with them elsewhere.
Fate made me what I am—may make me nothing—
But either that or nothing must I be:
I will not live degraded.

 Myr.   Hadst thou felt
Thus always, none would ever dare degrade thee. 630

 Sar. And who will do so now?

 Myr.   Dost thou suspect none?

 Sar. Suspect!—that's a spy's office. Oh! we lose
Ten thousand precious moments in vain words,
And vainer fears. Within there!—ye slaves, deck
The Hall of Nimrod for the evening revel;
If I must make a prison of our palace,
At least we'll wear our fetters jocundly;
If the Euphrates be forbid us, and
The summer-dwelling on its beauteous border,
Here we are still unmenaced. Ho! within there! 640
       [*Exit* SARDANAPALUS.

Myr. (*solus*). Why do I love this man? My country's
    daughters
Love none but heroes. But I have no country!
The slave hath lost all save her bonds. I love him;
And that's the heaviest link of the long chain—
To love whom we esteem not. Be it so:
The hour is coming when he'll need all love,
And find none. To fall from him now were baser
Than to have stabbed him on his throne when highest
Would have been noble in my country's creed:
I was not made for either. Could I save him,   650
I should not love *him* better, but myself;
And I have need of the last, for I have fallen
In my own thoughts, by loving this soft stranger:
And yet, methinks, I love him more, perceiving
That he is hated of his own barbarians,
The natural foes of all the blood of Greece.
Could I but wake a single thought like those
Which even the Phrygians felt when battling long
'Twixt Ilion and the sea, within his heart,
He would tread down the barbarous crowds, and triumph.
He loves me, and I love him; the slave loves   661
Her master, and would free him from his vices.
If not, I have a means of freedom still,
And if I cannot teach him how to reign,
May show him how alone a King can leave
His throne. I must not lose him from my sight. [*Exit.*

ACT II.

SCENE I.—*The Portal of the same Hall of the Palace.*

Beleses (*solus*). The Sun goes down: methinks he sets
    more slowly,
Taking his last look of Assyria's Empire.
How red he glares amongst those deepening clouds,
Like the blood he predicts. If not in vain,
Thou Sun that sinkest, and ye stars which rise,

I have outwatched ye, reading ray by ray
The edicts of your orbs, which make Time tremble[i.]
For what he brings the nations, 'tis the furthest
Hour of Assyria's years.   And yet how calm !
An earthquake should announce so great a fall—   10
A summer's sun discloses it.   Yon disk,
To the star-read Chaldean, bears upon
Its everlasting page the end of what
Seemed everlasting; but oh! thou true Sun !
The burning oracle of all that live,
As fountain of all life, and symbol of
Him who bestows it, wherefore dost thou limit
Thy lore unto calamity ?   Why not
Unfold the rise of days more worthy thine
All-glorious burst from ocean? why not dart   20
A beam of hope athwart the future years,
As of wrath to its days ?   Hear me ! oh, hear me !
I am thy worshipper, thy priest, thy servant—
I have gazed on thee at thy rise and fall,
And bowed my head beneath thy mid-day beams,
When my eye dared not meet thee.   I have watched
For thee, and after thee, and prayed to thee,
And sacrificed to thee, and read, and feared thee,
And asked of thee, and thou hast answered—but
Only to thus much : while I speak, he sinks—   30
Is gone—and leaves his beauty, not his knowledge,
To the delighted West, which revels in
Its hues of dying glory.   Yet what is
Death, so it be but glorious ?   'Tis a sunset ;
And mortals may be happy to resemble
The Gods but in decay.

Enter ARBACES *by an inner door.*

Arb.   Beleses, why
So wrapt in thy devotions ?   Dost thou stand
Gazing to trace thy disappearing God
Into some realm of undiscovered day ?
Our business is with night—'tis come.

i. *Each twinkle unto which Time trembles, and*
     Nations grow nothing ——.—[MS. M. erased.]

Bel.   But not   40
Gone.
  Arb. Let it roll on—we are ready.
  Bel.   Yes.
Would it were over !
  Arb.   Does the prophet doubt,
To whom the very stars shine Victory?
  Bel. I do not doubt of Victory—but the Victor.
  Arb. Well, let thy science settle that.   Meantime
I have prepared as many glittering spears
As will out-sparkle our allies—your planets.
There is no more to thwart us.   The she-king,
That less than woman, is even now upon
The waters with his female mates.   The order   50
Is issued for the feast in the pavilion.
The first cup which he drains will be the last
Quaffed by the line of Nimrod.
  Bel.   'Twas a brave one.
  Arb. And is a weak one—'tis worn out—we'll mend it.
  Bel. Art sure of that?
  Arb.   Its founder was a hunter—
I am a soldier—what is there to fear?
  Bel. The soldier.
  Arb.   And the priest, it may be : but
If you thought thus, or think, why not retain
Your king of concubines? why stir me up?
Why spur me to this enterprise? your own   60
No less than mine?
  Bel.   Look to the sky!
  Arb.   I look.
  Bel. What seest thou?
  Arb.   A fair summer's twilight, and
The gathering of the stars.
  Bel.   And midst them, mark
Yon earliest, and the brightest, which so quivers,
As it would quit its place in the blue ether.
  Arb. Well?
  Bel.   'Tis thy natal ruler—thy birth planet.
  Arb. (*touching his scabbard*). My star is in this scabbard :
    when it shines,
It shall out-dazzle comets.   Let us think

Of what is to be done to justify
Thy planets and their portents.   When we conquer,   70
They shall have temples—aye, and priests—and thou
Shalt be the pontiff of—what Gods thou wilt ;
For I observe that they are ever just,
And own the bravest for the most devout.
  Bel. Aye, and the most devout for brave—thou hast not
Seen me turn back from battle.
  Arb.   No ; I own thee
As firm in fight as Babylonia's captain,
As skilful in Chaldea's worship : now,
Will it but please thee to forget the priest,
And be the warrior ?
  Bel.   Why not both ?
  Arb.   The better ;   80
And yet it almost shames me, we shall have
So little to effect.   This woman's warfare
Degrades the very conqueror.   To have plucked
A bold and bloody despot from his throne,
And grappled with him, clashing steel with steel,
That were heroic or to win or fall ;
But to upraise my sword against this silkworm,[1]
And hear him whine, it may be——
  Bel.   Do not deem it :
He has that in him which may make you strife yet ;
And were he all you think, his guards are hardy,   90
And headed by the cool, stern Salemenes.
  Arb. They'll not resist.
  Bel.   Why not ? they are soldiers.
  Arb.   True,
And therefore need a soldier to command them.
  Bel. That Salemenes is.
  Arb.   But not their King.
Besides, he hates the effeminate thing that governs,
For the Queen's sake, his sister.   Mark you not
He keeps aloof from all the revels ?
  Bel.   But
Not from the council—there he is ever constant.
  Arb. And ever thwarted : what would you have more

  1. [Compare "these swoln silkworms," *Marino Faliero*, act ii. sc.
2, line 115, *Poetical Works*, 1901, iv. 386, *note* 4.]

To make a rebel out of?   A fool reigning,   100
His blood dishonoured, and himself disdained :
Why, it is *his* revenge we work for.
 Bel.   Could
He but be brought to think so : this I doubt of.
 Arb. What, if we sound him?
 Bel.   Yes —if the time served.

Enter BALEA.

 Bal. Satraps !   The king commands your presence at
The feast to-night.
 Bel.   To hear is to obey.
In the pavilion ?
 Bal.   No ; here in the palace.
 Arb. How ! in the palace ? it was not thus ordered.
 Bal. It is so ordered now.
 Arb.   And why ?
 Bal.   I know not.
May I retire?
 Arb. Stay.
 Bel. (*to Arb. aside*). Hush ! let him go his way.   110
(*Alternately to Bal.*) Yes, Balea, thank the Monarch, kiss
   the hem
Of his imperial robe, and say, his slaves
Will take the crumbs he deigns to scatter from
His royal table at the hour—was't midnight?
 Bal. It was : the place, the hall of Nimrod.   Lords,
I humble me before you, and depart.   [*Exit* BALEA.
 Arb. I like not this same sudden change of place ;
There is some mystery : wherefore should he change it ?
 Bel. Doth he not change a thousand times a day ?
Sloth is of all things the most fanciful—   120
And moves more parasangs in its intents
Than generals in their marches, when they seek
To leave their foe at fault.—Why dost thou muse ?
 Arb. He loved that gay pavilion,—it was ever
His summer dotage.
 Bel.   And he loved his Queen —
And thrice a thousand harlotry besides—
And he has loved all things by turns, except

Wisdom and Glory.

Arb.   Still—I like it not.
If he has changed—why, so must we : the attack
Were easy in the isolated bower,   130
Beset with drowsy guards and drunken courtiers;
But in the hall of Nimrod——

Bel.   Is it so ?
Methought the haughty soldier feared to mount
A throne too easily—does it disappoint thee
To find there is a slipperier step or two
Than what was counted on ?

Arb.   When the hour comes,
Thou shalt perceive how far I fear or no.
Thou hast seen my life at stake—and gaily played for :
But here is more upon the die—a kingdom.

Bel. I have foretold already—thou wilt win it :   140
Then on, and prosper.

Arb.   Now were I a soothsayer,
I would have boded so much to myself.
But be the stars obeyed—I cannot quarrel
With them, nor their interpreter.   Who's here?

Enter SALEMENES.

Sal. Satraps !
Bel.   My Prince !
Sal.   Well met—I sought ye both,
But elsewhere than the palace.

Arb.   Wherefore so ?
Sal. 'Tis not the hour.
Arb.   The hour !—what hour?
Sal.   Of midnight.
Bel. Midnight, my Lord !
Sal.   What, are you not invited ?
Bel. Oh ! yes—we had forgotten.
Sal.   Is it usual
Thus to forget a Sovereign's invitation ?   150
Arb. Why—we but now received it.
Sal.   Then why here ?
Arb. On duty.
Sal.   On what duty ?
Bel.   On the state's.

We have the privilege to approach the presence;
But found the Monarch absent.[i]

 Sal.   And I too
Am upon duty.

  Arb.   May we crave its purport?

  Sal. To arrest two traitors. Guards! Within there!

      Enter Guards.

  Sal. (*continuing*).   Satraps,
Your swords.

  Bel. (*delivering his*). My lord, behold my scimitar.

  Arb. (*drawing his sword*). Take mine.

  Sal. (*advancing*).   I will.

  Arb.   But in your heart the blade—
The hilt quits not this hand.[ii]

  Sal. (*drawing*).   How! dost thou brave me?
'Tis well—this saves a trial, and false mercy.   160
Soldiers, hew down the rebel!

  Arb.   Soldiers! Aye—
Alone you dare not.

  Sal.   Alone! foolish slave—
What is there in thee that a Prince should shrink from
Of open force? We dread thy treason, not
Thy strength: thy tooth is nought without its venom—
The serpent's, not the lion's. Cut him down.

  Bel. (*interposing*). Arbaces! Are you mad? Have I
   not rendered
My sword? Then trust like me our Sovereign's justice.

  Arb. No—I will sooner trust the stars thou prat'st of,
And this slight arm, and die a king at least   170
Of my own breath and body—so far that
None else shall chain them.

  Sal. (*to the Guards*). You hear *him* and *me.*
Take him not,—kill.

   [*The Guards attack* ARBACES, *who defends himself*
    valiantly and dexterously till they waver.

 i. *But found the Monarch claimed his privacy.*—[*MS. M. erased.*]
 ii.   —— *not else*
   It quits this living hand.—[*MS. M. erased.*]

Sal.   Is it even so ; and must
I do the hangman's office ?   Recreants ! see
How you should fell a traitor.

> [SALEMENES *attacks* ARBACES.

Enter SARDANAPALUS *and Train.*

Sar.   Hold your hands—
Upon your lives, I say.   What, deaf or drunken ?
My sword !   O fool, I wear no sword : here, fellow,
Give me thy weapon.   [*To a Guard.*

> [SARDANAPALUS *snatches a sword from one of the
> soldiers, and rushes between the combatants—they
> separate.*

Sar.   In my very palace !
What hinders me from cleaving you in twain,
Audacious brawlers ?
    Bel.   Sire, your justice.
    Sal.   Or—   180
Your weakness.
    Sar. (*raising the sword*).   How ?
    Sal.   Strike ! so the blow's repeated
Upon yon traitor—whom you spare a moment,
I trust, for torture—I'm content.
    Sar.   What—him !
Who dares assail Arbaces ?
    Sal.   I !
    Sar.   Indeed !
Prince, you forget yourself.   Upon what warrant ?
    Sal. (*showing the signet*).   Thine.
    Arb. (*confused*).   The King's !
    Sal.   Yes ! and let the King confirm it.
    Sar. I parted not from this for such a purpose.
    Sal. You parted with it for your safety—I
Employed it for the best.   Pronounce in person.
Here I am but your slave—a moment past   190
I was your representative.
    Sar.   Then sheathe
Your swords.

> [ARBACES *and* SALEMENES *return their swords to the
> scabbards.*

Sal.   Mine's sheathed : I pray you sheathe *not* yours :
'Tis the sole sceptre left you now with safety.

Sar. A heavy one ; the hilt, too, hurts my hand.
(*To a Guard.*) Here, fellow, take thy weapon back. Well,
    sirs,
What doth this mean ?

Bel.   The Prince must answer that.

Sal. Truth upon my part, treason upon theirs.

Sar. Treason—Arbaces ! treachery and Beleses !
That were an union I will not believe.

Bel. Where is the proof ?

Sal.   I'll answer that, if once   200
The king demands your fellow-traitor's sword.

Arb. (to Sal.). A sword which hath been drawn as oft
    as thine
Against his foes.

Sal.   And now against his brother,
And in an hour or so against himself.

Sar. That is not possible : he dared not ; no—
No—I'll not hear of such things. These vain bickerings
Are spawned in courts by base intrigues, and baser
Hirelings, who live by lies on good men's lives.
You must have been deceived, my brother.

Sal.   First
Let him deliver up his weapon, and   210
Proclaim himself your subject by that duty,
And I will answer all.

Sar.   Why, if I thought so—
But no, it cannot be : the Mede Arbaces—
The trusty, rough, true soldier—the best captain
Of all who discipline our nations——No,
I'll not insult him thus, to bid him render
The scimitar to me he never yielded
Unto our enemies. Chief, keep your weapon.

Sal. (delivering back the signet). Monarch, take back
    your signet.

Sar.   No, retain it ;
But use it with more moderation.

Sal.   Sire,   220
I used it for your honour, and restore it
Because I cannot keep it with my own.

Bestow it on Arbaces.
 Sar.   So I should :
He never asked it.
 Sal.   Doubt not, he will have it,
Without that hollow semblance of respect.
 Bel. I know not what hath prejudiced the Prince
So strongly 'gainst two subjects, than whom none
Have been more zealous for Assyria's weal.
 Sal. Peace, factious priest, and faithless soldier ! thou
Unit'st in thy own person the worst vices   230
Of the most dangerous orders of mankind.
Keep thy smooth words and juggling homilies
For those who know thee not. Thy fellow's sin
Is, at the least, a bold one, and not tempered
By the tricks taught thee in Chaldea.
 Bel.   Hear him,
My liege—the son of Belus ! he blasphemes
The worship of the land, which bows the knee
Before your fathers.
 Sar.   Oh ! for that I pray you
Let him have absolution. I dispense with
The worship of dead men ; feeling that I   240
Am mortal, and believing that the race
From whence I sprung are—what I see them—ashes.
 Bel. King ! Do not deem so : they are with the stars,
And——
 Sar. You shall join them ere they will rise,
If you preach farther—Why, *this* is rank treason.
 Sal. My lord !
 Sar.   To school me in the worship of
Assyria's idols ! Let him be released—
Give him his sword.
 Sal.   My Lord, and King, and Brother,
I pray ye pause.
 Sar.   Yes, and be sermonised,
And dinned, and deafened with dead men and Baal, 250
And all Chaldea's starry mysteries.
 Bel. Monarch ! respect them.
 Sar.   Oh ! for that—I love them ;
I love to watch them in the deep blue vault,
And to compare them with my Myrrha's eyes ;

I love to see their rays redoubled in
The tremulous silver of Euphrates' wave,
As the light breeze of midnight crisps the broad
And rolling water, sighing through the sedges
Which fringe his banks : but whether they may be
Gods, as some say, or the abodes of Gods,   260
As others hold, or simply lamps of night,
Worlds—or the lights of Worlds—I know nor care not.
There's something sweet in my uncertainty
I would not change for your Chaldean lore ;
Besides, I know of these all clay can know
Of aught above it, or below it—nothing.
I see their brilliancy and feel their beauty—ᴸ
When they shine on my grave I shall know neither.
    Bel. For *neither*, Sire, say *better*.
    Sar.   I will wait,
If it so please you, Pontiff, for that knowledge.   270
In the mean time receive your sword, and know
That I prefer your service militant
Unto your ministry—not loving either.
    Sal. (aside). His lusts have made him mad. Then
    must I save him,
Spite of himself.
    Sar.   Please you to hear me, Satraps !
And chiefly thou, my priest, because I doubt thee
More than the soldier ; and would doubt thee all
Wert thou not half a warrior : let us part
In peace—I'll not say pardon—which must be
Earned by the guilty ; this I'll not pronounce ye,   280
Although upon this breath of mine depends
Your own ; and, deadlier for ye, on my fears.
But fear not—for that I am soft, not fearful—
And so live on.   Were I the thing some think me,
Your heads would now be dripping the last drops
Of their attainted gore from the high gates
Of this our palace, into the dry dust,
Their only portion of the coveted kingdom
They would be crowned to reign o'er—let that pass.
As I have said, I will not *deem* ye guilty,   290
Nor *doom* ye guiltless.   Albeit better men

  ᴸ *I know them beautiful, and see them brilliant.*—[*MS. M. erased.*]

Than ye or I stand ready to arraign you;
And should I leave your fate to sterner judges,
And proofs of all kinds, I might sacrifice
Two men, who, whatsoe'er they now are, were
Once honest.   Ye are free, sirs.
    Arb.   Sire, this clemency——
    Bel. (interrupting him). Is worthy of yourself; and,
       although innocent,
We thank——
    Sar.   Priest! keep your thanksgivings for Belus;
His offspring needs none.
    Bel.   But being innocent——
    Sar. Be silent.—Guilt is loud.   If ye are loyal,   300
Ye are injured men, and should be sad, not grateful.
    Bel. So we should be, were justice always done
By earthly power omnipotent; but Innocence
Must oft receive her right as a mere favour.
    Sar. That's a good sentence for a homily,
Though not for this occasion.   Prithee keep it
To plead thy Sovereign's cause before his people.
    Bel. I trust there is no cause.
    Sar.   No *cause,* perhaps;
But many causers :—if ye meet with such
In the exercise of your inquisitive function   310
On earth, or should you read of it in heaven
In some mysterious twinkle of the stars,
Which are your chronicles, I pray you note,
That there are worse things betwixt earth and heaven
Than him who ruleth many and slays none;
And, hating not himself, yet loves his fellows
Enough to spare even those who would not spare him
Were they once masters—but that's doubtful.   Satraps!
Your swords and persons are at liberty
To use them as ye will—but from this hour   320
I have no call for either.   Salemenes!
Follow me.
    [*Exeunt* SARDANAPALUS, SALEMENES, *and the Train,*
      etc., leaving ARBACES *and* BELESES.
    Arb.   Beleses!
    Bel.   Now, what think you?
    Arb. That we are lost.

Bel.   That we have won the kingdom.
Arb. What? thus suspected—with the sword slung
   o'er us
But by a single hair, and that still wavering,
To be blown down by his imperious breath
Which spared us—why, I know not.
   Bel.   Seek not why;
But let us profit by the interval.[i.]
The hour is still our own—our power the same—
The night the same we destined. He hath changed 330
Nothing except our ignorance of all
Suspicion into such a certainty
As must make madness of delay.
   Arb.   And yet——
   Bel. What, doubting still?
   Arb.   He spared our lives, nay, more,
Saved them from Salemenes.
   Bel.   And how long
Will he so spare? till the first drunken minute.
   Arb. Or sober, rather. Yet he did it nobly;
Gave royally what we had forfeited
Basely——
   Bel.   Say bravely.
   Arb.   Somewhat of both, perhaps—
But it has touched me, and, whate'er betide,   340
I will no further on.
   Bel.   And lose the world!
   Arb. Lose any thing except my own esteem.
   Bel. I blush that we should owe our lives to such
A king of distaffs!
   Arb.   But no less we owe them;
And I should blush far more to take the grantor's![1]
   Bel. Thou may'st endure whate'er thou wilt—the stars
Have written otherwise.
   Arb.   Though they came down,
And marshalled me the way in all their brightness,
I would not follow.

i. —— *by the foolish confidence.*—[*MS. M. erased.*]

1. [The first edition reads "grantor." In the MS. the word may be
either "granter" or "grantor." "Grantor" is a technical term, in
law, for one "who grants a conveyance."]

Bel.   This is weakness—worse
Than a scared beldam's dreaming of the dead,   35c
And waking in the dark.—Go to—go to.

Arb. Methought he looked like Nimrod as he spoke,
Even as the proud imperial statue stands
Looking the monarch of the kings around it,
And sways, while they but ornament, the temple.

Bel. I told you that you had too much despised him,
And that there was some royalty within him—
What then? he is the nobler foe.

Arb.   But we
The meaner.—Would he had not spared us!

Bel.   So—
Wouldst thou be sacrificed thus readily?   360

Arb. No—but it had been better to have died
Than live ungrateful.

Bel.   Oh, the souls of some men!
Thou wouldst digest what some call treason, and
Fools treachery—and, behold, upon the sudden,
Because for something or for nothing, this
Rash reveller steps, ostentatiously,
'Twixt thee and Salemenes, thou art turned
Into—what shall I say?—Sardanapalus!
I know no name more ignominious.

Arb.   But
An hour ago, who dared to term me such   370
Had held his life but lightly—as it is,
I must forgive you, even as he forgave us—
Semiramis herself would not have done it.

Bel. No—the Queen liked no sharers of the kingdom,
Not even a husband.[1]

Arb.   I must serve him truly——

Bel. And humbly?

Arb.   No, sir, proudly—being honest.
I shall be nearer thrones than you to heaven;
And if not quite so haughty, yet more lofty.
You may do your own deeming—you have codes,

---

1. [According to Ælian, *Var. Hist.*, vii. 1, Semiramis, having
obtained from her husband permission to rule over Asia for five days,
thrust him into a dungeon, and obtained the sovereign power for
herself (ed. Paris, 1858, p. 355).]

And mysteries, and corollaries of   380
Right and wrong, which I lack for my direction,
And must pursue but what a plain heart teaches.
And now you know me.
  Bel.   Have you finished?
  Arb.   Yes—
With you.
  Bel. And would, perhaps, betray as well
As quit me?
  Arb.   That's a sacerdotal thought,
And not a soldier's.
  Bel.   Be it what you will—
Truce with these wranglings, and but hear me.
  Arb.   No—
There is more peril in your subtle spirit
Than in a phalanx.
  Bel.   If it must be so—
I'll on alone.
  Arb.   Alone!
  Bel.   Thrones hold but one.   390
  Arb. But this is filled.
  Bel.   With worse than vacancy—
A despised monarch. Look to it, Arbaces:
I have still aided, cherished, loved, and urged you;
Was willing even to serve you, in the hope
To serve and save Assyria.   Heaven itself
Seemed to consent, and all events were friendly,
Even to the last, till that your spirit shrunk
Into a shallow softness; but now, rather
Than see my country languish, I will be
Her saviour or the victim of her tyrant—   400
Or one or both—for sometimes both are one;
And if I win—Arbaces is my servant.
  Arb. Your servant!
  Bel.   Why not? better than be slave,
The *pardoned* slave of *she* Sardanapalus!

     Enter PANIA.

  Pan. My Lords, I bear an order from the king.
  Arb. It is obeyed ere spoken.

Bel.   Notwithstanding,
Let's hear it.
    Pan.   Forthwith, on this very night,
Repair to your respective satrapies
Of Babylon and Media.
    Bel.   With our troops?
    Pan. My order is unto the Satraps and   410
Their household train.
    Arb.   But——
    Bel.   It must be obeyed :
Say, we depart.
    Pan.   My order is to see you
Depart, and not to bear your answer.
    Bel. (aside).   Aye !^L
Well, Sir—we will accompany you hence.
    Pan. I will retire to marshal forth the guard
Of honour which befits your rank, and wait
Your leisure, so that it the hour exceeds not.
                  [*Exit* PANIA.

    Bel. Now then obey !
    Arb.   Doubtless.
    Bel.   Yes, to the gates
That grate the palace, which is now our prison—
No further.
    Arb.   Thou hast harped the truth indeed !   420
The realm itself, in all its wide extension,
Yawns dungeons at each step for thee and me.
    Bel. Graves !
    Arb.   If I thought so, this good sword should dig
One more than mine.
    Bel.   It shall have work enough.
Let me hope better than thou augurest ;
At present, let us hence as best we may.
Thou dost agree with me in understanding
This order as a sentence ?
    Arb.   Why, what other
Interpretation should it bear ? it is
The very policy of Orient monarchs—   430
Pardon and poison—favours and a sword—

---

    i. *Aye—that's earnest !—[MS. M. erased.]*

A distant voyage, and an eternal sleep.
How many Satraps in his father's time—
For he I own is, or at least *was*, bloodless—
  Bel. But *will* not—*can* not be so now.
  Arb.   I doubt it.
How many Satraps have I seen set out
In his Sire's day for mighty Vice-royalties,
Whose tombs are on their path!   I know not how,
But they all sickened by the way, it was
So long and heavy.
  Bel.   Let us but regain   440
The free air of the city, and we'll shorten
The journey.
  Arb.   'Twill be shortened at the gates,
It may be.
  Bel.   No; they hardly will risk that.
They mean us to die privately, but not
Within the palace or the city walls,
Where we are known, and may have partisans :
If they had meant to slay us here, we were
No longer with the living.   Let us hence.
  Arb. If I but thought he did not mean my life—
  Bel. Fool ! hence — what else should despotism
    alarmed   450
Mean?   Let us but rejoin our troops, and march.
  Arb. Towards our provinces?
  Bel.   No; towards your kingdom.
There 's time—there 's heart, and hope, and power, and
    means—
Which their half measures leave us in full scope.—
Away !
  Arb. And I even yet repenting must
Relapse to guilt !
  Bel.   Self-defence is a virtue,
Sole bulwark of all right.   Away, I say !
Let's leave this place, the air grows thick and choking,
And the walls have a scent of night-shade—hence !
Let us not leave them time for further council.   460
Our quick departure proves our civic zeal ;
Our quick departure hinders our good escort,
The worthy Pania, from anticipating

The orders of some parasangs from hence :
Nay, there 's no other choice, but ―― hence, I say.[i.]
     [*Exit with* ARBACES, *who follows reluctantly.*

    Enter SARDANAPALUS *and* SALEMENES.

  Sar. Well, all is remedied, and without bloodshed,
That worst of mockeries of a remedy ;
We are now secure by these men's exile.
  Sal.   Yes,
As he who treads on flowers is from the adder
Twined round their roots.
  Sar.   Why, what wouldst have me do ? 470
  Sal. Undo what you have done.
  Sar.   Revoke my pardon ?
  Sal. Replace the crown now tottering on your temples.
  Sar. That were tyrannical.
  Sal.   But sure.
  Sar.   We are so.
What danger can they work upon the frontier?
  Sal. They are not there yet—never should they be so,
Were I well listened to.
  Sar.   Nay, I *have* listened
Impartially to thee—why not to them ?
  Sal. You may know that hereafter ; as it is,
I take my leave to order forth the guard.
  Sar. And you will join us at the banquet ?
  Sal.   Sire, 480
Dispense with me—I am no wassailer :
Command me in all service save the Bacchant's.
  Sar. Nay, but 'tis fit to revel now and then.
  Sal. And fit that some should watch for those who revel
Too oft. Am I permitted to depart ?
  Sar. Yes――Stay a moment, my good Salemenes,
My brother—my best subject—better Prince
Than I am King. You should have been the monarch,
And I—I know not what, and care not ; but
Think not I am insensible to all   490
Thine honest wisdom, and thy rough yet kind,
Though oft-reproving sufferance of my follies.

      i. *Nay, if thou **wilt not** ――.—*[*MS. M. erased.*]

If I have spared these men against thy counsel,
That is, their lives—it is not that I doubt
The advice was sound; but, let them live : we will not
Cavil about their lives—so let them mend them.
Their banishment will leave me still sound sleep,
Which their death had not left me.
  Sal.   Thus you run
The risk to sleep for ever, to save traitors—
A moment's pang now changed for years of crime. 500
Still let them be made quiet.
  Sar.   Tempt me not;
My word is past.
  Sal.   But it may be recalled.
  Sar. 'Tis royal.
  Sal.   And should therefore be decisive.
This half-indulgence of an exile serves
But to provoke—a pardon should be full,
Or it is none.
  Sar.   And who persuaded me
After I had repealed them, or at least
Only dismissed them from our presence, who
Urged me to send them to their satrapies ?
  Sal. True; that I had forgotten; that is, Sire, 510
If they e'er reached their Satrapies—why, then,
Reprove me more for my advice.
  Sar.   And if
They do not reach them—look to it !—in safety,
In safety, mark me—and security—
Look to thine own.
  Sal.   Permit me to depart ;
Their *safety* shall be cared for.
  Sar.   Get thee hence, then ;
And, prithee, think more gently of thy brother.
  Sal. Sire, I shall ever duly serve my sovereign.
         [*Exit* SALEMENES.
  Sar. (*solus*). That man is of a temper too severe ;
Hard but as lofty as the rock, and free 520
From all the taints of common earth—while I
Am softer clay, impregnated with flowers :
But as our mould is, must the produce be.
If I have erred this time, 'tis on the side

Where Error sits most lightly on that sense,
I know not what to call it; but it reckons
With me ofttimes for pain, and sometimes pleasure;
A spirit which seems placed about my heart
To count its throbs, not quicken them, and ask
Questions which mortal never dared to ask me,   530
Nor Baal, though an oracular deity— [i.]
Albeit his marble face majestical
Frowns as the shadows of the evening dim
His brows to changed expression, till at times
I think the statue looks in act to speak.
Away with these vain thoughts, I will be joyous—
And here comes Joy's true herald.

Enter MYRRHA.

Myr.   King! the sky
Is overcast, and musters muttering thunder,
In clouds that seem approaching fast, and show
In forkéd flashes a commanding tempest. [ii.]   540
Will you then quit the palace?
Sar.   Tempest, say'st thou?
Myr. Aye, my good lord.
Sar.   For my own part, I should be
Not ill content to vary the smooth scene,
And watch the warring elements; but this
Would little suit the silken garments and
Smooth faces of our festive friends.   Say, Myrrha,
Art thou of those who dread the roar of clouds?
Myr. In my own country we respect their voices
As auguries of Jove. [iii.]
Sar.   Jove!—aye, your Baal—
Ours also has a property in thunder,   550
And ever and anon some falling bolt
Proves his divinity,—and yet sometimes

---

i. *Nor silent Baal, our imaged deity,*
   Although his marble face looks frowningly,
   As the dusk shadows of the evening cast
   His brow in coming dimness and at times.—[MS. M. erased.]

ii. *In distant flashes* { *a wide-spread* / *the approaching* } *tempest.*—[MS. M. erased.]

iii. *As from the Gods to augur.*—[MS. M. erased.]

Strikes his own altars.

    Myr.   That were a dread omen.

    Sar. Yes—for the priests. Well, we will not go forth
Beyond the palace walls to-night, but make
Our feast within.

    Myr.   Now, Jove be praised ! that he
Hath heard the prayer thou wouldst not hear. The Gods
Are kinder to thee than thou to thyself,
And flash this storm between thee and thy foes,
To shield thee from them.

    Sar.   Child, if there be peril, 560
Methinks it is the same within these walls
As on the river's brink.

    Myr.   Not so ; these walls
Are high and strong, and guarded. Treason has
To penetrate through many a winding way,
And massy portal ; but in the pavilion
There is no bulwark.

    Sar.   No, nor in the palace,
Nor in the fortress, nor upon the top
Of cloud-fenced Caucasus, where the eagle sits
Nested in pathless clefts, if treachery be :
Even as the arrow finds the airy king,   570
The steel will reach the earthly. But be calm ;
The men, or innocent or guilty, are
Banished, and far upon their way.

    Myr.   They live, then ?

    Sar. So sanguinary ? *Thou !*

    Myr.   I would not shrink
From just infliction of due punishment
On those who seek your life : were't otherwise,
I should not merit mine. Besides, you heard
The princely Salemenes.

    Sar.   This is strange ;
The gentle and the austere are both against me,
And urge me to revenge.

    Myr.   'Tis a Greek virtue. 580

    Sar. But not a kingly one—I'll none on't ; or
If ever I indulge in't, it shall be
With kings—my equals.

    Myr.   These men sought to be so.

Sar. Myrrha, this is too feminine, and springs
From fear——
  Myr.   For you.
  Sar.   No matter, still 'tis fear.
I have observed your sex, once roused to wrath,
Are timidly vindictive to a pitch
Of perseverance, which I would not copy.
I thought you were exempt from this, as from
The childish helplessness of Asian women.[i.]   590
  Myr. My Lord, I am no boaster of my love,
Nor of my attributes; I have shared your splendour,
And will partake your fortunes. You may live
To find one slave more true than subject myriads :
But this the Gods avert ! I am content
To be beloved on trust for what I feel,
Rather than prove it to you in your griefs,[ii.]
Which might not yield to any cares of mine.
  Sar. Grief cannot come where perfect love exists,
Except to heighten it, and vanish from   600
That which it could not scare away. Let's in—
The hour approaches, and we must prepare
To meet the invited guests who grace our feast.
                              [*Exeunt.*

ACT III.

SCENE I.—*The Hall of the Palace illuminated*—SARDANA-
PALUS *and his Guests at Table.—A storm without,
and Thunder occasionally heard during the Banquet.*

  Sar. Fill full ! why this is as it should be : here
Is my true realm, amidst bright eyes and faces
Happy as fair ! Here sorrow cannot reach.
  Zam. Nor elsewhere—where the King is, pleasure
      sparkles.
  Sar. Is not this better now than Nimrod's huntings,
Or my wild Grandam's chase in search of kingdoms
She could not keep when conquered ?

---

    i. *The weaker merit of our Asian women.*—[*MS. M. erased.*]
    ii. *Rather than prove that love to you in griefs.*—[*MS. M. erased.*]

Alt.   Mighty though
They were, as all thy royal line have been,
Yet none of those who went before have reached
The acmé of Sardanapalus, who   10
Has placed his joy in peace—the sole true glory.
   Sar. And pleasure, good Altada, to which glory
Is but the path.   What is it that we seek?
Enjoyment !   We have cut the way short to it,
And not gone tracking it through human ashes,
Making a grave with every footstep.
   Zam.   No;
All hearts are happy, and all voices bless
The King of peace—who holds a world in jubilee.
   Sar. Art sure of that?   I have heard otherwise;
Some say that there be traitors.
   Zam.   Traitors they   20
Who dare to say so !—'Tis impossible.
What cause?
   Sar.   What cause? true,—fill the goblet up;
We will not think of them : there are none such,
Or if there be, they are gone.
   Alt.   Guests, to my pledge !
Down on your knees, and drink a measure to
The safety of the King—the monarch, say I?
The God Sardanapalus !
            [ZAMES *and the Guests kneel, and exclaim—*
                        Mightier than
His father Baal, the God Sardanapalus !
      [*It thunders as they kneel ; some start up in confusion.*
   Zam. Why do you rise, my friends? in that strong
                        peal
His father gods consented.
   Myr.   Menaced, rather.   30
King, wilt thou bear this mad impiety?
   Sar. Impiety !—nay, if the sires who reigned
Before me can be Gods, I'll not disgrace
Their lineage.   But arise, my pious friends ;
Hoard your devotion for the Thunderer there :
I seek but to be loved, not worshipped.
   Alt.   Both—
Both you must ever be by all true subjects.

Sar. Methinks the thunders still increase : it is
An awful night.
    Myr.   Oh yes, for those who have
No palace to protect their worshippers.   40
    Sar. That 's true, my Myrrha ; and could I convert
My realm to one wide shelter for the wretched,
I'd do it.
    Myr.   Thou'rt no God, then—not to be
Able to work a will so good and general,
As thy wish would imply.
    Sar.   And your Gods, then,
Who can, and do not ?
    Myr.   Do not speak of that,
Lest we provoke them.
    Sar.   True—, they love not censure
Better than mortals.   Friends, a thought has struck
      me :
Were there no temples, would there, think ye, be
Air worshippers ? [i.] that is, when it is angry,   50
And pelting as even now.
    Myr.   The Persian prays
Upon his mountain.
    Sar.   Yes, when the Sun shines.
    Myr. And I would ask if this your palace were
Unroofed and desolate, how many flatterers
Would lick the dust in which the King lay low ?
    Alt. The fair Ionian is too sarcastic
Upon a nation whom she knows not well ;
The Assyrians know no pleasure but their King's,
And homage is their pride.
    Sar.   Nay, pardon, guests,
The fair Greek's readiness of speech.
    Alt.   *Pardon !* sire :
We honour her of all things next to thee.   61
Hark ! what was that?
    Zam.   That ! nothing but the jar
Of distant portals shaken by the wind.
    Alt. It sounded like the clash of—hark again !
    Zam. The big rain pattering on the roof.
    Sar.   No more.

      i. *Worshippers in the air.*—[*MS. M. erased.*]

Myrrha, my love, hast thou thy shell in order ?
Sing me a song of Sappho ;[1] her, thou know'st,
Who in thy country threw——

Enter PANIA, *with his sword and garments bloody, and
disordered. The guests rise in confusion.*

   Pan. (to the Guards).   Look to the portals ;
And with your best speed to the walls without.
Your arms ! To arms ! The King's in danger. Monarch
Excuse this haste,—'tis faith.
   Sar.   Speak on.
   Pan.   It is   71
As Salemenes feared ; the faithless Satraps——
   Sar. You are wounded—give some wine. Take breath,
      good Pania.
   Pan. 'Tis nothing—a mere flesh wound. I am worn
More with my speed to warn my sovereign,
Than hurt in his defence.
   Myr.   Well, Sir, the rebels ?
   Pan. Soon as Arbaces and Beleses reached
Their stations in the city, they refused
To march ; and on my attempt to use the power
Which I was delegated with, they called   80
Upon their troops, who rose in fierce defiance.
   Myr. All ?
   Pan.   Too many.
   Sar.   Spare not of thy free speech,
To spare mine ears—the truth.
   Pan.   My own slight guard
Were faithful, and what's left of it is still so.
   Myr. And are these all the force still faithful ?
   Pan.   No—
The Bactrians, now led on by Salemenes,
Who even then was on his way, still urged
By strong suspicion of the Median chiefs,
Are numerous, and make strong head against
The rebels, fighting inch by inch, and forming   90

   1. [Perhaps Grillparzer's *Sappho* was responsible for the anachronism.
See "Extracts from a Diary," January 12, 1821, *Letters*, 1901, v. 171,
note 1.]

An orb around the palace, where they mean
To centre all their force, and save the King.
(*He hesitates.*) I am charged to——
    Myr.   'Tis no time for hesitation.
    Pan. Prince Salemenes doth implore the King
To arm himself, although but for a moment,
And show himself unto the soldiers : his
Sole presence in this instant might do more
Than hosts can do in his behalf.
    Sar.   What, ho !
My armour there.
    Myr.   And wilt thou ?
    Sar.   Will I not ?
Ho, there !—but seek not for the buckler : 'tis   100
Too heavy :—a light cuirass and my sword.
Where are the rebels?
    Pan.   Scarce a furlong's length
From the outward wall the fiercest conflict rages.
    Sar. Then I may charge on horseback. Sfero, ho !
Order my horse out.—There is space enough
Even in our courts, and by the outer gate,
To marshal half the horsemen of Arabia.
                    [*Exit* SFERO *for the armour.*
    Myr. How I do love thee !
    Sar.   I ne'er doubted it.
    Myr. But now I know thee.
    Sar. (*to his Attendant*).   Bring down my spear too—
Where 's Salemenes?
    Pan.   Where a soldier should be,   110
In the thick of the fight.
    Sar.   Then hasten to him——Is
The path still open, and communication
Left 'twixt the palace and the phalanx ?
    Pan.   'Twas
When I late left him, and I have no fear ;
Our troops were steady, and the phalanx formed.
    Sar. Tell him to spare his person for the present,
And that I will not spare my own—and say,
I come.
    Pan. There 's victory in the very word. [*Exit* PANIA.
    Sar. Altada—Zames—forth, and arm ye ! There

Is all in readiness in the armoury.   120
See that the women are bestowed in safety
In the remote apartments : let a guard
Be set before them, with strict charge to quit
The post but with their lives—command it, Zames.
Altada, arm yourself, and return here ;
Your post is near our person.

> [*Exeunt* ZAMES, ALTADA, *and all save* MYRRHA.

Enter SFERO *and others with the King's Arms, etc.*

Sfe.   King ! your armour.
Sar. (arming himself). Give me the cuirass—so : my
    baldric ; now
My sword : I had forgot the helm—where is it ?
That 's well—no, 'tis too heavy ; you mistake, too—
It was not this I meant, but that which bears   130
A diadem around it.
Sfe.   Sire, I deemed
That too conspicuous from the precious stones
To risk your sacred brow beneath—and trust me,
This is of better metal, though less rich.
    Sar. You deemed ! Are you too turned a rebel ?
        Fellow !
Your part is to obey : return, and—no—
It is too late—I will go forth without it.
    Sfe. At least, wear this.
    Sar.   Wear Caucasus ! why, 'tis
A mountain on my temples.
    Sfe.   Sire, the meanest
Soldier goes not forth thus exposed to battle.   140
All men will recognise you—for the storm
Has ceased, and the moon breaks forth in her brightness.
    Sar. I go forth to be recognised, and thus
Shall be so sooner. Now—my spear ! I'm armed.

> [*In going stops short, and turns to* SFERO.

Sfero—I had forgotten—bring the mirror.[1]

---

1. [" In the third act, when Sardanapalus calls for a *mirror* to look
at himself in his *armour*, recollect to quote the Latin passage from
Juvenal upon Otho (a similar character, who did the same thing :
Gifford will help you to it). The trait is, perhaps, too familiar, but it

Sfe. The mirror, Sire?
Sar.   Yes, sir, of polished brass,
Brought from the spoils of India—but be speedy.
                                        [*Exit* SFERO.
Sar. Myrrha, retire unto a place of safety.
Why went you not forth with the other damsels?
Myr. Because my place is here.
Sar.   And when I am gone——
Myr. I follow.
Sar.   *You!* to battle?
Myr.   If it were so,   151
'Twere not the first Greek girl had trod the path.
I will await here your *return*.
Sar.   The place
Is spacious, and the first to be sought out,
If they prevail; and, if it be so,
And I return not——
Myr.   Still we meet again.
Sar. How?
Myr.   In the spot where all must meet at last—
In Hades! if there be, as I believe,
A shore beyond the Styx; and if there be not,
In ashes.
Sar.   Darest thou so much?
Myr.   I dare all things   16c
Except survive what I have loved, to be
A rebel's booty: forth, and do your bravest.

---

is historical (of Otho, at least), and natural in an effeminate character."—Letter to Murray, May 30, 1821, *Letters*, 1901, v. 301.   The
quotation was not made in the first edition, 1821, nor in any subsequent issue, till 1832.   It is from Juvenal, *Sat.* ii. lines 199-203—

> " Ille tenet speculum, pathici gestamen Othonis,
> Actoris Aurunci spolium, quo se ille videbat
> Armatum, cum jam tolli vexilla juberet.
> Res memoranda novis annalibus, atque recenti
> Historia, speculum civilis sarcina belli."

> "This grasps a mirror—pathic Otho's boast
> (Auruncan Actor's spoil), where, while his host,
> With shouts, the signal of the fight required,
> He viewed his mailed form; viewed, and admired!
> Lo, a new subject for the historic page,
> A MIRROR, midst the arms of civil rage!"
>   Gifford.]

Re-enter SFERO *with the mirror.*

Sar. (*looking at himself*). This cuirass fits me well, the
 baldric better,
And the helm not at all. Methinks I seem
   [*Flings away the helmet after trying it again.*
Passing well in these toys; and now to prove them.
Altada! Where's Altada?
 Sfe.   Waiting, Sire,
Without : he has your shield in readiness.
 Sar. True—I forgot—he is my shield-bearer
By right of blood, derived from age to age.
Myrrha, embrace me;—yet once more—once more—
Love me, whate'er betide. My chiefest glory   171
Shall be to make me worthier of your love.
 Myr. Go forth, and conquer!
    [*Exeunt* SARDANAPALUS *and* SFERO.
      Now, I am alone:
All are gone forth, and of that all how few
Perhaps return! Let him but vanquish, and
Me perish! If he vanquish not, I perish;
For I will not outlive him. He has wound
About my heart, I know not how nor why.
Not for that he is King; for now his kingdom
Rocks underneath his throne, and the earth yawns   180
To yield him no more of it than a grave;
And yet I love him more. Oh, mighty Jove!
Forgive this monstrous love for a barbarian,
Who knows not of Olympus! yes, I love him
Now—now—far more than——Hark—to the war shout!
Methinks it nears me. If it should be so,
    [*She draws forth a small vial.*
This cunning Colchian poison, which my father
Learned to compound on Euxine shores, and taught me
How to preserve, shall free me! It had freed me
Long ere this hour, but that I loved, until   190
I half forgot I was a slave:—where all
Are slaves save One, and proud of servitude,
So they are served in turn by something lower
In the degree of bondage: we forget
That shackles worn like ornaments no less

Are chains.   Again that shout ! and now the clash
Of arms—and now—and now——

Enter ALTADA.

Alt.   Ho, Sfero, ho !
Myr. He is not here ; what wouldst thou with him ?
         How
Goes on the conflict ?
     Alt.   Dubiously and fiercely.
   Myr. And the King ?
     Alt.   Like a king.   I must find Sfero,
And bring him a new spear with his own helmet.ᴸ   201
He fights till now bare-headed, and by far
Too much exposed.   The soldiers knew his face,
And the foe too ; and in the moon's broad light,
His silk tiara and his flowing hair
Make him a mark too royal.   Every arrow
Is pointed at the fair hair and fair features,
And the broad fillet which crowns both.
     Myr.   Ye Gods,
Who fulminate o'er my father's land, protect him !
Were you sent by the King ?
     Alt.   By Salemenes,   210
Who sent me privily upon this charge,
Without the knowledge of the careless sovereign.
The King ! the King fights as he revels ! ho !
What, Sfero ! I will seek the armoury—
He must be there.   [*Exit* ALTADA.
     Myr.   'Tis no dishonour—no—
'Tis no dishonour to have loved this man.
I almost wish now, what I never wished
Before—that he were Grecian.   If Alcides
Were shamed in wearing Lydian Omphale's
She-garb, and wielding her vile distaff; surely   220
He, who springs up a Hercules at once,
Nursed in effeminate arts from youth to manhood,
And rushes from the banquet to the battle,
As though it were a bed of love, deserves

ᴸ *—— and his own helmet.—[MS. M. erased.]*

That a Greek girl should be his paramour,
And a Greek bard his minstrel—a Greek tomb
His monument.   How goes the strife, sir?

Enter an Officer.

Officer.   Lost,
Lost almost past recovery.   Zames!   Where
Is Zames?
   Myr.   Posted with the guard appointed
To watch before the apartment of the women.   230
                               [*Exit Officer.*
   Myr. (*sola*). He 's gone; and told no more than that
    all 's lost!
What need have I to know more?   In those words,
Those little words, a kingdom and a king,
A line of thirteen ages, and the lives
Of thousands, and the fortune of all left
With life, are merged; and I, too, with the great,
Like a small bubble breaking with the wave
Which bore it, shall be nothing.   At the least,
My fate is in my keeping : no proud victor
Shall count me with his spoils.

Enter PANIA.

   Pan.   Away with me,   240
Myrrha, without delay; we must not lose
A moment—all that 's left us now.
   Myr.   The King?
   Pan. Sent me here to conduct you hence, beyond
The river, by a secret passage.
   Myr.   Then
He lives——
   Pan.   And charged me to secure your life,
And beg you to live on for his sake, till
He can rejoin you.
   Myr.   Will he then give way?
   Pan. Not till the last.   Still, still he does whate'er
Despair can do; and step by step disputes
The very palace.
   Myr.   They are here, then :—aye,   250

Their shouts come ringing through the ancient halls,
Never profaned by rebel echoes till
This fatal night.   Farewell, Assyria's line ι
Farewell to all of Nimrod!   Even the name
Is now no more.
  Pan.   Away with me—away!
  Myr. No: I'll die here!—Away, and tell your King
I loved him to the last.

Enter SARDANAPALUS *and* SALEMENES *with Soldiers.*
PANIA *quits* MYRRHA, *and ranges himself with them.*

  Sar.   Since it is thus,
We'll die where we were born—in our own halls.[i.]
Serry your ranks—stand firm.   I have despatched
A trusty satrap for the guard of Zames,   260
All fresh and faithful; they'll be here anon.
All is not over.—Pania, look to Myrrha.
       [PANIA *returns towards* MYRRHA.
  Sal. We have breathing time; yet once more charge,
    my friends—
One for Assyria!
  Sar.   Rather say for Bactria!
My faithful Bactrians, I will henceforth be
King of your nation, and we'll hold together
This realm as province.
  Sal.   Hark! they come—they come.

Enter BELESES *and* ARBACES *with the Rebels.*

  Arb. Set on, we have them in the toil.   Charge!
   charge!
  Bel. On! on!—Heaven fights for us, and with us—On!
   [*They charge the King and* SALEMENES *with their
    troops, who defend themselves till the arrival of*
    ZAMES *with the Guard before mentioned.   The
    Rebels are then driven off, and pursued by*
    SALEMENES, *etc.   As the King is going to join
    the pursuit,* BELESES *crosses him.*
  Bel. Ho! tyrant—*I* will end this war.

  i. *We'll die where we were raised* ——.—[*MS. M. erased.*]

Sar.   Even so, 270
My warlike priest, and precious prophet, and
Grateful and trusty subject : yield, I pray thee.
I would reserve thee for a fitter doom,
Rather than dip my hands in holy blood.
     Bel. Thine hour is come.
     Sar.   No, thine.—I've lately read,
Though but a young astrologer, the stars ;
And ranging round the zodiac, found thy fate
In the sign of the Scorpion, which proclaims
That thou wilt now be crushed.
     Bel.   But not by thee.
          [*They fight;* BELESES *is wounded and disarmed.*
     Sar. (*raising his sword to despatch him, exclaims*)—
Now call upon thy planets, will they shoot   280
From the sky to preserve their seer and credit ?
          [*A party of Rebels enter and rescue* BELESES. *They
               assail the King, who in turn, is rescued by a Party
               of his Soldiers, who drive the Rebels off.*
The villain was a prophet after all.
Upon them—ho ! there—victory is ours.
                                   [*Exit in pursuit.*
     Myr. (*to Pan.*). Pursue ! Why stand'st thou here, and
          leavest the ranks
Of fellow-soldiers conquering without thee ?
     Pan. The King's command was not to quit thee.
     Myr.   *Me !*
Think not of me—a single soldier's arm
Must not be wanting now. I ask no guard,
I need no guard : what, with a world at stake,
Keep watch upon a woman ? Hence, I say,   290
Or thou art shamed ! Nay, then, *I* will go forth,
A feeble female, 'midst their desperate strife,
And bid thee guard me *there*—where thou shouldst shield
Thy sovereign.   [*Exit* MYRRHA.
     Pan.   Yet stay, damsel !—She 's gone.
If aught of ill betide her, better I
Had lost my life. Sardanapalus holds her
Far dearer than his kingdom, yet he fights
For that too ; and can I do less than he,
Who never flashed a scimitar till now ?

Myrrha, return, and I obey you, though   300
In disobedience to the monarch.   [*Exit* PANIA.

Enter ALTADA *and* SFERO *by an opposite door.*

Alt.   Myrrha!
What, gone? yet she was here when the fight raged,
And Pania also.   Can aught have befallen them?
     Sfe. I saw both safe, when late the rebels fled;
They probably are but retired to make
Their way back to the harem.
     Alt.   If the King
Prove victor, as it seems even now he must,
And miss his own Ionian, we are doomed
To worse than captive rebels.
     Sfe.   Let us trace them:
She cannot be fled far; and, found, she makes   310
A richer prize to our soft sovereign
Than his recovered kingdom.
     Alt.   Baal himself
Ne'er fought more fiercely to win empire, than
His silken son to save it: he defies
All augury of foes or friends; and like
The close and sultry summer's day, which bodes
A twilight tempest, bursts forth in such thunder
As sweeps the air and deluges the earth.
The man 's inscrutable.
     Sfe.   Not more than others.
All are the sons of circumstance: away—   320
Let's seek the slave out, or prepare to be
Tortured for his infatuation, and [i]
Condemned without a crime.   [*Exeunt.*

Enter SALEMENES *and Soldiers, etc.*

     Sal.   The triumph is
Flattering: they are beaten backward from the palace,
And we have opened regular access
To the troops stationed on the other side
Euphrates, who may still be true; nay, must be,

     i. *Tortured because his mind is tortured.*—[*MS. M. erased.*]

When they hear of our victory.   But where
Is the chief victor? where 's the King?

 Enter SARDANAPALUS, *cum suis, etc., and* MYRRHA.

Sar.   Here, brother.
Sal. Unhurt, I hope.
 Sar.   Not quite; but let it pass. 330
We've cleared the palace——
 Sal.   And I trust the city.
Our numbers gather; and I've ordered onward
A cloud of Parthians, hitherto reserved,
All fresh and fiery, to be poured upon them
In their retreat, which soon will be a flight.
 Sar. It is already, or at least they marched
Faster than I could follow with my Bactrians,
Who spared no speed.   I am spent: give me a seat.
 Sal. There stands the throne, Sire.
 Sar.   'Tis no place to rest on,
For mind nor body : let me have a couch, 340
         [*They place a seat.*
A peasant's stool, I care not what : so—now
I breathe more freely.
 Sal.   This great hour has proved
The brightest and most glorious of your life.
 Sar. And the most tiresome.   Where 's my cupbearer?
Bring me some water.
 Sal. (*smiling*). 'Tis the first time he
Ever had such an order : even I,[i.]
Your most austere of counsellors, would now
Suggest a purpler beverage.
 Sar.   Blood—doubtless.
But there 's enough of that shed; as for wine,
I have learned to-night the price of the pure element :
Thrice have I drank of it, and thrice renewed, 351
With greater strength than the grape ever gave me,
My charge upon the rebels.   Where 's the soldier
Who gave me water in his helmet?[1]

  i. *He ever such an order* ——.—[*MS. M. erased.*]
   He ever had that order ——.—[*MS. M. erased.*]

 1. ["When 'the king was almost dying with thirst' . . . the eunuch

   One of the Guards.   Slain, Sire !
An arrow pierced his brain, while, scattering [i.]
The last drops from his helm, he stood in act
To place it on his brows.
   Sar.   Slain ! unrewarded !
And slain to serve my thirst : that's hard, poor slave !
Had he but lived, I would have gorged him with
Gold : all the gold of earth could ne'er repay   360
The pleasure of that draught ; for I was parched
As I am now.   [*They bring water—he drinks.*
       I live again—from henceforth
The goblet I reserve for hours of love,
But war on water.
   Sal.   And that bandage, Sire,
Which girds your arm ?
   Sar.   A scratch from brave Beleses.
   Myr. Oh ! he is wounded ! [ii.]
   Sar.   Not too much of that ;
And yet it feels a little stiff and painful,
Now I am cooler.
   Myr.   You have bound it with——
   Sar. The fillet of my diadem : the first time
That ornament was ever aught to me,   370

---

    i.   *—— ere they had time*
       To place his helm again.—[*MS. M. erased.*]
    ii. *O ye Gods ! wounded.*—[*MS. M.*]

Satibarzanes sought every place for water. . . . After much search he
found one of those poor Caunians had about two quarts of bad water
in a mean bottle, and he took it and carried it to the king. After the
king had drawn it all up, the eunuch asked him, ' If he did not find it a
disagreeable beverage?' Upon which he swore by all the gods, 'That
he had never drunk the most delicious wine, nor the lightest and
clearest water with so much pleasure. I wish only,' continued he, ' that
I could find the man who gave it thee, that I might make him a recompense. In the mean time I entreat the gods to make him happy and
rich.'"—Plutarch's *Artaxerxes*, Langhorne's translation, 1838, p. 694.
Poetry as well as history repeats itself. Compare the " water green "
which Gunga Din brought, at the risk of his own life, to fill the
wounded soldier's helmet (*Barrack-Room Ballads*, by Rudyard Kipling,
1892, p. 25). Compare, too—

        " *Arn.*   'Tis a scratch. . . .
     In the shoulder, not the sword arm—
     And that's enough. I am thirsty : would I had
     A helm of water ! "
  The Deformed Transformed, part ii. sc. ii. 44, *seq., vide post*, p. 518.]

Save an incumbrance.

    Myr. (*to the Attendants*). Summon speedily
A leech of the most skilful : pray, retire :
I will unbind your wound and tend it.
    Sar.   Do so,
For now it throbs sufficiently : but what
Know'st thou of wounds ? yet wherefore do I ask ?
Know'st thou, my brother, where I lighted on
This minion ?
    Sal.   Herding with the other females,
Like frightened antelopes.
    Sar.   No : like the dam
Of the young lion, femininely raging
(And femininely meaneth furiously,   380
Because all passions in excess are female,)
Against the hunter flying with her cub,
She urged on with her voice and gesture, and
Her floating hair and flashing eyes,[1] the soldiers,
In the pursuit.
    Sal.   Indeed !
    Sar.   You see, this night
Made warriors of more than me. I paused
To look upon her, and her kindled cheek ;
Her large black eyes, that flashed through her long hair
As it streamed o'er her ; her blue veins that rose
Along her most transparent brow ; her nostril   390
Dilated from its symmetry ; her lips
Apart ; her voice that clove through all the din,
As a lute pierceth through the cymbal's clash,
Jarred but not drowned by the loud brattling ; her
Waved arms, more dazzling with their own born whiteness
Than the steel her hand held, which she caught up
From a dead soldier's grasp ;—all these things made
Her seem unto the troops a prophetess
Of victory, or Victory herself,
Come down to hail us hers.[2]

---

1. [Compare—

          "His flashing eyes, his floating hair."

                         Kubla Khan, line 49.]

  2. [Compare *Childe Harold*, Canto I. stanzas lv., lvi., *Poetical
Works*, 1898, i. 57, 58, and *note* 11, pp. 91, 92.]

Sal. (aside).   This is too much.   400
Again the love-fit 's on him, and all 's lost,
Unless we turn his thoughts. (*Aloud.*) But pray thee, Sire,
Think of your wound—you said even now 'twas painful.
　　Sar. That 's true, too ; but I must not think of it.
　　Sal. I have looked to all things needful, and will now
Receive reports of progress made in such
Orders as I had given, and then return
To hear your further pleasure.
　　Sar.   Be it so.
　　Sal. (in retiring). Myrrha !
　　Myr.   Prince !
　　Sal.   You have shown a soul to-night,
Which, were he not my sister's lord—— But now   410
I have no time : thou lovest the King ?
　　Myr.   I love
Sardanapalus.
　　Sal.   But wouldst have him King still ?
　　Myr. I would not have him less than what he should
　　　be.
　　Sal. Well then, to have him King, and yours, and all
He should, or should not be ; to have him *live*,
Let him not sink back into luxury.
You have more power upon his spirit than
Wisdom within these walls, or fierce rebellion
Raging without : look well that he relapse not.
　　Myr. There needed not the voice of Salemenes   420
To urge me on to this : I will not fail.
All that a woman's weakness can——
　　Sal.   Is power
Omnipotent o'er such a heart as his :
Exert it wisely.   [*Exit* SALEMENES.
　　Sar.   Myrrha ! what, at whispers
With my stern brother ? I shall soon be jealous.
　　Myr. (smiling). You have cause, Sire ; for on the earth
　　　there breathes not
A man more worthy of a woman's love,
A soldier's trust, a subject's reverence,
A king's esteem—the whole world's admiration !
　　Sar. Praise him, but not so warmly. I must not   430
Hear those sweet lips grow eloquent in aught

That throws me into shade; yet you speak truth.
Myr. And now retire, to have your wound looked to,
Pray lean on me.
    Sar.   Yes, love! but not from pain.
                                      [*Exeunt omnes.*

ACT IV.

SCENE I.—SARDANAPALUS *discovered sleeping upon a
Couch, and occasionally disturbed in his slumbers,
with* MYRRHA *watching.*

   Myr. (*sola, gazing*). I have stolen upon his rest, if rest
      it be,
Which thus convulses slumber: shall I wake him?
No, he seems calmer.   Oh, thou God of Quiet!
Whose reign is o'er sealed eyelids and soft dreams,
Or deep, deep sleep, so as to be unfathomed,
Look like thy brother, Death,[1]—so still, so stirless—
For then we are happiest, as it may be, we
Are happiest of all within the realm
Of thy stern, silent, and unwakening Twin.
Again he moves—again the play of pain   10
Shoots o'er his features, as the sudden gust
Crisps the reluctant lake that lay so calm [i.]
Beneath the mountain shadow; or the blast
Ruffles the autumn leaves, that drooping cling
Faintly and motionless to their loved boughs.
I must awake him—yet not yet; who knows
From what I rouse him?   It seems pain; but if
I quicken him to heavier pain?   The fever
Of this tumultuous night, the grief too of
His wound, though slight, may cause all this, and shake
Me more to see than him to suffer.   No: 21
Let Nature use her own maternal means,

      i. *Crisps the unswelling wave.*—[*MS. M. erased.*]

   1. [Compare—

         "How wonderful is Death,
         Death and his brother Sleep!"
               Shelley's *Queen Mab*, i. lines 1, 2.]

And I await to second, not disturb her.
    Sar. (*awakening*). Not so—although he multiplied the
        stars,
And gave them to me as a realm to share
From you and with you! I would not so purchase
The empire of Eternity. Hence—hence—
Old Hunter of the earliest brutes! and ye,[i.]
Who hunted fellow-creatures as if brutes!
Once bloody mortals—and now bloodier idols,   30
If your priests lie not! And thou, ghastly Beldame!
Dripping with dusky gore, and trampling on
The carcasses of Inde—away! away!
Where am I? Where the spectres? Where——No—that
Is no false phantom: I should know it 'midst
All that the dead dare gloomily raise up
From their black gulf to daunt the living. Myrrha!
    Myr. Alas! thou art pale, and on thy brow the drops
Gather like night dew. My beloved, hush—
Calm thee. Thy speech seems of another world,   40
And thou art lord of this. Be of good cheer;
All will go well.
    Sar.   Thy *hand*—so—'tis thy hand;
'Tis flesh; grasp—clasp—yet closer, till I feel
Myself that which I was.
    Myr.   At least know me
For what I am, and ever must be—thine.
    Sar. I know it now. I know this life again.
Ah, Myrrha! I have been where we shall be.
    Myr. My lord!
    Sar.   I've been i' the grave—where worms are lords
And kings are——But I did not deem it so;
I thought 'twas nothing.
    Myr.   So it is; except   50
Unto the timid, who anticipate
That which may never be.
    Sar.   Oh, Myrrha! if
Sleep shows such things, what may not Death disclose?
    Myr. I know no evil Death can show, which Life
Has not already shown to those who live

---

    i. *Old Hunter of mankind when baited and ye*
      All brutal who pursued both brutes and men.—[*MS. M. erased.*]

Embodied longest.   If there be indeed
A shore where Mind survives, 'twill be as Mind
All unincorporate: or if there flits
A shadow of this cumbrous clog of clay,
Which stalks, methinks, between our souls and heaven,
And fetters us to earth—at least the phantom,   61
Whate'er it have to fear, will not fear Death.
   Sar. I fear it not; but I have felt—have seen—
A legion of the dead.
   Myr.   And so have I.
The dust we tread upon was once alive,
And wretched.   But proceed: what hast thou seen?
Speak it, 'twill lighten thy dimmed mind.
   Sar.   Methought——
   Myr. Yet pause, thou art tired—in pain—exhausted;
    all
Which can impair both strength and spirit: seek
Rather to sleep again.
   Sar.   Not now—I would not   70
Dream; though I know it now to be a dream
What I have dreamt:—and canst thou bear to hear it?
   Myr. I can bear all things, dreams of life or death,
Which I participate with you in semblance
Or full reality.
   Sar.   And this looked real,
I tell you: after that these eyes were open,
I saw them in their flight—for then they fled.
   Myr. Say on.
   Sar.   I saw, that is, I dreamed myself
Here—here—even where we are, guests as we were,
Myself a host that deemed himself but guest,   80
Willing to equal all in social freedom;
But, on my right hand and my left, instead
Of thee and Zames, and our customed meeting,
Was ranged on my left hand a haughty, dark,
And deadly face; I could not recognise it,
Yet I had seen it, though I knew not where:
The features were a Giant's, and the eye
Was still, yet lighted; his long locks curled down
On his vast bust, whence a huge quiver rose
With shaft-heads feathered from the eagle's wing,   90

That peeped up bristling through his serpent hair.[i]
I invited him to fill the cup which stood
Between us, but he answered not; I filled it;
He took it not, but stared upon me, till
I trembled at the fixed glare of his eye:
I frowned upon him as a king should frown;
He frowned not in his turn, but looked upon me
With the same aspect, which appalled me more,
Because it changed not; and I turned for refuge
To milder guests, and sought them on the right,   100
Where thou wert wont to be. But——   [*He pauses.*
   Myr.   What instead?
   Sar. In thy own chair—thy own place in the banquet—
I sought thy sweet face in the circle—but
Instead—a grey-haired, withered, bloody-eyed,
And bloody-handed, ghastly, ghostly thing,
Female in garb, and crowned upon the brow,
Furrowed with years, yet sneering with the passion
Of vengeance, leering too with that of lust,
Sate :—my veins curdled.[1]
   Myr.   Is this all?
   Sar.   Upon
Her right hand—her lank, bird-like, right hand— stood
A goblet, bubbling o'er with blood; and on   111
Her left, another, filled with—what I saw not,
But turned from it and her.   But all along
The table sate a range of crownéd wretches,
Of various aspects, but of one expression.
   Myr. And felt you not this a mere vision?
   Sar.   No:
It was so palpable, I could have touched them.
I turned from one face to another, in
The hope to find at last one which I knew
Ere I saw theirs: but no—all turned upon me,   120
And stared, but neither ate nor drank, but stared,

---

i. *With arrows peeping through his falling hair.*—[*MS. M. erased.*]

1. [In the diary for November 23, 1813 (*Letters*, 1898, ii. 334, 335),
Byron alludes to a dream which "chilled his blood" and shook his
nerves. Compare Coleridge's *Pains of Sleep*, lines 23-26—

    "Desire with loathing strangely mixed,
      On wild or hateful objects fixed.
      Fantastic passions! maddening brawl!
      And shame and terror over all!"]

Till I grew stone, as they seemed half to be,
Yet breathing stone, for I felt life in them,
And life in me : there was a horrid kind
Of sympathy between us, as if they
Had lost a part of death to come to me,
And I the half of life to sit by them.
We were in an existence all apart
From heaven or earth——And rather let me see
Death all than such a being !

Myr.   And the end ?   130

Sar. At last I sate, marble, as they, when rose
The Hunter and the Crone ; and smiling on me—
Yes, the enlarged but noble aspect of
The Hunter smiled upon me—I should say,
His lips, for his eyes moved not—and the woman's
Thin lips relaxed to something like a smile.
Both rose, and the crowned figures on each hand
Rose also, as if aping their chief shades—
Mere mimics even in death—but I sate still :
A desperate courage crept through every limb,   140
And at the last I feared them not, but laughed
Full in their phantom faces. But then—then
The Hunter laid his hand on mine : I took it,
And grasped it—but it melted from my own ;
While he too vanished, and left nothing but
The memory of a hero, for he looked so.

Myr. And was : the ancestor of heroes, too,
And thine no less.

Sar.   Aye, Myrrha, but the woman,
The female who remained, she flew upon me,
And burnt my lips up with her noisome kisses ;   150
And, flinging down the goblets on each hand,
Methought their poisons flowed around us, till
Each formed a hideous river. Still she clung ;
The other phantoms, like a row of statues,
Stood dull as in our temples, but she still
Embraced me, while I shrunk from her, as if,
In lieu of her remote descendant, I
Had been the son who slew her for her incest.[1]

1. [For the story of Semiramis and Ninya, see *Justinus Hist.*, lib. i.
cap. ii.]

Then—then—a chaos of all loathsome things
Thronged thick and shapeless : I was dead, yet feeling—
Buried, and raised again—consumed by worms,   161
Purged by the flames, and withered in the air !
I can fix nothing further of my thoughts,
Save that I longed for thee, and sought for thee,
In all these agonies,—and woke and found thee.
   Myr. So shalt thou find me ever at thy side,
Here and hereafter, if the last may be.
But think not of these things—the mere creations
Of late events, acting upon a frame
Unused by toil, yet over-wrought by toil—   170
Such as might try the sternest.
   Sar.   I am better.
Now that I see thee once more, *what was seen*
Seems nothing.

Enter SALEMENES.

   Sal.   Is the king so soon awake ?
   Sar. Yes, brother, and I would I had not slept ;
For all the predecessors of our line
Rose up, methought, to drag me down to them.
My father was amongst them, too ; but he,
I know not why, kept from me, leaving me
Between the hunter-founder of our race,
And her, the homicide and husband-killer,   180
Whom you call glorious.
   Sal.   So I term you also,
Now you have shown a spirit like to hers.
By day-break I propose that we set forth,
And charge once more the rebel crew, who still
Keep gathering head, repulsed, but not quite quelled.
   Sar. How wears the night ?
   Sal.   There yet remain some hours
Of darkness : use them for your further rest.
   Sar. No, not to-night, if 'tis not gone : methought
I passed hours in that vision.
   Myr.   Scarcely one ;
I watched by you : it was a heavy hour,   190
But an hour only.

Sar.   Let us then hold council ;
To-morrow we set forth.
    Sal.   But ere that time,
I had a grace to seek.
    Sar.   'Tis granted.
    Sal.   Hear it
Ere you reply too readily ; and 'tis
For *your* ear only.
    Myr.   Prince, I take my leave.
                         [*Exit* MYRRHA.
    Sal. That slave deserves her freedom.
    Sar.   Freedom only !
That slave deserves to share a throne.
    Sal.   Your patience—
'Tis not yet vacant, and 'tis of its partner
I come to speak with you.
    Sar.   How ! of the Queen ?
    Sal. Even so. I judged it fitting for their safety, 200
That, ere the dawn, she sets forth with her children
For Paphlagonia, where our kinsman Cotta [1]
Governs ; and there, at all events, secure
My nephews and your sons their lives, and with them
Their just pretensions to the crown in case——
    Sar. I perish—as is probable : well thought—
Let them set forth with a sure escort.
    Sal.   That
Is all provided, and the galley ready
To drop down the Euphrates ; but ere they
Depart, will you not see——
    Sar.   My sons ? It may 210
Unman my heart, and the poor boys will weep ;
And what can I reply to comfort them,
Save with some hollow hopes, and ill-worn smiles ?
You know I cannot feign.
    Sal.   But you can feel !
At least, I trust so : in a word, the Queen
Requests to see you ere you part—for ever.
    Sar. Unto what end ? what purpose ? I will grant
Aught—all that she can ask—but such a meeting.

    1. [See Diod. Siculi *Bibl. Hist.*, lib. ii. 80 c. Cotta was not a kins-
man, but a loyal tributary.]

Sal. You know, or ought to know, enough of women,
Since you have studied them so steadily,[i]   220
That what they ask in aught that touches on
The heart, is dearer to their feelings or
Their fancy, than the whole external world.
I think as you do of my sister's wish;
But 'twas her wish—she is my sister—you
Her husband—will you grant it?
   Sar.   'Twill be useless:
But let her come.
   Sal.   I go.   [*Exit* SALEMENES.
   Sar.   We have lived asunder
Too long to meet again—and *now* to meet!
Have I not cares enow, and pangs enow,
To bear alone, that we must mingle sorrows,   230
Who have ceased to mingle love?

Re-enter SALEMENES *and* ZARINA.

   Sal.   My sister! Courage:
Shame not our blood with trembling, but remember
From whence we sprung. The Queen is present, Sire.
   Zar. I pray thee, brother, leave me.
   Sal.   Since you ask it.
                       [*Exit* SALEMENES.
   Zar. Alone with him! How many a year has passed,[1]
Though we are still so young, since we have met,
Which I have worn in widowhood of heart.
He loved me not: yet he seems little changed—
Changed to me only—would the change were mutual!
He speaks not—scarce regards me—not a word,   240
Nor look—yet he *was* soft of voice and aspect,
Indifferent, not austere. My Lord!

i. The MS. inserts—

    (*But I speak only of such as are virtuous.*)

   1. [Byron must often have pictured to himself an unexpected meeting
with his wife. In certain moods he would write letters to her which
were never sent, or never reached her hands. The scene between
Sardanapalus and Zarina reflects the sentiments contained in one such
letter, dated November 17, 1821, which Moore printed in his *Life*,
pp. 581, 582. See *Letters*, 1901, v. 479.]

Sar.   Zarina !
Zar. No, *not* Zarina—do not say Zarina.
That tone—That word—annihilate long years,
And things which make them longer.
   Sar.   'Tis too late
To think of these past dreams. Let's not reproach—
That is, reproach me not—for the *last* time——
   Zar. And *first.* I ne'er reproached you.
   Sar.   'Tis most true ;
And that reproof comes heavier on my heart
Than——But our hearts are not in our own power. 250
   Zar. Nor hands ; but I gave both.
   Sar.   Your brother said
It was your will to see me, ere you went
From Nineveh with——(*He hesitates.*)
   Zar.   Our children : it is true.
I wish to thank you that you have not divided
My heart from all that 's left it now to love—
Those who are yours and mine, who look like you,
And look upon me as you looked upon me
Once——but *they* have not changed.
   Sar.   Nor ever will.
I fain would have them dutiful.
   Zar.   I cherish
Those infants, not alone from the blind love   260
Of a fond mother, but as a fond woman.
They are now the only tie between us.
   Sar.   Deem not
I have not done you justice : rather make them
Resemble your own line than their own Sire.
I trust them with you—to you : fit them for
A throne, or, if that be denied——You have heard
Of this night's tumults ?
   Zar.   I had half forgotten,
And could have welcomed any grief save yours,
Which gave me to behold your face again.
   Sar. The throne—I say it not in fear—but 'tis   270
In peril : they perhaps may never mount it ;
But let them not for this lose sight of it.
I will dare all things to bequeath it them ;
But if I fail, then they must win it back

Bravely—and, won, wear it wisely, not as I [l]
Have wasted down my royalty.
  Zar.   They ne'er
Shall know from me of aught but what may honour
Their father's memory.
  Sar.   Rather let them hear
The truth from you than from a trampling world.
If they be in adversity, they'll learn   280
Too soon the scorn of crowds for crownless Princes,
And find that all their father's sins are theirs.
My boys!—I could have borne it were I childless.
  Zar. Oh! do not say so—do not poison all
My peace left, by unwishing that thou wert
A father. If thou conquerest, they shall reign,
And honour him who saved the realm for them,
So little cared for as his own; and if——
  Sar. 'Tis lost, all Earth will cry out, " thank your
   father ! "
And they will swell the echo with a curse. 290
  Zar. That they shall never do; but rather honour
The name of him, who, dying like a king,
In his last hours did more for his own memory
Than many monarchs in a length of days,
Which date the flight of time, but make no annals.
  Sar. Our annals draw perchance unto their close ;
But at the least, whate'er the past, their end
Shall be like their beginning—memorable.
  Zar. Yet, be not rash—be careful of your life,
Live but for those who love.
  Sar.   And who are they ? 300
A slave, who loves from passion—I'll not say
Ambition—she has seen thrones shake, and loves ;
A few friends who have revelled till we are
As one, for they are nothing if I fall ;
A brother I have injured—children whom
I have neglected, and a spouse——
  Zar.   Who loves.
  Sar. And pardons?
  Zar.   I have never thought of this,
And cannot pardon till I have condemned.

  l. *Bravely and won wear wisely—not as I.*—[*MS. M. erased.*]

Sar. My wife!

Zar.   Now blessings on thee for that word!
I never thought to hear it more—from thee.   310

Sar. Oh! thou wilt hear it from my subjects.   Yes—
These slaves whom I have nurtured, pampered, fed,
And swoln with peace, and gorged with plenty, till
They reign themselves—all monarchs in their mansions—
Now swarm forth in rebellion, and demand
His death, who made their lives a jubilee;
While the few upon whom I have no claim
Are faithful!   This is true, yet monstrous.

Zar.   'Tis
Perhaps too natural; for benefits
Turn poison in bad minds.

Sar.   And good ones make   320
Good out of evil.   Happier than the bee,
Which hives not but from wholesome flowers.

Zar.   Then reap
The honey, nor inquire whence 'tis derived.
Be satisfied—you are not all abandoned.

Sar. My life insures me that.   How long, bethink you,
Were not I yet a king, should I be mortal;
That is, where mortals *are*, not where they must be?

Zar. I know not.   But yet live for my—that is,
Your children's sake!

Sar.   My gentle, wronged Zarina!
I am the very slave of Circumstance
And Impulse—borne away with every breath!   330
Misplaced upon the throne—misplaced in life.
I know not what I could have been, but feel
I am not what I should be—let it end.
But take this with thee: if I was not formed
To prize a love like thine, a mind like thine,
Nor dote even on thy beauty—as I've doted
On lesser charms, for no cause save that such
Devotion was a duty, and I hated.
All that looked like a chain for me or others   340
(This even Rebellion must avouch); yet hear
These words, perhaps among my last—that none
E'er valued more thy virtues, though he knew not
To profit by them—as the miner lights

Upon a vein of virgin ore, discovering
That which avails him nothing : he hath found it,
But 'tis not his—but some superior's, who
Placed him to dig, but not divide the wealth
Which sparkles at his feet; nor dare he lift
Nor poise it, but must grovel on, upturning   350
The sullen earth.

  Zar.   Oh ! if thou hast at length
Discovered that my love is worth esteem,
I ask no more—but let us hence together,
And *I*—let me say *we*—shall yet be happy.
Assyria is not all the earth—we'll find
A world out of our own—and be more blessed
Than I have ever been, or thou, with all
An empire to indulge thee.

Enter SALEMENES.

  Sal.   I must part ye—
The moments, which must not be lost, are passing.

  Zar. Inhuman brother ! wilt thou thus weigh out 360
Instants so high and blest?

  Sal.   Blest !

  Zar.   He hath been
So gentle with me, that I cannot think
Of quitting.

  Sal. So—this feminine farewell
Ends as such partings end, in *no* departure.
I thought as much, and yielded against all
My better bodings. But it must not be.

  Zar. Not be?

  Sal.   Remain, and perish——

  Zar.   With my husband——

  Sal. And children.

  Zar.   Alas !

  Sal.   Hear me, sister, like
My sister :—all 's prepared to make your safety
Certain, and of the boys too, our last hopes ;   370
'Tis not a single question of mere feeling,
Though that were much—but 'tis a point of state :
The rebels would do more to seize upon

The offspring of their sovereign, and so crush——
    Zar. Ah! do not name it.
    Sal.   Well, then, mark me: when
They are safe beyond the Median's grasp, the rebels
Have missed their chief aim—the extinction of
The line of Nimrod. Though the present King
Fall, his sons live—for victory and vengeance.
    Zar. But could not I remain, alone?
    Sal.   What! leave 380
Your children, with two parents and yet orphans—
In a strange land—so young, so distant?
    Zar.   No—
My heart will break.
    Sal.   Now you know all—decide.
    Sar. Zarina, he hath spoken well, and we
Must yield awhile to this necessity.
Remaining here, you may lose all; departing,
You save the better part of what is left,
To both of us, and to such loyal hearts
As yet beat in these kingdoms.
    Sal.   The time presses.
    Sar. Go, then. If e'er we meet again, perhaps   390
I may be worthier of you—and, if not,
Remember that my faults, though not atoned for,
Are *ended.* Yet, I dread thy nature will
Grieve more above the blighted name and ashes
Which once were mightiest in Assyria—than——
But I grow womanish again, and must not;
I must learn sternness now. My sins have all
Been of the softer order——*hide* thy tears—
I do not bid thee *not* to shed them—'twere
Easier to stop Euphrates at its source   400
Than one tear of a true and tender heart—
But let me not behold them; they unman me
Here when I had remanned myself. My brother,
Lead her away.
    Zar.   Oh, God! I never shall
Behold him more!
    Sal. (*striving to conduct her*). Nay, sister, I *must* be
        obeyed.
    Zar. I must remain—away! you shall not hold me.

What, shall he die alone?—*I* live alone?
  Sal. He shall *not die alone;* but lonely you
Have lived for years.
    Zar.   That's false! I knew *he* lived,
And lived upon his image—let me go!   410
  Sal. (conducting her off the stage). Nay, then, I must
       use some fraternal force,
Which you will pardon.
    Zar.   Never. Help me! Oh!
Sardanapalus, wilt thou thus behold me
Torn from thee?
    Sal.   Nay—then all is lost again,
If that this moment is not gained.
    Zar.   My brain turns—
My eyes fail—where is he?   [*She faints.*
  Sar. (advancing).   No—set her down;
She's dead—and you have slain her.
    Sal.   'Tis the mere
Faintness of o'erwrought passion: in the air
She will recover. Pray, keep back.—[*Aside.*] I must
Avail myself of this sole moment to   420
Bear her to where her children are embarked,
I' the royal galley on the river.
                [SALEMENES *bears her off.*
    Sar. (solus).   This, too—
And this too must I suffer—I, who never
Inflicted purposely on human hearts
A voluntary pang! But that is false—
She loved me, and I loved her.—Fatal passion!
Why dost thou not expire at *once* in hearts
Which thou hast lighted up at once? Zarina![L]
I must pay dearly for the desolation
Now brought upon thee. Had I never loved   430
But thee, I should have been an unopposed
Monarch of honouring nations. To what gulfs
A single deviation from the track
Of human duties leads even those who claim
The homage of mankind as their born due,
And find it, till they forfeit it themselves!

---

   i. *Which thou hast lighted up at once? but leavest*
     One to grieve o'er the other's change—Zarina.—[MS. M. *erased.*]

Enter MYRRHA.

Sar.   You here!   Who called you?

Myr.   No one—but I heard
Far off a voice of wail and lamentation,
And thought——

   Sar.   It forms no portion of your duties
To enter here till sought for.

   Myr.   Though I might,   440
Perhaps, recall some softer words of yours
(Although they *too were chiding*), which reproved me,
Because I ever dreaded to intrude ;
Resisting my own wish and your injunction
To heed no time nor presence, but approach you
Uncalled for :—I retire.

   Sar.   Yet stay—being here.
I pray you pardon me : events have soured me
Till I wax peevish—heed it not : I shall
Soon be myself again.

   Myr.   I wait with patience,
What I shall see with pleasure.

   Sar.   Scarce a moment   450
Before your entrance in this hall, Zarina,
Queen of Assyria, departed hence.

   Myr. Ah!

   Sar.   Wherefore do you start?

   Myr.   Did I do so?

   Sar. 'Twas well you entered by another portal,
Else you had met.   That pang at least is spared her !

   Myr. I know to feel for her.

   Sar.   That is too much,
And beyond nature—'tis nor mutual [i.]
Nor possible.   You cannot pity her,
Nor she aught but——

   Myr.   Despise the favourite slave?
Not more than I have ever scorned myself.   460

   Sar. Scorned ! what, to be the envy of your sex,
And lord it o'er the heart of the World's lord?

   Myr. Were you the lord of twice ten thousand worlds—
As you are like to lose the one you swayed—

i. —— *natural.*—[*MS. M.*   The first edition reads "mutual."]

I did abase myself as much in being
Your paramour, as though you were a peasant—
Nay, more, if that the peasant were a Greek.
   Sar. You talk it well——
   Myr.   And truly.
   Sar.   In the hour
Of man's adversity all things grow daring
Against the falling ; but as I am not   470
Quite fall'n, nor now disposed to bear reproaches,
Perhaps because I merit them too often,
Let us then part while peace is still between us.
   Myr. Part !
   Sar.   Have not all past human beings parted,
And must not all the present one day part ?
   Myr. Why ?
   Sar.   For your safety, which I will have looked to,
With a strong escort to your native land ;
And such gifts, as, if you had not been all
A Queen, shall make your dowry worth a kingdom.
   Myr. I pray you talk not thus.
   Sar.   The Queen is gone:
You need not shame to follow.   I would fall   481
Alone—I seek no partners but in pleasure.
   Myr. And I no pleasure but in parting not.
You shall not force me from you.
   Sar.   Think well of it—
It soon may be too late.
   Myr.   So let it be ;
For then you cannot separate me from you.
   Sar. And will not ; but I thought you wished it.
   Myr.   I !
   Sar. You spoke of your abasement.
   Myr.   And I feel it
Deeply—more deeply than all things but love.
   Sar. Then fly from it.
   Myr.   'Twill not recall the past—
'Twill not restore my honour, nor my heart.   491
No—here I stand or fall.   If that you conquer,
I live to joy in your great triumph : should
Your lot be different, I'll not weep, but share it.
You did not doubt me a few hours ago.

Sar. Your courage never—nor your love till now;
And none could make me doubt it save yourself.
Those words——
    Myr.   Were words.   I pray you, let the proofs
Be in the past acts you were pleased to praise
This very night, and in my further bearing,   500
Beside, wherever you are borne by fate.
    Sar. I am content: and, trusting in my cause,
Think we may yet be victors and return
To peace—the only victory I covet.
To me war is no glory—conquest no
Renown.   To be forced thus to uphold my right
Sits heavier on my heart than all the wrongs ^{i.}
These men would bow me down with.   Never, never
Can I forget this night, even should I live
To add it to the memory of others.   510
I thought to have made mine inoffensive rule
An era of sweet peace 'midst bloody annals,
A green spot amidst desert centuries,
On which the Future would turn back and smile,
And cultivate, or sigh when it could not
Recall Sardanapalus' golden reign.
I thought to have made my realm a paradise,
And every moon an epoch of new pleasures.
I took the rabble's shouts for love—the breath
Of friends for truth—the lips of woman for   520
My only guerdon—so they are, my Myrrha:
                              [*He kisses her.*
Kiss me.   Now let them take my realm and life!
They shall have both, but never *thee!*
    Myr.   No, never!
Man may despoil his brother man of all
That 's great or glittering—kingdoms fall, hosts yield,
Friends fail—slaves fly—and all betray—and, more
Than all, the most indebted—but a heart
That loves without self-love!   'Tis here—now prove it.

i. *Is heavier sorrow than the wrong which.*—[*MS. M. erased.*]

Enter SALEMENES.

Sal. I sought you—How ! *she* here again ?
 Sar.   Return not
Now to reproof: methinks your aspect speaks 530
Of higher matter than a woman's presence.
 Sal. The only woman whom it much imports me
At such a moment now is safe in absence—
The Queen 's embarked.
 Sar.   And well ? say that much.
 Sal.   Yes.
Her transient weakness has passed o'er ; at least,
It settled into tearless silence : her
Pale face and glittering eye, after a glance
Upon her sleeping children, were still fixed
Upon the palace towers as the swift galley
Stole down the hurrying stream beneath the starlight ;
But she said nothing.
 Sar.   Would I felt no more 541
Than she has said !
 Sal.   'Tis now too late to feel.
Your feelings cannot cancel a sole pang :
To change them, my advices bring sure tidings
That the rebellious Medes and Chaldees, marshalled
By their two leaders, are already up
In arms again ; and, serrying their ranks,
Prepare to attack : they have apparently
Been joined by other Satraps.
 Sar.   What ! more rebels ?
Let us be first, then.
 Sal.   That were hardly prudent 550
Now, though it was our first intention. If
By noon to-morrow we are joined by those
I've sent for by sure messengers, we shall be
In strength enough to venture an attack,
Aye, and pursuit too ; but, till then, my voice
Is to await the onset.
 Sar.   I detest
That waiting ; though it seems so safe to fight
Behind high walls, and hurl down foes into
Deep fosses, or behold them sprawl on spikes

Strewed to receive them, still I like it not—   560
My soul seems lukewarm; but when I set on them,
Though they were piled on mountains, I would have
A pluck at them, or perish in hot blood!—
Let me then charge.
  Sal.   You talk like a young soldier.
 Sar. I am no soldier, but a man: speak not
Of soldiership, I loathe the word, and those
Who pride themselves upon it; but direct me
Where I may pour upon them.
  Sal.   You must spare
To expose your life too hastily; 'tis not
Like mine or any other subject's breath: 570
The whole war turns upon it—with it; this
Alone creates it, kindles, and may quench it—
Prolong it—end it.
  Sar.   Then let us end both!
'Twere better thus, perhaps, than prolong either;
I'm sick of one, perchance of both.
        [*A trumpet sounds without.*
  Sal.   Hark!
  Sar.   Let us
Reply, not listen.
  Sal.   And your wound!
  Sar.   'Tis bound—
'Tis healed—I had forgotten it.   Away!
A leech's lancet would have scratched me deeper;[i.]
The slave that gave it might be well ashamed
To have struck so weakly.
  Sal.   Now, may none this hour
Strike with a better aim!
  Sar.   Aye, if we conquer;   581
But if not, they will only leave to me
A task they might have spared their king.   Upon them!
        [*Trumpet sounds again.*
  Sal. I am with you.
  Sar.   Ho, my arms! again, my arms!
        [*Exeunt.*

  i. *A leech's lancet would have done as much.*—[*MS. M. erased.*]

ACT V.

SCENE I.—*The same Hall in the Palace.*

MYRRHA *and* BALEA.

Myr. (at a window).[1] The day at last has broken.
    What a night
Hath ushered it !   How beautiful in heaven !
Though varied with a transitory storm,
More beautiful in that variety !
How hideous upon earth ! where Peace and Hope,
And Love and Revel, in an hour were trampled
By human passions to a human chaos,
Not yet resolved to separate elements—
'Tis warring still !   And can the sun so rise,
So bright, so rolling back the clouds into   10
Vapours more lovely than the unclouded sky,
With golden pinnacles, and snowy mountains,
And billows purpler than the Ocean's, making
In heaven a glorious mockery of the earth,
So like we almost deem it permanent ;
So fleeting, we can scarcely call it aught

---

1. [Myrrha's apostrophe to the sunrise may be compared with the famous waking vision of the "Solitary" in the Second Book of the *Excursion* (*Works of Wordsworth*, 1889, p. 439)—

> "The appearance, instantaneously disclosed,
> Was of a mighty city—boldly say
> A wilderness of building, sinking far
> And self-withdrawn into a boundless depth,
> Far sinking into splendour—without end !
> Fabric it seemed of diamond and of gold,
> With alabaster domes, and silver spires,
> And blazing terrace upon terrace, high
> Uplifted."

But the difference, even in form, between the two passages is more remarkable than the resemblance, and the interpretation, the moral of Byron's vision is distinct from, if not alien to, Wordsworth's.   The "Solitary" sees all heaven opened ; the revealed abode of spirits in beatitude—a refuge and a redemption from "this low world of care ;" while Myrrha drinks in "enough of heaven," a medicament of "Sorrow and of Love," for the invigoration of "the common, heavy, human hours" of mortal existence.   For a charge of "imitation," see *Works of Lord Byron*, 1832, xiii. 172, *note* 1.   See, too, *Poetical Works, etc.*, 1891, p. 271, *note* 2.]

Beyond a vision, 'tis so transiently
Scattered along the eternal vault : and yet
It dwells upon the soul, and soothes the soul,
And blends itself into the soul, until   20
Sunrise and sunset form the haunted epoch
Of Sorrow and of Love ; which they who mark not,
Know not the realms where those twin genii [i.]
(Who chasten and who purify our hearts,
So that we would not change their sweet rebukes
For all the boisterous joys that ever shook
The air with clamour) build the palaces
Where their fond votaries repose and breathe
Briefly ;—but in that brief cool calm inhale
Enough of heaven to enable them to bear   30
The rest of common, heavy, human hours,
And dream them through in placid sufferance,
Though seemingly employed like all the rest
Of toiling breathers in allotted tasks [ii.]
Of pain or pleasure, *two* names for *one* feeling,
Which our internal, restless agony
Would vary in the sound, although the sense
Escapes our highest efforts to be happy.
 Bal. You muse right calmly : and can you so watch
The sunrise which may be our last?
 Myr.   It is   40
Therefore that I so watch it, and reproach
Those eyes, which never may behold it more,
For having looked upon it oft, too oft,
Without the reverence and the rapture due
To that which keeps all earth from being as fragile
As I am in this form.   Come, look upon it,
The Chaldee's God, which, when I gaze upon,
I grow almost a convert to your Baal.
 Bal. As now he reigns in heaven, so once on earth
He swayed.
 Myr. He sways it now far more, then ; never

i. *Sunrise and sunset form the epoch of*
 Sorrow and love ; and they who mark them not
 { *Are fit for neither of those*
 { *Can ne'er hold converse with these two.*—[*MS. M. erased.*]
ii. *Of labouring wretches in allotted tasks.*—[*MS. M. erased.*]

Had earthly monarch half the power and glory   51
Which centres in a single ray of his.

   Bal. Surely he is a God !

   Myr.   So we Greeks deem too ;
And yet I sometimes think that gorgeous orb
Must rather be the abode of Gods than one
Of the immortal sovereigns.   Now he breaks
Through all the clouds, and fills my eyes with light
That shuts the world out.   I can look no more.

   Bal. Hark ! heard you not a sound ?

   Myr.   No, 'twas mere fancy ;
They battle it beyond the wall, and not   60
As in late midnight conflict in the very
Chambers : the palace has become a fortress
Since that insidious hour ; and here, within
The very centre, girded by vast courts
And regal halls of pyramid proportions,
Which must be carried one by one before
They penetrate to where they then arrived,
We are as much shut in even from the sound
Of peril as from glory.

   Bal.   But they reached
Thus far before.

   Myr.   Yes, by surprise, and were   70
Beat back by valour : now at once we have
Courage and vigilance to guard us.

   Bal.   May they
Prosper !

   Myr.   That is the prayer of many, and
The dread of more : it is an anxious hour ;
I strive to keep it from my thoughts.   Alas !
How vainly !

   Bal.   It is said the King's demeanour
In the late action scarcely more appalled
The rebels than astonished his true subjects.

   Myr. 'Tis easy to astonish or appal
The vulgar mass which moulds a horde of slaves ;   80
But he did bravely.

   Bal.   Slew he not Beleses ?
I heard the soldiers say he struck him down.

   Myr. The wretch was overthrown, but rescued to

Triumph, perhaps, o'er one who vanquished him
In fight, as he had spared him in his peril;
And by that heedless pity risked a crown.
   Bal.   Hark !
   Myr. You are right; some steps approach, but slowly.

Enter Soldiers, bearing in SALEMENES *wounded, with a
broken javelin in his side : they seat him upon one
of the couches which furnish the Apartment.*

   Myr. Oh, Jove !
   Bal.   Then all is over.
   Sal.   That is false.
Hew down the slave who says so, if a soldier.
   Myr. Spare him—he's none : a mere court butterfly,
That flutter in the pageant of a monarch.   91
   Sal. Let him live on, then.
   Myr.   So wilt thou, I trust.
   Sal. I fain would live this hour out, and the event,
But doubt it.   Wherefore did ye bear me here ?
   Sol. By the King's order. When the javelin struck
    you,
You fell and fainted : 'twas his strict command
To bear you to this hall.
   Sal.   'Twas not ill done :
For seeming slain in that cold dizzy trance,
The sight might shake our soldiers—but—'tis vain,
I feel it ebbing !
   Myr.   Let me see the wound ;   100
I am not quite skilless : in my native land
'Tis part of our instruction. War being constant,
We are nerved to look on such things.[i.]
   Sol.   Best extract
The javelin.
   Myr.   Hold ! no, no, it cannot be.
   Sal. I am sped, then !
   Myr.   With the blood that fast must follow
The extracted weapon, I do fear thy life.
   Sal. And I *not* death. Where was the King when you
Conveyed me from the spot where I was stricken ?

---

   i. *We are used to such inflictions.*—[*MS. M. erased.*]

Sol. Upon the same ground, and encouraging
With voice and gesture the dispirited troops   110
Who had seen you fall, and faltered back.
    Sal.   Whom heard ye
Named next to the command?
    Sol.   I did not hear.
    Sal. Fly, then, and tell him, 'twas my last request
That Zames take my post until the junction,
So hoped for, yet delayed, of Ofratanes,
Satrap of Susa.   Leave me here : our troops
Are not so numerous as to spare your absence.
    Sol. But Prince——
    Sal.   Hence, I say !   Here 's a courtier and
A woman, the best chamber company.
As you would not permit me to expire   120
Upon the field, I'll have no idle soldiers
About my sick couch.   Hence ! and do my bidding !
                      [*Exeunt the Soldiers.*

    Myr. Gallant and glorious Spirit ! must the earth
So soon resign thee ?
    Sal.   Gentle Myrrha, 'tis
The end I would have chosen, had I saved
The monarch or the monarchy by this ;
As 'tis, I have not outlived them.
    Myr.   You wax paler.
    Sal. Your hand ; this broken weapon but prolongs
My pangs, without sustaining life enough
To make me useful : I would draw it forth   130
And my life with it, could I but hear how
The fight goes.

Enter SARDANAPALUS *and Soldiers.*

    Sar.   My best brother !
    Sal.   And the battle
Is lost ?
    Sar. (*despondingly*). You see *me here.*
    Sal.   I'd rather see you *thus !*
        [*He draws out the weapon from the wound, and dies.*
    Sar. And *thus* I will be seen ; unless the succour,
The last frail reed of our beleagured hopes,

Arrive with Ofratanes.

   Myr.   Did you not
Receive a token from your dying brother,
Appointing Zames chief?

   Sar.   I did.

   Myr.   Where 's Zames?

   Sar. Dead.

   Myr.   And Altada?

   Sar.   Dying.

   Myr.   Pania?   Sfero?

   Sar. Pania yet lives; but Sfero's fled or captive.   140
I am alone.

   Myr.   And is all lost?

   Sar.   Our walls,
Though thinly manned, may still hold out against
Their present force, or aught save treachery :
But i' the field——

   Myr.   I thought 'twas the intent
Of Salemenes not to risk a sally
Till ye were strengthened by the expected succours.

   Sar. I over-ruled him.

   Myr.   Well, the *fault* 's a brave one.

   Sar. But fatal. Oh, my brother! I would give
These realms, of which thou wert the ornament,
The sword and shield, the sole-redeeming honour,   150
To call back——But I will not weep for thee ;
Thou shalt be mourned for as thou wouldst be mourned.
It grieves me most that thou couldst quit this life
Believing that I could survive what thou
Hast died for—our long royalty of race.
If I redeem it, I will give thee blood
Of thousands, tears of millions, for atonement,
(The tears of all the good are thine already).
If not, we meet again soon,—if the spirit
Within us lives beyond :—thou readest mine,   160
And dost me justice now. Let me once clasp
That yet warm hand, and fold that throbless heart
                  [*Embraces the body.*
To this which beats so bitterly. Now, bear
The body hence.

   Sol.   Where?

Sar.   To my proper chamber.
Place it beneath my canopy, as·though
The King lay there : when this is done, we will
Speak further of the rites due to such ashes.

       [*Exeunt Soldiers with the body of* SALEMENES.

Enter PANIA.

   Sar. Well, Pania ! have you placed the guards, and
     issued
The orders fixed on ?
   Pan.   Sire, I have obeyed.
   Sar. And do the soldiers keep their hearts up ?
   Pan.   Sire ?
   Sar. I am answered ! When a king asks twice, and
     has   171
A question as an answer to *his* question,
It is a portent. What ! they are disheartened ?
   Pan. The death of Salemenes, and the shouts
Of the exulting rebels on his fall,
Have made them——
   Sar.   *Rage*—not droop—it should have been.
We'll find the means to rouse them.
   Pan.   Such a loss
Might sadden even a victory.
   Sar.   Alas !
Who can so feel it as I feel ? but yet,
Though cooped within these walls, they are strong, and we
Have those without will break their way through hosts, 181
To make their sovereign's dwelling what it was—
A palace, not a prison—nor a fortress.

Enter an Officer, hastily.

   Sar. Thy face seems ominous. Speak !
   Offi.   I dare not.
   Sar.   Dare not ?
While millions dare revolt with sword in hand !
That 's strange. I pray thee break that loyal silence
Which loathes to shock its sovereign ; we can hear
Worse than thou hast to tell.
   Pan.   Proceed—thou hearest.

Offi. The wall which skirted near the river's brink
Is thrown down by the sudden inundation   190
Of the Euphrates, which now rolling, swoln
From the enormous mountains where it rises,
By the late rains of that tempestuous region,
O'erfloods its banks, and hath destroyed the bulwark.

Pan. That's a black augury! it has been said
For ages, "That the City ne'er should yield
"To man, until the River grew its foe."

Sar. I can forgive the omen, not the ravage.
How much is swept down of the wall?

Offi.   About
Some twenty stadia.[1]

Sar.   And all this is left   200
Pervious to the assailants?

Offi.   For the present
The River's fury must impede the assault;
But when he shrinks into his wonted channel,
And may be crossed by the accustomed barks,
The palace is their own.

Sar.   That shall be never.
Though men, and gods, and elements, and omens,
Have risen up 'gainst one who ne'er provoked them,
My father's house shall never be a cave
For wolves to horde and howl in.

Pan.   With your sanction,
I will proceed to the spot, and take such measures.   210
For the assurance of the vacant space
As time and means permit.

Sar.   About it straight,
And bring me back, as speedily as full
And fair investigation may permit,
Report of the true state of this irruption
Of waters.   [*Exeunt* PANIA *and the Officer*

Myr.   Thus the very waves rise up
Against you.

Sar.   They are not my subjects, girl,
And may be pardoned, since they can't be punished.

Myr. I joy to see this portent shakes you not.

Sar. I am past the fear of portents: they can tell me

          1. About two miles and a half.

Nothing I have not told myself since midnight :　　221
Despair anticipates such things.
　　Myr.　　　　　　　　　　Despair !
　　Sar. No ; not despair precisely. When we know
All that can come, and how to meet it, our
Resolves, if firm, may merit a more noble
Word than this is to give it utterance.
But what are words to us ? we have well nigh done
With them and all things.
　　Myr.　　　　　　Save *one deed*—the last
And greatest to all mortals ; crowning act
Of all that was, or is, or is to be—　　　　　　230
The only thing common to all mankind,
So different in their births, tongues, sexes, natures,
Hues, features, climes, times, feelings, intellects,[i.]
Without one point of union save in this—
To which we tend, for which we're born, and thread
The labyrinth of mystery, called life.
　　Sar. Our clue being well nigh wound out, let's be
　　　　cheerful.
They who have nothing more to fear may well
Indulge a smile at that which once appalled ;
As children at discovered bugbears.

Re-enter PANIA.

　　Pan.　　　　　　　　　　'Tis　　　240
As was reported : I have ordered there
A double guard, withdrawing from the wall,
Where it was strongest, the required addition
To watch the breach occasioned by the waters.
　　Sar. You have done your duty faithfully, and as
My worthy Pania ! further ties between us
Draw near a close—I pray you take this key :
　　　　　　　　　　　　　　[*Gives a key.*

It opens to a secret chamber, placed
Behind the couch in my own chamber—(Now
Pressed by a nobler weight than e'er it bore—　　250
Though a long line of sovereigns have lain down
Along its golden frame—as bearing for

　　i. *Complexions, climes, æras, and intellects.*—[*MS. M. erased.*]

A time what late was Salemenes.)—Search
The secret covert to which this will lead you;
'Tis full of treasure; [1] take it for yourself
And your companions : [i.] there's enough to load ye,
Though ye be many.   Let the slaves be freed, too;
And all the inmates of the palace, of
Whatever sex, now quit it in an hour.
Thence launch the regal barks, once formed for pleasure,
And now to serve for safety, and embark.   261
The river 's broad and swoln, and uncommanded,
(More potent than a king) by these besiegers.
Fly ! and be happy !

Pan.   Under your protection !
So you accompany your faithful guard.

Sar. No, Pania ! that must not be ; get thee hence,
And leave me to my fate.

Pan.   'Tis the first time
I ever disobeyed : but now——

Sar.   So all men
Dare beard me now, and Insolence within
Apes Treason from without.   Question no further ;   270
'Tis my command, my last command.   Wilt *thou*
Oppose it ? *thou !*

Pan.   But yet—not yet.

Sar.   Well, then,
Swear that you will obey when I shall give
The signal.

Pan.   With a heavy but true heart,
I promise.

Sar.   'Tis enough.   Now order here
Faggots, pine-nuts, and withered leaves, and such
Things as catch fire and blaze with one sole spark ;
Bring cedar, too, and precious drugs, and spices,
And mighty planks, to nourish a tall pile ;
Bring frankincense and myrrh, too, for it is   280
For a great sacrifice I build the pyre !

---

i.   *Ye will find the crevice*
   To which the key fits, with a little care.—[*MS. M. erased.*]

1. [Athenæus represents the treasures which Sardanapalus placed in
the chamber erected on his funeral pile as amounting to a thousand
myriads of talents of gold, and ten times as many talents of silver.]

And heap them round yon throne.
 Pan.   My Lord !
 Sar.   I have said it,
And *you* have sworn.
 Pan.   And could keep my faith
Without a vow.   [*Exit* PANIA.
 Myr.   What mean you?
 Sar.   You shall know
Anon—what the whole earth shall ne'er forget.

    PANIA, *returning with a Herald.*

 Pan. My King, in going forth upon my duty,
This herald has been brought before me, craving
An audience.
 Sar.   Let him speak.
 Her.   The *King* Arbaces——
 Sar. What, crowned already?—But, proceed.
 Her.   Beleses,
The anointed High-priest——
 Sar.   Of what god or demon?
With new kings rise new altars. But, proceed; 291
You are sent to prate your master's will, and not
Reply to mine.
 Her.   And Satrap Ofratanes——
 Sar. Why, *he* is *ours.*
 Her. (*showing a ring*). Be sure that he is now
In the camp of the conquerors; behold
His signet ring.
 Sar.   'Tis his. A worthy triad !
Poor Salemenes ! thou hast died in time
To see one treachery the less : this man
Was thy true friend and my most trusted subject.
Proceed.
 Her. They offer thee thy life, and freedom 300
Of choice to single out a residence
In any of the further provinces,
Guarded and watched, but not confined in person,
Where thou shalt pass thy days in peace ; but on
Condition that the three young princes are
Given up as hostages.

Sar. (*ironically*).   The generous Victors !

Her. I wait the answer.

Sar.   Answer, slave !   How long
Have slaves decided on the doom of kings?

Her. Since they were free.

Sar.   Mouthpiece of mutiny !
Thou at the least shalt learn the penalty   310
Of treason, though its proxy only.   Pania !
Let his head be thrown from our walls within
The rebels' lines, his carcass down the river.
Away with him !   [PANIA *and the Guards seizing him.*

Pan.   I never yet obeyed
Your orders with more pleasure than the present.
Hence with him, soldiers ! do not soil this hall
Of royalty with treasonable gore ;
Put him to rest without.

Her.   A single word :
My office, King, is sacred.

Sar.   And what 's *mine ?*
That thou shouldst come and dare to ask of me   320
To lay it down?

Her.   I but obeyed my orders,
At the same peril if refused, as now
Incurred by my obedience.

Sar.   So there are
New monarchs of an hour's growth as despotic
As sovereigns swathed in purple, and enthroned
From birth to manhood !

Her.   My life waits your breath.
Yours (I speak humbly)—but it may be—yours
May also be in danger scarce less imminent :
Would it then suit the last hours of a line
Such as that of Nimrod, to destroy   330
A peaceful herald, unarmed, in his office ;
And violate not only all that man
Holds sacred between man and man—but that
More holy tie which links us with the Gods ?

Sar. He 's right.—Let him go free.—My life's last act
Shall not be one of wrath.   Here, fellow, take
          [*Gives him a golden cup from a table near.*
This golden goblet, let it hold your wine,

And think of *me;* or melt it into ingots,
And think of nothing but their weight and value.

 Her. I thank you doubly for my life, and this 340
Most gorgeous gift, which renders it more precious.
But must I bear no answer?

 Sar.   Yes,—I ask
An hour's truce to consider.

 Her.   But an hour's?

 Sar. An hour's: if at the expiration of
That time your masters hear no further from me,
They are to deem that I reject their terms,
And act befittingly.

 Her.   I shall not fail
To be a faithful legate of your pleasure.

 Sar. And hark! a word more.

 Her.   I shall not forget it,
Whate'er it be.

 Sar.   Commend me to Beleses; 350
And tell him, ere a year expire, I summon
Him hence to meet me.

 Her.   Where?

 Sar.   At Babylon.
At least from thence he will depart to meet me.

 Her. I shall obey you to the letter. [*Exit Herald.*

 Sar.   Pania!—
Now, my good Pania!—quick—with what I ordered.

 Pan. My Lord,—the soldiers are already charged.
And see! they enter.

  Soldiers enter, and form a Pile about the Throne, etc.[1]

 Sar.   Higher, my good soldiers,
And thicker yet; and see that the foundation

---

 1. ["Then the king caused a huge pile of wood to be made in the palace court, and heaped together upon it all his gold, silver, and royal apparel, and enclosing his eunuchs and concubines in an apartment within the pile, caused it to be set on fire, and burned himself and them together."—Diod. Siculi *Bibl. Hist.*, lib. ii. cap. 81A.

 "And he also erected on the funeral pile a chamber 100 feet long, made of wood, and in it he had couches spread, and there he himself lay down with his wife, and his concubines lay on other couches around. . . . And he made the roof of the apartment of large stout

Be such as will not speedily exhaust
Its own too subtle flame; nor yet be quenched   360
With aught officious aid would bring to quell it.
Let the throne form the *core* of it; I would not
Leave that, save fraught with fire unquenchable,
To the new comers.   Frame the whole as if
'Twere to enkindle the strong tower of our
Inveterate enemies.   Now it bears an aspect!
How say you, Pania, will this pile suffice
For a King's obsequies?

 Pan.   Aye, for a kingdom's.
I understand you, now.

 Sar.   And blame me?

 Pan.   No—
Let me but fire the pile, and share it with you.   370

 Myr. That *duty* 's mine.

 Pan.   A woman's!

 Myr.   'Tis the soldier's
Part to die *for* his sovereign, and why not
The woman's with her lover?

 Pan.   'Tis most strange!

 Myr. But not so rare, my Pania, as thou think'st it.
In the mean time, live thou.—Farewell! the pile
Is ready.

beams, and there all the walls of it he made of numerous thick planks,
so that it was impossible to escape out of it. . . . And . . . he bade
the slaves set fire to the pile; and it was fifteen days burning.   And
those who saw the smoke wondered, and thought that he was cele-
brating a great sacrifice, but the eunuchs alone knew what was really
being done.   And in this way Sardanapalus, who had spent his life in
extraordinary luxury, died with as much magnanimity as possible."—
Athenæus, *Deipnosophistæ*, bk. xii. cap. 38.

 See *Abydenus apud Eusebium*, Præp. Ev. 9. 41. 4; Euseb., *Chron.*,
1878, p. 42, ed. A. Schoene.

 Saracus was the last king of Assyria, and being invaded by
Cyaxares and a faithless general Nabopolassar . . . "unable to resist
them, took counsel of despair, and after all means of resistance were
exhausted, burned himself in his palace."

 "The self-immolation of Saracus has a parallel in the conduct of the
Israelitish king Zimri, who, 'when he saw that the city was taken,
went into the palace of the king's house, and burnt the king's house
over him, and died' (1 Kings xvi. 18); and again in that of the Persian
governor Boges, who burnt himself with his wives and children at Eion
(Herod., vii. 107)."—*The Five Great Monarchies, etc.*, by Rev. G.
Rawlinson, 1871, ii. 232, *note* 4.]

Pan.   I should shame to leave my sovereign
With but a single female to partake
His death.
      Sar.   Too many far have heralded
Me to the dust already.   Get thee hence ;
Enrich thee.
      Pan.   And live wretched !
      Sar.   Think upon   380
Thy vow :—'tis sacred and irrevocable.
      Pan. Since it is so, farewell.
      Sar.   Search well my chamber,
Feel no remorse at bearing off the gold ;
Remember, what you leave you leave the slaves
Who slew me : and when you have borne away
All safe off to your boats, blow one long blast
Upon the trumpet as you quit the palace.
The river's brink is too remote, its stream
Too loud at present to permit the echo
To reach distinctly from its banks.   Then fly,—   390
And as you sail, turn back ; but still keep on
Your way along the Euphrates : if you reach
The land of Paphlagonia, where the Queen
Is safe with my three sons in Cotta's court,
Say what you *saw* at parting, and request
That she remember what I *said* at one
Parting more mournful still.
      Pan.   That royal hand !
Let me then once more press it to my lips ;
And these poor soldiers who throng round you, and
Would fain die with you !
      [*The Soldiers and* PANIA *throng round him, kissing
          his hand and the hem of his robe.*
      Sar.   My best ! my last friends ! 400
Let 's not unman each other : part at once :
All farewells should be sudden, when for ever,
Else they make an eternity of moments,
And clog the last sad sands of life with tears.
Hence, and be happy : trust me, I am not
Now to be pitied ; or far more for what
Is past than present ;—for the future, 'tis
In the hands of the deities, if such

There be : I shall know soon.   Farewell—Farewell.

      [*Exeunt* PANIA *and Soldiers.*

 Myr. These men were honest : it is comfort still 410
That our last looks should be on loving faces.

 Sar. And *lovely* ones, my beautiful !—but hear me !
If at this moment,—for we now are on
The brink,—thou feel'st an inward shrinking from
This leap through flame into the future, say it :
I shall not love thee less ; nay, perhaps more,
For yielding to thy nature : and there 's time
Yet for thee to escape hence.

 Myr.   Shall I light
One of the torches which lie heaped beneath
The ever-burning lamp that burns without, 420
Before Baal's shrine, in the adjoining hall ?

 Sar. Do so.   Is that thy answer ?

 Myr.   Thou shalt see.

      [*Exit* MYRRHA.

 Sar. (solus). She 's firm.   My fathers ! whom I will
  rejoin,
It may be, purified by death from some
Of the gross stains of too material being,
I would not leave your ancient first abode
To the defilement of usurping bondmen ;
If I have not kept your inheritance
As ye bequeathed it, this bright part of it,
Your treasure—your abode—your sacred relics 430
Of arms, and records—monuments, and spoils,
In which *they* would have revelled, I bear with me
To you in that absorbing element,
Which most personifies the soul as leaving
The least of matter unconsumed before
Its fiery workings :—and the light of this
Most royal of funereal pyres shall be [i.]
Not a mere pillar formed of cloud and flame,
A beacon in the horizon for a day,
And then a mount of ashes—but a light [ii.] 440
To lesson ages, rebel nations, and
Voluptuous princes.   Time shall quench full many

  i. *Funeral* ——.—[*MS. M.*]
  ii. *And strew the earth with ashes* ——.—[*MS. M. erased.*]

A people's records, and a hero's acts;
Sweep empire after empire, like this first
Of empires, into nothing; but even then
Shall spare this deed of mine, and hold it up
A problem few dare imitate, and none
Despise—but, it may be, avoid the life
Which led to such a consummation.

MYRRHA *returns with a lighted Torch in one Hand, and*
a Cup in the other.

   Myr.   Lo!
I've lit the lamp which lights us to the stars.   450
   Sar. And the cup?
   Myr.   'Tis my country's custom to
Make a libation to the Gods.
   Sar.   And mine
To make libations amongst men.   I've not
Forgot the custom; and although alone,
Will drain one draught in memory of many
A joyous banquet past.
      [SARDANAPALUS *takes the cup, and after drinking*
           and tinkling the reversed cup, as a drop falls,
           exclaims—
                  And this libation
Is for the excellent Beleses.
   Myr.   Why
Dwells thy mind rather upon that man's name
Than on his mate's in villany?
   Sar.   The other
Is a mere soldier, a mere tool, a kind   460
Of human sword in a friend's hand; the other
Is master-mover of his warlike puppet;
But I dismiss them from my mind.—Yet pause,
My Myrrha! dost thou truly follow me,
Freely and fearlessly?
   Myr.   And dost thou think
A Greek girl dare not do for love, that which
An Indian widow braves for custom? [i.]

     i.   —— *And what is there*
       An Indian widow dares for custom which
       A Greek girl ——.—[*MS. M. erased.*]

Sar.   Then
We but await the signal.
　Myr.   It is long
In sounding.
　Sar.   Now, farewell; one last embrace.
　Myr. Embrace, but *not* the last; there is one more. 470
Sar. True, the commingling fire will mix our ashes.
　Myr. And pure as is my love to thee, shall they,
Purged from the dross of earth, and earthly passion,
Mix pale with thine.   A single thought yet irks me.
　Sar. Say it.
　Myr.   It is that no kind hand will gather
The dust of both into one urn.
　Sar.   The better:
Rather let them be borne abroad upon
The winds of heaven, and scattered into air,
Than be polluted more by human hands
Of slaves and traitors.   In this blazing palace,   480
And its enormous walls of reeking ruin,
We leave a nobler monument than Egypt
Hath piled in her brick mountains, o'er dead kings,[1]
Or *kine*—for none know whether those proud piles
Be for their monarch, or their ox-god Apis:
So much for monuments that have forgotten
Their very record!
　Myr.   Then farewell, thou earth!
And loveliest spot of earth! farewell, Ionia!
Be thou still free and beautiful, and far
Aloof from desolation!   My last prayer   490
Was for thee, my last thoughts, save *one*, were of thee!
　Sar. And that?
　Myr.   Is yours.
                          [*The trumpet of* PANIA *sounds without.*

1. [Bishop Heber (*Quarterly Review*, July, 1821, vol. xxvii. p. 503)
takes exception to these lines on the ground that they "involve an
anachronism, inasmuch as, whatever date be assigned to the erection
of the earlier pyramids, there can be no reason for apprehending that,
at the fall of Nineveh, and while the kingdom and hierarchy of Egypt
subsisted in their full splendour, the destination of those immense
fabrics could have been a matter of doubt. . . . Herodotus, three
hundred years later, may have been misinformed on these points," etc.,
etc.   According to modern Egyptology, the erection of the "earlier
pyramids" was an event of remotest antiquity when the Assyrian
Empire was in its infancy.]

Sar.   Hark !
Myr.   *Now !*
Sar.   Adieu, Assyria !
I loved thee well, my own, my fathers' land,
And better as my country than my kingdom.
I sated thee with peace and joys ; and this
Is my reward ! and now I owe thee nothing,
Not even a grave.   [*He mounts the pile.*
                        Now, Myrrha !
Myr.   Art thou ready ?
Sar. As the torch in thy grasp.
                                [MYRRHA *fires the pile.*
                                      'Tis fired ! I come.
Myr.
      [*As* MYRRHA *springs forward to throw herself into
            the flames, the Curtain falls.*[1]

1.   End of Act fifth.—B.
                                                  Ravenne.
                                            May 27th 1821.

Mem.—I began the drama on the 13th of January, 1821, and continued the two first acts very slowly and at long intervals. The three
last acts were written since the 13th of May, 1821 (this present month,
that is to say in a fortnight).

THE TWO FOSCARI:[1]

AN HISTORICAL TRAGEDY.[2]

"The *father* softens, but the *governor's* resolved."—*Critic.*[3]

1. [The MS. of *The Two Foscari* is now in the possession of H.R.H. the Princess of Wales.]

2. [Begun June the 12th, completed July the 9th, Ravenna, 1821.—*Byron MS.*]

3. [*Gov.* "*The father softens—but the governor is fixed.*"
Dingle. "Aye that antithesis of persons is a most established figure."
—*Critic*, act ii. sc. 2.

Byron may have guessed that this passage would be quoted against him, and, by taking it as a motto, hoped to anticipate or disarm ridicule; or he may have selected it out of bravado, as though, forsooth, the public were too stupid to find him out.]

[*The Two Foscari* was produced at Drury Lane Theatre April 7, and again on April 18 and April 25, 1838. Macready played " Frances Foscari," Mr. Anderson " Jacopo Foscari," and Miss Helen Faucit " Marina."

According to the *Times*, April 9, 1838, " Miss Faucit's Marina, the most energetic part of the whole, was clever, and showed a careful attention to the points which might be made."

Macready notes in his diary, April 7, 1838 (*Reminiscences*, 1875, ii. 106): " Acted Foscari very well. Was very warmly received ... was called for at the end of the tragedy, and received by the whole house standing up and waving hand-kerchiefs with great enthusiasm. Dickens, Forster, Procter, Browning, Talfourd, all came into my room."]

INTRODUCTION TO *THE TWO FOSCARI*.

THE *Two Foscari* was begun on June 12, and finished, within the month, on July 9, 1821. Byron was still in the vein of the historic drama, though less concerned with "ancient chroniclers" and original "authorities" (*vide ante*, Preface to *Marino Faliero*, vol. iv. p. 332) than heretofore. "The Venetian play," he tells Murray, July 14, 1821, is "rigidly historical;" but he seems to have depended for his facts, not on Sanudo or Navagero, but on Daru's *Histoire de la République de Venise* (1821, ii. 520–537), and on Sismondi's *Histoire des Républiques . . . du Moyen Âge* (1815, x. 36–46). The story of the Two Doges, so far as it concerns the characters and action of Byron's play, may be briefly re-told. It will be found to differ in some important particulars from the extracts from Daru and Sismondi which Byron printed in his "Appendix to the *Two Foscari*" (*Sardanapalus, etc.*, 1821, pp. 305–324), and no less from a passage in Smedley's *Sketches from Venetian History* (1832, ii. 93–105), which was substituted for the French "Pièces justificatives," in the collected edition of 1832–1835, xiii. 198–202, and the octavo edition of 1837, etc., pp. 790, 791.

Francesco, son of Nicolò Foscari, was born in 1373. He was nominated a member of the Council of Ten in 1399, and, after holding various offices of state, elected Doge in 1423. His dukedom, the longest on record, lasted till 1457. He was married, in 1395, to Maria, daughter of Andrea Priuli, and, *en secondes noces*, to Maria, or Marina, daughter of Bartolommeo Nani. By his two wives he was the father of ten children—five sons and five daughters. Of the five sons, four died of the plague, and the fifth, Jacopo, lived to be the cause, if not the hero, of a tragedy.

The younger of the "Two Foscari" was a man of some cultivation, a collector and student of Greek manuscripts, well-mannered, and of ready wit, a child and lover of Venice, but indifferent to her ideals and regardless of her prejudices and restrictions. He seems to have begun life in a blaze of popularity, the admired of all admirers. His wedding with Lucrezia Contarini (January, 1441) was celebrated with a novel and peculiar splendour. Gorgeous youths, Companions of the Hose (*della calza*), in jackets of crimson velvet, with slashed sleeves lined with squirrel fur, preceded and followed the bridegroom's train. A hundred bridesmaids accompanied the bride. Her dowry exceeded 16,000 ducats, and her jewels, which included a necklace worn by a Queen of Cyprus, were " rich and rare." And the maiden herself was a pearl of great price. " She behaved," writes her brother, " and does behave, so well beyond what could have been looked for. I believe she is inspired by God ! "

Jacopo had everything which fortune could bestow, but he lacked a capacity for right conduct. Four years after his marriage (February 17, 1445) an accusation was laid before the Ten (Romanin, *Storia*, *etc.*, iv. 266) that, contrary to the law embodied in the Ducal *Promissione*, he had accepted gifts of jewels and money, not only from his fellow-citizens, but from his country's bitterest enemy, Filippo Visconti, Duke of Milan. Jacopo fled to Trieste, and in his absence the Ten, supported by a giunta of ten, on their own authority and independently of the Doge, sentenced him to perpetual banishment at Nauplia, in Roumania. One of the three *Capi di' dieci* was Ermolao (or *Veneticè* Almoro) Donato, of whom more hereafter. It is to be noted that this sentence was never carried into effect. At the end of four months, thanks to the intervention of five members of the Ten, he was removed from Trieste to Treviso, and, two years later (September 13, 1447), out of consideration to the Doge, who pleaded that the exile of his only son prevented him from giving his whole heart and soul to the Republic, permitted to return to Venice. So ends the first chapter of Jacopo's misadventures. He stands charged with unlawful, if not criminal, appropriation of gifts and moneys He had been punished, but less than he deserved, and, for his father's sake, the sentence of exile had been altogether remitted.

Three years went by, and once again, January, 1451, a charge was preferred against Jacopo Foscari, and on this occasion he was arrested and brought before the Ten. He was accused of being implicated in the murder of Ermolao Donato, who was assassinated November 5, 1450, on leaving the Ducal Palace, where he had been attending the Council of the Pregadi. On the morning after the murder Benedetto Gritti, one of the " avvogadori di Commun," was at Mestre, some five miles from Venice, and, happening to accost a servant of Jacopo's who was loading a barge with wood, asked for the latest news from Venice, and got as answer, " Donato has been murdered ! " The possession of the news some hours before it had been made public, and the fact that the newsmonger had been haunting the purlieus of the Ducal Palace on the previous afternoon, enabled the Ten to convict Jacopo. They alleged (Decree of X., March 26, 1451) that other evidence ("*testificationes et scripturæ*") was in their possession, and they pointed to the prisoner's obstinate silence on the rack—a silence unbroken save by "several incantations and magic words which fell from him," as a confirmation of his guilt. Moreover, it was "for the advantage of the State from many points of view" that convicted and condemned he should be. The question of his innocence or guilt (complicated by the report or tradition that one Nicolò Erizzo confessed on his death-bed that he had assassinated Donato for reasons of his own) is still under discussion. Berlan (*I due Foscari*, etc., 1852, p. 36) sums up against him. It may, however, be urged in favour of Jacopo that the Ten did not produce or quote the *scripturæ et testificationes* which convinced them of his guilt; that they stopped short of the death-penalty, and pronounced a sentence inadequate to the crime ; and, lastly, that not many years before they had taken into consideration the possibility and advisability of poisoning Filippo Visconti, an event which would, no doubt, have been "to the advantage of the State from many points of view."

Innocent or guilty, he was sentenced to perpetual banishment to the city of Candia, on the north coast of the island of Crete ; and, guilty or innocent, Jacopo was not the man to make the best of what remained to him and submit to fate. Intrigue he must, and, five years later (June, 1456), a report reached Venice that papers had been found in his possession, some relating to the Duke of Milan, calculated to excite "nuovi scandali e disordini," and others in cypher, which the Ten could not read. Over and above these papers there was direct evidence that Jacopo had written to the *Imperatore dei Turchi*, imploring him to send his galley and take him away from Candia. Here was a fresh instance of treachery to the Republic, and, July 21, 1456, Jacopo returned to Venice under the custody of Lorenzo Loredano.

According to Romanin (*Storia*, etc., iv. 284), he was not put to the torture, but confessed his guilt spontaneously, pleading, by way of excuse, that the letter to the Duke of Milan had been allowed to fall into the hands of spies, with a view to his being recalled to Venice and obtaining a glimpse of his parents and family, even at a risk of a fresh trial. On the other hand, the *Dolfin Cronaca*, the work of a kinsman of the Foscari, which records Jacopo's fruitless appeal to the sorrowful but inexorable Doge, and other incidents of a personal nature, testifies, if not to torture on

the rack, "to mutilation by thirty strokes of the lash." Be
that as it may, he was once more condemned to lifelong
exile, with the additional penalty that he should be imprisoned for a year. He sailed from Venice July 31, 1456, and
died at Candia, January 12, 1457. Jacopo's misconduct
and consequent misfortune overshadowed the splendour of
his father's reign, and, in very truth "brought his gray hairs
with sorrow to the grave."

After his son's death, the aged Doge, now in his eighty-
fifth year, retired to his own apartments, and refused to
preside at Councils of State. The Ten, who in 1446 had
yielded to the Doge's plea that a father fretting for an exiled
son could not discharge his public duties, were instant that
he should abdicate the dukedom on the score of decrepitude.
Accounts differ as to the mode in which he received the
sentence of deposition. It is certain that he was compelled
to abdicate on Sunday morning, October 23, 1457, but was
allowed a breathing-space of a few days to make his arrange-
ments for quitting the Ducal Palace.

On Monday, October 24, the Great Council met to elect his
successor, and sat with closed doors till Sunday, October 30.

On Thursday, October 27, Francesco, heedless of a suggestion that he should avoid the crowd, descended the Giants'
Staircase for the last time, and, says the *Dolfin Cronaca*,
"after crossing the courtyard, went out by the door leading
to the prisons, and entered his boat by the Ponte di Paglia."
"He was dressed," says another chronicle (*August. Cod.* 1,
cl. vii.), "in a scarlet mantle, from which the fur lining had
been taken," surmounted by a scarlet hood, an old friend
which he had worn when his ducal honours were new, and
which he had entrusted to his wife's care to be preserved for
"red" days and festivals of State. "In his hand he held
his staff, as he walked very slowly. His brother Marco was
by his side, behind him were cousins and grandsons . . .
and in this way he went to his own house."

On Sunday, October 30, Pasquale Malipiero was declared
Doge, and two days after, All Saints' Day, at the first hour
of the morning, Francesco Foscari died. If the interval
between ten o'clock on Sunday night and one o'clock on
Tuesday morning disproves the legend that the discrowned
Doge ruptured a blood-vessel at the moment when the bell
was tolling for the election of his successor, the truth remains
that, old as he was, he died of a broken heart.

His predecessor, Tomaso Mocenigo, had prophesied on
his death-bed that if the Venetians were to make Foscari
Doge they would forfeit their "gold and silver, their honour
and renown." "From your position of lords," said he, "you

will sink to that of vassals and servants to men of arms."
The prophecy was fulfilled. "If we look," writes Mr. H. F.
Brown (*Venice, etc.,* 1893, p. 306), "at the sum-total of
Foscari's reign . . . we find that the Republic had increased
her land territory by the addition of two great provinces,
Bergamo and Brescia . . . But the price had been enormous
. . . her debt rose from 6,000,000 to 13,000,000 ducats.
Venetian funds fell to 18½. . . . Externally there was much
pomp and splendour. . . . But underneath this bravery there
lurked the official corruption of the nobles, the suspicion of
the Ten, the first signs of bank failures, the increase in the
national debt, the fall in the value of the funds. Land
wars and landed possessions drew the Venetians from the
sea to *terra ferma.* . . . The beginning of the end had
arrived." (See *Two Doges of Venice,* by Alethea Wiel, 1891 ;
I due Foscari, Memorie Storicho Critiche, di Francesco
Berlan, 1852 ; *Storia Documentata di Venezia,* di S. Romanin,
1855, vol. iv. ; *Die beiden Foscari,* von Richard Senger, 1878.
For reviews, etc., of *The Two Foscari, vide ante,* "Introduction to *Sardanapalus,*" p. 5.)

Both Jeffrey in the *Edinburgh,* and Heber in the *Quarterly
Review,* took exception to the character of Jacopo Foscari,
in accordance with the Horatian maxim, "Incredulus odi."
"If," said Jeffrey, "he had been presented to the audience
wearing out his heart in exile, . . . we might have caught
some glimpse of the nature of his motives." As it is (in
obedience to the "unities ") "we first meet with him led from
the 'Question,' and afterwards . . . clinging to the dungeon
walls of his native city, and expiring from his dread of
leaving them." The situation lacks conviction.

"If," argued Heber, "there ever existed in nature a case
so extraordinary as that of a man who gravely preferred
tortures and a dungeon at home, to a temporary residence
in a beautiful island and a fine climate ; it is what few can
be made to believe, and still fewer to sympathize with."

It was, no doubt, with reference to these criticisms that
Byron told Medwin (*Conversations,* 1824, p. 173) that it was
no invention of his that the "young Foscari should have a
sickly affection for his native city. . . . I painted the men as
I found them, as they were—not as the critics would have
them. . . . But no painting, however highly coloured, can
give an idea of the intensity of a Venetian's affection for his
native city."

Goethe, on the other hand, was "not careful" to note
these inconsistencies and perplexities. He thought that the
dramatic handling of *The Two Foscari* was "worthy of great
praise," was "admirable !" (*Conversations with Goethe*
1874, p. 265).

DRAMATIS PERSONÆ.

MEN.

FRANCIS FOSCARI, *Doge of Venice.*

JACOPO FOSCARI, *Son of the Doge.*

JAMES LOREDANO, *a Patrician.*

MARCO MEMMO, *a Chief of the Forty.*

BARBARIGO, *a Senator.*

Other Senators, The Council of Ten, Guards, Attendants, etc., etc.

WOMAN.

MARINA, *Wife of young* FOSCARI.

SCENE—The Ducal Palace, Venice.

THE TWO FOSCARI.

ACT I.

SCENE I.—*A Hall in the Ducal Palace.*

Enter LOREDANO *and* BARBARIGO, *meeting.*

Lor. WHERE is the prisoner?
Bar.   Reposing from
The Question.
Lor.   The hour's past—fixed yesterday
For the resumption of his trial.—Let us
Rejoin our colleagues in the council, and
Urge his recall.
Bar.   Nay, let him profit by
A few brief minutes for his tortured limbs;
He was o'erwrought by the Question yesterday,
And may die under it if now repeated.[i] [1]

i. —— *too soon repeated.*—[*MS. erased.*]

1. [It is a moot point whether Jacopo Foscari was placed on the rack on the occasion of his third trial. The original document of the X. (July 23, 1456) runs thus : "Si videtur vobis per ea quæ dicta et lecta sunt, quod *procedatur* contra Ser Jacobum Foscari ; " and it is argued (see F. Berlan, *I due Foscari, etc.*, 1852, p. 57), (1) that the word *procedatur* is not a euphemism for "tortured," but should be rendered "judgment be given against ; " (2) that if the X. had decreed torture, torture would have been expressly enjoined ; and (3) that as the decrees of the Council were not divulged, there was no motive for ambiguity. S. Romanin (*Storia Documentata, etc.*, 1853, iv. 284) and R. Senger (*Die beiden Foscari*, 1878, p. 116) take the same view. On the other hand, Miss A. Wiel (*Two Doges of Venice*, 1891, p. 107) points out that, according to the *Dolfin Cronaca*, which Berlan did not consult, Jacopo was in a "mutilated" condition when the trial was over, and he was permitted to take a last farewell of his wife and

Lor. Well?

Bar.   I yield not to you in love of justice,
Or hate of the ambitious Foscari,   10
Father and son, and all their noxious race;
But the poor wretch has suffered beyond Nature's
Most stoical endurance.

Lor.   Without owning
His crime?

Bar.   Perhaps without committing any.
But he avowed the letter to the Duke
Of Milan, and his sufferings half atone for
Such weakness

Lor.   We shall see.

Bar.   You, Loredano,
Pursue hereditary hate too far.

Lor. How far?

Bar.   To extermination.

Lor.   When they are
Extinct, you may say this.—Let 's in to council.   20

Bar. Yet pause—the number of our colleagues is not
Complete yet; two are wanting ere we can
Proceed.

Lor.   And the chief judge, the Doge?

Bar.   No—he,
With more than Roman fortitude, is ever
First at the board in this unhappy process
Against his last and only son.[1]

Lor.   True—true—
His *last.*

children in Torricella. Goethe (*Conversations*, 1874, pp. 264, 265) did
not share Eckermann's astonishment that Byron "could dwell so long
on this torturing subject." "He was always a self-tormentor, and
hence such subjects were his darling theme."]

1. [It is extremely improbable that Francesco Foscari was present in
person at the third or two preceding trials of his son. As may be
gathered from the *parte* of the Council of Ten relating to the first trial,
there was a law which prescribed the contrary : " In ipsius Domini
Ducis præsentiâ de rebus ad ipsum, vel ad filios suos tangentibus non
tractetur, loquatur vel consulatur, sicut non potest (*fieri*) quando tracta-
tur de rebus tangentibus ad attinentes Domini Ducis." The fact that
" Nos Franciscus Foscari," etc., stood at the commencement of the
decree of exile may have given rise to the tradition that the Doge, like a
Roman father, tried and condemned his son. (See Berlan's *I due
Foscari*, p. 13.)]

Bar.   Will nothing move you?

Lor.   *Feels he*, think you?

Bar. He shows it not.

Lor.   I have marked *that*—the wretch!

Bar. But yesterday, I hear, on his return
To the ducal chambers, as he passed the threshold   30
The old man fainted.

Lor.   It begins to work, then.

Bar. The work is half your own.

Lor.   And should be *all* mine—
My father and my uncle are no more.

Bar. I have read their epitaph, which says they died
By poison.[1]

Lor.   When the Doge declared that he
Should never deem himself a sovereign till
The death of Peter Loredano, both
The brothers sickened shortly:—he *is* Sovereign.

Bar. A wretched one.

Lor.   What should they be who make
Orphans?

Bar.   But *did* the Doge make you so?

Lor.   Yes.   40

Bar. What solid proofs?

Lor.   When Princes set themselves
To work in secret, proofs and process are

---

1. [Pietro Loredano, admiral of the Venetian fleet, died November
11, 1438. His death was sudden and suspicious, for he was taken with
violent pains and spasms after presiding at a banquet in honour of his
victories over the Milanese; and, when his illness ended fatally it was
remembered that the Doge had publicly declared that so long as the
admiral lived he would never be *de facto* Prince of the Republic.
Jacopo Loredano chose to put his own interpretation on this outburst
of impatience, and inscribed on his father's monument in the Church
of the Monastery of Sant' Elena, in the Isola della Santa Lena, the
words, " Per insidias hostium veneno sublatus." (See *Ecclesiæ Venetæ*,
by Flaminio Cornaro, 1749, ix. 193, 194 ; see, too, Cicogna's *Inscri-
zioni Veneziane*, 1830, iii. 381.)
Not long afterwards Marco Loredano, the admiral's brother, met
with a somewhat similar fate. He had been despatched by the X. to
Legnano, to investigate the conduct of Andrea Donato, the Doge's
brother-in-law, who was suspected of having embezzled the public
moneys. His report was unfavourable to Donato, and, shortly after,
he too fell sick and died. It is most improbable that the Doge was
directly or indirectly responsible for the death of either brother ; but
there was an hereditary feud, and the libellous epitaph was a move in
the game.]

Alike made difficult; but I have such
Of the first, as shall make the second needless.
 Bar. But you will move by law?
 Lor.   By all the laws
Which he would leave us.
 Bar.   They are such in this
Our state as render retribution easier
Than 'mongst remoter nations. Is it true
That you have written in your books of commerce,
(The wealthy practice of our highest nobles)   50
" Doge Foscari, my debtor for the deaths
Of Marco and Pietro Loredano,
My sire and uncle?"[1]
 Lor.   It is written thus.
 Bar. And will you leave it unerased?
 Lor.   Till balanced.
 Bar. And how?
   [*Two Senators pass over the stage, as in their way to*
    " the Hall of the Council of Ten."
 Lor.   You see the number is complete.
Follow me.   [*Exit* LOREDANO.
 Bar. (*solus*). Follow *thee!* I have followed long
Thy path of desolation, as the wave
Sweeps after that before it, alike whelming[i.]
The wreck that creaks to the wild winds, and wretch
Who shrieks within its riven ribs, as gush   60
The waters through them; but this son and sire
Might move the elements to pause, and yet
Must I on hardily like them—Oh! would
I could as blindly and remorselessly!—
Lo, where he comes!—Be still, my heart! they are
Thy foes, must be thy victims: wilt thou beat
For those who almost broke thee?

    i. —— *checked by nought*
     The vessel that creaks ——.—[*MS. M. erased.*]

 1. [Daru gives Palazzi's *Fasti Ducales* and *L'Histoire Vénitienne* of
Vianolo as his authorities for this story.]

Enter Guards, with young FOSCARI *as Prisoner, etc.*

Guard.   Let him rest.
Signor, take time.
   Jac. Fos.   I thank thee, friend, I'm feeble;
But thou mayst stand reproved.
   Guard.   I'll stand the hazard.
   Jac. Fos. That's kind:—I meet some pity, but no
     mercy; [i.]   70
This is the first.
   Guard.   And might be the last, did they
Who rule behold us.
   Bar. (advancing to the Guard). There is one who does :
Yet fear not; I will neither be thy judge
Nor thy accuser; though the hour is past,
Wait their last summons—I am of " the Ten," [1]
And waiting for that summons, sanction you
Even by my presence : when the last call sounds,
We'll in together.—Look well to the prisoner !
   Jac. Fos. What voice is that?—'Tis Barbarigo's ! Ah !
Our House's foe, and one of my few judges.   80
   Bar. To balance such a foe, if such there be,
Thy father sits amongst thy judges.
   Jac. Fos.   True,
He judges.
   Bar.   Then deem not the laws too harsh
Which yield so much indulgence to a sire,
As to allow his voice in such high matter
As the state's safety——
   Jac. Fos.   And his son's.   I'm faint;
Let me approach, I pray you, for a breath
Of air, yon window which o'erlooks the waters.

---

i. —— *much pity.—[MS. M. erased.]*

   1. [" This whole episode in the private life of the Foscari family is
valuable chiefly for the light it throws upon the internal history of
Venice.   We are clearly in an atmosphere unknown before.   The
Council of Ten is all-powerful ; it even usurps functions which do not
belong to it by the constitution.   The air is charged with plots, suspicion, assassination, denunciation, spies,—all the paraphernalia which
went to confirm the popular legend as to the terrible nature of the
Dieci."—*Venice, etc.,* by Horatio F. Brown, 1893, p. 305.]

Enter an Officer, who whispers BARBARIGO.

Bar. (*to the Guard*). Let him approach.   I must not
    speak with him
Further than thus: I have transgressed my duty   90
In this brief parley, and must now redeem it [i.]
Within the Council Chamber.   [*Exit* BARBARIGO.
    [*Guard conducting* JACOPO FOSCARI *to the window.*
    Guard.   There, sir, 'tis
Open.—How feel you?
    Jac. Fos.   Like a boy—Oh Venice !
    Guard. And your limbs?
    Jac. Fos.   Limbs ! how often have they borne me [1]
Bounding o'er yon blue tide, as I have skimmed
The gondola along in childish race,
And, masqued as a young gondolier, amidst
My gay competitors, noble as I,
Raced for our pleasure, in the pride of strength ;
While the fair populace of crowding beauties,   100
Plebeian as patrician, cheered us on
With dazzling smiles, and wishes audible,
And waving kerchiefs, and applauding hands,
Even to the goal !—How many a time have I
Cloven with arm still lustier, breast more daring,
The wave all roughened ; with a swimmer's stroke
Flinging the billows back from my drenched hair,
And laughing from my lip the audacious brine,
Which kissed it like a wine-cup, rising o'er
The waves as they arose, and prouder still   110
The loftier they uplifted me ; and oft,
In wantonness of spirit, plunging down
Into their green and glassy gulfs, and making
My way to shells and sea-weed, all unseen
By those above, till they waxed fearful ; then

---

i. *In this brief colloquy, and must redeem it.*—[*MS. M.*]

1. [Compare—
       "And I have loved thee, Ocean ! and my joy
         Of youthful sports was on thy breast to be
         Borne, like thy bubbles, onward : from a boy
       I wantoned with thy breakers."
           Childe Harold, Canto IV. stanza clxxxiv. lines 1-4,
              Poetical Works, 1899, ii. 461, *note* 2.]

Returning with my grasp full of such tokens
As showed that I had searched the deep: exulting,
With a far-dashing stroke, and, drawing deep
The long-suspended breath, again I spurned
The foam which broke around me, and pursued   120
My track like a sea-bird.—I was a boy then.

Guard. Be a man now: there never was more need
Of manhood's strength.

Jac. Fos. (looking from the lattice). My beautiful, my
          own,
My only Venice—*this is breath!* Thy breeze,
Thine Adrian sea-breeze, how it fans my face!
Thy very winds feel native to my veins,
And cool them into calmness! How unlike
The hot gales of the horrid Cyclades,
Which howled about my Candiote dungeon,[1] and
Made my heart sick.

Guard.   I see the colour comes   130
Back to your cheek: Heaven send you strength to bear
What more may be imposed!—I dread to think on't.

Jac. Fos. They will not banish me again?—No—no,
Let them wring on; I am strong yet.

Guard.   Confess,
And the rack will be spared you.

Jac. Fos.   I confessed
Once—twice before: both times they exiled me.

Guard. And the third time will slay you.

Jac. Fos.   Let them do so,
So I be buried in my birth-place: better
Be ashes here than aught that lives elsewhere.

Guard. And can you so much love the soil which
          hates you?   140

Jac. Fos. The soil!—Oh no, it is the seed of the soil
Which persecutes me: but my native earth
Will take me as a mother to her arms.
I ask no more than a Venetian grave,
A dungeon, what they will, so it be here.

---

1. [The climate of Crete is genial and healthy; but the town of
Candia is exposed to winds from the north and north-west. Ulysses
was driven into Crete by a northerly wind (*Od.* xix. 186), and St. Paul
(Acts xxvii. 14) was driven by the same wind from the coast of Crete to
Clauda.]

Enter an Officer.

Offi. Bring in the prisoner!
Guard.   Signor, you hear the order.
Jac. Fos. Aye, I am used to such a summons; 'tis
The third time they have tortured me :—then lend me
Thine arm.   [*To the Guard.*
    Offi.   Take mine, sir; 'tis my duty to
Be nearest to your person.
    Jac. Fos.   You!—you are he   150
Who yesterday presided o'er my pangs—
Away!—I'll walk alone.
    Offi.   As you please, Signor;
The sentence was not of my signing, but
I dared not disobey the Council when
They——
    Jac. Fos. Bade thee stretch me on their horrid engine.
I pray thee touch me not—that is, just now;
The time will come they will renew that order,
But keep off from me till 'tis issued.   As
I look upon thy hands my curdling limbs
Quiver with the anticipated wrenching,   160
And the cold drops strain through my brow, as if——
But onward—I have borne it—I can bear it.—
How looks my father?
    Offi.   With his wonted aspect.
    Jac. Fos. So does the earth, and sky, the blue of
            Ocean,
The brightness of our city, and her domes,
The mirth of her Piazza—even now
Its merry hum of nations pierces here,
Even here, into these chambers of the unknown
Who govern, and the unknown and the unnumbered
Judged and destroyed in silence,—all things wear   170
The self-same aspect, to my very sire!
Nothing can sympathise with Foscari,
Not even a Foscari.—Sir, I attend you.
            [*Exeunt* JACOPO FOSCARI, *Officer, etc.*

Enter MEMMO *and another Senator.*

Mem. He 's gone—we are too late :—think you "the
 Ten"
Will sit for any length of time to-day?
 Sen. They say the prisoner is most obdurate,
Persisting in his first avowal; but
More I know not.
 Mem.   And that is much; the secrets
Of yon terrific chamber are as hidden
From us, the premier nobles of the state,   180
As from the people.
 Sen.   Save the wonted rumours,
Which—like the tales of spectres, that are rife
Near ruined buildings—never have been proved,
Nor wholly disbelieved : men know as little
Of the state's real acts as of the grave's
Unfathomed mysteries.
 Mem.   But with length of time
We gain a step in knowledge, and I look
Forward to be one day of the decemvirs.
 Sen. Or Doge?
 Mem.   Why, no; not if I can avoid it.
 Sen. 'Tis the first station of the state, and may   190
Be lawfully desired, and lawfully
Attained by noble aspirants.
 Mem.   To such
I leave it; though born noble, my ambition
Is limited : I'd rather be an unit
Of an united and Imperial "Ten,"
Than shine a lonely, though a gilded cipher.—
Whom have we here? the wife of Foscari?

Enter MARINA, *with a female Attendant.*

 Mar. What, no one?—I am wrong, there still are
 two;
But they are senators.
 Mem.   Most noble lady,
Command us.
 Mar.   *I command !*—Alas! my life   200
Has been one long entreaty, and a vain one.

Mem. I understand thee, but I must not answer.

Mar. (*fiercely*). True—none dare answer here save on
    the rack,
Or question save those——

Mem. (*interrupting her*). High-born dame![1] bethink
thee
Where thou now art.

Mar.   Where I now am!—It was
My husband's father's palace.

Mem.   The Duke's palace.

Mar. And his son's prison!—True, I have not for-
    got it;
And, if there were no other nearer, bitterer
Remembrances, would thank the illustrious Memmo
For pointing out the pleasures of the place.   210

Mem. Be calm!

Mar. (*looking up towards heaven*). I am; but oh, thou
    eternal God!
Canst *thou* continue so, with such a world?

Mem. Thy husband yet may be absolved.

Mar.   He is,
In Heaven. I pray you, Signor Senator,
Speak not of that; you are a man of office,
So is the Doge; he has a son at stake
Now, at this moment, and I have a husband,
Or had; they are there within, or were at least
An hour since, face to face, as judge and culprit:
Will *he* condemn *him*?

Mem.   I trust not.

1. [" She was a Contarini (her name was Lucrezia, not Marina)—
          "' A daughter of the house that now among
              Its ancestors in monumental brass
              Numbers eight Doges.'
On the occasion of her marriage the Bùcentaur came out in its
splendour; and a bridge of boats was thrown across the Canal Grande
for the bridegroom and his retinue of three hundred horse."—*Foscari*,
by Samuel Rogers, *Poems*, 1852, ii. 93, *note*.
      According to another footnote (*ibid.*, p. 90), "this story (*Foscari*)
and the tragedy of the *Two Foscari* were published within a few days
of each other, in November, 1821." The first edition of *Italy* was
published anonymously in 1822. According to the announcement of
a corrected and enlarged edition, which appeared in the *Morning
Chronicle*, April 11, 1823, "a few copies of this poem were printed off
the winter before last, while the author was abroad."]

Mar.   But if   220
He does not, there are those will sentence both.
  Mem. They can.
  Mar.   And with them power and will are one
In wickedness;—my *husband* 's lost !
  Mem.   Not so ;
Justice is judge in Venice.
  Mar.   If it were so,
There now would be no Venice.   But let it
Live on, so the good die not, till the hour
Of Nature's summons; but "the Ten 's" is quicker,
And we must wait on't.   Ah ! a voice of wail !
                              [*A faint cry within.*

  Sen. Hark !
  Mem.   'Twas a cry of—
  Mar.   No, no ; not my husband's—
Not Foscari's.
  Mem.   The voice was—
  Mar.   *Not his :* no.   230
He shriek !   No ; that should be his father's part,
Not his—not his—he'll die in silence.
                      [*A faint groan again within.*
  Mem.   What !
Again ?
  Mar. His voice ! it seemed so : I will not
Believe it.   Should he shrink, I cannot cease
To love ; but—no—no—no—it must have been
A fearful pang, which wrung a groan from him.
  Sen. And, feeling for thy husband's wrongs, wouldst
      thou
Have him bear more than mortal pain in silence ?
  Mar. We all must bear our tortures.   I have not
Left barren the great house of Foscari,   240
Though they sweep both the Doge and son from life ;
I have endured as much in giving life
To those who will succeed them, as they can
In leaving it : but mine were joyful pangs :
And yet they wrung me till I *could* have shrieked,
But did not ; for my hope was to bring forth
Heroes, and would not welcome them with tears.
  Mem. All 's silent now.

Mar.   Perhaps all's over; but
I will not deem it : he hath nerved himself,
And now defies them.

Enter an Officer hastily.

Mem.   How now, friend, what seek you?
Offi. A leech.   The prisoner has fainted. [*Exit Officer.*
Mem.   Lady, 251
'Twere better to retire.
    Sen. (*offering to assist her*). I pray thee do so.
    Mar. Off! *I* will tend him.
    Mem.   You !   Remember, lady !
Ingress is given to none within those chambers
Except " the Ten," and their familiars.
    Mar.   Well,
I know that none who enter there return
As they have entered—many never; but
They shall not balk my entrance.
    Mem.   Alas ! this
Is but to expose yourself to harsh repulse,
And worse suspense.
    Mar.   Who shall oppose me?
                                        They 260
    Mem.
Whose duty 'tis to do so.
    Mar.   'Tis *their* duty
To trample on all human feelings, all
Ties which bind man to man, to emulate
The fiends who will one day requite them in
Variety of torturing !   Yet I'll pass.
    Mem. It is impossible.
    Mar.   That shall be tried.[i.]
Despair defies even despotism : there is
That in my heart would make its way through hosts
With levelled spears; and think you a few jailors
Shall put me from my path?   Give me, then, way; 270
This is the Doge's palace; I am wife
Of the Duke's son, the *innocent* Duke's son,
And they shall hear this !
    Mem.   It will only serve

i. *Do not deem so.*—[*MS. M.*]

More to exasperate his judges.
 Mar.   What
Are *judges* who give way to anger ? they
Who do so are assassins. Give me way. [*Exit* MARINA.
 Sen. Poor lady !
 Mem.   'Tis mere desperation : she
Will not be admitted o'er the threshold.
 Sen.   And
Even if she be so, cannot save her husband.
But, see, the officer returns.
   [*The Officer passes over the stage with another person.*
 Mem.   I hardly   280
Thought that "the Ten" had even this touch of pity,
Or would permit assistance to this sufferer.
 Sen. Pity ! Is't pity to recall to feeling
The wretch too happy to escape to Death
By the compassionate trance, poor Nature's last
Resource against the tyranny of pain ?
 Mem. I marvel they condemn him not at once.
 Sen. That 's not their policy : they'd have him live,
Because he fears not death ; and banish him,
Because all earth, except his native land,   290
To him is one wide prison, and each breath
Of foreign air he draws seems a slow poison,
Consuming but not killing.
 Mem.   Circumstance
Confirms his crimes, but he avows them not.
 Sen. None, save the Letter, which, he says, was written
Addressed to Milan's duke, in the full knowledge
That it would fall into the Senate's hands,
And thus he should be re-conveyed to Venice.[1]

---

 1. [Jacopo's plea, that the letter to the Duke of Milan was written for
the express purpose of being recalled to Venice, is inadmissible for more
reasons than one. In the first place, if on suspicion of a letter written
but never sent, the Ten had thought fit to recall him, it by no means
followed that they would have granted him an interview with his wife
and family ; and, secondly, the fact that there were letters in cypher
found in his possession, and that a direct invitation to the Sultan to
rescue him by force was among the impounded documents (" Quod
requirebat dictum Teucrum ut mitteret ex galeis suis ad accipiendum et
levandum eum de dicto loco "), proves that the appeal to the Duke of
Milan was *bonâ fide*, and not a mere act of desperation. (See *The Two
Doges*, pp. 101, 102, and Berlan's *I due Foscari*, p. 53, etc.)]

Mem. But as a culprit.

Sen.   Yes, but to his country;
And that was all he sought,—so he avouches.   300

Mem. The accusation of the bribes was proved.

Sen. Not clearly, and the charge of homicide
Has been annulled by the death-bed confession
Of Nicolas Erizzo, who slew the late
Chief of "the Ten." [1]

Mem.   Then why not clear him?

Sen.   That
They ought to answer; for it is well known
That Almoro Donato, as I said,
Was slain by Erizzo for private vengeance.

Mem. There must be more in this strange process
      than
The apparent crimes of the accused disclose—   310
But here come two of "the Ten;" let us retire.

                              [*Exeunt* MEMMO *and Senator.*

                Enter LOREDANO *and* BARBARIGO.

Bar. (*addressing* LOR.). That were too much : believe
      me, 'twas not meet
The trial should go further at this moment.

Lor. And so the Council must break up, and Justice
Pause in her full career, because a woman
Breaks in on our deliberations?

Bar.   No,
That 's not the cause; you saw the prisoner's state.

Lor. And had he not recovered?

Bar.   To relapse
Upon the least renewal.

Lor.   'Twas not tried.

Bar. 'Tis vain to murmur; the majority   320
In council were against you.

Lor.   Thanks to *you*, sir,

1. [There is no documentary evidence for this "confession," which
rests on a mere tradition. (*Vide* Sanudo, *Vitæ Ducum Venetorum*,
apud Muratori, *Rerum Ital. Script.*, 1733, xxii. col. 1139; see, too,
Berlan, *I due Foscari*, p. 37.) Moreover, Almoro Donato was not
chief of the "Ten" at the date of his murder. The three "Capi" for
November, 1450, were Ermolao Vallaresso, Giovanni Giustiniani, and
Andrea Marcello (*vide ibid.*, p. 25).]

And the old ducal dotard, who combined
The worthy voices which o'er-ruled my own.
    Bar. I am a judge ; but must confess that part
Of our stern duty, which prescribes the Question,[1]
And bids us sit and see its sharp infliction,
Makes me wish——
        Lor.   What ?
        Bar.   That *you* would *sometimes* feel,
As I do always.
        Lor.   Go to, you're a child,
Infirm of feeling as of purpose, blown
About by every breath, shook[2] by a sigh,   330
And melted by a tear—a precious judge
For Venice ! and a worthy statesman to
Be partner in my policy.
        Bar.   He shed
No tears.
        Lor.   He cried out twice.
        Bar.   A Saint had done so,
Even with the crown of Glory in his eye,
At such inhuman artifice of pain
As was forced on him ; but he did not cry [i]
For pity ; not a word nor groan escaped him,
And those two shrieks were not in supplication,
But wrung from pangs, and followed by no prayers. 340
    Lor. He muttered many times between his teeth,
But inarticulately.[3]
        Bar.   That I heard not :
You stood more near him.
        Lor.   I did so.

----

i. *As was proved on him* ——.—[*MS.* *M.*]

1. ["Examination by torture : 'Such presumption is only sufficient
to put the person to the rack or torture' (Ayliffe's *Parergon*)."—*Cent.
Dict.*, art. " Question."]

2. [Shakespeare, Milton, Thompson, and others, use " shook " for
" shaken."]

3. [The inarticulate mutterings are probably an echo of the " incantation and magic words " ("incantationem et verba quæ sibi reperta
sunt de quibus ad funem utitur . . . quoniam in fune aliquam nec
vocem nec gemitum emittit sed solum inter dentes ipse videtur et
auditur loqui" [*Die beiden Foscari*, pp. 160, 161]), which, according to
the decree of the Council of Ten, dated March 26, 1451, Jacopo let fall
" while under torture" during his second trial.]

Bar.   Methought,
To my surprise too, you were touched with mercy,
And were the first to call out for assistance
When he was failing.
    Lor.   I believed that swoon
His last.
    Bar.   And have I not oft heard thee name
His and his father's death your nearest wish?
    Lor. If he dies innocent, that is to say,
With his guilt unavowed, he'll be lamented.   350
    Bar. What, wouldst thou slay his memory?
    Lor.   Wouldst thou have
His state descend to his children, as it must,
If he die unattainted?
    Bar.   War with *them* too?
    Lor. With all their house, till theirs or mine are
        nothing.
    Bar. And the deep agony of his pale wife,
And the repressed convulsion of the high
And princely brow of his old father, which
Broke forth in a slight shuddering, though rarely,
Or in some clammy drops, soon wiped away
In stern serenity; these moved you not?   360
                  [*Exit* LOREDANO.
He 's silent in his hate, as Foscari
Was in his suffering; and the poor wretch moved me
More by his silence than a thousand outcries
Could have effected.   'Twas a dreadful sight
When his distracted wife broke through into
The hall of our tribunal, and beheld
What we could scarcely look upon, long used
To such sights.   I must think no more of this,
Lest I forget in this compassion for
Our foes, their former injuries, and lose   370
The hold of vengeance Loredano plans
For him and me; but mine would be content
With lesser retribution than he thirsts for,
And I would mitigate his deeper hatred
To milder thoughts; but, for the present, Foscari
Has a short hourly respite, granted at
The instance of the elders of the Council,

Moved doubtless by his wife's appearance in
The hall, and his own sufferings.—Lo ! they come :
How feeble and forlorn ! I cannot bear   380
To look on them again in this extremity :
I'll hence, and try to soften Loredano.[i.]

[*Exit* BARBARIGO.

ACT II.

SCENE I.—*A hall in the* DOGE's *Palace.*

The DOGE *and a Senator.*

Sen. Is it your pleasure to sign the report
Now, or postpone it till to-morrow ?
    Doge.   Now ;
I overlooked it yesterday : it wants
Merely the signature.   Give me the pen—

[*The* DOGE *sits down and signs the paper.*
There, Signor.
    Sen. (*looking at the paper*).   You have forgot ; it is not
    signed.
    Doge. Not signed ?   Ah, I perceive my eyes begin
To wax more weak with age.   I did not see
That I had dipped the pen without effect.[ii.]
    Sen. (*dipping the pen into the ink, and placing the paper
        before the* DOGE).   Your hand, too, shakes, my
        Lord : allow me, thus—
    Doge. 'Tis done, I thank you. .
    Sen.   Thus the act confirmed
By you and by " the Ten " gives peace to Venice.   11
    Doge. 'Tis long since she enjoyed it : may it be
As long ere she resume her arms !
    Sen.   'Tis almost
Thirty-four years of nearly ceaseless warfare

---

    i. *I'll hence and follow Loredano home.*—[*MS. M.*]
    ii. *That I had dipped the pen too heedlessly.*—[*MS. M.*]

With the Turk, or the powers of Italy;
The state had need of some repose.
 Doge.   No doubt:
I found her Queen of Ocean, and I leave her
Lady of Lombardy; it is a comfort [L]
That I have added to her diadem
The gems of Brescia and Ravenna; Crema [1]   20
And Bergamo no less are hers; her realm
By land has grown by thus much in my reign,
While her sea-sway has not shrunk.
 Sen.   'Tis most true,
And merits all our country's gratitude.
 Doge. Perhaps so.
 Sen.   Which should be made manifest.
 Doge. I have not complained, sir.
 Sen.   My good Lord, forgive me.
 Doge. For what?
 Sen.   My heart bleeds for you.
 Doge.   For me, Signor?
 Sen. And for your——
 Doge.   Stop!
 Sen.   It must have way, my Lord:
I have too many duties towards you
And all your house, for past and present kindness, 30
Not to feel deeply for your son.
 Doge.   Was this
In your commission?
 Sen.   What, my Lord?
 Doge.   This prattle
Of things you know not: but the treaty's signed;
Return with it to them who sent you.
 Sen.   I
Obey. I had in charge, too, from the Council,
That you would fix an hour for their reunion.
 Doge. Say, when they will—now, even at this moment,

---

i. *Mistress of Lombardy—'tis some comfort to me.*—[*MS. M.*]

1. [Compare " Ce fut l'époque, où Vénise étendit son empire sur
Brescia, Bergame, Ravenne, et Crème; où elle fonda sa domination de
Lombardie," etc. (Sismondi's *Histoire des Républiques*, x. 38). Brescia
fell to the Venetians, October, 1426; Bergamo, in April, 1428; Ravenna,
in August, 1440; and Crema, in 1453.]

The Lion of St. Mark.

If it so please them : I am the State's servant.

Sen. They would accord some time for your repose.

Doge. I have no repose, that is, none which shall cause
The loss of an hour's time unto the State.   41
Let them meet when they will, I shall be found
Where I should be, and *what* I have been ever.

[*Exit Senator. The* DOGE *remains in silence.*

Enter an Attendant.

Att. Prince !

Doge.   Say on.

Att.   The illustrious lady Foscari
Requests an audience.

Doge.   Bid her enter.   Poor
Marina !

[*Exit Attendant. The* DOGE *remains in silence as
before.*

Enter MARINA.

Mar.   I have ventured, father, on
Your privacy.

Doge.   I have none from you, my child.
Command my time, when not commanded by
The State.

Mar.   I wished to speak to you of *him*.

Doge. Your husband ?

Mar.   And your son.

Doge.   Proceed, my daughter !

Mar. I had obtained permission from " the Ten "   51
To attend my husband for a limited number
Of hours.

Doge.   You had so.

Mar.   'Tis revoked.

Doge.   By whom ?

Mar. " The   Ten."—When   we   had   reached " the
Bridge of Sighs," [1]

1. [The Bridge of Sighs was not built till the end of the sixteenth
century. (*Vide ante, Marino Faliero*, act i. sc. 2, line 508, *Poetical
Works*, 1901, iv. 363, *note* 2; see, too, *Childe Harold*, Canto IV.
stanza i. line 1, *et post*, act iv. sc. 1, line 75.)]

Which I prepared to pass with Foscari,
The gloomy guardian of that passage first
Demurred : a messenger was sent back to
" The Ten ; "—but as the Court no longer sate,
And no permission had been given in writing,
I was thrust back, with the assurance that   60
Until that high tribunal reassembled
The dungeon walls must still divide us.

 Doge.   True,
The form has been omitted in the haste
With which the court adjourned ; and till it meets,
'Tis dubious.

 Mar. Till it meets ! and when it meets,
They'll torture him again ; and he and I
Must purchase by renewal of the rack
The interview of husband and of wife,
The holiest tie beneath the Heavens !—Oh God !
Dost thou see this ?

 Doge. Child—child——

 Mar. (abruptly). Call *me* not " child ! "
You soon will have no children—you deserve none— 71
You, who can talk thus calmly of a son
In circumstances which would call forth tears
Of blood from Spartans ! Though these did not weep
Their boys who died in battle, is it written
That they beheld them perish piecemeal, nor
Stretched forth a hand to save them ?

 Doge. You behold me :
I cannot weep—I would I could ; but if
Each white hair on this head were a young life,
This ducal cap the Diadem of earth,   80
This ducal ring with which I wed the waves
A talisman to still them—I'd give all
For him.

 Mar. With less he surely might be saved.

 Doge. That answer only shows you know not Venice.
Alas ! how should you ? she knows not herself,
In all her mystery. Hear me—they who aim
At Foscari, aim no less at his father ;
The sire's destruction would not save the son ;
They work by different means to the same end,

And that is—but they have not conquered yet.   90
    Mar. But they have crushed.
    Doge.   Nor crushed as yet—I live.
    Mar. And your son,—how long will he live?
    Doge.   I trust,
For all that yet is past, as many years
And happier than his father.   The rash boy,
With womanish impatience to return,
Hath ruined all by that detected letter:
A high crime, which I neither can deny
Nor palliate, as parent or as Duke:
Had he but borne a little, little longer
His Candiote exile, I had hopes——he has quenched
     them—   100
He must return.
    Mar.   To exile?
    Doge.   I have said it.
    Mar. And can I not go with him?
    Doge.   You well know
This prayer of yours was twice denied before
By the assembled "Ten," and hardly now
Will be accorded to a third request,
Since aggravated errors on the part
Of your Lord renders them still more austere.
    Mar. Austere? Atrocious! The old human fiends,
With one foot in the grave, with dim eyes, strange
To tears save drops of dotage, with long white [i.]   110
And scanty hairs, and shaking hands, and heads
As palsied as their hearts are hard, they counsel,
Cabal, and put men's lives out, as if Life
Were no more than the feelings long extinguished
In their accursèd bosoms.
    Doge.   You know not——
    Mar. I do—I do—and so should you, methinks—
That these are demons: could it be else that
Men, who have been of women born and suckled—
Who have loved, or talked at least of Love—have given
Their hands in sacred vows—have danced their babes 120
Upon their knees, perhaps have mourned above them—
In pain, in peril, or in death—who are,

    i. *To tears save those of dotage* ——.—[*MS. M.*]

Or were, at least in seeming, human, could
Do as they have done by yours, and you yourself—
You, who abet them?
    Doge.   I forgive this, for
You know not what you say.
    Mar.   *You* know it well,
And feel it nothing.
    Doge.   I have borne so much,
That words have ceased to shake me.
    Mar.   Oh, no doubt!
You have seen your son's blood flow, and your flesh
        shook not;
And after that, what are a woman's words?   130
No more than woman's tears, that they should shake you.
    Doge. Woman, this clamorous grief of thine, I tell thee,
Is no more in the balance weighed with that
Which——but I pity thee, my poor Marina!
    Mar. Pity my husband, or I cast it from me;
Pity thy son! *Thou* pity!—'tis a word
Strange to thy heart—how came it on thy lips?
    Doge. I must bear these reproaches, though they
        wrong me.
Couldst thou but read——
    Mar.   'Tis not upon thy brow,
Nor in thine eyes, nor in thine acts,—where then   140
Should I behold this sympathy? or shall?
    Doge (pointing downwards). There.
    Mar.   In the earth?
    Doge.   To which I am tending: when
It lies upon this heart, far lightlier, though
Loaded with marble, than the thoughts which press it
Now, you will know me better.
    Mar.   Are you, then,
Indeed, thus to be pitied?
    Doge.   Pitied! None
Shall ever use that base word, with which men
Cloak their soul's hoarded triumph, as a fit one
To mingle with my name; that name shall be,
As far as *I* have borne it, what it was   150
When I received it.
    Mar.   But for the poor children

Of him thou canst not, or thou wilt not save,
You were the last to bear it.
   Doge.   Would it were so!
Better for him he never had been born;
Better for me.—I have seen our house dishonoured.
   Mar. That 's false! A truer, nobler, trustier heart,
More loving, or more loyal, never beat
Within a human breast. I would not change
My exiled, persecuted, mangled husband,
Oppressed but not disgraced, crushed, overwhelmed, 160
Alive, or dead, for Prince or Paladin
In story or in fable, with a world
To back his suit. Dishonoured!—*he* dishonoured!
I tell thee, Doge, 'tis Venice is dishonoured;
His name shall be her foulest, worst reproach,
For what he suffers, not for what he did.
'Tis ye who are all traitors, Tyrant!—ye!
Did you but love your Country like this victim
Who totters back in chains to tortures, and
Submits to all things rather than to exile,   170
You'd fling yourselves before him, and implore
His grace for your enormous guilt.
   Doge.   He was
Indeed all you have said. I better bore
The deaths of the two sons [1] Heaven took from me,
Than Jacopo's disgrace.
   Mar.   That word again?
   Doge. Has he not been condemned?
   Mar.   Is none but guilt so?
   Doge. Time may restore his memory—I would hope so.
He was my pride, my——but 'tis useless now—
I am not given to tears, but wept for joy
When he was born: those drops were ominous.   180
   Mar. I say he 's innocent! And were he not so,
Is our own blood and kin to shrink from us
In fatal moments?
   Doge.   I shrank not from him:
But I have other duties than a father's;
The state would not dispense me from those duties;

   1. [Five sons were born to the Doge, of whom four died of the plague (*Two Doges, etc.*, by A. Wiel, 1891, p. 77).]

Twice I demanded it, but was refused : [1]
They must then be fulfilled.

Enter an Attendant.

  Att.   A message from
" The Ten."
  Doge. Who bears it ?
  Att.   Noble Loredano.
  Doge. He !—but admit him. [*Exit Attendant.*
  Mar.   Must I then retire ?
  Doge. Perhaps it is not requisite, if this 190
Concerns your husband, and if not——Well, Signor,
         [*To* LOREDANO *entering.*

Your pleasure ?
  Lor. I bear that of " the Ten."
  Doge.   They
Have chosen well their envoy.
  Lor.   'Tis *their* choice
Which leads me here.
  Doge.   It does their wisdom honour,
And no less to their courtesy.—Proceed.
  Lor. We have decided.
  Doge.   We ?
  Lor.   " The Ten " in council.
  Doge, What ! have they met again, and met without
Apprising me ?
  Lor.   They wished to spare your feelings,
No less than age.
  Doge.   That 's new—when spared they either ?
I thank them, notwithstanding.
  Lor.   You know well 200
That they have power to act at their discretion,
With or without the presence of the Doge.
  Doge. 'Tis some years since I learned this, long before
I became Doge, or dreamed of such advancement.
You need not school me, Signor ; I sate in
That Council when you were a young patrician.
  Lor. True, in my father's time ; I have heard him and

---

1. [The Doge offered to abdicate in June, 1433, in June, 1442, and
again in 1446 (see Romanin, *Storia, etc.*, 1855, iv. 170, 171, *note* 1).]

The Admiral, his brother, say as much.
Your Highness may remember them ; they both
Died suddenly.[1]

Doge.   And if they did so, better   210
So die than live on lingeringly in pain.

Lor. No doubt : yet most men like to live their days
     out.

Doge. And did not they ?

Lor.   The Grave knows best : they died,
As I said, suddenly.

Doge.   Is that so strange,
That you repeat the word emphatically ?

Lor. So far from strange, that never was there death
In my mind half so natural as theirs.
Think *you* not so ?

Doge.   What should I think of mortals ?

Lor. That they have mortal foes.

Doge.   I understand you ;
Your sires were mine, and you are heir in all things.   220

Lor. You best know if I should be so.

Doge.   I do.
Your fathers were my foes, and I have heard
Foul rumours were abroad ; I have also read
Their epitaph, attributing their deaths
To poison.   'Tis perhaps as true as most
Inscriptions upon tombs, and yet no less
A fable.

Lor.   Who dares say so ?

Doge.   I !——'Tis true
Your fathers were mine enemies, as bitter
As their son e'er can be, and I no less
Was theirs ; but I was *openly* their foe :   230
I never worked by plot in Council, nor
Cabal in commonwealth, nor secret means
Of practice against life by steel or drug.
The proof is—your existence.

Lor.   I fear not.

Doge. You have no cause, being what I am ; but
     were I
That you would have me thought, you long ere now

1. [*Vide ante*, p. 123.]

Were past the sense of fear.   Hate on; I care not.

   Lor.   I never yet knew that a noble's life
In Venice had to dread a Doge's frown,
That is, by open means.

     Doge.   But I, good Signor,   240
Am, or at least *was*, more than a mere duke,
In blood, in mind, in means; and that they know
Who dreaded to elect me, and have since
Striven all they dare to weigh me down: be sure,
Before or since that period, had I held you
At so much price as to require your absence,
A word of mine had set such spirits to work
As would have made you nothing.   But in all things
I have observed the strictest reverence;
Not for the laws alone, for those *you* have strained   250
(I do not speak of *you* but as a single
Voice of the many) somewhat beyond what
I could enforce for my authority,
Were I disposed to brawl; but, as I said,
I have observed with veneration, like
A priest's for the High Altar, even unto
The sacrifice of my own blood and quiet,
Safety, and all save honour, the decrees,
The health, the pride, and welfare of the State.
And now, sir, to your business.

   Lor.   'Tis decreed,   260
That, without further repetition of
The Question, or continuance of the trial,
Which only tends to show how stubborn guilt is,
("The Ten," dispensing with the stricter law
Which still prescribes the Question till a full
Confession, and the prisoner partly having
Avowed his crime in not denying that
The letter to the Duke of Milan 's his),
James Foscari return to banishment,
And sail in the same galley which conveyed him.   270

   Mar. Thank God!   At least they will not drag him
      more
Before that horrible tribunal.   Would he
But think so, to my mind the happiest doom,
Not he alone, but all who dwell here, could

Desire, were to escape from such a land.
   Doge. That is not a Venetian thought, my daughter.
   Mar. No, 'twas too human.   May I share his exile?
   Lor. Of this "the Ten" said nothing.
   Mar.   So I thought !
That were too human, also.   But it was not
Inhibited ?
   Lor.   It was not named.
   Mar. (to the Doge).   Then, father,   280
Surely you can obtain or grant me thus much :
                      [*To* LOREDANO.
And you, sir, not oppose my prayer to be
Permitted to accompany my husband.
   Doge. I will endeavour.
   Mar.   And you, Signor?
   Lor.   Lady !
'Tis not for me to anticipate the pleasure
Of the tribunal.
   Mar.   Pleasure ! what a word
To use for the decrees of——
   Doge.   Daughter, know you
In what a presence you pronounce these things ?
   Mar. A Prince's and his subject's.
   Lor.   Subject !
   Mar.   Oh !
It galls you :—well, you are his equal, as   290
You think ; but that you are not, nor would be,
Were he a peasant :—well, then, you're a Prince,
A princely noble ; and what then am I ?
   Lor. The offspring of a noble house.
   Mar.   And wedded
To one as noble.   What, or whose, then, is
The presence that should silence my free thoughts ?
   Lor. The presence of your husband's Judges.
   Doge.   And
The deference due even to the lightest word
That falls from those who rule in Venice.
   Mar.   Keep
Those maxims for your mass of scared mechanics,   300
Your merchants, your Dalmatian and Greek slaves,
Your tributaries, your dumb citizens,

And masked nobility, your sbirri, and
Your spies, your galley and your other slaves,
To whom your midnight carryings off and drownings,
Your dungeons next the palace roofs, or under
The water's level;[1] your mysterious meetings,
And unknown dooms, and sudden executions,
Your " Bridge of Sighs," your strangling chamber, and
Your torturing instruments, have made ye seem   310
The beings of another and worse world!
Keep such for them : I fear ye not.   I know ye ;[i.]
Have known and proved your worst, in the infernal
Process of my poor husband !   Treat me as
Ye treated him :—you did so, in so dealing
With him.   Then what have I to fear *from* you,
Even if I were of fearful nature, which
I trust I am not?
    Doge.   You hear, she speaks wildly.
    Mar. Not wisely, yet not wildly.
    Lor.   Lady ! words
Uttered within these walls I bear no further   320
Than to the threshold, saving such as pass
Between the Duke and me on the State's service.
Doge ! have you aught in answer?
    Doge.   Something from
The Doge ; it may be also from a parent.
    Lor. My mission *here* is to the *Doge.*
    Doge.   Then say
The Doge will choose his own ambassador,
Or state in person what is meet ; and for
The father——
    Lor.   I remember *mine.*—Farewell !
I kiss the hands of the illustrious Lady,
And bow me to the Duke.   [*Exit* LOREDANO.
    Mar.   Are you content ?   330
    Doge. I am what you behold.
    Mar.   And that 's a mystery.
    Doge. All things are so to mortals ; who can read them
Save he who made? or, if they can, the few

i. *Keep this for them* ——.—[*MS. M.*]

1. [For the *Pozzi* and *Piombi*, see *Marino Faliero*, act i. sc. 2,
Poetical Works, 1901, iv. 363, *note* 2.]

And gifted spirits, who have studied long
That loathsome volume—man, and pored upon
Those black and bloody leaves, his heart and brain,[i.]
But learn a magic which recoils upon
The adept who pursues it : all the sins
We find in others, Nature made our own ;
All our advantages are those of Fortune ;   340
Birth, wealth, health, beauty, are her accidents,
And when we cry out against Fate, 'twere well
We should remember Fortune can take nought
Save what she *gave*—the rest was nakedness,
And lusts, and appetites, and vanities,
The universal heritage, to battle
With as we may, and least in humblest stations,[ii.]
Where Hunger swallows all in one low want,[iii.]
And the original ordinance, that man
Must sweat for his poor pittance, keeps all passions   350
Aloof, save fear of famine !   All is low,
And false, and hollow—clay from first to last,
The Prince's urn no less than potter's vessel.
Our Fame is in men's breath, our lives upon
Less than their breath ; our durance upon days,[iv.]
Our days on seasons ; our whole being on
Something which is not *us* /[1]—So, we are slaves,
The greatest as the meanest—nothing rests
Upon our will ; the will itself no less[v.]
Depends upon a straw than on a storm ;   360
And when we think we lead, we are most led,[2]

i. *The blackest leaf, his heart, and blankest, his brain.*—[*MS. M.*
ii. —— *and best in humblest stations.*—[*MS. M.*]
iii. *Where hunger swallows all—where ever was*
     The monarch who could bear a three days' fast ?—[*MS. M.*]
iv. *Their disposition* ——.—[*MS. M.*].
v.   —— *the will itself dependent*
     Upon a storm, a straw, and both alike
     Leading to death ——.—[*MS. M.*]

1. [It would seem that Byron's "not ourselves" by no means
"made for" righteousness.]
2. [Compare—

        " The boldest steer but where their ports invite."

Childe Harold, Canto III. stanza lxx. lines 7–9 ; and Canto IV. stanza
xxxiv., *Poetical Works*, 1899, ii. 260, 353, and 74, *note* 1.]

And still towards Death, a thing which comes as much
Without our act or choice as birth, so that
Methinks we must have sinned in some old world,
And *this* is Hell: the best is, that it is not
Eternal.
    Mar.   These are things we cannot judge
On earth.
    Doge.   And how then shall we judge each other,
Who are all earth, and I, who am called upon
To judge my son? I have administered
My country faithfully—victoriously—   370
I dare them to the proof, the *chart* of what
She was and is: my reign has doubled realms;
And, in reward, the gratitude of Venice
Has left, or is about to leave, *me* single.
    Mar. And Foscari? I do not think of such things,
So I be left with him.
    Doge.   You shall be so;
Thus much they cannot well deny.
    Mar.   And if
They should, I will fly with him.
    Doge.   That can ne'er be.
And whither would you fly?
    Mar.   I know not, reck not—
To Syria, Egypt, to the Ottoman—   380
Any where, where we might respire unfettered,
And live nor girt by spies, nor liable
To edicts of inquisitors of state.
    Doge. What, wouldst thou have a renegade for
        husband,
And turn him into traitor?
    Mar.   He is none!
The Country is the traitress, which thrusts forth
Her best and bravest from her. Tyranny
Is far the worst of treasons. Dost thou deem
None rebels except subjects? The Prince who
Neglects or violates his trust is more   390
A brigand than the robber-chief.
    Doge.   I cannot
Charge me with such a breach of faith.
    Mar.   No; thou

Observ'st, obey'st such laws as make old Draco's
A code of mercy by comparison.
   Doge. I found the law; I did not make it.   Were I
A subject, still I might find parts and portions
Fit for amendment; but as Prince, I never
Would change, for the sake of my house, the charter
Left by our fathers.
   Mar.   Did they make it for
The ruin of their children?
   Doge.   Under such laws, Venice
Has risen to what she is—a state to rival   401
In deeds, and days, and sway, and, let me add,
In glory (for we have had Roman spirits
Amongst us), all that history has bequeathed
Of Rome and Carthage in their best times, when
The people swayed by Senates.
   Mar.   Rather say,
Groaned under the stern Oligarchs.
   Doge.   Perhaps so;
But yet subdued the World: in such a state
An individual, be he richest of
Such rank as is permitted, or the meanest,   410
Without a name, is alike nothing, when
The policy, irrevocably tending
To one great end, must be maintained in vigour.
   Mar. This means that you are more a Doge than
      father.
   Doge. It means, I am more citizen than either.
If we had not for many centuries
Had thousands of such citizens, and shall,
I trust, have still such, Venice were no city.
   Mar. Accursèd be the city where the laws
Would stifle Nature's!
   Doge.   Had I as many sons   420
As I have years, I would have given them all,
Not without feeling, but I would have given them
To the State's service, to fulfil her wishes,
On the flood, in the field, or, if it must be,
As it, alas! has been, to ostracism,
Exile, or chains, or whatsoever worse
She might decree.

Mar.   And this is Patriotism?
To me it seems the worst barbarity.
Let me seek out my husband : the sage "Ten,"
With all its jealousy, will hardly war   430
So far with a weak woman as deny me
A moment's access to his dungeon.
    Doge.   I'll
So far take on myself, as order that
You may be admitted.
    Mar.   And what shall I say
To Foscari from his father?
    Doge.   That he obey
The laws.
    Mar.   And nothing more? Will you not see him
Ere he depart? It may be the last time.
    Doge. The last!—my boy!—the last time I shall see
My last of children! Tell him I will come.   [*Exeunt.*

ACT III.

Scene I.—*The prison of* Jacopo Foscari.

Jac. Fos. (*solus*). No light, save yon faint gleam which
        shows me walls
Which never echoed but to Sorrow's sounds,[1]
The sigh of long imprisonment, the step
Of feet on which the iron clanked the groan
Of Death, the imprecation of Despair!
And yet for this I have returned to Venice,
With some faint hope, 'tis true, that Time, which wears

---

1. [Compare—

"Our voices took a dreary tone,
An echo of the dungeon stone."
Prisoner of Chillon, lines 63, 64.

Compare, too—

"—— prisoned solitude.
And the Mind's canker in its savage mood,
When the impatient thirst of light and air
Parches the heart."
Lament of Tasso, lines 4-7.]

The marble down, had worn away the hate
Of men's hearts; but I knew them not, and here
Must I consume my own, which never beat   10
For Venice but with such a yearning as
The dove has for her distant nest, when wheeling
High in the air on her return to greet
Her callow brood.   What letters are these which
                           [*Approaching the wall.*
Are scrawled along the inexorable wall?
Will the gleam let me trace them?   Ah! the names
Of my sad predecessors in this place,[1]
The dates of their despair, the brief words of
A grief too great for many.   This stone page
Holds like an epitaph their history;   20
And the poor captive's tale is graven on
His dungeon barrier, like the lover's record
Upon the bark of some tall tree,[2] which bears
His own and his belovéd's name.   Alas!
I recognise some names familiar to me,
And blighted like to mine, which I will add,
Fittest for such a chronicle as this,
Which only can be read, as writ, by wretches.[l.]
                           [*He engraves his name.*

Enter a Familiar of "the Ten."

   Fam. I bring you food.
   Jac. Fos.   I pray you set it down;
I am past hunger: but my lips are parched—   30
The water!
   Fam.   There.

          l. *Which never can be read but, as 'twas written,*
               By wretched beings.—[*MS.*]

   1. [For inscriptions on the walls of the *Pozzi*, see *note* 1 to *Childe
Harold's Pilgrimage*, Canto IV., *Poetical Works*, 1899, ii. 465–467.
Hobhouse transferred these "scratchings" to his pocket-books, and
thence to his *Historical Notes*; but even as prison inscriptions they
lack both point and style.]
   2. [Compare—

          " Run, run, Orlando; carve on every tree
            The fair, the chaste and unexpressive she."
                    As You Like It, act iii. sc. 2, lines 9, 10.]

Jac. Fos. (after drinking). I thank you : I am better.
   Fam. I am commanded to inform you that
Your further trial is postponed.
   Jac. Fos.   Till when?
   Fam. I know not.—It is also in my orders
That your illustrious lady be admitted.
   Jac. Fos. Ah! they relent, then—I had ceased to
          hope it:
'Twas time.

Enter MARINA.

   Mar.   My best belovéd!
   Jac. Fos. (embracing her).   My true wife,
And only friend! What happiness!
   Mar.   We'll part
No more.
   Jac. Fos. How! would'st thou share a dungeon?
   Mar.   Aye,
The rack, the grave, all—any thing with thee,   40
But the tomb last of all, for there we shall
Be ignorant of each other, yet I will
Share that—all things except new separation;
It is too much to have survived the first.
How dost thou? How are those worn limbs? Alas!
Why do I ask? Thy paleness——
   Jac. Fos.   'Tis the joy
Of seeing thee again so soon, and so
Without expectancy, has sent the blood
Back to my heart, and left my cheeks like thine,
For thou art pale too, my Marina!
   Mar.   'Tis   50
The gloom of this eternal cell, which never
Knew sunbeam, and the sallow sullen glare
Of the familiar's torch, which seems akin [i.]
To darkness more than light, by lending to
The dungeon vapours its bituminous smoke,
Which cloud whate'er we gaze on, even thine eyes—
No, not thine eyes—they sparkle—how they sparkle!

   i. *Of the familiar's torch, which seems to love*
      Darkness far more than light.—[MS.]

Jac. Fos. And thine !—but I am blinded by the torch.
Mar. As I had been without it. Couldst thou see here ?
Jac. Fos. Nothing at first; but use and time had
    taught me   60
Familiarity with what was darkness;
And the grey twilight of such glimmerings as
Glide through the crevices made by the winds
Was kinder to mine eyes than the full Sun,
When gorgeously o'ergilding any towers
Save those of Venice ; but a moment ere
Thou camest hither I was busy writing.
    Mar. What ?
    Jac. Fos.   My name : look, 'tis there—recorded
    next
The name of him who here preceded me—
If dungeon dates say true.
    Mar.   And what of him ?   70
    Jac. Fos. These walls are silent of men's ends; they
    only
Seem to hint shrewdly of them. Such stern walls
Were never piled on high save o'er the dead,
Or those who soon must be so.— *What of him ?*
Thou askest.—What of me ? may soon be asked,
With the like answer—doubt and dreadful surmise—
Unless thou tell'st my tale.
    Mar.   *I speak* of thee !
    Jac. Fos. And wherefore not ? All then shall speak
    of me :
The tyranny of silence is not lasting,
And, though events be hidden, just men's groans   80
Will burst all cerement, even a living grave's !
I do not *doubt* my memory, but my life ;
And neither do I fear.
    Mar.   Thy life is safe.
    Jac. Fos. And liberty ?
    Mar.   The mind should make its own !
    Jac. Fos. That has a noble sound ; but 'tis a sound,
A music most impressive, but too transient :
The Mind is much, but is not all. The Mind
Hath nerved me to endure the risk of death,
And torture positive, far worse than death

(If death be a deep sleep), without a groan,   90
Or with a cry which rather shamed my judges
Than me; but 'tis not all, for there are things
More woful—such as this small dungeon, where
I may breathe many years.
  Mar.   Alas! and this
Small dungeon is all that belongs to thee
Of this wide realm, of which thy sire is Prince.
  Jac. Fos. That thought would scarcely aid me to
   endure it.
My doom is common; many are in dungeons,
But none like mine, so near their father's palace;
But then my heart is sometimes high, and hope   100
Will stream along those moted rays of light
Peopled with dusty atoms, which afford
Our only day; for, save the gaoler's torch,
And a strange firefly, which was quickly caught
Last night in yon enormous spider's net,
I ne'er saw aught here like a ray.   Alas!
I know if mind may bear us up, or no,
For I have such, and shown it before men;
It sinks in solitude: my soul is social.
  Mar. I will be with thee.
  Jac. Fos.   Ah! if it were so!   110
But *that* they never granted—nor will grant,
And I shall be alone: no men; no books—
Those lying likenesses of lying men.
I asked for even those outlines of their kind,
Which they term annals, history, what you will,
Which men bequeath as portraits, and they were
Refused me,—so these walls have been my study,
More faithful pictures of Venetian story,
With all their blank, or dismal stains, than is
The Hall not far from hence, which bears on high   120
Hundreds of Doges, and their deeds and dates.
  Mar. I come to tell thee the result of their
Last council on thy doom.
  Jac. Fos.   I know it—look!
  [*He points to his limbs, as referring to the Question*
    which he had undergone.
  Mar. No—no—no more of that: even they relent

From that atrocity.

Jac. Fos.   What then ?

Mar.   That you
Return to Candia.

Jac. Fos.   Then my last hope 's gone.
I could endure my dungeon, for 'twas Venice ;
I could support the torture, there was something
In my native air that buoyed my spirits up
Like a ship on the Ocean tossed by storms,   130
But proudly still bestriding [1] the high waves,
And holding on its course ; but *there*, afar,
In that accurséd isle of slaves and captives,
And unbelievers, like a stranded wreck,
My very soul seemed mouldering in my bosom,
And piecemeal I shall perish, if remanded.

Mar. And *here ?*

Jac. Fos.   At once—by better means, as briefer.[i]
What ! would they even deny me my Sire's sepulchre,
As well as home and heritage ?

Mar.   My husband !
I have sued to accompany thee hence,   140
And not so hopelessly.   This love of thine
For an ungrateful and tyrannic soil
Is Passion, and not Patriotism ; for me,
So I could see thee with a quiet aspect,
And the sweet freedom of the earth and air,
I would not cavil about climes or regions.
This crowd of palaces and prisons is not
A Paradise ; its first inhabitants
Were wretched exiles.

Jac. Fos.   Well I know *how* wretched !

Mar. And yet you see how, from their banishment 150
Before the Tartar into these salt isles,
Their antique energy of mind, all that

---

i. *At once by briefer means and better.*—[*MS.*]

1. [Compare—

     "Once more upon the waters ! yet once more !
       And the waves bound beneath me as a steed
       That knows his rider."
            Childe Harold, Canto III. stanza ii. lines 1-3,
                Poetical Works, 1899, ii. 217, *note* 1.]

Remained of Rome for their inheritance,
Created by degrees an ocean Rome ; [1]
And shall an evil, which so often leads
To good, depress thee thus ?
    Jac. Fos.   Had I gone forth
From my own land, like the old patriarchs, seeking
Another region, with their flocks and herds ;
Had I been cast out like the Jews from Zion,
Or like our fathers, driven by Attila [2]   160
From fertile Italy, to barren islets,
I would have given some tears to my late country
And many thoughts ; but afterwards addressed
Myself, with those about me, to create
A new home and fresh state : perhaps I could
Have borne this—though I know not.
    Mar.   Wherefore not ?
It was the lot of millions, and must be
The fate of myriads more.
    Jac. Fos.   Aye—we but hear
Of the survivors' toil in their new lands,

---

1. In Lady Morgan's fearless and excellent work upon Italy, I perceive the expression of " Rome of the Ocean " applied to Venice. The same phrase occurs in the "Two Foscari." My publisher can vouch for me, that the tragedy was written and sent to England some time before I had seen Lady Morgan's work, which I only received on the 16th of August. I hasten, however, to notice the coincidence, and to yield the originality of the phrase to her who first placed it before the public.

[Byron calls Lady Morgan's *Italy* "fearless" on account of her strictures on the behaviour of Great Britain to Genoa in 1814. " England personally stood pledged to Genoa. . . . When the British officers rode into their gates bearing the white flag consecrated by the holy word of '*independence*,' the people . . . '*kissed their garments*.' . . . Every heart was open. . . . Lord William Bentinck's flag of '*Independenza*' was taken down from the steeples and high places at sunrise ; before noon the arms of Sardinia blazoned in their stead ; and yet the Genoese did not rise *en masse* and massacre the English " (*Italy*, 1821, i. 245, 246). The passage which Byron feared might be quoted to his disparagement runs as follows : " As the bark glides on, as the shore recedes, and the city of waves, the Rome of the ocean, rises on the horizon, the spirits rally ; . . . and as the spires and cupolas of Venice come forth in the lustre of the mid-day sun, and its palaces, half-veiled in the aërial tints of distance, gradually assume their superb proportions, then the dream of many a youthful vigil is realized " (*ibid.*, ii. 449).]

2. [Compare *Marino Faliero*, act ii. sc. 2, line 110, *Poetical Works*, 1901, iv. 386, *note* 3.]

Their numbers and success; but who can number   170
The hearts which broke in silence at that parting,
Or after their departure; of that malady [1]
Which calls up green and native fields to view
From the rough deep, with such identity
To the poor exile's fevered eye, that he
Can scarcely be restrained from treading them?
That melody, [2] which out of tones and tunes [i.]
Collects such pasture for the longing sorrow
Of the sad mountaineer, when far away
From his snow canopy of cliffs and clouds,   180
That he feeds on the sweet, but poisonous thought,
And dies. [3] You call this *weakness!* It is strength,
I say,—the parent of all honest feeling.
He who loves not his Country, can love nothing.
  Mar. Obey her, then: 'tis she that puts thee forth.

---

i. *That malady, which* ——.—[*MS. M.*]

1. The Calenture.—[From the Spanish *Calentura*, a fever peculiar to sailors within the tropics—

> "So, by a calenture misled,
>   The mariner with rapture sees,
> On the smooth ocean's azure bed,
>   Enamelled fields and verdant trees:
> With eager haste he longs to rove
>   In that fantastic scene, and thinks
> It must be some enchanted grove;
>   And in he leaps, and down he sinks."
>   Swift, *The South-Sea Project*, 1721, ed. 1824, xiv. 147.]

2. Alluding to the Swiss air and its effects.—[The *Ranz des Vaches*, played upon the bag-pipe by the young cowkeepers on the mountains: —"An air," says Rousseau, "so dear to the Swiss, that it was forbidden, under the pain of death, to play it to the troops, as it immediately drew tears from them, and made those who heard it desert, or die of what is called *la maladie du pais*, so ardent a desire did it excite to return to their country. It is in vain to seek in this air for energetic accents capable of producing such astonishing effects, for which strangers are unable to account from the music, which is in itself uncouth and wild. But it is from habit, recollections, and a thousand circumstances, retraced in this tune by those natives who hear it, and reminding them of their country, former pleasures of their youth, and all their ways of living, which occasion a bitter reflection at having lost them." Compare Byron's Swiss "Journal" for September 19, 1816, *Letters*, 1899, ii. 355.]

3. [Compare *Don Juan*, Canto XVI. stanza xlvi. lines 6, 7—

> "The calentures of music which o'ercome
> The mountaineers with dreams that they are highlands."]

Jac. Fos. Aye, there it is; 'tis like a mother's curse
Upon my soul—the mark is set upon me.
The exiles you speak of went forth by nations,
Their hands upheld each other by the way,
Their tents were pitched together—I'm alone.   190
   Mar. You shall be so no more—I will go with thee.
   Jac. Fos. My best Marina !—and our children?
   Mar.   They,
I fear, by the prevention of the state's
Abhorrent policy, (which holds all ties
As threads, which may be broken at her pleasure),
Will not be suffered to proceed with us.
   Jac. Fos. And canst thou leave them?
   Mar.   Yes—with many a pang !
But—I *can* leave them, children as they are,
To teach you to be less a child.   From this
Learn you to sway your feelings, when exacted   200
By duties paramount; and 'tis our first
On earth to bear.
   Jac. Fos.   Have I not borne?
   Mar.   Too much
From tyrannous injustice, and enough
To teach you not to shrink now from a lot,
Which, as compared with what you have undergone
Of late, is mercy.
   Jac. Fos.   Ah ! you never yet
Were far away from Venice, never saw
Her beautiful towers in the receding distance,
While every furrow of the vessel's track
Seemed ploughing deep into your heart; you never   210
Saw day go down upon your native spires [i.]
So calmly with its gold and crimson glory,
And after dreaming a disturbéd vision
Of them and theirs, awoke and found them not.
   Mar. I will divide this with you.   Let us think
Of our departure from this much-loved city,
(Since you must *love* it, as it seems,) and this
Chamber of state, her gratitude allots you.
Our children will be cared for by the Doge,   220
And by my uncles; we must sail ere night.—[*MS. M.*]

     i. —— *upon your native towers.—*[*MS. M.*]

Jac. Fos. That 's sudden. Shall I not behold my
father ?
Mar. You will.
Jac. Fos. Where ?
Mar. Here, or in the ducal
chamber—
He said not which. I would that you could bear
Your exile as he bears it.
Jac. Fos. Blame him not.
I sometimes murmur for a moment ; but
He could not now act otherwise. A show
Of feeling or compassion on his part
Would have but drawn upon his agéd head
Suspicion from " the Ten," and upon mine
Accumulated ills.
Mar. Accumulated ! 230
What pangs are those they have spared you ?
Jac. Fos. That of leaving
Venice without beholding him or you,
Which might have been forbidden now, as 'twas
Upon my former exile.
Mar. That is true,
And thus far I am also the State's debtor,
And shall be more so when I see us both
Floating on the free waves—away—away—
Be it to the earth's end, from this abhorred,
Unjust, and——
Jac. Fos. Curse it not. If I am silent,
Who dares accuse my Country ?
Mar. Men and Angels ! 240
The blood of myriads reeking up to Heaven,
The groans of slaves in chains, and men in dungeons,
Mothers, and wives, and sons, and sires, and subjects,
Held in the bondage of ten bald-heads ; and
Though last, not least, *thy silence ! Couldst thou* say
Aught in its favour, who would praise like *thee ?*
Jac. Fos. Let us address us then, since so it must be,
To our departure. Who comes here ?

Enter LOREDANO *attended by Familiars.*

Lor. (*to the Familiars*).   Retire,
But leave the torch.   [*Exeunt the two Familiars.*
    Jac. Fos.   Most welcome, noble Signor.
I did not deem this poor place could have drawn   250
Such presence hither.
    Lor.   'Tis not the first time
I have visited these places.
    Mar.   Nor would be
The last, were all men's merits well rewarded.
Came you here to insult us, or remain[i.]
As spy upon us, or as hostage for us?
    Lor. Neither are of my office, noble Lady!
I am sent hither to your husband, to
Announce " the Ten's " decree.
    Mar.   That tenderness
Has been anticipated : it is known.
    Lor. As how?
    Mar.   I have informed him, not so gently, 260
Doubtless, as your nice feelings would prescribe,
The indulgence of your colleagues ; but he knew it.
If you come for our thanks, take them, and hence!
The dungeon gloom is deep enough without you,
And full of reptiles, not less loathsome, though
Their sting is honester.
    Jac. Fos.   I pray you, calm you :
What can avail such words?
    Mar.   To let him know
That he is known.
    Lor.   Let the fair dame preserve
Her sex's privilege.
    Mar.   I have some sons, sir,
Will one day thank you better.
    Lor.   You do well   270
To nurse them wisely. Foscari—you know
Your sentence, then?
    Jac. Fos.   Return to Candia?
    Lor.   True—
For life.

i. *Come you here to insult us ——.—[MS. M.]*

Jac. Fos. Not long.

Lor.   I said—for *life.*

Jac. Fos.   And I
Repeat—not long.

Lor.   A year's imprisonment
In Canea—afterwards the freedom of
The whole isle.

Jac. Fos.   Both the same to me : the after
Freedom as is the first imprisonment.
Is't true my wife accompanies me ?

Lor.   Yes,
If she so wills it.

Mar.   Who obtained that justice ?

Lor. One who wars not with women.

Mar.   But oppresses
Men : howsoever let him have *my* thanks   281
For the only boon I would have asked or taken
From him or such as he is.

Lor.   He receives them
As they are offered.

Mar.   May they thrive with him
So much !—no more.

Jac. Fos.   Is this, sir, your whole mission ?
Because we have brief time for preparation,
And you perceive your presence doth disquiet
This lady, of a house noble as yours.

Mar. Nobler !

Lor.   How nobler ?

Mar.   As more generous !
We say the " generous steed " to express the purity   290
Of his high blood.   Thus much I've learnt, although
Venetian (who see few steeds save of bronze),[1]
From those Venetians who have skirred [2] the coasts
Of Egypt and her neighbour Araby :
And why not say as soon the " *generous man ?* "
If race be aught, it is in qualities

---

1. [For " steeds of brass," compare *Childe Harold*, Canto IV. stanza xiii. line 1, *Poetical Works*, 1899, ii. 338, and 336, *note* 1.]
2. [The first and all subsequent editions read " skimmed the coasts." Byron wrote " skirred," a word borrowed from Shakespeare.   Compare *Siege of Corinth*, line 692, *Poetical Works*, 1900, iii. 480, *note* 4.]

More than in years ; and mine, which is as old
As yours, is better in its product, nay—
Look not so stern—but get you back, and pore
Upon your genealogic tree's most green   300
Of leaves and most mature of fruits, and there
Blush to find ancestors, who would have blushed
For such a son—thou cold inveterate hater !

   Jac. Fos. Again, Marina !

   Mar.   Again ! *still*, Marina.
See you not, he comes here to glut his hate
With a last look upon our misery ?
Let him partake it !

   Jac. Fos.   That were difficult.

   Mar. Nothing more easy.   He partakes it now—
Aye, he may veil beneath a marble brow
And sneering lip the pang, but he partakes it.   310
A few brief words of truth shame the Devil's servants
No less than Master ; I have probed his soul
A moment, as the Eternal Fire, ere long,
Will reach it always.   See how he shrinks from me !
With death, and chains, and exile in his hand,
To scatter o'er his kind as he thinks fit ;
They are his weapons, not his armour, for
I have pierced him to the core of his cold heart.
I care not for his frowns !   We can but die,
And he but live, for him the very worst   320
Of destinies : each day secures him more
His tempter's.

   Jac. Fos.   This is mere insanity.

   Mar. It may be so ; and *who* hath made us *mad ?*

   Lor. Let her go on ; it irks not me.

   Mar.   That 's false !
You came here to enjoy a heartless triumph
Of cold looks upon manifold griefs !   You came
To be sued to in vain—to mark our tears,
And hoard our groans—to gaze upon the wreck
Which you have made a Prince's son—my husband ;
In short, to trample on the fallen—an office   330
The hangman shrinks from, as all men from him !
How have you sped ?   We are wretched, Signor, as
Your plots could make, and vengeance could desire us,

And how *feel you*?
 Lor.   As rocks.
 Mar.   By thunder blasted:
They feel not, but no less are shivered.   Come,
Foscari ; now let us go, and leave this felon,
The sole fit habitant of such a cell,
Which he has peopled often, but ne'er fitly
Till he himself shall brood in it alone.

Enter the DOGE.

 Jac. Fos. My father !
 Doge (embracing him). Jacopo ! my son—my son ! 340
 Jac. Fos. My father still !   How long it is since I
Have heard thee name my name—*our* name !
 Doge.   My boy !
Couldst thou but know——
 Jac. Fos.   I rarely, sir, have murmured.
 Doge. I feel too much thou hast not.
 Mar.   Doge, look there !
     [*She points to* LOREDANO.
 Doge. I see the man—what mean'st thou ?
 Mar.   Caution !
 Lor.   Being
The virtue which this noble lady most [L]
May practise, she doth well to recommend it.
 Mar. Wretch ! 'tis no virtue, but the policy
Of those who fain must deal perforce with vice :
As such I recommend it, as I would   350
To one whose foot was on an adder's path.
 Doge. Daughter, it is superfluous ; I have long
Known Loredano.
 Lor.   You may know him better.
 Mar. Yes ; *worse* he could not.
 Jac. Fos.   Father, let not these
Our parting hours be lost in listening to
Reproaches, which boot nothing.   Is it—is it,
Indeed, our last of meetings ?
 Doge.   You behold
These white hairs !

  L —— *which this noble lady worst.*—[*MS. M.*]

Jac. Fos.   And I feel, besides, that mine
Will never be so white.   Embrace me, father !
I loved you ever—never more than now.   360
Look to my children—to your last child's children :
Let them be all to you which he was once,
And never be to you what I am now.
May I not see *them* also ?
     Mar.   No—not *here.*
     Jac. Fos. They might behold their parent any where.
     Mar. I would that they beheld their father in
A place which would not mingle fear with love,
To freeze their young blood in its natural current.
They have fed well, slept soft, and knew not that
Their sire was a mere hunted outlaw.   Well,   370
I know his fate may one day be their heritage,
But let it only be their *heritage,*
And not their present fee.   Their senses, though
Alive to love, are yet awake to terror ;
And these vile damps, too, and yon *thick green* wave
Which floats above the place where we now stand—
A cell so far below the water's level,
Sending its pestilence through every crevice,
Might strike them : *this is not their* atmosphere,
However you—and you—and most of all,   380
As worthiest—*you*, sir, noble Loredano !
May breathe it without prejudice.
     Jac. Fos.   I had not
Reflected upon this, but acquiesce.
I shall depart, then, without meeting them ?
     Doge. Not so : they shall await you in my chamber.
     Jac. Fos. And must I leave them—*all ?*
     Lor.   You must.
     Jac. Fos.   Not one ?
     Lor. They are the State's.
     Mar.   I thought they had been mine.
     Lor. They are, in all maternal things.
     Mar.   That is,
In all things painful.   If they're sick, they will
Be left to me to tend them ; should they die,   390
To me to bury and to mourn ; but if
They live, they'll make you soldiers, senators,

Slaves, exiles—what *you* will ; or if they are
Females with portions, brides and *bribes* for nobles !
Behold the State's care for its sons and mothers !
    Lor. The hour approaches, and the wind is fair.
    Jac. Fos. How know you that here, where the genial
        wind
Ne'er blows in all its blustering freedom ?
    Lor.   'Twas so
When I came here.   The galley floats within
A bow-shot of the " Riva di Schiavoni."   400
    Jac. Fos. Father ! I pray you to precede me, and
Prepare my children to behold their father.
    Doge. Be firm, my son !
    Jac. Fos.   I will do my endeavour.
    Mar. Farewell ! at least to this detested dungeon,
And him to whose good offices you owe
In part your past imprisonment.
    Lor.   And present
Liberation.
    Doge.   He speaks truth.
    Jac. Fos.   No doubt ! but 'tis
Exchange of chains for heavier chains I owe him.
He knows this, or he had not sought to change them,
But I reproach not.
    Lor.   The time narrows, Signor.   410
    Jac. Fos. Alas ! I little thought so lingeringly
To leave abodes like this : but when I feel
That every step I take, even from this cell,
Is one away from Venice, I look back
Even on these dull damp walls, and——
    Doge.   Boy ! no tears.
    Mar. Let them flow on : he wept not on the rack
To shame him, and they cannot shame him now.
They will relieve his heart—that too kind heart—
And I will find an hour to wipe away
Those tears, or add my own.   I could weep now,   420
But would not gratify yon wretch so far.
Let us proceed.   Doge, lead the way.
    Lor. (*to the Familiar*).   The torch, there !
    Mar. Yes, light us on, as to a funeral pyre,
With Loredano mourning like an heir.

Doge. My son, you are feeble ; take this hand.
 Jac. Fos.   Alas !
Must youth support itself on age, and I
Who ought to be the prop of yours ?
 Lor.   Take mine.
 Mar. Touch it not, Foscari ; 'twill sting you. Signor,
Stand off ! be sure, that if a grasp of yours
Would raise us from the gulf wherein we are plunged, 430
No hand of ours would stretch itself to meet it.
Come, Foscari, take the hand the altar gave you ;
It could not save, but will support you ever. [*Exeunt.*

ACT IV.

Scene I.—*A Hall in the Ducal Palace.*

Enter Loredano *and* Barbarigo.

 Bar. And have you confidence in such a project ?
 Lor. I have.
 Bar.   'Tis hard upon his years.
 Lor.   Say rather
Kind to relieve him from the cares of State.
 Bar. 'Twill break his heart.
 Lor.   Age has no heart to break.
He has seen his son's half broken, and, except
A start of feeling in his dungeon, never
Swerved.
 Bar. In his countenance, I grant you, never ;
But I have seen him sometimes in a calm
So desolate, that the most clamorous grief
Had nought to envy him within. Where is he ? 10
 Lor. In his own portion of the palace, with
His son, and the whole race of Foscaris.
 Bar. Bidding farewell.
 Lor.   A last ! as, soon, he shall
Bid to his Dukedom.
 Bar.   When embarks the son ?
 Lor. Forthwith—when this long leave is taken. 'Tis
Time to admonish them again.

Bar.   Forbear;
Retrench not from their moments.
   Lor.   Not I, now
We have higher business for our own.   This day
Shall be the last of the old Doge's reign,
As the first of his son's last banishment,   20
And that is vengeance.
   Bar.   In my mind, too deep.
   Lor. 'Tis moderate—not even life for life, the rule
Denounced of retribution from all time;
They owe me still my father's and my uncle's.
   Bar. Did not the Doge deny this strongly?
   Lor.   Doubtless.
   Bar. And did not this shake your suspicion?
   Lor.   No.
   Bar. But if this deposition should take place
By our united influence in the Council,
It must be done with all the deference
Due to his years, his station, and his deeds.   30
   Lor. As much of ceremony as you will,
So that the thing be done.   You may, for aught
I care, depute the Council on their knees,
(Like Barbarossa to the Pope,) to beg him
To have the courtesy to abdicate.
   Bar. What if he will not?
   Lor.   We'll elect another,
And make him null.
   Bar.   But will the laws uphold us?[1]
   Lor. What laws?—" The Ten " are laws; and if they
      were not,
I will be legislator in this business.
   Bar. At your own peril?
   Lor.   There is none, I tell you, 40
Our powers are such.
   Bar.   But he has twice already
Solicited permission to retire,
And twice it was refused.

   1. [According to the law, it rested with the six councillors of the
Doge and a majority of the Grand Council to insist upon the abdication
of a Doge.   The action of the Ten was an usurpation of powers to
which they were not entitled by the terms of the Constitution.]

Lor.   The better reason
To grant it the third time.
    Bar.   Unasked ?
    Lor.   It shows
The impression of his former instances :
If they were from his heart, he may be thankful :
If not, 'twill punish his hypocrisy.
Come, they are met by this time ; let us join them,
And be *thou* fixed in purpose for this once.
I have prepared such arguments as will not   50
Fail to move them, and to remove him : since
Their thoughts, their objects, have been sounded, do not
You, with your wonted scruples, teach us pause,
And all will prosper.
    Bar.   Could I but be certain
This is no prelude to such persecution
Of the sire as has fallen upon the son,
I would support you.
    Lor.   He is safe, I tell you ;
His fourscore years and five may linger on
As long as he can drag them : 'tis his throne
Alone is aimed at.
    Bar.   But discarded Princes   60
Are seldom long of life.
    Lor.   And men of eighty
More seldom still.
    Bar.   And why not wait these few years?
    Lor. Because we have waited long enough, and he
Lived longer than enough.   Hence ! in to council !
            [*Exeunt* LOREDANO *and* BARBARIGO.

Enter MEMMO [1] *and a Senator.*

Sen. A summons to "the Ten !" why so ?
Mem.   "The Ten"

   1. [A touching incident is told concerning an interview between the
Doge and Jacopo Memmo, head of the Forty. The Doge had just
learnt (October 21, 1457) the decision of the Ten with regard to his
abdication, and noticed that Memmo watched him attentively. "Foscari
called to him, and, touching his hand, asked him whose son he was.
He answered, 'I am the son of Messer Marin Memmo.'—'He is my
dear friend,' said the Doge ; 'tell him from me that it would be
pleasing to me if he would come and see me, so that we might go at

Alone can answer ; they are rarely wont
To let their thoughts anticipate their purpose
By previous proclamation.   We are summoned—
That is enough.
 Sen.   For them, but not for us ;
I would know why.
 Mem.   You will know why anon, 70
If you obey : and, if not, you no less
Will know why you should have obeyed.
 Sen.   I mean not
To oppose them, *but——*
 Mem.   In Venice " *but* "'s a traitor.
But me no " *buts*," unless you would pass o'er
The Bridge which few repass.[1]
 Sen.   I am silent.
 Mem.   Why
Thus hesitate ?   " The Ten " have called in aid
Of their deliberation five and twenty
Patricians of the Senate—you are one,
And I another ; and it seems to me
Both honoured by the choice or chance which leads us 80
To mingle with a body so august.
 Sen. Most true.   I say no more.
 Mem.   As we hope, Signor,
And all may honestly, (that is, all those
Of noble blood may,) one day hope to be
Decemvir, it is surely for the Senate's [i.]
Chosen delegates, a school of wisdom, to
Be thus admitted, though as novices,
To view the mysteries.
 Sen.   Let us view them : they,
No doubt, are worth it.
 Mem.   Being worth our lives
If we divulge them, doubtless they are worth 90
Something, at least to you or me.
 Sen.   I sought not
A place within the sanctuary ; but being

   i. *Decemvirs, it is surely* ——.—[*MS. M.*]

our leisure in our boats to visit the monasteries ' " (*The Two Doges*, by
A. Weil, 1891, p. 124 ; see, too, Romanin, *Storia, etc.*, 1855, iv. 291).]
 1. [*Vide ante*, p. 139, *note* 1.]

Chosen, however reluctantly so chosen,
I shall fulfil my office.
    Mem.   Let us not
Be latest in obeying " the Ten's " summons.
    Sen. All are not met, but I am of your thought
So far—let 's in.
    Mem.   The earliest are most welcome
In earnest councils—we will not be least so.   [*Exeunt.*

      Enter the DOGE, JACOPO FOSCARI, *and* MARINA.

    Jac. Fos. Ah, father! though I must and will depart,
Yet—yet—I pray you to obtain for me   100
That I once more return unto my home,
Howe'er remote the period. Let there be
A point of time, as beacon to my heart,
With any penalty annexed they please,
But let me still return.
    Doge.   Son Jacopo,
Go and obey our Country's will :[1] 'tis not
For us to look beyond.
    Jac. Fos.   But still I must
Look back. I pray you think of me.
    Doge.   Alas!
You ever were my dearest offspring, when
They were more numerous, nor can be less so   110
Now you are last ; but did the State demand
The exile of the disinterréd ashes
Of your three goodly brothers, now in earth,[2]
And their desponding shades came flitting round
To impede the act, I must no less obey
A duty, paramount to every duty.
    Mar. My husband! let us on : this but prolongs

---

1. [Romanin (*Storia, etc.*, 1855, iv. 285, 286) quotes the following
anecdote from the *Cronaca Dolfin :*—
"Alla commozione, alle lagrime, ai singulti che accompagnavano gli
ultimi abbraciamenti, Jacopo più che mai sentendo il dolore di quel
distacco, diceva : *Padre ve priego, procurè per mi, che ritorni a casa
mia.* E messer lo doxe : *Jacomo va e obbedisci quel che vuol la terra
e non cercar piu oltre.* Ma, uscito l'infelice figlio dalla stanza, più non
resistendo alla piena degli affetti, si gettò piangendo sopra una sedia e
lamentando diceva : *O pietà grande!*"]
    2. [*Vide ante,* act ii. sc. 1, line 174, p. 143, *note* 1.]

Our sorrow.

Jac. Fos.   But we are not summoned yet;
The galley's sails are not unfurled :—who knows?
The wind may change.

Mar.   And if it do, it will not   120
Change *their* hearts, or your lot : the galley's oars
Will quickly clear the harbour.

Jac. Fos.   O, ye Elements !
Where are your storms?

Mar.   In human breasts.   Alas !
Will nothing calm you?

Jac. Fos.   Never yet did mariner
Put up to patron saint such prayers for prosperous
And pleasant breezes, as I call upon you,
Ye tutelar saints of my own city ! which
Ye love not with more holy love than I,
To lash up from the deep the Adrian waves,
And waken Auster, sovereign of the Tempest !   130
Till the sea dash me back on my own shore
A broken corse upon the barren Lido,
Where I may mingle with the sands which skirt
The land I love, and never shall see more !

Mar. And wish you this with *me* beside you?

Jac. Fos.   No—
No—not for thee, too good, too kind !   May'st thou
Live long to be a mother to those children
Thy fond fidelity for a time deprives
Of such support !   But for myself alone,
May all the winds of Heaven howl down the Gulf,   140
And tear the vessel, till the mariners,
Appalled, turn their despairing eyes on me,
As the Phenicians did on Jonah, then
Cast me out from amongst them, as an offering
To appease the waves.   The billow which destroys me
Will be more merciful than man, and bear me
Dead, but *still bear* me to a native grave,
From fishers' hands, upon the desolate strand,
Which, of its thousand wrecks, hath ne'er received
One lacerated like the heart which then   150
Will be.—But wherefore breaks it not? why live I?

Mar. To man thyself, I trust, with time, to master

Such useless passion.   Until now thou wert
A sufferer, but not a loud one : why
What is this to the things thou hast borne in silence—
Imprisonment and actual torture ?
   Jac. Fos.   Double,
Triple, and tenfold torture !   But you are right,
It must be borne.   Father, your blessing.
   Doge.   Would
It could avail thee ! but no less thou hast it.
   Jac. Fos.   Forgive——
   Doge.   What ?
   Jac. Fos.   My poor mother, for my birth,
And me for having lived, and you yourself   161
(As I forgive you), for the gift of life,
Which you bestowed upon me as my sire.
   Mar.   What hast thou done ?
   Jac. Fos.   Nothing.   I cannot charge
My memory with much save sorrow : but
I have been so beyond the common lot
Chastened and visited, I needs must think
That I was wicked.   If it be so, may
What I have undergone here keep me from
A like hereafter !
   Mar.   Fear not : *that*'s reserved   170
For your oppressors.
   Jac. Fos.   Let me hope not.
   Mar.   Hope not ?
   Jac. Fos.   I cannot wish them *all* they have inflicted.
   Mar. All! the consummate fiends !   A thousandfold
May the worm which never dieth feed upon them !
   Jac. Fos.   They may repent.
   Mar.   And if they do, Heaven will not
Accept the tardy penitence of demons.

Enter an Officer and Guards.

   Off.   Signor ! the boat is at the shore—the wind
Is rising—we are ready to attend you.
   Jac. Fos.   And I to be attended.   Once more, father,
Your hand !
   Doge.   Take it.   Alas ! how thine own trembles !   180

Jac. Fos. No—you mistake; 'tis yours that shakes, my
  father.
Farewell !
  Doge.   Farewell !   Is there aught else?
  Jac. Fos.   No—nothing.
                                    [*To the Officer.*
Lend me your arm, good Signor.
  Offi.   You turn pale—
Let me support you—paler—ho ! some aid there !
Some water !
  Mar.   Ah, he is dying !
  Jac. Fos.   Now, I'm ready—
My eyes swim strangely—where 's the door?
  Mar.   Away !
Let me support him—my best love !   Oh, God !
How faintly beats this heart—this pulse !
  Jac. Fos.   The light !
Is it the light?—I am faint.
                        [*Officer presents him with water.*
  Offi.   He will be better,
Perhaps, in the air.
  Jac. Fos.   I doubt not.   Father—wife—   190
Your hands !
  Mar.   There 's death in that damp, clammy grasp.[1]
Oh, God !—My Foscari, how fare you?
  Jac. Fos.   Well ! [*He dies.*
  Offi. He 's gone !
  Doge.   He 's free.
  Mar.   No—no, he is not dead ;
There must be life yet in that heart—he could not [i]
Thus leave me.
  Doge.   Daughter !
  Mar.   Hold thy peace, old man !

---

i. —— *he would not*
  Thus leave me.—[*MS. M.*]

1. [So, too, Coleridge of Keats: "There is death in that hand;"
and of Adam Steinmetz: "Alas! there is *death* in that dear hand."
See *Table Talk* for August 14, 1832, and *Letter to John Peirse Kennard,*
August 13, 1832, *Letters of S. T. C.,* 1895, ii. 764. Jacopo Foscari was
sent back to exile in Crete, and did not die till February, 1457. His
death at Venice, immediately after his sentence, is contrived for the
sake of observing " the unities."]

I am no daughter now—thou hast no son.
Oh, Foscari!
  Offi.   We must remove the body.
  Mar. Touch it not, dungeon miscreants! your base
    office
Ends with his life, and goes not beyond murder,
Even by your murderous laws. Leave his remains 200
To those who know to honour them.
  Offi.   I must
Inform the Signory, and learn their pleasure.
  Doge. Inform the Signory from *me*, the Doge,
They have no further power upon those ashes:
While he lived, he was theirs, as fits a subject—
Now he is *mine*—my broken-hearted boy! [*Exit Officer.*
  Mar. And I must live!
  Doge.   Your children live, Marina.
  Mar. My children! true—they live, and I must live
To bring them up to serve the State, and die
As died their father. Oh! what best of blessings 210
Were barrenness in Venice! Would my mother
Had been so!
  Doge.   My unhappy children!
  Mar.   What!
You feel it then at last—*you !*—Where is now
The Stoic of the State?
  Doge (*throwing himself down by the body*). *Here !*
  Mar.   Aye, weep on!
I thought you had no tears—you hoarded them
Until they are useless; but weep on! he never
Shall weep more—never, never more.

Enter LOREDANO *and* BARBARIGO.

  Lor.   What's here?
  Mar. Ah! the Devil come to insult the dead! Avaunt
Incarnate Lucifer! 'tis holy ground.
A martyr's ashes now lie there, which make it 220
A shrine. Get thee back to thy place of torment!
  Bar. Lady, we knew not of this sad event,
But passed here merely on our path from council.
  Mar. Pass on.

Lor.   We sought the Doge.

Mar. (pointing to the Doge, who is still on the ground
        by his son's body).   He 's busy, look,
About the business *you* provided for him.
Are ye content?

Bar.   We will not interrupt
A parent's sorrows.

Mar.   No, ye only make them,
Then leave them.

Doge (rising).   Sirs, I am ready.

Bar.   No—not now.

Lor. Yet 'twas important.

Doge.   If 'twas so, I can
Only repeat—I am ready.

Bar.   It shall not be   230
Just now, though Venice tottered o'er the deep
Like a frail vessel.   I respect your griefs.

Doge. I thank you.   If the tidings which you bring
Are evil, you may say them; nothing further
Can touch me more than him thou look'st on there;
If they be good, say on; you need not *fear*
That they can *comfort* me.

Bar.   I would they could!

Doge. I spoke not to *you*, but to Loredano.
He understands me.

Mar.   Ah! I thought it would be so.

Doge. What mean you?

Mar.   Lo! there is the blood beginning   240
To flow through the dead lips of Foscari—
The body bleeds in presence of the assassin.
                                        [*To* LOREDANO.
Thou cowardly murderer by law, behold
How Death itself bears witness to thy deeds!

Doge. My child! this is a phantasy of grief.
Bear hence the body. [*To his attendants.*] Signors, if
        it please you,
Within an hour I'll hear you.
        [*Exeunt* DOGE, MARINA, *and attendants with the*
            body. Manent LOREDANO *and* BARBARIGO.

Bar.   He must not
Be troubled **now.**

Lor.   He said himself that nought
Could give him trouble farther.
  Bar.   These are words;
But Grief is lonely, and the breaking in   250
Upon it barbarous.
  Lor.   Sorrow preys upon
Its solitude, and nothing more diverts it
From its sad visions of the other world,
Than calling it at moments back to this.
The busy have no time for tears.
  Bar.   And therefore
You would deprive this old man of all business?
  Lor. The thing 's decreed. The Giunta[1] and " the
   Ten "
Have made it law—who shall oppose that law?
  Bar. Humanity!
  Lor.   Because his son is dead?
  Bar. And yet unburied.
  Lor.   Had we known this when 260
The act was passing, it might have suspended
Its passage, but impedes it not—once passed.
  Bar. I'll not consent.
  Lor.   You have consented to
All that 's essential—leave the rest to me.
  Bar. Why press his abdication now?
  Lor.   The feelings
Of private passion may not interrupt
The public benefit; and what the State
Decides to-day must not give way before
To-morrow for a natural accident.
  Bar. You have a son.
  Lor.   I *have*—and *had* a father. 270
  Bar. Still so inexorable?
  Lor.   Still.
  Bar.   But let him
Inter his son before we press upon him

---

1. [It is to be noted that the " Giunta " was demanded by Loredano himself—a proof of his *bona fides*, as the addition of twenty-five nobles to the original Ten would add to the chance of opposition on the part of the supporters and champions of the Doge (see *The Two Doges*, p. 116, and Romanin, *Storia, etc.*, iv. 286, *note* 3).]

This edict.
    Lor.   Let him call up into life
My sire and uncle—I consent.   Men may,
Even agéd men, be, or appear to be,
Sires of a hundred sons, but cannot kindle
An atom of their ancestors from earth.
The victims are not equal ; he has seen
His sons expire by natural deaths, and I
My sires by violent and mysterious maladies.   280
I used no poison, bribed no subtle master
Of the destructive art of healing, to
Shorten the path to the eternal cure.
His sons—and he had four—are dead, without
My dabbling in vile drugs.
    Bar.   And art thou sure
He dealt in such ?
    Lor.   Most sure.
    Bar.   And yet he seems
All openness.
    Lor.   And so he seemed not long
Ago to Carmagnuola.
    Bar.   The attainted
And foreign traitor ?
    Lor.   Even so : when *he*,
After the very night in which " the Ten "   290
(Joined with the Doge) decided his destruction,
Met the great Duke at daybreak with a jest,
Demanding whether he should augur him
" The good day or good night ? " his Doge-ship answered,
" That he in truth had passed a night of vigil,
" In which " (he added with a gracious smile)
" There often has been question about you." [1]
'Twas true ; the question was the death resolved
Of Carmagnuola, eight months ere he died ;
And the old Doge, who knew him doomed, smiled on
       him   300

    1. An historical fact.   See DARU [1821], tom. ii. [pp. 398, 399.
Daru quotes as his authorities Sabellicus and Pietro Giustiniani.   As
a matter of fact, the Doge did his utmost to save Carmagnola,
pleading that his sentence should be commuted to imprisonment for
life (see *The Two Doges*, p. 66; and Romanin, *Storia, etc.*, iv.
161).]

With deadly cozenage, eight long months beforehand—
Eight months of such hypocrisy as is
Learnt but in eighty years.   Brave Carmagnuola
Is dead; so is young Foscari and his brethren—
I never *smiled* on *them*.
    Bar.   Was Carmagnuola
Your friend?
    Lor.   He was the safeguard of the city.
In early life its foe, but in his manhood,
Its saviour first, then victim.
    Bar.   Ah! that seems
The penalty of saving cities.   He
Whom we now act against not only saved   310
Our own, but added others to her sway.
    Lor. The Romans (and we ape them) gave a crown
To him who took a city: and they gave
A crown to him who saved a citizen
In battle: the rewards are equal.   Now,
If we should measure forth the cities taken
By the Doge Foscari, with citizens
Destroyed by him, or *through* him, the account
Were fearfully against him, although narrowed
To private havoc, such as between him   320
And my dead father.
    Bar.   Are you then thus fixed?
    Lor. Why, what should change me?
    Bar.   That which changes me.
But you, I know, are marble to retain
A feud.   But when all is accomplished, when
The old man is deposed, his name degraded,
His sons all dead, his family depressed,
And you and yours triumphant, shall you sleep?
    Lor. More soundly.
    Bar.   That's an error, and you'll find it
Ere you sleep with your fathers.
    Lor.   They sleep not
In their accelerated graves, nor will   330
Till Foscari fills his.   Each night I see them
Stalk frowning round my couch, and, pointing towards
The ducal palace, marshal me to vengeance.
    Bar. Fancy's distemperature!   There is no passion

More spectral or fantastical than Hate ,
Not even its opposite, Love, so peoples air
With phantoms, as this madness of the heart.

Enter an Officer.

　Lor. Where go you, sirrah?
　Offi.　　　　　　　By the ducal order
To forward the preparatory rites
For the late Foscari's interment.
　Bar.　　　　　　Their　　　　340
Vault has been often opened of late years.
　Lor. 'Twill be full soon, and may be closed for ever !
　Offi. May I pass on?
　Lor.　　　　You may.
　Bar.　　　　　　How bears the Doge
This last calamity?
　Offi.　　　　With desperate firmness.
In presence of another he says little,
But I perceive his lips move now and then ;
And once or twice I heard him, from the adjoining
Apartment, mutter forth the words—" My son ! "
Scarce audibly.　I must proceed.　　*[Exit Officer.*
　Bar.　　　　　This stroke
Will move all Venice in his favour.
　Lor.　　　　　　Right !　　　350
We must be speedy : let us call together
The delegates appointed to convey
The Council's resolution.
　Bar.　　　　　I protest
Against it at this moment.
　Lor.　　　　　As you please—
I'll take their voices on it ne'ertheless,
And see whose most may sway them, yours or mine.
　　　　　　[Exeunt BARBARIGO *and* LOREDANO

ACT V.

SCENE I.—*The* DOGE'S *Apartment.*

The DOGE *and Attendants.*

Att. My Lord, the deputation is in waiting;
But add, that if another hour would better
Accord with your will, they will make it theirs.
   Doge. To me all hours are like. Let them approach.
                                [Exit Attendant.
   An Officer. Prince! I have done your bidding.
   Doge.   What command?
   Offi. A melancholy one—to call the attendance
Of——
   Doge. True—true—true: I crave your pardon. I
Begin to fail in apprehension, and
Wax very old—old almost as my years.
Till now I fought them off, but they begin   10
To overtake me.

*Enter the Deputation, consisting of six of the Signory
and the Chief of the Ten.*

                   Noble men, your pleasure!
   Chief of the Ten. In the first place, the Council doth
        condole
With the Doge on his late and private grief.
   Doge. No more—no more of that.
   Chief of the Ten.   Will not the Duke
Accept the homage of respect?
   Doge.   I do
Accept it as 'tis given—proceed.
   Chief of the Ten.   " The Ten,"
With a selected giunta from the Senate
Of twenty-five of the best born patricians,
Having deliberated on the state
Of the Republic, and the o'erwhelming cares   20
Which, at this moment, doubly must oppress
Your years, so long devoted to your Country,

Have judged it fitting, with all reverence,
Now to solicit from your wisdom (which
Upon reflection must accord in this),
The resignation of the ducal ring,
Which you have worn so long and venerably:
And to prove that they are not ungrateful, nor
Cold to your years and services, they add
An appanage of twenty hundred golden   30
Ducats, to make retirement not less splendid
Than should become a Sovereign's retreat.

Doge. Did I hear rightly?
Chief of the Ten.   Need I say again?
Doge. No.—Have you done?
Chief of the Ten.   I have spoken.   Twenty four [1]
Hours are accorded you to give an answer.

Doge. I shall not need so many seconds.
Chief of the Ten.   We
Will now retire.

Doge.   Stay! four and twenty hours
Will alter nothing which I have to say.
Chief of the Ten. Speak!
Doge.   When I twice before reiterated
My wish to abdicate, it was refused me: 40
And not alone refused, but ye exacted
An oath from me that I would never more
Renew this instance.   I have sworn to die
In full exertion of the functions, which
My Country called me here to exercise,
According to my honour and my conscience—
I cannot break *my* oath.
Chief of the Ten.   Reduce us not
To the alternative of a decree,
Instead of your compliance.

Doge.   Providence
Prolongs my days to prove and chasten me;   50
But ye have no right to reproach my length

---

1. [By the terms of the "parte," or act of deposition drawn up by
the Ten, October 21, 1457, the time granted for deliberation was " till
the third hour of the following day."   This limitation as to time was
designed to prevent the Doge from summoning the Grand Council,
" to whom alone belonged the right of releasing him from the dukedom " (*The Two Doges*, p. 118; *Die beiden Foscari*, 1878, pp. 174-176).]

Of days, since every hour has been the Country's.
I am ready to lay down my life for her,
As I have laid down dearer things than life:
But for my dignity—I hold it of
The *whole* Republic: when the *general* will
Is manifest, then you shall all be answered.

    Chief of the Ten. We grieve for such an answer; but
      it cannot
Avail you aught.

    Doge.   I can submit to all things,
But nothing will advance; no, not a moment.   60
What you decree—decree.

    Chief of the Ten.   With this, then, must we
Return to those who sent us?

    Doge.   You have heard me.

    Chief of the Ten. With all due reverence we retire.

                   [Exeunt the Deputation, etc.

Enter an Attendant.

    Att.   My Lord,
The noble dame Marina craves an audience.

    Doge. My time is hers.

Enter MARINA.

    Mar.   My Lord, if I intrude—
Perhaps you fain would be alone?

    Doge.   Alone!
Alone, come all the world around me, I
Am now and evermore. But we will bear it.

    Mar. We will, and for the sake of those who are,
Endeavour——Oh, my husband!

    Doge.   Give it way: 70
I cannot comfort thee.

    Mar.   He might have lived,
So formed for gentle privacy of life,
So loving, so beloved; the native of
Another land, and who so blest and blessing
As my poor Foscari? Nothing was wanting
Unto his happiness and mine save not
To be Venetian.

Doge.   Or a Prince's son.

Mar. Yes; all things which conduce to other men's
Imperfect happiness or high ambition,
By some strange destiny, to him proved deadly.   80
The Country and the People whom he loved,
The Prince of whom he was the elder born,
And——

 Doge.   Soon may be a Prince no longer.

 Mar.   How?

 Doge. They have taken my son from me, and now aim
At my too long worn diadem and ring.
Let them resume the gewgaws!

 Mar.   Oh, the tyrants!
In such an hour too!

 Doge.   'Tis the fittest time;
An hour ago I should have felt it.

 Mar.   And
Will you not now resent it?—Oh, for vengeance!
But he, who, had he been enough protected,   90
Might have repaid protection in this moment,
Cannot assist his father.

 Doge.   Nor should do so
Against his Country, had he a thousand lives
Instead of that——

 Mar.   They tortured from him.   This
May be pure patriotism.   I am a woman:
To me my husband and my children were
Country and home.   I loved *him*—how I loved him!
I have seen him pass through such an ordeal as
The old martyrs would have shrunk from: he is gone,
And I, who would have given my blood for him,   100
Have nought to give but tears!   But could I compass
The retribution of his wrongs!—Well, well!
I have sons, who shall be men.

 Doge.   Your grief distracts you.

 Mar. I thought I could have borne it, when I saw him
Bowed down by such oppression; yes, I thought
That I would rather look upon his corse
Than his prolonged captivity:—I am punished
For that thought now.   Would I were in his grave!

 Doge. I must look on him once more.

Mar.   Come with me !
Doge. Is he——
Mar.   Our bridal bed is now his bier. 110
Doge. And he is in his shroud !
Mar.   Come, come, old man !
                    [*Exeunt the* DOGE *and* MARINA.

Enter BARBARIGO *and* LOREDANO.

Bar. (*to an Attendant*). Where is the Doge?
Att.   This instant retired hence,
With the illustrious lady his son's widow.
Lor. Where?
Att.   To the chamber where the body lies.
Bar. Let us return, then.
Lor.   You forget, you cannot.
We have the implicit order of the Giunta
To await their coming here, and join them in
Their office : they'll be here soon after us.
Bar. And will they press their answer on the Doge?
Lor. 'Twas his own wish that all should be done
                    promptly.   120
He answered quickly, and must so be answered ;
His dignity is looked to, his estate
Cared for—what would he more ?
Bar.   Die in his robes :
He could not have lived long ; but I have done
My best to save his honours, and opposed
This proposition to the last, though vainly.
Why would the general vote compel me hither?
Lor. 'Twas fit that some one of such different thoughts
From ours should be a witness, lest false tongues
Should whisper that a harsh majority   130
Dreaded to have its acts beheld by others.
Bar. And not less, I must needs think, for the sake
Of humbling me for my vain opposition.
You are ingenious, Loredano, in
Your modes of vengeance, nay, poetical,
A very Ovid in the art of *hating ;*
'Tis thus (although a secondary object,
Yet hate has microscopic eyes), to you

I owe, by way of foil to the more zealous,
This undesired association in   140
Your Giunta's duties.
 Lor.   How !—*my* Giunta !
 Bar.   *Yours !*
They speak your language, watch your nod, approve
Your plans, and do your work. Are they not *yours ?*
 Lor. You talk unwarily. 'Twere best they hear not
This from you.
 Bar.   Oh ! they'll hear as much one day
From louder tongues than mine ; they have gone beyond
Even their exorbitance of power : and when
This happens in the most contemned and abject
States, stung humanity will rise to check it.
 Lor. You talk but idly.
 Bar.   That remains for proof. 150
Here come our colleagues.

    Enter the Deputation as before.

 Chief of the Ten.   Is the Duke aware
We seek his presence ?
 Att.   He shall be informed.
           [*Exit Attendant.*
 Bar. The Duke is with his son.
 Chief of the Ten.   If it be so,
We will remit him till the rites are over.
Let us return. 'Tis time enough to-morrow.
 Lor. (*aside to Bar.*). Now the rich man's hell-fire upon
   your tongue,
Unquenched, unquenchable ! I'll have it torn
From its vile babbling roots, till you shall utter
Nothing but sobs through blood, for this ! Sage Signors,
I pray ye be not hasty.   [*Aloud to the others.*
 Bar.   But be human ! 160
 Lor. See, the Duke comes !

    Enter the DOGE.

 Doge.   I have obeyed your summons.
 Chief of the Ten. We come once more to urge our past
   request.

Doge. And I to answer.
Chief of the Ten.　　　　What?
Doge.　　　　　　　My only answer.
You have heard it.
　　Chief of the Ten. Hear *you* then the last decree,
Definitive and absolute!
　　Doge.　　　　　To the point—
To the point! I know of old the forms of office,
And gentle preludes to strong acts.—Go on!
　　Chief of the Ten. You are no longer Doge; you are
　　　released
From your imperial oath as Sovereign;
Your ducal robes must be put off; but for　　　170
Your services, the State allots the appanage
Already mentioned in our former congress.
Three days are left you to remove from hence,
Under the penalty to see confiscated
All your own private fortune.
　　Doge.　　　　　That last clause,
I am proud to say, would not enrich the treasury.
　　Chief of the Ten. Your answer, Duke!
　　Lor.　　　　　Your answer, Francis
　　　Foscari!
　　Doge. If I could have foreseen that my old age
Was prejudicial to the State, the Chief
Of the Republic never would háve shown　　　180
Himself so far ungrateful, as to place
His own high dignity before his Country;
But this *life* having been so many years
Not useless to that Country, I would fain
Have consecrated my last moments to her.
But the decree being rendered, I obey.[i][1]
　　Chief of the Ten. If you would have the three days
　　　named extended,
We willingly will lengthen them to eight,
As sign of our esteem.
　　Doge.　　　Not eight hours, Signor,

---

i. *The act is passed—I will obey it.—*[MS. M.]

1. [For this speech, see Daru (who quotes from Pietro Giustiniani
Histoire, etc., 1821, ii. 534).]

Not even eight minutes—there 's the ducal ring,   190
           [*Taking off his ring and cap.*
And there the ducal diadem !   And so
The Adriatic 's free to wed another.
    Chief of the Ten. Yet go not forth so quickly.
    Doge.   I am old, sir,
And even to move but slowly must begin
To move betimes.   Methinks I see amongst you
A face I know not.—Senator ! your name,
You, by your garb, Chief of the Forty !
    Mem.   Signor,
I am the son of Marco Memmo.
    Doge.   Ah !
Your father was my friend.—But *sons* and *fathers !*—
What, ho ! my servants there !
    Atten.   My Prince !
    Doge.   No Prince—   200
There are the princes of the Prince ! [*Pointing to the
      Ten's Deputation.*]—Prepare
To part from hence upon the instant.
    Chief of the Ten.   Why
So rashly ? 'twill give scandal.
    Doge.   Answer that ;
                 [*To the Ten.*
It is your province.—Sirs, bestir yourselves :
                 [*To the Servants.*
There is one burthen which I beg you bear
With care, although 'tis past all farther harm—
But I will look to that myself.
    Bar.   He means
The body of his son.
    Doge.   And call Marina,
My daughter !

Enter MARINA.

    Doge.   Get thee ready, we must mourn
Elsewhere.
    Mar.   And everywhere.
    Doge.   True ; but in freedom, 210
Without these jealous spies upon the great.
Signors, you may depart : what would you more ?

We are going : do you fear that we shall bear
The palace with us ?   Its *old* walls, ten times
As *old* as I am, and I'm very old,
Have served you, so have I, and I and they
Could tell a tale ; but I invoke them not
To fall upon you ! else they would, as erst
The pillars of stone Dagon's temple on
The Israelite and his Philistine foes.   220
Such power I do believe there might exist
In such a curse as mine, provoked by such
As you ; but I curse not.   Adieu, good Signors !
May the next Duke be better than the present !
   Lor. The *present* Duke is Paschal Malipiero.
   Doge. Not till I pass the threshold of these doors.
   Lor. Saint Mark's great bell is soon about to toll
For his inauguration.
   Doge.   Earth and Heaven !
Ye will reverberate this peal ; and I
Live to hear this !—the first Doge who e'er heard   230
Such sound for his successor : happier he,
My attainted predecessor, stern Faliero—
This insult at the least was spared him.
   Lor.   What !
Do you regret a traitor ?
   Doge.   No—I merely
Envy the dead.
   Chief of the Ten. My Lord, if you indeed
Are bent upon this rash abandonment
Of the State's palace, at the least retire
By the private staircase, which conducts you towards
The landing-place of the canal.
   Doge.   No. I
Will now descend the stairs by which I mounted   240
To sovereignty—the Giants' Stairs, on whose
Broad eminence I was invested Duke.
My services have called me up those steps,
The malice of my foes will drive me down them.[1]
There five and thirty years ago was I
Installed, and traversed these same halls, from which

---

1. [See Daru's *Histoire, etc.*, 1821, ii. 535. The *Cronaca Augustini*
is the authority for the anecdote (see *The Two Doges*, 1891, p. 126).]

I never thought to be divorced except
A corse—a corse, it might be, fighting for them—
But not pushed hence by fellow-citizens.
But come; my son and I will go together—   250
He to his grave, and I to pray for mine.
    Chief of the Ten. What ! thus in public ?
    Doge.   I was publicly
Elected, and so will I be deposed.
Marina ! art thou willing ?
    Mar.   Here 's my arm !
    Doge. And here my *staff :* thus propped will I go
    forth.
    Chief of the Ten. It must not be—the people will
    perceive it.
    Doge. The people !—There 's no people, you well
    know it,
Else you dare not deal thus by them or me.
There is a *populace*, perhaps, whose looks
May shame you; but they dare not groan nor curse
    you,   260
Save with their hearts and eyes.
    Chief of the Ten.   You speak in passion,
Else——
    Doge. You have reason.   I have spoken much
More than my wont : it is a foible which
Was not of mine, but more excuses you,
Inasmuch as it shows, that I approach
A dotage which may justify this deed
Of yours, although the law does not, nor will.
Farewell, sirs !
    Bar.   You shall not depart without
An escort fitting past and present rank.
We will accompany, with due respect,   270
The Doge unto his private palace.   Say !
My brethren, will we not?
    Different voices.   Aye !—Aye !
    Doge.   You shall not
Stir—in my train, at least.   I entered here
As Sovereign—I go out as citizen
By the same portals, but as citizen.
All these vain ceremonies are base insults,

Which only ulcerate the heart the more,
Applying poisons there as antidotes.
Pomp is for Princes—I am none !—That 's false,
I *am*, but only to these gates.—Ah !

    Lor.   Hark !   280
                       [*The great bell of St. Mark's tolls.*

    Bar. The bell !
    Chief of the Ten. St. Mark's, which tolls for the
         election
Of Malipiero.
    Doge.   Well I recognise
The sound ! I heard it once, but once before,
And that is five and thirty years ago ;
Even *then* I *was not young.*
    Bar.   Sit down, my Lord !
You tremble.
    Doge.   'Tis the knell of my poor boy !
My heart aches bitterly.
    Bar.   I pray you sit.
    Doge. No ; my seat here has been a throne till now.
Marina ! let us go.
    Mar.   Most readily.
    Doge (*walks a few steps, then stops*). I feel athirst—
         will no one bring me here   290
A cup of water ?
    Bar.   I——
    Mar.   And I——
    Lor.   And I——
       [*The Doge takes a goblet from the hand of* LOREDANO.
    Doge. I take *yours*, Loredano, from the hand
Most fit for such an hour as this.[i]
    Lor.   Why so ?
    Doge. 'Tis said that our Venetian crystal has
Such pure antipathy to poisons as
To burst, if aught of venom touches it.
You bore this goblet, and it is not broken.
    Lor. Well, sir !
    Doge.   Then it is false, or you are true
For my own part, I credit neither ; 'tis

        i. *I take yours, Loredano—'tis the draught*
          Most fitting such an hour as this.—[*MS. M.*]

An idle legend.

 Mar.   You talk wildly, and   300
Had better now be seated, nor as yet
Depart. Ah! now you look as looked my husband!

 Bar. He sinks!—support him!—quick—a chair—
  support him!

 Doge. The bell tolls on!—let's hence—my brain 's on
  fire!

 Bar. I do beseech you, lean upon us!

 Doge.   No!
A Sovereign should die standing. My poor boy!
Off with your arms!—*That bell!* [1]

      [*The* DOGE *drops down and dies.*

 Mar.   My God! My God!

 Bar. (*to Lor.*). Behold! your work 's completed!

 Chief of the Ten.   Is there then
No aid? Call in assistance!

 Att.   'Tis all over.

 Chief of the Ten. If it be so, at least his obsequies 310
Shall be such as befits his name and nation,
His rank and his devotion to the duties
Of the realm, while his age permitted him
To do himself and them full justice. Brethren,
Say, shall it not be so?

 Bar.   He has not had
The misery to die a subject where [i]
He reigned: then let his funeral rites be princely.[2]

 Chief of the Ten. We are agreed, then?

 All, except Lor., answer,   Yes.

---

    i. *The wretchedness to die* ——.—[*MS. M.*]

  1. [*Vide ante*, Introduction to *The Two Foscari*, p. 118.]
  2. ["A decree was at once passed that a public funeral should be
accorded to Foscari, . . . and the bells of St. Mark were ordered to peal
nine times. . . . The same Council also determined that on Thursday
night, November 3, the corpse should be carried into the room of the
'Signori di notte,' dressed in a golden mantle, with the ducal bonnet on
his head, golden spurs on his feet, . . . the gold sword by his side."
But Foscari's wife, Marina (or Maria) Nani, opposed. "She declined to
give up the body, which she had caused to be dressed in plain clothes,
and she maintained that no one but herself should provide for the
funeral expenses, even should she have to give up her dower." It is
needless to add that her protest was unavailing, and that the decree of
the Ten carried into effect.—*The Two Doges*, 1891, pp. 129, 130.]

Chief of the Ten. Heaven's peace be with him !
  Mar. Signors, your pardon : this is mockery.   320
Juggle no more with that poor remnant, which,
A moment since, while yet it had a soul,
(A soul by whom you have increased your Empire,
And made your power as proud as was his glory),
You banished from his palace and tore down
From his high place, with such relentless coldness ;
And now, when he can neither know these honours,
Nor would accept them if he could, you, Signors,
Purpose, with idle and superfluous pomp,
To make a pageant over what you trampled.   330
A princely funeral will be your reproach,
And not his honour.
  Chief of the Ten.   Lady, we revoke not
Our purposes so readily.
  Mar.   I know it,
As far as touches torturing the living.
I thought the dead had been beyond even *you*,
Though (some, no doubt) consigned to powers which may
Resemble that you exercise on earth.
Leave him to me ; you would have done so for
His dregs of life, which you have kindly shortened :
It is my last of duties, and may prove   340
A dreary comfort in my desolation.[i.]
Grief is fantastical, and loves the dead,
And the apparel of the grave.
  Chief of the Ten.   Do you
Pretend still to this office ?
  Mar.   I do, Signor.
Though his possessions have been all consumed
In the State's service, I have still my dowry,
Which shall be consecrated to his rites,
And those of——   [*She stops with agitation.*
  Chief of the Ten. Best retain it for your children.
  Mar. Aye, they are fatherless, I thank you.
  Chief of the Ten.   We
Cannot comply with your request.   His relics   350
Shall be exposed with wonted pomp, and followed
Unto their home by the new Doge, not clad

i. —— *comfort to my desolation.*—[*MS. M.*]

As *Doge*, but simply as a senator.

Mar. I have heard of murderers, who have interred
Their victims ; but ne'er heard, until this hour,
Of so much splendour in hypocrisy
O'er those they slew.[1] I've heard of widows' tears—
Alas ! I have shed some—always thanks to you !
I've heard of *heirs* in sables—you have left none
To the deceased, so you would act the part   360
Of such. Well, sirs, your will be done ! as one day,
I trust, Heaven's will be done too !ⁱ

    Chief of the Ten.   Know you, Lady,
To whom ye speak, and perils of such speech ?

    Mar. I know the former better than yourselves ;
The latter—like yourselves ; and can face both.
Wish you more funerals ?

    Bar.   Heed not her rash words ;
Her circumstances must excuse her bearing.

    Chief of the Ten. We will not note them down.

    Bar. (turning to Lor., who is writing upon his tablets).
                     What art thou writing,
With such an earnest brow, upon thy tablets ?

    Lor. (pointing to the Doge's body). That *he* has paid
    me ![2]

---

    i. *I trust Heaven's will be done also.*—[*MS.*]

    1. The Venetians appear to have had a particular turn for breaking the hearts of their Doges. The following is another instance of the kind in the Doge Marco Barbarigo : he was succeeded by his brother Agostino Barbarigo, whose chief merit is here mentioned.—"Le doge, blessé de trouver constamment un contradicteur et un censeur si amer dans son frère, lui dit un jour en plein conseil : 'Messire Augustin, vous faites tout votre possible pour hâter ma mort ; vous vous flattez de me succéder ; mais, si les autres vous connaissent aussi bien que je vous connais, ils n'auront garde de vous élire.' Là-dessus il se leva, ému de colère, rentra dans son appartement, et mourut quelques jours après. Ce frère, contre lequel il s'était emporté, fut précisément le successeur qu'on lui donna. C'était un mérite dont on aimait à tenir compte ; surtout à un parent, de s'être mis en opposition avec le chef de la république."—DARU, *Hist. de Vénise*, 1821, iii. 29.
    2. "*L'ha pagata.*" An historical fact. See *Hist. de Vénise*, par P. DARU, 1821, ii. 528, 529.
    [Daru quotes Palazzi's *Fasti Ducales* as his authority for this story. According to Pietro Giustiniani (*Storia*, lib. viii.), Jacopo Loredano was at pains to announce the decree of the Ten to the Doge in courteous and considerate terms, and begged him to pardon him for what it was his duty to do. Romanin points out that this version of the interview is inconsistent with the famous " *l'ha pagata.*"—*Storia, etc.*, iv. 290, *note* 1.]

Chief of the Ten.   What debt did he owe you? 370
Lor. A long and just one; Nature's debt and *mine.*[1]
                                                    [*Curtain falls.*[2]

1. [Here the original MS. ends. The two lines which follow, were
added by Gifford. In the margin of the MS. Byron has written,
"If the last line should appear obscure to those who do not recollect
the historical fact mentioned in the first act of Loredano's inscription
in his book, of ' Doge Foscari, debtor for the deaths of my father and
uncle,' you may add the following lines to the conclusion of the last
act :—

> *Chief of the Ten.* For what has he repaid thee?
> *Lor.*   For my father's
> And father's brother's death—by his son's and own!

Ask Gifford about this."]

2. [The *Appendix* to the First Edition of *The Two Foscari* consisted
of (i.) an extract from P. Daru's *Histoire de la République Française*,
1821, ii. 520–537; (ii.) an extract from J. C. L. Simonde de Sismondi's
Histoire des Républiques Italiennes du Moyen Age, 1815, x. 36–46; and
(iii.) a note in response to certain charges of plagiarism brought against
the author in the *Literary Gazette* and elsewhere; and to Southey's
indictment of the "Satanic School," which had recently appeared in
the Preface to the Laureate's *Vision of Judgement* (*Poetical Works of
Robert Southey*, 1838, x. 202-207). See, too, the Introduction to *The
Vision of Judgment, Poetical Works*, 1901, iv. 475-480.]

CAIN:

A MYSTERY.

"Now the Serpent was more subtil than any beast of the field which
the Lord God had made."

Genesis,
Chapter 3rd, verse 1.

INTRODUCTION TO *CAIN*.

CAIN was begun at Ravenna, July 16, and finished September 9, 1821 (*vide* MS. M.). Six months before, when he was at work on the first act of *Sardanapalus*, Byron had "pondered" *Cain*, but it was not till *Sardanapalus* and a second historical play, *The Two Foscari*, had been written, copied out, and sent to England, that he indulged his genius with a third drama—on "a metaphysical subject, something in the style of *Manfred*" (*Letters*, 1901, v. 189).

Goethe's comment on reading and reviewing *Cain* was that he should be surprised if Byron did not pursue the treatment of such "biblical subjects," as the destruction of Sodom and Gomorrah (*Conversations, etc.*, 1879, p. 62); and, many years after, he told Crabb Robinson (*Diary*, 1869, ii. 435) that Byron should have lived " to execute his vocation . . . to dramatize the Old Testament." He was better equipped for such a task than might have been imagined. A Scottish schoolboy, "from a child he had known the Scriptures," and, as his *Hebrew Melodies* testify, he was not unwilling to turn to the Bible as a source of poetic inspiration. Moreover, he was born with the religious temperament. Questions "of Providence, foreknowledge, will and fate," exercised his curiosity because they appealed to his imagination and moved his spirit. He was eager to plunge into controversy with friends and advisers who challenged or rebuked him, Hodgson, for instance, or Dallas; and he responded with remarkable amenity to the strictures and exhortations of such orthodox professors as Mr. Sheppard and Dr. Kennedy. He was, no doubt, from first to last a *heretic*, impatient, not to say contemptuous, of authority, but he was by no means indifferent to religion altogether. To " argue about it and about" was a necessity, if not an agreeable relief, to his intellectual energies. It would appear from the Ravenna diary (January 28, 1821, *Letters*, 1901, v. 190, 191), that the conception of Lucifer was working in his brain

before the " tragedy of Cain " was actually begun. He had
been recording a "thought" which had come to him, that
"at the very height of human desire and pleasure, a certain
sense of doubt and sorrow"—an *amari aliquid* which links
the future to the past, and so blots out the present—"mingles
with our bliss," making it of none effect, and, by way of
moral or corollary to his soliloquy, he adds three lines of
verse headed, "Thought for a speech of Lucifer in the
Tragedy of *Cain*"—

> "Were Death an *Evil*, would *I* let thee live?
> Fool! live as I live—as thy father lives,
> And thy son's sons shall live for evermore."

In these three lines, which were not inserted in the play,
and in the preceding "thought," we have the key-note to
Cain. "Man walketh in a vain shadow"—a shadow which
he can never overtake, the shadow of an eternally postponed
fruition. With a being capable of infinite satisfaction, he is
doomed to realize failure in attainment. In all that is best
and most enjoyable, "the rapturous moment and the placid
hour," there is a foretaste of "Death the Unknown"! The
tragedy of *Manfred* lies in remorse for the inevitable past;
the tragedy of *Cain*, in revolt against the limitations of the
inexorable present.

The investigation of the "sources" of *Cain* does not lead
to any very definite conclusion (see *Lord Byron's Cain und
Seine Quellen*, von Alfred Schaffner, 1880). He was pleased
to call his play "a Mystery," and, in his Preface (*vide post*,
p. 207), Byron alludes to the Old Mysteries as "those very
profane productions, whether in English, French, Italian, or
Spanish." The first reprint of the *Chester Plays* was published by the Roxburghe Club in 1818, but Byron's knowledge
of Mystery Plays was probably derived from *Dodsley's
Plays* (ed. 1780, l., xxxiii.-xlii.), or from John Stevens's Continuation of Dugdale's *Monasticon* (*vide post*, p. 207), or
possibly, as Herr Schaffner suggests, from Warton's *History
of English Poetry*, ed. 1871, ii. 222–230. He may, too, have
witnessed some belated *Rappresentazione* of the Creation
and Fall at Ravenna, or in one of the remoter towns or
villages of Italy. There is a superficial resemblance between
the treatment of the actual encounter of Cain and Abel, and
the conventional rendering of the same incident in the
Ludus Coventriæ, and in the *Mistére du Viel Testament;*
but it is unlikely that he had closely studied any one Mystery
Play at first hand. On the other hand, his recollections of
Gessner's *Death of Abel*, which "he had never read since he
was eight years old," were clearer than he imagined. Not

only in such minor matters as the destruction of Cain's altar by a whirlwind, and the substitution of the Angel of the Lord for the *Deus* of the Mysteries, but in the Teutonic domesticities of Cain and Adah, and the evangelical piety of Adam and Abel, there is a reflection, if not an imitation, of the German idyll (see Gessner's *Death of Abel*, ed. 1797, pp. 80, 102).

Of his indebtedness to Milton he makes no formal acknowledgment, but he was not ashamed to shelter himself behind Milton's shield when he was attacked on the score of blasphemy and profanity. "If *Cain* be blasphemous, *Paradise Lost* is blasphemous" (letter to Murray, Pisa, February 8, 1822), was, he would fain believe, a conclusive answer to his accusers. But apart from verbal parallels or coincidences, there is a genuine affinity between Byron's Lucifer and Milton's Satan. Lucifer, like Satan, is "not less than Archangel ruined," a repulsed but "unvanquished Titan," marred by a demonic sorrow, a confessor though a rival of Omnipotence. He is a majestic and, as a rule, a serious and solemn spirit, who compels the admiration and possibly the sympathy of the reader. There is, however, another strain in his ghostly attributes, which betrays a more recent consanguinity : now and again he gives token that he is of the lineage of Mephistopheles. He is sometimes, though rarely, a mocking as well as a rebellious spirit, and occasionally indulges in a grim *persiflage* beneath the dignity if not the capacity of Satan. It is needless to add that Lucifer has a most lifelike personality of his own. The conception of the spirit of evil justifying an eternal antagonism to the Creator from the standpoint of a superior morality, may, perhaps, be traced to a Manichean source, but it has been touched with a new emotion. Milton's devil is an abstraction of infernal pride—

> "Sole Positive of Night!
> Antipathist of Light!
> Fate's only essence! primal scorpion rod—
> The one permitted opposite of God!"

Goethe's devil is an abstraction of scorn. He "maketh a mock" alike of good and evil! But Byron's devil is a spirit, yet a mortal too—the traducer, because he has suffered for his sins ; the deceiver, because he is self-deceived ; the hoper against hope that there is a ransom for the soul in perfect self-will and not in perfect self-sacrifice. Byron did not uphold Lucifer, but he "had passed that way," and could imagine a spiritual warfare not only against the *Deus* of the Mysteries or of the Book of Genesis, but against what he believed and acknowledged to be the Author and Principle of good.

Autres temps, autres mœurs! It is all but impossible for the modern reader to appreciate the audacity of *Cain,* or to realize the alarm and indignation which it aroused by its appearance. Byron knew that he was raising a tempest, and pleads, in his Preface, "that with regard to the language of Lucifer, it was difficult for me to make him talk like a clergyman," and again and again he assures his correspondents (*e.g.* to Murray, November 23, 1821, "*Cain* is nothing more than a drama ;" to Moore, March 4, 1822, "With respect to Religion, can I never convince you that *I* have no such opinions as the characters in that drama, which seems to have frightened everybody?" *Letters,* 1901, v. 469; vi. 30) that it is Lucifer and not Byron who puts such awkward questions with regard to the "politics of paradise" and the origin of evil. Nobody seems to have believed him. It was taken for granted that Lucifer was the mouthpiece of Byron, that the author of *Don Juan* was not "on the side of the angels."

Little need be said of the "literature," the pamphlets and poems which were evoked by the publication of *Cain: A Mystery.* One of the most prominent assailants (said to be the Rev. H. J. Todd (1763–1845), Archdeacon of Cleveland, 1832, author *inter alia* of *Original Sin, Free Will,* etc., 1818) issued *A Remonstrance to Mr. John Murray, respecting a Recent Publication,* 1822, signed "Oxoniensis." The sting of the *Remonstrance* lay in the exposure of the fact that Byron was indebted to Bayle's *Dictionary* for his rabbinical legends, and that he had derived from the same source his Manichean doctrines of the *Two Principles, etc.,* and other "often-refuted sophisms" with regard to the origin of evil. Byron does not borrow more than a poet and a gentleman is at liberty to acquire by way of raw material, but it cannot be denied that he had read and inwardly digested more than one of Bayle's "most objectionable articles" (*e.g.* "Adam," "Eve," "Abel," "Manichees," "Paulicians," etc.). The *Remonstrance* was answered in *A Letter to Sir Walter Scott, etc.,* by "Harroviensis." Byron welcomed such a "Defender of the Faith," and was anxious that Murray should print the letter together with the poem. But Murray belittled the "defender," and was upbraided in turn for his slowness of heart (letter to Murray, June 6, 1822, *Letters,* 1901, vi. 76).

Fresh combatants rushed into the fray : "Philo-Milton," with a *Vindication of the "Paradise Lost" from the charge of exculpating "Cain: A Mystery,"* London, 1822 ; "Britannicus," with a pamphlet entitled, *Revolutionary Causes, etc., and A Postscript containing Strictures on "Cain," etc.,* London, 1822, etc. ; but their works, which hardly deserve to be catalogued, have perished with them. Finally, in 1830, a barrister named Harding Grant, author of *Chancery Practice,* compiled a work (*Lord Byron's "Cain," etc., with Notes*) of more than four hundred pages, in which he treats "the proceedings and speeches of Lucifer with the same earnestness as if they were existing and earthly personages." But it was "a week too late." The "Coryphæus of the Satanic School" had passed away, and the tumult had "dwindled to a calm."

Cain "appeared in conjunction with " *Sardanapalus* and *The Two Foscari,* December 19, 1821. Last but not least of the three plays, it had been announced "by a separate advertisement (*Morning Chronicle,* November 24, 1821), for the purpose of exciting the greater curiosity " (*Memoirs of the Life, etc.* [by John Watkins], 1822, p. 383), and it was no sooner published than it was pirated. In the following January, "*Cain : A Mystery,* by the author of *Don Juan,*" was issued by W. Benbow, at Castle Street, Leicester Square (the notorious " Byron Head," which Southey described as "one of those preparatory schools for the brothel and the gallows, where obscenity, sedition, and blasphemy are retailed in drams for the vulgar " !).

Murray had paid Byron £2710 for the three tragedies, and in order to protect the copyright, he applied, through counsel (Lancelot Shadwell, afterwards Vice-Chancellor), for an injunction in Chancery to stop the sale of piratical editions of *Cain.* In delivering judgment (February 12, 1822), the Chancellor, Lord Eldon (see *Courier,* Wednesday, February 13), replying to Shadwell, drew a comparison between *Cain* and *Paradise Lost,* "which he had read from beginning to end during the course of the last Long Vacation—*solicitæ jucunda oblivia vitæ.*" No one, he argued, could deny that the object and effects of *Paradise Lost* were "not to bring into disrepute," but "to promote reverence for our religion," and, *per contra,* no one could affirm that it was impossible to arrive at an opposite conclusion with regard to "the Preface, the poem, the general tone and manner of *Cain.*" It was a question for a jury. A jury might decide that *Cain* was blasphemous, and void of copyright ; and as there was a reasonable doubt in his mind as to the character of the book, and a doubt as to the conclusion at which a jury would arrive, he was compelled to refuse the injunction. According to Dr. Smiles (*Memoir of John Murray,* 1891, i. 428), the decision of a jury was taken, and an injunction eventually granted. If so, it was ineffectual, for Benbow issued another edition of *Cain* in 1824 (see Jacob's *Reports*, p. 474, *note*). See, too, the case of Murray *v.* Benbow and Another, as reported in the *Examiner*, February 17, 1822 ; and cases of Wolcot *v.* Walker, Southey *v.* Sherwood, Murray *v.* Benbow, and Lawrence *v.* Smith [*Quarterly Review*, April, 1822, vol. xxvii. pp. 120–138].

"*Cain*," said Moore (February 9, 1822), "has made a sensation." Friends and champions, the press, the public "turned up their thumbs." Gifford shook his head ; Hobhouse "launched out into a most violent invective" (letter to Murray, November 24, 1821) ; Jeffrey, in the *Edinburgh*, was regretful and hortatory ; Heber, in the *Quarterly*, was fault-finding and contemptuous. The "parsons preached at it from Kentish Town to Pisa" (letter to Moore, February 20, 1822). Even "the very highest authority in the land," his Majesty King George IV., "expressed his disapprobation of the blasphemy and licentiousness of Lord Byron's writings" (*Examiner*, February 17, 1822). Byron himself was forced to admit that "my Mont Saint Jean seems Cain" (*Don Juan*, Canto XI. stanza lvi. line 2). The many were unanimous in their verdict, but the higher court of the few reversed the judgment.

Goethe said that "Its beauty is such as we shall not see a second time in the world" (*Conversations, etc.*, 1874, p. 261) ; Scott, in speaking of "the very grand and tremendous drama of *Cain*," said that the author had "matched Milton on his own ground" (letter to Murray, December 4, 1821, *vide post*, p. 206) ; "*Cain*," wrote Shelley to Gisborne (April 10, 1822), "is apocalyptic ; it is a revelation never before communicated to man."

Uncritical praise, as well as uncritical censure, belongs to the past ; but the play remains, a singular exercise of "poetic energy," a confession, *ex animo*, of "the burthen of the mystery, . . . the heavy and the weary weight Of all this unintelligible world."

For reviews of *Cain: A Mystery*, *vide ante*, "Introduction to *Sardanapalus*," p. 5 ; see, too, *Eclectic Review*, May, 1822, N.S. vol. xvii. pp. 418–427 ; *Examiner*, June 2, 1822 ; *British Review*, 1822, vol. xix. pp. 94–102.

For O'Doherty's parody of the "Pisa" Letter, February 8, 1822, see *Blackwood's Edinburgh Magazine*, February, 1822, vol. xi. pp. 215–217 ; and for a review of Harding Grant's *Lord Byron's Cain, etc.*, see *Fraser's Magazine*, April, 1831, iii. 285–304.

TO

SIR WALTER SCOTT, BART.,

THIS MYSTERY OF CAIN

IS INSCRIBED,

BY HIS OBLIGED FRIEND

AND FAITHFUL SERVANT,

THE AUTHOR.[1]

1. [On the 13th December [1821] Sir Walter received a copy of *Cain*, as yet unpublished, from Murray, who had been instructed to ask whether he had any objection to having the "Mystery" dedicated to him. He replied in these words—

"*Edinburgh, 4th December*, 1821.

"MY DEAR SIR,—I accept, with feelings of great obligation, the flattering proposal of Lord Byron to prefix my name to the very grand and tremendous drama of 'Cain.' * I may be partial to it, and you will

---

* ["However, the praise often given to Byron has been so exaggerated as to provoke, perhaps, a reaction in which he is unduly disparaged. 'As various in composition as Shakespeare himself, Lord Byron has embraced,' says Sir Walter Scott, 'every topic of human life, and sounded every string on the divine harp, from its slightest to its most powerful and heart-astounding tones. . . . In the very grand and tremendous drama of Cain,' etc. . . . 'And Lord Byron has done all this,' Scott adds, 'while managing his pen with the careless and negligent ease of a man of quality.'"—*Poetry of Byron, chosen and arranged by Matthew Arnold*, 1881, p. xiii.

Scott does not *add* anything of the kind. The comparison with Shakespeare was written after Byron's death in May, 1824; the appreciation of *Cain* in December, 1821 (*vide supra*); while the allusion to "a man of quality" is to be found in an article contributed to the *Quarterly Review* in 1816!]

allow I have cause ; but I do not know that his Muse has ever taken so lofty a flight amid her former soarings. He has certainly matched Milton on his own ground. Some part of the language is bold, and may shock one class of readers, whose line will be adopted by others out of affectation or envy. But then they must condemn the ' Paradise Lost,' if they have a mind to be consistent. The fiend-like reasoning and bold blasphemy of the fiend and of his pupil lead exactly to the point which was to be expected,—the commission of the first murder, and the ruin and despair of the perpetrator.

"I do not see how any one can accuse the author himself of Manicheism. The Devil talks the language of that sect, doubtless ; because, not being able to deny the existence of the Good Principle, he endeavours to exalt himself—the Evil Principle—to a seeming equality with the Good ; but such arguments, in the mouth of such a being, can only be used to deceive and to betray. Lord Byron might have made this more evident, by placing in the mouth of Adam, or of some good and protecting spirit, the reasons which render the existence of moral evil consistent with the general benevolence of the Deity. The great key to the mystery is, perhaps, the imperfection of our own faculties, which see and feel strongly the partial evils which press upon us, but know too little of the general system of the universe, to be aware how the existence of these is to be reconciled with the benevolence of the great Creator.

"To drop these speculations, you have much occasion for some mighty spirit, like Lord Byron, to come down and trouble the waters ; for, excepting 'The John Bull,' * you seem stagnating strangely in London.

"Yours, my dear Sir,
"Very truly,
"WALTER SCOTT.

"To John Murray, Esq."—*Memoirs of the Life of Sir Walter Scott*, by J. G. Lockhart, Esq., 1838, iii. 92, 93.]

---

* [The first number of *John Bull*, "For God, the King, and the People," was published Sunday, December 17, 1820. Theodore Hook was the editor, and it is supposed that he owed his appointment to the intervention of Sir Walter Scott. The *raison d'être* of *John Bull* was to write up George IV., and to write down Queen Caroline. "The national movement (in favour of the Queen) was arrested ; and George IV. had mainly *John Bull* to thank for that result."—*A Sketch*, [by J. G. Lockhart], 1852, p. 45.]

PREFACE.

THE following scenes are entitled "A Mystery;" in
conformity with the ancient title annexed to dramas
upon similar subjects, which were styled " Mysteries, or
Moralities." [1] The author has by no means taken the
same liberties with his subject which were common
formerly, as may be seen by any reader curious enough
to refer to those very profane productions, whether in
English, French, Italian, or Spanish. The author has
endeavoured to preserve the language adapted to his
characters ; and where it is (and this is but rarely) taken
from actual *Scripture*, he has made as little alteration,
even of words, as the rhythm would permit. The reader
will recollect that the book of Genesis does not state

1. [" Mysteries," or Mystery Plays, were prior to and distinct from
"Moralities." Byron seems to have had some acquaintance with the
archæology of the drama, but it is not easy to divine the source or
extent of his knowledge. He may have received and read the Roxburghe
reprint of the *Chester Plays*, published in 1818 ; but it is most probable
that he had read the pages devoted to mystery plays in Warton's
History of Poetry, or that he had met with a version of the *Ludus
Coventriæ* (reprinted by J. O. Halliwell Phillipps, in 1841), printed in
Stevens's continuation of Dugdale's *Monasticon*, 1722, i. 139-153. There
is a sixteenth-century edition of *Le Mistère du Viel Testament*, which
was reprinted by the Baron James de Rothschild, in 1878 (see for " De
la Mort d'Abel et de la Malediction Cayn," pp. 103-113) ; but it is
improbable that it had come under Byron's notice. For a quotation
from an Italian Mystery Play, *vide post*, p. 264 ; and for Spanish
"Mystery Plays," see *Teatro Completo de Juan del Encina*, "Proemio,"
Madrid, 1893, and *History of Spanish Literature*, by George Ticknor,
1888, i. 257. For instances of the profanity of Mystery Plays, see the
Towneley Plays (" Mactacio Abel," p. 7), first published by the Surtees
Society in 1836, and republished by the Early English Text Society,
1897, E.S. No. lxxi.]

that Eve was tempted by a demon, but by "the Serpent;"[1] and that only because he was "the most subtil of all the beasts of the field." Whatever interpretation the Rabbins and the Fathers may have put upon this, I take the words as I find them, and reply, with Bishop Watson[2] upon similar occasions, when the Fathers were quoted to him as Moderator in the schools of Cambridge, "Behold the Book!"—holding up the Scripture. It is to be recollected, that my present subject has nothing to do with the *New Testament*, to which no reference can be here made without anachronism.[3] With the poems upon similar topics I have not been recently familiar. Since I was twenty I have never read Milton; but I had read him so frequently before, that this may make little difference. Gesner's "Death of Abel" I have never read since I was eight years of age, at Aberdeen. The

1. [For the contention that "the snake was the snake"—no more (*vide post*, p. 211), see *La Bible enfin Expliquée*, etc.; *Œuvres Complètes de Voltaire*, Paris, 1837, vi. 338, *note*. "La conversation de la femme et du serpent n'est point racontée comme une chose surnaturelle et incroyable, comme un miracle, ou comme une allégorie." See, too, Bayle (*Hist.* and *Crit. Dictionary*, 1735, ii. 851, art. "Eve," *note* A), who quotes Josephus, Paracelsus, and "some Rabbins," to the effect that it was an actual serpent which tempted Eve; and compare *Critical Remarks on the Hebrew Scriptures*, by the Rev. Alexander Geddes, LL.D., 1800, p. 42.]

2. [Richard Watson (1737-1816), Bishop of Llandaff, 1782, was appointed Moderator of the Schools in 1762, and Regius Professor of Divinity October 31, 1771. According to his own story (*Anecdotes of the Life of Richard Watson*, 1817, p. 39), "I determined to study nothing but my Bible. . . . I had no prejudice against, no predilection for, the Church of England, but a sincere regard for the *Church of Christ*, and an insuperable objection to every degree of dogmatical intolerance. I never troubled myself with answering any arguments which the opponents in the Divinity Schools brought against the articles of the Church, . . . but I used on such occasions to say to them, holding the New Testament in my hand, '*En sacrum codicem!* Here is the foundation of truth! Why do you follow the streams derived from it by the sophistry, or polluted by the passions, of man?'" It may be conceived that Watson's appeal to "Scripture" was against the sentence of orthodoxy. His authority as "a school Divine" is on a par with that of the author of *Cain*, or of an earlier theologian who "quoted Genesis like a very learned clerk"!]

3. [Byron breaks through his self-imposed canon with regard to the New Testament. There are allusions to the doctrine of the Atonement, act i. sc. 1, lines 163-166: act iii. sc. 1, lines 85-88; to the descent into Hades, act i. sc. 1, lines 541, 542; and to the miraculous walking on the Sea of Galilee, act ii. sc. 1, lines 16-20.]

general impression of my recollection is delight; but of the contents I remember only that Cain's wife was called Mahala, and Abel's Thirza; in the following pages I have called them "Adah" and "Zillah," the earliest female names which occur in Genesis. They were those of Lamech's wives: those of Cain and Abel are not called by their names. Whether, then, a coincidence of subject may have caused the same in expression, I know nothing, and care as little. [I [1] am prepared to be accused of Manicheism,[2] or some other hard name ending in *ism*, which makes a formidable figure and awful sound in the eyes and ears of those who would be as much puzzled to explain the terms so bandied about, as the liberal and pious indulgers in such epithets. Against such I can defend myself, or, if necessary, I can attack in turn. "Claw for claw, as Conan said to Satan, and the deevil take the shortest nails" (Waverley).[3]]

The reader will please to bear in mind (what few choose to recollect), that there is no allusion to a future state in any of the books of Moses, nor indeed in the Old Testament. For a reason for this extraordinary omission he may consult Warburton's "Divine Legation;"[4]

---

1. [The words enclosed in brackets are taken from an original draft of the Preface.]

2. [The Manichæans (the disciples of Mani or Manes, third century A.D.) held that there were two co-eternal Creators—a God of Darkness who made the body, and a God of Light who was responsible for the soul—and that it was the aim and function of the good spirit to rescue the soul, the spiritual part of man, from the possession and grasp of the body, which had been created by and was in the possession of the spirit of evil. St. Augustine passed through a stage of Manicheism, and in after-life exposed and refuted the heretical tenets which he had advocated, and with which he was familiar. See, for instance, his account of the Manichæan heresy " de duplici terrâ, de regno lucis et regno tenebrarum " (*Opera*, 1700, viii. 484, *c ; vide ibid.*, i. 693, 717 ; x. 893, *d.* etc.).]

3. [Conan the Jester, a character in the Irish ballads, was "a kind of Thersites, but brave and daring even to rashness. He had made a vow that he would never take a blow without returning it ; and having . . . descended to the infernal regions, he received a cuff from the arch-fiend, which he instantly returned, using the expression in the text ('blow for blow')." Sometimes the proverb is worded thus : "'Claw for claw, and the devil take the shortest nails,' as Conan said to the devil."—*Waverley Novels*, 1829 (notes to chap. xxii. of *Waverley*), i. 241, *note* 1 ; see, too, *ibid.*, p. 229.]

4. [The full title of Warburton's book runs thus : *The Divine*

whether satisfactory or not, no better has yet been assigned. I have therefore supposed it new to Cain, without, I hope, any perversion of Holy Writ.

With regard to the language of Lucifer, it was difficult for me to make him talk like a clergyman upon the same subjects; but I have done what I could to restrain him within the bounds of spiritual politeness. If he disclaims having tempted Eve in the shape of the Serpent, it is only because the book of Genesis has not the most distant allusion to anything of the kind, but merely to the Serpent in his serpentine capacity.

Note.—The reader will perceive that the author has partly adopted in this poem the notion of Cuvier,[1] that the world had been destroyed several times before the creation of man. This speculation, derived from the different strata and the bones of enormous and unknown animals found in them, is not contrary to the Mosaic account, but rather confirms it; as no human bones have yet been discovered in those strata, although those of many known animals are found near the remains of the unknown. The assertion of Lucifer, that the pre-Adamite world was also peopled by rational beings much more intelligent than man, and proportionably powerful to the mammoth, etc., etc., is, of course, a poetical fiction to help him to make out his case.

I ought to add, that there is a " tramelogedia " of

Legation of Moses Demonstrated on the Principles of a Religious Deist; from the omission of the Doctrine of a Future State of Reward and Punishment in the Jewish Dispensation. (See, more particularly (ed. 1741), Vol. II. pt. ii. bk. v. sect. 5, pp. 449–461, and bk. vi. pp. 569–678.) Compare the following passage from *Dieu et les Hommes* (*Œuvres, etc.,* de Voltaire, 1837, vi. 236, chap. xx.) : " Notre Warburton s'est épuisé à ramasser dans son fatras de la Divine légation, toutes les preuves que l'auteur du *Pentateuque,* n'a jamais parlé d'une vie à venir, et il n'a pas eu grande peine ; mais il en tire une plaisante conclusion, et digne d'un esprit aussi faux que le sien."]

1. [See *Recherches sur les Ossemens Fossiles,* par M. le Bon G. Cuvier, Paris, 1821, i., " Discours Préliminaire," pp. iv., vii. ; and for the thesis, " Il n'y a point d'os humaines fossiles," see p. lxiv. ; see, too, Cuvier's *Discours sur les révolutions de la surface du globe,* ed. 1825, p. 282 : " Si l'on peut en juger par les differens ordres d'animaux dont on y trouve les dépouilles, ils avaient peut-être subi jusqu' à deux ou trois irruptions de la mer." It is curious to note that Moore thought that Cuvier's book was " a most desolating one in the conclusions to which it may lead some minds " (*Life,* p. 554).]

Alfieri, called "Abele."[1] I have never read that, nor any other of the posthumous works of the writer, except his Life.

RAVENNA, *Sept.* 20, 1821.

1. [Alfieri's *Abele* was included in his *Opere inediti*, published by the Countess of Albany and the Abbé Calma in 1804.

"In a long Preface . . . dated April 25, 1796, Alfieri gives a curious account of the reasons which induced him to call it . . . 'Tramelogedy.' He says that *Abel* is neither a tragedy, a comedy, a drama, a tragi-comedy, nor a Greek tragedy, which last would, he thinks, be correctly described as melo-tragedy. Opera-tragedy would, in his opinion, be a fitting name for it ; but he prefers interpolating the word 'melo' into the middle of the word 'tragedy,' so as not to spoil the ending, although by so doing he has cut in two . . . the root of the word— τραγος."—*The Tragedies of Vittorio Alfieri*, edited by E. A. Bowring, C.B., 1876, ii. 472.

There is no resemblance whatever between Byron's *Cain* and Alfieri's *Abele*.]

DRAMATIS PERSONÆ.

MEN.

ADAM.

CAIN.

ABEL.

SPIRITS.

ANGEL OF THE LORD.

LUCIFER.

WOMEN.

EVE.

ADAH.

ZILLAH.

CAIN:

A MYSTERY.

ACT I.

SCENE I.—*The Land without Paradise.*—*Time, Sunrise.*

ADAM, EVE, CAIN, ABEL, ADAH, ZILLAH, *offering a Sacrifice.*

Adam. GOD, the Eternal! Infinite! All-wise!—
Who out of darkness on the deep didst make
Light on the waters with a word—All Hail!
Jehovah! with returning light—All Hail!
  Eve. God! who didst name the day, and separate
Morning from night, till then divided never—
Who didst divide the wave from wave, and call
Part of thy work the firmament—All Hail!
  Abel. God! who didst call the elements into
Earth, ocean, air and fire—and with the day   10
And night, and worlds which these illuminate,
Or shadow, madest beings to enjoy them,
And love both them and thee—All Hail! All Hail!
  Adah. God! the Eternal parent of all things!
Who didst create these best and beauteous beings,
To be belovéd, more than all, save thee—
Let me love thee and them:—All Hail! All Hail!
  Zillah. Oh, God! who loving, making, blessing all,
Yet didst permit the Serpent to creep in,
And drive my father forth from Paradise,   20

Keep us from further evil :—Hail ! All Hail !

Adam. Son Cain ! my first-born—wherefore art thou
    silent?

Cain. Why should I speak ?

Adam.   To pray.

Cain.   Have ye not prayed ?

Adam. We have, most fervently.

Cain.   And loudly : I

Have heard you.

Adam.   So will God, I trust.

Abel.   Amen !

Adam. But thou my eldest born? art silent still?

Cain. 'Tis better I should be so.

Adam.   Wherefore so?

Cain. I have nought to ask.

Adam.   Nor aught to thank for?

Cain.   No.

Adam. Dost thou not *live?*

Cain.   Must I not die?

Eve.   Alas !

The fruit of our forbidden tree begins   30

To fall.

Adam.   And we must gather it again.

Oh God ! why didst thou plant the tree of knowledge?

Cain. And wherefore plucked ye not the tree of life?

Ye might have then defied him.

Adam.   Oh ! my son,

Blaspheme not : these are Serpent's words.

Cain.   Why not ?

The snake spoke *truth ;* it *was* the Tree of Knowledge ;

It *was* the Tree of Life : knowledge is good,

And Life is good ; and how can both be evil ?

Eve. My boy ! thou speakest as I spoke in sin,

Before thy birth : let me not see renewed   40

My misery in thine. I have repented.

Let me not see my offspring fall into

The snares beyond the walls of Paradise,

Which even in Paradise destroyed his parents.

Content thee with what *is.* Had we been so,

Thou now hadst been contented.—Oh, my son !

Adam. Our orisons completed, let us hence,

Each to his task of toil—not heavy, though
Needful : the earth is young, and yields us kindly
Her fruits with little labour.
   Eve.   Cain—my son—   50
Behold thy father cheerful and resigned—
And do as he doth.   [*Exeunt* ADAM *and* EVE.
   Zillah.   Wilt thou not, my brother?
   Abel. Why wilt thou wear this gloom upon thy brow,
Which can avail thee nothing, save to rouse
The Eternal anger?
   Adah.   My belovéd Cain
Wilt thou frown even on me?
   Cain.   No, Adah! no ;
I fain would be alone a little while.
Abel, I'm sick at heart; but it will pass ;
Precede me, brother—I will follow shortly.
And you, too, sisters, tarry not behind ;   60
Your gentleness must not be harshly met :
I'll follow you anon.
   Adah.   If not, I will
Return to seek you here.
   Abel.   The peace of God
Be on your spirit, brother !
         [*Exeunt* ABEL, ZILLAH, *and* ADAH.
   Cain (*solus*).   And this is
Life ?—Toil ! and wherefore should I toil?—because
My father could not keep his place in Eden?
What had *I* done in this?—I was unborn :
I sought not to be born; nor love the state
To which that birth has brought me. Why did he
Yield to the Serpent and the woman? or   70
Yielding—why suffer? What was there in this?
The tree was planted, and why not for him?
If not, why place him near it, where it grew
The fairest in the centre? They have but
One answer to all questions, " 'Twas *his* will,
And *he* is good." How know I that? Because
He is all-powerful, must all-good, too, follow?
I judge but by the fruits—and they are bitter—
Which I must feed on for a fault not mine.
Whom have we here ?—A shape like to the angels   80

Yet of a sterner and a sadder aspect
Of spiritual essence : why do I quake ?
Why should I fear him more than other spirits,
Whom I see daily wave their fiery swords
Before the gates round which I linger oft,
In Twilight's hour, to catch a glimpse of those
Gardens which are my just inheritance,
Ere the night closes o'er the inhibited walls
And the immortal trees which overtop
The Cherubim-defended battlements ?   90
If I shrink not from these, the fire-armed angels,
Why should I quail from him who now approaches ?
Yet—he seems mightier far than them, nor less
Beauteous, and yet not all as beautiful
As he hath been, and might be : sorrow seems
Half of his immortality.[1]   And is it
So ? and can aught grieve save Humanity ?
He cometh.

Enter LUCIFER.

Lucifer.   Mortal !
Cain.   Spirit, who art thou ?
Lucifer. Master of spirits.
Cain.   And being so, canst thou
Leave them, and walk with dust ?
Lucifer.   I know the thoughts   100
Of dust, and feel for it, and with you.
Cain.   How !
You know my thoughts ?
Lucifer.   They are the thoughts of all
Worthy of thought ;—'tis your immortal part [2]

1. [Compare—
              " . . . his form had not yet lost
        All her original brightness, nor appears
        Less than Arch-angel ruined, and the excess
        Of glory obscure."
                              Paradise Lost, i. 591–593.

Compare, too—
                        " . . . but his face
        Deep scars of thunder had intrenched, and care
        Sat on his faded cheek."
                              Ibid., i. 600–602.]

2. [According to the Manichæans, the divinely created and immortal

Which speaks within you.
    Cain.   What immortal part?
This has not been revealed : the Tree of Life
Was withheld from us by my father's folly,
While that of Knowledge, by my mother's haste,
Was plucked too soon; and all the fruit is Death!
    Lucifer. They have deceived thee; thou shalt live.
    Cain.   I live,
But live to die; and, living, see no thing   110
To make death hateful, save an innate clinging,
A loathsome, and yet all invincible
Instinct of life, which I abhor, as I
Despise myself, yet cannot overcome—
And so I live.   Would I had never lived!
    Lucifer. Thou livest—and must live for ever.   Think
      not
The Earth, which is thine outward cov'ring, is
Existence—it will cease—and thou wilt be—
No less than thou art now.
    Cain.   No *less!* and why
No more?
    Lucifer. It may be thou shalt be as we.   120
    Cain. And ye?
    Lucifer.   Are everlasting.
    Cain.   Are ye happy?
    Lucifer. We are mighty.
    Cain.   Are ye happy?
    Lucifer.   No: art thou?
    Cain. How should I be so?   Look on me!
    Lucifer.   Poor clay!
And thou pretendest to be wretched!   Thou!
    Cain. I am:—and thou, with all thy might, what art
    thou?
    Lucifer. One who aspired to be what made thee, and
Would not have made thee what thou art.
    Cain.   Ah!
Thou look'st almost a god; and——
    Lucifer.   I am none:
And having failed to be one, would be nought

soul is imprisoned in an alien and evil body. There can be no harmony
between soul and body.]

Save what I am.   He conquered; let him reign!   130
   Cain. Who?
   Lucifer.   Thy Sire's maker—and the Earth's.
   Cain.   And Heaven's,
And all that in them is.   So I have heard
His Seraphs sing; and so my father saith.
   Lucifer. They say—what they must sing and say, on
      pain
Of being that which I am,—and thou art—
Of spirits and of men.
   Cain.   And what is that?
   Lucifer. Souls who dare use their immortality—
Souls who dare look the Omnipotent tyrant in
His everlasting face, and tell him that
His evil is not good!   If he has made,   140
As he saith—which I know not, nor believe—
But, if he made us—he cannot unmake:
We are immortal!—nay, he'd *have* us so,
That he may torture:—let him!   He is great—
But, in his greatness, is no happier than
We in our conflict!   Goodness would not make
Evil; and what else hath he made?   But let him
Sit on his vast and solitary throne—
Creating worlds, to make eternity
Less burthensome to his immense existence   150
And unparticipated solitude;[1]
Let him crowd orb on orb: he is alone
Indefinite, Indissoluble Tyrant;
Could he but crush himself, 'twere the best boon
He ever granted: but let him reign on!
And multiply himself in misery!
Spirits and Men, at least we sympathise—
And, suffering in concert, make our pangs

1. [Compare—
      " Let him unite above
        Star upon star, moon, Sun ;
        And let his God-head toil
        To re-adorn and re-illume his Heaven,
        Since in the end derision
        Shall prove his works and all his efforts vain."
   Adam, a Sacred Drama, by Giovanni Battista Andreini ;
             Cowper's *Milton*, 1810, iii. 24, *sqq.*]

Innumerable, more endurable,
By the unbounded sympathy of all   160
With all !   But *He* ! so wretched in his height,
So restless in his wretchedness, must still
Create, and re-create—perhaps he'll make [1]
One day a Son unto himself—as he
Gave you a father—and if he so doth,
Mark me ! that Son will be a sacrifice !
   Cain. Thou speak'st to me of things which long have
     swum
In visions through my thought : I never could
Reconcile what I saw with what I heard.
My father and my mother talk to me   170
Of serpents, and of fruits and trees : I see
The gates of what they call their Paradise
Guarded by fiery-sworded Cherubim,
Which shut them out—and me : I feel the weight
Of daily toil, and constant thought : I look
Around a world where I seem nothing, with
Thoughts which arise within me, as if they
Could master all things—but I thought alone
This misery was *mine.*   My father is
Tamed down ; my mother has forgot the mind   180
Which made her thirst for knowledge at the risk
Of an eternal curse ; my brother is
A watching shepherd boy,[2] who offers up
The firstlings of the flock to him who bids
The earth yield nothing to us without sweat ; [i]
My sister Zillah sings an earlier hymn
Than the birds' matins ; and my Adah—my
Own and belovéd—she, too, understands not
The mind which overwhelms me : never till

i. *A drudging husbandman who offers up*
   The first fruits of the earth to him who made
   That earth ——.—[*MS. M. erased.*]

   1. [Lines 163-166 ("perhaps" . . . "sacrifice"), which appear in the
MS., were omitted from the text in the first and all subsequent editions.
In the edition of 1832, etc. (xiv. 27), they are printed as a variant in a
footnote.   The present text follows the MS.]
   2. [According to the *Encyclopædia Biblica*, the word "Abel" signifies
"shepherd" or "herdman."   The Massorites give "breath," or
"vanity," as an equivalent.]

Now met I aught to sympathise with me.   190
'Tis well—I rather would consort with spirits.
   Lucifer. And hadst thou not been fit by thine own soul
For such companionship, I would not now
Have stood before thee as I am : a serpent
Had been enough to charm ye, as before.[i.]
   Cain. Ah! didst *thou* tempt my mother?
   Lucifer.   I tempt none,
Save with the truth : was not the Tree, the Tree
Of Knowledge? and was not the Tree of Life
Still fruitful?   Did *I* bid her pluck them not?
Did I plant things prohibited within   200
The reach of beings innocent, and curious
By their own innocence?   I would have made ye
Gods; and even He who thrust ye forth, so thrust ye
Because " ye should not eat the fruits of life,
" And become gods as we."   Were those his words?
   Cain. They were, as I have heard from those who
      heard them,
In thunder.
   Lucifer.   Then who was the Demon?   He
Who would not let ye live, or he who would
Have made ye live for ever, in the joy
And power of Knowledge?
   Cain.   Would they had snatched both 210
The fruits, or neither!
   Lucifer.   One is yours already,
The other may be still.
   Cain.   How so?
   Lucifer.   By being
Yourselves, in your resistance.   Nothing can
Quench the mind, if the mind will be itself
And centre of surrounding things—'tis made
To sway.
   Cain.   But didst thou tempt my parents?
   Lucifer.   I?
Poor clay—what should I tempt them for, or how?
   Cain. They say the Serpent was a spirit.
   Lucifer.   Who

     i. *Have stood before thee as I am ; but chosen*
       The serpent's charming symbol.—[*MS. M. erased.*]

Saith that? It is not written so on high:
The proud One will not so far falsify,   220
Though man's vast fears and little vanity
Would make him cast upon the spiritual nature
His own low failing. The snake *was* the snake—
No more; [1] and yet not less than those he tempted,
In nature being earth also—*more* in *wisdom*,
Since he could overcome them, and foreknew
The knowledge fatal to their narrow joys.
Think'st thou I'd take the shape of things that die?
 Cain. But the thing had a demon?
 Lucifer.   He but woke one
In those he spake to with his forky tongue.   230
I tell thee that the Serpent was no more
Than a mere serpent: ask the Cherubim
Who guard the tempting tree. When thousand ages
Have rolled o'er your dead ashes, and your seed's,
The seed of the then world may thus array
Their earliest fault in fable, and attribute
To me a shape I scorn, as I scorn all
That bows to him, who made things but to bend
Before his sullen, sole eternity;
But we, who see the truth, must speak it. Thy   240
Fond parents listened to a creeping thing,
And fell. For what should spirits tempt them? What
Was there to envy in the narrow bounds
Of Paradise, that spirits who pervade
Space——but I speak to thee of what thou know'st not,
With all thy Tree of Knowledge.
 Cain.   But thou canst not
Speak aught of Knowledge which I would not know,
And do not thirst to know, and bear a mind
To know.
 Lucifer. And heart to look on?
 Cain.   Be it proved.
 Lucifer. Darest thou look on Death?
 Cain.   He has not yet   250
Been seen.
 Lucifer. But must be undergone.
 Cain.   My father

1. [*Vide ante*, " Preface," p. 208.]

Says he is something dreadful, and my mother
Weeps when he 's named; and Abel lifts his eyes
To Heaven, and Zillah casts hers to the earth,
And sighs a prayer; and Adah looks on me,
And speaks not.
    Lucifer.   And thou?
    Cain.   Thoughts unspeakable
Crowd in my breast to burning, when I hear
Of this almighty Death, who is, it seems,
Inevitable.   Could I wrestle with him?
I wrestled with the lion, when a boy,   260
In play, till he ran roaring from my gripe.
    Lucifer. It has no shape; but will absorb all things
That bear the form of earth-born being.
    Cain.   Ah!
I thought it was a being: who could do
Such evil things to beings save a being?
    Lucifer. Ask the Destroyer.
    Cain.   Who?
    Lucifer.   The Maker—Call him
Which name thou wilt: he makes but to destroy.
    Cain. I knew not that, yet thought it, since I heard
Of Death: although I know not what it is—
Yet it seems horrible.   I have looked out   270
In the vast desolate night in search of him;
And when I saw gigantic shadows in
The umbrage of the walls of Eden, chequered
By the far-flashing of the Cherubs' swords,
I watched for what I thought his coming; for
With fear rose longing in my heart to know
What 'twas which shook us all—but nothing came.
And then I turned my weary eyes from off
Our native and forbidden Paradise,
Up to the lights above us, in the azure,   280
Which are so beautiful: shall they, too, die?
    Lucifer. Perhaps—but long outlive both thine and
        thee.
    Cain. I'm glad of that: I would not have them die—
They are so lovely.   What is Death?   I fear,
I feel, it is a dreadful thing; but what,
I cannot compass: 'tis denounced against us,

Both them who sinned and sinned not, as an ill—
What ill?
　　Lucifer. To be resolved into the earth.
　　Cain. But shall I know it?
　　Lucifer.　　　　　As I know not death,
I cannot answer.[1]
　　Cain.　　　　Were I quiet earth,　　　　290
That were no evil: would I ne'er had been
Aught else but dust!
　　Lucifer.　　　　That is a *grovelling* wish,
Less than thy father's—for he wished to know!
　　Cain. But not to live—or wherefore plucked he not
The Life-tree?
　　Lucifer.　　He was hindered.
　　Cain.　　　　　　Deadly error!
Not to snatch first that fruit:—but ere he plucked
The knowledge, he was ignorant of Death.
Alas! I scarcely now know what it is,
And yet I fear it—fear I know not what!
　　Lucifer. And I, who know all things, fear nothing;
see　　　　　300
What is true knowledge.
　　Cain.　　　　Wilt thou teach me all?
　　Lucifer. Aye, upon one condition.
　　Cain.　　　　Name it.
　　Lucifer.　　　　　　That
Thou dost fall down and worship me—thy Lord.
　　Cain. Thou art not the Lord my father worships.
　　Lucifer.　　　　　　No.
　　Cain. His equal?
　　Lucifer.　　No;—I have nought in common with him!
Nor would: I would be aught above—beneath—
Aught save a sharer or a servant of
His power. I dwell apart; but I am great:—
Many there are who worship me, and more
Who shall—be thou amongst the first.

1. [Compare—
　　　　" If, as thou sayst thine essence be as ours,
　　　　We have replied in telling thee, the thing
　　　　Mortals call Death hath nought to do with us."
Manfred, act i. sc. 1, lines 161-153, *Poetical Works,* 1901, iv. 90.]

Cain.   I never   310
As yet have bowed unto my father's God.
Although my brother Abel oft implores
That I would join with him in sacrifice :—
Why should I bow to thee?
    Lucifer.   Hast thou ne'er bowed
To him?
    Cain. Have I not said it?—need I say it?
Could not thy mighty knowledge teach thee that?
    Lucifer. He who bows not to him has bowed to me.[1]
    Cain. But I will bend to neither.
    Lucifer.   Ne'er the less,
Thou art my worshipper; not worshipping
Him makes thee mine the same.
    Cain.   And what is that? 320
    Lucifer. Thou'lt know here—and hereafter.
    Cain.   Let me but
Be taught the mystery of my being.
    Lucifer.   Follow
Where I will lead thee.
    Cain.   But I must retire
To till the earth—for I had promised——
    Lucifer.   What?
    Cain. To cull some first-fruits.
    Lucifer.   Why?
    Cain.   To offer up
With Abel on an altar.
    Lucifer.   Said'st thou not
Thou ne'er hadst bent to him who made thee?
    Cain.   Yes—
But Abel's earnest prayer has wrought upon me;
The offering is more his than mine—and Adah——
    Lucifer. Why dost thou hesitate?
    Cain.   She is my sister, 330

1. [Dr. Arnold, speaking of *Cain*, used to say, "There is something
to me almost awful in meeting suddenly, in the works of such a man,
so great and solemn a truth as is expressed in that speech of Lucifer,
"He who bows not to God hath bowed to me" (Stanley's *Life of
Arnold*, ed. 1887, i. 263, *note*). It may be awful, but it is not strange.
Byron was seldom at a loss for a text, and must have been familiar
with the words, "He that is not with Me is against Me." Moreover,
he was a man of genius!]

Born on the same day, of the same womb ; and
She wrung from me, with tears, this promise ; and
Rather than see her weep, I would, methinks,
Bear all—and worship aught.
   Lucifer.   Then follow me !
   Cain. I will.

Enter ADAH.

   Adah.   My brother, I have come for thee ;
It is our hour of rest and joy—and we
Have less without thee.   Thou hast laboured not
This morn ; but I have done thy task : the fruits
Are ripe, and glowing as the light which ripens :
Come away.
   Cain.   Seest thou not ?
   Adah.   I see an angel ;   340
We have seen many : will he share our hour
Of rest ?—he is welcome.
   Cain.   But he is not like
The angels we have seen.
   Adah.   Are there, then, others ?
But he is welcome, as they were : they deigned
To be our guests—will he ?
   Cain (to Lucifer).   Wilt thou ?
   Lucifer.   I ask
Thee to be mine.
   Cain.   I must away with him.
   Adah. And leave us ?
   Cain.   Aye.
   Adah.   And *me ?*
   Cain.   Belovéd Adah !
   Adah. Let me go with thee.
   Lucifer.   No, she must not.
   Adah.   Who
Art thou that steppest between heart and heart ?
   Cain. He is a God.
   Adah.   How know'st thou ?
   Cain.   He speaks like
A God.
   Adah. So did the Serpent, and it lied.   351

Lucifer. Thou errest, Adah!—was not the Tree
      that
Of Knowledge?
      Adah.   Aye—to our eternal sorrow.
      Lucifer. And yet that grief is knowledge—so he lied
      not:
And if he did betray you, 'twas with Truth;
And Truth in its own essence cannot be
But good.
      Adah.   But all we know of it has gathered
Evil on ill; expulsion from our home,
And dread, and toil, and sweat, and heaviness;
Remorse of that which was—and hope of that   360
Which cometh not.   Cain! walk not with this Spirit.
Bear with what we have borne, and love me—I
Love thee.
      Lucifer.   More than thy mother, and thy sire?
      Adah. I do.   Is that a sin, too?
      Lucifer.   No, not yet;
It one day will be in your children.
      Adah.   What!
Must not my daughter love her brother Enoch?
      Lucifer. Not as thou lovest Cain.
      Adah.   Oh, my God!
Shall they not love and bring forth things that love
Out of their love? have they not drawn their milk
Out of this bosom? was not he, their father,   370
Born of the same sole womb,[1] in the same hour
With me? did we not love each other? and
In multiplying our being multiply
Things which will love each other as we love
Them?—And as I love thee, my Cain! go not
Forth with this spirit; he is not of ours.
      Lucifer. The sin I speak of is not of my making,
And cannot be a sin in you—whate'er
It seem in those who will replace ye in

1. ["The most common opinion is that a son and daughter were
born together; and they go so far as to tell us the very name of
the daughters.   Cain's twin sister was called Calmana (see, too, *Le
Mistère du Viel Testament*, lines 1883–1926, ed. 1878), or Caimana, or
Debora, or Azzrum; that of Abel was named Delbora or Awina."—
Bayle's *Dictionary*, 1735, ii. 854, art. "Eve," D.]

Mortality.[1]
   Adah.   What is the sin which is not   380
Sin in itself?   Can circumstance make sin
Or virtue?—if it doth, we are the slaves
Of——
   Lucifer. Higher things than ye are slaves: and higher
Than them or ye would be so, did they not
Prefer an independency of torture
To the smooth agonies of adulation,
In hymns and harpings, and self-seeking prayers,
To that which is omnipotent, because
It is omnipotent, and not from love,
But terror and self-hope.
   Adah.   Omnipotence   390
Must be all goodness.
   Lucifer.   Was it so in Eden?
   Adah. Fiend! tempt me not with beauty; thou art
       fairer
Than was the Serpent, and as false.
   Lucifer.   As true.
Ask Eve, your mother: bears she not the knowledge
Of good and evil?
   Adah.   Oh, my mother! thou
Hast plucked a fruit more fatal to thine offspring
Than to thyself; thou at the least hast passed
Thy youth in Paradise, in innocent
And happy intercourse with happy spirits:
But we, thy children, ignorant of Eden,
Are girt about by demons, who assume   400
The words of God, and tempt us with our own
Dissatisfied and curious thoughts—as thou
Wert worked on by the snake, in thy most flushed
And heedless, harmless wantonness of bliss.
I cannot answer this immortal thing
Which stands before me; I cannot abhor him;
I look upon him with a pleasing fear,
And yet I fly not from him: in his eye
There is a fastening attraction which   410

---

1. [It is impossible not to be struck with the resemblance between
many of these passages and others in *Manfred, e.g.* act ii. sc. 1, lines
24-28, *Poetical Works*, 1901, iv. 99, *note* 1.]

Fixes my fluttering eyes on his; my heart
Beats quick; he awes me, and yet draws me near,
Nearer and nearer :—Cain—Cain—save me from him !
 Cain. What dreads my Adah? This is no ill spirit.
 Adah. He is not God—nor God's : I have beheld
The Cherubs and the Seraphs; he looks not
Like them.
 Cain. But there are spirits loftier still—
The archangels.
 Lucifer. And still loftier than the archangels.
 Adah. Aye—but not blesséd.
 Lucifer.   If the blessedness
Consists in slavery—no.
 Adah.   I have heard it said, 420
The Seraphs *love most*—Cherubim *know most*— [1]
And this should be a Cherub—since he loves not.
 Lucifer. And if the higher knowledge quenches love,
What must *he be* you cannot love when known ? [i.]
Since the all-knowing Cherubim love least,
The Seraphs' love can be but ignorance :
That they are not compatible, the doom
Of thy fond parents, for their daring, proves.
Choose betwixt Love and Knowledge—since there is
No other choice : your sire hath chosen already : 430
His worship is but fear.
 Adah.   Oh, Cain ! choose Love.
 Cain. For thee, my Adah, I choose not—It was
Born with me—but I love nought else.
 Adah.   Our parents ?
 Cain. Did they love us when they snatched from the
    Tree
That which hath driven us all from Paradise ?
 Adah. We were not born then—and if we had been,
Should we not love them—and our children, Cain ?

---

 i. *What can* he be *who places love in ignorance ?—*[*MS. M.*]

 1. ["One of the second order of angels of the Dionysian hierarchy,
reputed to excel specially in knowledge (as the seraphim in love). See
Bacon's *Advancement of Learning*, i. 28 : 'The first place is given to
the Angels of loue, which are tearmed Seraphim, the second to the
Angels of light, which are tearmed Cherubim.'"—*N. Eng. Dict.*, art.
"Cherub."]

  Cain. My little Enoch ! and his lisping sister !
Could I but deem them happy, I would half
Forget——but it can never be forgotten   440
Through thrice a thousand generations ! never
Shall men love the remembrance of the man
Who sowed the seed of evil and mankind
In the same hour ! They plucked the tree of science
And sin—and, not content with their own sorrow,
Begot *me—thee*—and all the few that are,
And all the unnumbered and innumerable
Multitudes, millions, myriads, which may be,
To inherit agonies accumulated
By ages !—and *I* must be sire of such things ! 450
Thy beauty and thy love—my love and joy,
The rapturous moment and the placid hour,
All we love in our children and each other,
But lead them and ourselves through many years
Of sin and pain—or few, but still of sorrow,
Interchecked with an instant of brief pleasure,
To Death—the unknown ! Methinks the Tree of Know-
   ledge
Hath not fulfilled its promise :—if they sinned,
At least they ought to have known all things that are
Of knowledge—and the mystery of Death.[i] 460
What do they know ?—that they are miserable.
What need of snakes and fruits to teach us that ?
  Adah. I am not wretched, Cain, and if thou
Wert happy——
  Cain.   Be thou happy, then, alone—
I will have nought to do with happiness,
Which humbles me and mine.
  Adah.   Alone I could not,
Nor *would* be happy ; but with those around us
I think I could be so, despite of Death,
Which, as I know it not, I dread not, though
It seems an awful shadow—if I may   470
Judge from what I have heard.
  Lucifer.   And thou couldst not
Alone, thou say'st, be happy ?
  Adah.   Alone ! Oh, my God !

   i. *But it was a lie no doubt.*—[*MS. M. erased.*]

Who could be happy and alone, or good?
To me my solitude seems sin; unless
When I think how soon I shall see my brother,
His brother, and our children, and our parents.

    Lucifer. Yet thy God is alone; and is he happy?
Lonely, and good?

    Adah.   He is not so; he hath
The angels and the mortals to make happy,
And thus becomes so in diffusing joy.   480
What else can joy be, but the spreading joy?[L]

    Lucifer. Ask of your sire, the exile fresh from Eden;
Or of his first-born son: ask your own heart;
It is not tranquil.

    Adah.   Alas! no! and you—
Are you of Heaven?

    Lucifer.   If I am not, enquire
The cause of this all-spreading happiness
(Which you proclaim) of the all-great and good
Maker of life and living things; it is
His secret, and he keeps it.   *We* must bear,
And some of us resist—and both in vain,   490
His Seraphs say: but it is worth the trial,
Since better may not be without: there is
A wisdom in the spirit, which directs
To right, as in the dim blue air the eye
Of you, young mortals, lights at once upon
The star which watches, welcoming the morn.

    Adah. It is a beautiful star; I love it for
Its beauty.

    Lucifer. And why not adore?

    Adah.   Our father
Adores the Invisible only.

    Lucifer.   But the symbols
Of the Invisible are the loveliest   500
Of what is visible; and yon bright star
Is leader of the host of Heaven.

    Adah.   Our father
Saith that he has beheld the God himself
Who made him and our mother.

    Lucifer.   Hast *thou* seen him?

        L. *What else can be joy?*——.—[*MS. M.*]

Adah. Yes—in his works.

Lucifer.   But in his being?

Adah.   No—
Save in my father, who is God's own image;
Or in his angels, who are like to thee—
And brighter, yet less beautiful and powerful
In seeming : as the silent sunny noon,
All light, they look upon us ; but thou seem'st   510
Like an ethereal night,[1] where long white clouds
Streak the deep purple, and unnumbered stars
Spangle the wonderful mysterious vault
With things that look as if they would be suns ;
So beautiful, unnumbered, and endearing,
Not dazzling, and yet drawing us to them,
They fill my eyes with tears, and so dost thou.
Thou seem'st unhappy : do not make us so,
And I will weep for thee.

Lucifer.   Alas ! those tears !
Couldst thou but know what oceans will be shed——   520

Adah. By me?

Lucifer.   By all.

Adah.   What all?

Lucifer.   The million millions—
The myriad myriads—the all-peopled earth—
The unpeopled earth—and the o'er-peopled Hell,
Of which thy bosom is the germ.

Adah.   O Cain !
This spirit curseth us.

Cain.   Let him say on ;
Him will I follow.

Adah.   Whither?

Lucifer.   To a place
Whence he shall come back to thee in an hour ;
But in that hour see things of many days.

Adah. How can that be?

Lucifer.   Did not your Maker make
Out of old worlds this new one in few days?   530
And cannot I, who aided in this work,

1. [Compare—
        " She walks in Beauty like the night."
        Hebrew Melodies, i. 1, *Poetical Works*, 1900, iii. 381.]

Show in an hour what he hath made in many,
Or hath destroyed in few?

Cain.　　　　　　　　　　Lead on.

Adah.　　　　　　　　　　　　　　Will he,
In sooth, return within an hour?

Lucifer.　　　　　　　　　　　He shall.
With us acts are exempt from time, and we
Can crowd eternity into an hour,
Or stretch an hour into eternity:
We breathe not by a mortal measurement—
But that's a mystery. Cain, come on with me.

Adah. Will he return?

Lucifer.　　　　　　　　Aye, woman! he alone　540
Of mortals from that place (the first and last
Who shall return, save ONE), shall come back to
　　thee,
To make that silent and expectant world
As populous as this: at present there
Are few inhabitants.

Adah.　　　　　　Where dwellest thou?

Lucifer. Throughout all space. Where should I dwell?
　　　Where are
Thy God or Gods—there am I: all things are
Divided with me: Life and Death—and Time—
Eternity—and heaven and earth—and that
Which is not heaven nor earth, but peopled with　550
Those who once peopled or shall people both—
These are my realms! so that I do divide
His, and possess a kingdom which is not
His.[1] If I were not that which I have said,
Could I stand here? His angels are within
Your vision.

Adah.　　　So they were when the fair Serpent
Spoke with our mother first.

Lucifer.　　　　　　　　Cain! thou hast heard.
If thou dost long for knowledge, I can satiate
That thirst; nor ask thee to partake of fruits
Which shall deprive thee of a single good　560

---

1. [Lucifer was evidently indebted to the Manichæans for his theory
of the *duplex terra*—an infernal as well as a celestial kingdom.]

The Conqueror has left thee.   Follow me.
   Cain. Spirit, I have said it.
                    [*Exeunt* LUCIFER *and* CAIN.
Adah (*follows exclaiming*). Cain! my brother! Cain!

ACT II.

SCENE I.—*The Abyss of Space.*

   Cain. I tread on air, and sink not—yet I fear
To sink.
   Lucifer. Have faith in me, and thou shalt be
Borne on the air,[1] of which I am the Prince.
   Cain. Can I do so without impiety?
   Lucifer. Believe—and sink not! doubt—and perish!
     thus
Would run the edict of the other God,
Who names me Demon to his angels; they
Echo the sound to miserable things,
Which, knowing nought beyond their shallow senses,
Worship the *word* which strikes their ear, and deem   10
Evil or good what is proclaimed to them
In their abasement.   I will have none such:
Worship or worship not, thou shalt behold
The worlds beyond thy little world, nor be
Amerced for doubts beyond thy little life,
With torture of *my* dooming.   There will come
An hour, when, tossed upon some water-drops,[i]
A man shall say to a man, " Believe in me,
And walk the waters;" and the man shall walk
The billows and be safe.   *I* will not say,   20
Believe in *me*, as a conditional creed
To save thee; but fly with me o'er the gulf
Of space an equal flight, and I will show
What thou dar'st not deny,—the history
Of past—and present, and of future worlds.

---

   i. *An hour, when walking on a petty lake.*—[*MS. M. erased.*]

   1. ["According to the prince of the power of the air" (*Eph.* ii. 2).]

Cain. Oh God ! or Demon ! or whate'er thou art,
Is yon our earth ?
    Lucifer.   Dost thou not recognise
The dust which formed your father?
    Cain.   Can it be ?
Yon small blue circle, swinging in far ether,[i]
With an inferior circlet purpler it still,[1]   30
Which looks like that which lit our earthly night ?
Is this our Paradise ?   Where are its walls,
And they who guard them ?
    Lucifer.   Point me out the site
Of Paradise.
    Cain.   How should I ?   As we move
Like sunbeams onward, it grows small and smaller,
And as it waxes little, and then less,
Gathers a halo round it, like the light
Which shone the roundest of the stars, when I
Beheld them from the skirts of Paradise :
Methinks they both, as we recede from them,   40
Appear to join the innumerable stars
Which are around us ; and, as we move on,
Increase their myriads.
    Lucifer.   And if there should be
Worlds greater than thine own—inhabited
By greater things—and they themselves far more
In number than the dust of thy dull earth,
Though multiplied to animated atoms,

----

    i. *Yon round blue circle swinging in far ether*
      With an inferior circlet dimmer still.—[*MS. M. erased.*]

  1. [Compare—

        " And, fast by, hanging in a golden chain,
         This pendent World, in bigness as a star
         Of smallest magnitude, close by the moon."
                         Paradise Lost, ii. 1051-1053.

Compare, too—

        " The magic car moved on.
         Earth's distant orb appeared
        The smallest light that twinkles in the heavens ;
         Whilst round the chariot's way
         Innumerable systems rolled,
         And countless spheres diffused
         An ever-varying glory."
        Shelley's *Queen Mab, Poetical Works*, 1829, p. 106.]

All living—and all doomed to death—and wretched,
What wouldst thou think?
   Cain.   I should be proud of thought
Which knew such things.
   Lucifer.   But if that high thought were 50
Linked to a servile mass of matter—and,
Knowing such things, aspiring to such things,
And science still beyond them, were chained down
To the most gross and petty paltry wants,
All foul and fulsome—and the very best
Of thine enjoyments a sweet degradation,
A most enervating and filthy cheat
To lure thee on to the renewal of
Fresh souls and bodies,[1] all foredoomed to be
As frail, and few so happy——
   Cain.   Spirit! I   60
Know nought of Death, save as a dreadful thing
Of which I have heard my parents speak, as of
A hideous heritage I owe to them
No less than life—a heritage not happy,
If I may judge, till now. But, Spirit! if
It be as thou hast said (and I within
Feel the prophetic torture of its truth),
Here let me die: for give birth to those
Who can but suffer many years, and die—
Methinks is merely propagating Death,   70
And multiplying murder.
   Lucifer.   Thou canst not
All die—there is what must survive.
   Cain.   The Other
Spake not of this unto my father, when
He shut him forth from Paradise, with death
Written upon his forehead. But at least
Let what is mortal of me perish, that
I may be in the rest as angels are.
   Lucifer. I am angelic: wouldst thou be as I am?

---

1. ["Several of the ancient Fathers, too much prejudiced in favour of virginity, have pretended that if Man had persevered in innocence he would not have entered into the carnal commerce of matrimony, and that the propagation of mankind would have been effected quite another way." (See St. Augustine, *De Civitate Dei*, xiv. cap. xxi. ; Bayle's *Dictionary*, art. " Eve," 1735, ii. 853, *note* C.)]

Cain. I know not what thou art : I see thy power,
And see thou show'st me things beyond *my* power,   80
Beyond all power of my born faculties,
Although inferior still to my desires
And my conceptions.
          Lucifer.   What are they which dwell
So humbly in their pride, as to sojourn
With worms in clay?
          Cain.   And what art thou who dwellest
So haughtily in spirit, and canst range
Nature and immortality—and yet
Seem'st sorrowful?
          Lucifer.   I seem that which I am;
And therefore do I ask of thee, if thou
Wouldst be immortal?
          Cain.   Thou hast said, I must be   90
Immortal in despite of me.   I knew not
This until lately—but since it must be,
Let me, or happy or unhappy, learn
To anticipate my immortality.
          Lucifer. Thou didst before I came upon thee.
          Cain.   How?
          Lucifer. By suffering.
          Cain.   And must torture be immortal?
          Lucifer. We and thy sons will try.   But now, behold!
Is it not glorious?
          Cain.   Oh thou beautiful
And unimaginable ether! and
Ye multiplying masses of increased   100
And still-increasing lights! what are ye? what
Is this blue wilderness of interminable
Air, where ye roll along, as I have seen
The leaves along the limpid streams of Eden?
Is your course measured for ye? Or do ye
Sweep on in your unbounded revelry
Through an aërial universe of endless
Expansion—at which my soul aches to think—
Intoxicated with eternity?[1]

          1. [Compare—
                    "Below lay stretched the universe!
                    There, far as the remotest line

Oh God ! Oh Gods ! or whatsoe'er ye are !   110
How beautiful ye are ! how beautiful
Your works, or accidents, or whatsoe'er
They may be !   Let me die, as atoms die,
(If that they die), or know ye in your might
And knowledge !   My thoughts are not in this hour
Unworthy what I see, though my dust is ;
Spirit ! let me expire, or see them nearer.
    Lucifer. Art thou not nearer? look back to thine
      earth !
    Cain. Where is it ?   I see nothing save a mass
Of most innumerable lights.
    Lucifer.   Look there !   120
    Cain. I cannot see it.
    Lucifer.   Yet it sparkles still.
    Cain. That !—yonder !
    Lucifer.   Yea.
    Cain.   And wilt thou tell me so ?
Why, I have seen the fire-flies and fire-worms
Sprinkle the dusky groves and the green banks
In the dim twilight, brighter than yon world
Which bears them.
    Lucifer.   Thou hast seen both worms and worlds,
Each bright and sparkling—what dost think of them ?
    Cain. That they are beautiful in their own sphere,
And that the night, which makes both beautiful,
The little shining fire-fly in its flight,   130
And the immortal star in its great course,
Must both be guided.
    Lucifer.   But by whom or what ?
    Cain. Show me.
    Lucifer.   Dar'st thou behold ?
    Cain.   How know I what
I *dare* behold ?   As yet, thou hast shown nought
I dare not gaze on further.
    Lucifer.   On, then, with me.

> That bounds imagination's flight,
>   Countless and unending orbs
> In many motions intermingled,
> Yet still fulfilled immutably
>   Eternal Nature's laws."
>   Shelley's *Queen Mab*, ii, *ibid.*, p. 107.]

Wouldst thou behold things mortal or immortal?

   Cain. Why, what are things?

   Lucifer.   *Both* partly : but what doth
Sit next thy heart?

   Cain.   The things I see.

   Lucifer.   But what
Sate nearest it?

   Cain.   The things I have not seen,
Nor ever shall—the mysteries of Death.   140

   Lucifer. What, if I show to thee things which have
      died,
As I have shown thee much which cannot die?

   Cain. Do so.

   Lucifer.   Away, then! on our mighty wings!

   Cain. Oh! how we cleave the blue! The stars fade
      from us!
The earth! where is my earth? Let me look on it,
For I was made of it.

   Lucifer.   'Tis now beyond thee,
Less, in the universe, than thou in it;
Yet deem not that thou canst escape it; thou
Shalt soon return to earth, and all its dust :
'Tis part of thy eternity, and mine.   150

   Cain. Where dost thou lead me?

   Lucifer.   To what was before thee!
The phantasm of the world; of which thy world
Is but the wreck.

   Cain.   What! is it not then new?

   Lucifer. No more than life is; and that was ere thou
Or *I* were, or the things which seem to us
Greater than either: many things will have
No end; and some, which would pretend to have
Had no beginning, have had one as mean
As thou; and mightier things have been extinct
To make way for much meaner than we can   160
Surmise; for *moments* only and the *space*
Have been and must be all *unchangeable.*
But changes make not death, except to clay;
But thou art clay—and canst but comprehend
That which was clay, and such thou shalt behold.

   Cain. Clay—Spirit—what thou wilt—I can survey.

Lucifer. Away, then!
Cain.   But the lights fade from me fast,
And some till now grew larger as we approached,
And wore the look of worlds.
Lucifer.   And such they are.
Cain. And Edens in them?
Lucifer.   It may be.
Cain.   And men? 170
Lucifer. Yea, or things higher.
Cain.   Aye! and serpents too? [i.]
Lucifer. Wouldst thou have men without them? must
      no reptiles
Breathe, save the erect ones?
Cain.   How the lights recede!
Where fly we?
Lucifer.   To the world of phantoms, which
Are beings past, and shadows still to come.
Cain. But it grows dark, and dark—the stars are gone!
Lucifer. And yet thou seest.
Cain.   'Tis a fearful light!
No sun—no moon—no lights innumerable—
The very blue of the empurpled night
Fades to a dreary twilight—yet I see   180
Huge dusky masses; but unlike the worlds
We were approaching, which, begirt with light,
Seemed full of life even when their atmosphere
Of light gave way, and showed them taking shapes
Unequal, of deep valleys and vast mountains;
And some emitting sparks, and some displaying
Enormous liquid plains, and some begirt
With luminous belts, and floating moons, which took,
Like them, the features of fair earth:—instead,
All here seems dark and dreadful.
Lucifer.   But distinct.   190
Thou seekest to behold Death, and dead things?
Cain. I seek it not; but as I know there are
Such, and that my sire's sin makes him and me,
And all that we inherit, liable
To such, I would behold, at once, what I
Must one day see perforce.

i. *And with serpents too?*—[MS. M.

Lucifer.   Behold !
Cain.   'Tis darkness !
Lucifer. And so it shall be ever—but we will
Unfold its gates !
    Cain.   Enormous vapours roll
Apart—what's this?
    Lucifer.   Enter !
    Cain.   Can I return ?
    Lucifer. Return ! be sure : how else should Death be
        peopled?   200
Its present realm is thin to what it will be,
Through thee and thine.
    Cain.   The clouds still open wide
And wider, and make widening circles round us !
    Lucifer. Advance !
    Cain.   And thou !
    Lucifer.   Fear not—without me thou
Couldst not have gone beyond thy world.   On ! on !
                    [*They disappear through the clouds.*

                    SCENE II.—*Hades.*

                Enter LUCIFER *and* CAIN.

    Cain. How silent and how vast are these dim worlds !
For they seem more than one, and yet more peopled
Than the huge brilliant luminous orbs which swung
So thickly in the upper air, that I
Had deemed them rather the bright populace
Of some all unimaginable Heaven,
Than things to be inhabited themselves,[L]
But that on drawing near them I beheld
Their swelling into palpable immensity
Of matter, which seemed made for life to dwell on,   10
Rather than life itself.   But here, all is
So shadowy, and so full of twilight, that
It speaks of a day past.
    Lucifer.   It is the realm

        i. *Rather than things to be inhabited.*—[*MS. M.*]

Of Death.—Wouldst have it present?
   Cain.   Till I know
That which it really is, I cannot answer.
But if it be as I have heard my father
Deal out in his long homilies, 'tis a thing—
Oh God! I dare not think on't! Curséd be
He who invented Life that leads to Death!
Or the dull mass of life, that, being life,   20
Could not retain, but needs must forfeit it—
Even for the innocent!
   Lucifer.   Dost thou curse thy father?
   Cain. Cursed he not me in giving me my birth?
Cursed he not me before my birth, in daring
To pluck the fruit forbidden?
   Lucifer.   Thou say'st well:
The curse is mutual 'twixt thy sire and thee—
But for thy sons and brother?
   Cain.   Let them share it
With me, their sire and brother! What else is
Bequeathed to me? I leave them my inheritance!
Oh, ye interminable gloomy realms   30
Of swimming shadows and enormous shapes,
Some fully shown, some indistinct, and all
Mighty and melancholy—what are ye?
Live ye, or have ye lived?
   Lucifer.   Somewhat of both.
   Cain. Then what is Death?
   Lucifer.   What? Hath not he who made ye
Said 'tis another life?
   Cain.   Till now he hath
Said nothing, save that all shall die.
   Lucifer.   Perhaps
He one day will unfold that further secret.
   Cain. Happy the day!
   Lucifer.   Yes; happy! when unfolded,
Through agonies unspeakable, and clogged   40
With agonies eternal, to innumerable
Yet unborn myriads of unconscious atoms,
All to be animated for this only!
   Cain. What are these mighty phantoms which I see
Floating around me?—They wear not the form

Of the Intelligences I have seen
Round our regretted and unentered Eden;
Nor wear the form of man as I have viewed it
In Adam's and in Abel's, and in mine,
Nor in my sister-bride's, nor in my children's: 50
And yet they have an aspect, which, though not
Of men nor angels, looks like something, which,
If not the last, rose higher than the first,
Haughty, and high, and beautiful, and full
Of seeming strength, but of inexplicable
Shape; for I never saw such.   They bear not
The wing of Seraph, nor the face of man,
Nor form of mightiest brute, nor aught that is
Now breathing; mighty yet and beautiful
As the most beautiful and mighty which   60
Live, and yet so unlike them, that I scarce
Can call them living.[1]
    Lucifer.   Yet they lived.
    Cain.   Where?
    Lucifer.   Where
Thou livest.
    Cain.   When?
    Lucifer.   On what thou callest earth
They did inhabit.
    Cain.   Adam is the first.
    Lucifer. Of thine, I grant thee—but too mean to be
The last of these.
    Cain.   And what are they?
    Lucifer.   That which
Thou shalt be.
    Cain.   But what *were* they?
    Lucifer.   Living, high,
Intelligent, good, great, and glorious things,
As much superior unto all thy sire
Adam could e'er have been in Eden, as   70
The sixty-thousandth generation shall be,

---

1. ["I have . . . supposed Cain to be shown in the *rational* pre-
Adamites, beings endowed with a higher intelligence than man, but
totally unlike him in form, and with much greater strength of mind
and person.   You may suppose the small talk which takes place
between him and Lucifer upon these matters is not quite canonical."—
Letter to Moore, September 19, 1821, *Letters*, 1901, v. 368.]

In its dull damp degeneracy, to
Thee and thy son ;—and how weak they are, judge
By thy own flesh.
 Cain.   Ah me ! and did *they* perish ?
 Lucifer. Yes, from their earth, as thou wilt fade from
  thine.
 Cain. But was *mine* theirs ?
 Lucifer.   It was.
 Cain.   But not as now.
It is too little and too lowly to
Sustain such creatures.
 Lucifer. True, it was more glorious.
 Cain. And wherefore did it fall ?
 Lucifer.   Ask him who fells.[1]
 Cain. But how ?
 Lucifer. By a most crushing and inexorable
Destruction and disorder of the elements, 81
Which struck a world to chaos, as a chaos
Subsiding has struck out a world : such things,
Though rare in time, are frequent in eternity.—
Pass on, and gaze upon the past.
 Cain.   'Tis awful !
 Lucifer. And true. Behold these phantoms ! they were
  once
Material as thou art.
 Cain. And must I be
Like them ?
 Lucifer. Let He [2] who made thee answer that.
I show thee what thy predecessors are,
And what they *were* thou feelest, in degree 20
Inferior as thy petty feelings and
Thy pettier portion of the immortal part
Of high intelligence and earthly strength.
What ye in common have with what they had
Is Life, and what ye *shall* have—Death : the rest
Of your poor attributes is such as suits

---

1. [Compare the "jingle between king and kine," in *Sardanapalus*, act v. sc. 1, lines 483, 484. It is hard to say whether Byron inserted and then omitted to erase these blemishes from negligence and indifference, or whether he regarded them as permissible or even felicitous.]
2. ["*Let* He." There is no doubt that Byron wrote, or that he should have written, "Let Him."]

Reptiles engendered out of the subsiding
Slime of a mighty universe, crushed into
A scarcely-yet shaped planet, peopled with
Things whose enjoyment was to be in blindness—   100
A Paradise of Ignorance, from which
Knowledge was barred as poison.   But behold
What these superior beings are or were ;
Or, if it irk thee, turn thee back and till
The earth, thy task—I'll waft thee there in safety.
    Cain. No : I'll stay here.
    Lucifer.   How long ?
    Cain.   For ever !   Since
I must one day return here from the earth,
I rather would remain ; I am sick of all
That dust has shown me—let me dwell in shadows.
    Lucifer. It cannot be : thou now beholdest as   110
A vision that which is reality.
To make thyself fit for this dwelling, thou
Must pass through what the things thou seest have
      passed—
The gates of Death.
    Cain.   By what gate have we entered
Even now ?
    Lucifer.   By mine !   But, plighted to return,
My spirit buoys thee up to breathe in regions
Where all is breathless save thyself.   Gaze on ;
But do not think to dwell here till thine hour
Is come !
    Cain.   And these, too—can they ne'er repass
To earth again?
    Lucifer.   *Their* earth is gone for ever—   120
So changed by its convulsion, they would not
Be conscious to a single present spot
Of its new scarcely hardened surface—'twas—
Oh, what a beautiful world it *was !*
    Cain.   And is !
It is not with the earth, though I must till it,
I feel at war—but that I may not profit
By what it bears of beautiful, untoiling,
Nor gratify my thousand swelling thoughts
With knowledge, nor allay my thousand fears

Of Death and Life.

 Lucifer.　　　　　What thy world is, thou see'st,　130
But canst not comprehend the shadow of
That which it was.

 Cain.　　　　　And those enormous creatures,
Phantoms inferior in intelligence
(At least so seeming) to the things we have passed,
Resembling somewhat the wild habitants
Of the deep woods of earth, the hugest which
Roar nightly in the forest, but ten-fold
In magnitude and terror ; taller than
The cherub-guarded walls of Eden—with
Eyes flashing like the fiery swords which fence them—
And tusks projecting like the trees stripped of　141
Their bark and branches— what were they ?

 Lucifer.　　　　　　　　That which
The Mammoth is in thy world ;—but these lie
By myriads underneath its surface.

 Cain.　　　　　　　But
None on it ?

 Lucifer.　　No : for thy frail race to war
With them would render the curse on it useless—
'Twould be destroyed so early.

 Cain.　　　　　But why *war ?*

 Lucifer. You have forgotten the denunciation
Which drove your race from Eden—war with all things,
And death to all things, and disease to most things,　150
And pangs, and bitterness ; these were the fruits
Of the forbidden tree.

 Cain.　　　　　But animals—
Did they, too, eat of it, that they must die?

 Lucifer. Your Maker told ye, *they* were made for you,
As you for him.—You would not have their doom
Superior to your own ?　Had Adam not
Fallen, all had stood.

 Cain.　　　　　Alas ! the hopeless wretches !
They too must share my sire's fate, like his sons ;
Like them, too, without having shared the apple ;
Like them, too, without the so dear-bought *knowledge !*
It was a lying tree—for we *know* nothing.　161
At least it *promised knowledge* at the *price*

Of death—but *knowledge* still : but what *knows* man ?

   Lucifer. It may be death leads to the *highest* knowledge;
And being of all things the sole thing certain,[i.]
At least leads to the *surest* science : therefore
The Tree was true, though deadly.

   Cain.   These dim realms !
I see them, but I know them not.

   Lucifer.   Because
Thy hour is yet afar, and matter cannot
Comprehend spirit wholly—but 'tis something   **170**
To know there are such realms.

   Cain.   We knew already
That there was Death.

   Lucifer.   But not what was beyond it.

   Cain. Nor know I now.

   Lucifer.   Thou knowest that there is
A state, and many states beyond thine own—
And this thou knewest not this morn.

   Cain.   But all
Seems dim and shadowy.

   Lucifer.   Be content ; it will
Seem clearer to thine immortality.

   Cain. And yon immeasurable liquid space
Of glorious azure which floats on beyond us,
Which looks like water, and which I should deem[ii.] **180**
The river which flows out of Paradise
Past my own dwelling, but that it is bankless
And boundless, and of an ethereal hue—
What is it ?

   Lucifer. There is still some such on earth,
Although inferior, and thy children shall
Dwell near it—'tis the phantasm of an Ocean.

   Cain. 'Tis like another world ; a liquid sun—
And those inordinate creatures sporting o'er
Its shining surface ?

   Lucifer.   Are its inhabitants,
The past Leviathans.

   Cain.   And yon immense   **190**

   i. *And being of all things the sole thing sure.*—[*MS. M.*]
  ii. *Which seems like water and which I should deem.*—[*MS. M.*]

Serpent, which rears his dripping mane and vasty
Head, ten times higher than the haughtiest cedar,
Forth from the abyss, looking as he could coil
Himself around the orbs we lately looked on—
Is he not of the kind which basked beneath
The Tree in Eden?
    Lucifer.   Eve, thy mother, best
Can tell what shape of serpent tempted her.
    Cain. This seems too terrible.   No doubt the other
Had more of beauty.
    Lucifer.   Hast thou ne'er beheld him?
    Cain. Many of the same kind (at least so called)
But never that precisely, which persuaded   201
The fatal fruit, nor even of the same aspect.
    Lucifer. Your father saw him not?
    Cain.   No: 'twas my mother
Who tempted him—she tempted by the serpent.
    Lucifer. Good man! whene'er thy wife, or thy sons'
        wives,
Tempt thee or them to aught that 's new or strange,
Be sure thou seest first who hath tempted *them!*
    Cain. Thy precept comes too late: there is no more
For serpents to tempt woman to.
    Lucifer.   But there
Are some things still which woman may tempt man to, 210
And man tempt woman:—let thy sons look to it!
My counsel is a kind one; for 'tis even
Given chiefly at my own expense; 'tis true,
'Twill not be followed, so there 's little lost.[1]
    Cain. I understand not this.
    Lucifer.   The happier thou!—
Thy world and thou are still too young!   Thou thinkest
Thyself most wicked and unhappy—is it
Not so?
    Cain.   For crime, I know not; but for pain,
I have felt much.
    Lucifer.   First-born of the first man!
Thy present state of sin—and thou art evil,   220
Of sorrow—and thou sufferest, are both Eden

    1. [Lucifer's candour and disinterested advice are " after " and in the manner of Mephistopheles.]

In all its innocence compared to what
Thou shortly may'st be ; and that state again,
In its redoubled wretchedness, a Paradise
To what thy sons' sons' sons, accumulating
In generations like to dust (which they
In fact but add to), shall endure and do.—
Now let us back to earth !
  Cain.   And wherefore didst thou
Lead me here only to inform me this ?
  Lucifer. Was not thy quest for knowledge ?
  Cain.   Yes—as being 230
The road to happiness !
  Lucifer.   If truth be so,
Thou hast it.
  Cain.   Then my father's God did well
When he prohibited the fatal Tree.
  Lucifer. But had done better in not planting it.
But ignorance of evil doth not save
From evil; it must still roll on the same,
A part of all things.
  Cain.   Not of all things. No—
I'll not believe it—for I thirst for good.
  Lucifer. And who and what doth not? *Who* covets
    evil
For its own bitter sake ?—*None*—nothing ! 'tis 240
The leaven of all life, and lifelessness.
  Cain. Within those glorious orbs which we behold,
Distant, and dazzling, and innumerable,
Ere we came down into this phantom realm,
Ill cannot come : they are too beautiful.
  Lucifer. Thou hast seen them from afar.
  Cain.   And what of that ?
Distance can but diminish glory—they,
When nearer, must be more ineffable.
  Lucifer. Approach the things of earth most beautiful,
And judge their beauty near.
  Cain.   I have done this— 250
The loveliest thing I know is loveliest nearest.
  Lucifer. Then there must be delusion.—What is that
Which being nearest to thine eyes is still
More beautiful than beauteous things remote ?

   Cain. My sister Adah.—All the stars of heaven,
The deep blue noon of night, lit by an orb
Which looks a spirit, or a spirit's world—
The hues of twilight—the Sun's gorgeous coming—
His setting indescribable, which fills
My eyes with pleasant tears as I behold   260
Him sink, and feel my heart float softly with him
Along that western paradise of clouds—
The forest shade, the green bough, the bird's voice—
The vesper bird's, which seems to sing of love,
And mingles with the song of Cherubim,
As the day closes over Eden's walls;—
All these are nothing, to my eyes and heart,
Like Adah's face: I turn from earth and heaven
To gaze on it.
   Lucifer.   'Tis fair as frail mortality,
In the first dawn and bloom of young creation,   270
And earliest embraces of earth's parents,
Can make its offspring; still it is delusion.
   Cain. You think so, being not her brother.
   Lucifer.   Mortal!
My brotherhood's with those who have no children.
   Cain. Then thou canst have no fellowship with us.
   Lucifer. It may be that thine own shall be for me.
But if thou dost possess a beautiful
Being beyond all beauty in thine eyes,
Why art thou wretched?
   Cain.   Why do I exist?
Why art *thou* wretched? why are all things so?   280
Ev'n he who made us must be, as the maker
Of things unhappy! To produce destruction
Can surely never be the task of joy,
And yet my sire says he 's omnipotent:
Then why is Evil—he being Good? I asked
This question of my father; and he said,
Because this Evil only was the path
To Good. Strange Good, that must arise from out
Its deadly opposite. I lately saw
A lamb stung by a reptile: the poor suckling   290
Lay foaming on the earth, beneath the vain
And piteous bleating of its restless dam;

My father plucked some herbs, and laid them to
The wound; and by degrees the helpless wretch
Resumed its careless life, and rose to drain
The mother's milk, who o'er it tremulous
Stood licking its reviving limbs with joy.
Behold, my son! said Adam, how from Evil
Springs Good![1]
 Lucifer. What didst thou answer?
 Cain.   Nothing; for
He is my father: but I thought, that 'twere 300
A better portion for the animal
Never to have been *stung at all*, than to
Purchase renewal of its little life
With agonies unutterable, though
Dispelled by antidotes.
 Lucifer.   But as thou saidst
Of all belovéd things thou lovest her
Who shared thy mother's milk, and giveth hers
Unto thy children——
 Cain.   Most assuredly:
What should I be without her?
 Lucifer.   What am I?
 Cain. Dost thou love nothing?
 Lucifer.   What does thy God love? 310
 Cain. All things, my father says; but I confess
I see it not in their allotment here.
 Lucifer. And, therefore, thou canst not see if *I* love
Or no—except some vast and general purpose,
To which particular things must melt like snows.
 Cain. Snows! what are they?
 Lucifer.   Be happier in not knowing
What thy remoter offspring must encounter;

---

1. ["If you say that God permitted sin to manifest His wisdom,
which shines the more brightly by the disorders which the wickedness
of men produces every day, than it would have done in a state of innocence, it may be answered that this is to compare the Deity to a father
who should suffer his children to break their legs on purpose to show
to all the city his great art in setting their broken bones; or to a king
who should suffer seditions and factions to increase through all his
kingdom, that he might purchase the glory of quelling them. . . . This
is that doctrine of a Father of the Church who said, ' Felix culpa quæ
talem Redemptorem meruit!' "—Bayle's *Dictionary*, 1737, art. " Paulicians," *note* B, 25, iv. 515.]

But bask beneath the clime which knows no winter.
 Cain. But dost thou not love something like thyself?
 Lucifer. And dost thou love *thyself?*
 Cain.   Yes, but love more 320
What makes my feelings more endurable,
And is more than myself, because I love it!
 Lucifer. Thou lovest it, because 'tis beautiful,
As was the apple in thy mother's eye;
And when it ceases to be so, thy love
Will cease, like any other appetite.[1]
 Cain. Cease to be beautiful! how can that be?
 Lucifer. With time.
 Cain.   But time has passed, and hitherto
Even Adam and my mother both are fair:
Not fair like Adah and the Seraphim—   330
But very fair.
 Lucifer.   All that must pass away
In them and her.
 Cain.   I'm sorry for it; but
Cannot conceive my love for her the less:
And when her beauty disappears, methinks
He who creates all beauty will lose more
Than me in seeing perish such a work.
 Lucifer. I pity thee who lovest what must perish.
 Cain. And I thee who lov'st nothing.
 Lucifer.   And thy brother—
Sits he not near thy heart?
 Cain.   Why should he not?
 Lucifer. Thy father loves him well—so does thy God. 340
 Cain. And so do I.
 Lucifer.   'Tis well and meekly done.
 Cain. Meekly!
 Lucifer.   He is the second born of flesh,
And is his mother's favourite.

---

 1. [Lucifer does not infect Cain with his cynical theories as to the origin and endurance of love. For the antidote, compare Wordsworth's sonnet "To a Painter" (No. 11), written in 1841—

> " Morn into noon did pass, noon into eve,
> And the old day was welcome as the young,
> As welcome, and as beautiful—in sooth
> More beautiful, as being a thing more holy,' etc.
>   *Works,* 1889, p. 772.]

Cain.   Let him keep
Her favour, since the Serpent was the first
To win it.
    Lucifer. And his father's?
    Cain.   What is that
To me? should I not love that which all love?
    Lucifer. And the Jehovah—the indulgent Lord,
And bounteous planter of barred Paradise—
He, too, looks smilingly on Abel.
    Cain.   I
Ne'er saw him, and I know not if he smiles.   350
    Lucifer. But you have seen his angels.
    Cain.   Rarely.
    Lucifer.   But
Sufficiently to see they love your brother :
His sacrifices are acceptable.
    Cain. So be they! wherefore speak to me of this?
    Lucifer. Because thou hast thought of this ere now.
    Cain.   And if
I *have* thought, why recall a thought that——(*he pauses
    as agitated*)—Spirit!
Here we are in *thy* world; speak not of *mine.*
Thou hast shown me wonders : thou hast shown me those
Mighty Pre-Adamites who walked the earth
Of which ours is the wreck : thou hast pointed out   360
Myriads of starry worlds, of which our own
Is the dim and remote companion, in
Infinity of life : thou hast shown me shadows
Of that existence with the dreaded name
Which my sire brought us—Death;[i] thou hast shown
    me much
But not all : show me where Jehovah dwells,
In his especial Paradise—or *thine :*
Where is it?
    Lucifer.   *Here,* and o'er all space.
    Cain.   But ye
Have some allotted dwelling—as all things ;
Clay has its earth, and other worlds their tenants ;   370
All temporary breathing creatures their
Peculiar element; and things which have

    i. *Which my sire shrinks from—Death* ——.—[*MS. erased.*]

Long ceased to breathe *our* breath, have theirs, thou
     say'st;
And the Jehovah and thyself have thine—
Ye do not dwell together?
    Lucifer.   No, we reign
Together; but our dwellings are asunder.
    Cain. Would there were only one of ye! perchance
An unity of purpose might make union
In elements which seem now jarred in storms.
How came ye, being Spirits wise and infinite,   380
To separate?   Are ye not as brethren in
Your essence—and your nature, and your glory?
    Lucifer. Art not thou Abel's brother?
    Cain.   We are brethren,
And so we shall remain; but were it not so,
Is spirit like to flesh? can it fall out—
Infinity with Immortality?
Jarring and turning space to misery—
For what?
    Lucifer. To reign.
    Cain.   Did ye not tell me that
Ye are both eternal?
    Lucifer.   Yea!
    Cain.   And what I have seen—
Yon blue immensity, is boundless?
    Lucifer.   Aye.   390
    Cain. And cannot ye both *reign*, then?—is there not
Enough?—why should ye differ?
    Lucifer.   We *both* reign.
    Cain. But one of you makes evil.
    Lucifer.   Which?
    Cain.   Thou! for
If thou canst do man good, why dost thou not?
    Lucifer. And why not he who made? *I* made ye
    not;
Ye are *his* creatures, and not mine.
    Cain.   Then leave us
His creatures, as thou say'st we are, or show me
Thy dwelling, or *his* dwelling.
    Lucifer.   I could show thee
Both; but the time will come thou shalt see one

Of them for evermore.[1]
    Cain.   And why not now?   400
    Lucifer. Thy human mind hath scarcely grasp to gather
The little I have shown thee into calm
And clear thought: and *thou* wouldst go on aspiring
To the great double Mysteries! the *two Principles*! [2]
And gaze upon them on their secret thrones!
Dust! limit thy ambition; for to see
Either of these would be for thee to perish!
    Cain. And let me perish, so I see them!
    Lucifer.   There
The son of her who snatched the apple spake!
But thou wouldst only perish, and not see them;   410
That sight is for the other state.
    Cain.   Of Death?
    Lucifer. That is the prelude.
    Cain.   Then I dread it less,
Now that I know it leads to something definite.
    Lucifer. And now I will convey thee to thy world,
Where thou shalt multiply the race of Adam,
Eat, drink, toil, tremble, laugh, weep, sleep—and die!
    Cain. And to what end have I beheld these things
Which thou hast shown me?
    Lucifer.   Didst thou not require
Knowledge? And have I not, in what I showed,
Taught thee to know thyself?
    Cain.   Alas! I seem   420
Nothing.[3]

---

1. [In Byron's Diary for January 28, 1821, we find the following entry—

    "*Thought for a speech of Lucifer, in the Tragedy of Cain.*

      "Were *Death* an *evil*, would *I* let thee *live* ?
      Fool! live as I live—as thy father lives,
      And thy sons' sons shall live for evermore!"
               Letters, 1901, v. 191.]

2. [Matthew Arnold (*Poetry of Byron,* 1881, p. xxii.) quotes these lines as an instance of Byron's unknowingness and want of humour. It cannot be denied that he leaves imbedded in his fabric lumps of unshapen material, which mar the symmetry of his art. Lucifer's harangue involves a reference to "hard words ending in *ism.*" The *spirit* of error, not the Manichæan heresy, should have proceeded out of his lips.]

3. ["Cain is a proud man: if Lucifer promised him kingdoms, etc.,

Lucifer. And this should be the human sum
Of knowledge, to know mortal nature's nothingness;
Bequeath that science to thy children, and
'Twill spare them many tortures.
　　Cain.　　　　　　　　　Haughty spirit!
Thou speak'st it proudly; but thyself, though proud,
Hast a superior.
　　Lucifer.　　　　No! By heaven, which he
Holds, and the abyss, and the immensity
Of worlds and life, which I hold with him—No!
I have a Victor—true; but no superior.[1]
Homage he has from all—but none from me:　　　　430
I battle it against him, as I battled
In highest Heaven—through all Eternity,
And the unfathomable gulfs of Hades,
And the interminable realms of space,
And the infinity of endless ages,
All, all, will I dispute! And world by world,
And star by star, and universe by universe,
Shall tremble in the balance, till the great
Conflict shall cease, if ever it shall cease,
Which it ne'er shall, till he or I be quenched!　　　440
And what can quench our immortality,
Or mutual and irrevocable hate?
He as a conqueror will call the conquered

it would *elate* him: the object of the Demon is to *depress* him still
further in his own estimation than he was before, by showing him
infinite things and his own abasement, till he falls into the frame of
mind that leads to the catastrophe, from mere *internal* irritation, *not*
premeditation, or envy of Abel (which would have made him contemptible), but from the rage and fury against the inadequacy of his
state to his conceptions, and which discharges itself rather against Life,
and the author of Life, than the mere living."—Letter to Moore,
November 3, 1821, *Letters*, 1901, v. 470. Here, no doubt, Byron is
speaking *in propriâ personâ.* It was this sense of limitation, of human
nothingness, which provoked an "internal irritation . . . a rage and
fury against the inadequacy of his state to his conceptions." His
"spirit beats its mortal bars," not, like Galahad, to be possessed by,
but to possess the Heavenly Vision.]
　　1. [Compare—

　　　　　　　"What though the field be lost,
　　　　All is not lost; th' unconquerable will
　　　　And study of revenge, immortal hate,
　　　　And courage never to submit or yield."
　　　　　　　　　　　　Paradise Lost, i. 105-108.]

Evil; but what will be the *Good* he gives?
Were I the victor, *his* works would be deemed
The only evil ones. And you, ye new
And scarce-born mortals, what have been his gifts
To you already, in your little world?
 Cain. But few; and some of those but bitter.
 Lucifer.   Back
With me, then, to thine earth, and try the rest   450
Of his celestial boons to you and yours.
Evil and Good are things in their own essence,
And not made good or evil by the Giver;
But if he gives you good—so call him; if
Evil springs from *him,* do not name it *mine,*
Till ye know better its true fount; and judge
Not by words, though of Spirits, but the fruits
Of your existence, such as it must be.
One good gift has the fatal apple given,—   460
Your *reason :*—let it not be overswayed
By tyrannous threats to force you into faith
'Gainst all external sense and inward feeling :
Think and endure,—and form an inner world
In your own bosom—where the outward fails;
So shall you nearer be the spiritual
Nature, and war triumphant with your own.
            [*They disappear.*

ACT III.

Scene I.—*The Earth, near Eden, as in Act I.*

Enter Cain *and* Adah.

 Adah. Hush! tread softly, Cain!
 Cain.   I will—but wherefore?
 Adah. Our little Enoch sleeps upon yon bed
Of leaves, beneath the cypress.
 Cain.   Cypress! 'tis
A gloomy tree, which looks as if it mourned
O'er what it shadows; wherefore didst thou choose it
For our child's canopy?

Adah.   Because its branches
Shut out the sun like night, and therefore seemed
Fitting to shadow slumber.
   Cain.   Aye, the last—
And longest ; but no matter—lead me to him.
                      [*They go up to the child.*
How lovely he appears ! his little cheeks,   10
In their pure incarnation,[1] vying with
The rose leaves strewn beneath them.
   Adah.   And his lips, too,
How beautifully parted !   No ; you shall not
Kiss him, at least not now : he will awake soon—
His hour of mid-day rest is nearly over ;
But it were pity to disturb him till
'Tis closed.
   Cain.   You have said well ; I will contain
My heart till then.   He smiles, and sleeps !—sleep on,
And smile, thou little, young inheritor
Of a world scarce less young : sleep on, and smile ! 20
Thine are the hours and days when both are cheering
And innocent ! *thou* hast not plucked the fruit—
Thou know'st not thou art naked !   Must the time
Come thou shalt be amerced for sins unknown,
Which were not thine nor mine ?   But now sleep on !
His cheeks are reddening into deeper smiles,
And shining lids are trembling o'er his long
Lashes,[2] dark as the cypress which waves o'er them ;
Half open, from beneath them the clear blue
Laughs out, although in slumber.   He must dream— 30
Of what ?   Of Paradise !—Aye ! dream of it,
My disinherited boy !   'Tis but a dream ;
For never more thyself, thy sons, nor fathers,
Shall walk in that forbidden place of joy !
   Adah. Dear Cain !   Nay, do not whisper o'er our son
Such melancholy yearnings o'er the past :

---

1. [An obsolete form of *carnation*, the colour of " flesh."]
2. [Compare—

      " Her dewy eyes are closed,
     And on their lids, whose texture fine
     Scarce hides the dark-blue orbs beneath,
       The baby Sleep is pillowed."
           Shelley's *Queen Mab*, i., *ibid.*, p. 104.]

Why wilt thou always mourn for Paradise?
Can we not make another?
   Cain.   Where?
   Adah.   Here, or
Where'er thou wilt: where'er thou art, I feel not
The want of this so much regretted Eden.   40
Have I not thee—our boy—our sire, and brother,
And Zillah—our sweet sister, and our Eve,
To whom we owe so much besides our birth?
   Cain. Yes—Death, too, is amongst the debts we owe
     her.
   Adah. Cain! that proud Spirit, who withdrew thee
     hence,
Hath saddened thine still deeper. I had hoped
The promised wonders which thou hast beheld,
Visions, thou say'st, of past and present worlds,
Would have composed thy mind into the calm
Of a contented knowledge; but I see   50
Thy guide hath done thee evil: still I thank him,
And can forgive him all, that he so soon
Hath given thee back to us.
   Cain.   So soon?
   Adah.   'Tis scarcely
Two hours since ye departed: two *long* hours
To *me*, but only *hours* upon the sun.
   Cain. And yet I have approached that sun, and seen
Worlds which he once shone on, and never more
Shall light; and worlds he never lit: methought
Years had rolled o'er my absence.
   Adah.   Hardly hours.
   Cain. The mind then hath capacity of time,   60
And measures it by that which it beholds,
Pleasing or painful;[1] little or almighty.

---

1. ["Time is our consciousness of the succession of ideas in our mind. . . . One man is stretched on the rack during twelve hours, another sleeps soundly in his bed. The difference of time perceived by these two persons is immense: one hardly will believe that half an hour has elapsed, the other could credit that centuries had flown during his agony."—Shelley's note to the lines—
             "... the thoughts that rise
      In time-destroying infiniteness."
           Queen Mab, viii., *ibid.*, p. 136.]

I had beheld the immemorial works
Of endless beings; skirred extinguished worlds;
And, gazing on eternity, methought
I had borrowed more by a few drops of ages
From its immensity: but now I feel
My littleness again.　Well said the Spirit,
That I was nothing!
　　Adah.　　　　　　　Wherefore said he so?
Jehovah said not that.
　　Cain.　　　　　　　No: *he* contents him　　　70
With making us the *nothing* which we are;
And after flattering dust with glimpses of
Eden and Immortality, resolves
It back to dust again—for what?
　　Adah.　　　　　　　Thou know'st—
Even for our parents' error.
　　Cain.　　　　　　　What is that
To us? they sinned, then *let them* die!
　　Adah. Thou hast not spoken well, nor is that thought
Thy own, but of the Spirit who was with thee.
Would *I* could die for them, so *they* might live!
　　Cain. Why, so say I—provided that one victim　　80
Might satiate the Insatiable of life,
And that our little rosy sleeper there
Might never taste of death nor human sorrow,
Nor hand it down to those who spring from him.
　　Adah. How know we that some such atonement one
　　　　day
May not redeem our race?
　　Cain.　　　　　　　By sacrificing
The harmless for the guilty? what atonement [1]
Were there? why, *we* are innocent: what have we
Done, that we must be victims for a deed
Before our birth, or need have victims to　　90
Atone for this mysterious, nameless sin—
If it be such a sin to seek for knowledge?
　　Adah. Alas! thou sinnest now, my Cain: thy words
Sound impious in mine ears.
　　Cain.　　　　　　　Then leave me!
　　Adah.　　　　　　　　　Never,

1. [*Vide ante*, p. 208.]

Though thy God left thee.
 Cain.   Say, what have we here?
 Adah. Two altars, which our brother Abel made
During thine absence, whereupon to offer
A sacrifice to God on thy return.
 Cain. And how knew *he*, that *I* would be so ready
With the burnt offerings, which he daily brings 100
With a meek brow, whose base humility
Shows more of fear than worship—as a bribe
To the Creator?
 Adah.   Surely, 'tis well done.
 Cain. One altar may suffice; *I* have no offering.
 Adah. The fruits of the earth,[1] the early, beautiful,
Blossom and bud—and bloom of flowers and fruits—
These are a goodly offering to the Lord,
Given with a gentle and a contrite spirit.
 Cain. I have toiled, and tilled, and sweaten in the
  sun,
According to the curse:—must I do more?   110
For what should I be gentle? for a war
With all the elements ere they will yield
The bread we eat? For what must I be grateful?
For being dust, and grovelling in the dust,
Till I return to dust? If I am nothing—
For nothing shall I be an hypocrite,
And seem well-pleased with pain? For what should I
Be contrite? for my father's sin, already
Expiate with what we all have undergone,
And to be more than expiated by   120
The ages prophesied, upon our seed.
Little deems our young blooming sleeper, there,
The germs of an eternal misery
To myriads is within him! better 'twere
I snatched him in his sleep, and dashed him 'gainst
The rocks, than let him live to——
 Adah.   Oh, my God!

 1. [It is Adah, Cain's wife, who suggests the disastrous compromise,
not a " burnt-offering," but the " fruits of the earth," which would cost
the giver little or nothing—an instance in point of Lucifer's cynical
reminder (*vide ante*, act ii. sc. 2, line 210, p. 247) " that there are some
things still which woman may tempt man to."]

Touch not the child—my child! *thy* child! Oh, Cain!
   Cain. Fear not! for all the stars, and all the power
Which sways them, I would not accost yon infant
With ruder greeting than a father's kiss.   130
   Adah. Then, why so awful in thy speech?
   Cain.   I said,
'Twere better that he ceased to live, than give
Life to so much of sorrow as he must
Endure, and, harder still, bequeath; but since
That saying jars you, let us only say—
'Twere better that he never had been born.
   Adah. Oh, do not say so! Where were then the
     joys,
The mother's joys of watching, nourishing,
And loving him? Soft! he awakes. Sweet Enoch!
                    [*She goes to the child.*
Oh, Cain! look on him; see how full of life,   140
Of strength, of bloom, of beauty, and of joy—
How like to me—how like to thee, when gentle—
For *then* we are *all* alike; is't not so, Cain?
Mother, and sire, and son, our features are
Reflected in each other; as they are
In the clear waters, when *they* are *gentle*, and
When *thou* art *gentle*. Love us, then, my Cain!
And love thyself for our sakes, for we love thee.
Look! how he laughs and stretches out his arms,
And opens wide his blue eyes upon thine,   150
To hail his father; while his little form
Flutters as winged with joy. Talk not of pain!
The childless cherubs well might envy thee
The pleasures of a parent! Bless him, Cain!
As yet he hath no words to thank thee, but
His heart will, and thine own too.
   Cain.   Bless thee, boy!
If that a mortal blessing may avail thee,
To save thee from the Serpent's curse!
   Adah.   It shall.
Surely a father's blessing may avert
A reptile's subtlety.
   Cain.   Of that I doubt;   160
But bless him ne'er the less.

Adah.   Our brother comes.
Cain. Thy brother Abel.

Enter ABEL.

Abel.   Welcome, Cain! My brother,
The peace of God be on thee!
       Cain.   Abel, hail!
   Abel. Our sister tells me that thou hast been wandering,
In high communion with a Spirit, far
Beyond our wonted range.   Was he of those
We have seen and spoken with, like to our father?
   Cain. No.
   Abel.   Why then commune with him? he may be
A foe to the Most High.
   Cain.   And friend to man.
Has the Most High been so—if so you term him?   170
   Abel. Term him! your words are strange to-day, my
                brother.
My sister Adah, leave us for awhile—
We mean to sacrifice.[1]
   Adah.   Farewell, my Cain;
But first embrace thy son.   May his soft spirit,
And Abel's pious ministry, recall thee
To peace and holiness!   [*Exit* ADAH, *with her child.*
   Abel.   Where hast thou been?
   Cain. I know not.
   Abel.   Nor what thou hast seen?
   Cain.   The dead—
The Immortal—the Unbounded—the Omnipotent—
The overpowering mysteries of space—
The innumerable worlds that were and are—   180
A whirlwind of such overwhelming things,
Suns, moons, and earths, upon their loud-voiced spheres
Singing in thunder round me, as have made me
Unfit for mortal converse: leave me, Abel.
   Abel. Thine eyes are flashing with unnatural light—

---

   1. ["From the beginning" the woman is ineligible for the priesthood
—"He for God only, she for God in him" (*Paradise Lost*, iv. 299).
"Let the women keep silence in the churches" (*Corinthians*, i. xiv.
34).]

Thy cheek is flushed with an unnatural hue—
Thy words are fraught with an unnatural sound—
What may this mean ?
 Cain.   It means—I pray thee, leave me
 Abel. Not till we have prayed and sacrificed together.
 Cain. Abel, I pray thee, sacrifice alone— 190
Jehovah loves thee well.
 Abel.   *Both* well, I hope.
 Cain. But thee the better : I care not for that ;
Thou art fitter for his worship than I am ;
Revere him, then—but let it be alone—
At least, without me.
 Abel.   Brother, I should ill
Deserve the name of our great father's son,
If, as my elder, I revered thee not,
And in the worship of our God, called not
On thee to join me, and precede me in
Our priesthood—'tis thy place.
 Cain.   But I have ne'er 200
Asserted it.
 Abel. The more my grief; I pray thee
To do so now : thy soul seems labouring in
Some strong delusion ; it will calm thee.
 Cain.   No ;
Nothing can calm me more. *Calm !* say I ? Never
Knew I what calm was in the soul, although
I have seen the elements stilled. My Abel, leave me !
Or let me leave thee to thy pious purpose.
 Abel. Neither; we must perform our task together.
Spurn me not.
 Cain. If it must be so——well, then,
What shall I do ?
 Abel.   Choose one of those two altars. 210
 Cain. Choose for me : they to me are so much turf
And stone.
 Abel. Choose thou !
 Cain.   I have chosen.
 Abel.   'Tis the highest,
And suits thee, as the elder. Now prepare
Thine offerings.
 Cain.   Where are thine ?

   Abel.   Behold them here—
The firstlings of the flock, and ·fat thereof—
A shepherd's humble offering.
   Cain.   I have no flocks;
I am a tiller of the ground, and must
Yield what it yieldeth to my toil—its fruit:
                         [He gathers fruits.
Behold them in their various bloom and ripeness.
    [They dress their altars, and kindle a flame upon them.[1]
   Abel. My brother, as the elder, offer first   220
Thy prayer and thanksgiving with sacrifice.
   Cain. No—I am new to this; lead thou the way,
And I will follow—as I may.
   Abel (kneeling).   Oh, God!
Who made us, and who breathed the breath of life
Within our nostrils, who hath blessed us,
And spared, despite our father's sin, to make
His children all lost, as they might have been,
Had not thy justice been so tempered with
The mercy which is thy delight, as to
Accord a pardon like a Paradise,   230
Compared with our great crimes:—Sole Lord of light!
Of good, and glory, and eternity!
Without whom all were evil, and with whom
Nothing can err, except to some good end
Of thine omnipotent benevolence!
Inscrutable, but still to be fulfilled!
Accept from out thy humble first of shepherds'
First of the first-born flocks—an offering,
In itself nothing—as what offering can be
Aught unto thee?—but yet accept it for   240

---

   1. [Compare the following passage from· *La Rapresentatione di Abel
et di Caino* (in Firenze l'anno MDLIV.)—

                " Abel parla a dio fatto il sacrifitio,
                     Rendendogli laude.
            Signor per cui di tanti bene abondo
            Liquali tu sommamente mi concedi
            Tanto mi piace, et tanto me' giocondo
            Quanto delle mie greggie che tu vedi
            El piu grasso el migliore el piu mondo
            Ti do con lieto core come tu vedi
            Tu vedi la intentione con lequal vegno," etc.

The thanksgiving of him who spreads it in
The face of thy high heaven—bowing his own
Even to the dust, of which he is—in honour
Of thee, and of thy name, for evermore !
   Cain (standing erect during this speech). Spirit whate'er
        or whosoe'er thou art,
Omnipotent, it may be—and, if good,
Shown in the exemption of thy deeds from evil ;
Jehovah upon earth ! and God in heaven !
And it may be with other names, because
Thine attributes seem many, as thy works :—   250
If thou must be propitiated with prayers,
Take them !   If thou must be induced with altars,
And softened with a sacrifice, receive them ;
Two beings here erect them unto thee.
If thou lov'st blood, the shepherd's shrine, which smokes
On my right hand, hath shed it for thy service
In the first of his flock, whose limbs now reek
In sanguinary incense to thy skies ;
Or, if the sweet and blooming fruits of earth,
And milder seasons, which the unstained turf   260
I spread them on now offers in the face
Of the broad sun which ripened them, may seem
Good to thee—inasmuch as they have not
Suffered in limb or life—and rather form
A sample of thy works, than supplication
To look on ours !   If a shrine without victim,
And altar without gore, may win thy favour,
Look on it ! and for him who dresseth it,
He is—such as thou mad'st him ; and seeks nothing
Which must be won by kneeling : if he 's evil,[i.]   270
Strike him ! thou art omnipotent, and may'st—
For what can he oppose ?   If he be good,
Strike him, or spare him, as thou wilt ! since all
Rests upon thee ; and Good and Evil seem
To have no power themselves, save in thy will—
And whether that be good or ill I know not,
Not being omnipotent, nor fit to judge
Omnipotence—but merely to endure
Its mandate ; which thus far I have endured.

    i. *Which must be won with prayers—if he be evil.*—[*MS. M.*]

[*The fire upon the altar of* ABEL *kindles into a column
of the brightest flame, and ascends to heaven;
while a whirlwind throws down the altar of*
CAIN, *and scatters the fruits abroad upon the
earth.*[1]

Abel (*kneeling*). Oh, brother, pray! Jehovah 's wroth
   with thee.   280
  Cain. Why so?
  Abel.   Thy fruits are scattered on the earth.
  Cain. From earth they came, to earth let them return;
Their seed will bear fresh fruit there ere the summer:
Thy burnt flesh-offering prospers better; see
How Heaven licks up the flames, when thick with blood!
  Abel. Think not upon my offering's acceptance,
But make another of thine own—before
It is too late.
  Cain.   I will build no more altars,
Nor suffer any——
  Abel (*rising*).   Cain! what meanest thou?
  Cain. To cast down yon vile flatterer of the clouds,
The smoky harbinger of thy dull prayers—   291
Thine altar, with its blood of lambs and kids,
Which fed on milk, to be destroyed in blood.
  Abel (*opposing him*). Thou shalt not:—add not impious
   works to impious
Words! let that altar stand—'tis hallowed now
By the immortal pleasure of Jehovah,
In his acceptance of the victims.
  Cain.   *His!*
His pleasure! what was his high pleasure in
The fumes of scorching flesh and smoking blood,
To the pain of the bleating mothers, which   300
Still yearn for their dead offspring? or the pangs
Of the sad ignorant victims underneath
Thy pious knife? Give way! this bloody record
Shall not stand in the sun, to shame creation!
  Abel. Brother, give back! thou shalt not touch my
   altar
With violence: if that thou wilt adopt it,
To try another sacrifice, 'tis thine.

          1. [See Gessner's *Death of Abel.*]

Cain. Another sacrifice ! Give way, or else
That sacrifice may be——
 Abel.   What mean'st thou ?
 Cain.   Give——
Give way !—thy God loves blood !—then look to it :—
Give way, ere he hath *more!*
 Abel.   In *his* great name, 311
I stand between thee and the shrine which hath
Had his acceptance.
 Cain.   If thou lov'st thyself,
Stand back till I have strewed this turf along
Its native soil :—else——
 Abel (opposing him). I love God far more
Than life.
 *Cain (striking him with a brand, on the temples, which
   he snatches from the altar).* Then take thy life
   unto thy God,
Since he loves lives.
 Abel (falls). What hast thou done—my brother ?
 Cain. Brother !
 Abel.   Oh, God ! receive thy servant ! and
Forgive his slayer, for he knew not what
He did—Cain, give me—give me thy hand ; and tell 320
Poor Zillah—
 Cain (after a moment's stupefaction). *My* hand ! 'tis all
   red, and with——
What ?   [*A long pause.—Looking slowly round.*
   Where am I ? alone ! Where 's Abel ? where
Cain ? Can it be that I am he ? My brother,
Awake !—why liest thou so long on the green earth ?
'Tis not the hour of slumber :—why so pale ?
What hast thou !——thou wert full of life this morn !
Abel ! I pray thee, mock me not ! I smote
Too fiercely, but not fatally. Ah, why
Wouldst thou oppose me ? This is mockery ;
And only done to daunt me :—'twas a blow— 330
And but a blow. Stir—stir—nay, only stir !
Why, so—that 's well !—thou breathest ! breathe upon me !
Oh God ! Oh God !
 Abel (very faintly). What 's he who speaks of God ?
 Cain. Thy murderer.

Abel.   Then may God forgive him ! Cain,
Comfort poor Zillah :—she has but one brother
Now.   [ABEL *dies.*
    Cain. And I none !—Who makes me brotherless ?
His eyes are open ! then he is not dead !
Death is like sleep ;[1] and sleep shuts down our lids.
His lips, too, are apart ; why then he breathes ;
And yet I feel it not.—His heart !—his heart !—   340
Let me see, doth it beat ? methinks——No !—no !
This is a vision, else I am become
The native of another and worse world.
The earth swims round me :—what is this ?—'tis wet ;
        [*Puts his hand to his brow, and then looks at it.*
And yet there are no dews ! 'Tis blood—my blood—
My brother's and my own ! and shed by me !
Then what have I further to do with life,
Since I have taken life from my own flesh ?
But he can not be dead !—Is silence death ?
No ; he will wake ; then let me watch by him.   350
Life cannot be so slight, as to be quenched
Thus quickly !—he hath spoken to me since—
What shall I say to him ?—My brother !—No :
He will not answer to that name ; for brethren
Smite not each other.   Yet—yet—speak to me.
Oh ! for a word more of that gentle voice,
That I may bear to hear my own again !

                Enter ZILLAH.

    Zillah. I heard a heavy sound ; what can it be ?
'Tis Cain ; and watching by my husband.   What
Dost thou there, brother ? Doth he sleep ? Oh, Heaven !
What means this paleness, and yon stream ?—No, no ! 361
It is not blood ; for who would shed his blood ?
Abel ! what 's this ?—who hath done this ? He moves
        not ;
He breathes not : and his hands drop down from mine

    1. [Compare—
            " How wonderful is Death —
            Death and his brother Sleep ! "
                        Queen Mab, i. lines 1, 2.]

With stony lifelessness!   Ah! cruel Cain!
Why camest thou not in time to save him from
This violence?   Whatever hath assailed him,
Thou wert the stronger, and shouldst have stepped in
Between him and aggression!   Father!—Eve!—
Adah!—come hither!   Death is in the world!   370
          [*Exit* ZILLAH, *calling on her Parents, etc.*
    Cain (*solus*). And who hath brought him there?—I—
        who abhor
The name of Death so deeply, that the thought
Empoisoned all my life, before I knew
His aspect—I have led him here, and given
My brother to his cold and still embrace,
As if he would not have asserted his
Inexorable claim without my aid.
I am awake at last—a dreary dream
Had maddened me;—but *he* shall ne'er awake!

          Enter ADAM, EVE, ADAH, *and* ZILLAH.

    Adam. A voice of woe from Zillah brings me here—   380
What do I see?—'Tis true!—My son!—my son!
Woman, behold the Serpent's work, and thine! [*To* EVE.
    Eve. Oh! speak not of it now: the Serpent's fangs
Are in my heart!   My best beloved, Abel!
Jehovah! this is punishment beyond
A mother's sin, to take *him* from me!
    Adam.   Who,
Or what hath done this deed?—speak, Cain, since thou
Wert present; was it some more hostile angel,
Who walks not with Jehovah? or some wild
Brute of the forest?
    Eve.   Ah! a livid light   390
Breaks through, as from a thunder-cloud! yon brand
Massy and bloody! snatched from off the altar,
And black with smoke, and red with——
    Adam.   Speak, my son!
Speak, and assure us, wretched as we are,
That we are not more miserable still.
    Adah. Speak, Cain! and say it was not *thou!*
    Eve.   It was!

I see it now—he hangs his guilty head,
And covers his ferocious eye with hands
Incarnadine !
   Adah.   Mother, thou dost him wrong—
Cain ! clear thee from this horrible accusal,   400
Which grief wrings from our parent.
   Eve.   Hear, Jehovah !
May the eternal Serpent's curse be on him !
For he was fitter for his seed than ours.
May all his days be desolate ! May——
   Adah.   Hold !
Curse him not, mother, for he is thy son—
Curse him not, mother, for he is my brother,
And my betrothed.
   Eve.   He hath left thee no brother—
Zillah no husband—me *no son !* for thus
I curse him from my sight for evermore !
All bonds I break between us, as he broke   410
That of his nature, *in yon*——Oh Death ! Death !
Why didst thou not take *me*, who first incurred thee ?
Why dost thou not so now ?
   Adam.   Eve ! let not this,
Thy natural grief, lead to impiety !
A heavy doom was long forespoken to us ;
And now that it begins, let it be borne
In such sort as may show our God, that we
Are faithful servants to his holy will.
   Eve (pointing to Cain). His will ! the will of yon
            Incarnate Spirit
Of Death, whom I have brought upon the earth   420
To strew it with the dead. May all the curses
Of life be on him ! and his agonies
Drive him forth o'er the wilderness, like us
From Eden, till his children do by him
As he did by his brother ! May the swords
And wings of fiery Cherubim pursue him
By day and night—snakes spring up in his path—
Earth's fruits be ashes in his mouth—the leaves
On which he lays his head to sleep be strewed
With scorpions ! May his dreams be of his victim ! 430
His waking a continual dread of Death !

May the clear rivers turn to blood as he [1]
Stoops down to stain them with his raging lip !
May every element shun or change to him !
May he live in the pangs which others die with !
And Death itself wax something worse than Death
To him who first acquainted him with man !
Hence, fratricide ! henceforth that word is *Cain*,
Through all the coming myriads of mankind,
Who shall abhor thee, though thou wert their sire !   440
May the grass wither from thy feet ! the woods
Deny thee shelter ! earth a home ! the dust
A grave ! the sun his light ! and heaven her God ! [2]

                                        [*Exit* EVE.

   Adam. Cain ! get thee forth : we dwell no more
     together.
Depart ! and leave the dead to me—I am
Henceforth alone—we never must meet more.
   Adah. Oh, part not with him thus, my father : do not
Add thy deep curse to Eve's upon his head !
   Adam. I curse him not : his spirit be his curse.
Come, Zillah !
   Zillah.   I must watch my husband's corse.[3]   450
   Adam. We will return again, when he is gone
Who hath provided for us this dread office.
Come, Zillah !
   Zillah.   Yet one kiss on yon pale clay,

1. [Compare—

> " And Water shall hear me,
>   And know thee and fly thee ;
> And the Winds shall not touch thee
>   When they pass by thee. . . .
> And thou shalt seek Death
>   To release thee in vain."
> *The Curse of Kehama*, by R. Southey, Canto II.]

2. [The last three lines of this terrible denunciation were not in the
original MS.   In forwarding them to Murray (September 12, 1821,
Letters, 1901, v. 361), to be added to Eve's speech, Byron says,
" There's as pretty a piece of Imprecation for you, when joined to the
lines already sent, as you may wish to meet with in the course of your
business.   But don't forget the addition of these three lines, which are
clinchers to Eve's speech."]

3. [If Byron had read his plays aloud, or been at pains to revise the
proofs, he would hardly have allowed " corse " to remain in such close
proximity to " curse."]

And those lips once so warm—my heart! my heart!
        [*Exeunt* ADAM *and* ZILLAH *weeping.*
  Adah. Cain! thou hast heard, we must go forth.   I
    am ready,
So shall our children be.   I will bear Enoch,
And you his sister.   Ere the sun declines
Let us depart, nor walk the wilderness
Under the cloud of night.—Nay, speak to me.
To *me—thine own.*
    Cain.   Leave me!
    Adah.   Why, all have left thee. 460
    Cain. And wherefore lingerest thou? Dost thou not
    fear
To dwell with one who hath done this?
    Adah.   I fear
Nothing except to leave thee, much as I
Shrink from the deed which leaves thee brotherless.
I must not speak of this—it is between thee
And the great God.
    A Voice from within exclaims. Cain! Cain!
    Adah.   Hear'st thou that voice?
    The Voice within. Cain! Cain!
    Adah.   It soundeth like an angel's tone.

          Enter the ANGEL *of the Lord.*[1]

  Angel. Where is thy brother Abel?
    Cain.   Am I then
My brother's keeper?
    Angel.   Cain! what hast thou done?
The voice of thy slain brother's blood cries out,   470
Even from the ground, unto the Lord!—Now art thou
Cursed from the earth, which opened late her mouth

    1. ["I have avoided introducing the Deity, as in Scripture (though
Milton does, and not very wisely either); but have adopted his angel
as sent to Cain instead, on purpose to avoid shocking any feelings on
the subject, by falling short of what all uninspired men must fall short
in, viz. giving an adequate notion of the effect of the presence of
Jehovah.   The Old Mysteries introduced him liberally enough, and
this is avoided in the New."—Letter to Murray, February 8, 1822,
Letters, 1901, vi. 13.   Byron does not seem to have known that in
the older portions of the Bible "Angel of the Lord" is only a name for
the Second Person of the Trinity.]

To drink thy brother's blood from thy rash hand.
Henceforth, when thou shalt till the ground, it shall not
Yield thee her strength; a fugitive shalt thou
Be from this day, and vagabond on earth!
　Adah. This punishment is more than he can bear.
Behold thou drivest him from the face of earth,
And from the face of God shall he be hid.
A fugitive and vagabond on earth,   480
'Twill come to pass, that whoso findeth him
Shall slay him.
　Cain.　　　　Would they could! but who are they
Shall slay me? Where are these on the lone earth
As yet unpeopled?
　Angel.　　　　Thou hast slain thy brother,
And who shall warrant thee against thy son?
　Adah. Angel of Light! be merciful, nor say
That this poor aching breast now nourishes
A murderer in my boy, and of his father.
　Angel. Then he would but be what his father is.
Did not the milk of Eve give nutriment   490
To him thou now seest so besmeared with blood?
The fratricide might well engender parricides.—
But it shall not be so—the Lord thy God
And mine commandeth me to set his seal
On Cain, so that he may go forth in safety.
Who slayeth Cain, a sevenfold vengeance shall
Be taken on his head.　Come hither!
　Cain.　　　　　　　　What
Wouldst thou with me?
　Angel.　　　　　　To mark upon thy brow[L]
Exemption from such deeds as thou hast done.
　Cain. No, let me die!
　Angel.　　　　　　It must not be.
　　　　　　[*The* ANGEL *sets the mark on* CAIN's *brow.*
　Cain.　　　　　　　　It burns 500
My brow, but nought to that which is within it!
Is there more? let me meet it as I may.
　Angel. Stern hast thou been and stubborn from the
　　　　womb,
As the ground thou must henceforth till; but he

　　　　i. *On thy brow—— .—[MS.]*

Thou slew'st was gentle as the flocks he tended.
 Cain. After the fall too soon was I begotten;
Ere yet my mother's mind subsided from
The Serpent, and my sire still mourned for Eden.
That which I am, I am; I did not seek
For life, nor did I make myself; but could I   510
With my own death redeem him from the dust—
And why not so? let him return to day,
And I lie ghastly! so shall be restored
By God the life to him he loved; and taken
From me a being I ne'er loved to bear.
 Angel. Who shall heal murder? what is done, is done;
Go forth! fulfil thy days! and be thy deeds
Unlike the last!   [*The* ANGEL *disappears.*
 Adah.   He 's gone, let us go forth;
I hear our little Enoch cry within
Our bower.
 Cain. Ah! little knows he what he weeps for! 520
And I who have shed blood cannot shed tears!
But the four rivers[1] would not cleanse my soul.
Think'st thou my boy will bear to look on me?
 Adah. If I thought that he would not, I would——
 Cain (*interrupting her*).   No,
No more of threats: we have had too many of them:
Go to our children—I will follow thee.
 Adah. I will not leave thee lonely with the dead—
Let us depart together.
 Cain.   Oh! thou dead
And everlasting witness! whose unsinking
Blood darkens earth and heaven! what thou *now* art 530
I know not! but if *thou* seest what *I* am,
I think thou wilt forgive him, whom his God
Can ne'er forgive, nor his own soul.—Farewell!
I must not, dare not touch what I have made thee.
I, who sprung from the same womb with thee, drained
The same breast, clasped thee often to my own,
In fondness brotherly and boyish, I
Can never meet thee more, nor even dare
To do that for thee, which thou shouldst have done

---

 1. [The "four rivers" which flowed round Eden, and consequently
the only waters with which Cain was acquainted upon earth.]

For me—compose thy limbs into their grave—   540
The first grave yet dug for mortality.
But who hath dug that grave ?   Oh, earth !   Oh, earth !
For all the fruits thou hast rendered to me, I
Give thee back this.—Now for the wilderness !
        [ADAH *stoops down and kisses the body of* ABEL.
    Adah. A dreary, and an early doom, my brother,
Has been thy lot !   Of all who mourn for thee,
I alone must not weep.   My office is
Henceforth to dry up tears, and not to shed them ;
But yet of all who mourn, none mourn like me,
Not only for thyself, but him who slew thee.   550
Now, Cain ! I will divide thy burden with thee.
    Cain. Eastward from Eden will we take our way ;
'Tis the most desolate, and suits my steps.
    Adah. Lead ! thou shalt be my guide, and may our
        God
Be thine !   Now let us carry forth our children.
    Cain. And *he* who lieth there was childless !   I
Have dried the fountain of a gentle race,
Which might have graced his recent marriage couch,
And might have tempered this stern blood of mine,
Uniting with our children Abel's offspring !   560
O Abel !
    Adah.   Peace be with him !
    Cain.   But with *me !*——
                                        [*Exeunt.*

HEAVEN AND EARTH;

A MYSTERY.

FOUNDED ON THE FOLLOWING PASSAGE IN GENESIS, CHAP. VI. 1, 2.

" And it came to pass . . . that the sons of God saw the daughters of men that they were fair ; and they took them wives of all which they chose."

―――――――――

" And woman wailing for her demon lover."
Coleridge [*Kubla Khan*, line 16].

INTRODUCTION TO *HEAVEN AND EARTH.*

HEAVEN and Earth was begun at Ravenna October 9, 1821.
"It occupied about fourteen days" (Medwin's *Conversations,*
1824, p. 231), and was forwarded to Murray, November 9,
1821. "You will find *it,*" wrote Byron (*Letters,* 1901, v. 474),
"*pious* enough, I trust—at least some of the Chorus might
have been written by Sternhold and Hopkins themselves for
that, and perhaps for the melody." It was on "a scriptural
subject"—"less speculative than *Cain,* and very pious"
(*Letters,* 1901, v. 475 ; vi. 31). It was to be published, he
insists, at the same time, and, if possible, in the same volume
with the "others" (*Sardanapalus,* etc.), and would serve, so
he seems to have *reflected* ("The moment he reflects, he is a
child," said Goethe), as an antidote to the audacities, or, as
some would have it, the impieties of *Cain !*

He reckoned without his publisher, who understood the
temper of the public and of the Government, and was
naturally loth to awaken any more "reasonable doubts" in
the mind of the Chancellor with regard to whether a
"scriptural drama" was irreverent or profane. The new
"Mystery" was revised by Gifford and printed, but withheld
from month to month, till, at length, "the fire kindled," and,
on the last day of October, 1821, Byron instructed John
Hunt to "obtain from Mr. Murray *Werner: a Drama,* and
another dramatic poem called *Heaven and Earth.*" It was
published in the second number of *The Liberal* (pp. 165–
206), January 1, 1823.

The same subject, the unequal union of angelic lovers
with the daughters of men, had taken Moore's fancy a year
before Byron had begun to "dramatize the Old Testament."
He had designed a long poem, but having discovered that
Byron was at work on the same theme, he resolved to
restrict himself to the production of an "episode," to "give
himself the chance of . . . an *heliacal rising,*" before he was
outshone by the advent of a greater luminary. Thanks to

Murray's scruples, and the "translation" of MSS. to Hunt, the "episode" took the lead of the "Mystery" by eight days. The *Loves of the Angels* (see *Memoirs, etc.*, 1853, iv. 28) was published December 23, 1822. None the less, lyric and drama were destined to run in double harness. Critics found it convenient to review the two poems in the same article, and were at pains to draw a series of more or less pointed and pungent comparisons between the unwilling though not unwitting rivals.

Wilson, in *Blackwood*, writes, "The first [the *Loves, etc.*] is all glitter and point like a piece of Derbyshire spar, and the other is dark and massy like a block of marble. . . . Moore writes with a crow-quill, . . . Byron writes with an eagle's plume;" while Jeffrey, in the *Edinburgh*, likens Moore to "an *aurora borealis*" and Byron to "an eruption of Mount Vesuvius"!

There is, indeed, apart from the subject, nothing in common between Moore's tender and alluring lyric and Byron's gloomy and tumultuous rhapsody, while contrast is to be sought rather in the poets than in their poems. The *Loves of the Angels* is the finished composition of an accomplished designer of Amoretti, one of the best of his kind, *Heaven and Earth* is the rough and unpromising sketch thrown off by a great master.

Both the one and the other have passed out of the ken of readers of poetry, but, on the whole, the *Loves of the Angels* has suffered the greater injustice. It is opined that there may be possibilities in a half-forgotten work of Byron, but it is taken for granted that nothing worthy of attention is to be found in Moore. At the time, however, Moore scored a success, and Byron hardly escaped a failure. It is to be noted that within a month of publication (January 18, 1823) Moore was at work upon a revise for a fifth edition—consulting D'Herbelot "for the project of turning the poor 'Angels' into Turks," and so "getting rid of that connection with the Scriptures," which, so the Longmans feared, would "in the long run be a drag on the popularity of the poem" (*Memoirs, etc.*, 1853, iv. 41). It was no wonder that Murray was "timorous" with regard to Byron and his "scriptural dramas," when the Longmans started at the shadow of a scriptural allusion.

Byron, in his innocence, had taken for his motto the verse in *Genesis* (ch. vi. 2), which records the intermarriage of the "sons of God" with the "daughters of men." In *Heaven and Earth* the angels *are* angels, members, though erring members, of Jehovah's "thundering choir," and the daughters of men are the descendants of Cain. The question had come up for debate owing to the recent appearance of a translation of the *Book of Enoch* (by Richard Laurence, LL.D., Oxford, 1821); and Moore, by way of safeguarding himself against any suspicion of theological irregularity, is careful to assure his readers (" Preface " to *Loves of the Angels*, 1823, p. viii. and *note*, pp. 125–127) that the " sons of God " were the descendants of Seth, and not beings of a supernatural order, as a mis-translation by the LXX., assisted by Philo and the "rhapsodical fictions of the *Book of Enoch*," had induced the ignorant or the profane to suppose. Nothing is so dangerous as innocence, and a little more of that *empeiria* of which Goethe accused him, would have saved Byron from straying from the path of orthodoxy.

It is impossible to say for certain whether Laurence's translation of the whole of the *Book of Enoch* had come under Byron's notice before he planned his new " Mystery," but it is plain that he was, at any rate, familiar with the well-known fragment, " Concerning the ' Watchers ' " [Περὶ τῶν Ἐγρηγόρων], which is preserved in the *Chronographia* of Georgius Syncellus, and was first printed by J. J. Scaliger in *Thes. temp. Euseb.* in 1606. In the prophecy of the Deluge to which he alludes (*vide post*, p. 302, *note* 1), the names of the delinquent seraphs (Semjâzâ and Azâzèl), and of the archangelic monitor Raphael, are to be found in the fragment. The germ of *Heaven and Earth* is not in the *Book of Genesis*, but in the *Book of Enoch*.

Medwin, who prints (*Conversations*, 1824, pp. 234–238) what purports to be the prose sketch of a Second Part of *Heaven and Earth* (he says that Byron compared it to Coleridge's promised conclusion of *Christabel*—" that, and nothing more ! "), detects two other strains in the composition of the " Mystery," an echo of Goethe's Faust and a " movement" which recalls the *Eumenides* of Æschylus. Byron told Murray that his fourth tragedy was " more lyrical and Greek " than he at first intended, and there is no doubt that with the *Prometheus Vinctus* he was familiar, if not at first hand, at least through the medium of Shelley's rendering. But apart from the " Greek choruses," which " Shelley made such a fuss about," Byron was acquainted with, and was not untouched by, the metrical peculiarities of the *Curse of Kehama*, and might have traced a kinship between his " angels " and Southey's " Glendoveers," to say nothing of *their* collaterals, the " glumms " and " gawreys " of *Peter Wilkins* (see notes to Southey's *Curse of Kehama*, Canto VI., *Poetical Works*, 1838, viii. 231–233).

Goethe was interested in *Heaven and Earth*. " He preferred it," says Crabb Robinson (*Diary*, 1869, ii. 434), " to all the other serious poems of Byron. . . . 'A bishop,' he exclaimed, though it sounded almost like satire, 'might have written it.' Goethe must have been thinking of a *German* bishop! (For his daughter-in-law's translation of the speeches of Anah and Aholibamah with their seraph-lovers, see *Goethe-Jahrbuch*, 1899, pp. 18–21 [Letters, 1901, v. Appendix II. p. 518].)

Heaven and Earth was reviewed by Jeffrey in the *Edinburgh Review*, February, 1823, vol. 38, pp. 42–48; by Wilson in *Blackwood's Edinburgh Magazine*, January, 1823, vol. xiii. pp. 71, 72; and in the *New Monthly Magazine*, N.S., 1823, vol. 7, pp. 353–358.

D. Maclise. R.A. del.   Walker & Cockerell. ph. sc.

Goethe.

DRAMATIS PERSONÆ.

——•◦•——

ANGELS.

SAMIASA.

AZAZIEL.

RAPHAEL, THE ARCHANGEL.

MEN.

NOAH AND HIS SONS.

IRAD.

JAPHET.

WOMEN.

ANAH.

AHOLIBAMAH.

————————————

Chorus of Spirits of the Earth.—Chorus of Mortals.

HEAVEN AND EARTH.

PART I.

Scene I.—*A woody and mountainous district near Mount Ararat.—Time, midnight.*

Enter Anah *and* Aholibamah.[1]

Anah. Our father sleeps: it is the hour when they
Who love us are accustomed to descend
Through the deep clouds o'er rocky Ararat :—
How my heart beats !
   Aho.   Let us proceed upon
Our invocation.
   Anah.   But the stars are hidden.
I tremble.
   Aho.   So do I, but not with fear
Of aught save their delay.
   Anah.   My sister, though
I love Azaziel more than——oh, too much !
What was I going to say ? my heart grows impious.
   Aho. And where is the impiety of loving   10
Celestial natures ?
   Anah.   But, Aholibamah,
I love our God less since his angel loved me :
This cannot be of good ; and though I know not
That I do wrong, I feel a thousand fears

---

1. [Aholibamah ("tent of the highest") was daughter of Anah (a Hivite clan-name), the daughter of Zibeon, Esau's wife, *Gen.* xxxvi. 14. Irad was the son of Enoch, and grandson of Cain, *Gen.* iv. 18.]

Which are not ominous of right.
    Aho.   Then wed thee
Unto some son of clay, and toil and spin !
There 's Japhet loves thee well, hath loved thee long:
Marry, and bring forth dust !
    Anah.   I should have loved
Azaziel not less were he mortal ; yet
I am glad he is not.   I cannot outlive him.   20
And when I think that his immortal wings
Will one day hover o'er the sepulchre
Of the poor child of clay [1] which so adored him,
As he adores the Highest, death becomes
Less terrible ; but yet I pity him :
His grief will be of ages, or at least
Mine would be such for him, were I the Seraph,
And he the perishable.
    Aho.   Rather say,
That he will single forth some other daughter
Of earth, and love her as he once loved Anah.   30

    Anah. And if it should be so, and she loved him,
Better thus than that he should weep for me.

    Aho. If I thought thus of Samiasa's love,
All Seraph as he is, I'd spurn him from me.
But to our invocation !—'Tis the hour.
    Anah.   Seraph !
           From thy sphere !
Whatever star contain thy glory ;
    In the eternal depths of heaven
      Albeit thou watchest with " the seven," [2]   40

---

   1. [Compare *Manfred*, act i. sc. 1, line 131, *Poetical Works*, 1901, iv. 89, and *note* 1.]

   2. The archangels, said to be seven in number, and to occupy the eighth rank in the celestial hierarchy.

[Compare *Tobit* xii. 15, " I am Raphael, one of the seven holy angels which present the prayers of the saints." *The Book of Enoch* (ch. xx.) names the other archangels, " Uriel, Rufael, Raguel, Michael, Saraqâêl, and Gabriel, who is over Paradise and the serpents and the cherubin." In the *Celestial Hierarchy* of Dionysius the Areopagite, a chapter is devoted to archangels, but their names are not recorded, or their number given. On the other hand, " The teaching of the oracles concerning the angels affirms that they are thousand thousands and myriad myriads."—*Celestial Hierarchy, etc.*, translated by the Rev. J. Parker, 1894, cap. xiv. p. 43. It has been supposed that " the seven which are the eyes of the Lord " (*Zech.* iv. 10) are the seven archangels.]

Though through space infinite and hoary
  Before thy bright wings worlds be driven,
    Yet hear!
Oh! think of her who holds thee dear!
  And though she nothing is to thee,
Yet think that thou art all to her.
    Thou canst not tell,—and never be
    Such pangs decreed to aught save me,—
      The bitterness of tears.
      Eternity is in thine years,   50
Unborn, undying beauty in thine eyes;
With me thou canst not sympathise,
  Except in love, and there thou must
  Acknowledge that more loving dust
Ne'er wept beneath the skies.
Thou walk'st thy many worlds, thou see'st
  The face of him who made thee great,
As he hath made me of the least
  Of those cast out from Eden's gate:
      Yet, Seraph dear!   60
        Oh hear!
For thou hast loved me, and I would not die
  Until I know what I must die in knowing,
That thou forget'st in thine eternity
  Her whose heart Death could not keep from o'er-
    flowing
For thee, immortal essence as thou art!
  Great is their love who love in sin and fear;
And such, I feel, are waging in my heart
A war unworthy: to an Adamite
  Forgive, my Seraph! that such thoughts appear, 70
    For sorrow is our element;
        Delight
An Eden kept afar from sight,
    Though sometimes with our visions blent.
    The hour is near
Which tells me we are not abandoned quite.—
      Appear! Appear!
        Seraph!
    My own Azaziel! be but here,
And leave the stars to their own light!   80

Aho.   Samiasa !
                    Wheresoe'er
          Thou rulest in the upper air—
          Or warring with the spirits who may dare
                    Dispute with him
          Who made all empires, empire; or recalling
Some wandering star, which shoots through the abyss,
          Whose tenants dying, while their world is falling,
Share the dim destiny of clay in this ;
          Or joining with the inferior cherubim,   90
          Thou deignest to partake their hymn—
                    Samiasa !
I call thee, I await thee, and I love thee.
          Many may worship thee, that will I not :
If that thy spirit down to mine may move thee,
          Descend and share my lot !
          Though I be formed of clay,
               And thou of beams
          More bright than those of day
               On Eden's streams,   100
          Thine immortality can not repay
               With love more warm than mine
My love.   There is a ray
          In me, which, though forbidden yet to shine,
          I feel was lighted at thy God's and thine.
It may be hidden long : death and decay
          Our mother Eve bequeathed us—but my heart
Defies it : though this life must pass away,
          Is *that* a cause for thee and me to part ?
Thou art immortal—so am I : I feel—   110
          I feel my immortality o'ersweep
All pains, all tears, all fears, and peal,
          Like the eternal thunders of the deep,
Into my ears this truth—" Thou liv'st for ever !"
               But if it be in joy
I know not, nor would know ;
          That secret rests with the Almighty giver,
          Who folds in clouds the fonts of bliss and woe.
               But thee and me he never can destroy ;
          Change us he may, but not o'erwhelm ; we are   120
          Of as eternal essence, and must war

With him if he will war with us; with *thee*
   I can share all things, even immortal sorrow;
For thou hast ventured to share life with *me*,
And shall *I* shrink from thine eternity?
   No! though the serpent's sting should pierce me
      thorough,
And thou thyself wert like the serpent, coil
  Around me still! and I will smile,
    And curse thee not; but hold
    Thee in as warm a fold   130
    As —— but descend, and prove
    A mortal's love
For an immortal.   If the skies contain
More joy than thou canst give and take, remain!
  Anah. Sister! sister! I view them winging
Their bright way through the parted night.
  Aho. The clouds from off their pinions flinging,
As though they bore to-morrow's light.
  Anah. But if our father see the sight!
  Aho. He would but deem it was the moon   140
Rising unto some sorcerer's tune
  An hour too soon.[1]
  Anah. They come! *he* comes!—Azaziel!
  Aho.   Haste
To meet them!   Oh! for wings to bear
My spirit, while they hover there,
    To Samiasa's breast!
  Anah. Lo! they have kindled all the west,
Like a returning sunset;—lo!
    On Ararat's late secret crest
A mild and many-coloured bow,   150

---

1. ["The adepts of Incantation . . . enter the realms of air, and by
their spells they scatter the clouds, they gather the clouds, they still
the storm. . . . We may adduce Ovid (*Amor.*, bk. ii., El., i. 23), who
says, 'Charmers draw down the horns of the blood-red moon,' . . .
Here it is to be observed that in the opinion of simple-minded
persons, the moon could be actually drawn down from heaven. So
Aristophanes says (*Clouds*, lines 739, 740), 'If I should purchase a
Thessalian witch, and draw down the moon by night;' and Claudian
(*In Rufin.*, bk. i. 145), 'I know by what spell the Thessalian sorceress
snatches away the lunar beam.'"—*Magic Incantations*, by Christianus
Pazig (circ. 1700), edited by Edmund Goldsmid, F.R.H.S., F.S.A.
(Scot.), 1886, pp. 30, 31. See, too, Virgil, *Eclogues*, viii. 69, "Carmina
vel cœlo possunt deducere Lunam."]

The remnant of their flashing path,
Now shines! and now, behold! it hath
Returned to night, as rippling foam,
    Which the Leviathan hath lashed
From his unfathomable home,
When sporting on the face of the calm deep,
    Subsides soon after he again hath dashed
Down, down, to where the Ocean's fountains sleep.
    Aho. They have touched earth! Samiasa!
    Anah.   My Azaziel!
                                               [*Exeunt.*

SCENE II.—*Enter* IRAD *and* JAPHET.

Irad. Despond not: wherefore wilt thou wander thus
To add thy silence to the silent night,
And lift thy tearful eye unto the stars?
They cannot aid thee.
    Japh.   But they soothe me—now
Perhaps she looks upon them as I look.
Methinks a being that is beautiful
Becometh more so as it looks on beauty,
The eternal beauty of undying things.
Oh, Anah!
    Irad.   But she loves thee not.
    Japh.   Alas!
    Irad. And proud Aholibamah spurns me also.   10
    Japh. I feel for thee too.
    Irad.   Let her keep her pride,
Mine hath enabled me to bear her scorn:
It may be, time too will avenge it.
    Japh.   Canst thou
Find joy in such a thought?
    Irad.   Nor joy nor sorrow.
I loved her well; I would have loved her better,
Had love been met with love: as 'tis, I leave her
To brighter destinies, if so she deems them.
    Japh. What destinies?
    Irad.   I have some cause to think
She loves another.
    Japh.   Anah!

Irad.   No ; her sister.

Japh. What other ?

Irad.   That I know not ; but her air, 20
If not her words, tells me she loves another.

Japh. Aye, but not Anah : she but loves her God.

Irad. Whate'er she loveth, so she loves thee not,
What can it profit thee ?

Japh.   True, nothing ; but
I love.

Irad. And so did I.

Japh.   And now thou lov'st not,
Or think'st thou lov'st not, art thou happier ?

Irad.   Yes.

Japh. I pity thee.

Irad.   Me ! why ?

Japh.   For being happy,
Deprived of that which makes my misery.

Irad. I take thy taunt as part of thy distemper,
And would not feel as thou dost for more shekels   30
Than all our father's herds would bring, if weighed
Against the metal of the sons of Cain— [1]
The yellow dust they try to barter with us,
As if such useless and discoloured trash,
The refuse of the earth, could be received
For milk, and wool, and flesh, and fruits, and all
Our flocks and wilderness afford.—Go, Japhet,
Sigh to the stars, as wolves howl to the moon—
I must back to my rest.

Japh.   And so would I
If I could rest.

Irad.   Thou wilt not to our tents then ?   40

Japh. No, Irad ; I will to the cavern,[2] whose
Mouth they say opens from the internal world,

---

1. ["Tubal-Cain [the seventh in descent from Cain] was an in-
structor of every artificer of brass and iron" (*Gen.* iv. 22). According to the *Book of Enoch*, cap. viii., it was "Azâzêl," one of the "sons
of the heavens," who "taught men to make swords, and knives, and
skins, and coats of mail, and made known to them metals, and the art
of working them, bracelets and ornaments, and the use of antimony,
and the beautifying of the eyebrows, and the most costly and choicest
stones, and all colouring tincture, so that the world was changed."]

2. [*Vide post*, p. 294.]

To let the inner spirits of the earth
Forth when they walk its surface.
  Irad.   Wherefore so ?
What wouldst thou there ?
  Japh.   Soothe further my sad spirit
With gloom as sad : it is a hopeless spot,
And I am hopeless.
  Irad.   But 'tis dangerous ;
Strange sounds and sights have peopled it with terrors.
I must go with thee.
  Japh.   Irad, no ; believe me
I feel no evil thought, and fear no evil.   50
  Irad. But evil things will be thy foe the more
As not being of them : turn thy steps aside,
Or let mine be with thine.
  Japh.   No, neither, Irad ;
I must proceed alone.
  Irad.   Then peace be with thee !
           [*Exit* IRAD.
  Japh. (*solus*). Peace ! I have sought it where it should
   be found,
In love—with love, too, which perhaps deserved it ;
And, in its stead, a heaviness of heart,
A weakness of the spirit, listless days,
And nights inexorable to sweet sleep
Have come upon me. Peace ! what peace? the calm 60
Of desolation, and the stillness of
The untrodden forest, only broken by
The sweeping tempest through its groaning boughs ;
Such is the sullen or the fitful state
Of my mind overworn. The Earth 's grown wicked,
And many signs and portents have proclaimed
A change at hand, and an o'erwhelming doom
To perishable beings. Oh, my Anah !
When the dread hour denounced shall open wide
The fountains of the deep, how mightest thou 70
Have lain within this bosom, folded from
The elements ; this bosom, which in vain
Hath beat for thee, and then will beat more vainly,
While thine—Oh, God ! at least remit to her
Thy wrath ! for she is pure amidst the failing

As a star in the clouds, which cannot quench,
Although they obscure it for an hour.   My Anah !
How would I have adored thee, but thou wouldst not ;
And still would I redeem thee—see thee live
When Ocean is earth's grave, and, unopposed   80
By rock or shallow, the Leviathan,
Lord of the shoreless sea and watery world,
Shall wonder at his boundlessness of realm. [*Exit* JAPHET.

Enter NOAH *and* SHEM.

Noah. Where is thy brother Japhet ?
Shem.   He went forth,
According to his wont, to meet with Irad,
He said ; but, as I fear, to bend his steps
Towards Anah's tents, round which he hovers nightly,
Like a dove round and round its pillaged nest ;
Or else he walks the wild up to the cavern
Which opens to the heart of Ararat.   90
Noah. What doth he there ?   It is an evil spot
Upon an earth all evil ; for things worse
Than even wicked men resort there : he
Still loves this daughter of a fated race,
Although he could not wed her if she loved him,
And that she doth not.   Oh, the unhappy hearts
Of men ! that one of my blood, knowing well
The destiny and evil of these days,
And that the hour approacheth, should indulge
In such forbidden yearnings !   Lead the way ;   100
He must be sought for !
Shem.   Go not forward, father :
I will seek Japhet.
Noah.   Do not fear tor me :
All evil things are powerless on the man
Selected by Jehovah.—Let us on.
Shem. To the tents of the father of the sisters ?
Noah. No ; to the cavern of the Caucasus.
                    [*Exeunt* NOAH *and* SHEM.

SCENE III.—*The mountains.—A cavern,*[1] *and the rocks of Caucasus.*

Japh. (solus). Ye wilds, that look eternal; and thou cave,
Which seem'st unfathomable; and ye mountains,
So varied and so terrible in beauty;
Here, in your rugged majesty of rocks
And toppling trees that twine their roots with stone [2]
In perpendicular places, where the foot
Of man would tremble, could he reach them—yes,
Ye look eternal! Yet, in a few days,
Perhaps even hours, ye will be changed, rent, hurled
Before the mass of waters; and yon cave,   10
Which seems to lead into a lower world,
Shall have its depths searched by the sweeping wave,
And dolphins gambol in the lion's den!
And man —— Oh, men! my fellow-beings! Who
Shall weep above your universal grave,
Save I? Who shall be left to weep? My kinsmen,
Alas! what am I better than ye are,
That I must live beyond ye? Where shall be

1. [Byron's knowledge of Mount Ararat was probably derived from the following passage in Tournefort: "It is a most frightful sight; David might well say such sort of places show the grandeur of the Lord. One can't but tremble to behold it; and to look on the horrible precipices ever so little will make the head turn round. The noise made by a vast number of crows [hence the 'rushing sound,' *vide post*, p. 295], who are continually flying from one side to the other, has something in it very frightful. To form any idea of this place you must imagine one of the highest mountains in the world opening its bosom, only to show the most horrible spectacle that can be thought of. All the precipices are perpendicular, and the extremities are rough and blackish, as if a smoke came out of the sides and smutted them."—*A Voyage in the Levant*, by M. [Joseph Pitton de] Tournefort, 1741, iii. 205, 206.
  Kitto also describes this "vast chasm," which contained "an enormous mass of ice, which seems to have fallen from a cliff that overhangs the ice" (*Travels in Persia*, 1846, i. 34); but Professor Friedrich Parrot, who was the first to ascend Mount Ararat, does not enlarge upon the "abyss" or chasm.—*Journey to Ararat*, translated by W. D. Cowley, 1845, p. 134.]
  2. [Compare the description of the "roots like snakes," which "wind out from rock and sand," in the scene on the Hartz Mountains in Goethe's *Faust.*]

The pleasant places where I thought of Anah
While I had hope ? or the more savage haunts,   20
Scarce less beloved, where I despaired for her ?
And can it be !—Shall yon exulting peak,
Whose glittering top is like a distant star,
Lie low beneath the boiling of the deep ?
No more to have the morning sun break forth,
And scatter back the mists in floating folds
From its tremendous brow ? no more to have
Day's broad orb drop behind its head at even,
Leaving it with a crown of many hues ?
No more to be the beacon of the world,   30
For angels to alight on, as the spot
Nearest the stars ?   And can those words " *no more*"
Be meant for thee, for all things, save for us,
And the predestined creeping things reserved
By my sire to Jehovah's bidding ?   May
He preserve *them*, and I *not* have the power
To snatch the loveliest of earth's daughters from
A doom which even some serpent, with his mate,
Shall 'scape to save his kind to be prolonged,
To hiss and sting through some emerging world,   40
Reeking and dank from out the slime, whose ooze
Shall slumber o'er the wreck of this, until
The salt morass subside into a sphere
Beneath the sun, and be the monument,
The sole and undistinguished sepulchre,
Of yet quick myriads of all life ?   How much
Breath will be stilled at once !   All beauteous world !
So young, so marked out for destruction, I
With a cleft heart look on thee day by day,
And night by night, thy numbered days and nights.   50
I cannot save thee, cannot save even her
Whose love had made me love thee more ; but as
A portion of thy dust, I cannot think
Upon thy coming doom without a feeling
Such as—Oh God ! and canst thou—   [*He pauses.*
     [*A rushing sound from the cavern is heard, and shouts
          of laughter—afterwards a Spirit passes.*
  Japh.   In the name
Of the Most High, what art thou ?

Spirit (laughs).   Ha ! ha ! ha ! [1]
Japh. By all that earth holds holiest, speak !
Spirit (laughs).   Ha ! ha !
Japh. By the approaching deluge ! by the earth
Which will be strangled by the ocean ! by
The deep which will lay open all her fountains !   60
The heaven which will convert her clouds to seas,
And the Omnipotent who makes and crushes !
Thou unknown, terrible, and indistinct,
Yet awful Thing of Shadows, speak to me !
Why dost thou laugh that horrid laugh ?
    Spirit.   Why weep'st thou ?
Japh. For earth and all her children.
    Spirit.   Ha ! ha ! ha !
                              [*Spirit vanishes.*

Japh. How the fiend mocks the tortures of a world,
The coming desolation of an orb,
On which the sun shall rise and warm no life !
How the earth sleeps ! and all that in it is   70
Sleep too upon the very eve of death !
Why should they wake to meet it ?   What are here,
Which look like death in life, and speak like things
Born ere this dying world ?   They come like clouds !
               [*Various Spirits pass from the cavern.*
    Spirit.   Rejoice !
        The abhorréd race
Which could not keep in Eden their high place,
        But listened to the voice
Of knowledge without power,
        Are nigh the hour,   80
          Of Death !
Not slow, not single, not by sword, nor sorrow,
    Nor years, nor heart-break, nor Time's sapping
      motion,

---

    1. [Medwin (*Conversations*, 1824, p. 233) compares the laughter of
the fiends in the cave of Caucasus with the snoring of the Furies in
the *Eumenides* of Æschylus—

        'Ρέγκουσι δ' οὐ πλαστοῖσι φυσιάμασιν (line 53).
      (" Their snoring nostrils blow fearsome breath.")
There is a closer parallel with—

        Γελᾷ δὲ δαίμων ἐπ' ἀνδρὶ θερμῷ (line 560).
      (" The spirit mocketh the headlong soul.")]

Shall they drop off.   Behold their last to-morrow !
   Earth shall be Ocean !
        And no breath,
Save of the winds, be on the unbounded wave !
   Angels shall tire their wings, but find no spot :
Not even a rock from out the liquid grave
      Shall lift its point to save,   90
Or show the place where strong Despair hath died,
After long looking o'er the ocean wide
   For the expected ebb which cometh not :
      All shall be void,
        Destroyed ! [1]
Another element shall be the lord
  Of life, and the abhorred
Children of dust be quenched ; and of each hue
Of earth nought left but the unbroken blue ;
And of the variegated mountain   100
   Shall nought remain
   Unchanged, or of the level plain ;
   Cedar and pine shall lift their tops in vain :
All merged within the universal fountain,
   Man, earth, and fire, shall die,
     And sea and sky
Look vast and lifeless in the eternal eye.
    Upon the foam
    Who shall erect a home ?
Japh. (*coming forward*). My sire !   110
    Earth's seed shall not expire ;
    Only the evil shall be put away
      From day.
  Avaunt ! ye exulting demons of the waste !
Who howl your hideous joy
When God destroys whom you dare not destroy :
     Hence ! haste !
  Back to your inner caves !
  Until the waves
Shall search you in your secret place,   120

---

1. [Matthew Arnold, *Poetry of Byron*, 1881, xiv., xv., quotes this
line in proof of Byron's barbarian insensibility "to the true artist's
fine passion for the correct use and consummate management of
words."]

And drive your sullen race
Forth, to be rolled upon the tossing winds,
    In restless wretchedness along all space !
Spirit.   Son of the saved !
    When thou and thine have braved
        The wide and warring element ;
    When the great barrier of the deep is rent,
Shall thou and thine be good or happy ?—No !
Thy new world and new race shall be of woe—
    Less goodly in their aspect, in their years   130
        Less than the glorious giants, who
        Yet walk the world in pride,
The Sons of Heaven by many a mortal bride.
    Thine shall be nothing of the past, save tears !
        And art thou not ashamed
            Thus to survive,
        And eat, and drink, and wive ?
With a base heart so far subdued and tamed,
As even to hear this wide destruction named,
Without such grief and courage, as should rather   140
    Bid thee await the world-dissolving wave,
Than seek a shelter with thy favoured father,
    And build thy city o'er the drowned earth's grave ?
        Who would outlive their kind,
        Except the base and blind ?
            Mine
            Hateth thine
As of a different order in the sphere,
        But not our own.
There is not one who hath not left a throne   150
    Vacant in heaven to dwell in darkness here,
Rather than see his mates endure alone.
        Go, wretch ! and give
A life like thine to other wretches—live !
    And when the annihilating waters roar
        Above what they have done,
Envy the giant patriarchs then no more,
And scorn thy sire as the surviving one !
        Thyself for being his son !

Chorus of Spirits issuing from the cavern.

Rejoice!   160
No more the human voice
Shall vex our joys in middle air
With prayer;
No more
Shall they adore;

And we, who ne'er for ages have adored
The prayer-exacting Lord,
To whom the omission of a sacrifice
Is vice;
We, we shall view the deep's salt sources poured   170
Until one element shall do the work
Of all in chaos; until they,
The creatures proud of their poor clay,
Shall perish, and their bleached bones shall lurk
In caves, in dens, in clefts of mountains, where
The deep shall follow to their latest lair;
Where even the brutes, in their despair,
Shall cease to prey on man and on each other,
And the striped tiger shall lie down to die
Beside the lamb, as though he were his brother;   180
Till all things shall be as they were,
Silent and uncreated, save the sky:
While a brief truce
Is made with Death, who shall forbear
The little remnant of the past creation,
To generate new nations for his use;
This remnant, floating o'er the undulation
Of the subsiding deluge, from its slime,
When the hot sun hath baked the reeking soil
Into a world, shall give again to Time   190
New beings—years, diseases, sorrow, crime—
With all companionship of hate and toil,
Until——
Japh. (*interrupting them*). The eternal Will
Shall deign to expound this dream
Of good and evil; and redeem
Unto himself all times, all things;
And, gathered under his almighty wings,

>   Abolish Hell !
>   And to the expiated Earth
>   Restore the beauty of her birth,   200
>   Her Eden in an endless paradise,
>   Where man no more can fall as once he fell,
>   And even the very demons shall do well !

Spirits. And when shall take effect this wondrous
>   spell?

Japh. When the Redeemer cometh; first in pain,
>   And then in glory.

Spirit. Meantime still struggle in the mortal chain,
>   Till Earth wax hoary;
>   War with yourselves, and Hell, and Heaven, in vain,
>   Until the clouds look gory   210
>   With the blood reeking from each battle-plain ;
>   New times, new climes, new arts, new men ; but still,
>   The same old tears, old crimes, and oldest ill,
>   Shall be amongst your race in different forms ;
>   But the same moral storms
>   Shall oversweep the future, as the waves
>   In a few hours the glorious giants' graves.[1]

>   *Chorus of Spirits.*

>   Brethren, rejoice !
>   Mortal, farewell !
>   Hark ! hark ! already we can hear the voice   220
>   Of growing Ocean's gloomy swell ;
>   The winds, too, plume their piercing wings ;
>   The clouds have nearly filled their springs ;
>   The fountains of the great deep shall be broken,
>   And heaven set wide her windows ;[2] while mankind
>   View, unacknowledged, each tremendous token—
>   Still, as they were from the beginning, blind.
>   We hear the sound they cannot hear,
>   The mustering thunders of the threatening sphere ;
>   Yet a few hours their coming is delayed ;   230

---

1. "[And] there were giants in the earth in those days ; and . . .
after, . . . mighty men, which were of old, men of renown."—*Genesis*
[vi. 4].
2. " The same day were all the fountains of the great deep broken
up, and the windows of heaven were opened."—*Genesis* [vii. 11].

Their flashing banners, folded still on high,
  Yet undisplayed,
Save to the Spirit's all-pervading eye.
   Howl! howl! oh Earth!
Thy death is nearer than thy recent birth;
Tremble, ye mountains, soon to shrink below
  The Ocean's overflow!
The wave shall break upon your cliffs; and shells,
 The little shells, of ocean's least things be
Deposed where now the eagle's offspring dwells—[1] 240
 How shall he shriek o'er the remorseless sea!
And call his nestlings up with fruitless yell,
Unanswered, save by the encroaching swell;—
While man shall long in vain for his broad wings,
 The wings which could not save:—
Where could he rest them, while the whole space brings
 Nought to his eye beyond the deep, his grave?
   Brethren, rejoice!
And loudly lift each superhuman voice—
   All die,   250
Save the slight remnant of Seth's seed—
  The seed of Seth,
Exempt for future sorrow's sake from death.
  But of the sons of Cain
   None shall remain;
 And all his goodly daughters
Must lie beneath the desolating waters;
Or, floating upward, with their long hair laid
Along the wave, the cruel heaven upbraid,
  Which would not spare   260
 Beings even in death so fair.
   It is decreed,
    All die!
And to the universal human cry
The universal silence shall succeed!
  Fly, brethren, fly!
  But still rejoice!
   We fell!

1. [Byron falls in with the popular theory as to the existence of fossil remains of marine animals at a height above the level of the sea. The "deluge" accounted for what was otherwise inexplicable.]

They fall!

So perish all   270

These petty foes of Heaven who shrink from Hell!

[*The Spirits disappear, soaring upwards.*

Japh. (solus). God hath proclaimed the destiny of
earth;

My father's ark of safety hath announced it;
The very demons shriek it from their caves;
The scroll[1] of Enoch prophesied it long

1. The book of Enoch, preserved by the Ethiopians, is said by them
to be anterior to the flood.

[Some fragments of the *Book of Enoch* (*vide ante*, Introduction to
Heaven and Earth, p. 281), which were included by Georgius Syncellus
(a Byzantine writer of the eighth century A.D.) in his *Chronographia*,
pp. 11, 26 (*Corpus Script. Hist. Byzantinæ*, 1829, i. 20), were printed
by J. J. Scaliger in 1606. They were, afterwards, included (i. 347-354)
in the *Spicilegium SS. Patrum* of Joannes Ernestus Grabius, which was
published at Oxford in 1714. A year after (1715) one of the fragments
was "made English," and published under the title of *The History of
the Angels and their Gallantry with the Daughters of Men*, written by
Enoch the Patriarch.

In 1785 James Bruce, the traveller, discovered three MSS. of the
Book of Enoch. One he conveyed to the library at Paris; a second
MS. he presented to the Bodleian Library at Oxford (*Travels*, ii. 422,
8vo ed. 1805). In 1801 an article entitled, "Notice du Libre d'Enoch,"
was contributed by Silvestre de Sacy to the *Magasin Encyclopédique*
(An. vi. tom. i. p. 369); and in 1821 Richard Laurence, LL.D., pub-
lished a translation "from the Ethiopic MS. in the Bodleian Library."
This was the first translation of the book as a whole.

The following extracts, which were evidently within Byron's recollec-
tion when he planned *Heaven and Earth*, are taken from *The Book of
Enoch*, translated from Professor Dillman's Ethiopic Text, by R. H.
Charles, Oxford, 1892:—

"Chap. vi. [1. And it came to pass when the children of men had
multiplied in those days that beautiful and comely daughters were born
unto them. [2. And the angels, the sons of the Heavens, saw and
lusted after them, and spake one to another, 'Come now, let us choose
us wives from among the children of men, and beget children.' [3.
And Semjâzâ, who was the leader, spake unto them: 'I fear ye will
not indeed agree to do this deed.' . . . [6. And they descended in the
days of Jared on the summit of Mount Hermon. . . .

"Chap. viii. [1. And Azâzêl taught men to make swords, etc.

"Chap. x. Then spake the Most High, the Great, the Holy One,
and sent Arsjalâljûr (= Uriel) to the son of Lamech, and said to him,
'Tell him in My Name to hide thyself!' and reveal to him that the end
is approaching; for the whole earth will be destroyed, and a deluge
will presently cover up the whole earth, and all that is in it will be
destroyed. [3. And now instruct him that he may escape, as his seed
may be preserved for all generations. [4. And again the Lord spake
to Rafael; Bind Azâzêl hand and foot, and place him in darkness;
make an opening in the desert which is in Dudâêl and place him
therein. [5. And place upon him rough and ragged rocks," etc.]

In silent books, which, in their silence, say
More to the mind than thunder to the ear:
And yet men listened not, nor listen; but
Walk darkling to their doom: which, though so nigh,
Shakes them no more in their dim disbelief,   280
Than their last cries shall shake the Almighty purpose,
Or deaf obedient Ocean, which fulfils it.
No sign yet hangs its banner in the air;
The clouds are few, and of their wonted texture;
The Sun will rise upon the Earth's last day
As on the fourth day of creation, when
God said unto him, " Shine !" and he broke forth
Into the dawn, which lighted not the yet
Unformed forefather of mankind—but roused
Before the human orison the earlier   290
Made and far sweeter voices of the birds,
Which in the open firmament of heaven
Have wings like angels, and like them salute
Heaven first each day before the Adamites:
Their matins now draw nigh—the east is kindling—
And they will sing ! and day will break !   Both near,
So near the awful close !   For these must drop
Their outworn pinions on the deep; and day,
After the bright course of a few brief morrows,—
Aye, day will rise; but upon what ?—a chaos,   300
Which was ere day; and which, renewed, makes Time
Nothing ! for, without life, what are the hours?
No more to dust than is Eternity
Unto Jehovah, who created both.
Without him, even Eternity would be
A void : without man, Time, as made for man,
Dies with man, and is swallowed in that deep
Which has no fountain; as his race will be
Devoured by that which drowns his infant world.—
What have we here ? Shapes of both earth and air ? 310
No—*all* of heaven, they are so beautiful.
I cannot trace their features; but their forms,
How lovelily they move along the side
Of the grey mountain, scattering its mist !
And after the swart savage spirits, whose
Infernal immortality poured forth

Their impious hymn of triumph, they shall be
Welcome as Eden.   It may be they come
To tell me the reprieve of our young world,
For which I have so often prayed.—They come !   320
Anah ! oh, God ! and with her——

Enter SAMIASA, AZAZIEL, ANAH, *and* AHOLIBAMAH.

Anah.   Japhet !
Sam.   Lo !
A son of Adam !
  Aza.   What doth the earth-born here,
While all his race are slumbering ?
  Japh.   Angel ! what
Dost thou on earth when thou should'st be on high ?
  Aza. Know'st thou not, or forget'st thou, that a part
Of our great function is to guard thine earth ?
  Japh. But all good angels have forsaken earth,
Which is condemned ; nay, even the evil fly
The approaching chaos.   Anah ! Anah ! my
In vain, and long, and still to be, beloved !   330
Why walk'st thou with this Spirit, in those hours
When no good Spirit longer lights below ?
  Anah. Japhet, I cannot answer thee ; yet, yet
Forgive me——
  Japh.   May the Heaven, which soon no more
Will pardon, do so ! for thou art greatly tempted.
  Aho. Back to thy tents, insulting son of Noah !
We know thee not.
  Japh.   The hour may come when thou
May'st know me better ; and thy sister know
Me still the same which I have ever been.
  Sam. Son of the patriarch, who hath ever been   340
Upright before his God, whate'er thy gifts,
And thy words seem of sorrow, mixed with wrath,
How have Azaziel, or myself, brought on thee
Wrong ?
  Japh. Wrong ! the greatest of all wrongs ! but, thou
Say'st well, though she be dust—I did not, could not,
Deserve her.   Farewell, Anah ! I have said
That word so often ! but now say it, ne'er

To be repeated.   Angel ! or whate'er
Thou art, or must be soon, hast thou the power
To save this beautiful—*these* beautiful   350
Children of Cain ?
   Aza.   From what ?
   Japh.   And is it so,
That ye too know not ?   Angels ! angels ! ye
Have shared man's sin, and, it may be, now must
Partake his punishment ; or, at the least,
My sorrow.
   Sam.   Sorrow ! I ne'er thought till now
To hear an Adamite speak riddles to me.
   Japh. And hath not the Most High expounded them ?
Then ye are lost as they are lost.
   Aho.   So be it !
If they love as they are loved, they will not shrink
More to be mortal, than I would to dare   360
An immortality of agonies
With Samiasa !
   Anah.   Sister ! sister ! speak not
Thus.
   Aza. Fearest thou, my Anah ?
   Anah.   Yes, for thee :
I would resign the greater remnant of
This little life of mine, before one hour
Of thine eternity should know a pang.
   Japh. It is for *him*, then ! for the Seraph thou
Hast left me !   That is nothing, if thou hast not
Left thy God too ! for unions like to these,
Between a mortal and an immortal, cannot   370
Be happy or be hallowed.   We are sent
Upon the earth to toil and die ; and they
Are made to minister on high unto
The Highest : but if he can *save* thee, soon
The hour will come in which celestial aid
Alone can do so.
   Anah.   Ah ! he speaks of Death.
   Sam. Of death to *us !* and those who are with us !
But that the man seems full of sorrow, I
Could smile.
   Japh.   I grieve not for myself, nor fear.

I am safe, not for my own deserts, but those   380
Of a well-doing sire, who hath been found
Righteous enough to save his children.   Would
His power was greater of redemption ! or
That by exchanging my own life for hers,
Who could alone have made mine happy, she,
The last and loveliest of Cain's race, could share
The ark which shall receive a remnant of
The seed of Seth !

   Aho.   And dost thou think that we,
With Cain's, the eldest born of Adam's, blood
Warm in our veins,—strong Cain ! who was begotten
In Paradise,[1]—would mingle with Seth's children ?   391
Seth, the last offspring of old Adam's dotage ?
No, not to save all Earth, were Earth in peril !
Our race hath always dwelt apart from thine
From the beginning, and shall do so ever.

   Japh. I did not speak to thee, Aholibamah !
Too much of the forefather whom thou vauntest
Has come down in that haughty blood which springs
From him who shed the first, and that a brother's !
But thou, my Anah ! let me call thee mine,   400
Albeit thou art not; 'tis a word I cannot
Part with, although I must from thee.   My Anah !
Thou who dost rather make me dream that Abel
Had left a daughter, whose pure pious race
Survived in thee, so much unlike thou art
The rest of the stern Cainites, save in beauty,
For all of them are fairest in their favour——

   Aho. (*interrupting him*).   And would'st thou have her
     like our father's foe
In mind, in soul?   If *I* partook thy thought,
And dreamed that aught of *Abel* was in *her !*—   410
Get thee hence, son of Noah ; thou makest strife.

   1. [This does not correspond with Cain's own statement—
     " After the fall too soon was I begotten."
       Cain, act iii. sc. 1, line 506 (*vide ante,* p. 274).

Bayle (*Hist. and Crit. Dict.,* 1735, ii. 853, art. " Eve," *note* B) has a
great deal to say with regard to the exact date of the birth of Cain.
He concludes with *Cornelius à Lapide,* who quotes Torniellus, " Cain
genitum esse mox post expulsionem Adæ et Evæ ex Paradiso."]

Japh. Offspring of Cain, thy father did so !
　Aho. 　　　　　　　　　　　But
He slew not Seth : and what hast thou to do
With other deeds between his God and him ?
　Japh. Thou speakest well: his God hath judged him, and
I had not named his deed, but that thyself
Didst seem to glory in him, nor to shrink
From what he had done.
　Aho. 　　　　　　　He was our father's father ;
The eldest born of man, the strongest, bravest,
And most enduring :—Shall I blush for him 　　　420
From whom we had our being ?　Look upon
Our race ; behold their stature and their beauty,
Their courage, strength, and length of days——
　Japh. 　　　　　　　　　They are numbered.
　Aho. Be it so ! but while yet their hours endure,
I glory in my brethren and our fathers.
　Japh. My sire and race but glory in their God,
Anah ! and thou ?——
　Anah. 　　　　　　　Whate'er our God decrees,
The God of Seth as Cain, I must obey,
And will endeavour patiently to obey.
But could I dare to pray in his dread hour 　　　430
Of universal vengeance (if such should be),
It would not be to live, alone exempt
Of all my house.　My sister ! oh, my sister !
What were the world, or other worlds, or all
The brightest future, without the sweet past—
Thy love, my father's, all the life, and all
The things which sprang up with me, like the stars,
Making my dim existence radiant with
Soft lights which were not mine ?　Aholibamah !
Oh ! if there should be mercy—seek it, find it : 　　440
I abhor Death, because that thou must die.
　Aho. What, hath this dreamer, with his father's ark,
The bugbear he hath built to scare the world,
Shaken *my* sister ?　Are *we* not the loved
Of Seraphs ? and if we were not, must we
Cling to a son of Noah for our lives ?
Rather than thus——But the enthusiast dreams
The worst of dreams, the fantasies engendered

By hopeless love and heated vigils.   Who
Shall shake these solid mountains, this firm earth,   450
And bid those clouds and waters take a shape
Distinct from that which we and all our sires
Have seen them wear on their eternal way?
Who shall do this?
    Japh.   He whose one word produced them.
    Aho. Who *heard* that word?
    Japh.   The universe, which leaped
To life before it.   Ah! smilest thou still in scorn?
Turn to thy Seraphs: if they attest it not,
They are none.
    Sam.   Aholibamah, own thy God!
    Aho. I have ever hailed our Maker, Samiasa,
As thine, and mine: a God of Love, not Sorrow.   460
    Japh. Alas! what else is Love but Sorrow?   Even
He who made earth in love had soon to grieve
Above its first and best inhabitants.
    Aho. 'Tis said so.
    Japh.   It is even so.

Enter NOAH *and* SHEM.

    Noah.   Japhet!   What
Dost thou here with these children of the wicked?
Dread'st thou not to partake their coming doom?
    Japh. Father, it cannot be a sin to seek
To save an earth-born being; and behold,
These are not of the sinful, since they have
The fellowship of angels.
    Noah.   These are they, then,   470
Who leave the throne of God, to take them wives
From out the race of Cain; the sons of Heaven,
Who seek Earth's daughters for their beauty?
    Aza.   Patriarch!
Thou hast said it.
    Noah.   Woe, woe, woe to such communion!
Has not God made a barrier between Earth
And Heaven, and limited each, kind to kind?
    Sam. Was not man made in high Jehovah's image?
Did God not love what he had made?   And what

Do we but imitate and emulate
His love unto created love?
 Noah.   I am   480
But man, and was not made to judge mankind,
Far less the sons of God; but as our God
Has deigned to commune with me, and reveal
His judgments, I reply, that the descent
Of Seraphs from their everlasting seat
Unto a perishable and perishing,
Even on the very *eve* of *perishing,*[1] world,
Cannot be good.
 Aza.   What! though it were to save?
 Noah. Not ye in all your glory can redeem
What he who made you glorious hath condemned. 490
Were your immortal mission safety, 'twould
Be general, not for two, though beautiful;
And beautiful they are, but not the less
Condemned.
 Japh. Oh, father! say it not.
 Noah.   Son! son!
If that thou wouldst avoid their doom, forget
That they exist: they soon shall cease to be,
While thou shalt be the sire of a new world,
And better.
 Japh. Let me die with *this,* and *them!*
 Noah. Thou *shouldst* for such a thought, but shalt
  not: he
Who *can,* redeems thee.
 Sam.   And why him and thee, 500
More than what he, thy son, prefers to both?
 Noah. Ask him who made thee greater than myself
And mine, but not less subject to his own
Almightiness. And lo! his mildest and
Least to be tempted messenger appears!

    Enter RAPHAEL[2] *the Archangel.*

 Raph. Spirits!
  Whose seat is near the throne,

 1. [Byron said that it was difficult to make Lucifer talk "like a
clergyman." He contrived to make Noah talk like a street-preacher.]
 2. [In the original MS. "Michael."—"I return you," says Byron,

What do ye here?
Is thus a Seraph's duty to be shown,
    Now that the hour is near   510
When Earth must be alone?
    Return!
    Adore and burn,
In glorious homage with the elected "Seven."
    Your place is Heaven.
Sam.   Raphael!
The first and fairest of the sons of God,
    How long hath this been law,
That Earth by angels must be left untrod?
    Earth! which oft saw   520
Jehovah's footsteps not disdain her sod!
    The world he loved, and made
    For love; and oft have we obeyed
His frequent mission with delighted pinions:
    Adoring him in his least works displayed;
Watching this youngest star of his dominions;
    And, as the latest birth of his great word,
    Eager to keep it worthy of our Lord.
    Why is thy brow severe?
And wherefore speak'st thou of destruction near? 530
Raph. Had Samiasa and Azaziel been
    In their true place, with the angelic choir,
        Written in fire
        They would have seen
        Jehovah's late decree,
And not enquired their Maker's breath of me:
        But ignorance must ever be
        A part of sin;
And even the Spirits' knowledge shall grow less
        As they wax proud within;   540
For Blindness is the first-born of Excess.
    When all good angels left the world, ye stayed,
Stung with strange passions, and debased
    By mortal feelings for a mortal maid:
But ye are pardoned thus far, and replaced

"the revise. I have softened the part to which Gifford objected, and
changed the name of Michael to Raphael, who was an angel of gentler
sympathies."—July 6, 1822, *Letters*, vi. 93.]

With your pure equals.   Hence ! away ! away !
          Or stay,
And lose Eternity by that delay !
Aza. And thou ! if Earth be thus forbidden
       In the decree   550
     To us until this moment hidden,
       Dost thou not err as we
         In being here ?
Raph. I came to call ye back to your fit sphere,
  In the great name and at the word of God,
Dear, dearest in themselves, and scarce less dear—
  That which I came to do : [1] till now we trod
Together the eternal space ; together
  Let us still walk the stars.[2] True, Earth must die !
Her race, returned into her womb, must wither, 560
  And much which she inherits : but oh ! why
Cannot this Earth be made, or be destroyed,
  Without involving ever some vast void
In the immortal ranks ? immortal still
  In their immeasurable forfeiture.
Our brother Satan fell ; his burning will
  Rather than longer worship dared endure !
  But ye who still are pure !
Seraphs ! less mighty than that mightiest one,—
  Think how he was undone !   570
And think if tempting man can compensate
  For Heaven desired too late ?
      Long have I warred,
      Long must I war
  With him who deemed it hard
To be created, and to acknowledge him
Who midst the cherubim
  Made him as suns to a dependent star,
Leaving the archangels at his right hand dim.
     I loved him—beautiful he was : oh, Heaven ! 580
Save *his* who made, what beauty and what power

1. [That is, "to call you back." His ministry and function of
clemency were almost as dear to him as his ministry and function of
adoration and obedience.]
   2. [For the connection of stars with angels, see *Book of Enoch.*
lxxv. 1.]

Was ever like to Satan's !   Would the hour
    In which he fell could ever be forgiven !
The wish is impious : but, oh ye !
Yet undestroyed, be warned !   Eternity
    With him, or with his God, is in your choice :
He hath not tempted you ; he cannot tempt
The angels, from his further snares exempt :
    But man hath listened to his voice,
And ye to woman's—beautiful she is,   590
The serpent's voice less subtle than her kiss.
The snake but vanquished dust ; but she will draw
A second host from heaven, to break Heaven's law.
        Yet, yet, oh fly !
        Ye cannot die ;
        But they
        Shall pass away,
While ye shall fill with shrieks the upper sky
    For perishable clay,
Whose memory in your immortality   600
    Shall long outlast the Sun which gave them day.
Think how your essence differeth from theirs
In all but suffering ! why partake
The agony to which they must be heirs—
Born to be ploughed with years, and sown with cares,
    And reaped by Death, lord of the human soil ?
Even had their days been left to toil their path
Through time to dust, unshortened by God's wrath,
    Still they are Evil's prey, and Sorrow's spoil.
Aho.   Let them fly !   610
I hear the voice which says that all must die,
Sooner than our white-bearded patriarchs died ;
        And that on high
        An ocean is prepared,
        While from below
The deep shall rise to meet Heaven's overflow—
        Few shall be spared,
It seems ; and, of that few, the race of Cain
Must lift their eyes to Adam's God in vain.
        Sister ! since it is so,   620
        And the eternal Lord
        In vain would be implored

For the remission of one hour of woe,
Let us resign even what we have adored,
And meet the wave, as we would meet the sword,
    If not unmoved, yet undismayed,
And wailing less for us than those who shall
Survive in mortal or immortal thrall,
    And, when the fatal waters are allayed,
Weep for the myriads who can weep no more.   630
Fly, Seraphs ! to your own eternal shore,
Where winds nor howl, nor waters roar.
      Our portion is to die,
    And yours to live for ever :
  But which is best, a dead Eternity,
Or living, is but known to the great Giver.
    Obey him, as we shall obey ;
  I would not keep this life of mine in clay
    An hour beyond his will ;
Nor see ye lose a portion of his grace,   640
For all the mercy which Seth's race
      Find still.
        Fly !
And as your pinions bear ye back to Heaven,
Think that my love still mounts with thee on high,
      Samiasa !
And if I look up with a tearless eye,
  'Tis that an angel's bride disdains to weep,—
Farewell !   Now rise, inexorable deep !
Anah.   And must we die ?   650
      And must I lose thee too,
      Azaziel ?
    Oh, my heart ! my heart !
      Thy prophecies were true !
    And yet thou wert so happy too !
The blow, though not unlooked for, falls as new :
      But yet depart !
      Ah ! why ?
    Yet let me not retain thee—fly !
My pangs can be but brief ; but thine would be   660
Eternal, if repulsed from Heaven for me.
    Too much already hast thou deigned
      To one of Adam's race !

Our doom is sorrow : not to us alone,
　But to the Spirits who have not disdained
To love us, cometh anguish with disgrace.
The first who taught us knowledge hath been hurled
　From his once archangelic throne
　Into some unknown world :
　　　And thou, Azaziel !　No—　　　　　　670
　　　Thou shalt not suffer woe
For me.　Away ! nor weep !
　Thou canst not weep ; but yet
　May'st suffer more, not weeping : then forget
Her, whom the surges of the all-strangling deep
Can bring no pang like this.　Fly ! fly !
Being gone, 'twill be less difficult to die.
　　Japh.　Oh say not so !
　　　　Father ! and thou, archangel, thou !
　Surely celestial mercy lurks below　　　680
That pure severe serenity of brow :
　Let them not meet this sea without a shore,
　Save in our ark, or let me be no more !
　　Noah.　Peace, child of passion, peace !
If not within thy heart, yet with thy tongue
　Do God no wrong !
Live as he wills it—die, when he ordains,
A righteous death, unlike the seed of Cain's.
　Cease, or be sorrowful in silence ; cease
To weary Heaven's ear with thy selfish plaint.　690
　Wouldst thou have God commit a sin for thee ?
　　　Such would it be
　　To alter his intent
For a mere mortal sorrow.　Be a man !
And bear what Adam's race must bear, and can.
　　Japh.　Aye, father ! but when they are gone,
　　　And we are all alone,
Floating upon the azure desert, and
The depth beneath us hides our own dear land,
　And dearer, silent friends and brethren, all　700
　Buried in its immeasurable breast,
Who, who, our tears, our shrieks, shall then command?
　Can we in Desolation's peace have rest ?
　　Oh God ! be thou a God, and spare

Yet while 'tis time !
   Renew not Adam's fall :
   Mankind were then but twain,
But they are numerous now as are the waves
   And the tremendous rain,
Whose drops shall be less thick than would their graves,
   Were graves permitted to the seed of Cain.   711
   Noah. Silence, vain boy ! each word of thine 's a crime.
Angel ! forgive this stripling's fond despair.
   Raph. Seraphs ! these mortals speak in passion : Ye !
Who are, or should be, passionless and pure,
May now return with me.
   Sam.   It may not be :
We have chosen, and will endure.
   Raph. Say'st thou ?
   Aza.   He hath said it, and I say, Amen !
   Raph.   Again !
      Then from this hour,   720
      Shorn as ye are of all celestial power,
And aliens from your God,
                  Farewell !
   Japh.   Alas ! where shall they dwell ?
Hark, hark !   Deep sounds, and deeper still,
   Are howling from the mountain's bosom :
There 's not a breath of wind upon the hill,
   Yet quivers every leaf, and drops each blossom :
Earth groans as if beneath a heavy load.
   Noah. Hark, hark ! the sea-birds cry !   730
   In clouds they overspread the lurid sky,
And hover round the mountain, where before
   Never a white wing, wetted by the wave,
      Yet dared to soar,
   Even when the waters waxed too fierce to brave.
      Soon it shall be their only shore,
      And then, no more !
   Japh.   The sun ! the sun ![1]
He riseth, but his better light is gone ;
      And a black circle, bound   740
      His glaring disk around,
Proclaims Earth's last of summer days hath shone !

   1. [Compare *Darkness*, lines 2-5, *Poetical Works*, 1891, iv. 42, 43.]

The clouds return into the hues of night,
Save where their brazen-coloured edges streak
The verge where brighter morns were wont to break.
 Noah. And lo ! yon flash of light,
The distant thunder's harbinger, appears !
  It cometh ! hence, away !
Leave to the elements their evil prey !
Hence to where our all-hallowed ark uprears 750
  Its safe and wreckless sides !
 Japh. Oh, father, stay !
Leave not my Anah to the swallowing tides !
 Noah. Must we not leave all life to such ? Begone !
 Japh.   Not I.
 Noah.   Then die
  With them !
How darest thou look on that prophetic sky,
And seek to save what all things now condemn,
  In overwhelming unison 760
  With just Jehovah's wrath !
 Japh. Can rage and justice join in the same path ?
 Noah. Blasphemer ! darest thou murmur even now !
 Raph. Patriarch, be still a father ! smooth thy brow :
Thy son, despite his folly, shall not sink :
He knows not what he says, yet shall not drink
 With sobs the salt foam of the swelling waters ;
But be, when passion passeth, good as thou,
 Nor perish like Heaven's children with man's daughters.
 Aho. The tempest cometh ; heaven and earth unite
  For the annihilation of all life. 771
  Unequal is the strife
Between our strength and the Eternal Might !
 Sam. But ours is with thee ; we will bear ye far
  To some untroubled star,
Where thou, and Anah, shalt partake our lot :
 And if thou dost not weep for thy lost earth,
Our forfeit Heaven shall also be forgot.
 Anah. Oh ! my dear father's tents, my place of birth,
And mountains, land, and woods ! when ye are not, 780
Who shall dry up my tears ?
 Aza.   Thy spirit-lord.
Fear not ; though we are shut from Heaven,

Yet much is ours, whence we can not be driven.
  Raph. Rebel! thy words are wicked, as thy deeds
Shall henceforth be but weak: the flaming sword,
Which chased the first-born out of Paradise,
Still flashes in the angelic hands.
  Aza. It cannot slay us: threaten dust with death,
And talk of weapons unto that which bleeds.
What are thy swords in our immortal eyes?   790
  Raph. The moment cometh to approve thy strength;
        And learn at length
How vain to war with what thy God commands:
Thy former force was in thy faith.

Enter Mortals, flying for refuge.

Chorus of Mortals.

_The heavens and earth are mingling—God! oh God!
What have we done? Yet spare!
Hark! even the forest beasts howl forth their prayer!
  The dragon crawls from out his den,
  To herd, in terror, innocent with men;
And the birds scream their agony through air.   800
Yet, yet, Jehovah! yet withdraw thy rod
Of wrath, and pity thine own world's despair!
Hear not man only but all nature plead!
  Raph. Farewell, thou earth! ye wretched sons of clay,
I cannot, must not, aid you. 'Tis decreed!
                   [*Exit* RAPHAEL.
  Japh. Some clouds sweep on as vultures for their prey.
While others, fixed as rocks, await the word
At which their wrathful vials shall be poured.
No azure more shall robe the firmament,
  Nor spangled stars be glorious: Death hath risen:
In the Sun's place a pale and ghastly glare   811
Hath wound itself around the dying air.
  Aza. Come, Anah! quit this chaos-founded prison,
To which the elements again repair,
To turn it into what it was: beneath
The shelter of these wings thou shalt be safe,
As was the eagle's nestling once within
Its mother's.—Let the coming chaos chafe

With all its elements! Heed not their din!
A brighter world than this, where thou shalt breathe   820
Ethereal life, will we explore :
These darkened clouds are not the only skies.
  [AZAZIEL *and* SAMIASA *fly off, and disappear with*
        ANAH *and* AHOLIBAMAH.
  Japh. They are gone! They have disappeared amidst
        the roar
Of the forsaken world; and never more,
Whether they live, or die with all Earth's life,
Now near its last, can aught restore
Anah unto these eyes.

                Chorus of Mortals.

Oh son of Noah! mercy on thy kind!
What! wilt thou leave us all—all—*all* behind?
While safe amidst the elemental strife,   830
Thou sitt'st within thy guarded ark?
  A Mother (offering her infant to JAPHET). Oh, let this
        child embark!
      I brought him forth in woe,
            But thought it joy
      To see him to my bosom clinging so.
            Why was he born?
            What hath he done—
            My unweaned son—
To move Jehovah's wrath or scorn?
What is there in this milk of mine, that Death   840
    Should stir all Heaven and Earth up to destroy
            My boy,
And roll the waters o'er his placid breath?
Save him, thou seed of Seth!
Or curséd be—with him who made
Thee and thy race, for which we are betrayed!
  Japh. Peace! 'tis no hour for curses, but for prayer!

                Chorus of Mortals.

        For prayer!!!
        And where

Shall prayer ascend,   850
When the swoln clouds unto the mountains bend
And burst,
And gushing oceans every barrier rend,
   Until the very deserts know no thirst?
Accursed
Be he who made thee and thy sire!
We deem our curses vain; we must expire;
      But as we know the worst,
Why should our hymns be raised, our knees be bent
Before the implacable Omnipotent,   860
Since we must fall the same?
If he hath made Earth, let it be his shame,
   To make a world for torture.—Lo! they come,
The loathsome waters, in their rage!
   And with their roar make wholesome nature dumb!
   The forest's trees (coeval with the hour
When Paradise upsprung,
   Ere Eve gave Adam knowledge for her dower,
Or Adam his first hymn of slavery sung),
   So massy, vast, yet green in their old age,   870
      Are overtopped,
Their summer blossoms by the surges lopped,
Which rise, and rise, and rise.
Vainly we look up to the lowering skies—
   They meet the seas,
And shut out God from our beseeching eyes.
   Fly, son of Noah, fly! and take thine ease,
In thine allotted ocean-tent;
And view, all floating o'er the element,
The corpses of the world of thy young days: 880
      Then to Jehovah raise
      Thy song of praise!
   A Mortal. Blesséd are the dead
      Who die in the Lord!
And though the waters be o'er earth outspread,
      Yet, as *his* word,
      Be the decree adored!
He gave me life—he taketh but
   The breath which is his own:
And though these eyes should be for ever shut,   890

Nor longer this weak voice before his throne
Be heard in supplicating tone,
  Still blesséd be the Lord,
   For what is past,
   For that which is :
   For all are his,
   From first to last—
Time—Space—Eternity—Life—Death—
 The vast known and immeasurable unknown.
He made, and can unmake ;   900
 And shall *I*, for a little gasp of breath,
Blaspheme and groan ?
 No ; let me die, as I have lived, in faith,
Nor quiver, though the Universe may quake !

Chorus of Mortals.

  Where shall we fly ?
  Not to the mountains high ;
For now their torrents rush, with double roar
 To meet the Ocean, which, advancing still
 Already grasps each drowning hill,
Nor leaves an unsearched cave.   910

Enter a Woman.

Woman. Oh, save me, save !
Our valley is no more :
 My father and my father's tent,
My brethren and my brethren's herds,
 The pleasant trees that o'er our noonday bent,
And sent forth evening songs from sweetest birds,
The little rivulet which freshened all
  Our pastures green,
  No more are to be seen.
When to the mountain cliff I climbed this morn, 920
 I turned to bless the spot,
 And not a leaf appeared about to fall ;—
 And now they are not !—
Why was I born ?
 Japh.   To die ! in youth to die !
And happier in that doom,

Than to behold the universal tomb,
                Which I
Am thus condemned to weep above in vain.
Why, when all perish, why must I remain?

[*The waters rise; Men fly in every direction; many
are overtaken by the waves: the Chorus of
Mortals disperses in search of safety up the
mountains:* JAPHET *remains upon a rock, while
the Ark floats towards him in the distance.*[1]

1. [Sketch of Second Part of *Heaven and Earth*, as reported by
Medwin (*Conversations*, 1824, pp. 234-237)—
   " Azazael and Samiasa . . . rise into the air with the two sisters. . . .
The appearance of the land strangled by the ocean will serve by way
of scenery and decorations.   The affectionate tenderness of Adah for
those from whom she is parted, and for ever, and her fears contrasting
with the loftier spirit of Aholibamah triumphing in the hopes of a new
and greater destiny will make the dialogue.   They, in the meantime,
continue their aërial voyage, everywhere denied admittance in those
floating islands over the sea of space, and driven back by guardian-
spirits of the different planets, till they are at length forced to alight on
the only peak of the earth uncovered by water.   Here a parting takes
place between the lovers. . . .   The fallen angels are suddenly called,
and condemned, their destination and punishment unknown.   The
sisters cling to the rock, the waters mounting higher and higher.   Now
enter Ark.   The scene draws up, and discovers Japhet endeavouring to
persuade the Patriarch, with very strong arguments of love and pity,
to receive the sisters, or at least Adah, on board.   Adah joins in his
entreaties, and endeavours to cling to the sides of the vessel.   The
proud and haughty Aholibamah scorns to pray either to God or man,
and anticipates the grave by plunging into the waters.   Noah is still
inexorable.   [Adah] is momentarily in danger of perishing before the
eyes of the Arkites.   Japhet is in despair.   The last wave sweeps her
from the rock, and her lifeless corpse floats past in all its beauty,
whilst a sea-bird screams over it, and seems to be the spirit of her
angel lord.   I once thought of conveying the lovers to the moon or one
of the planets; but it is not easy for the imagination to make any unknown world more beautiful than this; besides, I did not think they
would approve of the moon as a residence.   I remember what Fonte-
nelle said of its having no atmosphere, and the dark spots having
caverns where the inhabitants reside.   There was another objection:
all the human interest would have been destroyed, which I have even
endeavoured to give my angels."]

WERNER;

OR,

THE INHERITANCE:

A TRAGEDY.

[*Werner* was produced, for the first time, at the Park Theatre, New York, in 1826. Mr. Barry played "Werner."

Werner was brought out at Drury Lane Theatre, and played, for the first time, December 15, 1830. Macready appeared as "Werner," J. W. Wallack as "Ulric," Mrs. Faucit as "Josephine," and Miss Mordaunt as "Ida." According to the *Times*, December 16, 1830, "Mr. Macready appeared to very great advantage. We have never seen him exert himself more—we have never known him to exert himself with more powerful effect. Three of his scenes were masterpieces." Genest says that *Werner* was acted seventeen times in 1830-31.

There was a revival in 1833. Macready says (*Diary*, March 20) that he acted "'Werner' with unusual force, truth, and collectedness . . . finished off each burst of passion, and, in consequence, entered on the following emotion with clearness and earnestness" (Macready's *Reminiscences*, 1875, i. 366).

Werner was played in 1834, 5, 6, 7, 9 ; in 1841 ; in 1843-4 (New York, Boston, Baltimore, New Orleans, Cincinnati, Montreal); in 1845 (Paris, London, Glasgow, Belfast, Dublin); in 1846, 1847 ; in America in 1848 ; in the provinces in 1849 ; in 1850 ; and, for the last time, at the Theatre Royal, Haymarket, January 14, 1851. At the farewell performance Macready appeared as "Werner," Mr. Davenport as "Ulric," Mrs. Warner as "Josephine," Mrs. Ryder as "Ida." In the same year (1851) a portrait of Macready as "Werner," by Daniel Maclise, R.A., was on view at the Exhibition at the Royal Academy. The motto was taken from *Werner*, act i. sc. 1, lines 114, *sq.* (See, for a detailed criticism of Macready's "Werner," *Our Recent Actors*, by Westland Marston, 1881, i. 89-98 ; and for the famous "Macready *burst*," in act ii. sc. 2, and act v. sc. 1, *vide ibid.*, i. 97.)

Werner was brought out at Sadler's Wells Theatre, November 21, 1860, and repeated November 22, 23, 24, 28, 29 ; December, 3, 4, 11, 13, 14, 1860. Phelps appeared as "Werner," Mr. Edmund Phelps as "Ulric," Miss Atkinson as "Josephine." "Perhaps the old actor never performed the part so finely as he did on that night. The identity between the real and ideal relations of the characters was as vivid to him as to the audience, and gave a deeper intensity, on both sides, to the scenes between father and son." (See *The London Stage*, by H. Barton Baker, 1889, ii. 217.)

On the afternoon of June 1, 1887, *Werner* (four acts, arranged by Frank Marshall) was performed at the Lyceum Theatre for the benefit of Westland Marston. [Sir] Henry Irving appeared as "Werner," Miss Ellen Terry as "Josephine," Mr. Alexander as "Ulric." (See for an appreciation of Sir Henry Irving's presentation of *Werner*, the *Athenæum*, June 4, 1887.)]

INTRODUCTION TO *WERNER.*

————•————

WERNER; or, The Inheritance, was begun at Pisa, December 18, 1821, and finished January 20, 1822. At the end of the month, January 29, Byron despatched the MS., not to Murray, but to Moore, then in retreat at Paris, intending, no doubt, that it should be placed in the hands of another publisher; but a letter from Murray "melted him," and on March 6, 1822 (*Letters,* 1901, vi. 34), he desired Moore to forward the packet to Albemarle Street. The play was set up in type, and revised proofs were returned to Murray at the end of June; but, for various reasons, publication was withheld, and, on October 31, Byron informed John Hunt that he had empowered his friend Douglas Kinnaird to obtain *Werner,* with other MSS., from Murray. None the less, milder counsels again prevailed, and on Saturday, November 23, 1822, *Werner* was published, not in the same volume with *Heaven and Earth,* as Byron intended and expected, nor by John Hunt, as he had threatened, but by itself, and, as heretofore, by John Murray. *Werner* was "the last of all the flock" to issue from Murray's fold.

In his Preface to *Werner* (*vide post,* p. 337) Byron disclaims all pretensions to originality. "The following drama," he writes, "is taken entirely from the 'German's Tale, Kruitzner,' published . . . in Lee's *Canterbury Tales.* . . . I have adopted the characters, plan, and even the language, of many parts of this story." *Kruitzner* seems to have made a deep impression on his mind. When he was a boy of thirteen (*i.e.* in 1801, when the fourth volume of the *Canterbury Tales* was published), and again in 1815, he set himself to turn the tale into a drama. His first attempt, named *Ulric and Ilvina,* he threw into the fire, but he had nearly completed the first act of his second and maturer adaptation when he was "interrupted by circumstances," that is, no doubt, the circumstances which led up to and ended in the separation from his wife. (See letter of October 9, 1821, *Letters*, 1901, v. 391.)

On his leaving England for the Continent, April 25, 1816, the fragment was left behind. Most probably the MS. fell into his sister's hands, for in October, 1821, it was not forth-coming when Byron gave directions that Hobhouse should search for it "amongst my papers." Ultimately it came into the possession of the late Mr. Murray, and is now printed for the first time in its entirety (*vide post*, pp. 453–466 : selections were given in the *Nineteenth Century*, August, 1899). It should be borne in mind that this unprinted first act of *Werner*, which synchronizes with the *Siege of Corinth* and *Parisina*, was written when Byron was a member of the sub-committee of management of Drury Lane Theatre, and, as the numerous stage directions testify, with a view to stage-representation. The MS. is scored with corrections, and betrays an unusual elaboration, and, perhaps, some difficulty and hesitation in the choice of words and the construction of sentences. In the opening scene the situation is not caught and gripped, while the melancholy squalor of the original narrative is only too faithfully reproduced. The *Werner* of 1821, with all its shortcomings, is the production of a playwright. The *Werner* of 1815 is the attempt of a highly gifted amateur.

When Byron once more bethought himself of his old subject, he not only sent for the MS. of the first act, but desired Murray "to cut out Sophia Lee's" (*vide post*, p. 337) "*German's Tale* from the *Canterbury Tales*, and send it in a letter" (*Letters*, 1901, v. 390). He seems to have intended from the first to construct a drama out of the story, and, no doubt, to acknowledge the source of his inspiration. On the whole, he carried out his intention, taking places, characters, and incidents as he found them, but recasting the materials and turning prose into metre. But here and there, to save himself trouble, he "stole his brooms ready made," and, as he acknowledges in the Preface, "adopted even the language of the story." Act ii. sc. 2, lines 87–172 ; act iii. sc. 4 ; and act v. sc. 1, lines 94–479, are, more or less, faithful and exact reproductions of pp. 203–206, 228–232, and 252–271 of the novel (see *Canterbury Tales*, ed. 1832, vol. ii.). On the other hand, in the remaining three-fourths of the play, the language is not Miss Lee's, but Byron's, and the "conveyance" of inci-dents occasional and insignificant. Much, too, was imported into the play (*e.g.* almost the whole of the fourth act), of which there is neither hint nor suggestion in the story. Maginn's categorical statement (see " O'Doherty on *Werner*," *Miscel-lanies*, 1885, i. 189) that "here Lord Byron has *invented* nothing—absolutely, positively, undeniably NOTHING ; " that "there is not one incident in his play, not even the most trivial, that is not to be found in the novel," etc., is "positively and undeniably" a falsehood. Maginn read *Werner* for the purpose of attacking Byron, and, by printing selected passages from the novel and the play, in parallel columns, gives the reader to understand that he had made an exhaustive analysis of the original and the copy. The review, which is quoted as an authority in the editions of 1832 (xiv. pp. 113, 114) and 1837, etc., p. 341, is disingenuous and misleading.

The original story may be briefly retold. The prodigal and outlawed son of a Bohemian noble, Count Siegendorf, after various adventures, marries, under the assumed name of Friedrich Kruitzner, the daughter of an Italian scholar and man of science, of noble birth, but in narrow circumstances. A son, Conrad, is born to him, who, at eight years of age, is transferred to the charge of his grandfather. Twelve years go by, and, when the fortunes of the younger Siegendorf are at their lowest ebb, he learns, at the same moment, that his father is dead, and that a distant kinsman, the Baron Stralenheim, is meditating an attack on his person, with a view to claiming his inheritance. Of Conrad, who has disappeared, he hears nothing.

An accident compels the count and the baron to occupy adjoining quarters in a small town on the northern frontier of Silesia ; and, again, another accident places the usurping and intriguing baron at the mercy of his poverty-stricken and exiled kinsman. Stralenheim has fallen asleep near the fire in his easy-chair. Papers and several rouleaux of gold are ranged on a cabinet beside the bed. Kruitzner, who is armed with " a large and sharp knife," is suddenly confronted with his unarmed and slumbering foe, and though habit and conscience conspire to make murder impossible, he yields to a sudden and irresistible impulse, and snatches up "the portion of gold which is nearest." He has no sooner returned to his wife and confessed his deed, than Conrad suddenly appears on the scene, and at the very moment of an unexpected and joyous reunion with his parents, learns that his father is a thief. Kruitzner pleads " guilty with extenuating circumstances," and Conrad, who either is or pretends to be disgusted at his father's sophistries, makes the best of a bad business, and undertakes to conceal his father's dishonour and rescue him from the power of Stralenheim. The plot hinges on the unlooked-for and unsuspected action of Conrad. Unlike his father, he is not the man to let " I dare not wait upon I would," but murders Stralenheim in cold blood, and, at the same time, diverts suspicion from his father and

himself to the person of his comrade, a Hungarian soldier of
fortune, who is already supposed to be the thief, and who
had sought and obtained shelter in the apartments of the
conscience-stricken Kruitzner.

The scene changes to Prague. Siegendorf, no longer
Kruitzner, has regained his inheritance, and is once more
at the height of splendour and prosperity. A service of
thanksgiving is being held in the cathedral to commemorate
the signature of the Treaty of Prague (1635), and the count
is present in state. Suddenly he catches sight of the Hungarian, and, "like a flash of lightning," feels and remembers
that he *is* a thief, and that he might, however unjustly, be
suspected if not accused of the murder of Stralenheim. The
service is over, and the count is recrossing "Muldau's
Bridge," when he hears the fatal word *Kruitzner*, "the seal
of his shame," spoken in his ear. He returns to his castle,
and issues orders that the Hungarian should be arrested
and interrogated. An interview takes place, at which the
Hungarian denounces Conrad as the murderer of Stralenheim. The son acknowledges the deed, and upbraids the
father for his weakness and credulity in supposing that his
escape from Stralenheim's machinations could have been
effected by any other means. If, he argues, circumstances
can palliate dishonesty, they can compel and justify murder.
Common sense even now demands the immediate slaughter
of the Hungarian, as it compelled and sanctioned the
effectual silencing of Stralenheim. But Siegendorf knows
not "thorough," and shrinks at assassination. He repudiates
and denounces his son, and connives at the escape of the
Hungarian. Conrad, who is banished from Prague, rejoins
his former associates, the "black bands," which were the
scandal and terror of the neighbouring provinces, and is
killed in a skirmish with the regular troops. Siegendorf
dies of a broken heart.

The conception of *The German's Tale*, as Byron perceived,
is superior to the execution. The style is laboured and
involved, and the narrative long-winded and tiresome. It is,
perhaps, an adaptation, though not a literal translation, of a
German historical romance. But the *motif*—a son predestined to evil by the weakness and sensuality of his father,
a father punished for his want of rectitude by the passionate
criminality of his son, is the very key-note of tragedy.

If from haste or indolence Byron scamped his task, and
cut up whole cantles of the novel into nerveless and pointless
blank verse, here and there throughout the play, in scattered
lines and passages, he outdoes himself. The inspiration is
fitful, but supreme.

Werner was reviewed in *Blackwood's Edinburgh Maga-zine*, December, 1822, vol. xii. pp. 710–719 (republished in *Miscellanies* of W. Maginn, 1885, i. 189); in the *Scots Magazine*, December, 1822, N.S. vol. xi. pp. 688–694; the *European Magazine*, January, 1823, vol. 83, pp. 73–76; and in the *Eclectic Review*, February, 1823, N.S. vol. xix. pp. 148–155.

NOTE TO THE INTRODUCTION TO *WERNER*.

IN an article entitled, "Did Byron write *Werner?*" which appeared in the *Nineteenth Century* (August, 1899, vol. 46, pp. 243–250), the Hon. F. Leveson Gower undertakes to prove that *Werner* was not written by Lord Byron, but by Georgiana, Duchess of Devonshire (born June 9, 1757, died March 30, 1806). He adduces, in support of this claim, (1) a statement made to him by his sister, the late Lady Georgiana Fullerton, to the effect that their grandmother, the duchess, "wrote the poem and gave the MS. to her niece, Lady Caroline Ponsonby (better known as Lady Caroline Lamb), and that she, some years later, handed it over to Lord Byron, who, in 1822, published it in his own name;" (2) a letter written in 1822 by his mother, Lady Granville, to her sister, Lady Carlisle, which asserts that their mother, the duchess, "wrote an entire tragedy from Miss Lee's *Kreutzner the Hungarian* (*sic*)," and that the MS. had been sent to her by Lady Caroline's brother, Mr. William Ponsonby, and was in her possession; (3) another letter of Lady Granville's, dated December 3, 1822, in which she informs her sister that her husband, Lord Granville, had promised to read *Werner* aloud to her (*i.e.* Byron's *Werner*, published November 23, 1822), a promise which, if fulfilled, must have revealed one of two things—the existence of two dramas based on Miss Lee's *Kruitzner*, or the identity of Byron's version with that of the duchess. Now, argues Mr. Leveson Gower, if Lady Granville had known that two dramas were in existence, she would not have allowed her daughter, Lady Georgiana Fullerton, to believe "that the duchess was the author of the published poem."

I will deal with the external evidence first. Practically it amounts to this: (1) that Lady Granville knew that her

mother, the Duchess of Devonshire, dramatized Miss Lee's
Kruitzner ; and (2) that Lady Georgiana Fullerton believed
that the duchess gave the MS. of her play to Lady Caroline
Ponsonby, and that, many years after, Lady Caroline handed
it over to Byron.

The external evidence establishes the fact that the Duchess
of Devonshire dramatized *Kruitzner,* but it does not prove
that Byron purloined her adaptation. It records an unverified
impression on the part of the duchess's granddaughter, that
the MS. of a play written between the years 1801–1806,
passed into Byron's hands about the year 1813 ; that he took
a copy of the MS. ; and that in 1821–22 he caused his copy
to be retranscribed and published under his own name.

But Mr. Leveson Gower appeals to internal as well as
external evidence. (1) He regards the great inferiority of
Werner to Byron's published plays, and to the genuine
(hitherto) unpublished first act, together with the wholesale
plagiarisms from Miss Lee's story, as an additional proof that
the work was none of his. (2) He notes, as a suspicious circumstance, that " while the rough copies of his other poems
have been preserved, no rough copy of *Werner* is to be found."

In conclusion, he deals with two possible objections which
may be brought against his theory : (1) that Byron would
not have incurred the risk of detection at the hands of the
owners of the duchess's MS. ; and (2) that a great poet of
assured fame and reputation could have had no possible
motive for perpetrating a literary fraud. The first objection
he answers by assuming that Byron would have counted on
the reluctance of the " Ponsonby family and the daughters of
the Duchess " to rake up the ashes of old scandals ; the
second, by pointing out that, in 1822, he was making "frantic
endeavours to obtain money, not for himself, but to help the
cause of Greece."

(1) With regard to the marked inferiority of *Werner* to
Byron's other plays, and the relative proportion of adapted
to original matter, Mr. Leveson Gower appears to have been
misled by the disingenuous criticism of Maginn and other
contemporary reviewers (*vide* the Introduction, etc., p. 326).
There is no such inferiority, and the plagiarisms, which were
duly acknowledged, are confined to certain limited portions
of the play. (2) There is nothing unusual in the fact that
the rough draft of *Werner* cannot be found. In fact, but
few of the early drafts of the dramas and other poems written
in the later Italian days ever reached Murray's hands, or are
still in existence. The fair copy for the printer alone was
sent home. The time had gone by when Byron's publisher,
who was also his friend, would stipulate that " all the original

Walker & Cockerell. ph sc

Georgiana. 5th Duchess of Devonshire.

from the mezzotint by Valentine Green after Sir J. Reynolds. P. R. A.

MSS., copies and scraps" should fall to his share. But no argument can be founded on so insignificant a circumstance.

Finally, the argument on which Mr. Leveson Gower dwells at some length, that Byron's "motive" for perpetrating a literary fraud was the necessity for raising money for the cause of Greek independence, is refuted by the fact that *Werner* was begun in December, 1821, and finished in January, 1822, and that it was not till the spring of 1823 that he was elected a member of the Greek Committee, or had any occasion to raise funds for the maintenance of troops or the general expenses of the war. So far from attempting to raise money by *Werner*, in letters to Murray, dated March 6, October 24, November 18, 1822, he emphatically waives the question of "terms," and makes no demand or request for money whatever. It was not till December 23, 1823 (*Letters,* 1901, vi. 287), two years after the play had been written, that he speaks of applying the two or three hundred pounds which the copyright of *Werner* might be worth, to the maintenance of armed men in the service of the *Provisional Government.* He could not have "purloined" and palmed off as his own the duchess's version of Miss Lee's story in order to raise money for a purpose which had not arisen. He had no intention at first or last of presenting the copyright of *Werner* to Murray or Hunt, but he was willing to wait for his money, and had no motive for raising funds by an illegal and dishonourable trick.

That Byron did *not* write *Werner* is, surely, non-proven on the external and internal evidence adduced by Mr. Leveson Gower. On the other hand, there is abundant evidence, both external and internal, that, apart from his acknowledged indebtedness to Miss Lee's story, he did write *Werner.*

To take the external evidence first. On the first page of Mrs. Shelley's transcript of *Werner*, Byron inserted the date, "Dec. 18, 1821," and on the last he wrote "[The End] of fifth act of the Drama. B. P[isa]. Jy 21. 1822."

Turning to the journal of Edward Williams (Shelley's *Prose Works*, 1880, iv. 318), I find the following entries :—

"December 21, 1821. Lord B. told me that he had commenced a tragedy from Miss Lee's *German Tale* ('*Werner*'), and had been fagging at it all day."

"January 8, 1822. Mary read us the first two acts of Lord B.'s *Werner.*"

Again, in an unpublished diary of the same period it is recorded that Mrs. Shelley was engaged in the task of copying on January 17, 1822, and the eight following days, and that on January 25 she finished her transcript.

Again, Medwin (*Conversations*, 1824, p. 409) records the fact that Byron told him "that he had almost finished another play . . . called *Werner* ;" and (p. 412) "that *Werner* was written in twenty-eight days, and one entire act at a sitting." It is almost incredible that Byron should have recopied a copy of the duchess's play in order to impose on Mrs. Shelley and Williams and Medwin ; and it is quite incredible that they were in the plot, and lent themselves to the deception. It is certain that both Williams and Medwin believed that Byron was the author of *Werner*, and it is certain that nothing would have induced Mrs. Shelley to be *particeps criminis*—to copy a play which was not Byron's, to be published as Byron's, and to suffer her copy to be fraudulently endorsed by her guilty accomplice.

The internal evidence of the genuineness of *Werner* is still more convincing. In the first place, there are numerous "undesigned coincidences," allusions, and phrases to be found in *Werner* and elsewhere in Byron's *Poetical Works*, which bear his sign-manual, and cannot be attributed to another writer ; and, secondly, scattered through the play there are numerous lines, passages, allusions—"a cloud of witnesses" to their Byronic inspiration and creation.

Take the following parallels :—

Werner, act i. sc. 1, lines 693, 694—

> ". . . as parchment on a drum,
> Like Ziska's skin."

Age of Bronze, lines 133, 134—

> " The time may come,
> His name shall beat the alarm like Ziska's drum."

Werner, act ii. sc. 2, lines 177, 178—

> ". . . save your throat
> From the Raven-stone."

Manfred, act iii. (original version)—

> " The raven sits
> On the Raven-stone."

Werner, act ii. sc. 2, line 279—

> "Things which had made this silkworm cast his skin."

Marino Faliero, act ii. sc. 2, line 115—

> ". . . these swoln silkworms masters."

("Silkworm," as a term of contempt, is an Italianism.)

Werner, act iii. sc. 1, lines 288, 289—

> " I fear that men must draw their chariots, as
> They say kings did Sesostris'."

Age of Bronze, line 45—

> " The new Sesostris, whose unharnessed kings.'

Werner, act iii. sc. 3, lines 10, 11—

> ". . . while the knoll
> Of long-lived parents."

Childe Harold, Canto III. stanza xcvi. lines 5, 6—

> ". . . is the knoll
> Of what in me is sleepless."

(Wordsworth, in the *Excursion*, uses the archaic " knoll " as a substantive, but the repetition of so rare a word is significant.)

Or, compare the statement (see act i. sc. 1, line 213, *sq.*) that " A great personage . . . is drowned below the ford, with five post-horses, A monkey and a mastiff—and a valet," with the corresponding passage in *Kruitzner* and in Byron's unfinished fragment ; and note that " the monkey, the mastiff, and the valet," which formed part of Byron's retinue in 1821, are conspicuous by their absence from Miss Lee's story and the fragment.

Space precludes the quotation of further parallels, and for specimens of a score of passages which proclaim their author the following lines must suffice :—

Act i. sc. 1, lines 163–165—

> ". . . although then
> My passions were all living serpents, and
> Twined like the Gorgon's round me."

Act iii. sc. 1, lines 264–268—

> ". . . sound him with the gem ;
> 'Twill sink into his venal soul like lead
> Into the deep, and bring up slime and mud,
> And ooze, too, from the bottom, as the lead doth
> With its greased understratum."

Did Byron write *Werner*, or was it the Duchess of Devonshire ?

(For a correspondence on the subject, see *Literature*, August 12, 19, 26, September 9, 1899.)

PREFACE.

THE following drama is taken entirely from the *German's Tale, Kruitzner,* published many years ago in "Lee's *Canterbury Tales,*" written (I believe) by two sisters, of whom one furnished only this story and another, both of which are considered superior to the remainder of the collection.[1] I have adopted the characters, plan, and even the language of many parts of this story. Some of the characters are modified or altered, a few of the names changed, and one character (Ida of Stralenheim) added by myself: but in the rest

1. [This is not correct. *The Young Lady's Tale, or the Two Emilys* and *The Clergyman's Tale, or Pembroke,* were contributed by Sophia Lee. *Kruitzner, or The German's Tale,* was written by Harriet Lee (1757-1851), the younger of the sisters. Miss Lee began her literary career as a dramatist. A comedy, *The New Peerage; or, Our Eyes may deceive us,* was played at Drury Lane, November 10, 1787. In 1798 she published *The Mysterious Marriage; or, The Heirship of Rosalva.* After the publication of Byron's *Werner,* she wrote a dramatic version of *The German's Tale,* under the title of *The Three Strangers.* It was brought out at Covent Garden, December 10, 1825, and acted four times.

The first volume of the *Canterbury Tales,* by Harriet Lee, was published in 1797; the second volume, by Sophia Lee, in 1798 (a second edition of these volumes was published in 1799); a third volume (second edition), by Sophia and Harriet Lee, appeared in 1800; the fourth volume, by Harriet Lee (which contains *The German's Tale,* pp. 3-368), was published in 1801; and the fifth volume, by Harriet Lee, in 1805.

There can be little doubt that Byron's visit to Churchill's grave at Dover, which took place April 25, 1816 (see *Poetical Works,* 1901, iv. 45), was suggested by a passage in the *Introduction,* pp. vii.-ix., to the first volume (1797) of the *Canterbury Tales.* The author "wanders forth to note the *memorabilia* of Dover," is informed that "the greatest curiosity in the place is the tomb of a poet," and hastens "to a spot surrounded by ruined walls, in the midst of which stood the white marble tablet marked with Churchill's name," etc.]

the original is chiefly followed. When I was young
(about fourteen, I think,) I first read this tale, which
made a deep impression upon me; and may, indeed, be
said to contain the germ of much that I have since
written. I am not sure that it ever was very popular;
or, at any rate, its popularity has since been eclipsed by
that of other great writers in the same department. But
I have generally found that those who *had* read it, agreed
with me in their estimate of the singular power of mind
and conception which it developes. I should also add
conception, rather than execution; for the story might,
perhaps, have been developed with greater advantage.
Amongst those whose opinions agreed with mine upon
this story, I could mention some very high names: but
it is not necessary, nor indeed of any use; for every one
must judge according to his own feelings. I merely
refer the reader to the original story, that he may see to
what extent I have borrowed from it; and am not unwilling that he should find much greater pleasure in
perusing it than the drama which is founded upon its
contents.

I had begun a drama upon this tale so far back as
1815, (the first I ever attempted, except one at thirteen
years old, called "Ulric and Ilvina," which I had sense
enough to burn,) and had nearly completed an act,
when I was interrupted by circumstances. This is some-
where amongst my papers in England; but as it has not
been found, I have re-written the first, and added the
subsequent acts.

The whole is neither intended, nor in any shape
adapted, for the stage.[i]

i. [*Of England or any other country. It may seem unnecessary to
add this, but having seen a poem of mine never intended for representation, dragged in spite of my remonstrance upon the theatres of more than
one nation, I trust it will not be deemed impertinent if I once more
repeat my protest against [a gross] folly which may injure me—and [bene-
fit] no one. If it be understood that all dramatic writing is generically
intended for the stage, I deny it.*[1] With the exception of Shakespeare*

---

1. [Byron is replying to Jeffrey (*Edinburgh Review*, February, 1822,
vol. 36, p. 422). "A drama is not merely a dialogue, but *an action*:
and necessarily supposes that something is to pass before the eyes of
assembled spectators. . . . If an author does not bear this continually

(or Tate, Cibber, and Thompson under his name), not one in fifty plays of our dramatists is ever acted, however much they may be read. Only one of Massinger—none of Ford—none of Marlowe, one of Ben Jonson —none of Webster, none of Heywood: and, even in Comedy, Congreve is rarely acted, and that in only one of his plays. Neither is Joanna Baillie. I am far from attempting to raise myself to a level with the least of these names—I only wish to be [exempted] from a stage which is not theirs. Perhaps Mr. Lamb's essay upon the effects of dramatic representation on the intelligent auditor [1]—— marks are just with regard to this—plays of Shakespeare himself—the hundredfold to those of others.* —From a mutilated page of MS. M.]

---

in his mind, and does not write in the ideal presence of an eager and diversified assemblage, he may be a poet, perhaps, but assuredly he will never be a dramatist."]

1. ["It may seem a paradox, but I cannot help being of opinion that the plays of Shakespeare are less calculated for performance on a stage than those of almost any other dramatist whatever."—"On the Tragedies of Shakespeare," *Complete Works of Charles Lamb*, 1875, p. 255. It was, too, something of a paradox that Byron should be eager to shelter himself under the ægis of Charles Lamb. But unpopularity, like poverty, brings together strange bedfellows.]

DRAMATIS PERSONÆ.

—•◦•—

MEN.

WERNER.
ULRIC.
STRALENHEIM.
IDENSTEIN.
GABOR.
FRITZ.
HENRICK.
ERIC.
ARNHEIM.
MEISTER.
RODOLPH.
LUDWIG.

WOMEN.

JOSEPHINE.
IDA STRALENHEIM.

SCENE—Partly on the Frontier of Silesia, and partly in Siegendorf Castle, near Prague.

Time—*The Close of the Thirty Years' War.*[1]

1. [The Thirty Years' War dates from the capture of Pilsen by Mansfeld, November 21, 1618, and did not end till the Peace of Westphalia, October 24, 1648. The incident recorded in act v., a solemn commemoration of the Treaty of Prague, must have taken place in 1635. But in *Werner* there is little or no attempt "to follow history."]

WERNER;

THE INHERITANCE.

ACT I.

SCENE I.—*The Hall of a decayed Palace near a small Town on the Northern Frontier of Silesia—the Night tempestuous.*

WERNER *and* JOSEPHINE, *his Wife.*

Jos. MY love, be calmer!
Wer.   I am calm.
Jos.   To me—
Yes, but not to thyself: thy pace is hurried,
And no one walks a chamber like to ours,
With steps like thine, when his heart is at rest.
Were it a garden, I should deem thee happy,
And stepping with the bee from flower to flower;
But *here!*
Wer.   'Tis chill; the tapestry lets through
The wind to which it waves: my blood is frozen.
Jos. Ah, no!
Wer. (smiling). Why! wouldst thou have it so?
Jos.   I would
Have it a healthful current.
Wer.   Let it flow   10
Until 'tis spilt or checked—how soon, I care not.
Jos. And am I nothing in thy heart?

Wer.   All—all.

Jos. Then canst thou wish for that which must break
     mine?

Wer. (approaching her slowly). But for *thee* I had been
          —no matter what—
But much of good and evil; what I am,
Thou knowest; what I might or should have been,
Thou knowest not : but still I love thee, nor
Shall aught divide us.

          [WERNER *walks on abruptly, and then approaches*
               JOSEPHINE.
                              The storm of the night,
Perhaps affects me; I'm a thing of feelings,
And have of late been sickly, as, alas!   20
Thou know'st by sufferings more than mine, my Love!
In watching me.

     Jos.   To see thee well is much—
To see thee happy——

          Wer.   Where hast thou seen such?
Let me be wretched with the rest!

          Jos.   But think
How many in this hour of tempest shiver
Beneath the biting wind and heavy rain,
Whose every drop bows them down nearer earth,
Which hath no chamber for them save beneath
Her surface.

     Wer.   And that's not the worst: who cares
For chambers? rest is all. The wretches whom   30
Thou namest—aye, the wind howls round them, and
The dull and dropping rain saps in their bones
The creeping marrow. I have been a soldier,
A hunter, and a traveller, and am
A beggar, and should know the thing thou talk'st of.

     Jos. And art thou not now sheltered from them all?

     Wer. Yes. And from these alone.

     Jos.   And that is something.

     Wer. True—to a peasant.[i]

     Jos.   Should the nobly born
Be thankless for that refuge which their habits
Of early delicacy render more   40

          i. *Yea—to a peasant.—[MS. erased.]*

Needful than to the peasant, when the ebb
Of fortune leaves them on the shoals of life ?
    Wer. It is not that, thou know'st it is not : we
Have borne all this, I'll not say patiently,
Except in thee—but we have borne it.
    Jos.   Well ?
    Wer. Something beyond our outward sufferings (though
These were enough to gnaw into our souls)
Hath stung me oft, and, more than ever, *now*.
When, but for this untoward sickness, which
Seized me upon this desolate frontier, and   50
Hath wasted, not alone my strength, but means,
And leaves us—no ! this is beyond me !—but
For this I had been happy—*thou* been happy—
The splendour of my rank sustained—my name—
My father's name—been still upheld ; and, more
Than those——
    Jos. (abruptly). My son—our son—our Ulric,
Been clasped again in these long-empty arms,
And all a mother's hunger satisfied.
Twelve years ! he was but eight then :—beautiful
He was, and beautiful he must be now,   60
My Ulric ! my adored !
    Wer.   I have been full oft
The chase of Fortune ; now she hath o'ertaken
My spirit where it cannot turn at bay,—
Sick, poor, and lonely.
    Jos.   Lonely ! my dear husband ?
    Wer. Or worse—involving all I love, in this
Far worse than solitude. *Alone*, I had died,
And all been over in a nameless grave.
    Jos. And I had not outlived thee ; but pray take
Comfort ! We have struggled long ; and they who strive
With Fortune win or weary her at last,   70
So that they find the goal or cease to feel
Further. Take comfort,—we shall find our boy.
    Wer. We were in sight of him, of every thing
Which could bring compensation for past sorrow—
And to be baffled thus !
    Jos.   We are not baffled.

Wer. Are we not penniless?

Jos.   We ne'er were wealthy.

Wer. But I was born to wealth, and rank, and power;
Enjoyed them, loved them, and, alas! abused them,
And forfeited them by my father's wrath,
In my o'er-fervent youth: but for the abuse   80
Long-sufferings have atoned.   My father's death
Left the path open, yet not without snares.
This cold and creeping kinsman, who so long
Kept his eye on me, as the snake upon
The fluttering bird, hath ere this time outstept me,
Become the master of my rights, and lord
Of that which lifts him up to princes in
Dominion and domain.

Jos.   Who knows? our son
May have returned back to his grandsire, and
Even now uphold thy rights for thee?

Wer.   'Tis hopeless. 90
Since his strange disappearance from my father's,
Entailing, as it were, my sins upon
Himself, no tidings have revealed his course.
I parted with him to his grandsire, on
The promise that his anger would stop short
Of the third generation; but Heaven seems
To claim her stern prerogative, and visit
Upon my boy his father's faults and follies.

Jos. I must hope better still,—at least we have yet
Baffled the long pursuit of Stralenheim.—   100

Wer. We should have done, but for this fatal sickness;—
More fatal than a mortal malady,
Because it takes not life, but life's sole solace:
Even now I feel my spirit girt about
By the snares of this avaricious fiend :—
How do I know he hath not tracked us here?

Jos. He does not know thy person; and his spies,
Who so long watched thee, have been left at Hamburgh.
Our unexpected journey, and this change
Of name, leaves all discovery far behind :   110
None hold us here for aught save what we seem.

Wer. Save what we seem! save what we *are*—sick
      beggars,

Even to our very hopes.—Ha ! ha !

   Jos.　　　　　　　　　　　Alas !
That bitter laugh !

   Wer.　　　　　*Who* would read in this form
The high soul of the son of a long line ?
Who, in this garb, the heir of princely lands ?
Who, in this sunken, sickly eye, the pride
Of rank and ancestry ?　In this worn cheek
And famine-hollowed brow, the Lord of halls
Which daily feast a thousand vassals ?

   Jos.　　　　　　　　　　You　　　120
Pondered not thus upon these worldly things,
My Werner ! when you deigned to choose for bride
The foreign daughter of a wandering exile.

   Wer. An exile's daughter with an outcast son,
Were a fit marriage : but I still had hopes
To lift thee to the state we both were born for.
Your father's house was noble, though decayed ;
And worthy by its birth to match with ours.

   Jos. Your father did not think so, though 'twas noble ;
But had my birth been all my claim to match　　130
With thee, I should have deemed it what it is.

   Wer. And what is that in thine eyes ?

   Jos.　　　　　　　　　All which it
Has done in our behalf,—nothing.

   Wer.　　　　　　　　How,—nothing ?

   Jos. Or worse ; for it has been a canker in
Thy heart from the beginning : but for this,
We had not felt our poverty but as
Millions of myriads feel it—cheerfully ;
But for these phantoms of thy feudal fathers,
Thou mightst have earned thy bread, as thousands
　　earn it ;
Or, if that seem too humble, tried by commerce,　140
Or other civic means, to amend thy fortunes.

   Wer. (*ironically*). And been an Hanseatic burgher ?
　　Excellent !

   Jos. Whate'er thou mightest have been, to me thou art
What no state high or low can ever change,
My heart's first choice ;—which chose thee, knowing
　　neither

Thy birth, thy hopes, thy pride; nought, save thy
    sorrows:
While they last, let me comfort or divide them:
When they end—let mine end with them, or thee!
    Wer. My better angel! Such I have ever found thee;
This rashness, or this weakness of my temper,   150
Ne'er raised a thought to injure thee or thine.
Thou didst not mar my fortunes: my own nature
In youth was such as to unmake an empire,
Had such been my inheritance; but now,
Chastened, subdued, out-worn, and taught to know
Myself,—to lose this for our son and thee!
Trust me, when, in my two-and-twentieth spring,
My father barred me from my father's house,
The last sole scion of a thousand sires
(For I was then the last), it hurt me less   160
Than to behold my boy and my boy's mother
Excluded in their innocence from what
My faults deserved—exclusion; although then
My passions were all living serpents,[1] and
Twined like the Gorgon's round me.
                            [*A loud knocking is heard.*
    Jos.   Hark!
    Wer.   A knocking!
    Jos. Who can it be at this lone hour? We have
Few visitors.
    Wer.   And poverty hath none,
Save those who come to make it poorer still.
Well—I am prepared.
      [WERNER *puts his hand into his bosom, as if to search
          for some weapon.*
    Jos.   Oh! do not look so. I
Will to the door. It cannot be of import   170
In this lone spot of wintry desolation:—
The very desert saves man from mankind.
                         [*She goes to the door.*

---

    1. [Compare—
        "And still my passions wake and war."
              Lines "To ——" [Lady Blessington],
                  Poetical Works, 1901, iv. 564.]

Enter IDENSTEIN.

Iden. A fair good evening to my fair hostess
And worthy——What's your name, my friend?
　Wer.　　　　　　　　　　　　　　Are you
Not afraid to demand it?
　Iden.　　　　　　Not afraid?
Egad! I am afraid. You look as if
I asked for something better than your name,
By the face you put on it.
　Wer.　　　　　　　Better, sir!
　Iden. Better or worse, like matrimony : what
Shall I say more? You have been a guest this month
Here in the prince's palace—(to be sure,　　181
His Highness had resigned it to the ghosts
And rats these twelve years—but 'tis still a palace)—
I say you have been our lodger, and as yet
We do not know your name.
　Wer.　　　　　　　My name is Werner.[1]
　Iden. A goodly name, a very worthy name,
As e'er was gilt upon a trader's board :
I have a cousin in the lazaretto
Of Hamburgh, who has got a wife who bore
The same. He is an officer of trust,　　　190
Surgeon's assistant (hoping to be surgeon),
And has done miracles i' the way of business.
Perhaps you are related to my relative?
　Wer. To yours?
　Jos.　　　　　Oh, yes ; we are, but distantly.
(*Aside to* WERNER.) Cannot you humour the dull gossip
　　till
We learn his purpose?
　Iden.　　　　　Well, I'm glad of that ;
I thought so all along, such natural yearnings

---

　1. [It has been surmised that Byron had some knowledge of the
early life and history of the dramatist Friedrich Ludwig Zacharias
Werner (1768-1823), and that a similarity of character and incident
suggested the renaming of Kruitzner. But the change of name was
made in 1815, not in 1821, and it is far more probable that Byron
called his hero "Werner," because "Kruitzner" is unrhythmical, or
simply because "Werner," a common German surname, is not unlike
"Werther," which was "familiar as a household word."]

Played round my heart :—blood is not water, cousin ;
And so let's have some wine, and drink unto
Our better acquaintance : relatives should be   200
Friends.
  Wer. You appear to have drunk enough already ;
And if you have not, I've no wine to offer,
Else it were yours : but this you know, or should know :
You see I am poor, and sick, and will not see
That I would be alone ; but to your business !
What brings you here ?
  Iden.   Why, what should bring me here ?
  Wer. I know not, though I think that I could guess
That which will send you hence.
  Jos. (*aside*).   Patience, dear Werner !
  Iden. You don't know what has happened, then ?
  Jos.   How should we ?
  Iden. The river has o'erflowed.
  Jos.   Alas ! we have known
That to our sorrow for these five days ; since   211
It keeps us here.
  Iden.   But what you don't know is,
That a great personage, who fain would cross
Against the stream and three postilions' wishes,
Is drowned below the ford, with five post-horses,
A monkey, and a mastiff—and a valet.[1]
  Jos. Poor creatures ! are you sure ?
  Iden.   Yes, of the monkey,
And the valet, and the cattle ; but as yet
We know not if his Excellency 's dead
Or no ; your noblemen are hard to drown,   220
As it is fit that men in office should be ;
But what is certain is, that he has swallowed
Enough of the Oder [2] to have burst two peasants ;
And now a Saxon and Hungarian traveller,
Who, at their proper peril, snatched him from

---

 1. ["Lord Byron's establishment at Pisa was, like everything else
about him, somewhat singular ; it consisted of a monkey, a mastiff, a
bull-dog, two cats, . . . several servants in livery, and the trusty Fletcher
as *Major Domo*, or superintendant of the *Menagerie*."—*Life, Writings,
Opinions, etc.*, 1825, ii. 203, 204. See, too, Medwin, *Conversations*,
1824, pp. 1, 2.]
 2. [The Oder crosses and re-crosses the northern frontier of Silesia.]

The whirling river, have sent on to crave
A lodging, or a grave, according as
It may turn out with the live or dead body.
   Jos. And where will you receive him? here, I hope,
If we can be of service—say the word.   230
   Iden. Here? no; but in the Prince's own apartment,
As fits a noble guest:—'tis damp, no doubt,
Not having been inhabited these twelve years;
But then he comes from a much damper place,
So scarcely will catch cold in't, if he be
Still liable to cold—and if not, why
He'll be worse lodged to-morrow: ne'ertheless,
I have ordered fire and all appliances
To be got ready for the worst—that is,
In case he should survive.
   Jos.   Poor gentleman!   240
I hope he will, with all my heart.
   Wer.   Intendant,
Have you not learned his name? (*Aside to his wife.*)
     My Josephine,
Retire: I'll sift this fool.   [*Exit* JOSEPHINE.
   Iden.   His name? oh Lord!
Who knows if he hath now a name or no?
'Tis time enough to ask it when he 's able
To give an answer; or if not, to put
His heir's upon his epitaph. Methought
Just now you chid me for demanding names?
   Wer. True, true, I did so: you say well and wisely.

Enter GABOR.[1]

   Gab. If I intrude, I crave——
   Iden.   Oh, no intrusion!   250
This is the palace; this a stranger like
Yourself; I pray you make yourself at home:
But where 's his Excellency? and how fares he?
   Gab. Wetly and wearily, but out of peril:
He paused to change his garments in a cottage

---

   1. [In Miss Lee's *Kruitzner* Gabor is always spoken of as "The
Hungarian." He is no doubt named after Bethlen Gabor, Prince of
Transylvania, who was elected King of Hungary, August, 1620.]

(Where I doffed mine for these, and came on hither),
And has almost recovered from his drenching.
He will be here anon.
  Iden.   What ho, there! bustle!
Without there, Herman, Weilburg, Peter, Conrad!
    [*Gives directions to different servants who enter.*
A nobleman sleeps here to-night—see that   260
All is in order in the damask chamber—
Keep up the stove—I will myself to the cellar—
And Madame Idenstein (my consort, stranger,)
Shall furnish forth the bed-apparel; for,
To say the truth, they are marvellous scant of this
Within the palace precincts, since his Highness
Left it some dozen years ago. And then
His Excellency will sup, doubtless?
  Gab.   Faith!
I cannot tell; but I should think the pillow
Would please him better than the table, after 270
His soaking in your river: but for fear
Your viands should be thrown away, I mean
To sup myself, and have a friend without
Who will do honour to your good cheer with
A traveller's appetite.
  Iden.   But are you sure
His Excellency——But his name: what is it?
  Gab. I do not know.
  Iden.   And yet you saved his life.
  Gab. I helped my friend to do so.
  Iden.   Well, that's strange,
To save a man's life whom you do not know.
  Gab. Not so; for there are some I know so well, 280
I scarce should give myself the trouble.
  Iden.   Pray,
Good friend, and who may you be?
  Gab.   By my family,
Hungarian.
  Iden. Which is called?
  Gab.   It matters little.
  Iden. (*aside*). I think that all the world are grown
    anonymous,
Since no one cares to tell me what he's called!

Pray, has his Excellency a large suite?
 Gab.   Sufficient.
 Iden. How many?
 Gab.   I did not count them.
We came up by mere accident, and just
In time to drag him through his carriage window.
 Iden. Well, what would I give to save a great man! 290
No doubt you'll have a swingeing sum as recompense.
 Gab. Perhaps.
 Iden.   Now, how much do you reckon on?
 Gab. I have not yet put up myself to sale:
In the mean time, my best reward would be
A glass of your [1] Hockcheimer—a *green* glass,
Wreathed with rich grapes and Bacchanal devices,
O'erflowing with the oldest of your vintage:
For which I promise you, in case you e'er
Run hazard of being drowned, (although I own
It seems, of all deaths, the least likely for you,) 300
I'll pull you out for nothing. Quick, my friend,
And think, for every bumper I shall quaff,
A wave the less may roll above your head.
 Iden. (*aside*). I don't much like this fellow—close and
     dry
He seems,—two things which suit me not; however,
Wine he shall have; if that unlocks him not,
I shall not sleep to-night for curiosity. [*Exit* IDENSTEIN.
 Gab. (*to* WERNER). This master of the ceremonies is
The intendant of the palace, I presume:
'Tis a fine building, but decayed.
 Wer.   The apartment 310
Designed for him you rescued will be found
In fitter order for a sickly guest.
 Gab. I wonder then you occupied it not,
For you seem delicate in health.
 Wer. (*quickly*).   Sir!
 Gab.   Pray
Excuse me: have I said aught to offend you?
 Wer. Nothing: but we are strangers to each other.

---

 1. [Compare—
   "And so—for God's sake—hock and soda-water."
    Fragment written on MS. of Canto I. of *Don Juan.*]

Gab. And that 's the reason I would have us less so .
I thought our bustling guest without had said
You were a chance and passing guest, the counterpart
Of me and my companions.
　Wer.　　　　　　　　Very true.　　　　　320
　Gab. Then, as we never met before, and never,
It may be, may again encounter, why,
I thought to cheer up this old dungeon here
(At least to me) by asking you to share
The fare of my companions and myself.
　Wer. Pray, pardon me ; my health——
　Gab.　　　　　　　Even as you please.
I have been a soldier, and perhaps am blunt
In bearing.
　Wer.　　I have also served, and can
Requite a soldier's greeting.
　Gab.　　　　　　In what service?
The Imperial?
　Wer. (quickly, and then interrupting himself). I com-
　　　manded—no—I mean　　　　　330
I served ; but it is many years ago,
When first Bohemia [1] raised her banner 'gainst
The Austrian.
　Gab.　　　Well, that 's over now, and peace
Has turned some thousand gallant hearts adrift
To live as they best may : and, to say truth,
Some take the shortest.
　Wer.　　　　　What is that?
　Gab.　　　　　　　　Whate'er
They lay their hands on.　All Silesia and
Lusatia's woods are tenanted by bands
Of the late troops, who levy on the country
Their maintenance : the Chatelains must keep　340
Their castle walls—beyond them 'tis but doubtful
Travel for your rich Count or full-blown Baron.
My comfort is that, wander where I may,

---

1. [On the 18th of August, 1619, Bethlen Gabor threw in his lot
with the Bohemians, and "wrote the Directors at Prague that he would
march with his troops, and in September would, in their defence, enter
Moravia."—*History of the Thirty Years' War,* by A. Gindely, 1885, i.
166.　*Vide ibid.,* for portrait of "Gabriel Bethlem, D. G. Princeps
Transsylvaniæ, *etc.,* Ætatis suæ 40, A° Christi, 1620."]

I've little left to lose now.

Wer.   And I—nothing.

Gab. That's harder still. You say you were a soldier.

Wer. I was.

Gab.   You look one still. All soldiers are
Or should be comrades, even though enemies.
Our swords when drawn must cross, our engines aim
(While levelled) at each other's hearts; but when
A truce, a peace, or what you will, remits   350
The steel into its scabbard, and lets sleep
The spark which lights the matchlock, we are brethren.
You are poor and sickly—I am not rich, but healthy;
I want for nothing which I cannot want;
You seem devoid of this—wilt share it?

                    [GABOR *pulls out his purse.*

Wer.   Who
Told you I was a beggar?

Gab.   You yourself,
In saying you were a soldier during peace-time.

Wer. (*looking at him with suspicion*). You know me
     not.

Gab.   I know no man, not even
Myself: how should I then know one I ne'er
Beheld till half an hour since?

Wer.   Sir, I thank you.   360
Your offer's noble were it to a friend,
And not unkind as to an unknown stranger,
Though scarcely prudent; but no less I thank you.
I am a beggar in all save his trade;
And when I beg of any one, it shall be
Of him who was the first to offer what
Few can obtain by asking. Pardon me. [*Exit* WERNER.

Gab. (*solus*). A goodly fellow ·by his looks, though
     worn
As most good fellows are, by pain or pleasure,
Which tear life out of us before our time;   370
I scarce know which most quickly: but he seems
To have seen better days, as who has not
Who has seen yesterday?—But here approaches
Our sage intendant, with the wine: however,
For the cup's sake I'll bear the cupbearer.

Enter IDENSTEIN.

Iden. 'Tis here ! the *supernaculum !* [1] twenty years
Of age, if 'tis a day.
    Gab.   Which epoch makes
Young women and old wine ; and 'tis great pity,
Of two such excellent things, increase of years,
Which still improves the one, should spoil the other.
Fill full—Here 's to our hostess !—your fair wife !   381
                                       [*Takes the glass.*
    Iden. Fair !—Well, I trust your taste in wine is equal
To that you show for beauty ; but I pledge you
Nevertheless.
    Gab.   Is not the lovely woman
I met in the adjacent hall, who, with
An air, and port, and eye, which would have better
Beseemed this palace in its brightest days
(Though in a garb adapted to its present
Abandonment), returned my salutation—
Is not the same your spouse ?
    Iden.   I would she were !   390
But you're mistaken :—that 's the stranger's wife.
    Gab. And by her aspect she might be a Prince's ;
Though time hath touched her too, she still retains
Much beauty, and more majesty.
    Iden.   And that
Is more than I can say for Madame Idenstein,
At least in beauty : as for majesty,
She has some of its properties which might
Be spared—but never mind !
    Gab.   I don't. But who
May be this stranger? He too hath a bearing
Above his outward fortunes.
    Iden.   There I differ.   400
He 's poor as Job, and not so patient ; but
Who he may be, or what, or aught of him,

---

1. [From *super*, and *nagel*, "a nail." To drink *supernaculum* is to
empty the cup so thoroughly that the last drop or "pearl," drained on
to the nail, retains its shape, and does not run. If "the pearl" broke
and began to slide, the drinker was "sconced." Hence, good liquor.
See Rabelais' *Life of Gargantua, etc.,* Urquhart's Translation, 1863,
lib. i, ch. 5.]

Except his name (and that I only learned
To-night), I know not.
　　Gab.　　　　　　But how came he here?
　　Iden. In a most miserable old caleche,
About a month since, and immediately
Fell sick, almost to death.　He should have died.
　　Gab. Tender and true !—but why?
　　Iden.　　　　　　　　　Why, what is life
Without a living?　He has not a stiver.[i]
　　Gab. In that case, I much wonder that a person　410
Of your apparent prudence should admit
Guests so forlorn into this noble mansion.
　　Iden. That's true : but pity, as you know, *does* make
One's heart commit these follies ; and besides,
They had some valuables left at that time,
Which paid their way up to the present hour ;
And so I thought they might as well be lodged
Here as at the small tavern, and I gave them
The run of some of the oldest palace rooms.
They served to air them, at the least as long　420
As they could pay for firewood.
　　Gab.　　　　　　Poor souls !
　　Iden.　　　　　　　　　　Aye,
Exceeding poor.
　　Gab.　　　　And yet unused to poverty,
If I mistake not.　Whither were they going?
　　Iden. Oh ! Heaven knows where, unless to Heaven
　　　　itself.
Some days ago that looked the likeliest journey
For Werner.
　　Gab.　　　　Werner ! I have heard the name.
But it may be a feigned one.
　　Iden.　　　　　　Like enough !
But hark ! a noise of wheels and voices, and
A blaze of torches from without.　As sure
As destiny, his Excellency's come.　　　　430
I must be at my post ; will you not join me,
To help him from his carriage, and present
Your humble duty at the door ?
　　Gab.　　　　　　I dragged him

----

i. *Without means and he has not a stiver left.*—[*MS. erased.*]

From out that carriage when he would have given
His barony or county to repel
The rushing river from his gurgling throat.
He has valets now enough : they stood aloof then,
Shaking their dripping ears upon the shore,
All roaring " Help ! " but offering none ; and as
For *duty* (as you call it)—I did mine *then*,   440
Now do *yours*.   Hence, and bow and cringe him here !
    Iden. I cringe !—but I shall lose the opportunity—
Plague take it ! he'll be *here*, and I *not there !*
                         [*Exit* IDENSTEIN *hastily.*

            Re-enter WERNER.

    Wer. (to himself). I heard a noise of wheels and
      voices.   How
All sounds now jar me !   [*Perceiving* GABOR.
                 Still here !   Is he not
A spy of my pursuer's ?   His frank offer
So suddenly, and to a stranger, wore
The aspect of a secret enemy ;
For friends are slow at such.
    Gab.   Sir, you seem rapt ;
And yet the time is not akin to thought.   450
These old walls will be noisy soon.   The baron,
Or count (or whatsoe'er this half drowned noble
May be), for whom this desolate village and
Its lone inhabitants show more respect
Than did the elements, is come.
    Iden. (without).   This way—
This way, your Excellency :—have a care,
The staircase is a little gloomy, and
Somewhat decayed ; but if we had expected
So high a guest—Pray take my arm, my Lord !

Enter STRALENHEIM, IDENSTEIN, *and Attendants—partly
    his own, and partly Retainers of the Domain of which
    *IDENSTEIN *is Intendant.*

    Stral. I'll rest here a moment.
    Iden. (to the servants).   Ho ! a chair !   460
Instantly, knaves.   [STRALENHEIM *sits down.*

Wer. (*aside*).　　'Tis he !

Stral.　　　　　　　　I'm better now.

Who are these strangers ?

Iden.　　　　　　　Please you, my good Lord,

One says he is no stranger.

Wer. (*aloud and hastily*).　*Who* says that?

　　　　　　　[*They look at him with surprise.*

Iden. Why, no one spoke *of you*, or *to you !*—but

Here 's one his Excellency may be pleased

To recognise.　　　　　[*Pointing to* GABOR.

Gab.　　　I seek not to disturb

His noble memory.

Stral.　　　　I apprehend

This is one of the strangers to whose aid[L]

I owe my rescue.　Is not that the other?

　　　　　　　　[*Pointing to* WERNER.

My state when I was succoured must excuse　　470

My uncertainty to whom I owe so much.

Iden. He !—no, my Lord ! he rather wants for rescue

Than can afford it.　'Tis a poor sick man,

Travel-tired, and lately risen from a bed

From whence he never dreamed to rise.

Stral.　　　　　　　Methought

That there were two.

Gab.　　　There were, in company ;

But, in the service rendered to your Lordship,

I needs must say but *one*, and he is absent.

The chief part of whatever aid was rendered

Was *his :* it was his fortune to be first.　　480

My will was not inferior, but his strength

And youth outstripped me ; therefore do not waste

Your thanks on me.　I was but a glad second

Unto a nobler principal.

Stral.　　　　Where is he ?

An Atten. My Lord, he tarried in the cottage where

Your Excellency rested for an hour,

And said he would be here to-morrow.

Stral.　　　　　　Till

That hour arrives, I can but offer thanks,

And then——

　　　i. *This is one of those to whom I owe aid.*—[*MS. erased.*]

   Gab.   I seek no more, and scarce deserve
So much.   My comrade may speak for himself.   490
   Stral. (*fixing his eyes upon* WERNER: *then aside*).   It
     cannot be! and yet he must be looked to.
'Tis twenty years since I beheld him with
These eyes; and, though my agents still have kept
Theirs on him, policy has held aloof
My own from his, not to alarm him into
Suspicion of my plan.   Why did I leave
At Hamburgh those who would have made assurance
If this be he or no?   I thought, ere now,
To have been lord of Siegendorf, and parted
In haste, though even the elements appear   500
To fight against me, and this sudden flood
May keep me prisoner here till——
       [*He pauses and looks at* WERNER: *then resumes.*
                 This man must
Be watched.   If it is he, he is so changed,
His father, rising from his grave again,
Would pass by him unknown.   I must be wary:
An error would spoil all.
   Iden.   Your Lordship seems
Pensive.   Will it not please you to pass on?
   Stral. 'Tis past fatigue, which gives my weighed-down
     spirit
An outward show of thought.   I will to rest.
   Iden. The Prince's chamber is prepared, with all   510
The very furniture the Prince used when
Last here, in its full splendour.
          (*Aside*).   Somewhat tattered,
And devilish damp, but fine enough by torch-light;
And that's enough for your right noble blood
Of twenty quarterings upon a hatchment;
So let their bearer sleep 'neath something like one
Now, as he one day will for ever lie.
   Stral. (*rising and turning to* GABOR).   Good night, good
     people!   Sir, I trust to-morrow
Will find me apter to requite your service.
In the meantime I crave your company   520
A moment in my chamber.
   Gab.   I attend you.

Stral. (*after a few steps, pauses, and calls* WERNER).
   Friend!
Wer. Sir!
Iden.   *Sir!* Lord—oh Lord! Why don't you say
His Lordship, or his Excellency? Pray,
My Lord, excuse this poor man's want of breeding:
He hath not been accustomed to admission
To such a presence.
   Stral. (*to* IDENSTEIN). Peace, intendant!
   Iden.   Oh!
I am dumb.
   Stral. (*to* WERNER). Have you been long here?
   Wer.   Long?
   Stral.   I sought
An answer, not an echo.
   Wer.   You may seek
Both from the walls. I am not used to answer
Those whom I know not.
   Stral.   Indeed! Ne'er the less, 530
You might reply with courtesy to what
Is asked in kindness.
   Wer.   When I know it such
I will requite—that is, *reply*—in unison.
   Stral. The intendant said, you had been detained by
       sickness—
If I could aid you—journeying the same way?
   Wer. (*quickly*). I am not journeying the same way!
   Stral.   How know ye
That, ere you know my route?
   Wer.   Because there is
But one way that the rich and poor must tread
Together. You diverged from that dread path
Some hours ago, and I some days: henceforth   540
Our roads must lie asunder, though they tend
All to one home.
   Stral.   Your language is above
Your station.
   Wer. (*bitterly*). Is it?
   Stral.   Or, at least, beyond
Your garb.
   Wer.   'Tis well that it is not beneath it,

As sometimes happens to the better clad.
But, in a word, what would you with me?
   Stral. (startled).   I?
   Wer. Yes—you! You know me not, and question
    me,
And wonder that I answer not—not knowing
My inquisitor. Explain what you would have,
And then I'll satisfy yourself, or me.   550
   Stral. I knew not that you had reasons for reserve.
   Wer. Many have such :—Have you none?
   Stral.   None which can
Interest a mere stranger.
   Wer.   Then forgive
The same unknown and humble stranger, if
He wishes to remain so to the man
Who can have nought in common with him.
   Stral.   Sir,
I will not balk your humour, though untoward :
I only meant you service—but good night!
Intendant, show the way! (*To* GABOR.) Sir, you will
    with me?
      [*Exeunt* STRALENHEIM *and Attendants;* IDENSTEIN
        and GABOR.
   Wer. (*solus*). 'Tis he! I am taken in the toils.
    Before   560
I quitted Hamburg, Giulio, his late steward,
Informed me, that he had obtained an order
From Brandenburg's elector, for the arrest
Of Kruitzner (such the name I then bore) when
I came upon the frontier; the free city
Alone preserved my freedom—till I left
Its walls—fool that I was to quit them! But
I deemed this humble garb, and route obscure,
Had baffled the slow hounds in their pursuit.
What's to be done? He knows me not by person; 570
Nor could aught, save the eye of apprehension,
Have recognised *him*, after twenty years—
We met so rarely and so coldly in
Our youth. But those about him! Now I can
Divine the frankness of the Hungarian, who
No doubt is a mere tool and spy of Stralenheim's,

To sound and to secure me.   Without means !
Sick, poor—begirt too with the flooding rivers,
Impassable even to the wealthy, with
All the appliances which purchase modes   580
Of overpowering peril, with men's lives,—
How can I hope !   An hour ago methought
My state beyond despair ; and now, 'tis such,
The past seems paradise.   Another day,
And I'm detected,—on the very eve
Of honours, rights, and my inheritance,
When a few drops of gold might save me still
In favouring an escape.

      Enter IDENSTEIN *and* FRITZ *in conversation.*

   Fritz.   Immediately.
   Iden. I tell you, 'tis impossible.
   Fritz.   It must
Be tried, however ; and if one express   590
Fail, you must send on others, till the answer
Arrives from Frankfort, from the commandant.
   Iden. I will do what I can.
   Fritz.   And recollect
To spare no trouble ; you will be repaid
Tenfold.
   Iden.   The Baron is retired to rest ?
   Fritz. He hath thrown himself into an easy chair
Beside the fire, and slumbers ; and has ordered
He may not be disturbed until eleven,
When he will take himself to bed.
   Iden.   Before
An hour is past I'll do my best to serve him.   600
   Fritz. Remember !   [*Exit* FRITZ.
   Iden.   The devil take these great men ! they
Think all things made for them.   Now here must I
Rouse up some half a dozen shivering vassals
From their scant pallets, and, at peril of
Their lives, despatch them o'er the river towards
Frankfort.   Methinks the Baron's own experience
Some hours ago might teach him fellow-feeling :
But no, " it *must*." and there 's an end.   How now ?

Are you there, Mynheer Werner?
   Wer.   You have left
Your noble guest right quickly.
   Iden.   Yes—he 's dozing, 610
And seems to like that none should sleep besides.
Here is a packet for the Commandant
Of Frankfort, at all risks and all expenses;
But I must not lose time : Good night!   [*Exit* IDEN.
   Wer.   " To Frankfort!"
So, so, it thickens!   Aye, " the Commandant!"
This tallies well with all the prior steps
Of this cool, calculating fiend, who walks
Between me and my father's house.   No doubt
He writes for a detachment to convey me
Into some secret fortress.—Sooner than   620
This——
      [WERNER *looks around, and snatches up a knife lying*
        on a table in a recess.
               Now I am master of myself at least.
Hark,—footsteps!   How do I know that Stralenheim
Will wait for even the show of that authority
Which is to overshadow usurpation?
That he suspects me 's certain.   I'm alone—
He with a numerous train : I weak—he strong
In gold, in numbers, rank, authority.
I nameless, or involving in my name
Destruction, till I reach my own domain;
He full-blown with his titles, which impose   630
Still further on these obscure petty burghers
Than they could do elsewhere.   Hark ! nearer still !
I'll to the secret passage, which communicates
With the——No ! all is silent—'twas my fancy !—
Still as the breathless interval between
The flash and thunder :—I must hush my soul
Amidst its perils.   Yet I will retire,
To see if still be unexplored the passage
I wot of : it will serve me as a den
Of secrecy for some hours, at the worst.   640
      [WERNER *draws a panel, and exit, closing it after*
        him.

Enter GABOR *and* JOSEPHINE.

Gab. Where is your husband?

Jos.   *Here*, I thought : I left him
Not long since in his chamber.   But these rooms
Have many outlets, and he may be gone
To accompany the Intendant.

Gab.   Baron Stralenheim
Put many questions to the Intendant on
The subject of your lord, and, to be plain,
I have my doubts if he means well.

Jos.   Alas !
What can there be in common with the proud
And wealthy Baron, and the unknown Werner ?

Gab. That you know best.

Jos.   Or, if it were so, how 650
Come you to stir yourself in his behalf,
Rather than that of him whose life you saved?

Gab. I helped to save him, as in peril ; but
I did not pledge myself to serve him in
Oppression.   I know well these nobles, and
Their thousand modes of trampling on the poor.
I have proved them ; and my spirit boils up when
I find them practising against the weak :—
This is my only motive.

Jos.   It would be
Not easy to persuade my consort of   660
Your good intentions.

Gab.   Is he so suspicious?

Jos. He was not once ; but time and troubles have
Made him what you beheld.

Gab.   I'm sorry for it.
Suspicion is a heavy armour, and
With its own weight impedes more than protects.
Good night ! I trust to meet with him at day-break.

                           [*Exit* GABOR.

Re-enter IDENSTEIN *and some Peasants.* JOSEPHINE
              retires up the Hall.

First Peasant. But if I'm drowned ?

Iden.   Why, you will be well paid for 't,

And have risked more than drowning for as much,
I doubt not.
    Second Peasant. But our wives and families?
    Iden. Cannot be worse off than they are, and may 670
Be better.
    Third Peasant. I have neither, and will venture.
    Iden. That's right. A gallant carle, and fit to be
A soldier. I'll promote you to the ranks
In the Prince's body-guard—if you succeed :
And you shall have besides, in sparkling coin,
Two thalers.
    Third Peasant. No more !
    Iden.   Out upon your avarice !
Can that low vice alloy so much ambition?
I tell thee, fellow, that two thalers in
Small change will subdivide into a treasure.
Do not five hundred thousand heroes daily   680
Risk lives and souls for the tithe of one thaler ?
When had you half the sum ?
    Third Peasant.   Never—but ne'er
The less I must have three.
    Iden.   Have you forgot
Whose vassal you were born, knave ?
    Third Peasant.   No—the Prince's,
And not the stranger's.
    Iden.   Sirrah ! in the Prince's
Absence, I am sovereign ; and the Baron is
My intimate connection ;—" Cousin Idenstein !
(Quoth he) you'll order out a dozen villains."
And so, you villains ! troop—march—march, I say ;
And if a single dog's ear of this packet   690
Be sprinkled by the Oder—look to it !
For every page of paper, shall a hide
Of yours be stretched as parchment on a drum,
Like Ziska's skin,[1] to beat alarm to all
Refractory vassals, who can not effect
Impossibilities.—Away, ye earth-worms !
                       [*Exit, driving them out.*
    Jos. (*coming forward*). I fain would shun these scenes,
        too oft repeated,

    1. [Compare *Age of Bronze*, line 130, *vide post*, p. 549.]

Of feudal tyranny o'er petty victims;
I cannot aid, and will not witness such.
Even here, in this remote, unnamed, dull spot,   700
The dimmest in the district's map, exist
The insolence of wealth in poverty
O'er something poorer still—the pride of rank
In servitude, o'er something still more servile;
And vice in misery affecting still
A tattered splendour.   What a state of being!
In Tuscany, my own dear sunny land,
Our nobles were but citizens and merchants,[1]
Like Cosmo.   We had evils, but not such
As these; and our all-ripe and gushing valleys   710
Made poverty more cheerful, where each herb
Was in itself a meal, and every vine
Rained, as it were, the beverage which makes glad
The heart of man; and the ne'er unfelt sun
(But rarely clouded, and when clouded, leaving
His warmth behind in memory of his beams)
Makes the worn mantle, and the thin robe, less
Oppressive than an emperor's jewelled purple.
But, here! the despots of the north appear
To imitate the ice-wind of their clime,   720
Searching the shivering vassal through his rags,
To wring his soul—as the bleak elements
His form.   And 'tis to be amongst these sovereigns
My husband pants! and such his pride of birth—
That twenty years of usage, such as no
Father born in a humble state could nerve
His soul to persecute a son withal,
Hath changed no atom of his early nature;
But I, born nobly also, from my father's
Kindness was taught a different lesson.   Father!   730
May thy long-tried and now rewarded spirit
Look down on us and our so long desired
Ulric! I love my son, as thou didst me!
What's that?   Thou, Werner! can it be? and thus?

---

1. [For the "merchant dukes" of Florence, see *Childe Harold*,
Canto IV. stanza lx. line 4.   See, too, *ibid.*, stanza xlviii. line 8,
Poetical Works, 1899, ii. 373, and 365, *note* 1.]

Enter WERNER *hastily, with the knife in his hand, by the
    secret panel, which he closes hurriedly after him.*

Wer. (*not at first recognising her*).   Discovered ! then
        I'll stab——(*recognising her*).

                                     Ah ! Josephine

Why art thou not at rest?
    Jos.   What rest ?   My God !
What doth this mean ?
    Wer. (*showing a rouleau*).   Here's *gold—gold*, Josephine,
Will rescue us from this detested dungeon.
    Jos.   And how obtained ?—that knife !
    Wer.   'Tis bloodless—*yet.*
Away—we must to our chamber.
    Jos.   But whence comest thou ?   740
    Wer.   Ask not ! but let us think where we shall go—
This—this will make us way—(*showing the gold*)—I'll fit
        them now.
    Jos.   I dare not think thee guilty of dishonour.
    Wer.   Dishonour !
    Jos.   I have said it.
    Wer.   Let us hence :
'Tis the last night, I trust, that we need pass here.
    Jos.   And not the worst, I hope.
    Wer.   Hope ! I make *sure.*
But let us to our chamber.
    Jos.   Yet one question—
What hast thou *done ?*
    Wer. (*fiercely*).   Left one thing *undone,* which
Had made all well : let me not think of it !
Away !
    Jos.   Alas that I should doubt of thee !   750
                                       [*Exeunt.*

ACT II.

SCENE I.—*A Hall in the same Palace.*

Enter IDENSTEIN *and Others.*

Iden. Fine doings ! goodly doings ! honest doings !
A Baron pillaged in a Prince's palace !
Where, till this hour, such a sin ne'er was heard of.
  Fritz. It hardly could, unless the rats despoiled
The mice of a few shreds of tapestry.
  Iden. Oh ! that I e'er should live to see this day !
The honour of our city 's gone for ever.
  Fritz. Well, but now to discover the delinquent :
The Baron is determined not to lose
This sum without a search.
  Iden.   And so am I.   10
  Fritz. But whom do you suspect ?
  Iden.   Suspect ! all people
Without—within—above—below—Heaven help me !
  Fritz. Is there no other entrance to the chamber ?
  Iden. None whatsoever.
  Fritz.   Are you sure of that ?
  Iden. Certain.   I have lived and served here since my
      birth,
And if there were such, must have heard of such,
Or seen it.
  Fritz.   Then it must be some one who
Had access to the antechamber.
  Iden.   Doubtless.
  Fritz. The man called *Werner 's* poor !
  Iden.   Poor as a miser.[1]
But lodged so far off, in the other wing,   20
By which there 's no communication with
The baron's chamber, that it can't be he.
Besides, I bade him " good night " in the hall,

---

1. ["Your printer has made one odd mistake :—' poor as a *Mouse*'
instead of ' poor as a *Miser.*' The expression may seem strange, but
it is only a translation of 'Semper avarus eget ! '" (Hor., *Epist. I.* ii.
56).—Letter to Murray, May 29, 1822, *Letters*, 1901, vi. 75.]

Almost a mile off, and which only leads
To his own apartment, about the same time
When this burglarious, larcenous felony
Appears to have been committed.
    Fritz.   There 's another,
The stranger——
    Iden.   The Hungarian?
    Fritz.   He who helped
To fish the baron from the Oder.
    Iden.   Not
Unlikely.   But, hold—might it not have been   30
One of the suite?
    Fritz.   How?   *We*, sir !
    Iden.   No—not *you*,
But some of the inferior knaves.   You say
The Baron was asleep in the great chair—
The velvet chair—in his embroidered night-gown ;
His toilet spread before him, and upon it
A cabinet with letters, papers, and
Several rouleaux of gold ; of which *one* only
Has disappeared :—the door unbolted, with
No difficult access to any.
    Fritz.   Good sir,
Be not so quick ; the honour of the corps   40
Which forms the Baron's household 's unimpeached
From steward to scullion, save in the fair way
Of peculation ; such as in accompts,
Weights, measures, larder, cellar, buttery,
Where all men take their prey ; as also in
Postage of letters, gathering of rents,
Purveying feasts, and understanding with
The honest trades who furnish noble masters ;[1]
But for your petty, picking, downright thievery,
We scorn it as we do board wages.   Then   50
Had one of our folks done it, he would not
Have been so poor a spirit as to hazard
His neck for *one* rouleau, but have swooped all ;
Also the cabinet, if portable.
    Iden. There is some sense in that——
    Fritz.   No, Sir, be sure

    1. —— *who furnish our good masters.*—[*MS. M.*]

'Twas none of our corps ; but some petty, trivial
Picker and stealer, without art or genius.
The only question is—Who else could have
Access, save the Hungarian and yourself?
 Iden. You don't mean me ?
 Fritz.   No, sir ; I honour more   60
Your talents——
 Iden.   And my principles, I hope.
 Fritz. Of course. But to the point: What 's to be
   done ?
 Iden. Nothing—but there 's a good deal to be said.
We'll offer a reward ; move heaven and earth,
And the police (though there 's none nearer than
Frankfort) ; post notices in manuscript
(For we've no printer) ; and set by my clerk
To read them (for few can, save he and I).
We'll send out villains to strip beggars, and
Search empty pockets ; also, to arrest   70
All gipsies, and ill-clothed and sallow people.
Prisoners we'll have at least, if not the culprit ;
And for the Baron's gold—if 'tis not found,
At least he shall have the full satisfaction
Of melting twice its substance in the raising
The ghost of this rouleau. Here 's alchemy
For your Lord's losses !
 Fritz.   He hath found a better.
 Iden. Where ?
 Fritz.   In a most immense inheritance.
The late Count Siegendorf, his distant kinsman,
Is dead near Prague, in his castle, and my Lord   80
Is on his way to take possession.
 Iden.   Was there
No heir ?
 Fritz. Oh, yes ; but he has disappeared
Long from the world's eye, and, perhaps, the world.
A prodigal son, beneath his father's ban
For the last twenty years ; for whom his sire
Refused to kill the fatted calf ; and, therefore,
If living, he must chew the husks still. But
The Baron would find means to silence him,
Were he to re-appear : he 's politic,

And has much influence with a certain court.   90
   Iden. He 's fortunate.
   Fritz.   'Tis true, there is a grandson,
Whom the late Count reclaimed from his son's hands,
And educated as his heir ; but, then,
His birth is doubtful.
   Iden.   How so ?
   Fritz.   His sire made
A left-hand, love, imprudent sort of marriage,
With an Italian exile's dark-eyed daughter :
Noble, they say, too ; but no match for such
A house as Siegendorf's.   The grandsire ill
Could brook the alliance ; and could ne'er be brought
To see the parents, though he took the son.   100
   Iden. If he 's a lad of mettle, he may yet
Dispute your claim, and weave a web that may
Puzzle your Baron to unravel.
   Fritz.   Why,
For mettle, he has quite enough : they say,
He forms a happy mixture of his sire
And grandsire's qualities,—impetuous as
The former, and deep as the latter ; but
The strangest is, that he too disappeared
Some months ago.
   Iden.   The devil he did !
   Fritz.   Why, yes :
It must have been at *his* suggestion, at   110
An hour so critical as was the eve
Of the old man's death, whose heart was broken by it.
   Iden. Was there no cause assigned ?
   Fritz.   Plenty, no doubt,
And none, perhaps, the true one.   Some averred
It was to seek his parents ; some because
The old man held his spirit in so strictly
(But that could scarce be, for he doted on him) ;
A third believed he wished to serve in war,
But, peace being made soon after his departure,
He might have since returned, were that the motive ; 120
A fourth set charitably have surmised,
As there was something strange and mystic in him,
That in the wild exuberance of his nature

He had joined the black bands,[1] who lay waste Lusatia,
The mountains of Bohemia and Silesia,
Since the last years of war had dwindled into
A kind of general condottiero system
Of bandit-warfare; each troop with its chief,
And all against mankind.

Iden.　　　　　　That cannot be.
A young heir, bred to wealth and luxury,　　　130
To risk his life and honours with disbanded
Soldiers and desperadoes!

Fritz.　　　　　Heaven best knows!.
But there are human natures so allied
Unto the savage love of enterprise,
That they will seek for peril as a pleasure.
I've heard that nothing can reclaim your Indian,
Or tame the tiger, though their infancy
Were fed on milk and honey.　After all,
Your Wallenstein, your Tilly and Gustavus,
Your Bannier, and your Torstenson and Weimar,[2]　140

1. [The Swedish garrisons did not evacuate Bohemia till 1649, and then, as their occupation was gone, with considerable reluctance. "It need not, therefore, be a matter of wonder that from the discharged soldiers numerous bands of robbers ['*bande nere*,' or 'black bands :' see *Deformed Transformed*, Part II. sc. i. line 65] were formed; that these pursued on their own account the trade that they had formerly carried on under the cover of military law, and that commerce became again unsafe on the highways."—*History of the Thirty Years' War*, by A. Gindely, 1885, ii. 382, 383.]

2. [Albrecht Wenceslaus Eusebius, Count of Waldstein, Duke of Mecklenburg, quartermaster of the Imperial Army in the Thirty Years' War, was born in Bohemia, September 15, 1583, and assassinated at Egra, February 25, 1634.

Johann Tsercläs Count von Tilly, born 1559, defeated the Bohemians at the battle of Prague, November 8, 1620, died April 30, 1632.

Gustavus Adolphus, the "Lion of the North," born December 9, 1594, succeeded his father, Charles IX., King of Sweden, in 1611. As head of the Protestant League, he invaded Germany, defeated the armies of Conti and Schaumburg, June—December, 1630; defeated Tilly at Leipzig and Breitenfeld, September 7, 1631; defeated Wallenstein at Lutzen; but was killed in battle, November 16, 1632.

Johan Bannier, or Baner, Swedish general, born June 23, 1595, defeated the Saxons near Chemnitz, April 4, 1639, died December, 1649.

Lennart Torstenson, Swedish general, born 1603, fought at the battle of Leipzig, and was taken prisoner at Nürnburg. In 1641 he was appointed General-in-Chief of the Swedes in Germany, and died at Stockholm, April, 1651.

Bernhard, Duke of Saxe-Weimar, born 1604, succeeded Gustavus

Were but the same thing upon a grand scale;
And now that they are gone, and peace proclaimed,
They who would follow the same pastime must
Pursue it on their own account.   Here comes
The Baron, and the Saxon stranger, who
Was his chief aid in yesterday's escape,
But did not leave the cottage by the Oder
Until this morning.

Enter STRALENHEIM *and* ULRIC.

   Stral.   Since you have refused
All compensation, gentle stranger, save
Inadequate thanks, you almost check even them,   150
Making me feel the worthlessness of words,
And blush at my own barren gratitude,
They seem so niggardly, compared with what
Your courteous courage did in my behalf——
   Ulr. I pray you press the theme no further.
   Stral.   But
Can I not serve you?   You are young, and of
That mould which throws out heroes; fair in favour;
Brave, I know, by my living now to say so;
And, doubtlessly, with such a form and heart,
Would look into the fiery eyes of War,   160
As ardently for glory as you dared
An obscure death to save an unknown stranger,
In an as perilous, but opposite, element.
You are made for the service: I have served;
Have rank by birth and soldiership, and friends,
Who shall be yours.   'Tis true this pause of peace
Favours such views at present scantily;
But 'twill not last, men's spirits are too stirring;
And, after thirty years of conflict, peace
Is but a petty war, as the time shows us   170
In every forest, or a mere armed truce.
War will reclaim his own; and, in the meantime,
You might obtain a post, which would ensure

Adolphus in command in Germany, November 16, 1632; defeated the
Imperialists at Rheinfeld, 1638; died at Huningen, 1639.
   Banier and Torstenson were living when the Peace of Westphalia
was proclaimed, November 3, 1648.]

A higher soon, and, by my influence, fail not
To rise.   I speak of Brandenburgh, wherein
I stand well with the Elector;[1] in Bohemia,
Like you, I am a stranger, and we are now
Upon its frontier.
    Ulr.   You perceive my garb
Is Saxon, and, of course, my service due
To my own Sovereign.   If I must decline   180
Your offer, 'tis with the same feeling which
Induced it.
    Stral.   Why, this is mere usury!
I owe my life to you, and you refuse
The acquittance of the interest of the debt,
To heap more obligations on me, till
I bow beneath them.
    Ulr.   You shall say so when
I claim the payment.
    Stral.   Well, sir, since you will not—
You are nobly born?
    Ulr.   I have heard my kinsmen say so.
    Stral. Your actions show it.   Might I ask your name?
    Ulr. Ulric.
    Stral.   Your house's?
    Ulr.   When I'm worthy of it, 190
I'll answer you.
    Stral. (*aside*). Most probably an Austrian,
Whom these unsettled times forbid to boast
His lineage on these wild and dangerous frontiers,
Where the name of his country is abhorred.
               [*Aloud to* FRITZ *and* IDENSTEIN.
So, sirs! how have ye sped in your researches?
    Iden. Indifferent well, your Excellency.
    Stral.   Then
I am to deem the plunderer is caught?
    Iden. Humph!—not exactly.
    Stral.   Or, at least, suspected?
    Iden. Oh! for that matter, very much suspected.
    Stral. Who may he be?

---

   1. [George William, Elector of Brandenburgh (1595–1640), was in
alliance with Gustavus Adolphus; John George, Elector of Saxony
(1585–1656) (*vide supra*, line 179), was on the side of the Imperialists.]

Iden.   Why, don't *you* know, my Lord? 200
Stral. How should I? I was fast asleep.
Iden.   And so
Was I—and that 's the cause I know no more
Than does your Excellency.
   Stral.   Dolt !
   Iden.   Why, if
Your Lordship, being robbed, don't recognise
The rogue; how should I, not being robbed, identify
The thief among so many? In the crowd,
May it please your Excellency, your thief looks
Exactly like the rest, or rather better :
'Tis only at the bar and in the dungeon,
That wise men know your felon by his features;   210
But I'll engage, that if seen there but once,
Whether he be found criminal or no,
His face shall be so.
   Stral. (*to* FRITZ).   Prithee, Fritz, inform me
What hath been done to trace the fellow?
   Fritz.   Faith !
My Lord, not much as yet, except conjecture.
   Stral. Besides the loss (which, I must own, affects me
Just now materially), I needs would find
The villain out of public motives; for
So dexterous a spoiler, who could creep
Through my attendants, and so many peopled   220
And lighted chambers, on my rest, and snatch
The gold before my scarce-closed eyes, would soon
Leave bare your borough, Sir Intendant !
   Iden.   True;
If there were aught to carry off, my Lord.
   Ulr. What is all this?
   Stral.   You joined us but this morning,
And have not heard that I was robbed last night.
   Ulr. Some rumour of it reached me as I passed
The outer chambers of the palace, but
I know no further.
   Stral.   It is a strange business :
The Intendant can inform you of the facts.   230
   Iden. Most willingly. You see——-
   Stral. (*impatiently*).   Defer your tale,

Till certain of the hearer's patience.
    Iden.   That
Can only be approved by proofs.   You see——
    Stral. (again interrupting him, and addressing ULRIC).
In short, I was asleep upon my chair,
My cabinet before me, with some gold
Upon it (more than I much like to lose,
Though in part only) : some ingenious person
Contrived to glide through all my own attendants,
Besides those of the place, and bore away
A hundred golden ducats, which to find   **240**
I would be fain, and there 's an end. Perhaps
You (as I still am rather faint) would add
To yesterday's great obligation, this,
Though slighter, yet not slight, to aid these men
(Who seem but lukewarm) in recovering it?
    Ulr. Most willingly, and without loss of time—
(*To* IDENSTEIN.) Come hither, mynheer !
    Iden.   But so much haste bodes
Right little speed, and——
    Ulr.   Standing motionless
None; so let's march : we'll talk as we go on.
    Iden. But——
    Ulr.   Show the spot, and then I'll answer you. **250**
    Fritz. I will, sir, with his Excellency's leave.
    Stral. Do so, and take yon old ass with you.
    Fritz.   Hence !
    Ulr. Come on, old oracle, expound thy riddle !
             [*Exit with* IDENSTEIN *and* FRITZ.
    Stral. (solus). A   stalwart, active, soldier-looking
       stripling,
Handsome as Hercules ere his first labour,
And with a brow of thought beyond his years
When in repose, till his eye kindles up
In answering yours. I wish I could engage him :
I have need of some such spirits near me now,
For this inheritance is worth a struggle.   **260**
And though I am not the man to yield without one,
Neither are they who now rise up between me
And my desire. The boy, they say, 's a bold one ;
But he hath played the truant in some hour

Of freakish folly, leaving fortune to
Champion his claims.   That's well.   The father, whom
For years I've tracked, as does the blood-hound, never
In sight, but constantly in scent, had put me
To fault; but *here* I *have* him, and that's better.
It must be *he!*   All circumstance proclaims it;   270
And careless voices, knowing not the cause
Of my enquiries, still confirm it.—Yes!
The man, his bearing, and the mystery
Of his arrival, and the time; the account, too,
The Intendant gave (for I have not beheld her)
Of his wife's dignified but foreign aspect;
Besides the antipathy with which we met,
As snakes and lions shrink back from each other
By secret instinct that both must be foes
Deadly, without being natural prey to either;   280
All—all—confirm it to my mind.   However,
We'll grapple, ne'ertheless.   In a few hours
The order comes from Frankfort, if these waters
Rise not the higher (and the weather favours
Their quick abatement), and I'll have him safe
Within a dungeon, where he may avouch
His real estate and name; and there's no harm done,
Should he prove other than I deem.   This robbery
(Save for the actual loss) is lucky also;
He's poor, and that's suspicious—he's unknown,   290
And that's defenceless.—True, we have no proofs
Of guilt—but what hath he of innocence?
Were he a man indifferent to my prospects,
In other bearings, I should rather lay
The inculpation on the Hungarian, who
Hath something which I like not; and alone
Of all around, except the Intendant, and
The Prince's household and my own, had ingress
Familiar to the chamber.

Enter GABOR.

                              Friend, how fare you?
  Gab. As those who fare well everywhere, when they
Have supped and slumbered, no great matter how— 301

And you, my Lord?
   Stral.   Better in rest than purse :
Mine inn is like to cost me dear.
   Gab.   I heard
Of your late loss ; but 'tis a trifle to
One of your order.
   Stral.   You would hardly think so,
Were the loss yours.
   Gab.   I never had so much
(At once) in my whole life, and therefore am not
Fit to decide. But I came here to seek you.
Your couriers are turned back—I have outstripped them,
In my return.
   Stral.   You !—Why?
   Gab.   I went at daybreak, 310
To watch for the abatement of the river,
As being anxious to resume my journey.
Your messengers were all checked like myself ;
And, seeing the case hopeless, I await
The current's pleasure.
   Stral.   Would the dogs were in it !
Why did they not, at least, attempt the passage?
I ordered this at all risks.
   Gab.   Could you order
The Oder to divide, as Moses did
The Red Sea (scarcely redder than the flood
Of the swoln stream), and be obeyed, perhaps 320
They might have ventured.
   Stral.   I must see to it :
The knaves ! the slaves !—but they shall smart for this.
                      [*Exit* STRALENHEIM.
   Gab. (*solus*). There goes my noble, feudal, self-willed
        Baron !
Epitome of what brave chivalry
The preux Chevaliers of the good old times
Have left us. Yesterday he would have given
His lands [1] (if he hath any), and, still dearer,

---

   1. [Compare *The Antiquary*, by Sir W. Scott, i. 366, chap. vii. **ed.**
1851 : " ' Good man,' said Sir Arthur, ' can you think of nothing?—of
no help?—I'll make you rich—I'll give you a farm—I'll——' ' Our
riches will soon be equal,' said the beggar, looking upon the strife of

His sixteen quarterings, for as much fresh air
As would have filled a bladder, while he lay
Gurgling and foaming half way through the window   330
Of his o'erset and water-logged conveyance ;
And now he storms at half a dozen wretches
Because they love their lives too !   Yet, he 's right :
'Tis strange they should, when such as he may put them
To hazard at his pleasure.   Oh, thou world !
Thou art indeed a melancholy jest !   [*Exit* GABOR.

SCENE II.—*The Apartment of* WERNER, *in the Palace.*

Enter JOSEPHINE *and* ULRIC.

Jos. Stand back, and let me look on thee again !
My Ulric !—my belovéd !—can it be—
After twelve years?
    Ulr.   My dearest mother !
    Jos.   Yes!
My dream is realised—how beautiful !—
How more than all I sighed for !   Heaven receive
A mother's thanks ! a mother's tears of joy !
This is indeed thy work !—At such an hour, too,
He comes not only as a son, but saviour.
    Ulr. If such a joy await me, it must double
What I now feel, and lighten from my heart   10
A part of the long debt of duty, not
Of love (for that was ne'er withheld)—forgive me !
This long delay was not my fault.
    Jos.   I know it,
But cannot think of sorrow now, and doubt
If I e'er felt it, 'tis so dazzled from
My memory by this oblivious transport !—
My son !

the waters, ' They are sae already ; for I hae nae land, and you would
give your fair bounds and barony for a square yard of rock that would
be dry for twal hours.' "—*The Antiquary* was published in 1816, six
years before the second version of *Werner* was written, and ten years
after the death of the Duchess of Devonshire.]

Enter WERNER.

Wer.　　What have we here,—more strangers?—
Jos.　　　　　　　　　　　　　　　　　　No!
Look upon him!　What do you see?
　Wer.　　　　　　　　　　　A stripling,
For the first time—
　Ulr. (*kneeling*).　For twelve long years, my father!
Wer. Oh, God!
Jos.　　　　　　He faints!
Wer.　　　　　　　　No—I am better now—　**20**
Ulric! (*Embraces him.*)
　Ulr. My father, Siegendorf!
　Wer. (*starting*).　　　　Hush! boy—
The walls may hear that name!
　Ulr.　　　　　　　What then?
　Wer.　　　　　　　　　　Why, then—
But we will talk of that anon.　Remember,
I must be known here but as Werner.　Come!
Come to my arms again!　Why, thou look'st all
I should have been, and was not.　Josephine!
Sure 'tis no father's fondness dazzles me;
But, had I seen that form amid ten thousand
Youth of the choicest, my heart would have chosen
This for my son!
　Ulr.　　　　　And yet you knew me not!　　**30**
　Wer. Alas! I have had that upon my soul
Which makes me look on all men with an eye
That only knows the evil at first glance.
　Ulr. My memory served me far more fondly: I
Have not forgotten aught; and oft-times in
The proud and princely halls of—(I'll not name them,
As you say that 'tis perilous)—but i' the pomp
Of your sire's feudal mansion, I looked back
To the Bohemian mountains many a sunset,
And wept to see another day go down　　**40**
O'er thee and me, with those huge hills between us.
They shall not part us more.
　Wer.　　　　　　　I know not that.
Are you aware my father is no more?
　Ulr. Oh, Heavens! I left him in a green old age,

And looking like the oak, worn, but still steady
Amidst the elements, whilst younger trees
Fell fast around him.   'Twas scarce three months since.
   Wer. Why did you leave him?
   Jos. (embracing ULRIC).   Can you ask that question?
Is he not *here?*
   Wer.   True; he hath sought his parents,
And found them; but, oh! *how*, and in what state! 50
   Ulr. All shall be bettered.   What we have to do
Is to proceed, and to assert our rights,
Or rather yours; for I waive all, unless
Your father has disposed in such a sort
Of his broad lands as to make mine the foremost,
So that I must prefer my claim for form:
But I trust better, and that all is yours.
   Wer. Have you not heard of Stralenheim?
   Ulr.   I saved
His life but yesterday: he's here.
   Wer.   You saved
The serpent who will sting us all!
   Ulr.   You speak   60
Riddles: what is this Stralenheim to us?
   Wer. Every thing.   One who claims our father's lands:
Our distant kinsman, and our nearest foe.
   Ulr. I never heard his name till now.   The Count,
Indeed, spoke sometimes of a kinsman, who,
If his own line should fail, might be remotely
Involved in the succession; but his titles
Were never named before me—and what then?
His right must yield to ours.
   Wer.   Aye, if at Prague:
But here he is all-powerful; and has spread   70
Snares for thy father, which, if hitherto
He hath escaped them, is by fortune, not
By favour.
   Ulr.   Doth he personally know you?
   Wer. No; but he guesses shrewdly at my person,
As he betrayed last night; and I, perhaps,
But owe my temporary liberty
To his uncertainty.
   Ulr.   I think you wrong him

(Excuse me for the phrase); but Stralenheim
Is not what you prejudge him, or, if so,
He owes me something both for past and present.   80
I saved his life, he therefore trusts in me.
He hath been plundered too, since he came hither:
Is sick, a stranger, and as such not now
Able to trace the villain who hath robbed him:
I have pledged myself to do so; and the business
Which brought me here was chiefly that:[1] but I
Have found, in searching for another's dross,
My own whole treasure—you, my parents!
   Wer. (*agitatedly*).   Who
Taught you to mouth that name of "villain?"
   Ulr.   What
More noble name belongs to common thieves?   90
   Wer. Who taught you thus to brand an unknown being
With an infernal stigma?
   Ulr.   My own feelings
Taught me to name a ruffian from his deeds.
   Wer. Who taught you, long-sought and ill-found boy!
      that
It would be safe for my own son to insult me?
   Ulr. I named a villain. What is there in common
With such a being and my father?
   Wer.   Every thing !
That ruffian is thy father![2]
   Jos.   Oh, my son !
Believe him not—and yet !—— (*her voice falters.*)

---

   1. [The following is the original passage in the novel :—"' 'Stralenheim,' said Conrad, 'does not appear to me altogether the man you
take him for :—but were it even otherwise, he owes me gratitude not
only for the past, but for what he supposes to be my present employment. I saved his life, and he therefore places confidence in me. He
has been robbed last night—is sick—a stranger—and in no condition
to discover the villain who has plundered him . . . . and the business
on which I sought the Intendant was chiefly that.' "—*Canterbury Tales,*
by Sophia and Harriet Lee, 1838, ii. 203, 204.]

   2. ["' 'And who,' said he, 'has entitled you to brand thus with
ignominious epithets a being you do not know? Who . . . has taught
you that it would be safe even for my son to insult me?'—'It is not
necessary to know the person of a ruffian,' replied Conrad, indignantly,
'to give him the appellation he merits :—and what is there in common
between my father and such a character?'—'*Everything,*' said Siegendorf, bitterly,—'for that ruffian was your father!' "—*Ibid.,* p. 204.]

Ulr. (*starts, looks earnestly at* WERNER *and then*
  says slowly).   And you avow it?
Wer. Ulric, before you dare despise your father,   100
Learn to divine and judge his actions.   Young,
Rash, new to life, and reared in Luxury's lap,
Is it for you to measure Passion's force,
Or Misery's temptation?   Wait—(not long,
It cometh like the night, and quickly)—Wait!—
Wait till, like me, your hopes are blighted [1] till
Sorrow and Shame are handmaids of your cabin—
Famine and Poverty your guests at table;
Despair your bed-fellow—then rise, but not
From sleep, and judge! Should that day e'er arrive—   110
Should you see then the Serpent, who hath coiled
Himself around all that is dear and noble
Of you and yours, lie slumbering in your path,
With but *his* folds between your steps and happiness,
When *he*, who lives but to tear from you name,
Lands, life itself, lies at your mercy, with
Chance your conductor—midnight for your mantle—
The bare knife in your hand, and earth asleep,
Even to your deadliest foe; and he as 'twere
Inviting death, by looking like it, while   120
His death alone can save you:—Thank your God!
If then, like me, content with petty plunder,
You turn aside——I did so.
    Ulr.   But——
    Wer. (*abruptly*).   Hear me!
I will not brook a human voice—scarce dare
Listen to my own (if that be human still)—

1. ["'Conrad . . . before you thus presume to chastise me with your
eye, learn to understand my actions! Young, and inexperienced in the
world—reposing hitherto in the bosom of indulgence and luxury, is it
for *you* to judge of the impulse of the passions, or the temptations of
misery? Wait till, like me, you have blighted your fairest hopes—
have endured humiliation and sorrow—poverty and insult—before you
pretend to judge of their effect on you! Should that miserable day
ever arrive—should *you* see the being at your mercy who stands between you and everything that is dear or noble in life!—who is ready to
tear from you your name—your inheritance—your very life itself—con-
gratulate your own heart, if, like me, you are content with petty
plunder, and are not tempted to exterminate a serpent, who now lives,
perhaps to sting us all.'"—*Canterbury Tales*, by Sophia and Harriet
Lee, 1838, ii. 204, 205.]

Hear me! you do not know this man—I do.[1]
He 's mean, deceitful, avaricious.   You
Deem yourself safe, as young and brave; but learn
None are secure from desperation, few
From subtilty.   My worst foe, Stralenheim,   130
Housed in a Prince's palace, couched within
A Prince's chamber, lay below my knife!
An instant—a mere motion—the least impulse—
Had swept him and all fears of mine from earth.
He was within my power—my knife was raised—
Withdrawn—and I'm in his:—are you not so?
Who tells you that he knows you *not?*   Who says
He hath not lured you here to end you? or
To plunge you, with your parents, in a dungeon?

                                        [*He pauses.*

  Ulr. Proceed—proceed!
  Wer.   *Me* he hath ever known, 140
And hunted through each change of time—name—
                fortune—
And why not *you?*   Are you more versed in men?
He wound snares round me; flung along my path
Reptiles, whom, in my youth, I would have spurned
Even from my presence; but, in spurning now,
Fill only with fresh venom.   Will you be
More patient?   Ulric!—Ulric!—there are crimes
Made venial by the occasion, and temptations
Which nature cannot master or forbear.[2]

  1. ["' You do not know this man,' continued he; ' I do!—I believe
him to be mean—sordid—deceitful!   You will conceive yourself safe,
because you are young and brave!   Learn, however, . . . none are so
secure but desperation or subtilty may reach them!   Stralenheim, in
the palace of a prince, was in my power!   My knife was held over him
—a single moment would have swept him from the face of the earth,
and with him all my future fears:—I forbore—and I am now in his.—
Are you certain that you are not so too?   Who assures you he does
not know you?—who tells you that he has not lured you into his
society, either to rid himself of you for ever, or to plunge you with
your family into a dungeon?"—*Canterbury Tales*, by Sophia and
Harriet Lee, 1838, ii. 205.   It should be noted that this and other
passages from Miss Lee's story, which have been selected for comparison with the text, are to be regarded as representative parallels—
samples of a far more extended adaptation.   *Vide ante,* "The Introduction to *Werner,*" p. 326.]
  2. [" '*Me* . . . he has known invariably through every change of fortune
or of name—and why not you?—*Me* he has entrapped—are you more

Ulr. (*who looks first at him and then at* JOSEPHINE).
   My mother !
Wer.   Ah ! I thought so : you have now 150
Only one parent. I have lost alike
Father and son, and stand alone.
   Ulr.   But stay !
            [WERNER *rushes out of the chamber.*
   Jos. (*to* ULRIC). Follow him not, until this storm of
       passion
Abates. Think'st thou, that were it well for him,
I had not followed ?
   Ulr.   I obey you, mother,
Although reluctantly. My first act shall not
Be one of disobedience.
   Jos.   Oh ! he is good !
Condemn him not from his own mouth, but trust
To me, who have borne so much with him, and for him,
That this is but the surface of his soul,   160
And that the depth is rich in better things.
   Ulr. These then are but my father's principles ? [1]
My mother thinks not with him ?
   Jos.   Nor doth he
Think as he speaks. Alas ! long years of grief
Have made him sometimes thus.
   Ulr.   Explain to me
More clearly, then, these claims of Stralenheim,
That, when I see the subject in its bearings,
I may prepare to face him, or at least
To extricate you from your present perils.
I pledge myself to accomplish this—but would   170
I had arrived a few hours sooner !
   Jos.   Aye !
Hadst thou but done so !

---

discreet ? He has wound the snares of Idenstein around me :—of a
reptile, whom, a few years ago, I would have spurned from my presence,
and whom, in spurning now, I have furnished with fresh venom :—will
you be more patient?—Conrad, Conrad, there are crimes rendered
venial by the occasion, and temptations too exquisite for human forti-
. tude to master or endure.' "—*Canterbury Tales*, by Sophia and Harriet
Lee, 1838, ii. 205.]
   1. [" ' These are only the systems of my father . . My mother thinks
not with him ? ' "—*Ibid.*, p. 206.]

Enter GABOR *and* IDENSTEIN, *with Attendants.*

Gab. (*to* ULRIC).   I have sought you, comrade.
So this is my reward!
    Ulr.   What do you mean?
    Gab. 'Sdeath! have I lived to these years, and for
        this!
(*To* IDENSTEIN.)   But for your age and folly, I
    would——
    Iden.   Help!
Hands off! Touch an Intendant!
    Gab.   Do not think
I'll honour you so much as save your throat
From the Ravenstone [1] by choking you myself.
    Iden. I thank you for the respite: but there are
Those who have greater need of it than me.   180
    Ulr. Unriddle this vile wrangling, or——
    Gab.   At once, then,
The Baron has been robbed, and upon me
This worthy personage has deigned to fix
His kind suspicions—me! whom he ne'er saw
Till yester evening.
    Iden.   Wouldst have me suspect
My own acquaintances? You have to learn
That I keep better company.
    Gab.   You shall
Keep the best shortly, and the last for all men,
The worms! You hound of malice!
                         [GABOR *seizes on him.*
    Ulr. (*interfering*).   Nay, no violence:
He's old, unarmed—be temperate, Gabor!
    Gab. (*letting go* IDENSTEIN).   True: 190
I am a fool to lose myself because
Fools deem me knave: it is their homage.
    Ulr. (*to* IDENSTEIN).   How
Fare you?
    Iden. Help!
    Ulr.   I *have* helped you.

---

1. The Ravenstone, "Rabenstein," is the *stone gibbet* of Germany,
and so called from the ravens perching on it. [Compare *Manfred*,
act iii., First Version, *Poetical Works*, 1901, iv. 122.]

Iden.   Kill him ! then
I'll say so.
 Gab. I am calm—live on !
 Iden.   That 's more
Than you shall do, if there be judge or judgment
In Germany. The Baron shall decide !
 Gab. Does *he* abet you in your accusation ?
 Iden. Does he not ?
 Gab.   Then next time let him go sink
Ere I go hang for snatching him from drowning.
But here he comes !

Enter STRALENHEIM.

 Gab. (*goes up to him*). My noble Lord, I'm here ! 200
 Stral. Well, sir !
 Gab.   Have you aught with me ?
 Stral.   What should I
Have with you ?
 Gab.   You know best, if yesterday's
Flood has not washed away your memory ;
But that 's a trifle. I stand here accused,
In phrases not equivocal, by yon
Intendant, of the pillage of your person
Or chamber :—is the charge your own or his ?
 Stral. I accuse no man.
 Gab.   Then you acquit me, Baron ?
 Stral. I know not whom to accuse, or to acquit,
Or scarcely to suspect.
 Gab.   But you at least 210
Should know whom *not* to suspect. I am insulted—
Oppressed here by these menials, and I look
To you for remedy—teach them their duty !
To look for thieves at home were part of it,
If duly taught ; but, in one word, if I
Have an accuser, let it be a man
Worthy to be so of a man like me.
I am your equal.
 Stral. You !
 Gab.   Aye, sir ; and, for
Aught that you know, superior ; but proceed—

I do not ask for hints, and surmises,   220
And circumstance, and proof: I know enough
Of what I have done for you, and what you owe me,
'To have at least waited your payment rather
Than paid myself, had I been eager of
Your gold.   I also know, that were I even
The villain I am deemed, the service rendered
So recently would not permit you to
Pursue me to the death, except through shame,
Such as would leave your scutcheon but a blank.
But this is nothing: I demand of you   230
Justice upon your unjust servants, and
From your own lips a disavowal of
All sanction of their insolence: thus much
You owe to the unknown, who asks no more,
And never thought to have asked so much.
　　Stral.   This tone
May be of innocence.
　　Gab.   'Sdeath ! who dare doubt it,
Except such villains as ne'er had it ?
　　Stral.   You
Are hot, sir.
　　Gab.   Must I turn an icicle
Before the breath of menials, and their master ?[i.]
　　Stral. Ulric ! you know this man ; I found him in
Your company.   241
　　Gab.   We found *you* in the Oder ;
Would we had left you there !
　　Stral.   I give you thanks, sir.
　　Gab. I've earned them ; but might have earned more
　　　　from others,
Perchance, if I had left you to your fate.
　　Stral. Ulric ! you know this man ?
　　Gab.   No more than you do
If he avouches not my honour.
　　Ulr.   I
Can vouch your courage, and, as far as my
Own brief connection led me, honour.
　　Stral.   Then
I'm satisfied.

　　　　　　　i. —— *and a master.*—[*MS   M.*]

Gab. (*ironically*). Right easily, methinks.
What is the spell in his asseveration   250
More than in mine?
   Stral.   I merely said that *I*
Was satisfied—not that you are absolved.
   Gab. Again! Am I accused or no?
   Stral.   Go to!
You wax too insolent. If circumstance
And general suspicion be against you,
Is the fault mine? Is't not enough that I
Decline all question of your guilt or innocence?
   Gab. My Lord, my Lord, this is mere cozenage,[1]
A vile equivocation; you well know
Your doubts are certainties to all around you—   260
Your looks a voice—your frowns a sentence; you
Are practising your power on me—because
You have it; but beware! you know not whom
You strive to tread on.
   Stral.   Threat'st thou?
   Gab.   Not so much
As you accuse. You hint the basest injury,
And I retort it with an open warning.
   Stral. As you have said, 'tis true I owe you something,
For which you seem disposed to pay yourself.
   Gab. Not with your gold.
   Stral.   With bootless insolence.
       [*To his Attendants and* IDENSTEIN.
You need not further to molest this man,   270
But let him go his way. Ulric, good morrow!
      [*Exit* STRALENHEIM, IDENSTEIN, *and Attendants.*
   Gab. (*following*). I'll after him and——
   Ulr. (*stopping him*).   Not a step.
   Gab.   Who shall
Oppose me?
   Ulr.   Your own reason, with a moment's
Thought.

    1. [Compare—
                "Cozenage, mere cozenage."
            Merry Wives of Windsor, act iv. sc. 5, line 58.

    If further proof were needed, the repetition or echo of Shakespearian
phrases, here and elsewhere in the play, would reveal Byron's handiwork.]

Gab.   Must I bear this?
Ulr.   Pshaw! we all must bear
The arrogance of something higher than
Ourselves—the highest cannot temper Satan,
Nor the lowest his vicegerents upon earth.
I've seen you brave the elements, and bear
Things which had made this silkworm [1] cast his skin—
And shrink you from a few sharp sneers and words? 280
  Gab. Must I bear to be deemed a thief? If 'twere
A bandit of the woods, I could have borne it—
There 's something daring in it :—but to steal
The moneys of a slumbering man !—
  Ulr.   It seems, then,
You are *not* guilty.
  Gab.   Do I hear aright?
You too !
  Ulr.   I merely asked a simple question.
  Gab. If the judge asked me, I would answer " No "—
To you I answer *thus.*   [*He draws.*
  Ulr. (drawing).   With all my heart !
  Jos. Without there ! Ho! help! help!—Oh, God !
      here 's murder !   [*Exit* JOSEPHINE, *shrieking.*

GABOR *and* ULRIC *fight.* GABOR *is disarmed just as*
  STRALENHEIM, JOSEPHINE, IDENSTEIN, *etc., re-enter.*

  Jos. Oh! glorious Heaven ! He 's safe !
  Stral. (to JOSEPHINE).   *Who* 's safe !
  Jos.   My——
  *Ulr. (interrupting her with a stern look, and turning
      afterwards to* STRALENHEIM).   Both ! 290
Here 's no great harm done.
  Stral.   What hath caused all this?
  Ulr. You, Baron, I believe ; but as the effect
Is harmless, let it not disturb you.—Gabor !
There is your sword ; and when you bare it next,

---

  1. [Compare *Marino Faliero*, act ii. sc. 2, line 115—

              " These swoln silkworms masters."

Silkworm ("mal bigatto") is an Italianism. See *Poetical Works*, 1901,
iv. 386, *note* 4.]

Let it not be against your *friends*.
    [ULRIC *pronounces the last words slowly and emphati-
        cally in a low voice to* GABOR.
   Gab.   I thank you
Less for my life than for your counsel.
   Stral.   These
Brawls must end here.
   Gab. (*taking his sword*). They *shall*. You've wronged
     me, Ulric,
More with your unkind thoughts than sword : I would
The last were in my bosom rather than
The first in yours. I could have borne yon noble's 300
Absurd insinuations—ignorance
And dull suspicion are a part of his
Entail will last him longer than his lands—
But I may fit *him* yet :—you have vanquished me.
I was the fool of passion to conceive
That I could cope with you, whom I had seen
Already proved by greater perils than
Rest in this arm. We may meet by and by,
However—but in friendship.   [*Exit* GABOR.
   Stral.   I will brook
No more ! This outrage following upon his insults, 310
Perhaps his guilt, has cancelled all the little
I owed him heretofore for the so-vaunted
Aid which he added to your abler succour.
Ulric, you are not hurt ?—
   Ulr.   Not even by a scratch.
   Stral. (*to* IDENSTEIN). Intendant ! take your measures
     to secure
Yon fellow : I revoke my former lenity.
He shall be sent to Frankfort with an escort,
The instant that the waters have abated.
   Iden. Secure him ! He hath got his sword again—
And seems to know the use on't ; 'tis his trade, 320
Belike ;—*I'm* a civilian.
   Stral.   Fool ! are not
Yon score of vassals dogging at your heels
Enough to seize a dozen such ? Hence ! after him !
   Ulr. Baron, I do beseech you !
   Stral.   I must be

Obeyed.   No words !

Iden.   Well, if it must be so—
March, vassals ! I'm your leader, and will bring
The rear up : a wise general never should
Expose his precious life—on which all rests.
I like that article of war.

                        [*Exit* IDENSTEIN *and Attendants.*

Stral.   Come hither,
Ulric ; what does that woman here ? Oh ! now   330
I recognise her, 'tis the stranger's wife
Whom they *name* " Werner."

Ulr.   'Tis his name.

Stral.   Indeed !
Is not your husband visible, fair dame ?—

Jos. Who seeks him ?

Stral.   No one—for the present : but
I fain would parley, Ulric, with yourself
Alone.

Ulr.   I will retire with you.

Jos.   Not so :
You are the latest stranger, and command
All places here.
(*Aside to* ULRIC, *as she goes out.*) O Ulric ! have a care—
Remember what depends on a rash word !

Ulr. (*to* JOSEPHINE).   Fear not !—

                        [*Exit* JOSEPHINE.

Stral. Ulric, I think that I may trust you ;   340
You saved my life—and acts like these beget
Unbounded confidence.

Ulr.   Say on.

Stral.   Mysterious
And long-engendered circumstances (not
To be now fully entered on) have made
This man obnoxious—perhaps fatal to me.

Ulr. Who ? Gabor, the Hungarian ?

Stral.   No—this " Werner "—
With the false name and habit.

Ulr.   How can this be ?
He is the poorest of the poor—and yellow
Sickness sits caverned in his hollow eye : [i.]

    i.   —— *and hollow*
    Sickness sits caverned in his yellow eye.—[*MS. M.*]

The man is helpless.
    Stral.   He is—'tis no matter;—   350
But if he be the man I deem (and that
He is so, all around us here—and much
That is not here—confirm my apprehension)
He must be made secure ere twelve hours further.
    Ulr. And what have I to do with this?
    Stral.   I have sent
To Frankfort, to the Governor, my friend,
(I have the authority to do so by
An order of the house of Brandenburgh),
For a fit escort—but this curséd flood
Bars all access, and may do for some hours.   360
    Ulr. It is abating.
    Stral.   That is well.
    Ulr.   But how
Am I concerned?
    Stral.   As one who did so much
For me, you cannot be indifferent to
That which is of more import to me than
The life you rescued.—Keep your eye on *him!*
The man avoids me, knows that I now know him.—
Watch him!—as you would watch the wild boar when
He makes against you in the hunter's gap—
Like him he must be speared.
    Ulr.   Why so?
    Stral.   He stands
Between me and a brave inheritance!   370
Oh! could you see it! But you shall.
    Ulr.   I hope so.
    Stral. It is the richest of the rich Bohemia,
Unscathed by scorching war. It lies so near
The strongest city, Prague, that fire and sword
Have skimmed it lightly: so that now, besides
Its own exuberance, it bears double value
Confronted with whole realms far and near
Made deserts.
    Ulr.   You describe it faithfully.
    Stral. Aye—could you see it, you would say so—but,
As I have said, you shall.
    Ulr.   I accept the omen.   380

Stral. Then claim a recompense from it and me,
Such as *both* may make worthy your acceptance
And services to me and mine for ever.
    Ulr. And this sole, sick, and miserable wretch—
This way-worn stranger—stands between you and
This Paradise?—(As Adam did between
The devil and his)—[*Aside*].
    Stral.   He doth.
    Ulr.   Hath he no right?
    Stral. Right! none. A disinherited prodigal,
Who for these twenty years disgraced his lineage
In all his acts—but chiefly by his marriage,   390
And living amidst commerce-fetching burghers,
And dabbling merchants, in a mart of Jews.
    Ulr. He has a wife, then?
    Stral.   You'd be sorry to
Call such your mother. You have seen the woman
He *calls* his wife.
    Ulr.   Is she not so?
    Stral.   No more
Than he 's your father:—an Italian girl,
The daughter of a banished man, who lives
On love and poverty with this same Werner.
    Ulr. They are childless, then?
    Stral.   There is or was a bastard,
Whom the old man—the grandsire (as old age   400
Is ever doting) took to warm his bosom,
As it went chilly downward to the grave:
But the imp stands not in my path—he has fled,
No one knows whither; and if he had not,
His claims alone were too contemptible
To stand.—Why do you smile?
    Ulr.   At your vain fears:
A poor man almost in his grasp—a child
Of doubtful birth—can startle a grandee!
    Stral. All 's to be feared, where all is to be gained.
    Ulr. True; and aught done to save or to obtain it.
    Stral. You have harped the very string next to my
        heart.[1]   411

---

1.   [" Thou hast harped my fear aright."
                     Macbeth, act iv. sc. 1, line 74.]

I may depend upon you?

 Ulr.   'Twere too late
To doubt it.

 Stral.   Let no foolish pity shake
Your bosom (for the appearance of the man
Is pitiful)—he is a wretch, as likely
To have robbed me as the fellow more suspected,
Except that circumstance is less against him;
He being lodged far off, and in a chamber
Without approach to mine; and, to say truth,
I think too well of blood allied to mine,   420
To deem he would descend to such an act:
Besides, he was a soldier, and a brave one
Once—though too rash.

 Ulr.   And they, my Lord, we know
By our experience, never plunder till
They knock the brains out first—which makes them
   heirs,
Not thieves. The dead, who feel nought, can lose
   nothing,
Nor e'er be robbed: their spoils are a bequest—
No more.

 Stral. Go to! you are a wag. But say
I may be sure you'll keep an eye on this man,
And let me know his slightest movement towards 430
Concealment or escape.

 Ulr.   You may be sure
You yourself could not watch him more than I
Will be his sentinel.

 Stral.   By this you make me
Yours, and for ever.

 Ulr.   Such is my intention. [*Exeunt.*

ACT III.

SCENE I.—*A Hall in the same Palace, from whence the secret Passage leads.*

Enter WERNER *and* GABOR.

Gab. Sir, I have told my tale : if it so please you
To give me refuge for a few hours, well—
If not, I'll try my fortune elsewhere.
    Wer.   How
Can I, so wretched, give to Misery
A shelter?—wanting such myself as much
As e'er the hunted deer a covert——
    Gab.   Or
The wounded lion his cool cave.   Methinks
You rather look like one would turn at bay,
And rip the hunter's entrails.
    Wer.   Ah !
    Gab.   I care not
If it be so, being much disposed to do   10
The same myself.   But will you shelter me ?
I am oppressed like you—and poor like you—
Disgraced——
    Wer. (*abruptly*). Who told you that I was disgraced ?
    Gab. No one ; nor did I say *you* were so : with
Your poverty my likeness ended ; but
I said *I* was so—and would add, with truth,
As undeservedly as *you.*
    Wer.   Again !
As *I*?
    Gab. Or any other honest man.
What the devil would you have ?   You don't believe me
Guilty of this base theft ?
    Wer.   No, no—I cannot.   20
    Gab. Why that 's my heart of honour ! yon young gallant—
Your miserly Intendant and dense noble—
All—all suspected me ; and why ? because
I am the worst clothed, and least named amongst them ;

Although, were Momus'[1] lattice in your breasts,
My soul might brook to open it more widely
Than theirs: but thus it is—you poor and helpless—
Both still more than myself.

    Wer.　　　　　　　How know you that?

    Gab. You're right: I ask for shelter at the hand
Which I call helpless; if you now deny it,　　　　30
I were well paid.　But you, who seem to have proved
The wholesome bitterness of life, know well,
By sympathy, that all the outspread gold
Of the New World the Spaniard boasts about
Could never tempt the man who knows its worth,
Weighed at its proper value in the balance,
Save in such guise (and there I grant its power,
Because I feel it,) as may leave no nightmare
Upon his heart o' nights.

    Wer.　　　　　　　What do you mean?

    Gab. Just what I say; I thought my speech was
        plain:　　　　　　　　　　　　40
You are no thief—nor I—and, as true men,
Should aid each other.

    Wer.　　　　　　It is a damned world, sir.

    Gab. So is the nearest of the two next, as
The priests say (and no doubt they should know best),
Therefore I'll stick by this—as being loth
To suffer martyrdom, at least with such
An epitaph as larceny upon my tomb.
It is but a night's lodging which I crave;
To-morrow I will try the waters, as
The dove did—trusting that they have abated.　　50

    Wer. Abated?　Is there hope of that?

    Gab.　　　　　　　　　　There was

At noontide.

    Wer.　　　Then we may be safe.

    Gab.　　　　　　　　　　Are *you*

---

1. ["Momus is the god of cruel mockery.　He is said to have found fault with the man formed by Hephæstus, because a little door had not been left in his breast, so as to enable his fellows to look into his secret thoughts." (See Lucian's *Hermotimus*, cap. xx.)　There was a proverb, Τῷ Μώμῳ ἀρέσκειν, *Momo satisfacere; vide Adagia* Variorum, 1643, p. 58.　Byron describes Suwarrow as "Now Mars, now Momus" (*Don Juan*, Canto VII. stanza lv. line 7).]

In peril?

Wer.   Poverty is ever so.

Gab. That I know by long practice.   Will you not
Promise to make mine less?

Wer.   Your poverty?

Gab. No—you don't look a leech for that disorder;
I meant my peril only: you've a roof,
And I have none; I merely seek a covert.

Wer. Rightly; for how should such a wretch as I
Have gold?

Gab.   Scarce honestly, to say the truth on't,   60
Although I almost wish you had the Baron's.

Wer. Dare you insinuate?

Gab.   What?

Wer.   Are you aware
To whom you speak?

Gab.   No; and I am not used
Greatly to care.   (*A noise heard without.*)   But hark!
     they come!

Wer.   Who come?

Gab. The Intendant and his man-hounds after me:
I'd face them—but it were in vain to expect
Justice at hands like theirs.   Where shall I go?
But show me any place.   I do assure you,
If there be faith in man, I am most guiltless:
Think if it were your own case!

Wer. (*aside*).   Oh, just God!   70
Thy hell is not hereafter!   Am I dust still?

Gab. I see you're moved; and it shows well in you:
I may live to requite it.

Wer.   Are you not
A spy of Stralenheim's?

Gab.   Not I! and if
I were, what is there to espy in you?
Although, I recollect, his frequent question
About you and your spouse might lead to some
Suspicion; but you best know—what—and why.
I am his deadliest foe.

Wer.   You?

Gab.   After such
A treatment for the service which in part   80

I rendered him, I am his enemy:
If you are not his friend you will assist me.

   Wer. I will.

   Gab.   But how?

   Wer. (*showing the panel*).   There is a secret spring:
Remember, I discovered it by chance,
And used it but for safety.

   Gab.   Open it,
And I will use it for the same.

   Wer.   I found it,
As I have said: it leads through winding walls,
(So thick as to bear paths within their ribs,
Yet lose no jot of strength or stateliness,)
And hollow cells, and obscure niches, to   90
I know not whither; you must not advance:
Give me your word.

   Gab.   It is unnecessary:
How should I make my way in darkness through
A Gothic labyrinth of unknown windings?

   Wer. Yes, but who knows to what place it may lead?
I know not—(mark you!)—but who knows it might
     not
Lead even into the chamber of your foe?
So strangely were contrived these galleries
By our Teutonic fathers in old days,
When man built less against the elements   100
Than his next neighbour. You must not advance
Beyond the two first windings; if you do
(Albeit I never passed them,) I'll not answer
For what you may be led to.

   Gab.   But I will.
A thousand thanks!

   Wer.   You'll find the spring more obvious
On the other side; and, when you would return,
It yields to the least touch.

   Gab.   I'll in—farewell!
              [GABOR *goes in by the secret panel.*

   Wer. (*solus*). What have I done? Alas! what *had*
     I done
Before to make this fearful? Let it be
Still some atonement that I save the man,   110

Whose sacrifice had saved perhaps my own—
They come! to seek elsewhere what is before them!

Enter IDENSTEIN *and Others.*

Iden. Is he not here?   He must have vanished then
Through the dim Gothic glass by pious aid
Of pictured saints upon the red and yellow
Casements, through which the sunset streams like sunrise
On long pearl-coloured beards and crimson crosses.
And gilded crosiers, and crossed arms, and cowls,
And helms, and twisted armour, and long swords,
All the fantastic furniture of windows   120
Dim with brave knights and holy hermits, whose
Likeness and fame alike rest in some panes
Of crystal, which each rattling wind proclaims
As frail as any other life or glory.
He 's gone, however.
 Wer.   Whom do you seek?
 Iden.   A villain.
 Wer. Why need you come so far, then?
 Iden.   In the search
Of him who robbed the Baron.
 Wer.   Are you sure
You have divined the man?
 Iden.   As sure as you
Stand there: but where 's he gone?
 Wer.   Who?
 Iden.   He we sought.
 Wer. You see he is not here.
 Iden.   And yet we traced him   130
Up to this hall.   Are you accomplices?
Or deal you in the black art?
 Wer.   I deal plainly,
To many men the blackest.
 Iden.   It may be
I have a question or two for yourself
Hereafter; but we must continue now
Our search for t'other.
 Wer.   You had best begin
Your inquisition now: I may not be

So patient always.
    Iden.   I should like to know,
In good sooth, if you really are the man
That Stralenheim 's in quest of.
    Wer.   Insolent!   140
Said you not that he was not here?
    Iden.   Yes, *one;*
But there 's another whom he tracks more keenly,
And soon, it may be, with authority
Both paramount to his and mine.   But come!
Bustle, my boys! we are at fault.
                [Exit IDENSTEIN *and Attendants.*
    Wer.   In what
A maze hath my dim destiny involved me!
And one base sin hath done me less ill than
The leaving undone one far greater.   Down,
Thou busy devil, rising in my heart!
Thou art too late! I'll nought to do with blood.   150

Enter ULRIC.

    Ulr. I sought you, father.
    Wer.   Is't not dangerous?
    Ulr. No ; Stralenheim is ignorant of all
Or any of the ties between us : more—
He sends me here a spy upon your actions,
Deeming me wholly his.
    Wer.   I cannot think it :
'Tis but a snare he winds about us both,
To swoop the sire and son at once.
    Ulr.   I cannot
Pause in each petty fear, and stumble at
The doubts that rise like briers in our path,
But must break through them, as an unarmed carle   160
Would, though with naked limbs, were the wolf rustling
In the same thicket where he hewed for bread.
Nets are for thrushes, eagles are not caught so :
We'll overfly or rend them.
    Wer.   Show me *how?*
    Ulr. Can you not guess?
    Wer.   I cannot.

Ulr.　　　　　　　　　　That is strange.
Came the thought ne'er into your mind *last night?*
　Wer. I understand you not.
　Ulr.　　　　　　　　Then we shall never
More understand each other.　But to change
The topic——
　Wer.　　　　You mean to *pursue* it, as
'Tis of our safety.
　Ulr.　　　　　Right; I stand corrected.　　170
I see the subject now more clearly, and
Our general situation in its bearings.
The waters are abating; a few hours
Will bring his summoned myrmidons from Frankfort,
When you will be a prisoner, perhaps worse,
And I an outcast, bastardised by practice
Of this same Baron to make way for him.
　Wer. And now your remedy!　I thought to escape
By means of this accursèd gold; but now
I dare not use it, show it, scarce look on it.　　180
Methinks it wears upon its face my guilt
For motto, not the mintage of the state;
And, for the sovereign's head, my own begirt
With hissing snakes, which curl around my temples,
And cry to all beholders, Lo! a villain!
　Ulr. You must not use it, at least now; but take
This ring.　　　　　　[*He gives* WERNER *a jewel.*
　Wer.　　A gem!　It was my father's!
　Ulr.　　　　　　　　　　And
As such is now your own.　With this you must
Bribe the Intendant for his old caleche
And horses to pursue your route at sunrise,　　190
Together with my mother.
　Wer.　　　　　And leave you,
So lately found, in peril too?
　Ulr.　　　　　　　Fear nothing!
The only fear were if we fled together,
For that would make our ties beyond all doubt.
The waters only lie in flood between
This burgh and Frankfort; so far 's in our favour.
The route on to Bohemia, though encumbered,
Is not impassable; and when you gain

A few hours' start, the difficulties will be
The same to your pursuers.   Once beyond   200
The frontier, and you're safe.
  Wer.   My noble boy!
  Ulr. Hush! hush! no transports: we'll indulge in them
In Castle Siegendorf!   Display no gold:
Show Idenstein the gem (I know the man,
And have looked through him): it will answer thus
A double purpose.   Stralenheim lost *gold*—
No jewel: therefore it could *not* be his;
And then the man who was possest of this
Can hardly be suspected of abstracting
The Baron's coin, when he could thus convert   210
This ring to more than Stralenheim has lost
By his last night's slumber.   Be not over timid
In your address, nor yet too arrogant,
And Idenstein will serve you.
  Wer.   I will follow
In all things your direction.
  Ulr.   I would have
Spared you the trouble; but had I appeared
To take an interest in you, and still more
By dabbling with a jewel in your favour,
All had been known at once.
  Wer.   My guardian angel!
This overpays the past.   But how wilt thou   220
Fare in our absence?
  Ulr.   Stralenheim knows nothing
Of me as aught of kindred with yourself.
I will but wait a day or two with him
To lull all doubts, and then rejoin my father.
  Wer. To part no more! .
  Ulr.   I know not that; but at
The least we'll meet again once more.
  Wer.   My boy!
My friend! my only child, and sole preserver!
Oh, do not hate me!
  Ulr.   Hate my father!
  Wer.   Aye,
My father hated me.   Why not my son?
  Ulr. Your father knew you not as I do.

Wer.   Scorpions **230**
Are in thy words! Thou know me? in this guise
Thou canst not know me, I am not myself;
Yet (hate me not) I will be soon.
      Ulr.   I'll *wait!*
In the mean time be sure that all a son
Can do for parents shall be done for mine.
      Wer. I see it, and I feel it; yet I feel
Further—that you despise me.
      Ulr.   Wherefore should I?
      Wer. Must I repeat my humiliation?
      Ulr.   No!
I have fathomed it and you.   But let us talk
Of this no more.   Or, if it must be ever,   **240**
Not *now.*   Your error has redoubled all
The present difficulties of our house
At secret war with that of Stralenheim:
All we have now to think of is to baffle
HIM.   I have shown *one* way.
      Wer.   The only one,
And I embrace it, as I did my son,
Who showed *himself* and father's *safety* in
One day.
      Ulr.   You *shall* be safe; let that suffice.
Would Stralenheim's appearance in Bohemia
Disturb your right, or mine, if once we were   **250**
Admitted to our lands?
      Wer.   Assuredly,
Situate as we are now; although the first
Possessor might, as usual, prove the strongest—
Especially the next in blood.
      Ulr.   *Blood!* 'tis
A word of many meanings; in the veins,
And out of them, it is a different thing—
And so it should be, when the same in blood
(As it is called) are aliens to each other,
Like Theban brethren:[1] when a part is bad,
A few spilt ounces purify the rest.   **260**

1. [For the "Theban brethren," Eteocles and Polynices, see the
Septem c. Thebas of Æschylus.   Byron had read and liked the "Seven
before Thebes."—*Letters*, 1900, iv. 174.]

Wer. I do not apprehend you.
　Ulr.　　　　　　　　　　That may be—
And should, perhaps—and yet—but get ye ready;
You and my mother must away to-night.
Here comes the Intendant: sound him with the gem;
'Twill sink into his venal soul like lead
Into the deep, and bring up slime and mud,
And ooze, too, from the bottom, as the lead doth
With its greased understratum;[1] but no less
Will serve to warn our vessels through these shoals.
The freight is rich, so heave the line in time!　　　270
Farewell! I scarce have time, but yet your *hand*,
My father!——
　　Wer.　　　　　Let me embrace thee!
　　Ulr.　　　　　　　　　　We may be
Observed: subdue your nature to the hour!
Keep off from me as from your foe!
　　Wer.　　　　　　　　　Accursed
Be he who is the stifling cause which smothers
The best and sweetest feeling of our hearts;
At such an hour too!
　　Ulr.　　　　　　Yes, curse—it will ease you!
Here is the Intendant.

Enter IDENSTEIN.

　　　　　　　　Master Idenstein,
How fare you in your purpose?　Have you caught
The rogue?
　　Iden.　　　No, faith!
　　Ulr.　　　　　　　Well, there are plenty more:　280
You may have better luck another chase.
Where is the Baron?
　　Iden.　　　　　Gone back to his chamber:
And now I think on't, asking after you
With nobly-born impatience.
　　Ulr.　　　　　　　　Your great men

---

　1. [A cavity at the lower end of the lead attached to a sounding-line
is partially filled with an *arming* (tallow), to which the bottom,
especially if it be sand, shells, or fine gravel, adheres.—Knights's
American Mechanical Dictionary, 1877, art. "Sounding-Apparatus."]

Must be answered on the instant, as the bound
Of the stung steed replies unto the spur :
'Tis well they have horses, too ; for if they had not,
I fear that men must draw their chariots, as
They say kings did Sesostris.[1]

   Iden.   Who was he ?

   Ulr. An old Bohemian—an imperial gipsy.   290

   Iden. A gipsy or Bohemian, 'tis the same,
For they pass by both names.   And was he one ?

   Ulr. I've heard so ; but I must take leave.   Intendant,
Your servant !—Werner (*to* WERNER *slightly*), if that be
      your name,
Yours.   [*Exit* ULRIC.

   Iden. A well-spoken, pretty-faced young man !
And prettily behaved !   He knows his station,
You see, sir : how he gave to each his due
Precedence !

   Wer.   I perceived it, and applaud
His just discernment and your own.

   Iden.   That 's well—
That 's very well.   You also know your place, too ; 300
And yet I don't know that *I* know your place.

   Wer. (*showing the ring*).   Would this assist your
      knowledge ?

   Iden.   How !—What !—Eh !
A jewel !

   Wer.   'Tis your own on one condition.

   Iden. Mine !—Name it !

   Wer.   That hereafter you permit me
At thrice its value to redeem it : 'tis
A family ring.

   Iden.   A family !—*yours !*—a gem !
I'm breathless !

   Wer.   You must also furnish me,
An hour ere daybreak, with all means to quit
This place.

   Iden.   But is it real ?   Let me look on **it** :
Diamond, by all that 's glorious !

---

   1. [Compare *The Age of Bronze*, line 45, for the story of Sesostris
being drawn by kings. (See Diodorus Siculus, *Bibl. Hist.*, lib. i.
p. 37, C., ed. 1604, p. 53.)]

Wer.   Come, I'll trust you : 310
You have guessed, no doubt, that I was born above
My present seeming.
    Iden.   I can't say I did,
Though this looks like it : this is the true breeding
Of gentle blood !
    Wer.   I have important reasons
For wishing to continue privily
My journey hence.
    Iden.   So then *you are* the man
Whom Stralenheim 's in quest of ?
    Wer.   I am not ;
But being taken for him might conduct
So much embarrassment to me just now,
And to the Baron's self hereafter—'tis   320
To spare both that I would avoid all bustle.
    Iden. Be you the man or no, 'tis not my business ;
Besides, I never could obtain the half
From this proud, niggardly noble, who would raise
The country for some missing bits of coin,
And never offer a precise reward— [l.]
But *this !*—another look !
    Wer.   Gaze on it freely ;
At day-dawn it is yours.
    Iden.   Oh, thou sweet sparkler !
Thou more than stone of the philosopher !
Thou touch-stone of Philosophy herself !   330
Thou bright eye of the Mine ! thou loadstar of
The soul ! the true magnetic Pole to which
All hearts point duly north, like trembling needles !
Thou flaming Spirit of the Earth ! which, sitting
High on the Monarch's Diadem, attractest
More worship than the majesty who sweats
Beneath the crown which makes his head ache, like
Millions of hearts which bleed to lend it lustre !
Shalt thou be mine ? I am, methinks, already
A little king, a lucky alchymist !—   340
A wise magician, who has bound the devil
Without the forfeit of his soul. But come,
Werner, or what else ?

    l. *And never offered aught as a reward.*—[*MS. M. erased.*]

Wer.   Call me Werner still;
You may yet know me by a loftier title.
    Iden. I do believe in thee! thou art the spirit
Of whom I long have dreamed in a low garb.—
But come, I'll serve thee; thou shalt be as free
As air, despite the waters; let us hence:
I'll show thee I am honest—(oh, thou jewel!)
Thou shalt be furnished, Werner, with such means   350
Of flight, that if thou wert a snail, not birds [i.]
Should overtake thee.—Let me gaze again!
I have a foster-brother in the mart
Of Hamburgh skilled in precious stones. How many
Carats may it weigh?—Come, Werner, I will wing thee.
                                        [*Exeunt.*

Scene II.—Stralenheim's *Chamber.*

Stralenheim *and* Fritz.

Fritz. All 's ready, my good Lord!
    Stral.   I am not sleepy,
And yet I must to bed: I fain would say
To rest, but something heavy on my spirit,
Too dull for wakefulness, too quick for slumber,
Sits on me as a cloud along the sky,
Which will not let the sunbeams through, nor yet
Descend in rain and end, but spreads itself
'Twixt earth and heaven, like envy between man
And man, an everlasting mist:—I will
Unto my pillow.
    Fritz.   May you rest there well   10
    Stral. I feel, and fear, I shall.
    Fritz.   And wherefore fear?
    Stral. I know not why, and therefore do fear more,
Because an undescribable——but 'tis
All folly. Were the locks as I desired
Changed, to-day, of this chamber? for last night's
Adventure makes it needful.
    Fritz.   Certainly,
According to your order, and beneath

---

i. —— *that if thou wert a snail, none else.—[MS. M.]*

The inspection of myself and the young Saxon
Who saved your life.   I think they call him " Ulric."
    Stral. You *think !* you supercilious slave ! what right
Have you to *tax your* memory, which should be   21
Quick, proud, and happy to retain the *name*
Of him who saved your master, as a litany
Whose daily repetition marks your duty.—
Get hence ; "*You think,*" indeed ! you, who stood still
Howling and dripping on the bank, whilst I
Lay dying, and the stranger dashed aside
The roaring torrent, and restored me to
Thank him—and despise you. " *You think !* " and scarce
Can recollect his name !   I will not waste   30
More words on you.   Call me betimes.
    Fritz.   Good night !
I trust to-morrow will restore your Lordship
To renovated strength and temper.   [*The scene closes.*

SCENE III.—*The secret Passage.*

    Gab. (*solus*).   Four—
Five—six hours have I counted, like the guard
Of outposts, on the never-merry clock,
That hollow tongue [1] of time, which, even when
It sounds for joy, takes something from enjoyment
With every clang.   'Tis a perpetual knell,
Though for a marriage-feast it rings : each stroke
Peals for a hope the less ; the funeral note
Of Love deep-buried, without resurrection,
In the grave of Possession ; while the knoll [2]   10
Of long-lived parents finds a jovial echo
To triple time in the son's ear.
                                I'm cold—
I'm dark ;—I've blown my fingers—numbered o'er
And o'er my steps—and knocked my head against
Some fifty buttresses—and roused the rats

----

1. [Compare—
                " The iron tongue of midnight."
                Midsummer Night's Dream, act v. sc. 1, line 352.]

  2. [Compare *Childe Harold*, Canto III. stanza xcvi. line 5, *Poetical
Works*, 1899, ii. 275, *note* 1.]

And bats in general insurrection, till
Their curséd pattering feet and whirling wings
Leave me scarce hearing for another sound.
A light! It is at distance (if I can
Measure in darkness distance) : but it blinks   20
As through a crevice or a key-hole, in
The inhibited direction : I must on,
Nevertheless, from curiosity.
A distant lamp-light is an incident
In such a den as this.   Pray Heaven it lead me
To nothing that may tempt me! Else—Heaven aid me
To obtain or to escape it!   Shining still!
Were it the star of Lucifer himself,
Or he himself girt with its beams, I could
Contain no longer.   Softly : mighty well!   30
That corner 's turned—so—ah! no ;—right! it draws
Nearer.   Here is a darksome angle—so,
That 's weathered.—Let me pause.—Suppose it leads
Into some greater danger than that which
I have escaped—no matter, 'tis a new one ;
And novel perils, like fresh mistresses,
Wear more magnetic aspects :—I will on,
And be it where it may—I have my dagger
Which may protect me at a pinch.—Burn still,
Thou little light!   Thou art my *ignis fatuus !*   40
My stationary Will-o'-the-wisp!¹—So! so!
He hears my invocation, and fails not.   [*The scene closes.*

SCENE IV.—*A Garden.*

Enter WERNER.

Wer. I could not sleep—and now the hour 's at hand!
All 's ready.   Idenstein has kept his word ;
And stationed in the outskirts of the town,
Upon the forest's edge, the vehicle
Awaits us.   Now the dwindling stars begin
To pale in heaven ; and for the last time I

1. [Compare—
    " With your leave, I will call a will-o'-the-wisp."
                                        Goethe's *Faust.*]

Look on these horrible walls.   Oh! never, never
Shall I forget them.   Here I came most poor,
But not dishonoured : and I leave them with
A stain,—if not upon my name, yet in   10
My heart!—a never-dying canker-worm,
Which all the coming splendour of the lands,
And rights, and sovereignty of Siegendorf
Can scarcely lull a moment.   I must find
Some means of restitution, which would ease
My soul in part: but how, without discovery?—
It must be done, however; and I'll pause
Upon the method the first hour of safety.
The madness of my misery led to this
Base infamy; repentance must retrieve it :   20
I will have nought of Stralenheim's upon
My spirit, though he would grasp all of mine;
Lands, freedom, life,—and yet he sleeps as soundly
Perhaps, as infancy,[1] with gorgeous curtains
Spread for his canopy, o'er silken pillows,
Such as when——Hark! what noise is that?   Again!
The branches shake; and some loose stones have fallen
From yonder terrace.
                              [ULRIC *leaps down from the terrace.*
                              Ulric! ever welcome!
Thrice welcome now! this filial——
     Ulr.   Stop! before
We approach, tell me——
     Wer.   Why look you so?
     Ulr.   Do I   30
Behold my father, or——
     Wer.   What?
     Ulr.   An assassin?
     Wer. Insane or insolent!
     Ulr.   Reply, sir, as
You prize your life, or mine!
     Wer.   To what must I
Answer?
     Ulr.   Are you or are you not the assassin

1. [Compare—
          " Sleep she as sound as careless infancy."
                    Merry Wives of Windsor, act v. sc. 5, line 50.]

Of Stralenheim?

Wer.   I never was as yet
The murderer of any man.   What mean you?

Ulr.   Did not you *this* night (as the night before)
Retrace the secret passage?   Did you not
Again revisit Stralenheim's chamber?   and——

                    [ULRIC *pauses.*

Wer.   Proceed.

Ulr.   *Died* he not by your hand?

Wer.   Great God!   40

Ulr.   You are innocent, then!   my father's innocent!
Embrace me!   Yes,—your tone—your look—yes, yes,—
Yet *say* so.

Wer.   If I e'er, in heart or mind,
Conceived deliberately such a thought,
But rather strove to trample back to hell
Such thoughts—if e'er they glared a moment through
The irritation of my oppressed spirit—
May Heaven be shut for ever from my hopes,
As from mine eyes!

Ulr.   But Stralenheim is dead.

Wer.   'Tis horrible!   'tis hideous, as 'tis hateful!—   50
But what have I to do with this?

Ulr.   No bolt
Is forced; no violence can be detected,
Save on his body.   Part of his own household
Have been alarmed; but as the Intendant is
Absent, I took upon myself the care
Of mustering the police.   His chamber has,
Past doubt, been entered secretly.   Excuse me,
If nature——

Wer.   Oh, my boy!   what unknown woes
Of dark fatality, like clouds, are gathering
Above our house!

Ulr.   My father!   I acquit you!   60
But will the world do so?   will even the judge,
If——but you must away this instant.

Wer.   No!
I'll face it.   Who shall dare suspect me?

Ulr.   Yet
You had *no* guests—*no* visitors—no life

Breathing around you, save my mother's?
 Wer.   Ah!
The Hungarian?
 Ulr.   He is gone! he disappeared
Ere sunset.
 Wer.   No; I hid him in that very
Concealed and fatal gallery.
 Ulr.   *There* I'll find him.
           [ULRIC *is going.*
 Wer. It is too late: he had left the palace ere
I quitted it. I found the secret panel   70
Open, and the doors which lead from that hall
Which masks it: I but thought he had snatched the silent
And favourable moment to escape
The myrmidons of Idenstein, who were
Dogging him yester-even.
 Ulr.   You reclosed
The panel?
 Wer.   Yes; and not without reproach
(And inner trembling for the avoided peril)
At his dull heedlessness, in leaving thus
His shelterer's asylum to the risk
Of a discovery.
 Ulr.   You are sure you closed it? 80
 Wer. Certain.
 Ulr.   That's well; but had been better, if
You ne'er had turned it to a den for—— [*He pauses.*
 Wer.   Thieves!
Thou wouldst say: I must bear it, and deserve it;
But not——
 Ulr.   No, father; do not speak of this:
This is no hour to think of petty crimes,
But to prevent the consequence of great ones.
Why would you shelter this man?
 Wer.   Could I shun it?
A man pursued by my chief foe; disgraced
For my own crime: a victim to *my* safety,
Imploring a few hours' concealment from   90
The very wretch who was the cause he needed
Such refuge. Had he been a wolf, I could not
Have in such circumstances thrust him forth.

Ulr. And like the wolf he hath repaid you.   But
It is too late to ponder thus :—you must
Set out ere dawn.   I will remain here to
Trace the murderer, if 'tis possible.
    Wer. But this my sudden flight will give the Moloch
Suspicion : two new victims in the lieu
Of one, if I remain.   The fled Hungarian,   100
Who seems the culprit, and——
    Ulr.   Who *seems?*   *Who* else
Can be so?
    Wer.   Not *I*, though just now you doubted—
You, my *son !*—doubted——
    Ulr.   And do you doubt of him
The fugitive?
    Wer.   Boy ! since I fell into
The abyss of crime (though not of *such* crime), I,
Having seen the innocent oppressed for me,
May doubt even of the guilty's guilt.   Your heart
Is free, and quick with virtuous wrath to accuse
Appearances ; and views a criminal
In Innocence's shadow, it may be,   110
Because 'tis dusky.
    Ulr.   And if I do so,
What will mankind, who know you not, or knew
But to oppress?   You must not stand the hazard.
Away !—I'll make all easy.   Idenstein
Will for his own sake and his jewel's hold
His peace—he also is a partner in
Your flight—moreover——
    Wer.   Fly ! and leave my name
Linked with the Hungarian's, or, preferred as poorest,
To bear the brand of bloodshed?
    Ulr.   Pshaw ! leave any thing
Except our fathers' sovereignty and castles,   120
For which you have so long panted, and in vain !
What *name?*   You have *no name*, since that you bear
Is feigned.
    Wer.   Most true : but still I would not have it
Engraved in crimson in men's memories,
Though in this most obscure abode of men——
Besides, the search——

Ulr.   I will provide against
Aught that can touch you.   No one knows you here
As heir of Siegendorf: if Idenstein
Suspects, 'tis *but suspicion*, and he is
A fool: his folly shall have such employment,   130
Too, that the unknown Werner shall give way
To nearer thoughts of self.   The laws (if e'er
Laws reached this village) are all in abeyance
With the late general war of thirty years,
Or crushed, or rising slowly from the dust,
To which the march of armies trampled them.
Stralenheim, although noble, is unheeded
Here, save as *such*—without lands, influence,
Save what hath perished with him.   Few prolong
A week beyond their funeral rites their sway   140
O'er men, unless by relatives, whose interest
Is roused : such is not here the case; he died
Alone, unknown,—a solitary grave,
Obscure as his deserts, without a scutcheon,
Is all he'll have, or wants.   If *I* discover
The assassin, 'twill be well—if not, believe me,
None else ; though all the full-fed train of menials
May howl above his ashes (as they did
Around him in his danger on the Oder),
Will no more stir a finger *now* than *then*.   150
Hence ! hence ! I must not hear your answer.—Look !
The stars are almost faded, and the grey
Begins to grizzle the black hair of night.
You shall not answer :—Pardon me that I
Am peremptory : 'tis your son that speaks,
Your long-lost, late-found son.—Let 's call my mother !
Softly and swiftly step, and leave the rest
To me : I'll answer for the event as far
As regards *you*, and that is the chief point,
As my first duty, which shall be observed.   160
We'll meet in Castle Siegendorf—once more
Our banners shall be glorious !   Think of that
Alone, and leave all other thoughts to me,
Whose youth may better battle with them—Hence !
And may your age be happy !—I will kiss
My mother once more, then Heaven's speed be with you !

Wer. This counsel 's safe—but is it honourable?
Ulr. To save a father is a child's chief honour.

[*Exeunt.*

ACT IV.

SCENE I.—*A Gothic Hall in the Castle of Siegendorf,
near Prague.*

Enter ERIC *and* HENRICK, *Retainers of the Count.*

Eric. So, better times are come at last; to these
Old walls new masters and high wassail—both
A long desideratum.
Hen.   Yes, for *masters,*
It might be unto those who long for novelty,
Though made by a new grave: but, as for wassail,
Methinks the old Count Siegendorf maintained
His feudal hospitality as high
As e'er another Prince of the empire.
Eric.   Why
For the mere cup and trencher, we no doubt
Fared passing well; but as for merriment   10
And sport, without which salt and sauces season
The cheer but scantily, our sizings were
Even of the narrowest.
Hen.   The old count loved not
The roar of revel; are you sure that *this* does?
Eric. As yet he hath been courteous as he 's bounteous,
And we all love him.
Hen.   His reign is as yet
Hardly a year o'erpast its honeymoon,
And the first year of sovereigns is bridal:
Anon, we shall perceive his real sway
And moods of mind.
Eric.   Pray Heaven he keep the present!   20
Then his brave son, Count Ulric—there 's a knight!
Pity the wars are o'er!
Hen.   Why so?
Eric.   Look on him!

And answer that yourself.
 Hen.   He 's very youthful,
And strong and beautiful as a young tiger.
 Eric. That 's not a faithful vassal's likeness.
 Hen.   But
Perhaps a true one.
 Eric.   Pity, as I said,
The wars are over : in the hall, who like
Count Ulric for a well-supported pride,
Which awes, but yet offends not ? in the field,
Who like him with his spear in hand, when gnashing 30
His tusks, and ripping up, from right to left,
The howling hounds, the boar makes for the thicket ?
Who backs a horse, or bears a hawk, or wears
A sword like him ? Whose plume nods knightlier ?
 Hen. No one's, I grant you. Do not fear, if war
Be long in coming, he is of that kind
Will make it for himself, if he hath not
Already done as much.
 Eric.   What do you mean ?
 Hen. You can't deny his train of followers
(But few our native fellow-vassals born   40
On the domain) are such a sort of knaves
As——   [*Pauses.*
 Eric. What ?
 Hen.   The war (you love so much) leaves living.
Like other parents, she spoils her worst children.
 Eric. Nonsense ! they are all brave iron-visaged
    fellows,
Such as old Tilly loved.
 Hen.   And who loved Tilly ?
Ask that at Magdebourg [1]—or, for that matter,
Wallenstein either ;—they are gone to——
 Eric.   Rest !
But what beyond 'tis not ours to pronounce.

---

1. [At the siege of Magdeburg, May 19, 1631, "soldiers and citizens,
with their wives, boys and girls, old and young, were all mercilessly
butchered." "The city was set fire to at more than twelve points, and,
except the cathedral and about fifty houses, sank into soot and ashes.
It was not Tilly and his men, but Magdeburg's own people, who
kindled the city to a conflagration."—*History of the Thirty Years' War,*
by Anton Gindeley, 1885, ii. 65, 66.]

Hen. I wish they had left us something of their rest :
The country (nominally now at peace)　　　　　　50
Is over-run with—God knows who : they fly
By night, and disappear with sunrise ; but
Leave us no less desolation, nay, even more,
Than the most open warfare.
　　　Eric.　　　　　　　　　But Count Ulric—
What has all this to do with him?
　　　Hen.　　　　　　　　　With him !
He——might prevent it.　As you say he 's fond
Of war, why makes he it not on those marauders?
　　　Eric. You'd better ask himself.
　　　Hen.　　　　　　　　　I would as soon
Ask the lion why he laps not milk.
　　　Eric. And here he comes !
　　　Hen.　　　　The devil ! you'll hold your tongue? 60
　　　Eric. Why do you turn so pale?
　　　Hen.　　　　　　　　　'Tis nothing—but
Be silent.
　　　Eric.　　I will, upon what you have said.
　　　Hen. I assure you I meant nothing,—a mere sport
Of words, no more ; besides, had it been otherwise,
He is to espouse the gentle Baroness
Ida of Stralenheim, the late Baron's heiress ;
And she, no doubt, will soften whatsoever
Of fierceness the late long intestine wars
Have given all natures, and most unto those
Who were born in them, and bred up upon　　　　　70
The knees of Homicide ; sprinkled, as it were,
With blood even at their baptism.　Prithee, peace
On all that I have said !

　　　　　Enter ULRIC *and* RODOLPH.

　　　　　　　　Good morrow, count.
　　　Ulr. Good morrow, worthy Henrick.　Eric, is
All ready for the chase?
　　　Eric.　　　　　　The dogs are ordered
Down to the forest, and the vassals out
To beat the bushes, and the day looks promising.
Shall I call forth your Excellency's suite?

What courser will you please to mount?
   Ulr.   The dun,
Walstein.
   Eric. I fear he scarcely has recovered   80
The toils of Monday : 'twas a noble chase :
You speared *four* with your own hand.
   Ulr.   True, good Eric ;
I had forgotten—let it be the grey, then,
Old Ziska : he has not been out this fortnight.
   Eric. He shall be straight caparisoned. How many
Of your immediate retainers shall
Escort you?
   Ulr.   I leave that to Weilburgh, our
Master of the horse.   [*Exit* ERIC.
               Rodolph !
   Rod.   My Lord !
   Ulr.   The news
Is awkward from the—— [RODOLPH *points to* HENRICK.
               How now, Henrick? why
Loiter you here?
   Hen.   For your commands, my Lord.   90
   Ulr. Go to my father, and present my duty,
And learn if he would aught with me before
I mount.   [*Exit* HENRICK.
        Rodolph, our friends have had a check
Upon the frontiers of Franconia,[1] and
'Tis rumoured that the column sent against them
Is to be strengthened. I must join them soon.
   Rod. Best wait for further and more sure advices.
   Ulr. I mean it—and indeed it could not well
Have fallen out at a time more opposite
To all my plans.
   Rod.   It will be·difficult   100
To excuse your absence to the Count your father.
   Ulr. Yes, but the unsettled state of our domain
In high Silesia will permit and cover
My journey. In the mean time, when we are
Engaged in the chase, draw off the eighty men
Whom Wolffe leads—keep the forests on your route :

---

   1. [In Miss Lee's *Kruitzner*, Conrad meets his death in a skirmish
on the frontiers of Franconia.]

You know it well?
   Rod.   As well as on that night
When we——
   Ulr.   We will not speak of that until
We can repeat the same with like success:
And when you have joined, give Rosenberg this letter. 110
                         [*Gives a letter.*
Add further, that I have sent this slight addition
To our force with you and Wolffe, as herald of
My coming, though I could but spare them ill
At this time, as my father loves to keep
Full numbers of retainers round the castle,
Until this marriage, and its feasts and fooleries,
Are rung out with its peal of nuptial nonsense.
   Rod. I thought you loved the lady Ida?
   Ulr.   Why,
I do so—but it follows not from that
I would bind in my youth and glorious years,   120
So brief and burning, with a lady's zone,
Although 'twere that of Venus :—but I love her,
As woman should be loved—fairly and solely.
   Rod. And constantly?
   Ulr.   I think so; for I love
Nought else.—But I have not the time to pause
Upon these gewgaws of the heart.   Great things
We have to do ere long.   Speed! speed! good Rodolph!
   Rod. On my return, however, I shall find
The Baroness Ida lost in Countess Siegendorf?
   Ulr. Perhaps: my father wishes it, and, sooth,   130
'Tis no bad policy: this union with
The last bud of the rival branch at once
Unites the future and destroys the past.
   Rod. Adieu.
   Ulr.   Yet hold—we had better keep together
Until the chase begins; then draw thou off,
And do as I have said.
   Rod.   I will.   But to
Return—'twas a most kind act in the count
Your father to send up to Konigsberg
For this fair orphan of the Baron, and
To hail her as his daughter.

Ulr.   Wondrous kind !   140
Especially as little kindness till
Then grew between them.
  Rod.   The late Baron died
Of a fever, did he not?
    Ulr.   How should I know?
    Rod. I have heard it whispered there was something
            strange
About his death—and even the place of it
Is scarcely known.
    Ulr.   Some obscure village on
The Saxon or Silesian frontier.
    Rod.   He
Has left no testament—no farewell words?
    Ulr. I am neither confessor nor notary,
So cannot say.
    Rod.   Ah ! here 's the lady Ida.   150

Enter IDA STRALENHEIM.

Ulr. You are early, my sweet cousin !
    Ida.   Not *too* early,
Dear Ulric, if I do not interrupt you.
Why do you call me " *Cousin* ? "
    Ulr. (smiling).   Are we not so ?
    Ida. Yes, but I do not like the name ; methinks
It sounds so cold, as if you thought upon
Our pedigree, and only weighed our blood.
    Ulr. (starting).   Blood !
    Ida. Why does yours start from your cheeks?
    Ulr.   Aye ! doth it ?
    Ida. It doth—but no ! it rushes like a torrent
Even to your brow again.
    Ulr. (recovering himself). And if it fled,
It only was because your presence sent it   160
Back to my heart, which beats for you, sweet Cousin !
    Ida. " Cousin " again.
    Ulr.   Nay, then, I'll call you sister.
    Ida. I like that name still worse.—Would we had ne'er
Been aught of kindred !
    Ulr. (gloomily).   Would we never had !

Ida. Oh, heavens! and can *you wish that?*
Ulr.   Dearest Ida!
Did I not echo your own wish?
   Ida.   Yes, Ulric,
But then I wished it not with such a glance,
And scarce knew what I said; but let me be
Sister, or cousin, what you will, so that
I still to you am something.
   Ulr.   You shall be   170
All—all——
   Ida.   And you to *me are* so already;
But I can wait.
   Ulr.   Dear Ida!
   Ida.   Call me Ida,
Your Ida, for I would be yours, none else's—
Indeed I have none else left, since my poor father—
                           [*She pauses.*

   Ulr. You have *mine*—you have *me.*
   Ida.   Dear Ulric, how I wish
My father could but view my happiness,
Which wants but this!
   Ulr.   Indeed!
   Ida.   You would have loved him,
He you; for the brave ever love each other:
His manner was a little cold, his spirit
Proud (as is birth's prerogative); but under   180
This grave exterior——Would you had known each other!
Had such as you been near him on his journey,
He had not died without a friend to soothe
His last and lonely moments.
   Ulr.   Who says *that?*
   Ida. What?
   Ulr.   That he *died alone.*
   Ida.   The general rumour,
And disappearance of his servants, who
Have ne'er returned: that fever was most deadly
Which swept them all away.
   Ulr.   If they were near him,
He could not die neglected or alone.
   Ida. Alas! what is a menial to a death-bed,   190
When the dim eye rolls vainly round for what

It loves?—They say he died of a fever.
 Ulr.   *Say!*
It *was* so.
 Ida. I sometimes dream otherwise.
 Ulr. All dreams are false.
 Ida.   And yet I see him as
I see you.
 Ulr. *Where?*
 Ida.   In sleep—I see him lie
Pale, bleeding, and a man with a raised knife
Beside him.
 Ulr. But you do not see his *face?*
 Ida (looking at him). No! Oh, my God! do *you?*
 Ulr.   Why do you ask?
 Ida. Because you look as if you saw a murderer!
 Ulr. (agitatedly). Ida, this is mere childishness; your
    weakness   200
Infects me, to my shame: but as all feelings
Of yours are common to me, it affects me.
Prithee, sweet child, change——
 Ida.   Child, indeed! I have
Full fifteen summers!   [*A bugle sounds*
 Rod.   Hark, my Lord, the bugle!
 Ida (peevishly to RODOLPH*).* Why need you tell him
    that? Can he not hear it
Without your echo?
 Rod.   Pardon me, fair Baroness!
 Ida. I will not pardon you, unless you earn it
By aiding me in my dissuasion of
Count Ulric from the chase to-day.
 Rod.   You will not,
Lady, need aid of mine.
 Ulr.   I must not now   210
Forgo it.
 Ida. But you shall
 Ulr.   *Shall!*
 Ida.   Yes, or be
No true knight.—Come, dear Ulric! yield to me
In this, for this one day: the day looks heavy,
And you are turned so pale and ill.
 Ulr.   You jest.

Ida. Indeed I do not :—ask of Rodolph.
Rod.   Truly,
My Lord, within this quarter of an hour
You have changed more than e'er I saw you change
In years.
    Ulr.   'Tis nothing ; but if 'twere, the air
Would soon restore me.   I'm the true cameleon,
And live but on the atmosphere ; [1] your feasts   220
In castle halls, and social banquets, nurse not
My spirit—I'm a forester and breather
Of the steep mountain-tops,[2] where I love all
The eagle loves.
    Ida.   Except his prey, I hope.
    Ulr. Sweet Ida, wish me a fair chase, and I
Will bring you six boars' heads for trophies home.
    Ida. And will you not stay, then ?   You shall not go !
Come ! I will sing to you.
    Ulr.   Ida, you scarcely
Will make a soldier's wife.
    Ida.   I do not wish
To be so ; for I trust these wars are over,   230
And you will live in peace on your domains.

Enter WERNER *as* COUNT SIEGENDORF.

    Ulr. My father, I salute you, and it grieves me
With such brief greeting.—You have heard our bugle ;
The vassals wait.
    Sieg.   So let them.—You forget
To-morrow is the appointed festival
In Prague [3] for peace restored.   You are apt to follow
The chase with such an ardour as will scarce
Permit you to return to-day, or if
Returned, too much fatigued to join to-morrow

---

   1. [Compare " Excellent, i' faith ; of the chameleon's dish : I eat the
air " (*Hamlet*, act iii. sc. 2, lines 88, 89).]
   2. [Compare—
              " Had his free breathing been denied
              The range of the steep mountain's side."
                     Prisoner of Chillon, lines 142, 143.]
   3. [The Treaty of Prague was signed May 30, 1635.]

The nobles in our marshalled ranks.

  Ulr.   You, Count, 240
Will well supply the place of both—I am not
A lover of these pageantries.

  Sieg.   No, Ulric;
It were not well that you alone of all
Our young nobility——

  Ida.   And far the noblest
In aspect and demeanour.

  Sieg. (*to* IDA).   True, dear child,
Though somewhat frankly said for a fair damsel.—
But, Ulric, recollect too our position,
So lately reinstated in our honours.
Believe me, 'twould be marked in any house,
But most in *ours*, that ONE should be found wanting 250
At such a time and place. Besides, the Heaven
Which gave us back our own, in the same moment
It spread its peace o'er all, hath double claims
On us for thanksgiving : first, for our country ;
And next, that we are here to share its blessings.

  Ulr. (*aside*). Devout, too ! Well, sir, I obey at once.
(*Then aloud to a servant.*) Ludwig, dismiss the train
   without !   [*Exit* LUDWIG.

  Ida.   And so
You yield, at once, to him what I for hours
Might supplicate in vain.

  Sieg. (*smiling*).   You are not jealous
Of me, I trust, my pretty rebel ! who   260
Would sanction disobedience against all
Except thyself ? But fear not ; thou shalt rule him
Hereafter with a fonder sway and firmer.

  Ida. But I should like to govern *now*.

  Sieg.   You shall,
Your *harp*, which by the way awaits you with
The Countess in her chamber. She complains
That you are a sad truant to your music :
She attends you.

  Ida.   Then good morrow, my kind kinsmen !
Ulric, you'll come and hear me ?

  Ulr.   By and by.

  Ida. Be sure I'll sound it better than your bugles ; 270

Then pray you be as punctual to its notes :
I'll play you King Gustavus' march.
   Ulr.   And why not
Old Tilly's?
   Ida.   Not that monster's ! I should think
My harp-strings rang with groans, and not with music,
Could aught of *his* sound on it :—but come quickly ;
Your mother will be eager to receive you.   [*Exit* IDA.
   Sieg. Ulric, I wish to speak with you alone.
   Ulr. My time 's your vassal.—
(*Aside to* RODOLPH.)   Rodolph, hence ! and do
As I directed : and by his best speed
And readiest means let Rosenberg reply.   280
   Rod. Count Siegendorf, command you aught? I am
       bound
Upon a journey past the frontier.
   Sieg. (*starts*).   Ah !—
Where ? on *what* frontier ?
   Rod.   The Silesian, on
My way—(*Aside to* ULRIC.)—*Where* shall I say ?
   Ulr. (*aside to* RODOLPH).   To Hamburgh.
                (*Aside to himself*). That
Word will, I think, put a firm padlock on
His further inquisition.
   Rod.   Count, to Hamburgh.
   Sieg. (*agitated*). Hamburgh ! No, I have nought to
       do there, nor
Am aught connected with that city.   Then
God speed you !
   Rod.   Fare ye well, Count Siegendorf !
               [*Exit* RODOLPH.
   Sieg. Ulric, this man, who has just departed, is   290
One of those strange companions whom I fain
Would reason with you on.
   Ulr.   My Lord, he is
Noble by birth, of one of the first houses
In Saxony.
   Sieg.   I talk not of his birth,
But of his bearing. Men speak lightly of him.
   Ulr. So they will do of most men. Even the monarch
Is not fenced from his chamberlain's slander, or

The sneer of the last courtier whom he has made
Great and ungrateful.
 Sieg.   If I must be plain,
The world speaks more than lightly of this Rodolph : 300
They say he is leagued with the " black bands" who still
Ravage the frontier.
 Ulr.   And will you believe
The world ?
 Sieg. In this case—yes.
 Ulr.   In *any* case,
I thought you knew it better than to take
An accusation for a sentence.
 Sieg.   Son !
I understand you : you refer to—— but
My destiny has so involved about me
Her spider web, that I can only flutter
Like the poor fly, but break it not. Take heed,
Ulric ; you have seen to what the passions led me : 310
Twenty long years of misery and famine
Quenched them not—twenty thousand more, perchance,
Hereafter (or even here in *moments* which
Might date for years, did Anguish make the dial),
May not obliterate or expiate
The madness and dishonour of an instant.
Ulric, be warned by a father !—I was not
By mine, and you behold me !
 Ulr.   I behold
The prosperous and belovéd Siegendorf,
Lord of a Prince's appanage, and honoured 320
By those he rules and those he ranks with.
 Sieg.   Ah !
Why wilt thou call me prosperous, while I fear
For thee ? Belovéd, when thou lovest me not !
All hearts but one may beat in kindness for me—
But if my son's is cold !——
 Ulr.   Who *dare* say that ?
 Sieg. None else but I, who see it—*feel* it—keener
Than would your adversary, who dared say so,
Your sabre in his heart ! But mine survives
The wound.
 Ulr. You err. My nature is not given

To outward fondling : how should it be so, 　　330
After twelve years' divorcement from my parents ?

Sieg. And did not *I* too pass those twelve torn years
In a like absence ?　But 'tis vain to urge you—
Nature was never called back by remonstrance.
Let 's change the theme.　I wish you to consider
That these young violent nobles of high name,
But dark deeds (aye, the darkest, if all Rumour
Reports be true), with whom thou consortest,
Will lead thee——

Ulr. (*impatiently*).　I'll be *led* by no man.

Sieg.　　　　　　　　　　　　　　Nor
Be leader of such, I would hope : at once 　　340
To wean thee from the perils of thy youth
And haughty spirit, I have thought it well
That thou shouldst wed the lady Ida—more
As thou appear'st to love her.

Ulr.　　　　　　　　　I have said
I will obey your orders, were they to
Unite with Hecate—can a son say more ?

Sieg. He says too much in saying this.　It is not
The nature of thine age, nor of thy blood,
Nor of thy temperament, to talk so coolly,
Or act so carelessly, in that which is 　　350
The bloom or blight of all men's happiness,
(For Glory's pillow is but restless, if
Love lay not down his cheek there) : some strong bias,
Some master fiend is in thy service, to
Misrule the mortal who believes him slave,
And makes his every thought subservient ; else
Thou'dst say at once—" I love young Ida, and
Will wed her ; " or, " I love her not, and all
The powers on earth shall never make me."—So
Would *I* have answered.

Ulr.　　　　　　　Sir, *you* wed for love. 　　360

Sieg. I did, and it has been my only refuge
In many miseries.

Ulr.　　　　　　Which miseries
Had never been but for this love-match.

Sieg.　　　　　　　　　　　　　Still
Against your age and nature !　Who at twenty

E'er answered thus till now ?
   Ulr.   Did you not warn me
Against your own example ?
   Sieg.   Boyish sophist !
In a word, do you love, or love not, Ida ?
   Ulr. What matters it, if I am ready to
Obey you in espousing her ?
   Sieg.   As far
As you feel, nothing—but all life for her.   370
She 's young—all-beautiful—adores you—is
Endowed with qualities to give happiness,
Such as rounds common life into a dream
Of something which your poets cannot paint,
And (if it were not wisdom to love virtue),
For which Philosophy might barter Wisdom ;
And giving so much happiness, deserves
A little in return. I would not have her
Break her heart with a man who has none to break !
Or wither on her stalk like some pale rose   380
Deserted by the bird she thought a nightingale,
According to the Orient tale.[1] She is——
   Ulr. The daughter of dead Stralenheim, your foe :
I'll wed her, ne'ertheless ; though, to say truth,
Just now I am not violently transported
In favour of such unions.
   Sieg.   But she loves you.
   Ulr. And I love her, and therefore would think *twice.*
   Sieg. Alas ! Love never did so.
   Ulr.   Then 'tis time
He should begin, and take the bandage from
His eyes, and look before he leaps ; till now   390
He hath ta'en a jump i' the dark.
   Sieg.   But you consent ?
   Ulr. I did, and do.
   Sieg.   Then fix the day.
   Ulr.   'Tis usual,
And, certes, courteous, to leave that to the lady.
   Sieg. I will engage for *her*
   Ulr.   So will not *I*

---

1. [For "the attachment of the nightingale to the rose," see *Giaour*,
lines 21-31, *Poetical Works*, 1900, iii. 86, *note* 1.]

For any woman : and as what I fix,
I fain would see unshaken, when she gives
Her answer, I'll give mine.
  Sieg.   But 'tis your office
To woo.
  Ulr. Count, 'tis a marriage of your making,
So be it of your wooing ; but to please you,
I will now pay my duty to my mother,   400
With whom, you know, the lady Ida is.—
What would you have ?   You have forbid my stirring
For manly sports beyond the castle walls,
And I obey ; you bid me turn a chamberer,
To pick up gloves, and fans, and knitting-needles,
And list to songs and tunes, and watch for smiles,
And smile at pretty prattle, and look into
The eyes of feminine, as though they were
The stars receding early to our wish
Upon the dawn of a world-winning battle— 410
What can a son or man do more ? [*Exit* ULRIC.
  Sieg. (solus).   Too much !—
Too much of duty, and too little love !
He pays me in the coin he owes me not :
For such hath been my wayward fate, I could not
Fulfil a parent's duties by his side
Till now ; but love he owes me, for my thoughts
Ne'er left him, nor my eyes longed without tears
To see my child again,—and now I have found him !
But how ! obedient, but with coldness ; duteous
In my sight, but with carelessness ; mysterious— 420
Abstracted—distant—much given to long absence,
And where—none know—in league with the most riotous
Of our young nobles ; though, to do him justice,
He never stoops down to their vulgar pleasures ;
Yet there 's some tie between them which I can not
Unravel.   They look up to him—consult him—
Throng round him as a leader : but with me
He hath no confidence !   Ah ! can I hope it
After—what ! doth my father's curse descend
Even to my child ?   Or is the Hungarian near 430
To shed more blood ? or—Oh ! if it should be !
Spirit of Stralenheim, dost thou walk these walls

To wither him and his—who, though they slew not,
Unlatched the door of Death for thee ? 'Twas not
Our fault, nor is our sin : thou wert our foe,
And yet I spared thee when my own destruction
Slept with thee, to awake with thine awakening !
And only took—Accurséd gold ! thou liest
Like poison in my hands; I dare not use thee,
Nor part from thee ; thou camest in such a guise,   440
Methinks thou wouldst contaminate all hands
Like mine.   Yet I have done, to atone for thee,
Thou villanous gold ! and thy dead master's doom,
Though he died not by me or mine, as much
As if he were my brother !   I have ta'en
His orphan Ida—cherished her as one
Who will be mine.

Enter an ATTENDANT.

   Atten.   The abbot, if it please
Your Excellency, whom you sent for, waits
Upon you.   [*Exit* ATTENDANT.

Enter the PRIOR ALBERT.

   Prior.   Peace be with these walls, and all
Within them !
   Sieg.   Welcome, welcome, holy father !   450
And may thy prayer be heard !—all men have need
Of such, and I——
   Prior.   Have the first claim to all
The prayers of our community.   Our convent,
Erected by your ancestors, is still
Protected by their children.
   Sieg.   Yes, good father ;
Continue daily orisons for us
In these dim days of heresies and blood,
Though the schismatic Swede, Gustavus, is
Gone home.
   Prior.   To the endless home of unbelievers,
Where there is everlasting wail and woe,   460
Gnashing of teeth, and tears of blood, and fire
Eternal, and the worm which dieth not !

Sieg. True, father : and to avert those pangs from one,
Who, though of our most faultless holy Church,
Yet died without its last and dearest offices,
Which smooth the soul through purgatorial pains,
I have to offer humbly this donation
In masses for his spirit.

    [SIEGENDORF *offers the gold which he had taken from*
        STRALENHEIM.

Prior.   Count, if I
Receive it, 'tis because I know too well
Refusal would offend you.   Be assured   470
The largess shall be only dealt in alms,
And every mass no less sung for the dead.
Our House needs no donations, thanks to yours,
Which has of old endowed it ; but from you
And yours in all meet things 'tis fit we obey.
For whom shall mass be said ?

    Sieg. (faltering).   For—for—the dead.
    Prior. His name ?
    Sieg.   'Tis from a soul, and not a name,
I would avert perdition.

    Prior.   I meant not
To pry into your secret.   We will pray
For one unknown, the same as for the proudest.   480

    Sieg. Secret ! I have none : but, father, he who 's gone
Might *have* one ; or, in short, he did bequeath—
No, not bequeath—but I bestow this sum
For pious purposes.

    Prior.   A proper deed
In the behalf of our departed friends.

    Sieg. But he who 's gone was not my friend, but foe,
The deadliest and the stanchest.

    Prior.   Better still !
To employ our means to obtain Heaven for the souls
Of our dead enemies is worthy those
Who can forgive them living.

    Sieg.   But I did not   490
Forgive this man.   I loathed him to the last,
As he did me.   I do not love him now,
But——

    Prior. Best of all ! for this is pure religion !

You fain would rescue him you hate from hell—
An evangelical compassion—with
Your own gold too !
 Sieg.   Father, 'tis not my gold.
 Prior. Whose, then ? You said it was no legacy.
 Sieg. No matter whose—of this be sure, that he
Who owned it never more will need it, save
In that which it may purchase from your altars : 500
'Tis yours, or theirs.
 Prior.   Is there no blood upon it ?
 Sieg. No ; but there 's worse than blood—eternal
   shame !
 Prior. Did he who owned it die in his *bed ?*
 Sieg.   Alas !
He did.
 Prior. Son ! you relapse into revenge,
If you regret your enemy's bloodless death.
 Sieg. His death was fathomlessly deep in blood.
 Prior. You said he died in his bed, not battle.
 Sieg.   He
Died, I scarce know—but—he was stabbed i' the dark,
And now you have it—perished on his pillow
By a cut-throat !—Aye !—you may look upon me ! 510
I am *not* the man. I'll meet your eye on that point,
As I can one day God's.
 Prior.   Nor did he die
By means, or men, or instrument of yours ?
 Sieg. No ! by the God who sees and strikes !
 Prior.   Nor know you
Who slew him ?
 Sieg.   I could only guess at *one,*
And he to me a stranger, unconnected,
As unemployed. Except by onė day's knowledge,
I never saw the man who was suspected.
 Prior. Then you are free from guilt.
 Sieg. (eagerly).   Oh ! *am* I ?—say !
 Prior. You have said so, and know best.
 Sieg.   Father ! I have spoken 520
The truth, and nought but truth, if *not* the *whole ;*
Yet say I am *not* guilty ! for the blood
Of this man weighs on me, as if I shed it,

Though, by the Power who abhorreth human blood,
I did not!—nay, once spared it, when I might
And *could*—aye, perhaps, *should* (if our self-safety
Be e'er excusable in such defences
Against the attacks of over-potent foes):
But pray for him, for me, and all my house;
For, as I said, though I be innocent,   530
I know not why, a like remorse is on me,
As if he had fallen by me or mine.   Pray for me,
Father! I have prayed myself in vain.
    Prior.   I will.
Be comforted!   You are innocent, and should
Be calm as innocence.
    Sieg.   But calmness is not
Always the attribute of innocence.
I feel it is not.
    Prior.   But it will be so,
When the mind gathers up its truth within it.
Remember the great festival to-morrow,
In which you rank amidst our chiefest nobles,   540
As well as your brave son; and smooth your aspect,
Nor in the general orison of thanks
For bloodshed stopt, let blood you shed not rise,
A cloud, upon your thoughts.   This were to be
Too sensitive.   Take comfort, and forget
Such things, and leave remorse unto the guilty.   [*Exeunt.*

ACT V.

SCENE I.—*A large and magnificent Gothic Hall in the
Castle of Siegendorf, decorated with Trophies, Banners,
and Arms of that Family.*

Enter ARNHEIM *and* MEISTER, *attendants of* COUNT
SIEGENDORF.

    Arn. Be quick! the Count will soon return: the ladies
Already are at the portal.   Have you sent
The messengers in search of him he seeks for?

Meis. I have, in all directions, over Prague,
As far as the man's dress and figure could
By your description track him.   The devil take
These revels and processions !   All the pleasure
(If such there be) must fall to the spectators,—
I'm sure none doth to us who make the show.
   Arn. Go to ! my Lady Countess comes.
   Meis.   I'd rather 10
Ride a day's hunting on an outworn jade,
Than follow in the train of a great man,
In these dull pageantries.
   Arn.   Begone ! and rail
Within.   [*Exeunt.*

Enter the COUNTESS JOSEPHINE SIEGENDORF *and*
IDA STRALENHEIM.

Jos.   Well, Heaven be praised ! the show is over.
   Ida. How can you say so ?   Never have I dreamt
Of aught so beautiful.   The flowers, the boughs,
The banners, and the nobles, and the knights,
The gems, the robes, the plumes, the happy faces,
The coursers, and the incense, and the sun
Streaming through the stained windows, even the *tombs,* 20
Which looked so calm, and the celestial hymns,
Which seemed as if they rather came from Heaven
Than mounted there—the bursting organ's peal
Rolling on high like an harmonious thunder ;
The white robes and the lifted eyes ; the world
At peace ! and all at peace with one another !
Oh, my sweet mother !   [*Embracing* JOSEPHINE.
   Jos.   My belovéd child !
For such, I trust, thou shalt be shortly.
   Ida.   Oh !
I am so already.   Feel how my heart beats !
   Jos. It does, my love ; and never may it throb   30
With aught more bitter.
   Ida.   Never shall it do so !
How should it ?   What should make us grieve ?   I hate
To hear of sorrow : how can we be sad,
Who love each other so entirely ?   You,

The Count, and Ulric, and your daughter Ida.
 Jos. Poor child !
 Ida.   Do you pity me?
 Jos.   No : I but envy,
And that in sorrow, not in the world's sense
Of the universal vice, if one vice be
More general than another.
 Ida.   I'll not hear
A word against a world which still contains 40
You and my Ulric.   Did you ever see
Aught like him ?   How he towered amongst them all !
How all eyes followed him !   The flowers fell faster—
Rained from each lattice at his feet, methought,
Than before all the rest ; and where he trod
I dare be sworn that they grow still, nor e'er
Will wither.
 Jos. You will spoil him, little flatterer,
If he should hear you.
 Ida.   But he never will.
I dare not say so much to him—I fear him.
 Jos. Why so? he loves you well.
 Ida.   But I can never 50
Shape my thoughts *of* him into words *to* him :
Besides, he sometimes frightens me.
 Jos.   How so?
 Ida. A cloud comes o'er his blue eyes suddenly,
Yet he says nothing.
 Jos.   It is nothing : all men,
Especially in these dark troublous times,
Have much to think of.
 Ida.   But I cannot think
Of aught save him.
 Jos.   Yet there are other men,
In the world's eye, as goodly.   There 's, for instance,
The young Count Waldorf, who scarce once withdrew
His eyes from yours to-day.
 Ida.   I did not see him, 60
But Ulric.   Did you not see at the moment
When all knelt, and I wept? and yet, methought,
Through my fast tears, though they were thick and warm,
I saw him smiling on me.

Jos.   I could not
See aught save Heaven, to which my eyes were raised,
Together with the people's.
    Ida.   I thought too
Of Heaven, although I looked on Ulric.
    Jos.   Come,
Let us retire ! they will be here anon,
Expectant of the banquet.   We will lay
Aside these nodding plumes and dragging trains.   70
    Ida. And, above all, these stiff and heavy jewels,
Which make my head and heart ache, as both throb
Beneath their glitter o'er my brow and zone.
Dear mother, I am with you.

Enter COUNT SIEGENDORF, *in full dress, from the
solemnity, and* LUDWIG.

    Sieg.   Is he not found ?
    Lud. Strict search is making every where ; and if
The man be in Prague, be sure he will be found.
    Sieg. Where 's Ulric ?
    Lud.   He rode round the other way
With some young nobles ; but he left them soon ;
And, if I err not, not a minute since
I heard his Excellency, with his train,   80
Gallop o'er the west drawbridge.

Enter ULRIC, *splendidly dressed.*

    Sieg. (to LUDWIG).   See they cease not
Their quest of him I have described.   [*Exit* LUDWIG.
                     Oh, Ulric !
How have I longed for thee !
    Ulr.   Your wish is granted—
Behold me !
    Sieg.   I have seen the murderer.
    Ulr. Whom ?   Where ?
    Sieg.   The Hungarian, who slew Stralenheim.
    Ulr. You dream.
    Sieg.   I live ! and as I live, I saw him—
Heard him ! he dared to utter even my name.
    Ulr. What name ?

Sieg.   Werner ! *'twas* mine.
Ulr.   It must be so
No more : forget it.
   Sieg.   Never ! never ! all
My destinies were woven in that name :   90
It will not be engraved upon my tomb,
But it may lead me there.
   Ulr.   To the point——the Hungarian ?
   Sieg. Listen !—The church was thronged : the hymn
      was raised ;
" *Te Deum* " pealed from nations rather than
From choirs, in one great cry of " God be praised "
For one day's peace, after thrice ten dread years,
Each bloodier than the former : I arose,
With all the nobles, and as I looked down
Along the lines of lifted faces,—from
Our bannered and escutcheoned gallery, I   100
Saw, like a flash of lightning (for I saw
A moment and no more), what struck me sightless
To all else—the Hungarian's face ! I grew
Sick ; and when I recovered from the mist
Which curled about my senses, and again
Looked down, I saw him not. The thanksgiving
Was over, and we marched back in procession.
   Ulr. Continue.
   Sieg.   When we reached the Muldau's bridge,
The joyous crowd above, the numberless
Barks manned with revellers in their best garbs,   110
Which shot along the glancing tide below,
The decorated street, the long array,
The clashing music, and the thundering
Of far artillery, which seemed to bid
A long and loud farewell to its great doings,
The standards o'er me, and the tramplings round,
The roar of rushing thousands,—all—all could not
Chase this man from my mind, although my senses
No longer held him palpable.
   Ulr.   You saw him
No more, then ?
   Sieg.   I looked, as a dying soldier   120
Looks at a draught of water, for this man ;

But still I saw him not; but in his stead——
   Ulr. What in his stead?
   Sieg.   My eye for ever fell
Upon your dancing crest; the loftiest.
As on the loftiest and the loveliest head,
It rose the highest of the stream of plumes,
Which overflowed the glittering streets of Prague.
   Ulr. What 's this to the Hungarian?
   Sieg.   Much! for I
Had almost then forgot him in my son;
When just as the artillery ceased, and paused   130
The music, and the crowd embraced in lieu
Of shouting, I heard in a deep, low voice,
Distinct and keener far upon my ear
Than the late cannon's volume, this word—"*Werner!*"
   Ulr. Uttered by——
   Sieg.   Him! I turned—and saw—and fell.
   Ulr. And wherefore? Were you seen?
   Sieg.   The officious care
Of those around me dragged me from the spot,
Seeing my faintness, ignorant of the cause:
You, too, were too remote in the procession
(The old nobles being divided from their children)   140
To aid me.
   Ulr.   But I'll aid you now.
   Sieg.   In what?
   Ulr. In searching for this man, or——When he's found,
What shall we do with him?
   Sieg.   I know not that.
   Ulr. Then wherefore seek?
   Sieg.   Because I cannot rest
Till he is found. His fate, and Stralenheim's,
And ours, seem intertwisted! nor can be
Unravelled, till——

Enter an ATTENDANT.

   Atten.   A stranger to wait on
Your Excellency.
   Sieg.   Who?
   Atten.   He gave no name.

Sieg. Admit him, ne'ertheless.
   [*The* ATTENDANT *introduces* GABOR, *and afterwards*
     exit.

                  Ah !
Gab.   'Tis then Werner !
Sieg. (*haughtily*). The same you knew, sir, by that
    name ; and *you !*   150
   Gab. (*looking round*). I recognise you both : father and
    son,
It seems.   Count, I have heard that you, or yours,
Have lately been in search of me : I am here.
   Sieg. I have sought you, and have found you : you
    are charged
(Your own heart may inform you why) with such
A crime as——   [*He pauses.*
   Gab.   Give it utterance, and then
I'll meet the consequences.
   Sieg.   You shall do so—
Unless——
   Gab.   First, who accuses me ?
   Sieg.   All things,
If not all men : the universal rumour—
My own presence on the spot—the place—the time— 160
And every speck of circumstance unite
To fix the blot on you.
   Gab.   And on *me only ?*
Pause ere you answer : is no other name,
Save mine, stained in this business ?
   Sieg.   Trifling villain !
Who play'st with thine own guilt ! Of all that breathe
Thou best dost know the innocence of him
'Gainst whom thy breath would blow thy bloody slander.
But I will talk no further with a wretch,
Further than justice asks. Answer at once,
And without quibbling, to my charge.
   Gab.   'Tis false ! 170
   Sieg. Who says so ?
   Gab.   I.
   Sieg.   And how disprove it ?
   Gab.   By
The presence of the murderer.

   Sieg.   Name him.
   Gab.   He
May have more names than one.   Your Lordship had so
Once on a time.
   Sieg.   If you mean me, I dare
Your utmost.
   Gab.   You may do so, and in safety ;
I know the assassin.
   Sieg.   Where is he ?
   Gab. (*pointing to* ULRIC).   Beside you !
     [ULRIC *rushes forward to attack* GABOR ; SIEGENDORF
       interposes.
   Sieg. Liar and fiend ! but you shall not be slain ;
These walls are mine, and you are safe within them.
Ulric, repel this calumny, as I   [*He turns to* ULRIC.
Will do.   I avow it is a growth so monstrous,   180
I could not deem it earth-born : but be calm ;
It will refute itself.   But touch him not.
         [ULRIC *endeavours to compose himself.*
   Gab. Look at *him*, Count, and then *hear me.*
   Sieg. (*first to* GABOR, *and then looking at* ULRIC).
                      I hear thee.
My God ! you look——
   Ulr.   How ?
   Sieg.   As on that dread night,
When we met in the garden.
   Ulr. (*composing himself*).   It is nothing.
   Gab. Count, you are bound to hear me.   I came
      hither
Not seeking you, but sought.   When I knelt down
Amidst the people in the church, I dreamed not
To find the beggared Werner in the seat
Of Senators and Princes ; but you have called me,   190
And we have met.
   Sieg.   Go on, sir.
   Gab.   Ere I do so,
Allow me to inquire, who profited
By Stralenheim's death ?   Was't I—as poor as ever ;
And poorer by suspicion on my name !
The Baron lost in that last outrage neither
Jewels nor gold ; his life alone was sought.—

A life which stood between the claims of others
To honours and estates scarce less than princely.
   Sieg. These hints, as vague as vain, attach no less
To me than to my son.
   Gab.   I can't help that.   200
But let the consequence alight on him
Who feels himself the guilty one amongst us
I speak to you, Count Siegendorf, because
I know you innocent, and deem you just.
But ere I can proceed—*dare* you protect me ?
Dare you command me ?
     [SIEGENDORF *first looks at the Hungarian, and then
        at* ULRIC, *who has unbuckled his sabre, and is
        drawing lines with it on the floor—still in its
        sheath.*
   Ulr. (*looks at his father, and says,*) Let the man go on !
   Gab. I am unarmed, Count, bid your son lay down
His sabre.
   Ulr. (*offers it to him contemptuously*). Take it.
   Gab.   No, sir, 'tis enough
That we are both unarmed—I would not choose
To wear a steel which may be stained with more   210
Blood than came there in battle.
   Ulr. (*casts the sabre from him in contempt*). It—or some
Such other weapon in my hand—spared yours
Once, when disarmed and at my mercy.
   Gab.   True—
I have not forgotten it : you spared me for
Your own especial purpose—to sustain
An ignominy not my own.
   Ulr.   Proceed.
The tale is doubtless worthy the relater.
But is it of my father to hear further ? [*To* SIEGENDORF.
   Sieg. (*takes his son by the hand*). My son, I know my
        own innocence, and doubt not
Of yours—but I have promised this man patience ;   220
Let him continue.
   Gab.   I will not detain you,
By speaking of myself much : I began
Life early—and am what the world has made me.
At Frankfort on the Oder, where I passed

A winter in obscurity, it was
My chance at several places of resort
(Which I frequented sometimes, but not often)
To hear related a strange circumstance
In February last.   A martial force,
Sent by the state, had, after strong resistance,   230
Secured a band of desperate men, supposed
Marauders from the hostile camp.—They proved,
However, not to be so—but banditti,
Whom either accident or enterprise
Had carried from their usual haunt—the forests
Which skirt Bohemia—even into Lusatia.
Many amongst them were reported of
High rank—and martial law slept for a time.
At last they were escorted o'er the frontiers,
And placed beneath the civil jurisdiction   240
Of the free town of Frankfort.   Of *their* fate
I know no more.
  Sieg.   And what is this to Ulric?
  Gab. Amongst them there was said to be one man
Of wonderful endowments :—birth and fortune,
Youth, strength, and beauty, almost superhuman,
And courage as unrivalled, were proclaimed
His by the public rumour; and his sway,
Not only over his associates, but
His judges, was attributed to witchcraft,
Such was his influence :—I have no great faith   250
In any magic save that of the mine—
I therefore deemed him wealthy.—But my soul
Was roused with various feelings to seek out
This prodigy, if only to behold him.
  Sieg. And did you so?
  Gab.   You'll hear.   Chance favoured me :
A popular affray in the public square
Drew crowds together—it was one of those
Occasions where men's souls look out of them,
And show them as they are—even in their faces :
The moment my eye met his, I exclaimed,   260
"This is the man!" though he was then, as since,
With the nobles of the city.   I felt sure
I had not erred, and watched him long and nearly;

I noted down his form—his gesture—features,
Stature, and bearing—and amidst them all,
'Midst every natural and acquired distinction,
I could discern, methought, the assassin's eye
And gladiator's heart.
    Ulr. (*smiling*).   The tale sounds well.
    Gab. And may sound better.—He appeared to me
One of those beings to whom Fortune bends,   270
As she doth to the daring—and on whom
The fates of others oft depend; besides,
An indescribable sensation drew me
Near to this man, as if my point of fortune
Was to be fixed by him.—There I was wrong.
    Sieg. And may not be right now.
    Gab.
                     I followed him,
Solicited his notice—and obtained it—
Though not his friendship :—it was his intention
To leave the city privately—we left it
Together—and together we arrived   280
In the poor town where Werner was concealed,
And Stralenheim was succoured——Now we are on
The verge—*dare* you hear further?
    Sieg.
                 I must do so—
Or I have heard too much.
    Gab.
                I saw in you
A man above his station—and if not
So high, as now I find you, in my then
Conceptions, 'twas that I had rarely seen
Men such as you appeared in height of mind,
In the most high of worldly rank ; you were
Poor, even to all save rags : I would have shared   290
My purse, though slender, with you—you refused it.
    Sieg. Doth my refusal make a debt to you,
That thus you urge it?
    Gab.
             Still you owe me something,
Though not for that; and I owed you my safety,
At least my seeming safety, when the slaves
Of Stralenheim pursued me on the grounds
That *I* had robbed him.
    Sieg.
             I concealed you—I,
Whom and whose house you arraign, reviving viper !

Gab. I accuse no man—save in my defence.
You, Count, have made yourself accuser—judge :   300
Your hall 's my court, your heart is my tribunal.
Be just, and *I'll* be merciful !
    Sieg.   You merciful ?—
You ! Base calumniator !
    Gab.   I. 'Twill rest
With me at last to be so. You concealed me—
In secret passages known to yourself,
You said, and to none else. At dead of night,
Weary with watching in the dark, and dubious
Of tracing back my way, I saw a glimmer,
Through distant crannies, of a twinkling light :
I followed it, and reached a door—a secret   310
Portal—which opened to the chamber, where,
With cautious hand and slow, having first undone
As much as made a crevice of the fastening,
I looked through and beheld a purple bed,
And on it Stralenheim !—
    Sieg.   Asleep ! And yet
You slew him !—Wretch !
    Gab.   He was already slain,
And bleeding like a sacrifice. My own
Blood became ice.
    Sieg.   But he was all alone !
You saw none else ? You did not see the——
                [*He pauses from agitation.*
                      No,
    Gab.   320
He, whom you dare not name, nor even I
Scarce dare to recollect, was not then in
The chamber.
    Sieg. (*to* ULRIC). Then, my boy ! thou art guiltless still—
Thou bad'st me say *I* was so once.—Oh ! now
Do thou as much.
    Gab.   Be patient ! I can *not*
Recede now, though it shake the very walls
Which frown above us. You remember,—or
If not, your son does,—that the locks were changed
Beneath *his* chief inspection on the morn
Which led to this same night : how he had entered
He best knows—but within an antechamber,   330

The door of which was half ajar, I saw
A man who washed his bloody hands, and oft
With stern and anxious glance gazed back upon—
The bleeding body—but it moved no more.
    Sieg. Oh ! God of fathers !
    Gab.   I beheld his features
As I see yours—but yours they were not, though
Resembling them—behold them in Count Ulric's !
Distinct as I beheld them, though the expression
Is not now what it then was !—but it was so
When I first charged him with the crime—so lately. 340
    Sieg. This is so——
    Gab. (interrupting him). Nay—but hear me to the end !
Now you must do so.—I conceived myself
Betrayed by you and *him* (for now I saw
There was some tie between you) into this
Pretended den of refuge, to become
The victim of your guilt ; and my first thought
Was vengeance : but though armed with a short poniard
(Having left my sword without), I was no match
For him at any time, as had been proved
That morning—either in address or force.   350
I turned and fled—i' the dark : chance rather than
Skill made me gain the secret door of the hall,
And thence the chamber where you slept : if I
Had found you *waking*, Heaven alone can tell
What vengeance and suspicion might have prompted ;
But ne'er slept guilt as Werner slept that night.
    Sieg. And yet I had horrid dreams ! and such brief
        sleep,
The stars had not gone down when I awoke.
Why didst thou spare me ? I dreamt of my father—
And now my dream is out !
    Gab.   'Tis not my fault,   360
If I have read it.—Well ! I fled and hid me—
Chance led me here after so many moons—
And showed me Werner in Count Siegendorf !
Werner, whom I had sought in huts in vain,
Inhabited the palace of a sovereign !
You sought me and have found me—now you know
My secret, and may weigh its worth.

Sieg. (*after a pause*).   Indeed !
Gab. Is it revenge or justice which inspires
Your meditation?
    Sieg.   Neither—I was weighing
The value of your secret.
    Gab.   You shall know it   370
At once :—When you were poor, and I, though poor,
Rich enough to relieve such poverty
As might have envied mine, I offered you
My purse—you would not share it :—I'll be franker
With you : you are wealthy, noble, trusted by
The imperial powers—you understand me?
    Sieg.   Yes.
    Gab. Not quite.   You think me venal, and scarce
        true :
'Tis no less true, however, that my fortunes
Have made me both at present.   You shall aid me :
I would have aided you—and also have   380
Been somewhat damaged in my name to save
Yours and your son's.   Weigh well what I have said.
    Sieg. Dare you await the event of a few minutes'
Deliberation?
    Gab. (*casts his eyes on* ULRIC, *who is leaning against a*
        pillar).   If I should do so?
    Sieg. I pledge my life for yours.   Withdraw into
This tower.   [*Opens a turret-door.*
    Gab. (*hesitatingly*). This is the second *safe* asylum
You have offered me.
    Sieg.   And was not the first so?
    Gab. I know not that even now—but will approve
The second.   I have still a further shield.—
I did not enter Prague alone; and should I   390
Be put to rest with Stralenheim, there are
Some tongues without will wag in my behalf.
Be brief in your decision ! [1]
    Sieg.   I will be so.—

---

1. [" *Gab.* I have yet an additional security—I did not enter Prague
a solitary individual ; and there are tongues without that will speak for
me, although I should even share the fate of Stralenheim ! Let your
deliberation be short.—*Sieg.* My promise is solemn—sacred—irrevocable : it extends not, however, beyond my own walls."—*Canterbury
Tales*, 1838, ii. 268 ; see, too, pp. 269, 270.]

My word is sacred and irrevocable
Within *these* walls, but it extends no further.

    Gab. I'll take it for so much.

    Sieg. (*points to* ULRIC'S *sabre, still upon the ground*).

                    Take also *that*—
I saw you eye it eagerly, and him
Distrustfully.

    Gab. (*takes up the sabre*). I will; and so provide
To sell my life—not cheaply.

    [GABOR *goes into the turret, which* SIEGENDORF *closes.*

    Sieg. (*advances to* ULRIC). Now, Count Ulric !
For son I dare not call thee—What say'st thou ?   400

    Ulr. His tale is true.

    Sieg.   True, monster !

    Ulr.   Most true, father !
And you did well to listen to it : what
We know, we can provide against. He must
Be silenced.

    Sieg.   Aye, with half of my domains ;
And with the other half, could he and thou
Unsay this villany.

    Ulr.   It is no time
For trifling or dissembling. I have said
His story 's true ; and he too must be silenced.

    Sieg. How so?

    Ulr.   As Stralenheim is. Are you so dull
As never to have hit on this before ?   410
When we met in the garden, what except
Discovery in the act could make me know
His death ? Or had the Prince's household been
Then summoned, would the cry for the police
Been left to such a stranger ? Or should I
Have loitered on the way ? Or could *you, Werner,*
The object of the Baron's hate and fears,
Have fled, unless by many an hour before
Suspicion woke ? I sought and fathomed you,
Doubting if you were false or feeble : I   420
Perceived you were the latter : and yet so
Confiding have I found you, that I doubted
At times your weakness.

    Sieg.   Parricide ! no less

Than common stabber !   What deed of my life,
Or thought of mine, could make you deem me fit
For your accomplice ?
    Ulr.   Father, do not raise
The devil you cannot lay between us.   This
Is time for union and for action, not
For family disputes.   While *you* were tortured,
Could *I* be calm ?   Think you that I have heard   430
This fellow's tale without some feeling ?—You
Have taught me feeling for *you* and myself ;
For whom or what else did you ever teach it ?
    Sieg. Oh ! my dead father's curse ! 'tis working now.
    Ulr. Let it work on ! the grave will keep it down !
Ashes are feeble foes : it is more easy
To baffle such, than countermine a mole,
Which winds its blind but living path beneath you.
Yet hear me still !—If *you* condemn me, yet,
Remember *who* hath taught me once too often   440
To listen to him !   *Who* proclaimed to me
That *there were crimes* made venial by the occasion ?
That passion was our nature ? that the goods
Of Heaven waited on the goods of fortune ?
Who showed me his humanity secured
By his *nerves* only ?   *Who* deprived me of
All power to vindicate myself and race
In open day ?   By his disgrace which stamped
(It might be) bastardy on me, and on
Himself—a *felon's* brand !   The man who is   45c
At once both warm and weak invites to deeds
He longs to do, but dare not.   Is it strange
That I should *act* what you could *think ?*   We have done
With right and wrong ; and now must only ponder
Upon effects, not causes.   Stralenheim,
Whose life I saved from impulse, as *unknown*,
I would have saved a peasant's or a dog's, I slew
Known as our foe—but not from vengeance.   He
Was a rock in our way which I cut through,
As doth the bolt, because it stood between us   460
And our true destination—but not idly.
As stranger I preserved him, and he *owed me*
His *life :* when due, I but resumed the debt.

He, you, and I stood o'er a gulf wherein
I have plunged our enemy.   *You* kindled first
The torch—*you* showed the path ; now trace me that
Of safety—or let me !
 Sieg.   I have done with life !
 Ulr. Let us have done with that which cankers life—
Familiar feuds and vain recriminations
Of things which cannot be undone.   We have 470
No more to learn or hide : I know no fear,
And have within these very walls men who
(Although you know them not) dare venture all things.
You stand high with the state ; what passes here
Will not excite her too great curiosity :
Keep your own secret, keep a steady eye,
Stir not, and speak not ;—leave the rest to me :
We must have no *third* babblers thrust between us.
        [*Exit* ULRIC.
 Sieg. (*solus*). Am I awake ? are these my father's halls ?
And *you*—my son ?   *My* son ! *mine !* who have ever 480
Abhorred both mystery and blood, and yet
Am plunged into the deepest hell of both !
I must be speedy, or more will be shed—
The Hungarian's !—Ulric—he hath partisans,
It seems : I might have guessed as much.   Oh fool !
Wolves prowl in company.   He hath the key
(As I too) of the opposite door which leads
Into the turret.   Now then ! or once more
To be the father of fresh crimes, no less
Than of the criminal !   Ho ! Gabor ! Gabor ! 490
   [*Exit into the turret, closing the door after him.*

SCENE II.—*The Interior of the Turret.*

GABOR *and* SIEGENDORF.

 Gab. Who calls ?
 Sieg.   I—Siegendorf !   Take these and fly !
Lose not a moment !
  [*Tears off a diamond star and other jewels, and thrusts
   them into* GABOR's *hand.*
 Gab.   What am I to do

With these ?

Sieg. Whate'er you will : sell them, or hoard,
And prosper ; but delay not, or you are lost !

Gab. You pledged your honour for my safety !

Sieg. And
Must thus redeem it. Fly ! I am not master,
It seems, of my own castle—of my own
Retainers—nay, even of these very walls,
Or I would bid them fall and crush me ! Fly !
Or you will be slain by——

Gab. Is it even so ? 10
Farewell, then ! Recollect, however, Count,
You sought this fatal interview !

Sieg. I did :
Let it not be more fatal still !—Begone !

Gab. By the same path I entered ?

Sieg. Yes ; that 's safe still ;
But loiter not in Prague ;—you do not know
With whom you have to deal.

Gab. I know too well—
And knew it ere yourself, unhappy Sire !
Farewell ! [*Exit* GABOR.

Sieg. (*solus and listening*). He hath cleared the staircase.
Ah ! I hear
The door sound loud behind him ! He is safe !
Safe !—Oh, my father's spirit !—I am faint—— 20
[*He leans down upon a stone seat, near the wall of the
tower, in a drooping posture.*

Enter ULRIC *with others armed, and with weapons drawn.*

Ulr. Despatch !—he 's there !

Lud. The Count, my Lord !

Ulr. (*recognizing* SIEGENDORF). *You* here, sir !

Sieg. Yes : if you want another victim, strike !

Ulr. (*seeing him stript of his jewels*). Where is the ruffian
who hath plundered you ?
Vassals, despatch in search of him ! You see
'Twas as I said—the wretch hath stript my father
Of jewels which might form a Prince's heir-loom !

Away ! I'll follow you forthwith.
     [*Exeunt all but* SIEGENDORF *and* ULRIC.
       What 's this ?
Where is the villain?
 Sieg.   There are *two*, sir : which
Are you in quest of?
 Ulr.   Let us hear no more
Of this : he must be found. You have not let him 30
Escape ?
 Sieg. He 's gone.
 Ulr.   With your connivance?
 Sieg.   With
My fullest, freest aid.
 Ulr.   Then fare you well !
       [ULRIC *is going.*
 Sieg. Stop ! I command—entreat—implore ! Oh, Ulric !
Will you then leave me?
 Ulr.   What ! remain to be
Denounced—dragged, it may be, in chains ; and all
By your inherent weakness, half-humanity,
Selfish remorse, and temporizing pity,
That sacrifices your whole race to save
A wretch to profit by our ruin ! No, Count,
Henceforth you have no son !
 Sieg.   I never had one ; 40
And would you ne'er had borne the useless name !
Where will you go ? I would not send you forth
Without protection.
 Ulr.   Leave that unto me.
I am not alone ; nor merely the vain heir
Of your domains ; a thousand, aye, ten thousand
Swords, hearts, and hands are mine.
 Sieg.   The foresters !
With whom the Hungarian found you first at Frankfort !
 Ulr. Yes—men—who are worthy of the name ! Go
  tell
Your Senators that they look well to Prague ;
Their Feast of Peace was early for the times ; 50
There are more spirits abroad than have been laid
With Wallenstein !

Enter JOSEPHINE *and* IDA.

Jos.   What is't we hear?   My Siegendorf!
Thank Heaven, I see you safe!
    Sieg.   Safe!
    Ida.   Yes, dear father!
    Sieg. No, no; I have no children: never more
Call me by that worst name of parent.
    Jos.   What
Means my good Lord?
    Sieg.   That you have given birth
To a demon!
    Ida (taking ULRIC'S *hand).* Who shall dare say this of
        Ulric?
    Sieg. Ida, beware! there's blood upon that hand.
    Ida (stooping to kiss it). I'd kiss it off, though it were
        mine.
    Sieg.   It is so!
    Ulr. Away! it is your father's!   [*Exit* ULRIC.
    Ida.   Oh, great God!   60
And I have loved this man!
        [IDA *falls senseless—*JOSEPHINE *stands speechless with
            horror.*
    Sieg.   The wretch hath slain
Them both!—My Josephine! we are now alone!
Would we had ever been so!—All is over
For me!—Now open wide, my sire, thy grave;
Thy curse hath dug it deeper for thy son
In mine!—The race of Siegendorf is past.

The end of the fifth act and the Drama.

B. P. Jy 20, 1822.

WERNER.

Nov. 1815.

[FIRST DRAFT.]

ACT I.

SCENE I.—*A ruinous chateau on the Silesian frontier of Bohemia.*

Josepha. THE storm is at it's height—how the wind
   howls,
Like an unearthly voice, through these lone chambers!
And the rain patters on the flapping casement
Which quivers in it's frame—the night is starless—
Yet cheerly Werner! still our hearts are warm:
The tempest is without, or should be so—
For we are sheltered here where Fortune's clouds
May roll all harmless o'er us as the wrath
Of these wild elements that menace now,
Yet do not reach us.
   Werner (without attending, and walking disturbedly,
      speaking to himself). No—'Tis past—'tis blighted,
The last faint hope to which my withered fortune   11
Clung with a feeble and a fluttering grasp,
Yet clung convulsively—for twas the *last*—
Is broken with the rest: would that my heart were
But there is pride, and passion's war within,
Which give my breast vitality to suffer,
As it hath suffered through long years till now.
My father's wrath extends beyond the grave,

And haunts me in the shape of Stralenheim !
He revels in my fathers palace—I—   20
Exiled—disherited—a nameless outcast !

                            [Werner pauses.

My boy, too, where and what is he ?—my father
Might well have limited his curse to me.
If that my heritage had passed to Ulric,
I had not mourned my own less happy lot.
No—No—all 's past—all torn away.
   Josepha.   Dear Werner,
Oh banish these discomfortable thoughts
That thus contend within you : we are poor,
So we have ever been—but I remember
The time when thy Josepha's smile could turn   30
Thy heart to hers—despite of every ill.
So let it now—alas ! you hear me not.
    Werner. What said you ?—let it pass—no matter
        what—
Think me not churlish, Sweet, I am not well.
My brain is hot and busy—long fatigue
And last night's watching have oppressed me much.
    Josepha. Then get thee to thy couch. I do perceive
In thy pale cheek and in thy bloodshot eye
A strange distemperature—nay, as a boon,
I do entreat thee to thy rest.
    Werner.   My *rest !*   40
Well—be it so—Good Night !
    Josepha.   Thy hand is burning ;
I will prepare a potion :—peace be with thee—
Tomorrow's dawn I trust will find thee healthful ;
And, then, our Ulric may perchance—
    Werner. Our Ulric—thine and mine—our only boy—
Curse on his father and his father's Sire !
(For, if it is so, I will render back
A curse that Heaven will hear as well as his),
Our Ulric by his father's fault or folly,
And by my father's unrelenting pride,   50
Is at this hour, perchance, undone. This night
That shelters us may shower it's wrath on him—
A homeless beggar for his parent's sin—
Thy sin and mine—Thy child and mine atones—

Our Ulric—Woman !—I'll to no bed to-night—
There is no pillow for my thoughts.
  Josepha.   What words,
What fearful words are these ! what may they mean ?
  Werner. Look on me—thou hast known me, hitherto,
As an oppressed, but yet a humble creature ;
By birth predestined to the yoke I've borne.   60
Till now I've borne it patiently, at least,
In bitter silence—but the hour is come,
That should and shall behold me as I was,
And ought again to be—
  Josepha.   I know not what
Thy mystery may tend to, but my fate—
My heart—my will—my love are linked with thine,
And I would share thy sorrow : lay it open.
  Werner. Thou see'st the son of Count—but let it
    pass—
I forfeited the name in wedding thee :
That fault of many faults a father's pride   70
Proclaimed the last and worst—and, from that hour,
He disavowed, disherited, debased
A wayward son — — tis a long tale—too long—
And I am heartsick of the heavy thought.
  Josepha. Oh, I could weep—but that were little solace :
Yet tell the rest—or, if thou wilt not, say—
Yet say—why, through long years, from me withheld,
This fearful secret that hath gnawed thy soul?
  Werner. Why ? had it not been base to call on thee
For patience and for pity—to awake   80
The thirst of grandeur in thy gentle spirit—
To tell thee what thou shouldst have been—the wife
Of one, in power—birth—wealth, preeminent—
Then, sudden quailing in that lofty tone,
To bid thee soothe thy husband—peasant Werner?
  Josepha. I would thou wert, indeed, the peasant
    Werner ;
For then thy soul had been of calmer mould,
And suited to thy lot——
  Werner.   Was it not so ?
Beneath a humble name and garb—the which
My youthful riot and a father's frown,   90

Too justly fixed upon me, had compelled
My bowed down spirit to assume too well—
Since it deceived the world, myself, and thee:
I linked my lot irrevocably with thine—
And I have loved thee deeply—long and dearly—
Even as I love thee still—but these late crosses,
And most of all the last,—have maddened me;
And I am wild and wayward as in youth,
Ere I beheld thee—
    Josepha.   Would thou never hadst!
Since I have been a blight upon thy hope,   100
And marred alike the present and the future.
    Werner. Yet say not so—for all that I have known
Of true and calm content—of love—of peace—
Has been with thee and from thee: wert thou not,
I were a lonely and self-loathing thing.
Ulric has left us! all, save thou, have left me!
Father and son—Fortune—Fame—Power—Ambition—
The ties of being—the high soul of man—
All save the long remorse—the consciousness,
The curse of living on, regretting life   110
Mispent in miserably gazing upward,
While others soared—Away, I'll think no more.
    Josepha. But Ulric—wherefore didst thou let him
        leave
His home and us? tis now three weary years.
    Werner (interrupting her quickly). Since my hard
        father, half-relenting, sent
The offer of a scanty stipend which
I needs must earn by rendering up my son—
Fool that I was—I thought this quick compliance,
And never more assuming in myself
The haught name of my house would soften him— 120
And for our child secure the heritage
Forfeit in me forever. Since that hour,
Till the last year, the wretched pittance came—
Then ceased with every tidings of my son
And Sire—till late I heard the last had ceased
To live—and unforgiving died—Oh God!
    Josepha. Was it for this our Ulric left us so?
Thou dids't deceive me then—he went not forth

To join the legions of Count Tilly's war?

Werner. I know not—he had left my father's castle, 130
Some months before his death—but why?—but why?
Left it as I did ere his birth, perchance,
Like me an outcast.   Old age had not made
My father meeker—and my son, Alas!
Too much his Sire resembled——

   Josepha.   Yet there 's comfort.
Restrain thy wandering Spirit—Ulric cannot
Have left his native land—thou dost not know,
Though it looks strangely, thy Sire and he
In anger parted—Hope is left us still.

   Werner. The best hope that I ever held in youth,
When every pulse was life, each thought a joy,   141
(Yet not irrationally sanguine, since
My birth bespoke high thoughts,) hath lured and left me.
I will not be a dreamer in mine age—
The hunter of a shadow—let *boys hope:*
Of Hope I now know nothing but the name—
And that 's a sound which jars upon my heart.
I've wearied thee—Good night—my patient Love

   Josepha. I must not leave thee thus—my husband—
     friend—
My heart is rent in twain for thee—I scarce   150
Dare greet thee as I would, lest that my love
Should seem officious and ill timed :—'tis early—
Yet rest were as a healing balm to thee—
Then once again—Good night!

   Voice Without. What Ho—lights ho!

Scene II.

   Josepha. What noise is that? 'tis nearer—hush! they
     knock.

   [*A knocking heard at the gate—*Werner *starts.*
   Werner (aside). It may be that the bloodhounds of
     the villain,
Who long has tracked me, have approached at last :
I'll not be taken tamely.

   Josepha.   'Twas the voice,

The single voice of some lone traveller.
I'll to the door.
  Werner.   No—stay thou here—again !
     [*Knocking repeated. Opens the door.*
Well—Sir—your pleasure ?

     Enter CARL *the Bavarian.*

  Carl.   Thanks most worthy Sir !
My pleasure, for to-night, depends on yours—
I'm weary, wet, and wayworn—without shelter,
Unless you please to grant it.
  Josepha.   You shall have it, 10
Such as this ruinous mansion may afford :
Tis spacious, but too cold and crazy now
For Hospitality's more cordial welcome :
But as it is 'tis yours.
  Werner (to his wife). Why say ye so ?
At once such hearty greeting to a stranger ?
At such a lonely hour, too—
  Josepha (in reply to Werner). Nay—he's honest.
There is trust-worthiness in his blunt looks.
  Werner (to Josepha). "Trustworthiness in looks !"
    I'll trust no looks !
I look into men's faces for their age,
Not for their actions—had he Adam's brow, 20
Open and goodly as before the fall,
I've lived too long to trust the frankest aspect.
  (*To Carl.*) Whence come you Sir ?
  Carl.   From Frankfort, on my way
To my own country—I've a companion too—
He tarries now behind :—an hour ago,
On reaching that same river on your frontier,
We found it swoln by storms—a stranger's carriage,
Despite the current, drawn by sturdy mules,
Essayed to pass, and nearly reached the middle
Of that which was the *ford* in gentler weather, 30
When down came driver, carriage, mules, and all—
You may suppose the worthy Lord within
Fared ill enough :—worse still he might have suffered,

But that my comrade and myself rushed in,
And with main strength and some good luck beside,
Dislodged and saved him : he'll be here anon.
His equipage by this time is at Dresden—
I left it floating that way.
    Werner.   Where is he ?
    Carl. Hitherward on his way, even like myself—
We saw the light and made for the nearest shelter :   40
You'll not deny us for a single night ?
You've room enough, methinks—and this vast ruin
Will not be worse for three more guests.
    Werner.   Two more :
And thou ?—well—be it so—(*aside*) (tonight will soon
Be overpast : they shall not stay tomorrow)—
Know you the name of him you saved ?
    Carl.   Not I !
I think I heard him called a Baron Something—
But was too chill to stay and hear his titles :
You know they are sometimes tedious in the reckoning,
If counted over by the noble wearer.   50
Has't any wine ? I'm wet, stung to the marrow—
My comrade waited to escort the Baron :
They will be here, anon—they, too, want cheering :
I'll taste for them, if it please you, courteous host !
    Josepha. Such as our vintage is shall give you
        welcome :
I'll bring you some anon.   *[goes out.*
    Carl (*looking round*).   A goodly mansion !
And has been nobly tenanted, I doubt not.
This worn magnificence some day has shone
On light hearts and long revels—those torn banners
Have waved o'er courtly guests—and yon huge lamp
High blazed through many a midnight—I could wish 61
My lot had led me here in those gay times !
Your days, my host, must pass but heavily.
Are you the vassal of these antient chiefs,
Whose heir wastes elsewhere their fast melting hoards,
And placed to keep their cobwebs company ?
    Werner (*who has been absorbed in thought till the latter
        part of his speech*). A Vassal !—I a vassal !—*who*
        accosts me

With such familiar question?—(*checks himself and says
  aside*)—Down startled pride !
Have not long years of wretchedness yet quenched thee,
And, suffering evil, wilt thou start at scorn?   70
 (*To Carl.*) Sir ! if I boast no birth—and, as you see,
My state bespeaks none—still, no being breathes
Who calls me slave or servant.—Like yourself
I am a stranger here—a lonely guest—
But, for a time, on sufferance. On my way,
From—a far distant city—Sickness seized,
And long detained me in the neighbouring hamlet.
The Intendant of the owner of this castle,
Then uninhabited, with kind intent,
Permitted me to wait returning health   80
Within these walls—more sheltered than the cot
Of humble peasants.
 Carl.   Worthy Sir, your mercy !
I meant not to offend you—plain of speech,
And blunt in apprehension, I do judge
Men's station from their seeming—but themselves
From acts alone. You bid me share your shelter,
And I am bound to you ; and had you been
The lowliest vassal had not thanked you less,
Than I do now, believing you his better,
Perhaps my own superior—
 Werner.   What imports it? 90
What—who I am—or whence—you are welcome—sit—
You shall have cheer anon. (*walks disturbedly aside*)
 Carl (*to himself*). Here's a strange fellow !
Wild, churlish, angry—*why,* I know not, seek not.
Would that the wine were come ! my doublet 's wet,
But my throat dry as Summer's drought in desarts.
Ah—here it sparkles !

Enter JOSEPHA *with wine in flask—and a cup. As she
  pours it out a Voice is heard without calling at a distance.* WERNER *starts—*JOSEPHA *listens tremulously.*

 Werner.   That voice—that voice—Hark !
No—no—tis silent—Sir—I say—that voice—
Whose is it—speak—

Carl (drinking unconcernedly). Whose is it? faith, I
    know not—
And, yet, 'tis my companion's : he 's like you,
And does not care to tell his name and station.   100
                [*The voice again and nearer.*
Josepha. 'Tis his—I knew it—Ulric!—Ulric!—Ulric!
                [*She drops the wine and rushes out.*
Carl. The flask 's unhurt—but every drop is spilt.
Confound the voice! I say—would he were dumb!
And faith! to me, he has been nearly so—
A silent and unsocial travelling mate.
    Werner (stands in agitation gazing towards the door).
        If it be he—I cannot move to meet him.
Yes—it must be so—there is no such voice
That so could sound and shake me : he is here,
And I am—

Enter STRALENHEIM.

Werner (turns and sees him). A curse upon thee,
    stranger!
Where dids't thou learn a tone so like my boy's?   110
Thou mock bird of my hopes—a curse upon thee!
Out! Out! I say.   Thou shalt not harbour here.
    Stralenheim. What means the peasant? knows he
        unto whom
He dares address this language?
    Carl.   Noble Sir!
Pray heed him not—he 's Phrenzy's next door neighbour,
And full of these strange starts and causeless jarrings.
    Werner. Oh, that long wished for voice!—I dreamed
        of it—
And then it did elude me—then—and now.

Enter ULRIC and JOSEPHA.   WERNER *falls on his neck.*

Oh God! forgive, for thou dids't not forget me.
Although I murmured—tis—it is my Son!   120
    Josepha. Aye, 'tis dear Ulric—yet, methinks, he 's
        changed, too :
His cheek is tanned, his frame more firmly knit!

That scar, too, dearest Ulric—I do fear me—
Thou hast been battling with these heretics,
And that 's a Swedish token on thy brow.
   Ulric. My heart is glad with yours—we meet like those
Who never would have parted :—of the past
You shall know more anon—but, here 's a guest
That asks a gentle welcome.   Noble Baron,
My father's silence looks discourtesy :   130
Yet must I plead his pardon—'tis his love
Of a long truant that has rapt him, thus,
From hospitable greeting—you'll be seated—
And, Father, we will sup like famished hunters.

JOSEPHA *goes out here.*

   Stralenheim. I have much need of rest: no more
        refreshment !
Were all my people housed within the hamlet,
Or can they follow ?
   Ulric.   Not to night I fear.
They staid in hope the damaged Cabriole
Might, with the dawn of day, have such repairs,
As circumstance admits of.
   Carl.   Nay—that 's hopeless.   140
They must not only mend but draw it too.
The mules are drowned—a murrain on them both !
One kicked me as I would have helped him on.
   Stralenheim. It is most irksome to me—this delay.
I was for Prague on business of great moment.
   Werner. For Prague—Sir—Say you ?—
   Stralenheim.   Yes, my host ! for Prague.
And these vile floods and villainous cross roads
Steal my time from it's uses—but—my people ?
Where do they shelter ?
   Ulric.   In the boatman's shed,
Near to the ferry : you mistook the ford—   150
Tis higher to the right :—their entertainment
Will be but rough—but 'tis a single night,
And they had best be guardians of the baggage.
The shed will hold the weather from their sleep,
The woodfire warm them—and, for beds, a cloak

Is swansdown to a seasoned traveller :
It has been mine for many a moon, and may
Tonight, for aught it recks me.
    Stralenheim.   And tomorrow
I must be on my journey—and betimes.
It is not more than three days travel, hence,   160
To Mansfeldt Castle.
    Werner and Ulric.   Mansfeldt Castle !—
    Stralenheim.   Aye !
For thither tends my progress—so, betimes,
Mine host I would be stirring—think of that !
And let me find my couch of rest at present.
    Werner. You shall Sir—but—to Mansfeldt !—
          [ULRIC *stops his father and says aside to him,*
                               Silence—father—
Whate'er it be that shakes you thus—*tread down*—
  (*To Stralenheim*) My father, Sir, was born not far
    from Prague,
And knows it's environs—and, when he hears,
The name endeared to him by native thoughts,
He would ask of it, and it's habitants—   170
You will excuse his plain blunt mode of question.
    Stralenheim. Indeed, perchance, then, he may aid my
        search.
Pray, know you aught of one named Werner ? who
(But he no doubt has passed through many names),
Lived long in Hamburgh—and has thence been traced
Into Silesia—and not far from hence—
But there we lost him ; he who can disclose
Aught of him, or his hiding-place, will find
Advantage in revealing it.
    Ulric.   Why so—Sir ?
    Stralenheim. There are strong reasons to suspect this
        man   180
Of crimes against the State—league with Swedes—
And other evil acts of moment :—he
Who shall deliver him, bound hand and foot,
Will benefit his country and himself :
I will reward him doubly too.
    Ulric.   You know him ?
    Stralenheim. He never met my eyes—but Circumstance

Has led me to near knowledge of the man.
He is a villain—and an enemy
To all men—most to me! If earth contain him,
He shall be found and fettered: I have hopes,   190
By traces which tomorrow will unravel,
A fresh clue to his lurking spot is nigh.

   Carl. And, if I find it, I will break the thread.
What, all the world against one luckless wight!
And he a fugitive—I would I knew him!

   Ulric. You'd help him to escape—is it not so?

   Carl. I would, indeed!

   Ulric.   The greater greenhorn you!
I would secure him—nay—I will do so.

   Stralenheim. If it be so—my gratitude for aid,
And rescue of my life from the wild waters,   200
Will double in it's strength and it's requital.
Your father, too, perhaps can help our search?

   Werner. *I* turn a spy—no—not for *Mansfeldt Castle,*
And all the broad domain it frowns upon.

   Stralenheim. Mansfeldt again!—you know it then?
     perchance,
You also know the story of it's lords?

   Werner. Whate'er I know, there is no bribe of thine
Can swerve me to the crooked path thou pointest.
The chamber's ready, which your rest demands.

   Stralenheim (aside). 'Tis strange—this peasant's tone
     is wondrous high,   210
His air imperious—and his eye shines out
As wont to look command with a quick glance—
His garb befits him not—why, he may be
The man I look for! now, I look again,
There is the very lip—short curling lip—
And the oerjutting eye-brow dark and large,
And the peculiar wild variety
Of feature, even unto the Viper's eye,
Of that detested race, and it's descendant
Who stands alone between me and a power,   220
Which Princes gaze at with unquiet eyes!
This is no peasant—but, whate'er he be,
Tomorrow shall secure him and unfold.

   Ulric. It will not please you, Sir, then to remain

With us beyond tomorrow?

   Stralenheim. Nay—I do not say so—there is no haste.
And now I think again—I'll tarry here—
Perhaps until the floods abate—we'll see—
In the mean time—to my chamber—so—Good Night!

                     [Exit with WERNER.

   Werner. This way, Sir.

   Carl. And I to mine : pray, where are we to rest? 230
We'll sup within—

   Ulric.   What matter where—there 's room.

   Carl. I would fain see my way through this vast
       ruin ;
Come take the lamp, and we'll explore together.

   Josepha (meeting them). And I will with my son.

   Ulric.   Nay—stay—dear mother!
These chilly damps and the cold rush of winds
Fling a rough paleness o'er thy delicate cheek—
And thou seem'st lovely in thy sickliness
Of most transparent beauty :—but it grieves me.
Nay ! tarry here by the blaze of the bright hearth :—
I will return anon—and we have much   240
To listen and impart. Come, Carl, we'll find
Some gorgeous canopy, and, thence, unroost
It's present bedfellows the bats—and thou
Shalt slumber underneath a velvet cloud
That mantles o'er the couch of some dead Countess.

                 [Exit CARL *and* ULRIC.

   Josepha (sola). It was my joy to see him—nothing
      more
I should have said—which sent my gush of blood
Back on my full heart with a dancing tide :
It was my weary hope's unthought fulfilment,
My agony of mother-feelings curdled   250
At once in gathered rapture—which did change
My cheek into the hue of fainting Nature.
I should have answered thus—and yet I could not :
For though 'twas true—it was not all the truth.
I have much suffered in the thought of Werner's
Late deep distemperature of mind and fortunes,
Which since have almost driven him into phrenzy :—
And though that I would soothe, not share, such passions,

And show not how they shake me :—when alone,
I feel them prey upon me by reflection,   260
And want the very solace I bestowed ;
And which, it seems, I cannot give and have.
Ulric must be my comforter—his father's
Hath long been the most melancholy soul
That ever hovered o'er the verge of Madness :
And, better, had he leapt into it's gulph :
Though to the Mad thoughts are realities,
Yet they can play with sorrow—and live on.
But with the mind of consciousness and care
The body wears to ruin, and the struggle,   270
However long, is deadly——   He is lost,
And all around him tasteless :—in his mirth
His very laughter moves me oft to tears,
And I have turned to hide them—for, in him,
As Sunshine glittering o'er unburied bones——
Soft—he is here.——

  Werner.   Josepha—where is Ulric?
 Josepha. Gone with the other stranger to gaze o'er
These shattered corridors, and spread themselves
A pillow with their mantles, in the least ruinous :
I must replenish the diminished hearth   280
In the inner chamber—the repast is ready,
And Ulric will be here again.—

THE
DEFORMED TRANSFORMED:

A DRAMA.

INTRODUCTION TO *THE DEFORMED TRANSFORMED*.

THE date of the original MS. of *The Deformed Transformed* is "Pisa, 1822." There is nothing to show in what month it was written, but it may be conjectured that it was begun and finished within the period which elapsed between the death of Allegra, April 20, and the death of Shelley, July 8, 1822. According to Medwin (*Conversations*, 1824, p. 227), an unfavourable criticism of Shelley's ("It is a bad imitation of *Faust*"), together with a discovery that "two entire lines" of Southey's—

> "And water shall see thee,
> And fear thee, and flee thee"—

were imbedded in one of his "Songs," touched Byron so deeply that he "threw the poem into the fire," and concealed the existence of a second copy for more than two years. It is a fact that Byron's correspondence does not contain the remotest allusion to *The Deformed Transformed;* but, with regard to the plagiarism from Southey, in the play as written in 1822 there is neither Song nor Incantation which could have contained two lines from *The Curse of Kehama*.

As a dramatist, Byron's function, or *métier*, was twofold. In *Manfred*, in *Cain*, in *Heaven and Earth*, he is concerned with the analysis and evolution of metaphysical or ethical notions ; in *Marino Faliero,* in *Sardanapalus*, and *The Two Foscari*, he set himself "to dramatize striking passages of history ; " in *The Deformed Transformed* he sought to combine the solution of a metaphysical puzzle or problem, the relation of personality to individuality, with the scenic rendering of a striking historical episode, the Sack of Rome in 1527.

In the note or advertisement prefixed to the drama, Byron acknowledges that "the production" is founded partly on the story of a forgotten novel, *The Three Brothers*, and partly on "the *Faust* of the great Goethe."

Arnaud, or Julian, the hero of *The Three Brothers* (by Joshua Pickersgill, jun., 4 vols., 1803), " sells his soul to the Devil, and becomes an arch-fiend in order to avenge himself for the taunts of strangers on the deformity of his person " (see *Gent. Mag.*, November, 1804, vol. 74, p. 1047 ; and *post*, pp. 473–479). The idea of an escape from natural bonds or disabilities by supernatural means and at the price of the soul or will, the *un*-Christlike surrender to the tempter, which is the *grund-stoff* of the Faust-legend, was brought home to Byron, in the first instance, not by Goethe, or Calderon, or Marlowe, but by Joshua Pickersgill. A fellow-feeling lent an intimate and peculiar interest to the theme. He had suffered all his life from a painful and inconvenient defect, which his proud and sensitive spirit had magnified into a deformity. He had been stung to the quick by his mother's taunts and his sweetheart's ridicule, by the jeers of the base and thoughtless, by slanderous and brutal paragraphs in newspapers. He could not forget that he was lame. If his enemies had but possessed the wit, they might have given him " the sobriquet of *Le Diable Boiteux* " (letter to Moore, April 2, 1823, *Letters*, 1901, vi. 179). It was no wonder that so poignant, so persistent a calamity should be " reproduced in his poetry " (*Life*, p. 13), or that his passionate impatience of such a " thorn in the flesh " should picture to itself a mysterious and unhallowed miracle of healing. It is true, as Moore says (*Life*, pp. 45, 306), that " the trifling deformity of his foot " was the embittering circumstance of his life," that it " haunted him like a curse ; " but it by no means follows that he seriously regarded his physical peculiarity as a stamp of the Divine reprobation, that " he was possessed by an *idée fixe* that every blessing would be ' turned into a curse' to him " (letter of Lady Byron to H. C. Robinson, *Diary, etc.*, 1869, iii. 435, 436). No doubt he indulged himself in morbid fancies, played with the extravagances of a restless imagination, and wedded them to verse ; but his intellect, " brooding like the day, a master o'er a slave," kept guard. He would never have pleaded on his own behalf that the tyranny of an *idée fixe*, a delusion that he was predestined to evil, was an excuse for his shortcomings or his sins.

Byron's very considerable obligations to *The Three Brothers* might have escaped notice, but the resemblance between his " Stranger," or " Cæsar," and the Mephistopheles of " the great Goethe " was open and palpable.

If Medwin may be trusted (*Conversations*, 1824, p. 210), Byron had read " *Faust* in a sorry French translation," and it is probable that Shelley's inspired rendering of " May-day

Night," which was published in *The Liberal* (No. i., October 14, 1822, pp. 123–137), had been read to him, and had attracted his attention. *The Deformed Transformed* is " a *Faustish* kind of drama ; " and Goethe, who maintained that Byron's play as a whole was "no imitation," but " new and original, close, genuine, and spirited," could not fail to perceive that "his devil was suggested by my Mephistopheles " (*Conversations*, 1874, p. 174). The tempter who cannot resist the temptation of sneering at his own wiles, who mocks for mocking's sake, is not Byron's creation, but Goethe's. Lucifer talked *at* the clergy, if he did not "talk like a clergyman ; " but the " bitter hunchback," even when he is *solus*, sneers as the river wanders, " at his own sweet will." He is not a doctor, but a spirit of unbelief !

The second part of *The Deformed Transformed* represents, in three scenes, the Siege and Sack of Rome in 1527. Byron had read Robertson's *Charles the Fifth* (ed. 1798, ii. 313–329) in his boyhood (*Life*, p. 47), but it is on record that he had studied, more or less closely, the narratives of contemporary authorities. A note to *The Prophecy of Dante* (*Poetical Works*, 1901, iv. 258) refers to the *Sacco di Roma*, descritto da Luigi Guicciardini, and the *Ragguaglio Storico . . . sacco di Roma dell' anno* MDXXVII. of Jacopo Buonaparte ; and it is evident that he was familiar with Cellini's story of the marvellous gests and exploits *quorum maxima pars fuit*, which were wrought at " the walls by the Campo Santo," or on the ramparts of the Castle of San Angelo.

The Sack of Rome was a great national calamity, and it was something more : it was a profanation and a sacrilege. The literature which it evoked was a cry of anguish, a prophetic burden of despair. " Chants populaires," writes M. Émile Gebhart (*De l'Italie*, " Le Sac de Rome en 1527," 1876, pp. 267, *sq*.), " *Nouvelles* de Giraldi Cintio, en forme de Décaméron . . . récits historiques . . . de César Grollier, *Dialogues* anonymes . . . poésies de Pasquin, toute une littérature se developpa sur ce thème douloureux. . . . Le *Lamento di Roma*, œuvre étrange, d'inspiration gibeline, rappelle les espérances politiques exprimées jadis par Dante . . . ' Bien que César m'ait dépouillée de liberté, nous avons toujours été d'accord dans une même volonté. Je ne me lamenterais pas si lui régnait ; mais je crois qu'il est ressuscité, ou qu'il ressuscitera véritablement, car souvent un Ange m'a annoncé qu'un César viendrait me délivrer.' . . . Enfin, voici une chanson française que répétaient en repassant les monts les soldats du Marquis de Saluces :—

" ' Parlons de la déffaicte
De ces pouvres Rommains,

Aussi de la complaincte
De notre père saint.

" ' O noble roy de France,
Regarde en pitié
L'Église en ballance . . .
Pour Dieu ! ne tarde plus,
C'est ta mère, ta substance ;
O fils, n'en faictz reffus.' "

"Le dernier monument," adds M. Gebhart, in a footnote, "de cette littérature, est le singulier drame de Byron, *The Deformed Transformed*, dont Jules César est le héros, et le Sac de Rome le cadre."

It is unlikely that Byron, who read everything he could lay his hands upon, and spared no trouble to master his "period," had not, either at first or second hand, acquainted himself with specimens of this popular literature. (For *La Presa e Lamento di Roma, Romæ Lamentatio*, etc., see *Lamenti Storici dei Secoli xiv., xv.* (Medin e Fratri), *Scelta di Curiosità*, etc., 235, 236, 237, Bologna, 1890, vol. iii. See, too, for "Chanson sur la Mort du Connétable de Bourbon," *Recueil de Chants historiques français*, par A. J. V. Le Roux de Lincy, 1842, ii. 99.)

The Deformed Transformed was published by John Hunt, February 20, 1824. A third edition appeared February 23, 1824.

It was reviewed, unfavourably, in the *London Magazine*, March, 1824, vol. 9, pp. 315-321 ; the *Scots Magazine*, March, 1824, N.S. vol. xiv. pp. 353-356 ; and in the *Monthly Review*, March, 1824, Enlarged Series, 103, pp. 321, 324. One reviewer, however (*London Magazine*), had the candour to admit that "Lord Byron may write below himself, but he can never write below us ! "

For the unfinished third part, *vide post*, pp. 532-534.

ADVERTISEMENT.

THIS production is founded partly on the story of a
novel called "The Three Brothers," [1] published many

1. [*The Three Brothers*, by Joshua Pickersgill, junior, was published
in 1803. There is no copy of *The Three Brothers* in the British
Museum. The following extracts are taken from a copy in the Bodleian
Library at Oxford (vol. 4, cap. xi. pp. 229–350) :—

"Arnaud, the natural son of the Marquis de Souvricour, was a child
'extraordinary in Beauty and Intellect.' When travelling with his
parents to Languedoc, Arnaud being 8 years old, he was shot at by
banditti, and forsaken by his parents. The Captain of the band nursed
him. 'But those perfections to which Arnaud owed his existence,
ceased to adorn it. The ball had gored his shoulder, and the fall had
dislocated it ; by the latter misadventure his spine likewise was so
fatally injured as to be irrecoverable to its pristine uprightness.
Injuries so compound confounded the Captain, who sorrowed to see a
creature so charming, at once deformed by a crooked back and an
excrescent shoulder.' Arnaud was found and taken back to his parents.
'The bitterest consciousness of his deformity was derived from their
indelicate, though, perhaps, insensible alteration of conduct. . . . Of
his person he continued to speak as of an abhorrent enemy. . . .
"Were a blessing submitted to my choice, I would say, [said Arnaud]
be it my immediate dissolution." "I think," said his mother, . . .
"that you could wish better." "Yes," adjoined Arnaud, "for that
wish should be that I ever had remained unborn."' He polishes the
broken blade of a sword, and views himself therein ; the sight so
horrifies him that he determines to throw himself over a precipice, but
draws back at the last moment. He goes to a cavern, and conjures up
the prince of hell. "Arnaud knew himself to be interrogated. What
he required. . . . What was that answer the effects explain. . . .
There passed in liveliest portraiture the various men distinguished for
that beauty and grace which Arnaud so much desired, that he was
ambitious to purchase them with his soul. He felt that it was his part
to chuse whom he would resemble, yet he remained unresolved, though
the spectator of an hundred shades of renown, among which glided by
Alexander, Alcibiades, and Hephestion : at length appeared the supernatural effigy of a man, whose perfections human artist never could
depict or insculp—Demetrius, the son of Antigonus. Arnaud's heart
heaved quick with preference, and strait he found within his hand the

years ago, from which M. G. Lewis's "Wood Demon"[1]
was also taken; and partly on the "Faust" of the great
Goëthe. The present publication[2] contains the two first
Parts only, and the opening chorus of the third. The
rest may perhaps appear hereafter.

resemblance of a poniard, its point inverted towards his breast. A
mere automaton in the hands of the Demon, he thrust the point
through his heart, and underwent a painless death. During his trance,
his spirit metempsychosed from the body of his detestation to that of
his admiration. . . . Arnaud awoke a Julian!'"]

1. [For a *résumé* of M. G. Lewis's *Wood Demon* (afterwards re-cast
as *One O'clock; or, The Knight and the Wood-Demon*, 1811), see
"First Visit to the Theatre in London," *Poems*, by Hartley Coleridge,
1851, i., Appendix C, pp. cxcix.–cciii. The *Wood Demon* in its original
form was never published.]

2. [Mrs. Shelley inscribed the following note on the fly-leaf of her
copy of *The Deformed Transformed :*—

"This had long been a favourite subject with Lord Byron. I think
that he mentioned it also in Switzerland. I copied it—he sending a
portion of it at a time, as it was finished, to me. At this time he had
a great horror of its being said that he plagiarised, or that he studied
for ideas, and wrote with difficulty. Thus he gave Shelley Aikins'
edition of the British poets, that it might not be found in his house by
some English lounger, and reported home; thus, too, he always dated
when he began and when he ended a poem, to prove hereafter how
quickly it was done. I do not think that he altered a line in this drama
after he had once written it down. He composed and corrected in his
mind. I do not know how he meant to finish it; but he said himself
that the whole conduct of the story was already conceived. It was at
this time that a brutal paragraph * alluding to his lameness appeared,
which he repeated to me lest I should hear it from some one else. No
action of Lord Byron's life—scarce a line he has written—but was
influenced by his personal defect."]

---

* It is possible that Mrs. Shelley alludes to a sentence in the
Memoirs, etc., of Lord Byron (by Dr. John Watkin), 1822, p. 46 : "A
malformation of one of his feet, and other indications of a rickety constitution, served as a plea for suffering him to range the hills and to
wander about at his pleasure on the seashore, that his frame might be
invigorated by air and exercise."

G. Rothwell, R. H. A. pinx. 1841.   Walker & Cockerell. ph. sc.

Mary Wollstonecraft Shelley.

DRAMATIS PERSONÆ.

—•◦•—

STRANGER, *afterwards* CÆSAR.
ARNOLD.
BOURBON.
PHILIBERT.
CELLINI.

BERTHA.
OLIMPIA.

Spirits, Soldiers, Citizens of Rome, Priests,
Peasants, etc.

THE
DEFORMED TRANSFORMED.[i.]

PART I.

SCENE I.—*A Forest.*

Enter ARNOLD *and his mother* BERTHA.

Bert. OUT, Hunchback!

Arn.   I was born so, Mother![1]

Bert.   Out,
Thou incubus! Thou nightmare! Of seven sons,

i. *The Deformed—a drama.—B. Pisa, 1822.*

1. [Moore (*Life*, p. 13) quotes these lines in connection with a
passage in Byron's "Memoranda," where, in speaking of his own
sensitiveness on the subject of his deformed foot, he described the
feeling of horror and humiliation that came over him, when his mother,
in one of her fits of passion, called him "*a lame brat!*" . . . "It may
be questioned," he adds, "whether that whole drama [*The Deformed
Transformed*] was not indebted for its origin to that single recollection."
Byron's early letters (*e.g.* November 2, 11, 17, 1804, *Letters*, 1898,
i. 41, 45, 48) are full of complaints of his mother's "eccentric behaviour," her "fits of phrenzy," her "caprices," "passions," and so
forth; and there is convincing proof—see *Life*, pp. 28, 306; *Letters*,
1898, ii. 122 (incident at Bellingham's execution); *Letters*, 1901, vi.
179 (*Le Diable Boiteux*)—that he regarded the contraction of the muscles
of his legs as a more or less repulsive deformity. And yet, to quote one
of a hundred testimonies,—" with regard to Lord Byron's features, Mr.
Mathews observed, that he was the only man he ever contemplated,
to whom he felt disposed to apply the word *beautiful*" (*Memoirs of
Charles Mathews*, 1838, ii. 380). The looker-on or the consoler
computes the magnitude and the liberality of the compensation. The
sufferer thinks only of his sufferings.]

The sole abortion !
 Arn.   Would that I had been so,
And never seen the light !
 Bert.   I would so, too !
But as thou *hast*—hence, hence—and do thy best !
That back of thine may bear its burthen ; 'tis
More high, if not so broad as that of others.
 Arn. It *bears* its burthen ;—but, my heart ! Will it
Sustain that which you lay upon it, Mother ?
I love, or, at the least, I loved you : nothing   10
Save You, in nature, can love aught like me.
You nursed me—do not kill me !
 Bert.   Yes—I nursed thee,
Because thou wert my first-born, and I knew not
If there would be another unlike thee,
That monstrous sport of Nature. But get hence,
And gather wood !¹
 Arn.   I will : but when I bring it,
Speak to me kindly. Though my brothers are
So beautiful and lusty, and as free
As the free chase they follow, do not spurn me :
Our milk has been the same.
 Bert.   As is the hedgehog's, 20
Which sucks at midnight from the wholesome dam
Of the young bull, until the milkmaid finds
The nipple, next day, sore, and udder dry.
Call not thy brothers brethren ! Call me not
Mother ; for if I brought thee forth, it was
As foolish hens at times hatch vipers, by
Sitting upon strange eggs. Out, urchin, out !
            [*Exit* BERTHA.

 Arn. (*solus*). Oh, mother !——She is gone, and I
   must do
Her bidding ;—wearily but willingly
I would fulfil it, could I only hope   30
A kind word in return. What shall I do ?
  [ARNOLD *begins to cut wood : in doing this he wounds*
    one of his hands.
My labour for the day is over now.
Accurséd be this blood that flows so fast ;

 1. [So, too, Prospero to Caliban, *Tempest*, act i. sc. 2, line 309, etc.]

For double curses will be my meed now
At home—What home? I have no home, no kin,
No kind—not made like other creatures, or
To share their sports or pleasures.   Must I bleed, too,
Like them? Oh, that each drop which falls to earth
Would rise a snake to sting them, as they have stung
    me!
Or that the Devil, to whom they liken me,   40
Would aid his likeness! If I must partake [1]
His form, why not his power? Is it because
I have not his will too? For one kind word
From her who bore me would still reconcile me
Even to this hateful aspect.   Let me wash
The wound.

     [ARNOLD *goes to a spring, and stoops to wash his*
       hand : he starts back.

They are right; and Nature's mirror shows me,
What she hath made me.   I will not look on it
Again, and scarce dare think on't.   Hideous wretch
That I am!   The very waters mock me with   50
My horrid shadow—like a demon placed
Deep in the fountain to scare back the cattle
From drinking therein.   [*He pauses.*
          And shall I live on,
A burden to the earth, myself, and shame
Unto what brought me into life?   Thou blood,
Which flowest so freely from a scratch, let me
Try if thou wilt not, in a fuller stream,
Pour forth my woes for ever with thyself
On earth, to which I will restore, at once,
This hateful compound of her atoms, and   60
Resolve back to her elements, and take
The shape of any reptile save myself,
And make a world for myriads of new worms!
This knife! now let me prove if it will sever
This withered slip of Nature's nightshade—my
Vile form—from the creation, as it hath

   1. [Compare—
            " Have not partook oppression."
              Marino Faliero, act i. sc. 2, line 468,
              Poetical Works, 1901, iv. 362, *note* 1.]

The green bough from the forest.
> [ARNOLD *places the knife in the ground, with the point upwards.*

                          Now 'tis set,
And I can fall upon it.   Yet one glance
On the fair day, which sees no foul thing like
Myself, and the sweet sun which warmed me, but   70
In vain.   The birds—how joyously they sing !
So let them, for I would not be lamented :
But let their merriest notes be Arnold's knell ;
The fallen leaves my monument ; the murmur
Of the near fountain my sole elegy.
Now, knife, stand firmly, as I fain would fall !
> [*As he rushes to throw himself upon the knife, his eye is suddenly caught by the fountain, which seems in motion.*

The fountain moves without a wind : but shall
The ripple of a spring change my resolve ?
No.   Yet it moves again !   The waters stir,
Not as with air, but by some subterrane   80
And rocking Power of the internal world.
What's here ?   A mist !   No more ?—
> [*A cloud comes from the fountain.   He stands gazing upon it : it is dispelled, and a tall black man comes towards him.*[1]

Arn.   What would you ?   Speak !
Spirit or man ?
   Stran.   As man is both, why not
Say both in one ?
   Arn.   Your form is man's, and yet
You may be devil.
   Stran.   So many men are that
Which is so called or thought, that you may add me
To which you please, without much wrong to either.
But come : you wish to kill yourself ;—pursue
Your purpose.
   Arn.   You have interrupted me.
   Stran. What is that resolution which can e'er   90

---

1. [Compare the story of the philosopher Jamblichus and the raising of Eros and Anteros from their "fountain-dwellings."—*Manfred*, act ii. sc. 2, line 93, *Poetical Works*, 1901, iv. 105, *note* 2.]

Be interrupted?   If I be the devil
You deem, a single moment would have made you
Mine, and for ever, by your suicide;
And yet my coming saves you.
    Arn.   I said not
You *were* the Demon, but that your approach
Was like one.
    Stran.   Unless you keep company
With him (and you seem scarce used to such high
Society) you can't tell how he approaches;
And for his aspect, look upon the fountain,
And then on me, and judge which of us twain   100
Looks likest what the boors believe to be
Their cloven-footed terror.
    Arn.   Do you—dare *you*
To taunt me with my born deformity?
    Stran. Were I to taunt a buffalo with this
Cloven foot of thine, or the swift dromedary
With thy Sublime of Humps, the animals
Would revel in the compliment.   And yet
Both beings are more swift, more strong, more mighty
In action and endurance than thyself,
And all the fierce and fair of the same kind   110
With thee.   Thy form is natural: 'twas only
Nature's mistaken largess to bestow
The gifts which are of others upon man.
    Arn. Give me the strength then of the buffalo's foot,[i.]
When he spurns high the dust, beholding his
Near enemy; or let me have the long
And patient swiftness of the desert-ship,
The helmless dromedary!—and I'll bear [ii.]
Thy fiendish sarcasm with a saintly patience.
    Stran. I will.
    Arn. (*with surprise*). Thou *canst?*
    Stran.   Perhaps.   Would you
      aught else?   120
    Arn. Thou mockest me.
    Stran.   Not I.   Why should I mock
What all are mocking?   That 's poor sport, methinks.

---

i. *Give me the strength of the buffalo's foot* (*which marks me*).—[*MS.*]
ii. *The sailless dromedary* ——.—[*MS.*]

To talk to thee in human language (for
Thou canst not yet speak mine), the forester
Hunts not the wretched coney, but the boar,
Or wolf, or lion—leaving paltry game
To petty burghers, who leave once a year
Their walls, to fill their household cauldrons with
Such scullion prey.   The meanest gibe at thee,—
Now *I* can mock the mightiest.[i.]

> *Arn.*   Then waste not   130
> Thy time on me: I seek thee not.
> *Stran.*   Your thoughts
> Are not far from me.   Do not send me back:
> I'm not so easily recalled to do
> Good service.
> *Arn.*   What wilt thou do for me?
> *Stran.*   Change
> Shapes with you, if you will, since yours so irks you;
> Or form you to your wish in any shape.
> *Arn.* Oh! then you are indeed the Demon, for
> Nought else would wittingly wear mine.
> *Stran.*   I'll show thee
> The brightest which the world e'er bore, and give thee
> Thy choice.
> *Arn.*   On what condition?
> *Stran.*   There 's a question!
> An hour ago you would have given your soul   141
> To look like other men, and now you pause
> To wear the form of heroes.
> *Arn.*   No; I will not.
> I must not compromise my soul.
> *Stran.*   What soul,
> Worth naming so, would dwell in such a carcase?
> *Arn.* 'Tis an aspiring one, whate'er the tenement
> In which it is mislodged.   But name your compact:
> Must it be signed in blood?
> *Stran.*   Not in your own.
> *Arn.* Whose blood then?
> *Stran.*   We will talk of that hereafter.
> But I'll be moderate with you, for I see   150
> Great things within you.   You shall have no bond

i. *Now I can gibe the mightiest.*—[*MS.*]

But your own will, no contract save your deeds.
Are you content ?
   Arn.   I take thee at thy word.
   Stran.   Now then !—
   [*The Stranger approaches the fountain, and turns to*
      ARNOLD.
                   A little of your blood.[1]
   Arn.   For what ?
   Stran. To mingle with the magic of the waters,
And make the charm effective.
   Arn. (*holding out his wounded arm*). Take it all.
   Stran. Not now. A few drops will suffice for this.
   [*The Stranger takes some of* ARNOLD'S *blood in his
      hand, and casts it into the fountain.*
      Shadows of Beauty !
        Shadows of Power !
      Rise to your duty—   160
        This is the hour !
      Walk lovely and pliant[i]
        From the depth of this fountain,
      As the cloud-shapen giant
        Bestrides the Hartz Mountain.[2]
      Come as ye were,
        That our eyes may behold
      The model in air
        Of the form I will mould,
      Bright as the Iris   170
        When ether is spanned ;—
      Such *his* desire is,   [*Pointing to* ARNOLD.
        Such *my* command ![ii]
      Demons heroic—
        Demons who wore
      The form of the Stoic
        Or sophist of yore—

    i. *Walk lively and pliant.*
      You shall rise up as pliant.—[*MS. erased.*]
    ii. *And such* my *command.*—[*MS.*]

    1. [So, too, in *The Tragical History of Dr. Faustus* (Marlowe's
Works, 1858, p. 112), Faustus stabs his arm, "and with his proper
blood Assures his soul to be great Lucifer's."]
    2. This is a well-known German superstition—a gigantic shadow
produced by reflection on the Brocken. [See Brewster's *Letters on
Natural Magic*, 1831, p. 128.]

      Or the shape of each victor—
        From Macedon's boy,
      To each high Roman's picture,   180
        Who breathed to destroy—
      Shadows of Beauty !
        Shadows of Power !
      Up to your duty—
        This is the hour !

    [*Various phantoms arise from the waters, and pass
        in succession before the Stranger and* ARNOLD.

Arn. What do I see?

Stran.   The black-eyed Roman,[1] with
The eagle's beak between those eyes which ne'er
Beheld a conqueror, or looked along
The land he made not Rome's, while Rome became
His, and all theirs who heired his very name.   190

    Arn. The phantom 's bald; *my* quest is beauty.
      Could I
Inherit but his fame with his defects !

    Stran. His brow was girt with laurels more than hairs.[2]
You see his aspect—choose it, or reject.
I can but promise you his form ; his fame
Must be long sought and fought for.

    Arn.   I will fight, too,
But not as a mock Cæsar. Let him pass :
His aspect may be fair, but suits me not.

    Stran. Then you are far more difficult to please
Than Cato's sister, or than Brutus's mother,   200
Or Cleopatra at sixteen [3]—an age
When love is not less in the eye than heart.
But be it so ! Shadow, pass on !

        [*The phantom of Julius Cæsar disappears.*

    Arn.   And can it
Be, that the man who shook the earth is gone,[i]

---

     i.   *And can*
       It be ? the man who shook the earth is gone.—[*MS.*]

    1. [" Nigris vegetisque oculis."—Suetonius, *Vitæ C. Julius Cæsar*,
cap. xlv., *Opera Omnia*, 1826, i. 105.]
    2. [*Vide post*, p. 501, *note* 1.]
    3. [" Sed ante alias [Julius Cæsar] dilexit M. Bruti matrem Serviliam
. . . dilexit et reginas . . . sed maxime Cleopatram" (*ibid.*, i. 113,
115). Cleopatra, born B.C. 69, was twenty-one years old when she
met Cæsar, B.C. 48.]

And left no footstep?
 Stran.   There you err. His substance
Left graves enough, and woes enough, and fame
More than enough to track his memory;
But for his shadow—'tis no more than yours,
Except a little longer and less crooked
I' the sun. Behold another! [*A second phantom passes.*
 Arn.   Who is he?   210
 Stran. He was the fairest and the bravest of
Athenians.[1] Look upon him well.
 Arn.   He is
More lovely than the last. How beautiful!
 Stran. Such was the curled son of Clinias;—wouldst
thou
Invest thee with his form?
 Arn.   Would that I had
Been born with it! But since I may choose further,
I will *look* further. [*The shade of Alcibiades disappears.*
 Stran.   Lo! behold again!
 Arn. What! that low, swarthy, short-nosed, round-
eyed satyr,
With the wide nostrils and Silenus' aspect,
The splay feet and low stature![2] I had better 220
Remain that which I am.
 Stran.   And yet he was
The earth's perfection of all mental beauty,
And personification of all virtue.
But you reject him?
 Arn.   If his form could bring me
That which redeemed it—no.
 Stran.   I have no power
To promise that; but you may try, and find it
Easier in such a form—or in your own.

---

1. ["Upon the whole, it may be doubted whether there be a name
of Antiquity which comes down with such a general charm as that
of *Alcibiades. Why?* I cannot answer: who can?"—*Detached
Thoughts* (1821), No. 108, *Letters*, 1901, v. 461. For Sir Walter Scott's
note on this passage, see *Letters*, 1900, iv. 77, 78, *note* 2.]

2. [The outside of Socrates was that of a satyr and buffoon, but his
soul was all virtue, and from within him came such divine and pathetic
things, as pierced the heart, and drew tears from the hearers.—Plato,
Symp., p. 216, D.]

Arn. No.   I was not born for philosophy,
Though I have that about me which has need on't.
Let him fleet on.
  Stran.   Be air, thou Hemlock-drinker ! 230
  [*The shadow of Socrates disappears : another rises.*
  Arn. What's here ? whose broad brow and whose curly
   beard
And manly aspect look like Hercules,[1]
Save that his jocund eye hath more of Bacchus
Than the sad purger of the infernal world,
Leaning dejected on his club of conquest,[2]
As if he knew the worthlessness of those
For whom he had fought.
  Stran.   It was the man who lost
The ancient world for love.
  Arn.   I cannot blame him,
Since I have risked my soul because I find not
That which he exchanged the earth for.
  Stran.   Since so far
You seem congenial, will you wear his features ? 241
  Arn. No. As you leave me choice, I am difficult.
If but to see the heroes I should ne'er
Have seen else, on this side of the dim shore,
Whence they float back before us.
  Stran.   Hence, Triumvir,
Thy Cleopatra's waiting.
    [*The shade of Antony disappears : another rises.*
  Arn.   Who is this?
Who truly looketh like a demigod,
Blooming and bright, with golden hair, and stature,
If not more high than mortal, yet immortal
In all that nameless bearing of his limbs, 250
Which he wears as the Sun his rays—a something
Which shines from him, and yet is but the flashing
Emanation of a thing more glorious still.
Was *he e'er human only ?*[3]

 1. ["Anthony had a noble dignity of countenance, a graceful length
of beard, a large forehead, an aquiline nose : and, upon the whole, the
same manly aspect that we see in the pictures and statues of Hercules."
—Plutarch's *Lives*, Langhorne's Translation, 1838, p. 634.]
 2. [As in the " Farnese " Hercules.]
 3. [The beauty and mien [of Demetrius Poliorcetes] were so inimitable

Stran.   Let the earth speak,
If there be atoms of him left, or even
Of the more solid gold that formed his urn.
    Arn. Who was this glory of mankind ?
    Stran.   The shame
Of Greece in peace, her thunderbolt in war—
Demetrius the Macedonian, and
Taker of cities.
    Arn.   Yet one shadow more.   260
    Stran. (*addressing the shadow*). Get thee to Lamia's
        lap !
    [*The shade of Demetrius Poliorcetes vanishes : another
        rises.*
                            I'll fit you still,
Fear not, my Hunchback : if the shadows of
That which existed please not your nice taste,
I'll animate the ideal marble, till
Your soul be reconciled to her new garment.
    Arn. Content ! I will fix here.
    Stran.   I must commend
Your choice. The godlike son of the sea-goddess,
The unshorn boy of Peleus, with his locks
As beautiful and clear as the amber waves
Of rich Pactolus, rolled o'er sands of gold,   270
Softened by intervening crystal, and
Rippled like flowing waters by the wind,

that no statuary or painter could hit off a likeness. His countenance
had a mixture of grace and dignity ; and was at once amiable and
awful ; and the unsubdued and eager air of youth was blended with the
majesty of the hero and the king.—Plutarch's *Lives,* Langhorne's
Translation, 1838, p. 616.
    Demetrius the Besieger rescued Greece from the sway of Ptolemy
and Cassander, B.C. 307. He passed the following winter at Athens,
where divine honours were paid to him under the title of "the Preserver" (ὁ Σωτήρ). He was "the shame of Greece in peace," by
reason of his profligacy—"the citadel was so polluted with his de-
baucheries, that it appeared to be kept sacred in some degree when he
indulged himself only with such *Hetæræ* as Chrysis, Lamia, Demo, and
Anticyra." He was the unspiritual ancestor of Charles the Second.
Once when his father, Antigonus, had been told that he was indisposed,
"he went to see him ; and when he came to the door, he met one of
his favourites going out. He went in, however, and, sitting down by
him, took hold of his hand. 'My fever,' said Demetrius, 'has left
me.' 'I knew it,' said Antigonus, 'for I met it this moment at the
door.' "—Plutarch's *Lives, ibid.,* pp. 621–623.]

All vowed to Sperchius [1] as they were—behold them !
And *him*—as he stood by Polixena,
With sanctioned and with softened love, before
The altar, gazing on his Trojan bride,
With some remorse within for Hector slain
And Priam weeping, mingled with deep passion
For the sweet downcast virgin, whose young hand
Trembled in *his* who slew her brother.   So   280
He stood i' the temple !   Look upon him as
Greece looked her last upon her best, the instant
Ere Paris' arrow flew.

   Arn.   I gaze upon him
As if I were his soul, whose form shall soon
Envelope mine.

   Stran.   You have done well.   The greatest
Deformity should only barter with
The extremest beauty—if the proverb 's true
Of mortals, that Extremes meet.

   Arn.   Come !   Be quick !
I am impatient.

   Stran.   As a youthful beauty
Before her glass.   *You both* see what is not,   290
But dream it is what must be.

   Arn.   Must I wait?

   Stran. No ; that were a pity.   But a word or two :
His stature is twelve cubits ; would you so far
Outstep these times, and be a Titan ?   Or
(To talk canonically) wax a son
Of Anak ?

   Arn.   Why not?

   Stran.   Glorious ambition !
I love thee most in dwarfs !   A mortal of
Philistine stature would have gladly pared
His own Goliath down to a slight David :
But thou, my manikin, wouldst soar a show   300
Rather than hero.   Thou shalt be indulged,

---

1. [Spercheus was a river-god, the husband of Polydora, the daughter
of Peleus. Peleus casts into the river the hair of his son Achilles, in
the pious hope that his son-in-law would accept the votive offering, and
grant the youth a safe return from the Trojan war. See *Iliad*, xxiii.
140, *sqq.*]

If such be thy desire; and, yet, by being
A little less removed from present men
In figure, thou canst sway them more; for all
Would rise against thee now, as if to hunt
A new-found Mammoth; and their curséd engines,
Their culverins, and so forth, would find way
Through our friend's armour there, with greater ease
Than the Adulterer's arrow through his heel
Which Thetis had forgotten to baptize   310
In Styx.
   Arn.   Then let it be as thou deem'st best.
   Stran. Thou shalt be beauteous as the thing thou seest,
And strong as what it was, and——
   Arn.   I ask not
For Valour, since Deformity is daring.[1]
It is its essence to o'ertake mankind
By heart and soul, and make itself the equal—
Aye, the superior of the rest.   There is
A spur in its halt movements, to become
All that the others cannot, in such things
As still are free to both, to compensate   320
For stepdame Nature's avarice at first.
They woo with fearless deeds the smiles of fortune,
And oft, like Timour the lame Tartar,[2] win them.
   Stran. Well spoken!   And thou doubtless wilt remain
Formed as thou art.   I may dismiss the mould
Of shadow, which must turn to flesh, to incase
This daring soul, which could achieve no less
Without it.

---

   1. ["Whosoever," says Bacon, "hath anything fixed in his person
that doth induce contempt, hath also a perpetual spur in himself
to rescue and deliver himself from scorn; therefore, all deformed
persons are extreme bold; first, as in their own defence, as being
exposed to scorn, but in process of time by a general habit; also it
stirreth in them industry, and especially of this kind, to watch and
observe the weakness of others, that they may have somewhat to repay"
(Essay xliv.).   Byron's "chief incentive, when a boy, to distinction
was that mark of deformity on his person, by an acute sense of which
he was first stung into the ambition of being great."—*Life*, p. 306.]
   2. [Timúr Bey, or Timúr Lang, *i.e.* "the lame Timúr" (A.D. 1336–
1405), was the founder of the Mogul dynasty.   He was the Tamerlane
of history and of legend.   Byron had certainly read the selections from
Marlowe's *Tamburlaine the Great*, in Lamb's *Specimens of English
Dramatic Poets*.]

Arn.   Had no power presented me
The possibility of change, I would
Have done the best which spirit may to make   330
Its way with all Deformity's dull, deadly,
Discouraging weight upon me, like a mountain,
In feeling, on my heart as on my shoulders—
A hateful and unsightly molehill to
The eyes of happier men.   I would have looked
On Beauty in that sex which is the type
Of all we know or dream of beautiful,
Beyond the world they brighten, with a sigh—
Not of love, but despair; nor sought to win,
Though to a heart all love, what could not love me   340
In turn, because of this vile crookéd clog,
Which makes me lonely.   Nay, I could have borne
It all, had not my mother spurned me from her.
The she-bear licks her cubs into a sort
Of shape;—my Dam beheld my shape was hopeless.
Had she exposed me, like the Spartan, ere
I knew the passionate part of life, I had
Been a clod of the valley,—happier nothing
Than what I am.   But even thus—the lowest,
Ugliest, and meanest of mankind—what courage   350
And perseverance could have done, perchance
Had made me something—as it has made heroes
Of the same mould as mine.   You lately saw me
Master of my own life, and quick to quit it;
And he who is so is the master of
Whatever dreads to die.
     Stran.   Decide between
What you have been, or will be.
     Arn.   I have done so.
You have opened brighter prospects to my eyes,
And sweeter to my heart.   As I am now,
I might be feared—admired—respected—loved   360
Of all save those next to me, of whom I
Would be belovéd.   As thou showest me
A choice of forms, I take the one I view.
Haste ! haste !
     Stran.   And what shall *I* wear ?
     Arn.   Surely, he

Who can command all forms will choose the highest,
Something superior even to that which was
Pelides now before us.   Perhaps *his*
Who slew him, that of Paris : or—still higher—
The Poet's God, clothed in such limbs as are
Themselves a poetry.
 Stran.   Less will content me ; 370
For I, too, love a change.
 Arn.   Your aspect is
Dusky, but not uncomely.[1]
 Stran.   If I chose,
I might be whiter ; but I have a *penchant*
For black—it is so honest, and, besides,
Can neither blush with shame nor pale with fear ;
But I have worn it long enough of late,
And now I'll take your figure.
 Arn.   Mine !
 Stran.   Yes.   You
Shall change with Thetis' son, and I with Bertha,
Your mother's offspring.   People have their tastes ;
You have yours—I mine.
 Arn.   Despatch ! despatch !
 Stran.   Even so.
 [*The Stranger takes some earth and moulds it along
  the turf, and then addresses the phantom of
  Achilles.*

    Beautiful shadow   381
     Of Thetis's boy !
    Who sleeps in the meadow
     Whose grass grows o'er Troy :
    From the red earth, like Adam,[2]
     Thy likeness I shape,
    As the Being who made him,
     Whose actions I ape.
    Thou Clay, be all glowing,
     Till the Rose in his cheek 390
    Be as fair as, when blowing,
     It wears its first streak !

1. ["I am black, but comely."—*Song of Solomon* i. 5.]
2. Adam means "*red earth*," from which the first man was formed.
[The word '*adām* is said to be analogous to the Assyrian *admu*,
"child"—*i.e.* "one made" by God.—*Encycl. Bibl.*, art. "Adam."]

Ye Violets, I scatter,
  Now turn into eyes !
And thou, sunshiny Water,
  Of blood take the guise !
Let these Hyacinth boughs
  Be his long flowing hair,
And wave o'er his brows,
  As thou wavest in air !   400
Let his heart be this marble
  I tear from the rock !
But his voice as the warble
  Of birds on yon oak !
Let his flesh be the purest
  Of mould, in which grew
The Lily-root surest,
  And drank the best dew !
Let his limbs be the lightest
  Which clay can compound,   410
And his aspect the brightest
  On earth to be found !
Elements, near me,
  Be mingled and stirred,
Know me, and hear me,
  And leap to my word !
Sunbeams, awaken
  This earth's animation ![1.]
'Tis done ! He hath taken
  His stand in creation !   420
[ARNOLD *falls senseless ; his soul passes into the shape
  of Achilles, which rises from the ground ; while
  the phantom has disappeared, part by part, as the
  figure was formed from the earth.*

Arn. (*in his new form*). I love, and I shall be beloved !
    Oh, life !
At last I feel thee ! Glorious Spirit !
    Stran.   Stop !
What shall become of your abandoned garment,
Yon hump, and lump, and clod of ugliness,
Which late you wore, or were ?
    Arn.   Who cares ? Let wolves

i. *This shape into Life.*—[*MS.*]

And vultures take it, if they will.

Stran.   And if
They do, and are not scared by it, you'll say
It must be peace-time, and no better fare
Abroad i' the fields.

Arn.   Let us but leave it there;
No matter what becomes on't.

Stran.   That's ungrateful; 430
If not ungrateful.   Whatsoe'er it be,
It hath sustained your soul full many a day.

Arn. Aye, as the dunghill may conceal a gem
Which is now set in gold, as jewels should be.

Stran. But if I give another form, it must be
By fair exchange, not robbery.   For they [1]
Who make men without women's aid have long
Had patents for the same, and do not love
Your Interlopers.   The Devil may take men,[i.]
Not make them,—though he reap the benefit   440
Of the original workmanship :—and therefore
Some one must be found to assume the shape
You have quitted.

Arn.   Who would do so?

Stran.   That I know not,
And therefore I must.

Arn.   You !

Stran.   I said it ere
You inhabited your present dome of beauty.

Arn. True.   I forget all things in the new joy
Of this immortal change.

Stran.   In a few moments
I will be as you were, and you shall see

---

i. *Your Interloper* ——.—[*MS.*]

1. [The reference is to the *homunculi* of the alchymists. See Retzsch's
illustrations to Goethe's *Faust*, 1834, plates 3, 4, 5. Compare, too,
The Second Part of Faust, act ii.—

> "The glass rings low, the charming power that lives
>   Within it makes the music that it gives.
>   It dims ! it brightens ! it will shape itself.
>   And see ! a graceful dazzling little elf.
>   He lives ! he moves ! spruce mannikin of fire,
>   What more can we ? what more can earth desire?"
>   Anster's Translation, 1886, p. 91.]

Yourself for ever by you, as your shadow.
   Arn. I would be spared this.
   Stran.   But it cannot be.   450
What! shrink already, being what you are,
From seeing what you were?
   Arn.   Do as thou wilt.
   Stran. (*to the late form of* ARNOLD, *extended on the*
        earth).
        Clay! not dead, but soul-less!
          Though no man would choose thee,
        An Immortal no less
          Deigns not to refuse thee.
        Clay thou art; and unto spirit
        All clay is of equal merit.
        Fire! *without* which nought can live;
        Fire! but *in* which nought can live,   460
          Save the fabled salamander,
          Or immortal souls, which wander,
        Praying what doth not forgive,
        Howling for a drop of water,
           Burning in a quenchless lot:
        Fire! the only element
          Where nor fish, beast, bird, nor worm,
           Save the Worm which dieth not,
          Can preserve a moment's form,
        But must with thyself be blent: 470
        Fire! man's safeguard and his slaughter:
        Fire! Creation's first-born Daughter,
          And Destruction's threatened Son,
          When Heaven with the world hath done:
        Fire! assist me to renew
        Life in what lies in my view
          Stiff and cold!
        His resurrection rests with me and you!
        One little, marshy spark of flame—[1]
        And he again shall seem the same;   480
          But I his Spirit's place shall hold!

---

   1. [Compare *Prisoner of Chillon*, stanza ii. line 35, *Poetical Works*,
1901, iv. 15, *note* 1. Compare, too, the dialogue between Mephistopheles
and the Will-o'-the-Wisp, in the scene on the Hartz Mountains, in
Faust, Part I. (see Anster's Translation, 1886, p. 271).]

[*An ignis-fatuus flits through the wood and rests on
the brow of the body.   The Stranger disappears:
the body rises.*

Arn. (*in his new form*). Oh! horrible!
Stran. (*in* ARNOLD'S *late shape*). What! tremblest thou?
Arn.   Not so—
I merely shudder.   Where is fled the shape
Thou lately worest?
    Stran.   To the world of shadows.
But let us thread the present.   Whither wilt thou?
    Arn. Must thou be my companion?
    Stran.   Wherefore not?
Your betters keep worse company.
    Arn.   *My* betters!
    Stran. Oh! you wax proud, I see, of your new form:
I'm glad of that.   Ungrateful too!   That's well;
You improve apace;—two changes in an instant,   490
And you are old in the World's ways already.
But bear with me: indeed you'll find me useful
Upon your pilgrimage.   But come, pronounce
Where shall we now be errant?
    Arn.   Where the World
Is thickest, that I may behold it in
Its workings.
    Stran.   That's to say, where there is War
And Woman in activity.   Let's see!
Spain—Italy—the new Atlantic world—[1]
Afric with all its Moors.   In very truth,
There is small choice: the whole race are just now   500
Tugging as usual at each other's hearts.
    Arn. I have heard great things of Rome.
    Stran.   A goodly choice—
And scarce a better to be found on earth,
Since Sodom was put out.   The field is wide too;
For now the Frank, and Hun, and Spanish scion
Of the old Vandals, are at play along

---

1. [The immediate reference is to the composite forces, German,
French, and Spanish, of the Imperial Army under the command of
Charles de Bourbon; but there is in lines 498–507 a manifest allusion
to the revolutionary movements in South America, Italy, and Spain,
which were at their height in 1822. (See the *Age of Bronze*, section vi.
lines 260, *sq.*, *post*, pp. 555–557.)]

The sunny shores of the World's garden.
   Arn.   How
Shall we proceed?
   Stran.   Like gallants, on good coursers.
What, ho! my chargers! Never yet were better,
Since Phaeton was upset into the Po.[1]   510
Our pages too!

    Enter two Pages, with four coal-black horses.

   Arn.   A noble sight!
   Stran.   And of
A nobler breed. Match me in Barbary,
Or your Kochlini race of Araby,[i. 2]
With these!
   Arn.   The mighty steam, which volumes high
From their proud nostrils, burns the very air;
And sparks of flame, like dancing fire-flies wheel
Around their manes, as common insects swarm
Round common steeds towards sunset.
   Stran.   Mount, my lord:
They and I are your servitors.
   Arn.   And these
Our dark-eyed pages—what may be their names?   520
   Stran. You shall baptize them.
   Arn.   What! in holy water?
   Stran. Why not? The deeper sinner, better saint.
   Arn. They are beautiful, and cannot, sure, be demons.
   Stran. True; the devil's always ugly: and your beauty
Is never diabolical.
   Arn.   I'll call him
Who bears the golden horn, and wears such bright
And blooming aspect, *Huon;*[3] for he looks

i. *Kochlani* ——.—[*MS.*]

1. [See Euripides, *Hippolytus*, line 733.]
2. [Kochlani horses were bred in a central province of Arabia.]
3. [Byron's knowledge of Huon of Bordeaux was, most probably,
derived from Sotheby's *Oberon; or, Huon de Bourdeux: A Mask*,
published in 1802. For *The Boke of Duke Huon of Burdeux*, done
into English by Sir John Bourchier, Lord Berners, see the reprint
issued by the Early English Text Society (E.S., No. xliii. 1884); and
for *Analyse de Huon de Bordeaux, etc.*, see *Les Epopées Françaises*, by
Léon Gautier, 1880, ii. 719-773.]

Like to the lovely boy lost in the forest,
And never found till now.   And for the other
And darker, and more thoughtful, who smiles not,   530
But looks as serious though serene as night,
He shall be *Memnon*,[1] from the Ethiop king
Whose statue turns a harper once a day.
And you ?
    Stran.   I have ten thousand names, and twice
As many attributes ; but as I wear
A human shape, will take a human name.
    Arn. More human than the shape (though it was mine
        once)
I trust.
    Stran. Then call me Cæsar.
    Arn.   Why, that name
Belongs to Empire, and has been but borne
By the World's lords.
    Stran.   And therefore fittest for   540
The Devil in disguise—since so you deem me,
Unless you call me Pope instead.
    Arn.   Well, then,
Cæsar thou shalt be.   For myself, my name
Shall be plain Arnold still.
    Cæs.   We'll add a title—[i]
" Count Arnold : " it hath no ungracious sound,
And will look well upon a billet-doux.
    Arn. Or in an order for a battle-field.
    Cæs. (sings). To horse ! to horse ! my coal-black steed
        Paws the ground and snuffs the air !
There 's not a foal of Arab's breed   550
        More knows whom he must bear ;

        i. *We'll add a " Count " to it.*—[*MS.*]

    1. [The so-called statue of Memnon, the beautiful son of Tithonus
and Éos (Dawn), is now known to be that of Amenhotep III., who
reigned in the eighteenth dynasty, about 1430 B.C.   Strabo, ed. 1807,
p. 1155, was the first to record the musical note which sounded from
the statue when it was touched by the rays of the rising sun.   It used
to be argued (see Gifford's note to *Don Juan*, Canto XIII. stanza lxiv.
line 3, ed. 1837, p. 731) that the sounds were produced by a trick, but
of late years it has been maintained that the Memnon's wail was due
to natural causes, the pressure of suddenly-warmed currents of air
through the pores and crevices of the stone.   After the statue was restored, the phenomenon ceased.   (See *La statue vocale de Memnon*, par
J. A. Letronne, Paris, 1833, pp. 55, 56.)]

On the hill he will not tire,
Swifter as it waxes higher ;
In the marsh he will not slacken,
On the plain be overtaken ;
In the wave he will not sink,
Nor pause at the brook's side to drink ;
In the race he will not pant,
In the combat he'll not faint ;
On the stones he will not stumble,   560
Time nor toil shall make him humble ;
In the stall he will not stiffen,
But be wingèd as a Griffin,
Only flying with his feet :
And will not such a voyage be sweet ?
Merrily ! merrily ! never unsound,
Shall our bonny black horses skim over the ground !
From the Alps to the Caucasus, ride we, or fly !
For we'll leave them behind in the glance of an eye.
                    [*They mount their horses, and disappear.*

SCENE II.—*A Camp before the walls of Rome.*

ARNOLD *and* CÆSAR.

Cæs. You are well entered now.
    Arn.   Aye ; but my path
Has been o'er carcasses : mine eyes are full [i.]
Of blood.
    Cæs.   Then wipe them, and see clearly.   Why !
Thou art a conqueror ; the chosen knight
And free companion of the gallant Bourbon,
Late constable of France ; [1] and now to be

----

i. —— *my eyes are full.*—[*MS.*]

1. [Charles de Bourbon, Comte de Montpensier et de la Marche,
Dauphin d'Auvergne, was born February 17, 1490. He served in Italy
with Bayard, and helped to decide the victory of Agnadello (A.D. 1510).
He was appointed Constable of France by Francis I., January, 1515,
and fought at the battle of Marignano, September 13, 1515. Not long
afterwards he lost the king's favour, who was set against him by his
mother, Louise de Savoie ; was recalled from his command in Italy,
and superseded by Odet de Foix, brother of the king's mistress. It

Lord of the city which hath been Earth's Lord
Under its emperors, and—changing sex,
Not sceptre, an Hermaphrodite of Empire—
Lady of the old world.[1]

    Arn.   How *old?* What! are there 10
New worlds?

    Cæs.   To *you.* You'll find there are such shortly,
By its rich harvests, new disease, and gold;
From one *half* of the world named a *whole* new one,
Because you know no better than the dull
And dubious notice of your eyes and ears.

    Arn. I'll trust them.

    Cæs.   Do! They will deceive you sweetly,
And that is better than the bitter truth.

    Arn. Dog!

    Cæs.   Man!

    Arn.   Devil!

was not, however, till he became a widower (Susanne, Duchesse de Bourbon, died April 28, 1521) that he finally broke with Francis and attached himself to the Emperor Charles V. *Madame*, the king's mother, not only coveted the vast estates of the house of Bourbon, but was enamoured of the Constable's person, and, so to speak, gave him his choice between marriage and a suit for his fiefs. Charles would have nothing to say to the lady's proposals or to her son's entreaties, and seeing that rejection meant ruin, he " entered into a correspondence with the Emperor and the King [Henry VIII.] of England . . . and, finding this discovered, went into the Emperor's service."

After various and varying successes, both in the South of France and in Lombardy, he found himself, in the spring of 1527, not so much the commander-in-chief as the popular *capo* of a mixed body of German, Spanish, and Italian *condottieri*, unpaid and ill-disciplined, who had mutinied more than once, who could only be kept together by the prospect of unlimited booty, and a timely concession to their demands. "To Rome! to Rome!" cried the hungry and tumultuous *landsknechts*, and on May 5, 1527, the "late Constable of France," at the head of an army of 30,000 troops, appeared before the walls of the sacred city. On the morning of the 6th of May, he was killed by a shot from an arquebuse. His epitaph recounts his honours: " Aucto Imperio, Gallo victo, Superatâ Italiâ, Pontifice obsesso, Româ captâ, Borbonius, Hic Jacet; " but in Paris they painted the sill of his gate-way yellow, because he was a renegade and a traitor. He could not have said, with the dying Bayard, " Ne me plaignez pas—je meurs sans avoir servi contre *ma patrie, mon roy*, et mon serment." (See *Modern Universal History*, 1760, xxiv. 150–152, Note C ; *Nouvelle Biographie Universelle*, art. "Bourbon.")]

1. [The contrast is between imperial Rome, the Lord of the world, and papal Rome, " the great harlot which did corrupt the earth with her fornication " (*Rev.* xix. 2). Compare Part II. sc. iii. line 26, *vide post*, p. 521.]

Cæs.   Your obedient humble servant.
Arn. Say *master* rather.   Thou hast lured me on,
Through scenes of blood and lust, till I am here.   20
   Cæs. And where wouldst thou be?
   Arn.   Oh, *at* peace—*in* peace!
   Cæs. And where is that which is so?   From the star
To the winding worm, all life is motion; and
In life *commotion* is the extremest point
Of life.   The planet wheels till it becomes
A comet, and destroying as it sweeps
The stars, goes out.   The poor worm winds its way,
Living upon the death of other things,
But still, like them, must live and die, the subject
Of something which has made it live and die.   30
You must obey what all obey, the rule
Of fixed Necessity: against her edict
Rebellion prospers not.
   Arn.   And when it prospers——
   Cæs. 'Tis no rebellion.
   Arn.   Will it prosper now?
   Cæs. The Bourbon hath given orders for the assault,
And by the dawn there will be work.
   Arn.   Alas!
And shall the city yield?   I see the giant
Abode of the true God, and his true saint,
Saint Peter, rear its dome and cross into
That sky whence Christ ascended from the cross,   40
Which his blood made a badge of glory and
Of joy (as once of torture unto him),—
God and God's Son, man's sole and only refuge!
   Cæs. 'Tis there, and shall be.
   Arn.   What?
   Cæs.   The Crucifix
Above, and many altar shrines below.
Also some culverins upon the walls,
And harquebusses, and what not; besides
The men who are to kindle them to death
Of other men.
   Arn.   And those scarce mortal arches,[1]

1. [Compare *Manfred*, act iii. sc. 4, line 10; and *Childe Harold*, Canto IV. stanza cxxviii. line 1; *Poetical Works*, 1901, iv. 131, 1899, ii. 423, *note* 2.]

Pile above pile of everlasting wall,   50
The theatre where Emperors and their subjects
(Those subjects *Romans*) stood at gaze upon
The battles of the monarchs of the wild
And wood—the lion and his tusky rebels
Of the then untamed desert, brought to joust
In the arena—as right well they might,
When they had left no human foe unconquered—
Made even the forest pay its tribute of
Life to their amphitheatre, as well
As Dacia men to die the eternal death   60
For a sole instant's pastime, and " Pass on
To a new gladiator ! "—Must it fall ?
   Cæs. The city, or the amphitheatre ?
The church, or one, or all ? for you confound
Both them and me.
   Arn.   To-morrow sounds the assault
With the first cock-crow.
   Cæs.   Which, if it end with
The evening's first nightingale, will be
Something new in the annals of great sieges ;
For men must have their prey after long toil.
   Arn. The sun goes down as calmly, and perhaps   70
More beautifully, than he did on Rome
On the day Remus leapt her wall.
   Cæs.   I saw him.
   Arn. You !
   Cæs.   Yes, Sir !   You forget I am or was
Spirit, till I took up with your cast shape,
And a worse name.   I'm Cæsar and a hunch-back
Now.   Well ! the first of Cæsars was a bald-head,
And loved his laurels better as a wig
(So history says) than as a glory.[1]   Thus
The world runs on, but we'll be merry still.
I saw your Romulus (simple as I am)   80
Slay his own twin, quick-born of the same womb,
Because he leapt a ditch ('twas then no wall,

1. ["Calvitii vero deformitatem iniquissime ferret, sæpe obtrectatorum jocis obnoxiam expertus.   Ideoque et deficientem capillum revocare a vertice assuerat, et ex omnibus decretis sibi a Senatu populoque honoribus non aliud aut recepit aut usurpavit libentius, quam jus laureæ coronæ perpetuo gestandæ."—Suetonius, *Opera Omnia*, 1826, i. 105, 106.]

Whate'er it now be); and Rome's earliest cement
Was brother's blood; and if its native blood
Be spilt till the choked Tiber be as red
As e'er 'twas yellow, it will never wear
The deep hue of the Ocean and the Earth,
Which the great robber sons of fratricide
Have made their never-ceasing scene of slaughter,
For ages.

 Arn. But what have these done, their far 90
Remote descendants, who have lived in peace,
The peace of Heaven, and in her sunshine of
Piety?

 Cæs. And what had *they* done, whom the old
Romans o'erswept?—Hark !

 Arn.   They are soldiers singing
A reckless roundelay, upon the eve
Of many deaths, it may be of their own.

 Cæs. And why should they not sing as well as swans?
They are black ones, to be sure.

 Arn.   So, you are learned,
I see, too?

 Cæs. In my grammar, certes. I
Was educated for a monk of all times,   100
And once I was well versed in the forgotten
Etruscan letters, and—were I so minded—
Could make their hieroglyphics plainer than
Your alphabet.

 Arn.   And wherefore do you not?

 Cæs. It answers better to resolve the alphabet
Back into hieroglyphics. Like your statesman,
And prophet, pontiff, doctor, alchymist,
Philosopher, and what not, they have built
More Babels, without new dispersion, than
The stammering young ones of the flood's dull ooze, 110
Who failed and fled each other. Why? why, marry,
Because no man could understand his neighbour.
They are wiser now, and will not separate
For nonsense. Nay, it is their brotherhood,
Their Shibboleth—their Koran—Talmud—their
Cabala—their best brick-work, wherewithal
They build more——

Arn. (*interrupting him*). Oh, thou everlasting sneerer !
Be silent ! How the soldier's rough strain seems
Softened by distance to a hymn-like cadence !
Listen !

    Cæs. Yes. I have heard the angels sing.   120
    Arn. And demons howl.
    Cæs.   And man, too. Let us listen :
I love all music.

Song of the Soldiers within.

The black bands came over
    The Alps and their snow ;
With Bourbon, the rover,
    They passed the broad Po.
We have beaten all foemen,
    We have captured a King,[1]
We have turned back on no men,
    And so let us sing !   130
Here 's the Bourbon for ever !
    Though penniless all,
We'll have one more endeavour
    At yonder old wall.
With the Bourbon we'll gather
    At day-dawn before
The gates, and together
    Or break or climb o'er
The wall : on the ladder,
    As mounts each firm foot,[L]   140
Our shout shall grow gladder,
    And Death only be mute.[2]
With the Bourbon we'll mount o'er
    The walls of old Rome,
And who then shall count o'er [ii.]
    The spoils of each dome ?

    i. *With a soldier's firm foot.*—[*MS.*]
    ii. *With the Bourbon will count o'er.*—[*MS.*]

    1. [Francis the First was taken prisoner at the Battle of Pavia,
February 24, 1525.]
    2. [Compare *The Siege of Corinth*, line 752, *Poetical Works*, 1900,
iii. 483. There is a note of tragic irony in the soldiers' vain-glorious
prophecy.]

Up! up with the Lily!
    And down with the Keys!
In old Rome, the seven-hilly,
    We'll revel at ease.   150
Her streets shall be gory,
    Her Tiber all red,
And her temples so hoary
    Shall clang with our tread.
Oh, the Bourbon! the Bourbon![1]
    The Bourbon for aye!
Of our song bear the burden!
    And fire, fire away!
With Spain for the vanguard,
    Our varied host comes;   160
And next to the Spaniard
    Beat Germany's drums;
And Italy's lances
    Are couched at their mother;
But our leader from France is,
    Who warred with his brother.
Oh, the Bourbon! the Bourbon!
    Sans country or home,
We'll follow the Bourbon,
    To plunder old Rome.   170

Cæs.   An indifferent song
For those within the walls, methinks, to hear.
    Arn. Yes, if they keep to their chorus. But here comes
The general with his chiefs and men of trust.[i.]
A goodly rebel.

    Enter the Constable BOURBON *" cum suis," etc., etc.*

    Phil.   How now, noble Prince,
You are not cheerful?
    Bourb.   Why should I be so?
    Phil. Upon the eve of conquest, such as ours,
Most men would be so.

    i. *The General with his men of confidence.*—[MS.]

    1. [Brantôme (*Memoires, etc.,* 1722, i. 215) quotes a "chanson" of
" Les soldats Espagnols" as they marched Romewards. "Calla calla
Julio Cesar, Hannibal, y Scipion! Viva la fama de Bourbon."]

Bourb.   If I were secure !

Phil. Doubt not our soldiers. Were the walls of
    adamant,

They'd crack them. Hunger is a sharp artillery.   180

    Bourb. That they will falter is my least of fears.

That they will be repulsed, with Bourbon for

Their chief, and all their kindled appetites

To marshal them on—were those hoary walls

Mountains, and those who guard them like the gods

Of the old fables, I would trust my Titans ;—

But now——

    Phil.   They are but men who war with mortals.

    Bourb. True : but those walls have girded in great
    ages,

And sent forth mighty spirits. The past earth

And present phantom of imperious Rome [i]   190

Is peopled with those warriors ; and methinks

They flit along the eternal City's rampart,

And stretch their glorious, gory, shadowy hands,

And beckon me away !

    Phil.   So let them ! Wilt thou

Turn back from shadowy menaces of shadows ?

    Bourb. They do not menace me. I could have
    faced,

Methinks, a Sylla's menace ; but they clasp,

And raise, and wring their dim and deathlike hands,

And with their thin aspen faces and fixed eyes

Fascinate mine. Look there !

    Phil.   I look upon   200

A lofty battlement.

    Bourb.   And there !

    Phil.   Not even

A guard in sight ; they wisely keep below,

Sheltered by the grey parapet from some

Stray bullet of our lansquenets, who might

Practise in the cool twilight.

    Bourb.   You are blind.

    Phil. If seeing nothing more than may be seen

Be so.

    Bourb. A thousand years have manned the walls

    i. *And present phantom of that deathless world.*—[*MS.*]

With all their heroes,—the last Cato [1] stands
And tears his bowels, rather than survive
The liberty of that I would enslave.   210
And the first Cæsar with his triumphs flits
From battlement to battlement.
    Phil.   Then conquer
The walls for which he conquered and be greater!
    Bourb. True : so I will, or perish.
    Phil.   You can *not*.
In such an enterprise to die is rather
The dawn of an eternal day, than death.
           [*Count* ARNOLD *and* CÆSAR *advance.*
    Cæs. And the mere men—do they, too, sweat beneath
The noon of this same ever-scorching glory?
    Bourb.   Ah!
Welcome the bitter Hunchback! and his master,
The beauty of our host, and brave as beauteous,   220
And generous as lovely.   We shall find
Work for you both ere morning.
    Cæs.   You will find,
So please your Highness, no less for yourself.
    Bourb. And if I do, there will not be a labourer
More forward, Hunchback!
    Cæs.   You may well say so,
For *you* have seen that back—as general,
Placed in the rear in action—but your foes
Have never seen it.
    Bourb.   That 's a fair retort,
For I provoked it :—but the Bourbon's breast
Has been, and ever shall be, far advanced   230
In danger's face as yours, were you the *devil*.
    Cæs. And if I were, I might have saved myself
The toil of coming here.
    Phil.   Why so?
    Cæs.   One half

---

1. [When the Uticans decided not to stand a siege, but to send
deputies to Cæsar, Cato determined to put an end to his life rather
than fall into the hands of the conqueror. Accordingly, after he had
retired to rest he stabbed himself under the breast, and when the
physician sewed up the wound, he thrust him away, and plucked out
his own bowels.— Plutarch's *Lives*, Langhorne's Translation, 1838,
p. 553.]

Of your brave bands of their own bold accord
Will go to him, the other half be sent,
More swiftly, not less surely.
    Bourb.   Arnold, your
Slight crooked *friend*'s as snake-like in his words
As his deeds.
    Cæs.   Your Highness much mistakes me.
The first snake was a flatterer—I am none;
And for my deeds, I only sting when stung.   240
    Bourb. You are brave, and *that*'s enough for me; and
        quick
In speech as sharp in action—and that 's more.
I am not alone the soldier, but the soldiers'
Comrade.
    Cæs.   They are but bad company, your Highness;
And worse even for their friends than foes, as being
More permanent acquaintance.
    Phil.   How now, fellow!
Thou waxest insolent, beyond the privilege
Of a buffoon.
    Cæs.   You mean I speak the truth.
I'll lie—it is as easy: then you'll praise me
For calling you a hero.
    Bourb.   Philibert!   250
Let him alone; he 's brave, and ever has
Been first, with that swart face and mountain shoulder,
In field or storm, and patient in starvation;
And for his tongue, the camp is full of licence,
And the sharp stinging of a lively rogue
Is, to my mind, far preferable to
The gross, dull, heavy, gloomy execration
Of a mere famished sullen grumbling slave,[i.]
Whom nothing can convince save a full meal,
And wine, and sleep, and a few Maravedis,   260
With which he deems him rich.
    Cæs.   It would be well
If the earth's princes asked no more.
    Bourb.   Be silent!
    Cæs. Aye, but not idle.   Work yourself with words![ii.]

      i. *Of a mere starving* ——.—[*MS.*]
     ii. —— *Work away with words.*—[*MS.*]

You have few to speak.

Phil.   What means the audacious prater?

Cæs. To prate, like other prophets.

Bourb.   Philibert!
Why will you vex him?   Have we not enough
To think on?   Arnold! I will lead the attack
To-morrow.

Arn.   I have heard as much, my Lord.

Bourb. And you will follow?

Arn.   Since I must not lead.

Bourb. 'Tis necessary for the further daring   270
Of our too needy army, that their chief
Plant the first foot upon the foremost ladder's
First step.

Cæs.   Upon its topmost, let us hope:
So shall he have his full deserts.

Bourb.   The world's
Great capital perchance is ours to-morrow.[i.]
Through every change the seven-hilled city hath
Retained her sway o'er nations, and the Cæsars
But yielded to the Alarics, the Alarics
Unto the pontiffs.   Roman, Goth, or priest,
Still the world's masters!   Civilised, barbarian,   280
Or saintly, still the walls of Romulus
Have been the circus of an Empire.   Well!
'Twas *their* turn—now 'tis ours; and let us hope
That we will fight as well, and rule much better.

Cæs. No doubt, the camp's the school of civic rights.
What would you make of Rome?

Bourb.   That which it was.

Cæs. In Alaric's time?

Bourb.   No, slave! in the first Cæsar's,
Whose name you bear like other curs——

Cæs.   And kings!
'Tis a great name for blood-hounds.

Bourb.   There's a demon
In that fierce rattlesnake thy tongue.   Wilt never   290
Be serious?

Cæs.   On the eve of battle, no;—
That were not soldier-like.   'Tis for the general

i. *First City rests upon to-morrow's action.*—[MS.]

To be more pensive : we adventurers
Must be more cheerful.   Wherefore should we think ?
Our tutelar Deity, in a leader's shape,
Takes care of us.   Keep thought aloof from hosts !
If the knaves take to thinking, you will have
To crack those walls alone.
    Bourb.   You may sneer, since
'Tis lucky for you that you fight no worse for 't.
    Cæs. I thank you for the freedom ; 'tis the only   300
Pay I have taken in your Highness' service.
    Bourb. Well, sir, to-morrow you shall pay yourself.
Look on those towers ; they hold my treasury :
But, Philibert, we'll in to council.   Arnold,
We would request your presence.
    Arn.   Prince ! my service
Is yours, as in the field.
    Bourb.   In both we prize it,
And yours will be a post of trust at daybreak.
    Cæs. And mine ?
    Bourb.   To follow glory with the Bourbon.
Good night !
    Arn. (*to* CÆSAR). Prepare our armour for the assault,
And wait within my tent.
              [*Exeunt* BOURBON, ARNOLD, PHILIBERT, *etc.*
    Cæs. (*solus*).   Within thy tent !   310
Think'st thou that I pass from thee with my presence ?
Or that this crooked coffer, which contained
Thy principle of life, is aught to me
Except a mask ?   And these are men, forsooth !
Heroes and chiefs, the flower of Adam's bastards !
This is the consequence of giving matter
The power of thought.   It is a stubborn substance,
And thinks chaotically, as it acts,
Ever relapsing into its first elements.
Well ! I must play with these poor puppets : 'tis   320
The Spirit's pastime in his idler hours.
When I grow weary of it, I have business
Amongst the stars, which these poor creatures deem
Were made for them to look at.   'Twere a jest now
To bring one down amongst them, and set fire
Unto their anthill : how the pismires then

Would scamper o'er the scalding soil, and, ceasing
From tearing down each other's nests, pipe forth
One universal orison! ha! ha!   [*Exit* CÆSAR.

PART II.

SCENE I.—*Before the walls of Rome.*—*The Assault: the
Army in motion, with ladders to scale the walls;* [1]
BOURBON *with a white scarf over his armour, foremost.*

Chorus of Spirits in the air.

I.

'Tis the morn, but dim and dark.[i]
Whither flies the silent lark?
Whither shrinks the clouded sun?
Is the day indeed begun?
Nature's eye is melancholy
O'er the city high and holy:
But without there is a din
Should arouse the saints within,
And revive the heroic ashes
Round which yellow Tiber dashes.   10
Oh, ye seven hills! awaken,
Ere your very base be shaken!

II.

Hearken to the steady stamp!
Mars is in their every tramp!

---

i. *'Tis the morning—Hark! Hark! Hark!—[MS.]*

1. ["Dès l'aube du lundi 6 mai 1527, le connétable, à cheval, la
cuirasse couverte d'un manteau blanc, marcha vers le Borgo, dont les
murailles, à la hauteur de San-Spirito, étaient d'accès facile. . . .
Bourbon mit pied à terre, et, prenant lui-même une échelle l'appliqua
tout près de la porte Torrione."—*De l'Italie*, par Émile Gebhart,
1876, p. 255. Cæsar Grolierius (*Historia expugnatæ . . . Urbis*,
1637), who claims to speak as an eye-witness (p. 2), describes "Borbonius" as "insignemque veste et armis" (p. 62).]

Not a step is out of tune,
As the tides obey the moon !
On they march, though to self-slaughter,
Regular as rolling water,
Whose high-waves o'ersweep the border
Of huge moles, but keep their order,   20
Breaking only rank by rank.
Hearken to the armour's clank !
Look down o'er each frowning warrior,
How he glares upon the barrier :
Look on each step of each ladder,
As the stripes that streak an adder.

III.

Look upon the bristling wall,
Manned without an interval !
Round and round, and tier on tier,
Cannon's black mouth, shining spear,   30
Lit match, bell-mouthed Musquetoon,
Gaping to be murderous soon ;
All the warlike gear of old,
Mixed with what we now behold,
 In this strife 'twixt old and new,
Gather like a locusts' crew.
Shade of Remus ! 'tis a time
Awful as thy brother's crime !
Christians war against Christ's shrine :—
Must its lot be like to thine ?   40

IV.

Near—and near—and nearer still,
As the Earthquake saps the hill,
First with trembling, hollow motion,
Like a scarce awakened ocean,
Then with stronger shock and louder,
Till the rocks are crushed to powder,—
Onward sweeps the rolling host !
Heroes of the immortal boast !
Mighty Chiefs ! eternal shadows !
First flowers of the bloody meadows   50

Which encompass Rome, the mother
Of a people without brother !
Will you sleep when nations' quarrels
Plough the root up of your laurels ?
Ye who weep o'er Carthage burning,
Weep not—*strike !* for Rome is mourning ![1]

V.

Onward sweep the varied nations !
Famine long hath dealt their rations.
To the wall, with hate and hunger,
Numerous as wolves, and stronger,   60
On they sweep.   Oh, glorious City !
Must thou be a theme for pity ?
Fight, like your first sire, each Roman !
Alaric was a gentle foeman,
Matched with Bourbon's black banditti !
Rouse thee, thou eternal City ;
Rouse thee !   Rather give the torch
With thine own hand to thy porch,[L]
Than behold such hosts pollute
Your worst dwelling with their foot.   70

VI.

Ah ! behold yon bleeding spectre !
Ilion's children find no Hector ;
Priam's offspring loved their brother ;
Rome's great sire forgot his mother,
When he slew his gallant twin,
With inexpiable sin.
See the giant shadow stride
O'er the ramparts high and wide !
When the first o'erleapt thy wall,
Its foundation mourned thy fall.   80
Now, though towering like a Babel,
Who to stop his steps are able ?

i. *Than such victors should pollute.*—[*MS.*]

1. Scipio, the second Africanus, is said to have repeated a verse of
Homer [*Iliad*. vi. 448], and wept over the burning of Carthage [B.C.
146].   He had better have granted it a capitulation.

Stalking o'er thy highest dome,
Remus claims his vengeance, Rome !

VII.

Now they reach thee in their anger:
Fire and smoke and hellish clangour
Are around thee, thou world's wonder !
Death is in thy walls and under.
Now the meeting steel first clashes,
Downward then the ladder crashes,   90
With its iron load all gleaming,
Lying at its foot blaspheming !
Up again ! for every warrior
Slain, another climbs the barrier.
Thicker grows the strife : thy ditches
Europe's mingling gore enriches.
Rome ! although thy wall may perish,
Such manure thy fields will cherish,
Making gay the harvest-home ;
But thy hearths, alas ! oh, Rome !—   100
Yet be Rome amidst thine anguish,
Fight as thou wast wont to vanquish !

VIII.

Yet once more, ye old Penates !
Let not your quenched hearts be Atés !
Yet again, ye shadowy Heroes,
Yield not to these stranger Neros !
Though the son who slew his mother
Shed Rome's blood, he was your brother:
'Twas the Roman curbed the Roman ;—
Brennus was a baffled foeman.   110
Yet again, ye saints and martyrs,
Rise ! for yours are holier charters !
Mighty Gods of temples falling,
Yet in ruin still appalling !
Mightier Founders of those altars,
True and Christian,—strike the assaulters !
Tiber ! Tiber ! let thy torrent
Show even Nature 's self abhorrent.

Let each breathing heart dilated
Turn, as doth the lion baited!   120
Rome be crushed to one wide tomb,
But be still the Roman's Rome![1]

[BOURBON, ARNOLD, CÆSAR, *and others, arrive at the foot of the wall.* ARNOLD *is about to plant his ladder.*

Bourb. Hold, Arnold! I am first.
Arn.   Not so, my Lord.
Bourb. Hold, sir, I charge you! Follow! I am proud
Of such a follower, but will brook no leader.

[BOURBON *plants his ladder, and begins to mount.*

Now, boys! On! on!

[*A shot strikes him, and* BOURBON *falls.*

Cæs.   And off!
Arn.   Eternal powers!
The host will be appalled,—but vengeance! vengeance!
Bourb. 'Tis nothing—lend me your hand.

[BOURBON *takes* ARNOLD *by the hand, and rises; but as he puts his foot on the step, falls again.*

                          Arnold! I am sped.
Conceal my fall[2]—all will go well—conceal it!
Fling my cloak o'er what will be dust anon;   130
Let not the soldiers see it.
Arn.   You must be
Removed; the aid of——
Bourb.   No, my gallant boy!
Death is upon me. But what is *one* life?
The Bourbon's spirit shall command them still.
Keep them yet ignorant that I am but clay,
Till they are conquerors—then do as you may.

---

1. [Byron retains or adopts the old-fashioned pronunciation of the word "Rome" *metri gratiâ.* Compare *The Island,* Canto II. line 199.]

2. [" Le bouillant Bourbon, à la tête des plus intrepides assaillans tenoit, de la main gauche une échelle appuyée contre le mur, et de la droite faisoit signe à ses soldats de monter pour suivre leurs camarades; en ce moment il reçut dans le flanc une balle d'arquebuse qui le traversa de part en part; il tomba à terre, mortellement blessé. On rapporte qu'avant d'expirer il prononça ces mots : 'Officiers et soldats, cachez ma mort à l'ennemi et marchez toujours en avant; la victoire est à vous, mon trépas ne peut vous la ravir.'"—*Sac de Rome en* 1527, par Jacques Buonaparte, 1836, p. 201.]

Cæs. Would not your Highness choose to kiss the
cross?
We have no priest here, but the hilt of sword
May serve instead :—it did the same for Bayard.[1]
Bourb. Thou bitter slave! to name *him* at this time!
But I deserve it.
Arn. (*to* CÆSAR). Villain, hold your peace!   141
Cæs. What, when a Christian dies?   Shall I not offer
A Christian " Vade in pace ? "[2]
Arn.   Silence!   Oh!
Those eyes are glazing which o'erlooked the world,
And saw no equal.
Bourb.   Arnold, shouldst thou see
France——But hark! hark! the assault grows warmer—
          Oh!
For but an hour, a minute more of life,
To die within the wall!   Hence, Arnold, hence!
You lose time—they will conquer Rome without thee.
Arn. And without *thee.*
Bourb.   Not so; I'll lead them still 150
In spirit.   Cover up my dust, and breathe not
That I have ceased to breathe.   Away! and be
Victorious.
Arn.   But I must not leave thee thus.
Bourb. You must—farewell—Up! up! the world is
winning.   [BOURBON *dies.*
Cæs. (*to* ARNOLD). Come, Count, to business.
Arn.   True.   I'll weep hereafter.
      [ARNOLD *covers* BOURBON'S *body with a mantle,
            mounts the ladder, crying*
The Bourbon! Bourbon!   On, boys! Rome is ours!
Cæs. Good night, Lord Constable! thou wert a Man.
      [CÆSAR *follows* ARNOLD; *they reach the battlement;*
            ARNOLD *and* CÆSAR *are struck down.*

1. [" Quand il sentit le coup, se print à cryer : ' Jésus !' et puis il dist
' Hélas ! mon Dieu, je suis mort !' Si prit son espée par la poignée en
signe de croix en disant tout hault, ' Miserere mei, Deus, secundùm
magnam misericordiam tuam.'"—*Chronique de Bayart*, 1836, cap. lxiv.,
p. 119. For his rebuke of Charles de Bourbon, " Ne me plaignez
pas," etc., *vide ante*, p. 499.]
2. [" ' M. de Bourbon,' dit un contemporain, ' termina de vie par
mort, mais avant fist le devoir de bon Chrestien ; car il se confessa et
reçut son Créateur.'"—*De l'Italie*, par Émile Gebhart, 1876, p. 256.]

Cæs. A precious somerset ! Is your countship injured ?
Arn. No.   [*Remounts the ladder.*
Cæs.   A rare blood-hound, when his own is heated !
And 'tis no boy's play. Now he strikes them down ! 160
His hand is on the battlement—he grasps it
As though it were an altar ; now his foot
Is on it, and——What have we here ?—a Roman ?
The first bird of the covey ! he has fallen [*A man falls.*
On the outside of the nest. Why, how now, fellow ?
    Wounded Man. A drop of water !
    Cæs.   Blood 's the only liquid
Nearer than Tiber.
    Wounded Man.   I have died for Rome.   [*Dies.*
    Cæs. And so did Bourbon, in another sense.
Oh, these immortal men ! and their great motives !
But I must after my young charge. He is   170
By this time i' the Forum. Charge ! charge !
            [CÆSAR *mounts the ladder ; the scene closes.*

SCENE II.—*The City.*—*Combats between the Besiegers and
Besieged in the streets. Inhabitants flying in confusion.*

Enter CÆSAR.

    Cæs. I cannot find my hero ; he is mixed
With the heroic crowd that now pursue
The fugitives, or battle with the desperate.
What have we here ? A Cardinal or two
That do not seem in love with martyrdom.
How the old red-shanks scamper ! Could they doff
Their hose as they have doffed their hats, 'twould be
A blessing, as a mark [1] the less for plunder.
But let them fly ; the crimson kennels now
Will not much stain their stockings, since the mire   10
Is of the self-same purple hue.

    1. ["While I was at work upon that diabolical task of mine, there
came, from time to time, to watch me, some of the Cardinals who
were invested in the castle ; and most frequently the Cardinal of
Ravenna and the Cardinal de' Gaddi. I often told them not to show
themselves, since their nasty red caps gave a fair mark for the enemy."
—*Life of Benvenuto Cellini*, translated by J. A. Symonds, 1888, i. 112.
See, too, for the flight of the Cardinals, *Sac de Rome*, par Jacques
Buonaparte, Paris, 1836, p. 203.]

Enter a Party fighting—ARNOLD *at the head of the Besiegers.*

He comes,
Hand in hand with the mild twins—Gore and Glory.[L]
Holla! hold, Count!
Arn.   Away! they must not rally.
Cæs. I tell thee, be not rash; a golden bridge
Is for a flying enemy.   I gave thee
A form of beauty, and an
Exemption from some maladies of body,
But not of mind, which is not mine to give.
But though I gave the form of Thetis' son,
I dipped thee not in Styx; and 'gainst a foe   20
I would not warrant thy chivalric heart
More than Pelides' heel; why, then, be cautious,
And know thyself a mortal still.
Arn.   And who
With aught of soul would combat if he were
Invulnerable?   That were pretty sport.
Think'st thou I beat for hares when lions roar?
                    [ARNOLD *rushes into the combat.*
Cæs. A precious sample of humanity!
Well, his blood 's up; and, if a little 's shed,
'Twill serve to curb his fever.
        [ARNOLD *engages with a Roman, who retires towards
            a portico.*
Arn.   Yield thee, slave!
I promise quarter.
Rom.   That 's soon said.
Arn.   And done—— 30
My word is known.
Rom.   So shall be my deeds.
            [*They re-engage.* CÆSAR *comes forward.*
Cæs. Why, Arnold! hold thine own: thou hast in hand
A famous artisan, a cunning sculptor;
Also a dealer in the sword and dagger.
Not so, my musqueteer; 'twas he who slew
The Bourbon from the wall.[1]

i. *Covered with gore and glory—those good times.*—[*MS.*]

1. ["Directing my arquebuse where I saw the thickest and most

Arn.   Aye, did he so?
Then he hath carved his monument.
   Rom.   I yet
May live to carve your better's.
   Cæs. Well said, my man of marble! Benvenuto,
Thou hast some practice in both ways; and he   40
Who slays Cellini will have worked as hard
As e'er thou didst upon Carrara's blocks.

   [ARNOLD *disarms and wounds* CELLINI, *but slightly:*
        the latter draws a pistol, and fires; then retires,
        and disappears through the portico.

   Cæs. How farest thou? Thou hast a taste, methinks,
Of red Bellona's banquet.
   Arn. (*staggers*).   'Tis a scratch.
Lend me thy scarf. He shall not 'scape me thus.
   Cæs. Where is it?
   Arn.   In the shoulder, not the sword arm—
And that 's enough. I am thirsty: would I had
A helm of water!
   Cæs.   That 's a liquid now
In requisition, but by no means easiest
To come at.
   Arn.   And my thirst increases;—but   50
I'll find a way to quench it.
   Cæs.   Or be quenched
Thyself.
   Arn. The chance is even; we will throw
The dice thereon. But I lose time in prating;
Prithee be quick.   [CÆSAR *binds on the scarf.*
                 And what dost thou so idly?
Why dost not strike?

serried troop of fighting men, I aimed exactly at one whom I remarked
to be higher than the rest; the fog prevented me from being certain
whether he was on horseback or on foot. Then I turned to Alessandro
and Cecchino, and bade them discharge their arquebuses, showing
them how to avoid being hit by the besiegers. When we had fired two
rounds apiece, I crept cautiously up to the walls, and observing a most
extraordinary confusion, I discovered afterwards that one of our shots
had killed the Constable of Bourbon; and from what I subsequently
learned he was the man whom I had first noticed above the heads of
the rest." It is a fact "that Bourbon was shot dead near the spot
Cellini mentions. But the honour of flying the arquebuse . . . cannot
be assigned to any one in particular."—*Life of Benvenuto Cellini*, 1888,
i. 114, and *note*.]

Cæs. Your old philosophers
Beheld mankind, as mere spectators of
The Olympic games. When I behold a prize
Worth wrestling for, I may be found a Milo.[1]
 Arn. Aye, 'gainst an oak.
 Cæs. A forest, when it suits me :
I combat with a mass, or not at all.   60
Meantime, pursue thy sport as I do mine ;
Which is just now to gaze, since all these labourers
Will reap my harvest gratis.
 Arn. Thou art still
A fiend !
 Cæs. And thou—a man.
 Arn. Why, such I fain would show me.[i.]
 Cæs. True—as men are.
 Arn. And what is that ?
 Cæs. Thou feelest and thou see'st.
  [*Exit* ARNOLD, *joining in the combat which still
   continues between detached parties. The scene
   closes.*

SCENE III.—*St. Peter's—The interior of the Church—The
 Pope at the Altar—Priests, etc., crowding in confusion,
 and Citizens flying for refuge, pursued by Soldiery.*

Enter CÆSAR.

A Spanish Soldier. Down with them, comrades, seize
  upon those lamps !
Cleave yon bald-pated shaveling to the chine !
His rosary 's of gold !
 Lutheran Soldier. Revenge ! revenge !
Plunder hereafter, but for vengeance now—
Yonder stands Anti-Christ !
 Cæs. (*interposing*). How now, schismatic ?
What wouldst thou ?

i.   *'Tis the moment
  When such I fain would show me.*—[*MS.*]

 1. [Compare *Ode to Napoleon Buonaparte*, stanza vi. line **2**, *Poetical
Works*, 1900, iii. 307, *note* 3.]

Luth. Sold.   In the holy name of Christ,
Destroy proud Anti-Christ.[1]   I am a Christian.

Cæs.   Yea, a disciple that would make the founder
Of your belief renounce it, could he see
Such proselytes.   Best stint thyself to plunder.   10

Luth. Sold.   I say he is the Devil.

Cæs.   Hush! keep that secret,[i.]
Lest he should recognise you for his own.

Luth. Sold.   Why would you save him?   I repeat he is
The Devil, or the Devil's vicar upon earth.

Cæs.   And that 's the reason : would you make a quarrel
With your best friends?   You had far best be quiet;
His hour is not yet come.

Luth. Sold.   That shall be seen!

[*The Lutheran Soldier rushes forward : a shot strikes
him from one of the Pope's Guards, and he falls
at the foot of the Altar.*[2]

Cæs. (*to the Lutheran*).   I told you so.

Luth. Sold.   And will you not avenge me?

---

i. *Hush! don't let him hear you
Or he might take you off before your time.*—[*MS.*]

1. [Among the Imperial troops which Charles de Bourbon led against
Rome were at least six thousand Landsknechts, ardent converts to the
Reformed religion, and eager to prove their zeal by the slaughter of
Catholics and the destruction of altars and crucifixes. Their leader,
George Frundsberg, had set out for Rome with the pious intention of
hanging the Pope (see *The Popes of Rome*, by Leopold Ranke, translated
by Sarah Austen, 1866, i. 72). Brantôme (*Memoires de Messire Pierre
de Bourdeille*. . . . Leyde, 1722, i. 230) gives a vivid picture of their
fanatical savagery : " Leur cruauté ne s'estendit pas seulement sur les
personnes, mais sur les marbres et les anciennes statuës. Les Lansquenets, qui nouvellement estoient imbus de la nouvelle Religion, et les
Espagnols encore aussi bien que les autres, s'habilloient en Cardinaux
et evesques en leur habits Pontificaux et se pourmenoient ainsi parmy
la Ville."
In the Schmalkald articles, 1530, the pious belief that the Pope was
Antichrist became an article of the Lutheran creed. Compare the
following extracts, quoted by Hans Schultz in *Der Sacco di Roma*,
1894, p. 63, from the *Historia von der Romischen Bischof, etc.*, 1527 :
" Der Papst ist für den Verfasser der Antichrist, der durch Lug und
Trug seine Herrschaft in der Welt behauptet."]
2. [" Quant à l'armée impériale, on n'en vit jamais de plus étonnante.
. . . Allemands et Espagnols, luthériens iconoclastes qui brûlaient les
églises, ou furieux mystiques qui brûlaient Juifs et Maures, barbares
plus raffinés que *leur vieux ancêtres les Visigoths, les Vandales et les
Huns*, ils frappaient l'Italie d'une terreur sans exemple."—*De l'Italie*,
by E. Gebhart, chap. vii., " Le Sac de Rome en 1527," p. 245.]

Cæs. Not I! You know that "Vengeance is the
Lord's : "
You see he loves no interlopers.
　　Luth. Sold. (dying).　　　　　Oh!　　　　　20
Had I but slain him, I had gone on high,
Crowned with eternal glory! Heaven, forgive
My feebleness of arm that reached him not,
And take thy servant to thy mercy. 'Tis
A glorious triumph still; proud Babylon's
No more; the Harlot of the Seven Hills
Hath changed her scarlet raiment for sackcloth
And ashes!　　　　　　　　　[*The Lutheran dies.*
　　Cæs.　　　Yes, thine own amidst the rest.
Well done, old Babel!
　　　　[*The Guards defend themselves desperately, while the
　　　　　　Pontiff escapes, by a private passage, to the
　　　　　　Vatican and the Castle of St. Angelo.*[1]
　　Cæs.　　　　　　　Ha! right nobly battled!
Now, priest! now, soldier! the two great professions, 30
Together by the ears and hearts! I have not
Seen a more comic pantomime since Titus
Took Jewry. But the Romans had the best then;
Now they must take their turn.
　　Soldiers.　　　　　　He hath escaped!
Follow!
　　Another Sold. They have barred the narrow passage up,
And it is clogged with dead even to the door.
　　Cæs. I am glad he hath escaped : he may thank me for't
In part. I would not have his bulls abolished—
'Twere worth one half our empire : his indulgences
Demand some in return; no, no, he must not　　　40
Fall;—and besides, his now escape may furnish
A future miracle, in future proof

1. ["We got with the greatest difficulty to the gate of the castle.
... I ascended to the keep, and, at the same instant, Pope Clement
came in through the corridors into the castle; he had refused to leave
the palace of St. Peter earlier, being unable to believe that his enemies
would effect their entrance into Rome."—*Life of Benvenuto Cellini,*
translated by J. A. Symonds, 1888, i. 114, 115.
So, too, Jacques Buonaparte (*Le Sac de Rome,* 1836, p. 202) : "Le
Pape Clement, avoit entendu les cris des soldats ; il se sauvoit pré-
cipitamment par un long corridor pratiqué dans un mur double et se
laissoit emporter de son palais au château Saint-Ange."]

Of his infallibility.   [*To the Spanish Soldiery.*
                    Well, cut-throats !
What do you pause for ?   If you make not haste,
There will not be a link of pious gold left.
And *you*, too, Catholics !   Would ye return
From such a pilgrimage without a relic ?
The very Lutherans have more true devotion :
See how they strip the shrines !
    Soldiers.   By holy Peter !
He speaks the truth ; the heretics will bear   50
The best away.
    Cæs.   And that were shame !   Go to !
Assist in their conversion.
        [*The Soldiers disperse ; many quit the Church, others
            enter.*
    Cæs.   They are gone,
And others come : so flows the wave on wave
Of what these creatures call Eternity,
Deeming themselves the breakers of the Ocean,
While they are but its bubbles, ignorant
That foam is their foundation.   So, another !

    Enter OLIMPIA, *flying from the pursuit—She springs
            upon the Altar.*

Sold. She 's mine !
Another Sold. (*opposing the former*). You lie, I tracked
        her first : and were she
The Pope's niece, I'll not yield her.   [*They fight.*
    3d Sold. (*advancing towards* OLIMPIA). You may settle
Your claims ; I'll make mine good.
    Olimp.   Infernal slave !   60
You touch me not alive.
        3d Sold.   Alive or dead !
    Olimp. (*embracing a massive crucifix*). Respect your
        God !
    3d Sold.   Yes, when he shines in gold.
Girl, you but grasp your dowry.
        [*As he advances,* OLIMPIA, *with a strong and sudden
            effort, casts down the crucifix ; it strikes the
            Soldier, who falls.*

3d Sold. Oh, great God!

Olimp. Ah! now you recognise him.

3d Sold. My brain 's crushed!
Comrades, help, ho! All 's darkness! [*He dies.*

Other Soldiers (*coming up*). Slay her, although she had
 a thousand lives:
She hath killed our comrade.

Olimp. Welcome such a death!
You have no life to give, which the worst slave
Would take. Great God! through thy redeeming Son,
And thy Son's Mother, now receive me as   70
I would approach thee, worthy her, and him, and thee!

Enter ARNOLD.

Arn. What do I see? Accurséd jackals!
Forbear!

Cæs. (*aside and laughing*). Ha! ha! here 's equity!
 The dogs
Have as much right as he. But to the issue!

Soldiers. Count, she hath slain our comrade.

Arn. With what weapon?

Sold. The cross, beneath which he is crushed; behold
 him
Lie there, more like a worm than man; she cast it
Upon his head.

Arn. Even so: there is a woman
Worthy a brave man's liking. Were ye such,
Ye would have honoured her. But get ye hence, 80
And thank your meanness, other God you have none,
For your existence. Had you touched a hair
Of those dishevelled locks, I would have thinned
Your ranks more than the enemy. Away!
Ye jackals! gnaw the bones the lion leaves,
But not even these till he permits.

A Sold. (*murmuring*). The lion
Might conquer for himself then.

Arn. (*cuts him down*). Mutineer!
Rebel in hell—you shall obey on earth!
      [*The Soldiers assault* ARNOLD.

Arn. Come on! I'm glad on't! I will show you, slaves,

How you should be commanded, and who led you   90
First o'er the wall you were so shy to scale,
Until I waved my banners from its height,
As you are bold within it.

> [ARNOLD *mows down the foremost; the rest throw
> down their arms.*

Soldiers.   Mercy ! mercy !

Arn. Then learn to grant it.   Have I taught you *who*
Led you o'er Rome's eternal battlements ?

Soldiers. We saw it, and we know it; yet forgive
A moment's error in the heat of conquest—
The conquest which you led to.

Arn.   Get you hence !
Hence to your quarters ! you will find them fixed
In the Colonna palace.

Olimp. (aside).   In my father's   100
House !

Arn. (to the Soldiers). Leave your arms; ye have no
        further need
Of such : the city 's rendered.   And mark well
You keep your hands clean, or I'll find out a stream
As red as Tiber now runs, for your baptism.

Soldiers (deposing their arms and departing). We obey !

Arn. (to OLIMPIA*).* Lady, you are safe.

Olimp.   I should be so,
Had I a knife even; but it matters not—
Death hath a thousand gates; and on the marble,
Even at the altar foot, whence I look down
Upon destruction, shall my head be dashed,
Ere thou ascend it.   God forgive thee, man !   110

Arn. I wish to merit his forgiveness, and
Thine own, although I have not injured thee.

Olimp. No ! Thou hast only sacked my native land,—
No injury !—and made my father's house
A den of thieves !   No injury !—this temple—
Slippery with Roman and with holy gore !
No injury !   And now thou wouldst preserve me,
To be —— but that shall never be !

> [*She raises her eyes to Heaven, folds her robe round
> her, and prepares to dash herself down on the side
> of the Altar opposite to that where* ARNOLD *stands.*

Arn.   Hold ! hold !
I swear.

Olimp. Spare thine already forfeit soul
A perjury for which even Hell would loathe thee.   120
I know thee.

Arn.   No, thou know'st me not ; I am not
Of these men, though——

Olimp.   I judge thee by thy mates ;
It is for God to judge thee as thou art.
I see thee purple with the blood of Rome ;
Take mine, 'tis all thou e'er shalt have of me,
And here, upon the marble of this temple,
Where the baptismal font baptized me God's,
I offer him a blood less holy
But not less pure (pure as it left me then,
A redeeméd infant) than the holy water   130
The saints have sanctified !

> [OLIMPIA *waves her hand to* ARNOLD *with disdain,*
> *and dashes herself on the pavement from the*
> *Altar.*

Arn.   Eternal God !
I feel thee now ! Help ! help ! she 's gone.

Cæs. (approaches).   I am here.

Arn. Thou ! but oh, save her !

Cæs. (assisting him to raise OLIMPIA). She hath done
    it well !
The leap was serious.

Arn.   Oh ! she is lifeless !

Cæs.   If
She be so, I have nought to do with that :
The resurrection is beyond me.

Arn.   Slave !

Cæs. Aye, slave or master, 'tis all one : methinks
Good words, however, are as well at times.

Arn. Words !—Canst thou aid her ?

Cæs.   I will try. A sprinkling
Of that same holy water may be useful.   140

> [He brings some in his helmet from the font.

Arn. 'Tis mixed with blood.

Cæs.   There is no cleaner now
In Rome.

Arn. How pale! how beautiful! how lifeless!
Alive or dead, thou Essence of all Beauty,
I love but thee!
   Cæs.   Even so Achilles loved
Penthesilea;[1] with his form it seems
You have his heart, and yet it was no soft one.
   Arn. She breathes! But no, 'twas nothing, or the last
Faint flutter Life disputes with Death.
   Cæs.   She breathes.
   Arn. Thou say'st it? Then 'tis truth.
   Cæs.   You do me right—
The Devil speaks truth much oftener than he's deemed:
He hath an ignorant audience.   151
   Arn. (without attending to him). Yes! her heart beats.
Alas! that the first beat of the only heart
I ever wished to beat with mine should vibrate
To an assassin's pulse.
   Cæs.   A sage reflection,
But somewhat late i' the day. Where shall we bear her?
I say she lives.
   Arn.   And will she live?
   Cæs.   As much
As dust can.
   Arn.   Then she is dead!
   Cæs.   Bah! bah! You are so,
And do not know it. She will come to life—
Such as you think so, such as you now are;
But we must work by human means.
   Arn.   We will   160
Convey her unto the Colonna palace,
Where I have pitched my banner.
   Cæs.   Come then! raise her up!
   Arn. Softly!
   Cæs.   As softly as they bear the dead,
Perhaps because they cannot feel the jolting.
   Arn. But doth she live indeed?
   Cæs.   Nay, never fear!
But, if you rue it after, blame not me.

---

1. [Penthesilea, Queen of the Amazons, was slain by Achilles, who
wept over her as she lay a-dying, bewailing her beauty and her daring.
For the picture, see Pausanias, *Descriptio Græciæ*, lib. v. cap. 11, 2.]

Arn. Let her but live !

Cæs.   The Spirit of her life
Is yet within her breast, and may revive.
Count ! count ! I am your servant in all things,
And this is a new office :—'tis not oft   170
I am employed in such ; but you perceive
How staunch a friend is what you call a fiend.
On earth you have often only fiends for friends ;
Now *I* desert not mine.   Soft ! bear her hence,
The beautiful half-clay, and nearly spirit !
I am almost enamoured of her, as
Of old the Angels of her earliest sex.[1]

Arn. Thou !

Cæs.   I ! But fear not.   I'll not be your rival.

Arn. Rival !

Cæs.   I could be one right formidable ;
But since I slew the seven husbands of   180
Tobias' future bride (and after all
Was smoked out by some incense),[2] I have laid
Aside intrigue : 'tis rarely worth the trouble
Of gaining, or—what is more difficult—
Getting rid of your prize again ; for there 's
The rub ! at least to mortals.

Arn.   Prithee, peace !
Softly ! methinks her lips move, her eyes open !

Cæs. Like stars, no doubt ; for that 's a metaphor
For Lucifer and Venus.

Arn.   To the palace
Colonna, as I told you !

Cæs.   Oh ! I know   190
My way through Rome.

Arn.   Now onward, onward ! Gently !
               [*Exeunt, bearing* OLIMPIA.   *The scene closes.*

1. [See *Gen.* vi. 2, the motto of *Heaven and Earth, ante*, p, 277.]
2. ["It came to pass the same day, that in Ecbatane a city of
Media, Sara the daughter of Raguel was also reproached by her father's
maids ; because that she had been married to seven husbands, whom
Asmodeus the evil spirit had killed before they had lain with her. . . .
And as he went, he remembered the words of Raphael, and took the
ashes of the perfumes, and put the heart and the liver of the fish
thereupon, and made smoke therewith.   The which smell when the
evil spirit had smelled, he fled into the utmost parts of Egypt."—*Tobit*
iii. 7, 8 ; viii. 2, 3.]

PART III.

SCENE I.—*A Castle in the Apennines, surrounded by a wild but smiling Country. Chorus of Peasants singing before the Gates.*

Chorus.

I.

The wars are over,
 The spring is come;
The bride and her lover
 Have sought their home:
They are happy, we rejoice;
Let their hearts have an echo in every voice!

II.

The spring is come; the violet's gone,
The first-born child of the early sun:[i.]
With us she is but a winter's flower,
The snow on the hills cannot blast her bower, 10
And she lifts up her dewy eye of blue
To the youngest sky of the self-same hue.

III.

And when the spring comes with her host
Of flowers, that flower beloved the most
Shrinks from the crowd that may confuse
Her heavenly odour and virgin hues.

IV.

Pluck the others, but still remember
Their herald out of dim December—
The morning star of all the flowers,
The pledge of daylight's lengthened hours; 20
Nor, midst the roses, e'er forget
The virgin—virgin Violet.

i. *The first born who burst the winter sun.*—[MS.]

Enter Cæsar.

Cæs. (*singing*). The wars are all over,
  Our swords are all idle,
  The steed bites the bridle,
 The casque 's on the wall.
 There 's rest for the rover ;
  But his armour is rusty,
  And the veteran grows crusty,
As he yawns in the hall.   30
  He drinks—but what 's drinking ?
  A mere pause from thinking !
No bugle awakes him with life-and-death call.

Chorus.

  But the hound bayeth loudly,
   The boar 's in the wood,
  And the falcon longs proudly
   To spring from her hood
  On the wrist of the noble
   She sits like a crest,
  And the air is in trouble   40
   With birds from their nest.

Cæs. Oh ! shadow of Glory !
  Dim image of War !
 But the chase hath no story,
  Her hero no star,
 Since Nimrod, the founder
  Of empire and chase,
 Who made the woods wonder
  And quake for their race.
 When the lion was young,   50
  In the pride of his might,
 Then 'twas sport for the strong
  To embrace him in fight ;
 To go forth, with a pine
  For a spear, 'gainst the mammoth,
 Or strike through the ravine [i.]
  At the foaming behemoth ;

   i. —— *through the brine.*—[*MS.*]

While man was in stature
  As towers in our time,
The first born of Nature,   60
  And, like her, sublime !

Chorus.

But the wars are over,
  The spring is come;
The bride and her lover
  Have sought their home:
They are happy, and we rejoice;
Let their hearts have an echo from every voice!
            [*Exeunt the Peasantry, singing.*

FRAGMENT OF THE THIRD PART OF *THE DEFORMED TRANSFORMED.*

Chorus.

When the merry bells are ringing,
And the peasant girls are singing
And the early flowers are flinging
    Their odours in the air;
And the honey bee is clinging
To the buds; and birds are winging
    Their way, pair by pair:
Then the earth looks free from trouble
With the brightness of a bubble:
Though I did not make it,   10
I could breathe on and break it;
But too much I scorn it,
Or else I would mourn it,
To see despots and slaves
Playing o'er their own graves.

Enter COUNT ARNOLD.

> *Mem.* Jealous—Arnold of Cæsar.
> Olympia at first not liking Cæsar
> —then?—Arnold jealous of himself
> under his former figure, owing to
> the power of intellect, etc., etc., etc.

Arnold. You are merry, Sir—what? singing too?
Cæsar.   It is
The land of Song—and Canticles you know
Were once my avocation.
     Arn.   Nothing moves you;
You scoff even at your own calamity—

And such calamity! how wert thou fallen   20
Son of the Morning! and yet Lucifer
Can smile.
    Cæs.   His shape can—would you have me weep,
In the fair form I wear, to please you?
    Arn.   Ah!
    Cæs. You are grave—what have you on your spirit!
    Arn.   Nothing.
    Cæs. How mortals lie by instinct! If you ask
A disappointed courtier—What's the matter?
" Nothing "—an outshone Beauty what has made
Her smooth brow crisp—" Oh, Nothing!"—a young heir
When his Sire has recovered from the Gout,
What ails him? " Nothing!" or a Monarch who   30
Has heard the truth, and looks imperial on it—
What clouds his royal aspect? " Nothing," " Nothing!'
Nothing—eternal nothing—of these nothings
All are a lie—for all to them are much!
And they themselves alone the real " Nothings."
Your present Nothing, too, is something to you—
What is it?
    Arn.   Know you not?
    Cæs.   I only know
What I desire to know! and will not waste
Omniscience upon phantoms. Out with it!
If you seek aid from me—or else be silent.   40
And eat your thoughts—till they breed snakes within
        you.
    Arn. Olimpia!
    Cæs.   I thought as much—go on.
    Arn. I thought she had loved me.
    Cæs.   Blessings on your Creed!
What a good Christian you were found to be!
But what cold Sceptic hath appalled your faith
And transubstantiated to crumbs again
The *body* of your Credence?
    Arn.   No one—but—
Each day—each hour—each minute shows me more
And more she loves me not—
    Cæs.   Doth she rebel?
    Arn. No, she is calm, and meek, and silent with me,

And coldly dutiful, and proudly patient—   51
Endures my Love—not meets it.
  Cæs.   That seems strange.
You are beautiful and brave ! the first is much
For passion—and the rest for Vanity.
  Arn. I saved her life, too ; and her Father's life,
And Father's house from ashes.
  Cæs.   These are nothing.
You seek for Gratitude—the Philosopher's stone.
  Arn. And find it not.
  Cæs.   You cannot find what is not.
But *found* would it content you ? would you owe
To thankfulness what you desire from Passion ?   60
No ! No ! you would be *loved*—what you call loved—
Self-loved—loved for *yourself*—for neither health,
Nor wealth, nor youth, nor power, nor rank, nor beauty—
For these you may be stript of—but *beloved*
As an abstraction—for—you know not what !
These are the wishes of a moderate lover—
And *so* you love.
  Arn.   Ah ! could I be beloved,
Would I ask wherefore ?
  Cæs.   Yes ! and not believe
The answer—You are jealous.
  Arn.   And of whom ?
  Cæs. It may be of yourself,[1] for Jealousy   70
Is as a shadow of the Sun.   The Orb
Is mighty—as you mortals deem—and to
Your little Universe seems universal ;
But, great as He appears, and is to you,
The smallest cloud—the slightest vapour of
Your humid earth enables you to look
Upon a Sky which you revile as dull ;
Though your eyes dare not gaze on it when cloudless.
Nothing can blind a mortal like to light.
Now Love in you is as the Sun—a thing   80
Beyond you—and your Jealousy 's of Earth—

1. [Lucifer or Mephistopheles, renamed Cæsar, wears the shape of
the Deformed Arnold.   It may be that Byron intended to make Olimpia
bestow her affections, not on the glorious Achilles, but the witty and
interesting Hunchback.]

A cloud of your own raising.

   Arn.   Not so always!

There is a cause at times.

   Cæs.   Oh, yes! when atoms jostle,

The System is in peril.   But I speak

Of things you know not.   Well, to earth again!

This precious thing of dust—this bright Olimpia—

This marvellous Virgin, is a marble maid—

An Idol, but a cold one to your heat

Promethean, and unkindled by your torch.

   Arn.   Slave!

   Cæs.   In the victor's Chariot, when Rome triumphed,

There was a Slave of yore to tell him truth!   91

You are a Conqueror—command your Slave.

   Arn.   Teach me the way to win the woman's love.

   Cæs.   Leave her.

   Arn.   Were that the path—I'd not pursue it

   Cæs.   No doubt! for if you did, the remedy

Would be for a disease already cured.

   Arn.   All wretched as I am, I would not quit

My unrequited love, for all that's happy.

   Cæs.   You have possessed the woman—still possess.

What need you more?

   Arn.   To be myself possessed—   100

To be her heart as she is mine.

THE AGE OF BRONZE;

OR,

CARMEN SECULARE ET ANNUS HAUD MIRABILIS.[i.]

"Impar *Congressus* Achilli." [1]

i. [*Annus Mirabilis.*—*MS.*]

1. [It has been suggested by Dr. Garnett (late keeper of the Printed Books in the British Museum) that the motto to *The Age of Bronze* may, possibly, contain a reference to the statue of Achilles, "inscribed by the women of England to Arthur, Duke of Wellington, and his brave companions in arms," which was erected in Hyde Park, June 18, 1822.]

———

THE Age of Bronze was begun in December, 1822, and finished on January 10, 1823. " I have sent," he writes (letter to Leigh Hunt, *Letters*, 1901, vi. 160), " to Mrs. S[helley], for the benefit of being copied, a poem of about seven hundred and fifty lines length—The Age of Bronze,— or *Carmen Seculare et Annus haud Mirabilis*, with this Epigraph—' Impar *Congressus* Achilli.' It is calculated for the reading part of the million, being all on politics, etc., etc., etc., and a review of the day in general,—in my early *English Bards* style, but a little more stilted, and somewhat too full of ' epithets of war' and classical and historical allusions. If notes are necessary, they can be added."

On March 5th he forwarded the " Proof in Slips" ("and certainly the *Slips* are the most conspicuous part of it ") to his new publisher, John Hunt ; and, on April 1, 1823, *The Age of Bronze* was published, but not with the author's name.

Ten years had gone by since he had published, only to disclaim, the latest of his boyish satires, *The Waltz*, and more than six years since he had written, " at the request of Douglas Kinnaird," the stilted and laboured *Monody on the Death of . . . Sheridan.* In the interval (1816–1822) he had essayed any and every measure but the heroic, and, at length, as a tardy recognition of his allegiance to " the great moral poet of all times, of all climes, of all feelings, and of all stages of existence " (*Observations upon " Observations,"* *Letters*, 1901, v. 590), he reverts, as he believes, to his " early *English Bards* style," the style of Pope.

The brazen age, the " Annus Haud Mirabilis," which the satirist would hold up to scorn, was 1822, the year after Napoleon's death, which witnessed a revolution in Spain, and the Congress of Allied Sovereigns at Verona. Earlier in the year, the publication of Las Cases' *Mémorial de S*ʲᵉ *Hélène*, and of O'Meara's *Napoleon in Exile, or a Voice from St. Helena*, had created a sensation on both sides of the Channel. Public opinion had differed as to the system on which Napoleon should be treated—and, since his death, there had been a conflict of evidence as to the manner in which he had been treated, at St. Helena. Tories believed that an almost excessive lenience and indulgence had been wasted on a graceless and thankless intriguer, while the "Opposition," Liberals or Radicals, were moved to indignation at the hardships and restrictions which were ruthlessly and needlessly imposed on a fallen and powerless foe. It was, and is, a very pretty quarrel ; and Byron, whose lifelong admiration for his "Héros de Roman" was tempered by reason, approached the Longwood controversy somewhat in the spirit of a partisan.

In *The Age of Bronze* (sects. iii.–v.) he touches on certain incidents of the "Last Phase" of Napoleon's career, and proceeds to recapitulate, in a sort of *Memoria Technica*, the chief events of his history, from the dawn at Marengo to the sunset at "bloody and most bootless Waterloo," and draws the unimpeachable moral that "Honesty is the best policy," even when the "game is Empire" and "the stakes are thrones" !

From the rise and fall, the tyranny and captivity of Napoleon, he passes on to the Congress of Allied Powers, which met at Verona in November, 1822.

The "Congress" is the object of his satire. It had assembled with a parade of power and magnificence, and had dispersed with little or nothing accomplished. It was "impar Achilli" (*vide ante*, p. 535, *note* 1), an empty menace, ill-matched with the revolutionary spirit, and in pitiful contrast to the *Sic volo, sic jubeo* of the dead Napoleon.

The immediate and efficient cause of the Congress of Verona was the success of the revolution in Spain. The point at issue between Spanish Liberals and Royalists, or *serviles*, was the adherence to, or the evasion of, the democratic Constitution of 1812. At the moment the Liberals were in the ascendant, and, as Chateaubriand puts it, had driven King Ferdinand into captivity, at Urgel, in Catalonia, to the tune of the Spanish Marseillaise, " *Tragala, Tragala,*" "swallow it, swallow it," that is, " accept the Constitution." On July 7, 1822, a government was established under the name of the " Supreme Regency of Spain during the Captivity of the King," and, hence, the consternation of the partners of the Holy Alliance, especially France, who conceived, or feigned to conceive, that revolution next door was a source of danger to constitutional government at home. To meet the emergency, a Congress was summoned in the first instance at Vienna, and afterwards at Verona.

Thither came the sovereigns of Europe, great and small, accompanied by their chancellors and ministers. The Czar Alexander was attended by Count Nesselrode and Count Pozzo di Borgo ; the Emperor Francis of Austria, by Metternich and Prince Esterhazy ; the King of Prussia (Frederic William III.), by Count Bernstorff and Baron Humboldt. George IV. of Great Britain, and Louis XVIII. of France, being elderly and gouty, sent as their plenipotentiaries the Duke of Wellington and the Vicomte de Montmorenci, accompanied, and, finally, superseded by, the French ambassador, M. de Chateaubriand. Thither, too, came the smaller fry, Kings of the Two Sicilies and of Sardinia ; and last, but not least, Marie Louise of Austria, Archduchess of Parma, *ci-devant* widow of Napoleon, and wife *sub rosâ* of her one-eyed chamberlain, Count de Neipperg. They met, they debated, they went to the theatre in state, and finally decided to send monitory despatches to Spain, and to leave to France a free hand to look after her own interests, and to go to war or not, as she was pleased to determine. There was one dissentient, the Duke of Wellington, who refused to sign the *procès verbaux*. His Britannic Majesty had been advised to let the Spaniards alone, and not to meddle with their internal affairs. The final outcome of the Congress, the French invasion of Spain, could not be foreseen ; and, apparently, all that the Congress had accomplished was to refuse to prohibit the exportation of negroes from Africa to America, and to decline to receive the Greek deputies.

As the *Morning Chronicle* (November 7, 1822) was pleased to put it, " the Royal vultures have been deprived of their anticipated meal."

From the Holy Alliance and its antagonist, " the revolutionary stork," Byron turns to the landed and agricultural " interest " of Great Britain. With the cessation of war and the resumption of cash payments in 1819, prices had fallen some 50 per cent., and rents were beginning to fall. Wheat, which in 1818 had fetched 80s. a quarter, in December, 1822, was quoted at 39s. 11d. ; consols were at 80. Poor rates had risen from £2,000,000 in 1792 to £8,000,000 in 1822. How was the distress which these changes involved to be met? By retrenchment and reform, by the repeal of taxes, the reduction of salaries, by the landlords and farmers, who had profited by war prices, submitting to the inevitable reaction ; or by sliding scales, by a return to an inflated currency, perhaps by a repudiation of a portion of the funded debt?

The point of Byron's diatribe is that Squire Dives had enjoyed good things during the war, and, now that the war was over, he had no intention to let Lazarus have his turn ;

that, whoever suffered, it should not be Dives ; that patriotism had brought grist to his mill ; and that he proposed to
suck no small advantage out of peace.

> "Year after year they voted cent. per cent.,
> Blood, sweat, and tear-wrung millions—why? for rent?
> They roared, they dined, they drank, they swore they meant
> To die for England—why then live?—for rent ! "

It is easier to divine the " Sources " and the inspiration of
The Age of Bronze than to place the reader *au courant* with
the literary and political *causerie* of the day. Byron wrote
with O'Meara's book at his elbow, and with batches of
Galignani's Messenger, the *Morning Chronicle,* and *Cobbett's
Weekly Register* within his reach. He was under the impression that his lines would appear as an anonymous con-
tribution to *The Liberal,* and, in any case, he felt that he
could speak out, unchecked and uncriticized by friend or
publisher. He was, so to speak, unmuzzled.

With regard to the style and quality of his new satire,
Byron was under an amiable delusion. His couplets, he
imagined, were in his " early *English Bards* style," but
" more stilted." He did not realize that, whatever the intervening years had taken away, they had " left behind " experience and passion, and that he had learned to think and
to feel. The fault of the poem is that too much matter is
packed into too small a compass, and that, in parts, every
line implies a minute acquaintance with contemporary
events, and requires an explanatory note. But, even so, in
The Age of Bronze Byron has wedded " a striking passage
of history " to striking and imperishable verse.

The Age of Bronze was reviewed in the *Scots Magazine,*
April, 1823, N.S., vol. xii. pp. 483–488 ; the *Monthly Review,*
April, 1823, E.S., vol. 100, pp. 430–433 ; the *Monthly Maga-
zine,* May, 1823, vol. 55, pp. 322–325 ; the *Examiner,*
March 30, 1823 ; the *Literary Chronicle,* April 5, 1823 ; and
the *Literary Gazette,* April 5, 1823.

THE AGE OF BRONZE.

I.

The " good old times "—all times when old are good —
Are gone ; the present might be if they would ;
Great things have been, and are, and greater still
Want little of mere mortals but their will : [i.]
A wider space, a greener field, is given
To those who play their " tricks before high heaven." [1]
I know not if the angels weep, but men
Have wept enough—for what ?—to weep again !

II.

All is exploded—be it good or bad.
Reader ! remember when thou wert a lad,
Then Pitt was all ; or, if not all, so much,   10
His very rival almost deemed him such. [2]
We—we have seen the intellectual race
Of giants stand, like Titans, face to face—
Athos and Ida, with a dashing sea
Of eloquence between, which flowed all free,
As the deep billows of the Ægean roar
Betwixt the Hellenic and the Phrygian shore.
But where are they—the rivals ! a few feet
Of sullen earth divide each winding sheet. [3]   20

i. *Want nothing of the little, but their* will.—[*MS.*]

1. [*Measure for Measure*, act ii. sc. 2, line 121.]
2. [Fox used to say, " *I* never want *a* word, but Pitt never wants
the word."]
3. [The grave of Fox, in Westminster Abbey is within eighteen
inches of that of Pitt. Compare—

How peaceful and how powerful is the grave,
Which hushes all! a calm, unstormy wave,
Which oversweeps the World.   The theme is old
Of " Dust to Dust," but half its tale untold :
Time tempers not its terrors—still the worm
Winds its cold folds, the tomb preserves its form,
Varied above, but still alike below ;
The urn may shine—the ashes will not glow—
Though Cleopatra's mummy cross the sea [1]
O'er which from empire she lured Anthony ;   30
Though Alexander's urn [2] a show be grown

> " Nor yet suppress the generous sigh,
> Because his rival slumbers nigh ;
> Nor be thy *requiescat* dumb,
> Lest it be said o'er Fox's tomb.
> .   .   .   .   .
> Where,—taming thought to human pride !—
> The mighty chiefs sleep side by side.
> Drop upon Fox's grave the tear,
> 'Twill trickle to his rival's bier," etc.
>   *Marmion*, by Sir Walter Scott,
>   Introduction to Canto I. lines 125-128, 184-188.

Compare, too, Macaulay on Warren Hastings : "In that temple of
silence and reconciliation, where the enmities of twenty generations lie
buried, in the Great Abbey . . . the dust of the illustrious accused
should have mingled with the dust of the illustrious accusers.   This
was not to be."—*Critical and Historical Essays*, 1843, iii. 465.]

1. [The Cleopatra whose mummy is preserved in the British Museum
was a member of the Theban Archon family.   Her date was *circ.* A.D.
100.]

2. [According to Strabo (*Rerum Geog.*, xvii. ed. 1807, ii. 1127),
Ptolemæus Soter brought Alexander's body back from Babylon, and
buried it in Alexandria, in the spot afterwards known as the *Soma*.
There it lay, in Strabo's time, not in its original body-mask of golden
chase-work, which Ptolemæus Cocces had stolen, but in a casket of
glass.   Great men "turned to pilgrims" to visit Alexander's grave.
Augustus crowned the still life-like body with a golden laurel-wreath,
and scattered flowers over the tomb : Caligula stole the breastplate, and
wore it during his pantomimic triumphs ; Septimius Severus buried in
the sarcophagus the writings of the priests, and a clue to the hieroglyphics.   Finally, the sarcophagus and its sacred remains disappear,
and Alexander himself passes into the land of fable and romance.   In
1801 a sarcophagus came into the possession of the English Army, and
was presented by George III. to the British Museum.   Hieroglyphics
were as yet undeciphered, and, in 1805, the traveller Edward Daniel
Clarke published a quarto monograph (*The Tomb of Alexander, etc.*),
in which he proves, to his own satisfaction, that "this surprising
sarcophagus in one entire block of green Egyptian *breccia*," had once
contained the ashes of Alexander the Great.   Byron knew Clarke, and,
no doubt, respected his authority (see letter December 15, 1813,

On shores he wept to conquer, though unknow.ı— [1]
How vain, how worse than vain, at length appear
The madman's wish, the Macedonian's tear !
He wept for worlds to conquer—half the earth
Knows not his name, or but his death, and birth,
And desolation; while his native Greece
Hath all of desolation, save its peace.
He " wept for worlds to conquer ! " he who ne'er
Conceived the Globe, he panted not to spare !
With even the busy Northern Isle unknown,
Which holds his urn—and never knew his throne.

III.

But where is he, the modern, mightier far,
Who, born no king, made monarchs draw his car ;
The new Sesostris, whose unharnessed kings,[2]
Freed from the bit, believe themselves with wings,
And spurn the dust o'er which they crawled of late,
Chained to the chariot of the Chieftain's state ?

40

Letters, 1898, ii. 308) ; and, hence, the description of " Alexander's urn " as "a show." The sarcophagus which has, since 1844, been assigned to its rightful occupant, Nectanebus II. (Nekht-neb-f), is a conspicuous object in the Egyptian Gallery of the British Museum. It is a curious coincidence that in the Ethiopic version of the Pseudo-Callisthenes, Alexander is said to have been the son of Nectanebus II., who threw a spell over Olympias, the wife of Philip of Macedon, and won her love by the exercise of nefarious magic. (See the *Life and Exploits of Alexander the Great.* by E. A. Wallis Budge, Litt.D., F.S.A., Keeper of the Egyptian and Assyrian Antiquities in the British Museum, 1896, i. ix.)]

1. [Arrian (*Alexand. Anabasis*, vii. 1, 4, ed. 1849, p. 165) says that Alexander would never have rested content with what he had acquired ; "that if he had annexed Europe to Asia, and the British Isles to Europe, he would have sought out some no-man's-land to conquer." So insatiable was his ambition, that when the courtly philosopher Anaxarchus explained to him the theory of the plurality of worlds he bemoaned himself because as yet he was not master of one. " *Heu me,* inquit, *miserum, quod ne uno quidem adhuc potitus sum.*"—Valerius Maximus, *De Dictis, etc.,* lib. viii. cap. xiv. ex. 2. See, too, *Juvenal,* x. 168, 169. Burton (*Anatomy of Melancholy,* 1893, i. 64) denies that this was spoken like a prince, but, as wise Seneca censures him [on another occasion, however], 'twas *vox iniquissima et stultissima,* "'twas spoken like a bedlam fool."]

2. [Compare *Werner,* act iii. sc. 1, lines 288, 289, "When he [Sesostris] went into the temple or the city, his custom was to cause the horses to be unharnessed out of his chariot, and to yoke four kings and four princes to the chariot-pole."—Diodori Siculi *Bibl. Hist.,* lib. i. p. 37, C, ed. 1604, p. 53.]

Yes ! where is he, " the champion and the child " [1]
Of all that 's great or little—wise or wild ;   50
Whose game was Empire, and whose stakes were
      thrones ;
Whose table Earth—whose dice were human bones?
Behold the grand result in yon lone Isle,
And, as thy nature urges—weep or smile.
Sigh to behold the Eagle's lofty rage
Reduced to nibble at his narrow cage ;
Smile to survey the queller of the nations
Now daily squabbling o'er disputed rations ; [L]

i. Lines 55-58 not in MS.

1. [In a speech delivered in the House of Commons, February 17,
1800, " On the continuance of the War with France," Pitt described
Napoleon as the "child and champion of Jacobinism." Coleridge,
who was reporting for the *Morning Post*, took down Pitt's words as
" nursling and champion " (unpublished MS. note-book), a finer and
more original phrase, but substituted " child " for " nursling " in his
" copy." (See *Letters of S. T. Coleridge*, 1895, i. 327, *note* 1.) The
phrase was much in vogue, *e.g.* " All that survives of Jacobinism in
Europe looks up to him as its ' child and champion.' "—*Quarterly
Review*, xvi. 48. See, too, *Poetical Works*, 1898, ii. 400, *note* 1.]

2. [O'Meara, under the dates August 19, September 5, September 7,
13, etc. (see *Napoleon in Exile*, 1888, i. 95, 96, 114, 121, etc.), reports
complaints on the part of Napoleon with regard to the reduction of
expenses suggested or enforced by Sir Hudson Lowe, and gives
specimens of the nature and detail of these reductions. For a refuta-
tion of O'Meara's facts and figures (as given in *Napoleon in Exile*,
1822, ii. Appendix V.), see the *History of the Captivity of Napoleon*, by
William Forsyth, Q.C., 1853, iii. 121, *sq.* ; see, too, *Sir Hudson Lowe
and Napoleon*, by R. C. Seaton, 1898). It is a fact that Sir Hudson
Lowe, on his own responsibility, increased the allowance for the household expenses of Napoleon and his staff from £8000 to £12,000 a year,
and it is also perfectly true that opportunities for complaint were
welcomed by the ex-Emperor and his mimic court. It was *la politique
de Longwood* to make the worst of everything, on the off-chance that
England would get to hear, and that Radical indignation and Radical
sympathy would gild, perhaps unbar, the eagle's cage. It is true, too,
that a large sum of money was spent on behalf of a prisoner of war
whom the stalwarts of the Tory party would have executed in cold
blood. But it is also true that Napoleon had no need to manufacture
complaints, that he was exposed to unnecessary discomforts, that useless
and irritating precautions were taken to prevent his escape, that the
bottles of champagne and madeira, the fowls and the bundles of wood
were counted with an irritating preciseness, inconsistent with the
general scale of expenditure, which saved a little waste, and covered
both principals and agents with ridicule. It is said that O'Meara, in
his published volumes, manipulated his evidence, and that his own
letters give him the lie ; but there is a mass of correspondence, published
and unpublished, between him and Sir Thomas Reade, Sir Hudson

Weep to perceive him mourning, as he dines,
O'er curtailed dishes and o'er stinted wines ;   60
O'er petty quarrels upon petty things.
Is this the Man who scourged or feasted kings ?
Behold the scales in which his fortune hangs,
A surgeon's [1] statement, and an earl's [2] harangues !
A bust delayed,[3]—a book [4] refused, can shake
The sleep of Him who kept the world awake.
Is this indeed the tamer of the Great,[i.]
Now slave of all could tease or irritate—
The paltry gaoler [5] and the prying spy,

i. *Weep to survey the Tamer of the Great.*—[*MS.*]

Lowe, and Major Gorrequer (see Addit. MSS. Brit. Mus. 20,145),
which remains as it was written, and which testifies to facts which
might have been and were not refuted on the spot and at the moment.
With regard to "disputed rations," the Governor should have been
armed with a crushing answer to any and every complaint. As it was,
he was able to show that champagne was allowed to "Napoleon
Buonaparte," and that he did not exceed his allowance.]

1. [In his correspondence with Lord Bathurst, Sir Hudson Lowe
more than once quotes "statements" made by Dr. O'Meara (*vide post*,
p. 546). But the surgeon may be William Warden (1777-1849), whose
*Letters written on board His Majesty's Ship the Northumberland, and
at St. Helena*, were published in 1816.]

2. [Henry, Earl of Bathurst (1762-1834), Secretary for War and the
Colonies, replied to Lord Holland's motion "for papers connected
with the personal treatment of Napoleon Buonaparte at St. Helena,"
March 18, 1817.   *Parl. Deb.*, vol. 35, pp. 1137-1166.]

3. [A bust of Napoleon's son, the Duke of Reichstadt, had been
forwarded to St. Helena. O'Meara (*Napoleon in Exile, etc.*, 1822, i.
p. 100) says "that it had been in the island fourteen days, during
several of which it was at Plantation House," before it was transferred
to Longwood.   Forsyth (*History of Napoleon in Captivity*, 1853, ii.
146) denies this statement. It was, no doubt, detained on board ship
for inspection, but not at Plantation House.]

4. [The book in question was *The Substance of some Letters written
by an Englishman in Paris*, 1816 (by J. C. Hobhouse). It was inscribed
"To the Emperor Napoleon." Lowe's excuse was that Hobhouse had
submitted the work to his inspection, and suggested that if the Governor
did not think fit to give it to Napoleon, he might place it in his own
library. (See *Napoleon in Exile*, 1822, i. 85-87 ; and Forsyth, 1853, i.
193.)]

5. [Lieutenant-General Sir Hudson Lowe, K.C.B. (1769-1844), was
the son of an army surgeon, John Hudson Lowe. His mother was
Irish. He was appointed Governor of St. Helena, August 23, 1815,
and landed in the island April 14, 1816. Byron met him at Lord
Holland's, before he sailed for St. Helena, and was not impressed
by his remarks on Napoleon and Waterloo (*Letters*, 1901, v. 429).
He was well-intentioned, honourable, and, in essentials, humane, but
he was arrogant and tactless. The following sentence, from a letter

The staring stranger with his note-book nigh ? [1]   70
Plunged in a dungeon, he had still been great ;
How low, how little was this middle state,
Between a prison and a palace, where
How few could feel for what he had to bear !
Vain his complaint,—My Lord presents his bill,
His food and wine were doled out duly still ;
Vain was his sickness, never was a clime
So free from homicide—to doubt 's crime ;
And the stiff surgeon,[2] who maintained his cause,

written by Lowe to O'Meara, October 3, 1816 (Forsyth, i. 318, 319), is
characteristic : "With respect to the instructions I have received, and
my manner of making them known, never having regarded General
Bonaparte's opinions in any point whatever as to *matter* or *manner*, as
an oracle or criterion by which to regulate my own judgment, I am not
disposed to think the less favourably of the instructions, or my mode
of executing them." It must, however, be borne in mind that this was
written some time after Lowe's fifth and last interview with his captive
(Aug. 18, 1816) ; that Napoleon had abused him to his face and behind
his back, and was not above resorting to paltry subterfuges in order to
defy and exasperate his "paltry gaoler."]
    1. [There is reason to think that "the staring stranger" was the
traveller Captain Basil Hall (1788-1844), who called upon Byron at
Venice (see *Letters*, 1900, iv. 252), but did not see him. His account of
his interview with Napoleon is attached to his narrative of a *Voyage
to Java*, 1840. It is not included in the earlier editions of Hall's *Voyage
to the Corea and the Loochoo Islands*, but is quoted by Scott, in his
Life of Napoleon, 1827.]
    2. [Barry Edward O'Meara (1786-1836) began life as assistant-
surgeon to the 62nd Regiment, then stationed in Sicily and Calabria.
In 1815 he was surgeon on board the *Bellerophon*, under Captain
F. L. Maitland. Napoleon took a fancy to him because he could
speak Italian, and, as his own surgeon Mengeaud would not follow
him into exile, requested that O'Meara might accompany him, in the
Northumberland, to St. Helena. His position was an ambiguous one.
He was to act as Napoleon's medical and, *quoad hoc*, confidential
attendant, but he was not to be subservient to him or dependent on
him. At St. Helena Lowe expected him to be something between an
intermediary and a spy, and, for a time, O'Meara discharged both
functions to the Governor's satisfaction (statements by Dr. O'Meara
are quoted by Lowe in his letter to Lord Bathurst [*Life of Napoleon*,
etc., by Sir W. Scott, 1828, p. 763]). As time went on, the surgeon
yielded to the glamour of Napoleon's influence, and more and more
disliked and resented the necessity of communicating private conversations to Lowe. He "withheld his confidence," with the result that
the Governor became suspicious, and treated O'Meara with reprobation
and contempt. At length, on July 18, 1818, on a renewed accusation
of "irregularities," Lord Bathurst dismissed him from his post, and
ordered him to quit St. Helena. He returned to England, and,
October 28, 1818, addressed a letter (see Forsyth's *Napoleon, etc.*, iii.
132, 433) to J. W. Croker, the Secretary to the Admiralty, in which he

Hath lost his place, and gained the world's applause. 80
But smile—though all the pangs of brain and heart
Disdain, defy, the tardy aid of art;
Though, save the few fond friends and imaged face
Of that fair boy his Sire shall ne'er embrace,
None stand by his low bed—though even the mind
Be wavering, which long awed and awes mankind:
Smile—for the fettered Eagle breaks his chain,
And higher Worlds than this are his again.[1]

IV.

How, if that soaring Spirit still retain
A conscious twilight of his blazing reign,
How must he smile, on looking down, to see   90
The little that he was and sought to be !
What though his Name a wider empire found
Than his Ambition, though with scarce a bound;
Though first in glory, deepest in reverse,
He tasted Empire's blessings and its curse;
Though kings, rejoicing in their late escape
From chains, would gladly be *their* Tyrant's ape;
How must he smile, and turn to yon lone grave,
The proudest Sea-mark that o'ertops the wave !   100
What though his gaoler, duteous to the last,
Scarce deemed the coffin's lead could keep him fast,
Refusing one poor line[2] along the lid,

argued against the justice of his dismissal. One sentence which asserted that Lowe had dwelt upon the "benefit which would result to Europe from the death of Napoleon," was seized upon by Croker as calumnious, and in answer to his remonstrance, O'Meara's name was struck off the list of naval surgeons. He published, in 1819, a work entitled *Exposition of some of the Transactions that have taken place at St. Helena since the appointment of Sir Hudson Lowe as Governor*, which was afterwards expanded into *Napoleon in Exile, or a Voice from St. Helena* (2 vols., 1822). The latter work made a great sensation, and passed through five editions. It was republished in 1888. O'Meara was able, and generously disposed, but he was not "stiff" (*vide infra*, 489). "He was," says Lord Rosebery (*Napoleon, The Last Phase*, 1900, p. 31), "the confidential servant of Napoleon: unknown to Napoleon, he was the confidential agent of Lowe; and behind both their backs he was the confidential informant of the British Government. . . . Testimony from such a source is . . . tainted." Neither men nor angels will disentangle the wheat from the tares.]

1. [Buonaparte died the 5th of May, 1821.]
2. [At the end of vol. ii. of O'Meara's *Voice, etc.* (ed. 5), there is a

To date the birth and death of all it hid ;
That name shall hallow the ignoble shore,
A talisman to all save him who bore :
The fleets that sweep before the eastern blast
Shall hear their sea-boys [1] hail it from the mast ;
When Victory's Gallic column [2] shall but rise,
Like Pompey's pillar,[3] in a desert's skies,   110
The rocky Isle that holds or held his dust,
Shall crown the Atlantic like the Hero's bust,
And mighty Nature o'er his obsequies
Do more than niggard Envy still denies.
But what are these to him? Can Glory's lust
Touch the freed spirit or the fettered dust ?
Small care hath he of what his tomb consists ;
Nought if he sleeps—nor more if he exists :
Alike the better-seeing Shade will smile
On the rude cavern [4] of the rocky isle,   120
As if his ashes found their latest home
In Rome's Pantheon or Gaul's mimic dome.[5]

statement, signed by Count Montholon, to the effect that he wished the
following inscription to be placed on Napoleon's coffin—

" Napoléon.
Né à Ajaccio le 15 Août, 1769,
Mort à Ste. Hélène le 5 Mai, 1821 ; "

but that the Governor said, " that his instructions would not allow
him to sanction any other name being placed on the coffin than that
of 'General Bonaparte.'" Lowe would have sanctioned " Napoléon
Bonaparte," but, on his own admission, *did* refuse the inscription of the
one word " Napoléon."—Forsyth, iii. 295, 296, *note* 3.]

1. [Hall, in his interview with Napoleon at St. Helena, *Narrative of
a Voyage to Java*, 1840, p. 77, testifies that, weeks before the vessel
anchored at St. Helena, August 11, 1817, "the probability of seeing
him [Napoleon] had engrossed the thoughts of every one on board. . . .
Even those of our number who, from their situation, could have no
chance of seeing him, caught the fever of the moment, and the most
cold and indifferent person on board was roused on the occasion into
unexpected excitement."]

2. [The Colonne Vendôme, erected to commemorate the Battle of
Austerlitz, was inaugurated in 1810.]

3. [Pompey's, *i.e.* Diocletian's Pillar stands on a mound near the
Arabian cemetery, about three quarters of a mile from Alexandria,
between the city and Lake Mareotis.]

4. [Napoleon was buried, May 9, 1821, in a garden in the middle of
a deep ravine, under the shade of two willow trees.]

5. [Byron took for granted that Napoleon's remains would one day
rest under the dome of the Pantheon, where Mirabeau is buried, and
where cenotaphs have been erected to Voltaire and Rousseau. As it is

He wants not this ; but France shall feel the want
Of this last consolation, though so scant :
Her Honour—Fame—and Faith demand his bones,
To rear above a Pyramid of thrones ;
Or carried onward in the battle's van,
To form, like Guesclin's dust, her Talisman.[1]
But be it as it is—the time may come
His name shall beat the alarm, like Ziska's drum.[2] 130

V.

Oh Heaven ! of which he was in power a feature ;
Oh Earth ! of which he was a noble creature ;
Thou Isle ! to be remembered long and well,
That saw'st the unfledged eaglet chip his shell !
Ye Alps which viewed him in his dawning flights
Hover, the Victor of a hundred fights !

(since December 15, 1840) he sleeps under the Dôme des Invalides.
Above the entrance are these words, which are taken from his will : "Je
désire que mes cendres reposent sur les bords de la Seine, au milieu
de ce peuple Français que j'ai tant aimé."]
 1. Guesclin died during the siege of a city ; it surrendered, and the
keys were brought and laid upon his bier, so that the place might
appear rendered to his ashes. [Bertrand du Guesclin, born 1320, first
distinguished himself in the service of King John II. of France, in
defending Rennes against Henry Duke of Lancaster, 1356-57. He
was made Constable of France in 1370, and died before the walls of
Châteauneuf-de-Randon (Lozère), July 13, 1380. He was buried by
the order of Charles V. in Saint-Denis, hard by the tomb which the
king had built for himself. In *La Vie vaillant Bertran du Guesclin*
[*Chronique, etc.* (par E. Charrière), 1839, tom. ii. p. 321, lines 22716, *sq.*],
the English do not place the keys of the castle on Du Guesclin's bier,
but present them to him as he lies tossing on his death-bed (" à son lit
agité "). So, too, *Histoire de Messire Bertrand du Guesclin*, par
Claude Menard, 1618, 540 : "Et Engloiz se accorderent à ce faire.
Lors issirent dudit Chastel, et vindrent à Bertran, et lui presenterent
les clefs. Et ne demora guères, qu'il getta le souppir de la mort."]
 2. [John of Trocnow, surnamed Žižka, or the "One-eyed," was born
circ. 1360, and died while he was besieging a town on the Moravian
border, October 11, 1424. He was the hero of the Hussite or Taborite
crusade (1419-1422), the *malleus Catholicorum.* The story is that on
his death-bed he was asked where he wished to be buried, and replied,
"that it mattered not, that his flesh might be thrown to the vultures
and eagles ; but his skin was to be carefully preserved and made into
a drum, to be carried in the front of the battle, that the very sound
might disperse their enemies." Voltaire, in his *Essai sur Les Mœurs et
L'Esprit des Nations* (cap. lxxiii. s.f. *Œuvres Complètes, etc.*, 1836, iii.
256), mentions the legend as a fact, " Il ordonna qu' après sa mort on
fît un tambour de sa peau." Compare *Werner*, act i. sc. 1, lines 693,
694.]

Thou Rome, who saw'st thy Cæsar's deeds outdone !
Alas ! why passed he too the Rubicon—
The Rubicon of Man's awakened rights,
To herd with vulgar kings and parasites?   140
Egypt ! from whose all dateless tombs arose
Forgotten Pharaohs from their long repose,
And shook within their pyramids to hear
A new Cambyses thundering in their ear ;
While the dark shades of Forty Ages stood
Like startled giants by Nile's famous flood ; [1]
Or from the Pyramid's tall pinnacle
Beheld the desert peopled, as from hell,
With clashing hosts, who strewed the barren sand,
To re-manure the uncultivated land !   150
Spain ! which, a moment mindless of the Cid,
Beheld his banner flouting thy Madrid ! [2]
Austria ! which saw thy twice-ta'en capital [3]
Twice spared to be the traitress of his fall !
Ye race of Frederic !—Frederics but in name
And falsehood—heirs to all except his fame :
Who, crushed at Jena, crouched at Berlin, [4] fell
First, and but rose to follow !   Ye who dwell
Where Kosciusko dwelt, remembering yet
The unpaid amount of Catherine's bloody debt ! [5] 160

1. ["Au moment de la bataille Napoléon avait dit à ses troupes, en
leur montrant les Pyramides : 'Soldats, quarante siècles vous regar-
dent.'"—*Campagnes d'Égypte et de Syrie*, 1798-9, par le Général
Bertrand, 1847, i. 160.]

2. [Madrid was taken by the French, first in March, 1808, and
again December 2, 1808.].

3. [Vienna was taken by the French under Murat, November 14,
1805, evacuated January 12, 1806, captured by Napoleon, May, 1800,
and restored at the conclusion of peace, October 14, 1809.   Her
treachery consisted in her hospitality to the sovereigns at the Congress
of Vienna, November, 1814, and her share in the Treaty of Vienna,
March·25, 1815, which ratified the Treaties of Chaumont, March 1,
and of Paris, April 11, 1814.]

4. [At Jena Napoleon defeated Prince Hohenlohe, and at Auerstadt
General Davoust defeated the King of Prussia, October 14, 1806.
Napoleon then advanced to Berlin, October 27, from which he issued
his famous decree against British commerce, November 20, 1806.]

5. [The partition of Poland.   "Henry [of Prussia] arrived at St.
Petersburg, December 9, 1770 ; and it seems now to be certain that the
first open proposal of a dismemberment of Poland arose in his conversations with the Empress. . . . Catherine said to the Prince, 'I will
frighten Turkey and flatter England.   It is your business to gain

Poland ! o'er which the avenging Angel past,
But left thee as he found thee,[1] still a waste,
Forgetting all thy still enduring claim,
Thy lotted people and extinguished name,
Thy sigh for freedom, thy long-flowing tear,
That sound that crashes in the tyrant's ear—
Kosciusko ![2] On—on—on—the thirst of War
Gasps for the gore of serfs and of their Czar.
The half barbaric Moscow's minarets
Gleam in the sun, but 'tis a sun that sets !   170
Moscow ! thou limit of his long career,
For which rude Charles had wept his frozen tear[3]
To see in vain—*he* saw thee—how ? with spire
And palace fuel to one common fire.
To this the soldier lent his kindling match,
To this the peasant gave his cottage thatch,

Austria, that she may lull France to sleep ; ' and she became at length
so eager, that . . . she dipt her finger into ink, and drew with it
the lines of partition on a map of Poland which lay before them."—
Edinburgh Review, November, 1822 (art. x. on *Histoire des Trois
Démembremens de la Pologne*, par M. Ferrand, 1820, etc., vol. 37, pp.
479, 480.]

1. [Napoleon promised much, but did little for the Poles. "In
speaking of the business of Poland he . . . said it was a whim (*c'était
un caprice*)."—*Narrative of an Embassy to Warsaw*, by M. Dufour de
Pradt, 1816, p. 51. "The Polish question," says Lord Wolseley (*Decline
and Fall of Napoleon*, 1895, p. 19), "thrust itself most inconveniently
before him. In early life all his sympathies . . . were with the Poles,
and he had regarded the partition of their country as a crime. . . . As
a very young man liberty was his only religion ; but he had now learned
to hate and to fear that term. . . . He had no desire . . . to be the
Don Quixote of Poland by reconstituting it as a kingdom. To fight
Russia by the re-establishment of Polish independence was not, therefore, to be thought of."]

2. [The final partition of Poland took place after the Battle of
Maciejowice, October 12, 1794, when "Freedom shrieked when
Kosciusko fell." Tyrants, *e.g.* Napoleon in 1806, and Alexander in
1814 and again in 1815, approached Kosciusko with respect, and
loaded him with flattery and promises, and then "passed by on the
other side."]

3. [The reference is to Charles's chagrin when the Grand Vizier
allowed the Russians to retire in safety from the banks of the Pruth,
and assented to the Treaty of Jassy, July 21, 1711. Charles, "impatient
for the fight, and to behold the enemy in his power," had ridden above
fifty leagues from Bender to Jassy, swam the Pruth at the risk of his
life, and found that the Czar had marched off in triumph. He contrived
to rip up the Vizier's robe with his spur, "remonta à cheval, et re-
tourna à Bender le désespoir dans le cœur" (*Histoire de Charles XII.*,
Livre v. *s.f.*).]

To this the merchant flung his hoarded store,
The prince his hall—and Moscow was no more!
Sublimest of volcanoes! Etna's flame
Pales before thine, and quenchless Hecla 's tame;   180
Vesuvius shows his blaze,[1] an usual sight
For gaping tourists, from his hackneyed height:[L]
Thou stand'st alone unrivalled, till the Fire
To come, in which all empires shall expire!

Thou other Element! as strong and stern,
To teach a lesson conquerors will not learn!—
Whose icy wing flapped o'er the faltering foe,
Till fell a hero with each flake of snow;
How did thy numbing beak and silent fang,
Pierce, till hosts perished with a single pang!   190
In vain shall Seine look up along his banks
For the gay thousands of his dashing ranks!
In vain shall France recall beneath her vines
Her Youth—their blood flows faster than her wines;
Or stagnant in their human ice remains
In frozen mummies on the Polar plains.
In vain will Italy's broad sun awaken
Her offspring chilled; its beams are now forsaken.
Of all the trophies gathered from the war,
What shall return? the Conqueror's broken car![2]   200
The Conqueror's yet unbroken heart! Again

i. *For staring tourists* ——.—[*MS.*]

1. [" Naples, October 29, 1822. Le Vésuve continue à lancer des
pierres et des cendres."—From *Le Moniteur Universel*, November 21,
1822.]
2. [The material for this description of Napoleon on his return from
Moscow is drawn from De Pradt's *Narrative of an Embassy to Warsaw
and Wilna*, published in 1816, pp. 133-141. "I hurried out, and
arrived at the Hôtel d'Angleterre . . . [Warsaw, December 10, 1812].
I saw a small carriage body placed on a sledge made of four pieces of
fir: it had stood some crashes, and was much damaged. . . . The
ministers joined me in addressing to him . . . wishes for the preserva-
tion of his health and the prosperity of his journey. He replied, ' I
never was better; if I carried the devil with me, I should be all the
better for that [*Quand j'aurai le diable je ne m'en porterai que mieux*).'
These were his last words. He then mounted the humble sledge,
which bore Cæsar and his fortune, and disappeared." The passage
is quoted in the *Quarterly Review*, October, 1815, vol. xiv. pp. 64-68.]

The horn of Roland [1] sounds, and not in vain.
Lutzen, where fell the Swede of victory,[2]
Beholds him conquer, but, alas ! not die:
Dresden [3] surveys three despots fly once more
Before their sovereign,—sovereign as before ; [i.]
But there exhausted Fortune quits the field,
And Leipsic's [4] treason bids the unvanquished yield ;
The Saxon jackal leaves the lion's side
To turn the bear's, and wolf's, and fox's guide ;   210
And backward to the den of his despair
The forest monarch shrinks, but finds no lair !

Oh ye ! and each, and all ! Oh France ! who found
Thy long fair fields ploughed up as hostile ground,
Disputed foot by foot, till Treason, still
His only victor, from Montmartre's hill [5]
Looked down o'er trampled Paris ! and thou Isle,
Which seest Etruria from thy ramparts smile,
Thou momentary shelter of his pride,
Till wooed by danger, his yet weeping bride !   220
Oh, France ! retaken by a single march,

i. *Dresden beholds three nations fly once more*
   Before the lash they oft had felt before.—[MS. erased.]

1. ["Soldats Français ! Serrez vos rangs !
      Entendez Roland qui vous crie !
      Armez vous contre vos tyrans !
      Brisez les fers de la patrie."
   " L'Ombre de Roland," *Morning Chronicle*, October 10, 1822.]

2. [Gustavus Adolphus fell at the great battle of Lutzen, in November, 1632. Napoleon defeated the allied Russian and Prussian armies at Lutzen, May 2, 1813.]

3. [On June 26, 1813, Napoleon re-entered Dresden, and on the 27th repulsed the allied sovereigns, the Emperors of Russia and Prussia, with tremendous loss. Thousands of prisoners and a great quantity of cannon were taken.]

4. [At the battle of Leipsic, October 18, 1813, on the appearance of Bernadotte, the Saxon soldiers under Regnier deserted and went over to the Allies. Napoleon, whose army was already weakened, lost 30,000 men at Leipzig.]

5. [Joseph Buonaparte, who had been stationed on the heights of Montmartre, March 30, 1814, to witness if not direct the defence of Paris against the Allies under Blücher, authorized Marmont to capitulate. His action was, unjustly, regarded as a betrayal of his brother's capital.]

Whose path was through one long triumphal arch !
Oh bloody and most bootless Waterloo !
Which proves how fools may have their fortune too,
Won half by blunder, half by treachery :
Oh dull Saint Helen ! with thy gaoler nigh—
Hear ! hear Prometheus [1] from his rock appeal
To Earth,—Air,—Ocean,—all that felt or feel
His power and glory, all who yet shall hear
A name eternal as the rolling year ;   230
He teaches them the lesson taught so long,
So oft, so vainly—learn to do no wrong !
A single step into the right had made
This man the Washington of worlds betrayed :
A single step into the wrong has given
His name a doubt to all the winds of heaven ;
The reed of Fortune, and of thrones the rod,
Of Fame the Moloch or the demigod ;
His country's Cæsar, Europe's Hannibal,
Without their decent dignity of fall.   240
Yet Vanity herself had better taught
A surer path even to the fame he sought,
By pointing out on History's fruitless page
Ten thousand conquerors for a single sage.
While Franklin's quiet memory climbs to Heaven,
Calming the lightning which he thence hath riven,
Or drawing from the no less kindled earth
Freedom and peace to that which boasts his birth ; [2]
While Washington 's a watchword, such as ne'er

---

1. I refer the reader to the first address of Prometheus in Æschylus,
when he is left alone by his attendants, and before the arrival of the
chorus of Sea-nymphs.—*Prometheus Vinctus*, line 88, *sq.*

2. [Franklin published his *Opinions and Conjectures concerning the
Properties and Effects of the Electrical Matter and the Means of pre-
serving Buildings, Ships, etc., from Lightning*, in 1751, and in June,
1752, " the immortal kite was flown." It was in 1781, when he was
minister plenipotentiary at the Court of France, that the Latin hexa-
meter, " Eripuit cœlo fulmen sceptrumque tyrannis," first applied to him
by Turgot, was affixed to his portrait by Fragonard. The line, said to
be an adaptation of a line in the *Astronomicon* of Manilius (lib. i. 104),
descriptive of the Reason, " Eripuitque Jovi fulmen viresque tonandi,"
was turned into French by Nogaret, d'Alembert, and other wits and
scholars. It appears on the reverse of a medal by F. Dupré, dated
1786. (See *Works* of Benjamin Franklin, edited by Jared Sparks, 1840,
viii. 537–539 ; *Life and Times, etc.*, by James Parton, 1864, i. 285–291.)]

Shall sink while there 's an echo left to air : [1]   250
While even the Spaniard's thirst of gold and war
Forgets Pizarro to shout Bolivar ! [2]
Alas ! why must the same Atlantic wave
Which wafted freedom gird a tyrant's grave—
The king of kings, and yet of slaves the slave,
Who burst the chains of millions to renew
The very fetters which his arm broke through,
And crushed the rights of Europe and his own,
To flit between a dungeon and a throne ?

VI.

But 'twill not be—the spark 's awakened—lo !   260
The swarthy Spaniard feels his former glow ;
The same high spirit which beat back the Moor
Through eight long ages of alternate gore
Revives—and where ? in that avenging clime
Where Spain was once synonymous with crime,
Where Cortes' and Pizarro's banner flew,
The infant world redeems her name of " *New*."
'Tis the *old* aspiration breathed afresh,
To kindle souls within degraded flesh,
Such as repulsed the Persian from the shore   270
Where Greece *was*—No ! she still is Greece once more.
One common cause makes myriads of one breast,
Slaves of the East, or helots of the West :
On Andes' [3] and on Athos' peaks unfurled,

1. [" To be the first man—*not* the Dictator, not the Sylla, but the
Washington, or the Aristides, the leader in talent and truth—is next
to the Divinity."—Journal, November 24, 1813, *Letters*, 1898, ii. 340.]
   2. [Simon Bolivar (*El Libertador*), 1783-1830, was at the height of
his power and fame at the beginning of 1823. In 1821 he had united
New Grenada to Venezuela under the name of the Republic of
Columbia, and on the 1st of September he made a solemn entry into
Lima. He was greeted with acclaim, but in accepting the honours
which his fellow-citizens showered upon him, he warned them against
the dangers of tyranny. "Beware," he said, "of a Napoleon or an
Iturbide." Byron, at one time, had a mind to settle in "Bolivar's
country" (letter to Ellice, June 12, 1821, *Letters*, 1901, vi. 89) ; and he
christened his yacht *The Bolivar*.]
   3. [A proclamation of Bolivar's, dated June 8, 1822, runs thus :
"Columbians, now all your delightful country is free. . . . From the
banks of the Orinoco to the Andes of Peru, the . . . army marching
in triumph has covered with its protecting arms the entire extent of

The self-same standard streams o'er either world:
The Athenian [1] wears again Harmodius' sword;
The Chili chief [2] abjures his foreign lord;
The Spartan knows himself once more a Greek,[3]
Young Freedom plumes the crest of each cacique;
Debating despots, hemmed on either shore,   280
Shrink vainly from the roused Atlantic's roar;

Columbia."—"Jamaica Papers," *Morning Chronicle*, September 28, 1822.]

1. [The capitulation of Athens was signed June 21, 1822. "Three days after the Greeks had sworn to observe the capitulation, they commenced murdering their helpless prisoners. . . . The streets of Athens were stained with the blood of four hundred men, women, and children." —*History of Greece*, by George Finlay, 1877, vi. 283. The sword was hid in the myrtle bough. Hence the allusion. (Compare *Childe Harold*, Canto III. stanza xx. line 9, *Poetical Works*, 1899, ii. 228, and 291, *note* 2.)]

2. [The independence of Chili dated from April 5, 1818, when General José de San Martin routed the Spanish army on the plains of Maypo. On the 28th of July, 1821, the Independence of Peru was proclaimed. General San Martin assumed the title of Protector, and, August 3, 4, 1821, issued proclamations, in which he announced the independence of Peru, and bade the Spaniards tremble if they "abused his indulgence." *Extracts from a Journal written on the Coast of Chili, etc.*, by Captain Basil Hall, 1824, i. 266-272.]

3. [On the 8th of August, 1822, Niketas and Hypsilantes defeated the Turks under Dramali, near Lerna. The Moreotes attributed their good fortune to the generalship of Kolokotrones, a Messenian. Compare with the whole of section vi. the following quotations from an article on the "Numbers of the Greeks," which appeared in the *Morning Chronicle*, September 13, 1822—

> " 'Trust not for freedom to the Franks,
> They have a king who buys and sells;
> In native swords and native ranks
> The only hope of courage dwells.'
> Byron.

"As Russia has now removed her warlike projects, and the Greeks are engaged single-handed with the whole force of the Ottoman Empire, etc. . . . Byron's Grecian bard can no longer exclaim—

> 'My country! on thy voiceless shore
> The heroic lay is tuneless now—
> The heroic bosom beats no more.'

"Greece is no longer a 'nation's sepulchre,' the foul abode of slaves, but the living theatre of the patriot's toils and the hero's achievements. Her banners once more float on the mountains, and the battles she has already won show that in every glen and valley, as well as on

> 'Suli's rock and Parga's shore
> Exists the remnant of a line
> Such as the Doric mothers bore.' "]

Through Calpe's strait the rolling tides advance,
Sweep slightly by the half-tamed land of France,
Dash o'er the old Spaniard's cradle, and would fain
Unite Ausonia to the mighty main :
But driven from thence awhile, yet not for aye,
Break o'er th' Ægean, mindful of the day
Of Salamis !—there, there the waves arise,
Not to be lulled by tyrant victories.
Lone, lost, abandoned in their utmost need   290
By Christians, unto whom they gave their creed,
The desolated lands, the ravaged isle,
The fostered feud encouraged to beguile,
The aid evaded, and the cold delay,
Prolonged but in the hope to make a prey ;— [1]
These, these shall tell the tale, and Greece can show
The false friend worse than the infuriate foe.
But this is well : Greeks only should free Greece,
Not the barbarian, with his masque of peace.
How should the Autocrat of bondage be   300
The king of serfs, and set the nations free ?
Better still serve the haughty Mussulman,
Than swell the Cossaque's prowling caravan ;
Better still toil for masters, than await,
The slave of slaves, before a Russian gate,—
Numbered by hordes, a human capital,
A live estate, existing but for thrall,
Lotted by thousands, as a meet reward
For the first courtier in the Czar's regard ;
While their immediate owner never tastes   310
His sleep, *sans* dreaming of Siberia's wastes :
Better succumb even to their own despair,
And drive the Camel—than purvey the Bear.

VII.

But not alone within the hoariest clime
Where Freedom dates her birth with that of Time,
And not alone where, plunged in night, a crowd

1. [An account of these Russian intrigues in Greece is contained in
Thomas Gordon's *History of the Greek Revolution*, 1832, i. 194-204.]

Of Incas darken to a dubious cloud,[i]
The dawn revives : renowned, romantic Spain
Holds back the invader from her soil again.
Not now the Roman tribe nor Punic horde [ii]   320
Demands her fields as lists to prove the sword;
Not now the Vandal or the Visigoth
Pollute the plains, alike abhorring both; [iii.]
Nor old Pelayo [1] on his mountain rears
The warlike fathers of a thousand years.
That seed is sown and reaped, as oft the Moor
Sighs to remember on his dusky shore.
Long in the peasant's song or poet's page
Has dwelt the memory of Abencerrage;
The Zegri,[2] and the captive victors, flung   330
Back to the barbarous realm from whence they sprung.
But these are gone—their faith, their swords, their sway,
Yet left more anti-christian foes than they; [iv.]
The bigot monarch, and the butcher priest,[3]
The Inquisition, with her burning feast,
The Faith's red "Auto," fed with human fuel,
While sate the catholic Moloch, calmly cruel,
Enjoying, with inexorable eye,[v.]

i. *Of Incas known but as a cloud.*—[*MS. erased.*]
ii. *Not now the Roman or the Punic horde.*—[*MS.*]
iii. —— *abhorrent of them both.*—[*MS.*]
iv. *And yet have left worse enemies than they.*—[*MS. erased.*]
v. *As rose on his remorseless ear the cry.*—[*MS. erased.*]

1. [Pelayo, said to be the son of Favila, Duke of Cantabria, was elected king by the Christians of the Asturias in 718, and defeated the Arab generals Suleyman and Manurza. He died A.D. 737.]
2. [For the "fabulous sketches" of the Zegri and Abencerrages, rival Moorish tribes, whose quarrels, at the close of the fifteenth century, deluged Granada with blood, see the *Civil Wars of Granada*, a prose fiction, interspersed with ballads, by Ginés Perez de Hita, published in 1595. An opera, *Les Abencérages*, by Cherubini, was performed in Paris in 1813. Chateaubriand's *Les Aventures du dernier Abencerage* was not published till 1826.]
3. [Ferdinand VII. returned to Madrid in March, 1814. "No sooner was he established on his throne . . . than he set himself to restore the old absolutism with its worst abuses. The nobles recovered their privileges . . . the Inquisition resumed its activity ; and the Jesuits returned to Spain. . . . A *camarilla* of worthless courtiers and priests conducted the government, and urged the king to fresh acts of revolutionary violence. For six years Spain groaned under a royalist 'reign of terror.'"—*Encycl. Brit.*, art. "Spain," vol. 22, p. 34[c.]]

That fiery festival of Agony!
The stern or feeble sovereign, one or both   340
By turns; the haughtiness whose pride was sloth;
The long degenerate noble; the debased
Hidalgo, and the peasant less disgraced,
But more degraded; the unpeopled realm;
The once proud navy which forgot the helm;
The once impervious phalanx disarrayed;
The idle forge that formed Toledo's blade;
The foreign wealth that flowed on every shore,
Save hers who earned it with the native's gore;
The very language which might vie with Rome's,   350
And once was known to nations like their homes,
Neglected or forgotten :—such *was* Spain ;
But such she is not, nor shall be again.
These worst, these *home* invaders, felt and feel
The new Numantine soul of old Castile,[i.]
Up! up again! undaunted Tauridor!
The bull of Phalaris renews his roar ;[ii.]
Mount, chivalrous Hidalgo! not in vain
Revive the cry—" Iago! and close Spain!"[1]
Yes, close her with your arméd bosoms round,   360
And form the barrier which Napoleon found,—
The exterminating war, the desert plain,
The streets without a tenant, save the slain ;
The wild Sierra, with its wilder troop[iii.]
Of vulture-plumed Guerrillas, on the stoop[iv.]
For their incessant prey; the desperate wall
Of Saragossa, mightiest in her fall;
The Man nerved to a spirit, and the Maid
Waving her more than Amazonian blade ;[2]
The knife of Arragon, Toledo's steel ;   370

i. *The re-awakened virtue* ——.—[*MS. erased.*]
ii. —— *is on the shore.*—[*MS. erased.*]
iii. *The wild Guerilla on Morena* ——.—[*MS. erased.*]
iv. *Of eagle-eyed* ——.—[*MS. erased.*]

1. " 'St. Jago and close Spain !' the old Spanish war-cry." [" Santiago y serra España."]
2. [Compare *Childe Harold*, Canto I. stanzas liv.-lvi., *Poetical Works*, i. 57, 58, 91, 92 (*note 11*). The " man " was Tio Jorge (Jorge Ibort), *vide ibid.*, p. 94.]

The famous lance of chivalrous Castile; [1]
The unerring rifle of the Catalan;
The Andalusian courser in the van;
The torch to make a Moscow of Madrid;
And in each heart the spirit of the Cid:—
Such have been, such shall be, such are.   Advance,
And win—not Spain! but thine own freedom, France!

VIII.

But lo! a Congress! [2]   What! that hallowed name
Which freed the Atlantic!   May we hope the same
For outworn Europe?   With the sound arise,   380
Like Samuel's shade to Saul's monarchic eyes,
The prophets of young Freedom, summoned far
From climes of Washington and Bolivar;
Henry, the forest-born Demosthenes,
Whose thunder shook the Philip of the seas; [3]
And stoic Franklin's energetic shade,

1. The Arragonians are peculiarly dexterous in the use of this weapon,
and displayed it particularly in former French wars.

2. [*Vide ante*, the Introduction to the *Age of Bronze*, pp. 537-540.]

3. [Patrick Henry, born May 29, 1736, died June 6, 1799, was one
of the leading spirits of the American Revolution.   His father, John
Henry, a Scotchman, a cousin of the historian, William Robertson,
had acquired a small property in Virginia.   Patrick was not exactly
"forest born," but, as a child, loved to play truant "in the forest with
his gun or over his angle-rod."   He first came into notice as an orator
in the "Parson's Cause," a suit brought by a minister of the Established
Church to recover his salary, which had been fixed at 16,000 lbs. of
tobacco.   In his speech he is said to have struck the key-note of the
Revolution by arguing that "a king, by disallowing acts of a salutary
nature, from being the father of his people, degenerates into a tyrant,
and forfeits all right to his subjects' obedience."   His famous speech
against the "Stamps Act" was delivered in the House of Burgesses of
Virginia, May 29, 1765.   One passage, with which, no doubt, Byron
was familiar, has passed into history.   "Cæsar had his Brutus—Charles
the First had his Cromwell—and George the Third——"   Henry was
interrupted with a shout of "Treason! treason!!" but finished the
sentence with, and "George the Third *may profit by their example.*
If *this* be treason, make the most of it.'
Henry was delegate to the first Continental Congress, five times
Governor of Virginia, and was appointed U.S. Senator in 1794.
His contemporaries said that he was "the greatest orator that ever
lived."   He seems to have exercised a kind of magical influence over
his hearers, which they could not explain, which charmed and overwhelmed them, and has left behind a tradition of bewitching persuasive-
ness and almost prophetic sublimity."—See *Life of Patrick Henry*, by
William Wirt, 1845, *passim.*]

Robed in the lightnings which his hand allayed ;
And Washington, the tyrant-tamer, wake,
To bid us blush for these old chains, or break.
But *who* compose this Senate of the few   390
That should redeem the many?   *Who* renew
This consecrated name, till now assigned
To councils held to benefit mankind?
Who now assemble at the holy call?
The blest Alliance, which says three are all!
An earthly Trinity! which wears the shape
Of Heaven's, as man is mimicked by the ape.
A pious Unity! in purpose one—
To melt three fools to a Napoleon.[i.]
Why, Egypt's Gods were rational to these ;   400
Their dogs and oxen knew their own degrees,
And, quiet in their kennel or their shed,
Cared little, so that they were duly fed ;
But these, more hungry, must have something more —
The power to bark and bite, to toss and gore.
Ah, how much happier were good Æsop's frogs
Than we! for ours are animated logs,
With ponderous malice swaying to and fro,
And crushing nations with a stupid blow ;
All dully anxious to leave little work   410
Unto the revolutionary stork.

IX.

Thrice blest Verona! since the holy three
With their imperial presence shine on thee!
Honoured by them, thy treacherous site forgets [ii.]
The vaunted tomb of " all the Capulets ! "[1]

i. —— *to one Napoleon.—[MS. erased.]*
ii. —— *thy poor old wall forgets.—[MS. erased.]*

1. ["I have been over Verona. The amphitheatre is wonderful—
beats even Greece. Of the truth of Juliet's story they seem tenacious
to a degree, insisting on the fact, giving a date (1303), and showing a
tomb. It is a plain, open, and partly decayed sarcophagus, with
withered leaves in it, in a wild and desolate conventual garden, once a
cemetery, now ruined to the very graves. The situation struck me as
very appropriate to the legend, being blighted as their love. . . . The
Gothic monuments of the Scaliger princes pleased me, but 'a poor
virtuoso am I.'"—Letter to Moore, November 7, 1816, *Letters*, 1899,

Thy Scaligers—for what was " Dog the Great,"
" Can Grande," [1] (which I venture to translate,)
To these sublimer pugs ?   Thy poet too,
Catullus, whose old laurels yield to new ; [2]
Thine amphitheatre, where Romans sate ;   420
And Dante's exile sheltered by thy gate ;
Thy good old man, whose world was all within
Thy wall, nor knew the country held him in ; [3]
Would that the royal guests it girds about
Were so far like, as never to get out !
Aye, shout ! inscribe ! [4] rear monuments of shame,
To tell Oppression that the world is tame !

iii. 386, 387.   The tombs of the Scaligers are close to the Church of
Santa Maria l'Antica.   Juliet's tomb, " of red Verona marble," is in the
garden of the *Orfanotrofio*, between the Via Cappucini and the Adige.
It is not " that ancient vault where all the kindred of the Capulets lie,"
which has long since been destroyed.   Since 1814 Verona had been
under Austria's sway, and had " treacherously" forgotten her republican traditions.]
    1. [Francesco Can Grande della Scala died in 1329.   It was under
his roof that Dante learned

            ". . . how salt his food who fares
          Upon another's bread—how steep his path
        Who treadeth up and down another's stairs."

For anecdotes of Can Grande, see *Commedia, etc.*, by E. H. Plumptre,
D.D., 1886, I. cxx., cxxi. ; and compare *Dante at Verona*, by D. G.
Rossetti, *Works*, 1886, i. 1–17.]
    2. [Ippolito Pindemonte, the modern Tibullus (1753–1828).   (See
Letters, 1900, iv. 127, *note* 4.)]
    3. [Claudian's famous old man of Verona, "*qui suburbium nunquam
egressus est.*"

        " Indocilis rerum, vicinæ nescius urbis,
          Adspectu fruitur liberiore poli."

C. Claudiani *Opera*, lii., *Epigramma*, ii. lines 9, 10 (ed. 1821, iii.
427).]
    4. [" In the amphitheatre . . . crowds collected after the sittings
of the Congress, to witness dramatic representations. . . . But for the
costumes, a spectator might have imagined he was witnessing a resurrection of the ancient Romans."—*Congress, etc.*, by M. de Chateaubriand, 1838, i. 76.   This was on the 24th of November.   Catalani
sang.   Rossini's cantata was performed with tremendous applause.
On the next day the august visitors witnessed an illumination of the
city.   " Leur attention s'est principalement arrêtée sur le superbe
portail de l'église Sainte-Agnés, qui brillait de mille feux, au milieu
desquels se lisait l'inscription suivante en lettres de grandeur colossale :

        ' *A Cesare Augusto Verona esultante.*' "

—*Le Moniteur*, December 14, 1822.]

Crowd to the theatre with loyal rage,
The comedy is not upon the stage;
The show is rich in ribandry and stars,   430
Then gaze upon it through thy dungeon bars;
Clap thy permitted palms, kind Italy,
For thus much still thy fettered hands are free !

X.

Resplendent sight ! Behold the coxcomb Czar,[1]
The Autocrat of waltzes [2] and of war !
As eager for a plaudit as a realm,
And just as fit for flirting as the helm;
A Calmuck beauty with a Cossack wit,
And generous spirit, when 'tis not frost-bit;
Now half dissolving to a liberal thaw,[i]   440

i. *Now half inclining* ——.—[*MS.*]

1. [Alexander I. (Paulowitsch), 1777–1825, succeeded his father in
1801. He began his reign well. Taxation was diminished, judicial
penalties were remitted, universities were founded and reorganized,
personal servitude was abolished or restricted throughout the empire.
At the height of his power and influence, when he was regarded as the
Liberator of Europe, he granted a Constitution to Poland, based on
liberal if not democratic principles (June 21, 1815). But after a time
he reverted to absolutism. Autocracy at home, a mystical and senti-
mental alliance with autocrats abroad, were incompatible with the
indulgence of liberal proclivities. "After the Congresses of Aix-la-
Chapelle and Troppau," writes M. Rambaud (*History of Russia*, 1888,
ii. 384), "he was no longer the same man. . . . From that time he
considered himself the dupe of his generous ideas, . . . at Carlsbad, at
Laybach, and at Verona, Alexander was already the leader of the
European reaction." But even to the last he believed that he could run
with the hare and hunt with the hounds. "They may say of me,"
he exclaimed, "what they will; but I have lived and shall die
republican" (*ibid.*, p. 398).

Alexander was a man of ideas, a sentimentalist, and a *poseur*, but he
had an eye to the main chance. Whatever cause or dynasty suffered,
the Emperor Alexander was still triumphant. Byron's special grudge
against him at this time was due to his vacillation with regard to the
cause of Greek Independence. But he is too contemptuous. There
were points in common between the "Coxcomb Czar" and his satirist;
and it is far from certain that if the twain had changed places Byron
might not have proved just "*such* an Alexander." In one respect their
destiny was alike. The greatest sorrow of their lives was the death of
a natural daughter.]

2. [For Alexander's waltzing, see *Personal Reminiscences*, by Cornelia
Knight and Thomas Raikes, 1875, p. 286. See, too, Moore's *Fables
for the Holy Alliance*, Fable I., "A Dream."]

But hardened back whene'er the morning 's raw ;
With no objection to true Liberty,
Except that it would make the nations free.
How well the imperial dandy prates of peace !
How fain, if Greeks would be his slaves, free Greece !
How nobly gave he back the Poles their Diet,
Then told pugnacious Poland to be quiet !
How kindly would he send the mild Ukraine,
With all her pleasant Pulks,[1] to lecture Spain !
How royally show off in proud Madrid　　　　　450
His goodly person, from the South long hid !
A blessing cheaply purchased, the world knows,
By having Muscovites for friends or foes.
Proceed, thou namesake of great Philip's son !
La Harpe, thine Aristotle, beckons on ; [2]
And that which Scythia was to him of yore
Find with thy Scythians on Iberia's shore.
Yet think upon, thou somewhat agéd youth,
Thy predecessor on the banks of Pruth ;
Thou hast to aid thee, should his lot be thine,　　46
Many an old woman,[3] but not Catherine.[4]
Spain, too, hath rocks, and rivers, and defiles—

1. [" Pulk " is Polish for " regiment."　The allusion must be to the
military colonies planted by " the corporal of Gatchina," Araktchèef,
in the governments of Novgorod, Kharkof, and elsewhere.]
2. [Frédéric César La Harpe (1754–1838) was appointed by Catherine II. Governor to the Grand-Dukes Alexander and Constantine.
It was from La Harpe's teaching that Alexander imbibed his liberal
ideas.　In 1816, when Byron passed the summer in Switzerland, La
Harpe was domiciled at Lausanne, and it is possible that a meeting
took place.]
3. [Alexander's platonic attachment to the Baronne de Krüdener
(Barbe Julie de Wietenhoff), beauty, novelist, *illuminée*, was the source
of amusement rather than scandal.　The Baronne, then in her fiftieth
year, was the channel through which Franz Bader's theory or doctrine
of the " Holy Alliance " was conveyed to the enthusiastic and receptive
Czar.　It was only a passing whim.　Alexander's mysticism was for
ornament, not for use, and, before very long, Egeria and her Muscovite
Numa parted company.]
4. The dexterity of Catherine extricated Peter (called the Great by
courtesy), when surrounded by the Mussulmans on the banks of the
river Pruth.　[Catherine, who had long been Peter's mistress, had at
length been acknowledged as his wife.　Her " dexterity " took the
form of a bribe of money and jewels, conveyed to the Turkish grand-
vizier Baltazhi-Mahomet, who was induced to accede to the Treaty of
Pruth, July 20, 1711.]

The Bear may rush into the Lion's toils.
Fatal to Goths are Xeres' sunny fields ; [1]
Think'st thou to thee Napoleon's victor yields ?
Better reclaim thy deserts, turn thy swords
To ploughshares, shave and wash thy Bashkir [2] hordes,
Redeem thy realms from slavery and the knout,
Than follow headlong in the fatal route,
To infest the clime whose skies and laws are pure   470
With thy foul legions.   Spain wants no manure :
Her soil is fertile, but she feeds no foe :
Her vultures, too, were gorged not long ago ;
And wouldst thou furnish them with fresher prey ?
Alas ! thou wilt not conquer, but purvey.
I am Diogenes, though Russ and Hun [3]
Stand between mine and many a myriad's sun ;
But were I not Diogenes, I'd wander
Rather a worm than *such* an Alexander !   ·
Be slaves who will, the cynic shall be free ;   480
His tub hath tougher walls than Sinopè : [i.]
Still will he hold his lantern up to scan
The face of monarchs for an " honest man." [4]

XI.

And what doth Gaul, the all-prolific land
Of *ne plus ultra* ultras and their band
Of mercenaries ? and her noisy chambers
And tribune, which each orator first clambers

i. *Still will I roll my tub at Sinope*
   Be slaves who may ——.—[*MS.*]

1.   [" Eight thousand men had to Asturias march'd
        Beneath Count Julian's banner. . . . To revenge
     His quarrel, twice that number left their bones,
     Slain in unnatural battle, on the field
     Of Xeres, where the sceptre from the Goths
     By righteous Heaven was reft."
             Southey's *Roderick*, Canto XXV. lines 1, 2, 7-11.]

2. [The Bashkirs are a Turco-Mongolian tribe inhabiting the slopes
of the Ural Mountains.   They supply a body of irregular cavalry to the
Russian army.]

3. [The Austrian and Russian armies stood between the Greeks and
other peoples, and their independence, as Alexander the Great stood
between Diogenes and the sunshine.]

4. [Lines 482, 483, are not in the MS.]

Before he finds a voice, and when 'tis found,
Hears " the lie " echo for his answer round ?
Our British Commons sometimes deign to "hear !"   490
A Gallic senate hath more tongue than ear ;
Even Constant,[1] their sole master of debate,
Must fight next day his speech to vindicate.
But this costs little to true Franks, who'd rather
Combat than listen, were it to their father.
What is the simple standing of a shot,
To listening long, and interrupting not ?
Though this was not the method of old Rome,
When Tully fulmined o'er each vocal dome,
Demosthenes has sanctioned the transaction,   500
In saying eloquence meant " Action, action !"

XII.

But where 's the monarch?[2] hath he dined? or yet
Groans beneath indigestion's heavy debt?

1. [Constant (Henri Benjamin de Rebecque, 1767–1830) was the " stormy petrel" of debate in the French Chamber. For instance, in a discussion on secret service money for the police (July 27, 1822), he exclaimed, " Vous les représentez-vous payant d'une main le salaire du vol, et tenant peut-être un crucifix de l'autre?" No wonder that there were "violens murmures, cris d'indignation à droite." The duel, however, did not arise out of a speech in the Chamber, but from a letter of June 5, 1822, in *La Quotidienne*, in which the Marquis de Forbin des Issarts replied to some letters of Constant, which had appeared in the *Courrier* and *Constitutionnel*. Constant was lame, and accordingly both combatants "out été placés à dix petits pas sur des chaises." Both fired twice, but neither " was a penny the worse." (See *La Grande Encyclopédie*, art. "Constant;" and, for details, *La Quotidienne*, June 8, 1822. See, too, for "session de 1822," *Opinions et Discours* de M. Casimir Perrier, 1838, ii. 5–47.)]

1. [Louis XVIII. (Louis Stanislas Xavier, 1755–1824) passed several years of exile in England, at Goswell, Wanstead, and latterly at Hartwell, near Aylesbury, in Buckinghamshire. When he entered Paris as king, in May, 1814, he was in his fifty-ninth year, inordinately bulky and unwieldy—a king *pour rire*. " C'est ce gros goutteux," explained an *ouvrier* to a bystander, who had asked, "Which is the king?" Fifteen mutton cutlets, "sautées au jus," for breakfast ; fifteen mutton cutlets served with a "sauce à la champagne," for dinner ; to say nothing of strawberries, and sweet apple-puffs between meals, made digestion and locomotion difficult. It was no wonder that he was a martyr to the gout. But he cared for nature and for books as well as for eating. His *Lettres d'Artwell* (Paris, 1830), which profess to be selections from his correspondence with a friend, give a pleasant picture of the *roi en exil*. His wife, Louise de Savoie, died November,

Have revolutionary patés risen,
And turned the royal entrails to a prison?
Have discontented movements stirred the troops?
Or have *no* movements followed traitorous soups?
Have Carbonaro [1] cooks not carbonadoed
Each course enough? or doctors dire dissuaded
Repletion? Ah! in thy dejected looks   510
I read all France's treason in her cooks!
Good classic Louis! is it, canst thou say,
Desirable to be the "Desiré?"
Why wouldst thou leave calm Hartwell's green abode,
Apician table, and Horatian ode,
To rule a people who will not be ruled,
And love much rather to be scourged than schooled?
Ah! thine was not the temper or the taste
For thrones; the table sees thee better placed:
A mild Epicurean, formed, at best,   520
To be a kind host and as good a guest,
To talk of Letters, and to know by heart
One *half* the Poet's, *all* the Gourmand's art;
A scholar always, now and then a wit,
And gentle when Digestion may permit;—

1810, and in the following April he writes (*Lettres*, pp. 70, 71), "Mars
a maintenu le bien d'un hiver fort doux; point encore de goutte; *à
brebis tondue, Dieu mesure le vent*. Hélas! je l'éprouve bien qu'elle
est tondue cette pauvre brebis! . . . je me promène dans le jardin, je
vois mes rosiers qui poussent bien; à qui offrirai-je les roses? . . .
Eh bien! je ne voudrais pas que cette goutte d'absinthe cessât, car
pour cela il faudrait l'oublier. L'oublier! Ah Dieu! Je suis comme
les enfans d'Israël qui disaient: *Super flumina Babylonis* . . . *Sion*,
Mais ajoutons tout de suite: *Si oblitus fuero tui, Jerusalem, oblivioni
detur dextera mea*." In another letter, June 8, 1811, he criticizes some
translations of Horace, and laments that the good Père Sanadon has
confined himself to the *Opera Expurgata*. Not, he adds, that he
would not have excluded one or two odes, "mais on a impitoyable-
ment sabré des choses délicieuses" (*Lettres*, p. 98).

To his wit, Chateaubriand testifies (*The Congress, etc.*, 1838, i. 262).
At the council, when affairs of state were being discussed, the king
"would say in his clear shrill voice, 'I am going to make you laugh,
M. de Chateaubriand.' The other ministers fumed with impatience,
but Chateaubriand laughed, not as a courtier, but as a human being."]

1. [Louvel, who assassinated the Duc de Berri, and who was
executed June 7, 1820, was supposed to have been an agent of the
carbonari. La Fayette, Constant, Lafitte, and others were also suspected of being connected with secret societies.—*The Court of the
Tuileries*, 1815-1848, by Lady Jackson, 1883, ii. 19.]

But not to govern lands enslaved or free;
The gout was martyrdom enough for thee.

XIII.

Shall noble Albion pass without a phrase
From a bold Briton in her wonted praise?
" Arts—arms—and George—and glory—and the Isles,
And happy Britain, wealth, and Freedom's smiles,   531
White cliffs, that held invasion far aloof,
Contented subjects, all alike tax-proof,
Proud Wellington, with eagle beak so curled,[i.]
That nose, the hook where he suspends the world ![1]
And Waterloo, and trade, and——(hush ! not yet
A syllable of imposts or of debt)——
And ne'er (enough) lamented Castlereagh,[2]
Whose penknife slit a goose-quill t'other day—[ii.]
And, ' pilots who have weathered every storm'—[3]   540
(But, no, not even for rhyme's sake, name Reform)."
These are the themes thus sung so oft before,
Methinks we need not sing them any more;
Found in so many volumes far and near,

    i. *Immortal Wellington with beak so curled.*
      That foremost Corporal of all the World—
      Immortal Wellington—and flags unfurled.—[*MS. erased.*]
    ii. *Whose penknife saved some nation's t'other day.*
      Who shaved his throat by chance the other day.—[*MS. erased.*]

1.   " Naso suspendis adunco."—HORACE [*Sat.* i. 6, 5].
The Roman applies it to one who merely was imperious to his acquaintance.

2. [Robert Stewart, Viscount Castlereagh, afterwards Marquis of Londonderry (1769-1822), who had been labouring under a "mental delirium" (Letter of Duke of Wellington, August 9, 1822), committed suicide by cutting his throat with a penknife (August 12, 1822). He was the uncompromising and successful opponent of popular causes in Ireland, Italy, and elsewhere, and, as such, Byron assailed him, alive and dead, with the bitterest invective. (See, for instance, the " Dedication" to *Don Juan*, stanzas xi.-xvi., sundry epigrams, and an " Epitaph.") In the Preface to Cantos VI., VII., VIII., of *Don Juan*, he justifies the inclusion of a stanza or two on Castlereagh, which had been written " before his decease," and, again, alludes to his suicide. (For an estimate of his career and character, see *Letters*, 1900, iv. 108, 109, *note* 1; and for a full report of the inquest, *The Annual Biography*, 1823, pp. 56-62.)]

3. ["The Pilot that weathered the Storm" was written by Canning, to be recited at a dinner given on Pitt's birthday, May 28, 1802.]

There 's no occasion you should find them here.
Yet something may remain perchance to chime
With reason, and, what 's stranger still, with rhyme.[i.]
Even this thy genius, Canning![1] may permit,
Who, bred a statesman, still wast born a wit,
And never, even in that dull House, couldst tame 550
To unleavened prose thine own poetic flame ;
Our last, our best, our only orator,
Even I can praise thee—Tories do no more :
Nay, not so much ;—they hate thee, man, because
Thy Spirit less upholds them than it awes.
The hounds will gather to their huntsman's hollo,
And where he leads the duteous pack will follow ;
But not for love mistake their yelling cry ;
Their yelp for game is not an eulogy ;
Less faithful far than the four-footed pack, 560
A dubious scent would lure the bipeds back.
Thy saddle-girths are not yet quite secure,
Nor royal stallion's feet extremely sure ;
The unwieldy old white horse is apt at last
To stumble, kick—and now and then stick fast
With his great Self and Rider in the mud ;
But what of that ? the animal shows blood.

XIV.

Alas, the Country ! how shall tongue or pen
Bewail her now *un*country gentlemen ?
The last to bid the cry of warfare cease, 570
The first to make a malady of peace.

i. *With reason—whate'er it may with rhyme.*—[*MS. erased.*]

1. [George Canning (1770-1827) succeeded Lord Londonderry as
Foreign Secretary, September 8, 1822. He was not a *persona grata* to
George IV., who had been offended by Canning's neutral attitude, as
a minister, on the question of the Queen's message (June 7, 1820),
and by his avowal "of an unaltered regard and affection" for that
"illustrious personage" herself. There was, too, the prospect of
Catholic Emancipation. In 1821 he had spoken in favour of Plunket's
bills, and, the next year (April 30, 1822), he had brought in a bill to
remove the disabilities of Roman Catholic peers from sitting in the
House of Lords. If Canning persisted in his advocacy of Catholic
claims, the king's conscience might turn restive, and urge him to
effectual resistance. Hence the warning in lines 563-567.]

For what were all these country patriots born?
To hunt—and vote—and raise the price of corn?
But corn, like every mortal thing, must fall,
Kings—Conquerors—and markets most of all.
And must ye fall with every ear of grain?
Why would you trouble Buonaparté's reign?
He was your great Triptolemus;[1] his vices
Destroyed but realms, and still maintained your prices;
He amplified to every lord's content   580
The grand agrarian alchymy, high *rent*.[i.]
Why did the tyrant stumble on the Tartars,
And lower wheat to such desponding quarters?
Why did you chain him on yon Isle so lone?
The man was worth much more upon his throne.
True, blood and treasure boundlessly were spilt,
But what of that? the Gaul may bear the guilt;
But bread was high, the farmer paid his way,
And acres told upon the appointed day.[ii.]
But where is now the goodly audit ale?   590
The purse-proud tenant, never known to fail?
The farm which never yet was left on hand?
The marsh reclaimed to most improving land?
The impatient hope of the expiring lease?
The doubling rental?   What an evil 's peace!
In vain the prize excites the ploughman's skill,
In vain the Commons pass their patriot bill;[2]
The *Landed Interest*—(you may understand
The phrase much better leaving out the *land*)—
The land self-interest groans from shore to shore,   600

i. *The mighty monosyllable high* Rent !—[*MS.*]
ii. —— *upon the audit day.*—[*MS. M.*]

1. [Demeter gave Triptolemus a chariot drawn by serpents, and
bade him scatter wheat throughout the world. (See Ovid, *Met.*, lib. v.
lines 642-661.)]

2. [" Lord Londonderry proposed (April 29, 1822) that whenever
wheat should be under 60 shillings a quarter, Government should be
authorized to issue £1,000,000 in Exchequer bills to landed proprietors
on the security of their crops; that importation of foreign corn should
be permitted whenever the price of wheat should be at or above 70
shillings a quarter . . . that a sliding-scale should be fixed, that for
wheat being under 80s. a quarter at 12 shillings; above 80s. and below
85s., at 5 shillings; and above 85s., only one shilling."—Alison's *History
of Europe*, 1815-1852, *and* 1854, ii. 506. The first clause was thrown
out, but the rest of the bill passed May 13, 1822.]

For fear that plenty should attain the poor.[i.]
Up, up again, ye rents, exalt your notes,
Or else the Ministry will lose their votes,
And patriotism, so delicately nice,
Her loaves will lower to the market price;[ii.]
For ah! "the loaves and fishes," once so high,
Are gone—their oven closed, their ocean dry,[iii.]
And nought remains of all the millions spent,
Excepting to grow moderate and content.
They who are not so, *had* their turn—and turn   610
About still flows from Fortune's equal urn;
Now let their virtue be its own reward,
And share the blessings which themselves prepared.
See these inglorious Cincinnati swarm,
Farmers of war, dictators of the farm;
Their ploughshare was the sword in hireling hands,
Their fields manured by gore of other lands;
Safe in their barns, these Sabine tillers
Their brethren out to battle—why? for rent!
Year after year they voted cent. per cent.   620
Blood, sweat, and tear-wrung millions—why?—for rent!
They roared, they dined, they drank, they swore they meant
To die for England—why then live?—for rent!
The peace has made one general malcontent
Of these high-market patriots; war was rent!
Their love of country, millions all mis-spent,
How reconcile? by reconciling rent!
And will they not repay the treasures lent?
No: down with everything, and up with rent!
Their good, ill, health, wealth, joy, or discontent,   630
Being, end, aim, religion—*rent—rent—rent!*
Thou sold'st thy birthright, Esau! for a mess;
Thou shouldst have gotten more, or eaten less;
Now thou hast swilled thy pottage, thy demands
Are idle; Israel says the bargain stands.
Such, landlords! was your appetite for war,

i. *For fear that riches* ——.—[*MS. M.*]
ii. *Will sell the harvest at a market price.*—[*MS. M.*]
iii. *Are gone—their fields untilled.*—[*MS. M.*]

And gorged with blood, you grumble at a scar !
What ! would they spread their earthquake even o'er cash ?
And when land crumbles, bid firm paper crash ?[1]
So rent may rise, bid Bank and Nation fall,   640
And found on 'Change a *Fundling* Hospital ?
Lo; Mother Church, while all religion writhes,
Like Niobe, weeps o'er her offspring—Tithes ;[2]
The Prelates go to—where the Saints have gone,
And proud pluralities subside to one ;
Church, state, and faction wrestle in the dark,
Tossed by the deluge in their common ark.
Shorn of her bishops, banks, and dividends,
Another Babel soars—but Britain ends.
And why ? to pamper the self-seeking wants,   650
And prop the hill of these agrarian ants.
" Go to these ants, thou sluggard, and be wise ; "
Admire their patience through each sacrifice,
Till taught to feel the lesson of their pride,
The price of taxes and of homicide ;
Admire their justice, which would fain deny
The debt of nations :—pray *who made it high ?*[3]

1. [Peel's bill for the resumption of cash payments (Act 59 Geo. III. cap. 49) was passed June 14, 1819. The "landed interest" attributed the fall of prices and the consequent fall of rent to this measure, and hinted more or less plainly that the fund-holders should share the loss. They had lent their money when the currency was inflated, and should not now be paid off in gold.

" But *you*," exclaims Cobbett [Letter to Mr. Western (*Weekly Register*, November 23, 1822)], " what can induce you to stickle for the Pitt system [*i.e.* paper-money]? I will tell you what it is : you loved the *high prices*, and the domination that they gave you. . . . Besides this, you think that the *boroughs can be preserved* by a return to paper-money, and along with them the hare-and-pheasant law and justice. You loved the glorious times of paper-money, and you want them back again. You think that they could go on for ever. . . . The bill of 1819 was really a great relaxation of the Pitt system, and when you are crying out *spoliation* and *confiscation*, when you are bawling out so lustily about the robbery committed on you by the fund-holders and the placemen, and are praising the infernal Pitt system at the same time, . . . you say they are receiving, the fund-vagabonds in particular, *more* than they ought." It is evident that Byron's verse is a reverberation of Cobbett's prose.]

2. [Petitions were presented by the inhabitants of St. Andrew, Holborn ; St. Botolf, Bishopsgate ; and St. Gregory by St. Paul, to the Court of Common Council, against a tithe-charge of 2s. 9d. in the pound on their annual rents.—*Morning Chronicle*, November 1, 1822.]

3. [Lines 614–657 are not in the MS.]

XV.

Or turn to sail between those shifting rocks,
The new Symplegades [1]—the crushing Stocks,
Where Midas might again his wish behold   660
In real paper or imagined gold.
That magic palace of Alcina [2] shows
More wealth than Britain ever had to lose,
Were all her atoms of unleavened ore,
And all her pebbles from Pactolus' shore.
There Fortune plays, while Rumour holds the stake
And the World trembles to bid brokers break.
How rich is Britain ! not indeed in mines,
Or peace or plenty, corn or oil, or wines ;
No land of Canaan, full of milk and honey,   670
Nor (save in paper shekels) ready money :
But let us not to own the truth refuse,   ·
Was ever Christian land so rich in Jews ?
Those parted with their teeth to good King John,
And now, ye kings, they kindly draw your own ;
All states, all things, all sovereigns they control,
And waft a loan " from Indus to the pole."
The banker—broker—baron [3]—brethren, speed

1. [The Symplegades, or "justling rocks," Ovid's *instabiles Cyaneæ*, were supposed to crush the ships which sailed between them.]

2. [Alcina, the personification of carnal pleasure in the *Orlando Furioso*, is the counterpart of Homer's *Circe.* "She enjoyed her lovers for a time, and then changed them into trees, stones, fountains, or beasts, as her fancy dictated." (See Ariosto, *Orlando Furioso*, vi. 35, *seq.*)]

3. [There were five brothers Rothschild : Anselm, of Frankfort, 1773-1855 ; Salomon, of Vienna, 1774-1855 ; Nathan Mayer, of London, 1777-1836 ; Charles, of Naples, 1788-1855 ; and James, of Paris, 1792-1868. In 1821 Austria raised 37½ million guldens through the firm, and, as an acknowledgment of their services, the Emperor raised the brothers to the rank of baron, and appointed Baron Nathan Mayer Consul-General in London, and Baron James to the same post in Paris. In 1822 both Russia (see line 684) and England raised 3½ millions sterling through the Rothschilds. The "two Jews" (line 686, etc.) are, probably, the two Consuls-General. In 1822 their honours were new, and some mocked. There is the story that Talleyrand once presented the Parisian brother to Montmorenci as *M. le premier Baron Juif* to *M. le premier Baron Chrétien ;* while another tale, parent or off-spring of the preceding, which appeared in *La Quotidienne*, December 21, 1822, testifies to the fact, not recorded, that a Rothschild was at Verona during the Congress : " M. de Rotschild, baron et banquier

To aid these bankrupt tyrants in their need.
Nor these alone; Columbia feels no less   680
Fresh speculations follow each success;
And philanthropic Israel deigns to drain
Her mild per-centage from exhausted Spain.
Not without Abraham's seed can Russia march;
'Tis gold, not steel, that rears the conqueror's arch.
Two Jews, a chosen people, can command
In every realm their Scripture-promised land :—
Two Jews, keep down the Romans,[1] and uphold
The accurséd Hun, more brutal than of old:
Two Jews,—but not Samaritans—direct   690
The world, with all the spirit of their sect.
What is the happiness of earth to them ?
A congress forms their " New Jerusalem,"
Where baronies and orders both invite—
Oh, holy Abraham ! dost thou see the sight ?
Thy followers mingling with these royal swine,
Who spit not " on their Jewish gaberdine,"
But honour them as portion of the show—
(Where now, oh Pope ! is thy forsaken toe ?
Could it not favour Judah with some kicks ?   700
Or has it ceased to " kick against the pricks ? ")
On Shylock's shore behold them stand afresh,
To cut from Nation's hearts their " pound of flesh."

XVI.

Strange sight this Congress ! destined to unite
All that 's incongruous, all that 's opposite.
I speak not of the Sovereigns—they're alike,
A common coin as ever mint could strike ;
But those who sway the puppets, pull the strings,
Have more of motley than their heavy kings.

général des gouvernemens absolus, s'est, dit-on, rendu au congrès, il a
été présenté à l'empereur d'Autriche, et S.M., en lui remettant une
décoration, a daigné lui dire : ' Vous pouvez être assuré, Monsieur, que
la maison d'Autriche sera toujours disposée à reconnaître vos services
et à vous accorder ce qui pourra vous être agréable,'—' Votre Majesté,'
a répondu le baron financier, ' pourra toujours également compter sur
la maison Rotschild.' "—See The Rotschilds, by John Reeves, 1886.]

1. [In 1822 the Neapolitan Government raised 22,000,000 ducats
through the Rothschilds.]

Jews, authors, generals, charlatans, combine,   710
While Europe wonders at the vast design :
There Metternich, power's foremost parasite,
Cajoles ; there Wellington forgets to fight ;
There Chateaubriand [1] forms new books of martyrs ;
And subtle Greeks [2] intrigue for stupid Tartars ;
There Montmorenci, the sworn foe to charters,[3]
Turns a diplomatist of great éclat,
To furnish articles for the " Débats ; "
Of war so certain—yet not quite so sure
As his dismissal in the " Moniteur."   720
Alas ! how could his cabinet thus err !
Can Peace be worth an ultra-minister ?

1. Monsieur Chateaubriand, who has not forgotten the author in the minister, received a handsome compliment at Verona from a literary sovereign : "Ah ! Monsieur C., are you related to that Chateaubriand who—who—who has written *something ?*" (écrit *quelque chose !*) It is said that the author of Atala repented him for a moment of his legitimacy. [François René Vicomte de Chateaubriand (1768-1848) published *Les Martyrs ou le Triomphe de la religion chrétienne* in 1809.]

2. [Count Capo d'Istria (b. 1776)—afterwards President of Greece. The count was murdered, in September, 1831, by the brother and son of a Mainote chief whom he had imprisoned (*note* to ed. 1832). Byron may have believed that Capo d'Istria was still in the service of the Czar, but, according to Alison, his advocacy of his compatriots the Greeks had led to his withdrawal from the Russian Foreign Office, and prevented his taking part in the Congress. It was, however, stated in the papers that he had been summoned, and was on his way to Verona.]

3. [Jean Mathieu Félicité, Duc de Montmorenci (1766-1826), was, in his youth, a Jacobin. He proposed, August 4, 1789, to abrogate feudal rights, and June 15, 1790, to abolish the nobility. He was superseded as plenipotentiary by Chateaubriand, and on his return to Paris created a duke. Before the end of the year he was called upon to resign his portfolio as Minister of Foreign Affairs. The king disliked him, and there were personal disagreements between him and the Prime Minister, M. de Villêle.

The following " gazette " appeared in the *Moniteur :*—

" Ordonnance du Roi. Signé Louis. Art Ier Le Vicomte de Chateaubriand, pair de France, est nomme ministre secrétaire d'état au département des affaires étrangères. Louis par la grace de Dieu Roi de France et de Navarre.

" Art. Ier. Le Duc Mathieu de Montmorenci, pair de France, est nommé ministre d'Etat, et membre de notre Conseil privé.
    " Dimanche, 29 Décembre, 1822."
" On Tuesday, January 1, 1823," writes Chateaubriand, *Congress,* 1838, i. 258, " we crossed the bridges, and went to sleep in that minister's bed, which was not made for us,—a bed in which one sleeps but little, and in which one remains only for a short time."]

He falls indeed, perhaps to rise again,
" Almost as quickly as he conquered Spain." [1]

XVII.

Enough of this—a sight more mournful woos
The averted eye of the reluctant Muse.
The Imperial daughter, the Imperial bride,[2]
The imperial Victim—sacrifice to pride;
The mother of the Hero's hope, the boy,
The young Astyanax of Modern Troy;[3]   730
The still pale shadow of the loftiest Queen
That Earth has yet to see, or e'er hath seen;
She flits amidst the phantoms of the hour,
The theme of pity, and the wreck of power.
Oh, cruel mockery ! Could not Austria spare
A daughter? What did France's widow there ?
Her fitter place was by St. Helen's wave,
Her only throne is in Napoleon's grave.
But, no,—she still must hold a petty reign,
Flanked by her formidable chamberlain;   740
The martial Argus, whose not hundred eyes[4]
Must watch her through these paltry pageantries.

1. [From Pope's line on Lord Peterborough, *Imitations of Horace*, Sat. i. 132.]

2. [Marie Louise, daughter of Francis I. of Austria, was born December 12, 1791, and died December 18, 1849. She was married to Napoleon, April 2, 1810, and gave birth to a son, March 29, 1811. In accordance with the Treaty of Paris, she left France April 26, 1814, renounced the title of Empress, and was created Duchess of Parma, Placentia, and Guastalla. After Napoleon's death (May 5, 1821). "Proud Austria's mournful flower" did not long remain a widow, but speedily and secretly married her chamberlain and gentleman of honour, Count Adam de Neipperg (*ce polisson* Neipperg, as Napoleon called him), to whom she had long been attached. It was supposed that she attended the Congress of Verona in the interest of her son, the ex-King of Rome; to whom Napoleon had bequeathed money and heirlooms. She was a solemn stately personage, *tant soit peu déclassée*, and the other potentates whispered and joked at her expense. Chateaubriand says that when the Duke of Wellington was bored with the meetings of the Congress, he would while away the time in the company of the Orsini, who scribbled on the margin of intercepted French despatches, " Pas pour Mariée." Not for Madame de Neipperg.]

3. [Napoleon François Charles Joseph, Duke of Reichstadt, died at the palace of Schönbrunn, July 22, 1832, having just attained his twenty-first year.]

4. [Count Adam Albrecht de Neipperg had lost an eye from a wound in battle.]

What though she share no more, and shared in vain,
A sway surpassing that of Charlemagne,
Which swept from Moscow to the southern seas !
Yet still she rules the pastoral realm of cheese,
Where Parma views the traveller resort,
To note the trappings of her mimic court.
But she appears ! Verona sees her shorn
Of all her beams—while nations gaze and mourn— 750
Ere yet her husband's ashes have had time
To chill in their inhospitable clime ;
(If e'er those awful ashes can grow cold ;—
But no,—their embers soon will burst the mould ;)
She comes !—the Andromache (but not Racine's,
Nor Homer's,)—Lo ! on Pyrrhus' arm [1] she leans ! [L]
Yes ! the right arm, yet red from Waterloo,
Which cut her lord's half-shattered sceptre through,
Is offered and accepted ?   Could a slave
Do more ? or less ?—and *he* in his new grave ! 760
Her eye—her cheek—betray no inward strife,
And the *Ex*-Empress grows as *Ex* a wife !
So much for human ties in royal breasts !
Why spare men's feelings, when their own are jests ?

XVIII.

But, tired of foreign follies, I turn home,
And sketch the group—the picture 's yet to come.

i. *She comes the Andromache of Europe's Queens,*
And led by Pyrrhus' arm on which she leans.—[*MS. M.*]

1. [*La Quotidienne* of December 4, 1822, has a satirical reference to a passage in the *Courier*, which attached a diplomatic importance to the "galanterie respectueuse que le duc de Wellington aurait faite à cette jeune Princesse." We read, too, of another victorious foe, the King of Prussia, giving "la main à l'archduchesse Marie-Louise jusqu'à son carrosse" (*Le Constitutionnel*, November 19, 1822). "All the world wondered" what Andromache did, and how she would fare—*dans cette galère.* It is difficult to explain the allusion to Pyrrhus. Andromache was the unwilling bride of Pyrrhus or Neoptolemus, whose father had slain her husband, Hector ; Marie Louise the willing bride of Neipperg, who had certainly fought at Leipsic, but who could not be said to have given the final blow to Napoleon at Waterloo. Pyrrhus must stand for the victorious foe, and the right arm on which the too-forgiving Andromache leant, must have been offered by "the respectful gallantry" of the Duke of Wellington.]

My Muse 'gan weep, but, ere a tear was spilt,
She caught Sir William Curtis in a kilt ![1]
While thronged the chiefs of every Highland clan
To hail their brother, Vich Ian Alderman !   770
Guildhall grows Gael, and echoes with Erse roar,
While all the Common Council cry " Claymore ! "[2]
To see proud Albyn's tartans as a belt
Gird the gross sirloin of a city Celt,
She burst into a laughter so extreme,
That I awoke—and lo ! it was *no* dream !

Here, reader, will we pause :—if there 's no harm in
This first—you'll have, perhaps, a second " Carmen."

B. Jⁿ 10th 1823.

1. [Sir William Curtis (1752–1825), maker of sea-biscuits at Wapping,
was M.P. for the City of London 1790–1818, Lord Mayor 1795–6.
George IV. affected his society, visited him at Ramsgate, and sailed
with him in his gorgeously appointed yacht.   When the king visited
Scotland in August, 1822, Curtis followed in his train.   On first landing at Leith, "Sir William Curtis, who had *celtified* himself on the
occasion, marched joyously in his scanty longitude of kilt."   At the
Levee, August 17, "Sir William Curtis again appeared in the Royal
tartan, but he had forsaken the philabeg and addicted himself to the
trews " (*Morning Chronicle*, August 19, 20, 1822).   "The Fat Knight"
was seventy years of age, and there was much joking at his expense.
See, for instance, some lines in "Hudibrastic measure," *Gentleman's
Magazine*, vol. 92, Part II. p. 606—

"And who is he, that sleek and smart one
Pot-bellied pyramid of Tartan ?
     .   .
So mountainous in pinguitude,
Ponderibus librata Suis,
He stands like *pig* of lead, so true is,
That his abdomen throws alone
A *Body-guard* around the Throne ! "

2. [Lines 771, 772 are not in the MS.]

THE ISLAND;

OR,

CHRISTIAN AND HIS COMRADES.

INTRODUCTION TO *THE ISLAND.*

THE first canto of *The Island* was finished January 10, 1823. We know that Byron was still at work on "the poeshie," January 25 (*Letters*, 1901, vi. 164), and may reasonably conjecture that a somewhat illegible date affixed to the fourth canto, stands for February 14, 1823. The MS. had been received in London before April 9 (*ibid.*, p. 192); and on June 26, 1823, *The Island; or, The Adventures of Christian and his Comrades,* was published by John Hunt.

Byron's "Advertisement," or note, prefixed to *The Island* contains all that need be said with regard to the "sources" of the poem.

Two separate works were consulted : (1) *A Narrative of the Mutiny on board His Majesty's Ship Bounty, and the subsequent Voyage of . . . the Ship's Boat from Tofoa, one of the Friendly Islands, to Timor, a Dutch Settlement in the East Indies,* written by Lieutenant William Bligh, 1790 ; and (2) *An Account of the Natives of the Tonga Islands,* Compiled and Arranged from the Extensive Communications of Mr. William Mariner, by John Martin, M.D., 1817.

According to George Clinton (*Life and Writings of Lord Byron*, 1824, p. 656), Byron was profoundly impressed by Mariner's report of the scenery and folklore of the *Friendly Islands*, was "never tired of talking of it to his friends," and, in order to turn this poetic material to account, finally bethought him that Bligh's *Narrative* of the mutiny of the *Bounty* would serve as a framework or structure "for an embroidery of rare device"—the figures and foliage of a tropical pattern. That, at least, is the substance of Clinton's analysis of the "sources" of *The Island*, and whether he spoke, or only feigned to speak, with authority, his criticism is sound and to the point. The story of the mutiny of the *Bounty*, which is faithfully related in the first canto, is not, as the second title implies, a prelude to the "Adventures of Christian and his Comrades," but to a description of "The Island," an Ogygia of the South Seas.

It must be borne in mind that Byron's acquaintance with

the details of the mutiny of the *Bounty* was derived exclusively from Bligh's *Narrative;* that he does not seem to have studied the minutes of the court-martial on Peter Heyward and the other prisoners (September, 1792), or to have possessed the information that in 1809, and, again, in 1815, the Admiralty received authentic information with regard to the final settlement of Christian and his comrades on Pitcairn Island.   Articles, however, had appeared in the *Quarterly Review*, February, 1810, vol. iii. pp. 23, 24, and July, 1815, vol. xiii. pp. 376–378, which contained an extract from the log-book of Captain Mayhew Folger, of the American ship *Topaz*, dated September 29, 1808, and letters from Folger (March 1, 1813, and Sir Thomas Staines, October 18, 1814, which solved the mystery.   Moreover, the article of February, 1810, is quoted in the notes (pp. 313–318) affixed to Miss Mitford's *Christina, the Maid of the South Seas*, 1811, a poem founded on Bligh's *Narrative*, of which neither Byron nor his reviewers seem to have heard.

But whatever may have been his opportunities of ascertaining the facts of the case, it is certain (see his note to Canto IV. section vi. line 122) that he did not know what became of Christian, and that whereas in the first canto he follows the text of Bligh's *Narrative*, in the three last cantos he draws upon his imagination, turning Tahiti into Toobonai (Tubuai), and transporting Toobonai from one archipelago to another—from the Society to the Friendly Islands.

Another and still more surprising feature of *The Island* is that Byron accepts, without qualification or reserve, the guilt of the mutineers and the innocence and worth of Lieutenant Bligh.   It is true that by inheritance he was imbued with the traditions of the service, and from personal experience understood the necessity of discipline on board ship ; but it may be taken for granted that if he had known that the sympathy, if not the esteem, of the public had been transferred from Bligh to Christian, that in the opinion of grave and competent writers, the guilt of mutiny on the high seas had been almost condoned by the violence and brutality of the commanding officer, he would have sided with the oppressed rather than the oppressor.   As it is, he takes Bligh at his own valuation, and carefully abstains from "eulogizing mutiny." (Letter to L. Hunt, January 25, 1823.)

The story of the "mutiny of the *Bounty*" happened in this wise.   In 1787 it occurred to certain West India planters and merchants, resident in London, that it would benefit the natives, and perhaps themselves, if the bread-fruit tree, which flourished in Tahiti (the Otaheite of Captain Cook and Sir Joseph Banks, see *Poetical Works*, 1899, ii. 7, note 2) and other islands of the South Seas, could be acclimatized in the West Indies. A petition was addressed to the king, with the result that a vessel, with a burden of 215 tons, which Banks christened the *Bounty*, sailed from Spithead December 23, 1787. Lieutenant William Bligh, who had sailed with Cook in the *Resolution*, acted as commanding officer, and under him were five midshipmen, a master, two master's mates, etc.—forty-four persons all told. The *Bounty* arrived at Tahiti October 26, 1788, and there for six delightful months the ship's company tarried, " fleeting the time carelessly, as in the elder world." But " Scripture saith an ending to all fine things must be," and on April 4, 1789, the *Bounty*, with a cargo of over a thousand bread-fruit trees, planted in pots, tubs, and boxes (see for plate of the pots, etc., *A Voyage, etc.*, 1792, p. 1), sailed away westward for the Cape of Good Hope, and the West Indies. All went well at first, but "just before sun-rising" on Tuesday, April 28, 1789, "the north-westernmost of the Friendly Islands, called Tofoa, bearing north-east," Fletcher Christian, who was mate of the watch, assisted by Charles Churchill, master-at-arms, Alexander Smith (the John Adams of Pitcairn Island), and Thomas Burkitt, able seamen, seized the captain, tied his hands behind his back, hauled him out of his berth, and forced him on deck. The boatswain, William Cole, was ordered to hoist out the ship's launch, which measured twenty-three feet from stem to stern, and into this open boat Bligh, together with eighteen of the crew, who were or were supposed to be on his side, were thrust, on pain of instant death. When they were in the boat they were "veered round with a rope, and finally cast adrift." Bligh and his eighteen innocent companions sailed westward, and, after a voyage of "twelve hundred leagues," during which they were preserved from death and destruction by the wise ordering and patient heroism of the commander, safely anchored in Kœpang Bay, on the north-west coast of the Isle of Timor, June 14, 1789. (See Bligh's *Narrative, etc.*, 1790, pp. 11–88 ; and *The Island*, Canto I. section ix. lines 169–201.)

The *Bounty*, with the remainder of the crew, twenty-five in number, "the most able of the ship's company," sailed eastward, first to Toobooai, or Tubuai, an island to the south of the Society Islands, thence to Tahiti (June 6), back to Tubuai (June 26), and yet again, to Tahiti (September 20), where sixteen of the mutineers, including the midshipman George Stewart (the "Torquil" of *The Island*), were put on shore. Finally, September 21, 1789, Fletcher Christian, with the *Bounty* and eight of her crew, six Tahitian men, and twelve women, sailed away still further east to unknown shores, and, so it was believed, disappeared for good and all. Long afterwards it was known that they had landed on Pitcairn Island, broken up the *Bounty*, and founded a permanent settlement.

When Bligh returned to England (March 14, 1790), and acquainted the Government "with the atrocious act of piracy and mutiny" which had been committed on the high seas, the *Pandora* frigate, with Captain Edwards, was despatched to apprehend the mutineers, and bring them back to England for trial and punishment. The *Pandora* reached Tahiti March 23, 1791, set sail, with fourteen prisoners, May 8, and was wrecked on the "Great Barrier Reef" north-east of Queensland, August 29, 1791. Four of the prisoners, including George Stewart, who had been manacled, and were confined in "Pandora's box," perished in the wreck, and the remaining ten were brought back to England, and tried by court-martial. (See *The Eventful History of the Mutiny, etc.* (by Sir John Barrow), 1831, pp. 205-244.)

The story, which runs through the second, third, and fourth cantos, may possibly owe some of its details to a vague recollection of incidents which happened, or were supposed to happen, at Tahiti, in the interval between the final departure of the *Bounty*, September 21, 1789, and the arrival of the *Pandora*, March 23, 1791 ; but, as a whole, it is a work of fiction.

With the exception of the fifteenth and sixteenth cantos of *Don Juan*, *The Island* was the last poem of any importance which Byron lived to write, and the question naturally suggests itself—Is the new song as good as the old? Byron answers the question himself. He tells Leigh Hunt (January 25, 1823) that he hopes the "poem will be a little above the ordinary run of periodical poesy," and that, though portions of the Toobonai (*sic*) islanders are "pamby," he intends "to scatter some *un*common places here and there nevertheless." On the whole, in point of conception and execution, *The Island* is weaker and less coherent than the *Corsair* ; but it contains lines and passages (*e.g.* Canto I. lines 107–124, 133–140 ; Canto II. lines 272–297 ; Canto IV. lines 94–188) which display a finer feeling and a more "exalted wit" than the "purple patches" of *The Turkish Tales*.

The poetic faculty is somewhat exhausted, but the poetic vision has been purged and heightened by suffering and self-knowledge.

The Island was reviewed in the *Monthly Review*, July, 1823, E.S., vol. 101, pp. 316-319 ; the *New Monthly Magazine*, N.S., 1823, vol. 8, pp. 136-141 ; the *Atlantic Magazine*, April, 1826, vol. 2, pp. 333-337 ; in the *Literary Chronicle*, June 21, 1823 ; and the *Literary Gazette*, June 21, 1823.

ADVERTISEMENT.

THE foundation of the following story will be found partly in Lieutenant Bligh's "Narrative of the Mutiny and Seizure of the Bounty, in the South Seas (in 1789);" and partly in "Mariner's Account of the Tonga Islands."

GENOA, 1823.

THE ISLAND.

CANTO THE FIRST.

I.

THE morning watch was come; the vessel lay
Her course, and gently made her liquid way; [i]
The cloven billow flashed from off her prow
In furrows formed by that majestic plough;
The waters with their world were all before;
Behind, the South Sea's many an islet shore.
The quiet night, now dappling, 'gan to wane,
Dividing darkness from the dawning main;
The dolphins, not unconscious of the day,
Swam high, as eager of the coming ray;   10
The stars from broader beams began to creep,
And lift their shining eyelids from the deep; [ii]
The sail resumed its lately shadowed white,
And the wind fluttered with a freshening flight;
The purpling Ocean owns the coming Sun,
But ere he break—a deed is to be done.

II.

The gallant Chief [1] within his cabin slept,
Secure in those by whom the watch was kept:

i. —— *and made before the breeze her way.*—[*MS. D. erased.*]
ii. —— *their doubtful shimmer from the deep.*—[*MS. D. erased.*]

1. [William Bligh, the son of Cornish parents, was born September 9,

His dreams were of Old England's welcome shore,
Of toils rewarded, and of dangers o'er ;   20

1754 (? 1753). He served under Cook in his second voyage in the *Resolution,* 1772–75, as sailing-master ; and, in 1782, fought under Lord Howe at Gibraltar. He married a daughter of William Betham, first collector of customs in the Isle of Man, and hence his connection with Fletcher Christian, who belonged to a Manx family, and the midshipman Peter Hayward, who was the son of a Deemster. He was appointed to the *Bounty* in December, 1787, and in 1791 to the *Providence,* which was despatched to the Society Islands to obtain a fresh cargo of bread-fruit trees in place of those which were thrown overboard by the mutineers. He commanded the *Glatton* at Copenhagen, May 21, 1801, and on that and other occasions served with distinction. He was made Governor of New South Wales in 1805, but was forcibly deposed in an insurrection headed by Major Johnston, January, 1808. He was kept in prison till 1810, but on his return to England his administration of his office was approved, and Johnston was cashiered. He was advanced to the rank of Vice-Admiral of the Blue in 1814, and died, December 7, 1817.

In his *Narrative* Bligh describes the mutiny as " a close-planned act of villainy," and attributes the conspiracy not to his own harshness, or to disloyalty provoked by "real or imaginary grievances," but to the contrast of life on board ship, "in ever climbing up the climbing wave," with the unearned luxuries of Tahiti, "the allurements of dissipation . . . the female connections," which the sailors had left behind. Besides his own apology, there are the sworn statements of the two midshipmen, Hayward and Hallet, and others, which Bligh published in answer to a pamphlet which Edward Christian, afterwards Chief Justice of Ely, wrote in defence of his brother Fletcher. The evidence against Bligh is contained in the MS. journal of the boatswain's mate, James Morrison, which was saved, as by a miracle, from the wreck of the *Pandora,* and is quoted by Sir John Barrow, Lady Belcher, and other authorities. There is, too, the testimony of John Adams (Alexander Smith), as recorded by Captain Beachey, and, as additional proof of indifference and tyrannical behaviour, there are Bligh's own letters to Peter Hayward's mother and uncle (March 26, April 2, 1790), and W. C. Wentworth's account of his administration as Governor of New South Wales (see *A Statistical Description, etc.,* 1819, p. 166). It cannot be gainsaid that Bligh was a man of integrity and worth, and that he was upheld and esteemed by the Admiralty. Morrison's Journal, though in parts corroborated by Bligh's MS. Journal, is not altogether convincing, and the testimony of John Adams in his old age counts for little. But according to his own supporters he "damned" his men though not the officers, and his own *Narrative,* as well as Morrison's Journal, proves that he was suspicious, and that he underrated and misunderstood the character and worth of his subordinates. He was responsible for the prolonged sojourn at Tahiti, and he should have remembered that time and distance are powerful solvents, and that between Portsmouth Hard and the untracked waters of the Pacific, "all Arcadia" had intervened. He was a man of imperfect sympathies, wanting in tact and fineness, but in the hour of need he behaved like a hero, and saved himself and others by submission to duty and strenuous self-control. Moreover, he "helped England" not once or twice, "in the brave days of old." (See *A*

His name was added to the glorious roll
Of those who search the storm-surrounded Pole.
The worst was over, and the rest seemed sure,[1]
And why should not his slumber be secure ?
Alas ! his deck was trod by unwilling feet,
And wilder hands would hold the vessel's sheet ;
Young hearts, which languished for some sunny isle,
Where summer years and summer women smile ;
Men without country, who, too long estranged,
Had found no native home, or found it changed,   30
And, half uncivilised, preferred the cave
Of some soft savage to the uncertain wave—
The gushing fruits that nature gave untilled ;
The wood without a path—but where they willed ;
The field o'er which promiscuous Plenty poured
Her horn ; the equal land without a lord ;
The wish—which ages have not yet subdued
In man—to have no master save his mood ;[2]
The earth, whose mine was on its face, unsold,
The glowing sun and produce all its gold ;   40
The Freedom which can call each grot a home ;
The general garden, where all steps may roam,
Where Nature owns a nation as her child,
Exulting in the enjoyment of the wild ;[i.]

i. *And all enjoy the exuberance of the wild.*—[*MS. D. erased.*]

Narrative, etc., 1790 ; *The Naval History of Great Britain*, by E. P.
Brenton, 1823, i. 96, *sq.* ; *Royal Naval Biography*, by John Marshall,
1823-35, ii. pp. 747, *sq.* ; *Mutineers of the Bounty*, by Lady Belcher,
1870, p. 8 ; *Dictionary of National Biography*, art. " Bligh.")]

  1. [" A few hours before, my situation had been peculiarly flattering.
I had a ship in the most perfect order, and well stored with every
necessary, both for service and health ; . . . the voyage was two thirds
completed, and the remaining part in a very promising way."—*A
Narrative of the Mutiny, etc.*, by Lieut. W. Bligh, 1790, p. 9.]

  2. [" The women at Otaheite are handsome, mild, and cheerful in
their manners and conversation, possessed of great sensibility, and have
sufficient delicacy to make them admired and beloved. The chiefs
were so much attached to our people, that they rather encouraged their
stay among them than otherwise, and even made them promises of
large possessions. Under these and many other attendant circumstances
equally desirable, it is now, perhaps, not so much to be wondered at
. . . that a set of sailors, most of them void of connections, should be
led away, especially when they imagined it in their power to fix themselves, in the midst of plenty, . . . on the finest island in the world,
where they need not labour, and where the allurements of dissipation
are beyond anything that can be conceived."—*Ibid.*, p. 10.]

Their shells, their fruits, the only wealth they know,
Their unexploring navy, the canoe;[i.]
Their sport, the dashing breakers and the chase;
Their strangest sight, an European face:—
Such was the country which these strangers yearned
To see again—a sight they dearly earned.   50

III.

Awake, bold Bligh! the foe is at the gate!
Awake! awake!——Alas! it is too late!
Fiercely beside thy cot the mutineer
Stands, and proclaims the reign of rage and fear.
Thy limbs are bound, the bayonet at thy breast;
The hands, which trembled at thy voice, arrest;
Dragged o'er the deck, no more at thy command
The obedient helm shall veer, the sail expand;
That savage Spirit, which would lull by wrath
Its desperate escape from Duty's path,   60
Glares round thee, in the scarce believing eyes
Of those who fear the Chief they sacrifice:
For ne'er can Man his conscience all assuage,
Unless he drain the wine of Passion—Rage.

IV.

In vain, not silenced by the eye of Death,
Thou call'st the loyal with thy menaced breath:—
They come not; they are few, and, overawed,
Must acquiesce, while sterner hearts applaud.
In vain thou dost demand the cause: a curse
Is all the answer, with the threat of worse.   70
Full in thine eyes is waved the glittering blade,
Close to thy throat the pointed bayonet laid.
The levelled muskets circle round thy breast
In hands as steeled to do the deadly rest.
Thou dar'st them to their worst, exclaiming—" Fire!"
But they who pitied not could yet admire;
Some lurking remnant of their former awe
Restrained them longer than their broken law;

i. *Their formidable fleet the quick canoe.—*[*MS. D. erased.*]

They would not dip their souls at once in blood,
But left thee to the mercies of the flood.[1]   80

V.

" Hoist out the boat ! " was now the leader's cry ;
And who dare answer " No ! " to Mutiny,
In the first dawning of the drunken hour,
The Saturnalia of unhoped-for power ?
The boat is lowered with all the haste of hate,
With its slight plank between thee and thy fate ;
Her only cargo such a scant supply
As promises the death their hands deny ;
And just enough of water and of bread
To keep, some days, the dying from the dead :   90
Some cordage, canvass, sails, and lines, and twine,
But treasures all to hermits of the brine,
Were added after, to the earnest prayer
Of those who saw no hope, save sea and air ;
And last, that trembling vassal of the Pole—
The feeling compass—Navigation's soul.[2]

VI.

And now the self-elected Chief finds time
To stun the first sensation of his crime,

1. [" Just before sunrising Mr. Christian, with the master-at-arms,
gunner's mate, and Thomas Burkitt, seaman, came into my cabin while
I was asleep, and, seizing me, tied my hands with a cord behind my
back, and threatened me with instant death if I spoke or made the least
noise. I, however, called out so loud as to alarm every one ; but they
had already secured the officers who were not of their party, by
placing sentinels at their doors. There were three men at my cabin
door, besides the four within ; Christian had only a cutlass in his hand,
the others had muskets and bayonets. I was hauled out of bed, and
forced on deck in my shirt, suffering great pain from the tightness with
which they had tied my hands. . . . The boatswain was now ordered
to hoist the launch out. The boat being hoisted out, Mr. Hayward
and Mr. Hallet, midshipmen, were ordered into it ; upon which I demanded the cause of such an order, and endeavoured to persuade some
one to a sense of duty ; but it was to no effect : ' Hold your tongue,
sir, or you are dead this instant,' was constantly repeated to me."—
A Narrative of the Mutiny, etc., by Lieut. W. Bligh, 1790, pp. 1, 2.]

2. [" The boatswain, and seamen who were to go in the boat,
were allowed to collect twine, canvass, lines, sails, cordage, an eight-
and-twenty-gallon cask of water, and the carpenter to take his tool-
chest. Mr. Samuel got one hundred and fifty pounds of bread with a
small quantity of rum and wine . . . also a quadrant and compass."
—*Ibid.*, p. 3.]

And raise it in his followers—" Ho ! the bowl ! " [1]
Lest passion should return to reason's shoal.[i.]   100
" Brandy for heroes ! " [2] Burke could once exclaim—
No doubt a liquid path to Epic fame ;
And such the new-born heroes found it here,
And drained the draught with an applauding cheer.
" Huzza ! for Otaheite ! " [3] was the cry.
How strange such shouts from sons of Mutiny !
The gentle island, and the genial soil,
The friendly hearts, the feasts without a toil,
The courteous manners but from nature caught,
The wealth unhoarded, and the love unbought ;   110
Could these have charms for rudest sea-boys, driven
Before the mast by every wind of heaven ?
And now, even now prepared with others' woes
To earn mild Virtue's vain desire, repose ?
Alas ! such is our nature ! all but aim
At the same end by pathways not the same ;
Our means—our birth—our nation, and our name,
Our fortune—temper—even our outward frame,
Are far more potent o'er our yielding clay
Than aught we know beyond our little day.   120
Yet still there whispers the small voice within,

i. *And lull it in his followers—" Ho! the dram"*
Rebellion's sacrament, and paschal lamb.
(*A broken metaphor of flesh for wine*
But Catholics know the exchange is none of mine.—[MS. D. erased.]
And raise it in his followers—Ho ! the bowl
That sure Nepenthe for the wavering [*soul*].—[MS. D. erased.]

1. [" The mutineers now hurried those they meant to get rid of into
the boat, . . . Christian directed a dram to be served to each of his
own crew."—*A Narrative, etc.*, 1790, p. 3.]
2. [It was Johnson, not Burke, who upheld the claims of brandy.—
" He was persuaded," says Boswell, " to drink one glass of it [claret].
He shook his head, and said, ' Poor stuff !—No, Sir, claret is the liquor
for boys ; port for men ; but he who aspires to be a hero (smiling)
must drink brandy.' "—Boswell's *Life of Johnson*, 1848, p. 627.]
3. [" While the ship . . . was in sight she steered to the W.N.W.,
but I considered this only a feint ; for when we were sent away,
' Huzza for Otaheite ! ' was frequently heard among the mutineers."—
A Narrative, etc., 1790, pp. 4–8. This statement is questioned by Sir
John Barrow (*The Eventful History, etc.*, 1831, p. 91), on the grounds
that the mutiny was the result of a sudden determination on the part of
Christian, and that liberty, and not the delights of Tahiti, was the
object which the mutineers had in view.]

Heard through Gain's silence, and o'er Glory's din :
Whatever creed be taught, or land be trod,
Man's conscience is the Oracle of God.[1]

VII.

The launch is crowded with the faithful few
Who wait their Chief, a melancholy crew :
But some remained reluctant on the deck
Of that proud vessel—now a moral wreck—
And viewed their Captain's fate with piteous eyes ;
While others scoffed his augured miseries,   130
Sneered at the prospect of his pigmy sail,
And the slight bark so laden and so frail.
The tender nautilus, who steers his prow,
The sea-born sailor of his shell canoe,
The ocean Mab, the fairy of the sea,
Seems far less fragile, and, alas ! more free.
He, when the lightning-winged Tornados sweep
The surge, is safe—his port is in the deep—
And triumphs o'er the armadas of Mankind,
Which shake the World, yet crumble in the wind.   140

VIII.

When all was now prepared, the vessel clear
Which hailed her master in the mutineer,
A seaman, less obdurate than his mates,
Showed the vain pity which but irritates ;
Watched his late Chieftain with exploring eye,
And told, in signs, repentant sympathy ;
Held the moist shaddock to his parchéd mouth,
Which felt Exhaustion's deep and bitter drouth.
But soon observed, this guardian was withdrawn,
Nor further Mercy clouds Rebellion's dawn.[2]   150

1. [A variant of Pope's lines—

> "For modes of faith let graceless zealots fight,
> His can't be wrong, whose life is in the right."
> *Essay on Man*, iii. 305, 306.]

2. ["Isaac Martin, one of the guard over me, I saw, had an inclina-
tion to assist me ; and as he fed me with shaddock (my lips being quite
parched with my endeavours to bring about a change), we explained
our wishes to each other by our looks ; but this being observed, Martin
was instantly removed from me."—*A Narrative, etc.*, 1790, p. 4.]

Then forward stepped the bold and froward boy
His Chief had cherished only to destroy,
And, pointing to the helpless prow beneath,
Exclaimed, " Depart at once ! delay is death !"
Yet then, even then, his feelings ceased not all :
In that last moment could a word recall
Remorse for the black deed as yet half done,
And what he hid from many showed to one :
When Bligh in stern reproach demanded where
Was now his grateful sense of former care?   160
Where all his hopes to see his name aspire,
And blazon Britain's thousand glories higher?
His feverish lips thus broke their gloomy spell,
" 'Tis that ! 'tis that ! I am in hell ! in hell !" [1]
No more he said ; but urging to the bark
His Chief, commits him to his fragile ark ;
These the sole accents from his tongue that fell,
But volumes lurked below his fierce farewell.

1. ["Christian . . . then . . . said, 'Come, Captain Bligh, your
officers and men are now in the boat ; and you must go with them ;
if you attempt to make the least resistance you will instantly be put to
death ;' and without any farther ceremony, holding me by the cord that
tied my hands, with a tribe of armed ruffians about me, I was forced
over the side, where they untied my hands. Being in the boat, we
were veered astern by a rope. A few pieces of pork were thrown to me
and some clothes. . . . After having undergone a great deal of ridicule, and being kept for some time to make sport for these unfeeling
wretches, we were at length cast adrift in the open ocean. . . . When
they were forcing me out of the ship, I asked him [Christian] if this
treatment was a proper return for the many instances he had received of
my friendship? He appeared disturbed at the question, and answered,
with much emotion, 'That,—Captain Bligh,—that is the thing ;—I am
in hell—I am in hell.'"—*A Narrative, etc.*, 1790, pp. 4-8.

Bligh's testimony on this point does not correspond with Morrison's
journal, or with the evidence of the master, John Fryer, given at the
court-martial, September 12, 1792. According to Morrison, when the
boatswain tried to pacify Christian, he replied, " It is too late, I have
been in hell for this fortnight past, and am determined to bear it no
longer." The master's version is that he appealed to Christian, and
that Christian exclaimed, " Hold your tongue, sir, I have been in hell
for weeks past ; Captain Bligh has brought all this on himself." Bligh
seems to have flattered himself that in the act of mutiny Christian was
seized with remorse, but it is clear that the wish was father to the
thought. Moreover, on being questioned, Fryer, who was a supporter
of the captain, explained that Christian referred to quarrels, to abuse
in general, and more particularly to a recent accusation of stealing
cocoa-nuts. (See *The Eventful History, etc.*, 1831, pp. 84, 208, 209.)]

IX.

The arctic [1] Sun rose broad above the wave;
The breeze now sank, now whispered from his cave; 170
As on the Æolian harp, his fitful wings
Now swelled, now fluttered o'er his Ocean strings. [i.]
With slow, despairing oar, the abandoned skiff
Ploughs its drear progress to the scarce seen cliff,
Which lifts its peak a cloud above the main:
That boat and ship shall never meet again!

But 'tis not mine to tell their tale of grief,
Their constant peril, and their scant relief;
Their days of danger, and their nights of pain;
Their manly courage even when deemed in vain;   180
The sapping famine, rendering scarce a son
Known to his mother in the skeleton; [2]
The ills that lessened still their little store,
And starved even Hunger till he wrung no more;
The varying frowns and favours of the deep,
That now almost ingulfs, then leaves to creep
With crazy oar and shattered strength along
The tide that yields reluctant to the strong;
The incessant fever of that arid thirst [3]
Which welcomes, as a well, the clouds that burst   190
Above their naked bones, and feels delight
In the cold drenching of the stormy night,
And from the outspread canvass gladly wrings
A drop to moisten Life's all-gasping springs;
The savage foe escaped, to seek again
More hospitable shelter from the main;
The ghastly Spectres which were doomed at last

i. *Now swelled now sighed along* ——.—[*MS. D. erased.*]

1. [Byron must mean "antarctic." "Arctic" is used figuratively for "cold," but not as a synonym for "polar."]
2. ["At dawn of day some of my people seemed half dead; our appearances were horrible; and I could look no way, but I caught the eye of some one in distress."—*A Narrative, etc.*, p. 37. Later on, p. 80, when the launch reached Timor, he speaks of the crew as "so many spectres, whose ghastly countenances, if the cause had been unknown, would have excited terror rather than pity."]
3. [Bligh dwells on the misery caused to the luckless crew by drenching rains and by hunger, but says that no one suffered from thirst.]

To tell as true a tale of dangers past,
As ever the dark annals of the deep
Disclosed for man to dread or woman weep.   200

X.

We leave them to their fate, but not unknown
Nor unredressed.   Revenge may have her own : [i.]
Roused Discipline aloud proclaims their cause,
And injured Navies urge their broken laws.
Pursue we on his track the mutineer,
Whom distant vengeance had not taught to fear.
Wide o'er the wave—away ! away ! away !
Once more his eyes shall hail the welcome bay ;
Once more the happy shores without a law
Receive the outlaws whom they lately saw ;   210
Nature, and Nature's goddess—Woman—woos
To lands where, save their conscience, none accuse ;
Where all partake the earth without dispute, [ii.]
And bread itself is gathered as a fruit ; [1]
Where none contest the fields, the woods, the streams :—
The goldless Age, where Gold disturbs no dreams,
Inhabits or inhabited the shore,
Till Europe taught them better than before ;
Bestowed her customs, and amended theirs,
But left her vices also to their heirs. [2]   220
Away with this ! behold them as they were,
Do good with Nature, or with Nature err.
" Huzza ! for Otaheite ! " was the cry,
As stately swept the gallant vessel by.
The breeze springs up ; the lately flapping sail
Extends its arch before the growing gale ;

---

i. *Nor yet unpitied.   Vengeance had her own.*—[*MS. D. erased.*]
ii. —— *the undisputed root.*—[*MS. D. erased.*]

1. The now celebrated bread fruit, to transplant which Captain
Bligh's expedition was undertaken.
[The bread-fruit (*Autocarpus incisa*) was discovered by Dampier,
in 1688.   " Cook says that its taste is insipid, with a slight sweetness,
somewhat resembling that of the crumb of wheaten bread mixed with
a Jerusalem artichoke."—*The Eventful History*, etc., 1831, p. 43.]
2. [See *Letters from Mr. Fletcher Christian* (*pseud.*), 1796, pp. 48,
49.]

In swifter ripples stream aside the seas,
Which her bold bow flings off with dashing ease.
Thus Argo ploughed the Euxine's virgin foam,[i.]
But those she wafted still looked back to home;   230
These spurn their country with their rebel bark,
And fly her as the raven fled the Ark ;
And yet they seek to nestle with the dove,
And tame their fiery spirits down to Love.

End of Canto 1st, Jn 14.

i. *Thus Argo plunged into the Euxine's foam.*—[*MS. D. erased.*]

CANTO THE SECOND.

I.

How pleasant were the songs of Toobonai,[1]
When Summer's Sun went down the coral bay!
Come, let us to the islet's softest shade,
And hear the warbling birds! the damsels said:

1. The first three sections are taken from an actual song of the Tonga Islanders, of which a prose translation is given in "Mariner's Account of the Tonga Islands." Toobonai is *not* however one of them; but was one of those where Christian and the mutineers took refuge. I have altered and added, but have retained as much as possible of the original.

["Whilst we were talking of *Vavaoo tóoa Lico*, the women said to us, 'Let us repair to the back of the island to contemplate the setting sun: there let us listen to the warbling of the birds, and the cooing of the wood-pigeon. We will gather flowers from the burying-place at *Matáwto*, and partake of refreshments prepared for us at *Lico O'nĕ:* we will then bathe in the sea, and rinse ourselves in the *Váoo A'ca;* we will anoint our skins in the sun with sweet-scented oil, and will plait in wreaths the flowers gathered at *Matáwto.'* And now as we stand motionless on the eminence over *Anoo Mánoo*, the whistling of the wind among the branches of the lofty *toa* shall fill us with a pleasing melancholy; or our minds shall be seized with astonishment as we behold the roaring surf below, endeavouring but in vain to tear away the firm rocks. Oh! how much happier shall we be thus employed, than when engaged in the troublesome and insipid cares of life!

"Now as night comes on, we must return to the *Moóa*. But hark!— hear you not the sound of the mats?—they are practising a *bo-oóla* ['a kind of dance performed by torch-light'], to be performed to-night on the *malái*, at Tanéa. Let us also go there. How will that scene of rejoicing call to our minds the many festivals held there, before *Vavaoo* was torn to pieces by war! Alas! how destructive is war! Behold! how it has rendered the land productive of weeds, and opened untimely graves for departed heroes! Our chiefs can now no longer enjoy the sweet pleasure of wandering alone by moonlight in search of their mistresses. But let us banish sorrow from our hearts: since we are at war, we must think and act like the natives of *Fiji*, who first taught

The wood-dove from the forest depth shall coo,
Like voices of the Gods from Bolotoo; [1]
We'll cull the flowers that grow above the dead,
For these most bloom where rests the warrior's head ;
And we will sit in Twilight's face, and see
The sweet Moon glancing through the Tooa [2] tree,   10
The lofty accents of whose sighing bough
Shall sadly please us as we lean below ;
Or climb the steep, and view the surf in vain
Wrestle with rocky giants o'er the main,
Which spurn in columns back the baffled spray.
How beautiful are these ! how happy they,
Who, from the toil and tumult of their lives,
Steal to look down where nought but Ocean strives !
Even He too loves at times the blue lagoon,
And smooths his ruffled mane beneath the Moon.   20

II.

Yes—from the sepulchre we'll gather flowers,
Then feast like spirits in their promised bowers,
Then plunge and revel in the rolling surf,
Then lay our limbs along the tender turf,
And, wet and shining from the sportive toil,

us this destructive art. Let us therefore enjoy the present time, for
to-morrow perhaps, or the next day, we may die. We will dress ourselves with *chi coola*, and put bands of white *táppa* round our waists.
We will plait thick wreaths of *jiale* for our heads, and prepare strings
of *hooni* for our necks, that their whiteness may show off the colour of
our skins. Mark how the uncultivated spectators are profuse of their
applause ! But now the dance is over: let us remain here to-night and
feast and be cheerful, and to-morrow we will depart for the Mooa.
How troublesome are the young men, begging for our wreaths of
flowers ! while they say in their flattery, 'See how charming these
young girls look coming from *Licoo!*—how beautiful are their skins,
diffusing around a fragrance like the flowering precipice of *Mataloco:*—
Let us also visit *Licoo*. We will depart to-morrow.'"—*An Account of
the Natives of the Tonga Islands, etc.*, 1817, i. 307, 308. It should be
noted that John Martin, M.D. (1789–1869) compiled this work from
Mariner's "Communications."

   1. [Bolotoo is a visionary island to the north westward, the home of
the Gods. The souls of chieftains, priests, and, possibly, the gentry,
ascend to Bolotoo after death; but the souls of the lower classes
"come to dust" with their bodies.—*An Account, etc.*, 1817, ii. 104, 105.]

   2. [The toa, or drooping casuarina (*C. equisetifolia*). "Formerly
the toa was regarded as sacred, and planted in groves round the
'Morais' of Tahiti."—*Polynesia*, by G. F. Angas, 1866, p. 44.]

Anoint our bodies with the fragrant oil,
And plait our garlands gathered from the grave,
And wear the wreaths that sprung from out the brave.
But lo ! night comes, the Mooa [1] woos us back,
The sound of mats [2] are heard along our track ;   30
Anon the torchlight dance shall fling its sheen
In flashing mazes o'er the Marly's [3] green ;
And we too will be there ; we too recall
The memory bright with many a festival,
Ere Fiji blew the shell of war, when foes
For the first time were wafted in canoes.[i.]
Alas ! for them the flower of manhood bleeds ;
Alas ! for them our fields are rank with weeds :
Forgotten is the rapture, or unknown,[ii.]
Of wandering with the Moon and Love alone.   40
But be it so :—*they* taught us how to wield
The club, and rain our arrows o'er the field :
Now let them reap the harvest of their art !
But feast to-night ! to-morrow we depart.
Strike up the dance ! the Cava bowl [4] fill high !

i. *Ere Fiji's children blew the shell of war*
   And armed Canoes brought Fury from afar.—[*MS. D. erased.*]
ii. *Too long forgotten in the pleasure ground.*—[*MS. D. erased.*]

1. [The capital town of an island.]
2. ["The preparation of *gnatoo*, or *tappa*-cloth, from the inner bark of the paper mulberry tree, occupies much of the time of the Tongan women. The bark, after being soaked in water, is beaten out by means of wooden mallets, which are grooved longitudinally. . . . Early in the morning," says Mariner, "when the air is calm and still, the beating of the *gnatoo* at all the plantations about has a very pleasing effect ; some sounds being near at hand, and others almost lost by the distance, some a little more acute, others more grave, and all with remarkable regularity, produce a musical variety that is . . . heightened by the singing of the birds, and the cheerful influence of the scene."—*Polynesia*, 1846, pp. 249, 250.]
3. [Marly, or Malái, is an open grass plat set apart for public ceremonies.]
4. [Cava, "kava," or "ava," is an intoxicating drink, prepared from the roots and stems of a kind of pepper (*Piper methysticum*). Mariner (*An Account, etc.*, 1817, ii. 183–206) gives a highly interesting and suggestive account of the process of brewing the kava, and of the solemn "kava-drinking," which was attended with ceremonial rites. Briefly, a large wooden bowl, about three feet in diameter, and one foot in depth in the centre (see, for a typical specimen, King Thakombau's kava-bowl, in the British Museum), is placed in front of the king or chief, who sits in the midst, surrounded by his guests and courtiers. A

Drain every drop !—to-morrow we may die.
In summer garments be our limbs arrayed ;
Around our waists the Tappa's white displayed ;
Thick wreaths shall form our coronal,[1] like Spring's,
And round our necks shall glance the Hooni strings ; 50
So shall their brighter hues contrast the glow
Of the dusk bosoms that beat high below.

III.

But now the dance is o'er—yet stay awhile ;
Ah, pause ! nor yet put out the social smile.
To-morrow for the Mooa we depart,
But not to-night—to-night is for the heart.
Again bestow the wreaths we gently woo,
Ye young Enchantresses of gay Licoo ![2]
How lovely are your forms ! how every sense
Bows to your beauties, softened, but intense,[i]   60
Like to the flowers on Mataloco's steep,
Which fling their fragrance far athwart the deep !—

i. *How beauteous are their skins, how softly all*
   The forms of Beauty wrap them like a pall.—[*MS. D. erased.*]

portion of kava root is handed to each person present, who chews it to
a pulp, and then deposits his quid in the kava bowl. Water being
gradually added, the roots are well squeezed and twisted by various
"curvilinear turns" of the hands and arms through the "fow," *i.e.*
shavings of fibrous bark. When the "kava is in the cup," quaighs
made of the "unexpanded leaf of the banana" are handed round to
the guests, and the symposium begins. Mariner (*ibid.*, p. 205, *note*)
records a striking feature of the preliminary rites, a consecration or
symbolic "grace before" drinking. "When a god has no priest, as
Tali-y-Toobó [the Supreme Deity of the Tongans], no person . . .
presides at the head of his cava circle, the place being left . . . vacant,
but which it is supposed the god invisibly occupies. . . . And they go
through the usual form of words, as if the first cup was actually filled
and presented to the god : thus, before any cup is filled, the man by
the side of the bowl says . . . 'The cava is in the cup :' the mataboole
answers . . . 'Give it to our god :' but this is mere form, for there is
no cup filled for the god." (See, too, *The Making of Religion*, by
A. Lang, 1900, p. 279.)]
   1. [The gnatoo, which is a piece of tappa cloth, is worn in different
ways. "Twenty yards of fine cloth are required by a Tahitian woman
to make one dress, which is worn from the waist downwards."—
Polynesia, 1866, p. 45.]
   2. [*Licoo* is the name given to the back of or unfrequented part of
any island.]

We too will see Licoo ; but—oh ! my heart !—
What do I say ?—to-morrow we depart !

IV

Thus rose a song—the harmony of times
Before the winds blew Europe o'er these climes.
True, they had vices—such are Nature's growth—
But only the barbarian's—we have both ;
The sordor of civilisation, mixed
With all the savage which Man's fall hath fixed.   70
Who hath not seen Dissimulation's reign,
The prayers of Abel linked to deeds of Cain ?
Who such would see may from his lattice view
The Old World more degraded than the New,—
Now *new* no more, save where Columbia rears
Twin giants, born by Freedom to her spheres,
Where Chimborazo, over air,—earth,—wave,—
Glares with his Titan eye, and sees no slave.[i.][1]

v.

Such was this ditty of Tradition's days,
Which to the dead a lingering fame conveys   80
In song, where Fame as yet hath left no sign
Beyond the sound whose charm is half divine ;
Which leaves no record to the sceptic eye,
But yields young History all to Harmony ;
A boy Achilles, with the Centaur's lyre
In hand, to teach him to surpass his sire.
For one long-cherished ballad's[2] simple stave,
Rung from the rock, or mingled with the wave,

---

ii. *Glares with his mountain eye* ——.—[*MS. D. erased.*]

1. [The *Morning Chronicle*, November 6, 1822, prints the following proclamation of José Maria Carreno, Commandant-General of Panama: "Inhabitants of the Isthmus ! The Genius of History, which has everywhere crowned our arms, announces peace to Colombia. . . . From the banks of Orinoco to the towering summits of Chimborazo not a single enemy exists, and those who proudly marched towards the abode of the ancient children of the Sun have either perished or remain prisoners expecting our clemency."]

2. [Compare "a wise man's sentiment," as quoted by Andrew Fletcher of Saltoun : "He believed if a man were permitted to make all the Ballads, he need not care who should make the Laws."—*An Account of a Conversation, etc.*, 1704, p. 10.]

Or from the bubbling streamlet's grassy side,
Or gathering mountain echoes as they glide,   90
Hath greater power o'er each true heart and ear,
Than all the columns Conquest's minions rear; [i]
Invites, when Hieroglyphics [1] are a theme
For sages' labours, or the student's dream;
Attracts, when History's volumes are a toil,—
The first, the freshest bud of Feeling's soil.
Such was this rude rhyme—rhyme is of the rude—
But such inspired the Norseman's solitude,
Who came and conquered; such, wherever rise
Lands which no foes destroy or civilise,   100
Exist: and what can our accomplished art
Of verse do more than reach the awakened heart? [2]

VI.

And sweetly now those untaught melodies
Broke the luxurious silence of the skies,
The sweet siesta of a summer day,
The tropic afternoon of Toobonai,
When every flower was bloom, and air was balm,
And the first breath began to stir the palm,
The first yet voiceless wind to urge the wave
All gently to refresh the thirsty cave,   110
Where sat the Songstress with the stranger boy,
Who taught her Passion's desolating joy,
Too powerful over every heart, but most
O'er those who know not how it may be lost;
O'er those who, burning in the new-born fire,
Like martyrs revel in their funeral pyre,
With such devotion to their ecstacy,
That Life knows no such rapture as to die:
And die they do; for earthly life has nought
Matched with that burst of Nature, even in thought;

i. *Than all the records History's annals rear.—[MS. D. erased.]*

1. [Jean François Champollion (1790–1832), at a meeting of the
Académie des inscriptions, at Paris, September 17, 1822, announced
the discovery of the alphabet of hieroglyphics.]

2. [So, too, Shelley, in his Preface to the *Revolt of Islam,* speaks of
"that more essential attribute of Poetry, the power of awakening in
others sensations like those which animate my own bosom."]

And all our dreams of better life above 　　　　121
But close in one eternal gush of Love.

VII.

There sat the gentle savage of the wild,
In growth a woman, though in years a child,
As childhood dates within our colder clime,
Where nought is ripened rapidly save crime;
The infant of an infant world, as pure
From Nature—lovely, warm, and premature;
Dusky like night, but night with all her stars;
Or cavern sparkling with its native spars; 　　　　130
With eyes that were a language and a spell,
A form like Aphrodite's in her shell,
With all her loves around her on the deep,
Voluptuous as the first approach of sleep;
Yet full of life—for through her tropic cheek
The blush would make its way, and all but speak;
The sun-born blood suffused her neck, and threw
O'er her clear nut-brown skin a lucid hue,
Like coral reddening through the darkened wave,
Which draws the diver to the crimson cave. 　　　　140
Such was this daughter of the southern seas,
Herself a billow in her energies,[i]
To bear the bark of others' happiness,
Nor feel a sorrow till their joy grew less:
Her wild and warm yet faithful bosom knew
No joy like what it gave; her hopes ne'er drew
Aught from Experience, that chill touchstone, whose
Sad proof reduces all things from their hues:
She feared no ill, because she knew it not,
Or what she knew was soon—too soon—forgot: 　　　　150
Her smiles and tears had passed, as light winds pass
O'er lakes to ruffle, not destroy, their glass,
Whose depths unsearched, and fountains from the hill,
Restore their surface, in itself so still,
Until the Earthquake tear the Naiad's cave,
Root up the spring, and trample on the wave,

---

i. *And she herself the daughter of the Seas*
　　As full of gems and energy as these.—[*MS. D. erased.*]

And crush the living waters to a mass,
The amphibious desert of the dank morass !
And must their fate be hers ?   The eternal change
But grasps Humanity with quicker range ;   160
And they who fall but fall as worlds will fall,
To rise, if just, a Spirit o'er them all.

VIII.

And who is he ? the blue-eyed northern child [1]
Of isles more known to man, but scarce less wild ;
The fair-haired offspring of the Hebrides,
Where roars the Pentland with its whirling seas ;

1. [George Stewart was born at Ronaldshay (circ. 1764), but was living at Stromness in 1780 (where his father's house, "The White House," is still shown), when, on the homeward voyage of the *Resolution*, Cook and Bligh were hospitably entertained by his parents. He was of honourable descent. His mother's ancestors were sprung from a half-brother of Mary Stuart's, and his father's family dated back to 1400. When he was at Timor, Bligh gave a "description of the pirates" for purposes of identification by the authorities at Calcutta and elsewhere. "George Stewart, midshipman, aged 23 years, is five feet seven inches high, good complexion, dark hair, slender made . . . small face, and black eyes; tatowed on the left breast with a star," etc. Lieutenant Bligh took Stewart with him, partly in return for the "civilities" at Stromness, but also because "he was a seaman, and had always borne a good character." Alexander Smith told Captain Beachey (*Narrative of a Voyage to the Pacific*, 1831, Part I. p. 53) that it was Stewart who advised Christian "to take possession of the ship," but Peter Hayward, who survived to old age, strenuously maintained that this was a calumny, that Stewart was forcibly detained in his cabin, and that he would not, in any case, have taken part in the mutiny. He had, perhaps, already wooed and won a daughter of the isles, and when the *Bounty* revisited Tahiti, September 20, 1789, he was put ashore, and took up his quarters in her father's house. There he remained till March, 1791, when he "voluntarily surrendered himself" to the captain of the *Pandora*, and was immediately put in irons. The story of his parting from his bride is told in *A Missionary Voyage to the Southern Pacific Ocean in the Ship Duff* (by W. Wilson), 1799, p. 360: "The history of Peggy Stewart marks a tenderness of heart that never will be heard without emotion. . . . They had lived with the old chief in the most tender state of endearment ; a beautiful little girl had been the fruit of their union, and was at the breast when the *Pandora* arrived. . . . Frantic with grief, the unhappy Peggy . . . flew with her infant in a canoe to the arms of her husband. She was separated from him by violence, and conveyed on shore in a state of despair and grief too big for utterance . . . she sank into the deepest dejection, pined under a rapid decay . . . and fell a victim to her feelings, dying literally of a broken heart." Stewart was drowned or killed by an accident during the wreck of the *Pandora*, August 29, 1791. *Sunt lacrymæ rerum !* It is a mournful tale.]

Rocked in his cradle by the roaring wind,
The tempest-born in body and in mind,
His young eyes opening on the ocean-foam,
Had from that moment deemed the deep his home,   170
The giant comrade of his pensive moods,
The sharer of his craggy solitudes,
The only Mentor of his youth, where'er
His bark was borne ; the sport of wave and air ;
A careless thing, who placed his choice in chance,
Nursed by the legends of his land's romance ;
Eager to hope, but not less firm to bear,
Acquainted with all feelings save despair.
Placed in the Arab's clime he would have been
As bold a rover as the sands have seen,   180
And braved their thirst with as enduring lip
As Ishmael, wafted on his Desert-Ship ; [1]
Fixed upon Chili's shore, a proud cacique ;
On Hellas' mountains, a rebellious Greek ; [2]
Born in a tent, perhaps a Tamerlane ;
Bred to a throne, perhaps unfit to reign.
For the same soul that rends its path to sway,
If reared to such, can find no further prey
Beyond itself, and must retrace its way,[3]
Plunging for pleasure into pain : the same   190
Spirit which made a Nero, Rome's worst shame,
A humbler state and discipline of heart,
Had formed his glorious namesake's counterpart ; [4]

---

1. The "ship of the desert" is the Oriental figure for the camel or dromedary ; and they deserve the metaphor well,—the former for his endurance, the latter for his swiftness. [Compare *The Deformed Transformed*, Part I. sc. 1, line 117.]

2. [Compare *The Age of Bronze*, lines 271-279.]

3.   "Lucullus, when frugality could charm,
            Had roasted turnips in the Sabine farm."
                              POPE [*Moral Essays*, i. 218, 219.]

4. The consul Nero, who made the unequalled march which deceived Hannibal, and defeated Asdrubal ; thereby accomplishing an achievement almost unrivalled in military annals.   The first intelligence of his return, to Hannibal, was the sight of Asdrubal's head thrown into his camp.   When Hannibal saw this, he exclaimed with a sigh, that "Rome would now be the mistress of the world."   And yet to this victory of Nero's it might be owing that his imperial namesake reigned at all.   But the infamy of one has eclipsed the glory of the other. When the name of "Nero" is heard, who thinks of the consul ?—But

But grant his vices, grant them all his own,
How small their theatre without a throne!

IX.

Thou smilest :—these comparisons seem high
To those who scan all things with dazzled eye;
Linked with the unknown name of one whose doom
Has nought to do with glory or with Rome,
With Chili, Hellas, or with Araby;—   200
Thou smilest?—Smile; 'tis better thus than sigh;
Yet such he might have been; he was a man,
A soaring spirit, ever in the van,
A patriot hero or despotic chief,[i.]
To form a nation's glory or its grief,
Born under auspices which make us more
Or less than we delight to ponder o'er.
But these are visions; say, what was he here?
A blooming boy, a truant mutineer.
The fair-haired Torquil, free as Ocean's spray,   210
The husband of the bride of Toobonai.

X.

By Neuha's side he sate, and watched the waters,—
Neuha, the sun-flower of the island daughters,
Highborn, (a birth at which the herald smiles,
Without a scutcheon for these secret isles,)
Of a long race, the valiant and the free,
The naked knights of savage chivalry,
Whose grassy cairns ascend along the shore;
And thine—I've seen—Achilles! do no more.[1]
She, when the thunder-bearing strangers came,   220
In vast canoes, begirt with bolts of flame,
Topped with tall trees, which, loftier than the palm,
Seemed rooted in the deep amidst its calm:
But when the winds awakened, shot forth wings

---

i. *Tyrant or hero—patriot or a chief.*—[*MS. erased.*]

such are human things! [For Hannibal's cry of despair, "Agnoscere
se fortunam Carthaginis!" see Livy, lib. xxvii. cap. li. *s.f.*]
  1. [Compare *Childe Harold*, Canto II. stanza v. line 1, see *Poetical
Works*, 1899, ii. 102, and 99, *note* 1.]

Broad as the cloud along the horizon flings,
And swayed the waves, like cities of the sea,
Making the very billows look less free ;—
She, with her paddling oar and dancing prow,
Shot through the surf, like reindeer through the snow,
Swift-gliding o'er the breaker's whitening edge,   230
Light as a Nereid in her ocean sledge,
And gazed and wondered at the giant hulk,
Which heaved from wave to wave its trampling bulk.
The anchor dropped; it lay along the deep,
Like a huge lion in the sun asleep,
While round it swarmed the Proas' flitting chain,
Like summer bees that hum around his mane.

XI.

The white man landed !—need the rest be told ?
The New World stretched its dusk hand to the Old ;
Each was to each a marvel, and the tie   240
Of wonder warmed to better sympathy.
Kind was the welcome of the sun-born sires,
And kinder still their daughters' gentler fires.
Their union grew : the children of the storm
Found beauty linked with many a dusky form ;
While these in turn admired the paler glow,
Which seemed so white in climes that knew no snow.
The chace, the race, the liberty to roam,
The soil where every cottage showed a home ;
The sea-spread net, the lightly launched canoe,   250
Which stemmed the studded archipelago, ¡
O'er whose blue bosom rose the starry isles ;
The healthy slumber, earned by sportive toils ;
The palm, the loftiest Dryad of the woods,
Within whose bosom infant Bacchus broods,
While eagles scarce build higher than the crest
Which shadows o'er the vineyard in her breast ;
The Cava feast, the Yam, the Cocoa's root,
Which bears at once the cup, and milk, and fruit ;
The Bread-tree, which, without the ploughshare, yields
The unreaped harvest of unfurrowed fields,   261
And bakes its unadulterated loaves

Without a furnace in unpurchased groves,
And flings off famine from its fertile breast,
A priceless market for the gathering guest ;—
These, with the luxuries of seas and woods,
The airy joys of social solitudes,
Tamed each rude wanderer to the sympathies
Of those who were more happy, if less wise,
Did more than Europe's discipline had done,   270
And civilised Civilisation's son !

XII.

Of these, and there was many a willing pair,
Neuha [1] and Torquil were not the least fair :
Both children of the isles, though distant far ;
Both born beneath a sea-presiding star ;
Both nourished amidst Nature's native scenes,
Loved to the last, whatever intervenes
Between us and our Childhood's sympathy,
Which still reverts to what first caught the eye.
He who first met the Highlands' swelling blue   280
Will love each peak that shows a kindred hue,
Hail in each crag a friend's familiar face,
And clasp the mountain in his Mind's embrace.
Long have I roamed through lands which are not mine,
Adored the Alp, and loved the Apennine,
Revered Parnassus, and beheld the steep
Jove's Ida and Olympus crown the deep :
But 'twas not all long ages' lore, nor all
Their nature held me in their thrilling thrall ;
The infant rapture still survived the boy,   290
And Loch-na-gar with Ida looked o'er Troy,[2]

1. [Toobo Neuha is the name of a Tongan chieftain. See Mariner's
Account, etc., 1817, 141, *sq.*]
2. When very young, about eight years of age, after an attack of the
scarlet fever at Aberdeen, I was removed by medical advice into the
Highlands. Here I passed occasionally some summers, and from this
period I date my love of mountainous countries. I can never forget
the effect, a few years afterwards, in England, of the only thing I had
long seen, even in miniature, of a mountain, in the Malvern Hills.
After I returned to Cheltenham, I used to watch them every afternoon,
at sunset, with a sensation which I cannot describe. This was boyish
enough : but I was then only thirteen years of age, and it was in the

Mixed Celtic memories with the Phrygian mount,
And Highland linns with Castalie's clear fount.
Forgive me, Homer's universal shade !
Forgive me, Phœbus ! that my fancy strayed ;
The North and Nature taught me to adore
Your scenes sublime, from those beloved before.

XIII.

The love which maketh all things fond and fair,
The youth which makes one rainbow of the air,
The dangers past, that make even Man enjoy   300
The pause in which he ceases to destroy,
The mutual beauty, which the sternest feel
Strike to their hearts like lightning to the steel,
United the half savage and the whole,
The maid and boy, in one absorbing soul.
No more the thundering memory of the fight
Wrapped his weaned bosom in its dark delight ;
No more the irksome restlessness of Rest
Disturbed him like the eagle in her nest,
Whose whetted beak [1] and far-pervading eye   310
Darts for a victim over all the sky :
His heart was tamed to that voluptuous state,
At once Elysian and effeminate,
Which leaves no laurels o'er the Hero's urn ;—
These wither when for aught save blood they burn ;
Yet when their ashes in their nook are laid,
Doth not the myrtle leave as sweet a shade ?
Had Cæsar known but Cleopatra's kiss,
Rome had been free, the world had not been his.
And what have Cæsar's deeds and Cæsar's fame   320
Done for the earth ?   We feel them in our shame.
The gory sanction of his Glory stains
The rust which tyrants cherish on our chains.
Though Glory—Nature—Reason—Freedom, bid

holidays. [Byron spent his summer holidays, 1796–98, at the farm-
house of Ballatrich, on Deeside. (See *Poetical Works*, 1898, i. 192,
note 2.   For his visit to Cheltenham, in the summer of 1801, see *Life*,
pp. 8, 19.)]
    1. [For the eagle's beak, see *Childe Harold*, Canto III. stanza xviii.
line 6, *Poetical Works*, 1899, ii. 226, *note* 1.]

Roused millions do what single Brutus did—
Sweep these mere mock-birds of the Despot's song
From the tall bough where they have perched so long,—
Still are we hawked at by such mousing owls,[1]
And take for falcons those ignoble fowls,
When but a word of freedom would dispel   330
These bugbears, as their terrors show too well.

XIV.

Rapt in the fond forgetfulness of life,
Neuha, the South Sea girl, was all a wife,
With no distracting world to call her off
From Love; with no Society to scoff
At the new transient flame; no babbling crowd
Of coxcombry in admiration loud,
Or with adulterous whisper to alloy
Her duty, and her glory, and her joy:
With faith and feelings naked as her form,   340
She stood as stands a rainbow in a storm,
Changing its hues with bright variety,
But still expanding lovelier o'er the sky,
Howe'er its arch may swell, its colours move,
The cloud-compelling harbinger of Love.

XV.

Here, in this grotto of the wave-worn shore,
They passed the Tropic's red meridian o'er;
Nor long the hours—they never paused o'er time,
Unbroken by the clock's funereal chime,[2]
Which deals the daily pittance of our span,   350
And points and mocks with iron laugh at man.[L]
What deemed they of the future or the past?
The present, like a tyrant, held them fast:
Their hour-glass was the sea-sand, and the tide,
Like her smooth billow, saw their moments glide;

---

i. *Which knolls the knell of moments out of man.*—[*MS. D. erased.*]

1. [Compare *Macbeth*, act ii. sc. 4, line 13.]
2. [Compare—

> "The never-merry clock."
>> *Werner,* act iii. sc. 3, line 3.]

Their clock the Sun, in his unbounded tower;
They reckoned not, whose day was but an hour;
The nightingale, their only vesper-bell,
Sung sweetly to the rose the day's farewell;[1]
The broad Sun set, but not with lingering sweep,   360
As in the North he mellows o'er the deep;
But fiery, full, and fierce, as if he left
The World for ever, earth of light bereft,
Plunged with red forehead down along the wave,
As dives a hero headlong to his grave.
Then rose they, looking first along the skies,
And then for light into each other's eyes,
Wondering that Summer showed so brief a sun,
And asking if indeed the day were done.

XVI.

And let not this seem strange: the devotee   370
Lives not in earth, but in his ecstasy;
Around him days and worlds are heedless driven,
His Soul is gone before his dust to Heaven.
Is Love less potent?   No—his path is trod,
Alike uplifted gloriously to God;
Or linked to all we know of Heaven below,
The other better self, whose joy or woe
Is more than ours; the all-absorbing flame
Which, kindled by another, grows the same,[i.]
Wrapt in one blaze; the pure, yet funeral pile,   380
Where gentle hearts, like Bramins, sit and smile.
How often we forget all time, when lone,
Admiring Nature's universal throne,
Her woods—her wilds—her waters—the intense
Reply of *hers* to our intelligence!
Live not the Stars and Mountains?   Are the Waves
Without a spirit?   Are the dropping caves
Without a feeling in their silent tears?[2]

i.   *Which kindled by another's* ——.—[*MS. D.*]

1. The now well-known story of the loves of the nightingale and rose
need not be more than alluded to, being sufficiently familiar to the
Western as to the Eastern reader. [Compare *Werner*, act iv. sc. 1,
lines 380–382; and *The Giaour*, lines 21, 33.]
   2. [Compare *Childe Harold*, Canto III. stanzas lxxii., lxxv. Once

No, no ;—they woo and clasp us to their spheres,
Dissolve this clog and clod of clay before   390
Its hour, and merge our soul in the great shore.
Strip off this fond and false identity !—
Who thinks of self when gazing on the sky ?
And who, though gazing lower, ever thought,
In the young moments ere the heart is taught
Time's lesson, of Man's baseness or his own ?
All Nature is his realm, and Love his throne.

XVII.

Neuha arose, and Torquil : Twilight's hour
Came sad and softly to their rocky bower,
Which, kindling by degrees its dewy spars,   400
Echoed their dim light to the mustering stars.
Slowly the pair, partaking Nature's calm,
Sought out their cottage, built beneath the palm ;
Now smiling and now silent, as the scene ;
Lovely as Love—the Spirit !—when serene.
The Ocean scarce spoke louder with his swell,
Than breathes his mimic murmurer in the shell,[1]

again the language and the sentiment recall Wordsworth's *Tintern Abbey*. (See *Poetical Works*, 1899, ii. 261, *note 2.*)]

1. If the reader will apply to his ear the sea-shell on his chimney-piece, he will be aware of what is alluded to . If the text should appear obscure, he will find in *Gebir* the same idea better expressed in two lines. The poem I never read, but have heard the lines quoted, by a more recondite reader—who seems to be of a different opinion from the editor of the *Quarterly Review*, who qualified it in his answer to the Critical Reviewer of his *Juvenal*, as trash of the worst and most insane description. It is to Mr. Landor, the author of *Gebir*, so qualified, and of some Latin poems, which vie with Martial or Catullus in obscenity, that the immaculate Mr. Southey addresses his declamation against impurity !

[These are the lines in *Gebir* to which Byron alludes—

> " But I have sinuous shells of pearly hue.
> ·   ·   ·   ·
>
> Shake one and it awakens ; then apply
> Its polisht lips to your attentive ear,
> And it remembers its august abodes,
> And murmurs as the ocean murmurs there.

Compare, too, *The Excursion*, bk. iv.—

> " I have seen
> A curious child, who dwelt upon a tract
> Of inland ground, applying to his ear
> The convolutions of a smooth-lipped shell,

As, far divided from his parent deep,
The sea-born infant cries, and will not sleep,
Raising his little plaint in vain, to rave   410
For the broad bosom of his nursing wave :
The woods drooped darkly, as inclined to rest,
The tropic bird wheeled rockward to his nest,
And the blue sky spread round them like a lake
Of peace, where Piety her thirst might slake.

XVIII.

But through the palm and plantain, hark, a Voice !
Not such as would have been a lover's choice,
In such an hour, to break the air so still ;
No dying night-breeze, harping o'er the hill,
Striking the strings of nature, rock and tree,   420
Those best and earliest lyres of Harmony,
With Echo for their chorus ; nor the alarm
Of the loud war-whoop to dispel the charm ;
Nor the soliloquy of the hermit owl,
Exhaling all his solitary soul,
The dim though large-eyed wingéd anchorite,
Who peals his dreary Pæan o'er the night ;
But a loud, long, and naval whistle, shrill
As ever started through a sea-bird's bill ;
And then a pause, and then a hoarse " Hillo !   430
Torquil, my boy ! what cheer ?   Ho ! brother, ho ! "
" Who hails ? " cried Torquil, following with his eye
The sound.   " Here's one," was all the brief reply.

> To which, in silence hushed, his very soul
> Listened intently," etc.

Landor, in his *Satire upon Satirists*, 1836, p. 29, commenting on
Wordsworth's alleged remark that he " would not give five shillings for
all the poetry that Southey had written " (see *Letters*, 1900, iv. Appendix IX. pp. 483, 484), calls attention to this unacknowledged borrowing.
" It would have been honester," he says, " and more decorous if the
writer of the following verses had mentioned from what bar he drew his
wire."   According to H. C. Robinson (*Diary*, 1869, iii. 114), Wordsworth acknowledged no obligation to Landor's *Gebir* for the image of
the sea-shell.   " From his childhood the shell was familiar to him, etc.
The ' Satire ' seemed to give Wordsworth little annoyance."]

XIX.

But here the herald of the self-same mouth [1]
Came breathing o'er the aromatic south,
Not like a " bed of violets " on the gale,
But such as wafts its cloud o'er grog or ale,
Borne from a short frail pipe, which yet had blown
Its gentle odours over either zone,
And, puffed where'er winds rise or waters roll,   440
Had wafted smoke from Portsmouth to the Pole,
Opposed its vapour as the lightning flashed,
And reeked, 'midst mountain-billows, unabashed,
To Æolus a constant sacrifice,
Through every change of all the varying skies.
And what was he who bore it ?—I may err,
But deem him sailor or philosopher. [2]
Sublime Tobacco ! which from East to West
Cheers the tar's labour or the Turkman's rest ;
Which on the Moslem's ottoman divides   450
His hours, and rivals opium and his brides ;
Magnificent in Stamboul, but less grand,
Though not less loved, in Wapping or the Strand ;
Divine in hookas, glorious in a pipe,
When tipped with amber, mellow, rich, and ripe ;
Like other charmers, wooing the caress,
More dazzlingly when daring in full dress ;
Yet thy true lovers more admire by far [i]
Thy naked beauties—Give me a cigar ! [3]

i. *Yet they who love thee best prefer by far.*—[*MS. D. erased.*]

1. [In his Preface to Cantos I., II.'of *Childe Harold* (*Poetical Works*, 1899, ii. 5), Byron relies on the authority of "Ariosto Thomson and Beattie" for the inclusion of droll or satirical "variations" in a serious poem. Nevertheless, Dallas prevailed on him to omit certain "ludicrous stanzas." It is to be regretted that no one suggested the excision of sections xix.-xxi. from the second canto of *The Island.*]

2. Hobbes, the father of Locke's and other philosophy, was an inveterate smoker,—even to pipes beyond computation.

["Soon after dinner he [Hobbes] retired to his study, and had his candle, with ten or twelve pipes of tobacco laid by him ; then, shutting his door, he fell to smoking, and thinking, and writing for several hours."—*Memoirs of the Family of Cavendish*, by White Kennet, D.D., 1708, pp. 14, 15.]

3. ["I shall now smoke two cigars, and get me to bed. . . . The Havannah are the best ;—but neither are so pleasant as a hooka or chiboque."—*Journal*, December 6, 1813, *Letters*, 1898, ii. 368.]

XX.

Through the approaching darkness of the wood   460
A human figure broke the solitude,
Fantastically, it may be, arrayed,
A seaman in a savage masquerade ;
Such as appears to rise out from the deep,
When o'er the line the merry vessels sweep,
And the rough Saturnalia of the tar
Flock o'er the deck, in Neptune's borrowed car ; [1]
And, pleased, the God of Ocean sees his name
Revive once more, though but in mimic game
Of his true sons, who riot in the breeze   470
Undreamt of in his native Cyclades.
Still the old God delights, from out the main,
To snatch some glimpses of his ancient reign.
Our sailor's jacket, though in ragged trim,
His constant pipe, which never yet burned dim,
His foremast air, and somewhat rolling gait,
Like his dear vessel, spoke his former state ;
But then a sort of kerchief round his head,
Not over tightly bound, nor nicely spread ;
And, 'stead of trowsers (ah ! too early torn !   480
For even the mildest woods will have their thorn)
A curious sort of somewhat scanty mat
Now served for inexpressibles and hat ;
His naked feet and neck, and sunburnt face,
Perchance might suit alike with either race.
His arms were all his own, our Europe's growth,
Which two worlds bless for civilising both ;
The musket swung behind his shoulders broad,
And somewhat stooped by his marine abode,
But brawny as the boar's ; and hung beneath,   490
His cutlass drooped, unconscious of a sheath,
Or lost or worn away ; his pistols were
Linked to his belt, a matrimonial pair—
(Let not this metaphor appear a scoff,
Though one missed fire, the other would go off) ;
These, with a bayonet, not so free from rust

1. This rough but jovial ceremony, used in crossing the line, has been
so often and so well described, that it need not be more than alluded to.

As when the arm-chest held its brighter trust,
Completed his accoutrements, as Night
Surveyed him in his garb heteroclite.

XXI.

" What cheer, Ben Bunting ? " cried (when in full view
Our new acquaintance) Torquil.   " Aught of new ? " 501
" Ey, ey ! " quoth Ben, " not new, but news enow ;
A strange sail in the offing."—" Sail ! and how ?
What ! could you make her out ?   It cannot be ;
I've seen no rag of canvass on the sea."
" Belike," said Ben, " you might not from the bay,
But from the bluff-head, where I watched to-day,
I saw her in the doldrums ; for the wind
Was light and baffling."—" When the Sun declined
Where lay she ? had she anchored ? "—" No, but still 510
She bore down on us, till the wind grew still."
" Her flag ? "—" I had no glass ; but fore and aft,
Egad ! she seemed a wicked-looking craft."
" Armed ? "—" I expect so ;—sent on the look-out :
'Tis time, belike, to put our helm about."
" About ?—Whate'er may have us now in chase,
We'll make no running fight, for that were base ;
We will die at our quarters, like true men."
" Ey, ey ! for that 'tis all the same to Ben."
" Does Christian know this ? "—" Aye ; he has piped all
          hands
                                                    520
To quarters.   They are furbishing the stands
Of arms ; and we have got some guns to bear,
And scaled them.   You are wanted."—" That's but fair ;
And if it were not, mine is not the soul
To leave my comrades helpless on the shoal.
My Neuha ! ah ! and must my fate pursue
Not me alone, but one so sweet and true ?
But whatsoe'er betide, ah, Neuha ! now
Unman me not : the hour will not allow
A tear ; I am thine whatever intervenes ! "   530
" Right," quoth Ben ; " that will do for the marines." [1]

---

1. "That will do for the marines, but the sailors won't believe it," is
an old saying : and one of the few fragments of former jealousies which
still survive (in jest only) between these gallant services.

CANTO THE THIRD.

I.

THE fight was o'er; the flashing through the gloom,
Which robes the cannon as he wings a tomb,
Had ceased; and sulphury vapours upward driven
Had left the Earth, and but polluted Heaven:
The rattling roar which rung in every volley
Had left the echoes to their melancholy;
No more they shrieked their horror, boom for boom;
The strife was done, the vanquished had their doom;
The mutineers were crushed, dispersed, or ta'en,
Or lived to deem the happiest were the slain.   10
Few, few escaped, and these were hunted o'er
The isle they loved beyond their native shore.
No further home was theirs, it seemed, on earth,
Once renegades to that which gave them birth;
Tracked like wild beasts, like them they sought the wild,
As to a Mother's bosom flies the child;
But vainly wolves and lions seek their den,
And still more vainly men escape from men.

II.

Beneath a rock whose jutting base protrudes
Far over Ocean in its fiercest moods,   20
When scaling his enormous crag the wave
Is hurled down headlong, like the foremost brave,
And falls back on the foaming crowd behind,
Which fight beneath the banners of the wind,
But now at rest, a little remnant drew

Together, bleeding, thirsty, faint, and few;
But still their weapons in their hands, and still
With something of the pride of former will,
As men not all unused to meditate,
And strive much more than wonder at their fate.   30
Their present lot was what they had foreseen,
And dared as what was likely to have been;
Yet still the lingering hope, which deemed their lot
Not pardoned, but unsought for or forgot,
Or trusted that, if sought, their distant caves
Might still be missed amidst the world of waves,
Had weaned their thoughts in part from what they saw
And felt, the vengeance of their country's law.
Their sea-green isle, their guilt-won Paradise,
No more could shield their Virtue or their Vice: 40
Their better feelings, if such were, were thrown
Back on themselves,—their sins remained alone.
Proscribed even in their second country, they
Were lost; in vain the World before them lay;
All outlets seemed secured.   Their new allies
Had fought and bled in mutual sacrifice;
But what availed the club and spear, and arm
Of Hercules, against the sulphury charm,
The magic of the thunder, which destroyed
The warrior ere his strength could be employed?   50
Dug, like a spreading pestilence, the grave
No less of human bravery than the brave![1]
Their own scant numbers acted all the few
Against the many oft will dare and do;
But though the choice seems native to die free,
Even Greece can boast but one Thermopylæ,
Till *now*, when she has forged her broken chain
Back to a sword, and dies and lives again!

1. Archidamus, King of Sparta, and son of Agesilaus, when he saw
a machine invented for the casting of stones and darts, exclaimed that
it was the "grave of valour." The same story has been told of some
knights on the first application of gunpowder; but the original anecdote
is in Plutarch. [The Greek is "'Απόλωλεν, ἀνδρὸς ἀρετά." Plutarch's
Scripta Moralia, 1839, i. 230.]

III.

Beside the jutting rock the few appeared,
Like the last remnant of the red-deer's herd;   60
Their eyes were feverish, and their aspect worn,
But still the hunter's blood was on their horn.
A little stream came tumbling from the height,
And straggling into ocean as it might,
Its bounding crystal frolicked in the ray,
And gushed from cliff to crag with saltless spray;
Close on the wild, wide ocean, yet as pure
And fresh as Innocence, and more secure,
Its silver torrent glittered o'er the deep,
As the shy chamois' eye o'erlooks the steep,   70
While far below the vast and sullen swell
Of Ocean's alpine azure rose and fell.
To this young spring they rushed,—all feelings first
Absorbed in Passion's and in Nature's thirst,—
Drank as they do who drink their last, and threw
Their arms aside to revel in its dew;
Cooled their scorched throats, and washed the gory stains
From wounds whose only bandage might be chains;
Then, when their drought was quenched, looked sadly
          round,
As wondering how so many still were found   80
Alive and fetterless:—but silent all,
Each sought his fellow's eyes, as if to call
On him for language which his lips denied,
As though their voices with their cause had died.

IV.

Stern, and aloof a little from the rest,
Stood Christian, with his arms across his chest.
The ruddy, reckless, dauntless hue once spread
Along his cheek was livid now as lead;
His light-brown locks, so graceful in their flow,
Now rose like startled vipers o'er his brow.   90
Still as a statue, with his lips comprest
To stifle even the breath within his breast,
Fast by the rock, all menacing, but mute,
He stood; and, save a slight beat of his foot,

Which deepened now and then the sandy dint
Beneath his heel, his form seemed turned to flint.
Some paces further Torquil leaned his head
Against a bank, and spoke not, but he bled,—
Not mortally :—his worst wound was within ;
His brow was pale, his blue eyes sunken in,   100
And blood-drops, sprinkled o'er his yellow hair,
Showed that his faintness came not from despair,
But Nature's ebb.   Beside him was another,
Rough as a bear, but willing as a brother,—
Ben Bunting, who essayed to wash, and wipe,
And bind his wound—then calmly lit his pipe,
A trophy which survived a hundred fights,
A beacon which had cheered ten thousand nights.
The fourth and last of this deserted group
Walked up and down—at times would stand, then stoop
To pick a pebble up—then let it drop—   111
Then hurry as in haste—then quickly stop—
Then cast his eyes on his companions—then
Half whistle half a tune, and pause again—
And then his former movements would redouble,
With something between carelessness and trouble.
This is a long description, but applies
To scarce five minutes passed before the eyes ;
But yet *what* minutes !   Moments like to these
Rend men's lives into immortalities.   120

                              v.

At length Jack Skyscrape, a mercurial man,
Who fluttered over all things like a fan,
More brave than firm, and more disposed to dare
And die at once than wrestle with despair,
Exclaimed, " G—d damn ! "—those syllables intense,—
Nucleus of England's native eloquence,
As the Turk's " Allah ! " or the Roman's more
Pagan " Proh Jupiter ! " was wont of yore
To give their first impressions such a vent,
By way of echo to embarrassment.[i.]   130
Jack was embarrassed,—never hero more,

        i. *To people in a small embarrassment.*—[*MS. D. erased.*]

And as he knew not what to say, he swore:
Nor swore in vain; the long congenial sound
Revived Ben Bunting from his pipe profound;
He drew it from his mouth, and looked full wise,
But merely added to the oath his *eyes;*
Thus rendering the imperfect phrase complete,
A peroration I need not repeat.

VI.

But Christian,[1] of a higher order, stood
Like an extinct volcano in his mood;   140

1. [Fletcher Christian, born 1763, was the fourth son of Charles
Christian, an attorney, of Moreland Close, in the parish of Brigham,
Cumberland. His family, which was of Manx extraction, was connected
with the Christians of Ewanrigg, and the Curwens of Workington
Hall. His brother Edward became Chief Justice of Ely, and was well
known as the editor of *Blackstone's Commentaries.* For purposes of
verification (see *An Answer to certain Assertions, etc.,* 1794, p. 9),
Bligh described him as "aged 24 years, five feet nine inches high,
blackish or very dark brown complexioned, dark brown hair, strong
made, star tatowed on the left breast," etc. According to "Morrison's
Journal," high words had passed between Bligh and Christian on more
than one occasion, and, on the day before the mutiny, a question
having arisen with regard to the disappearance of some cocoa-nuts,
Christian was cross-examined by the captain as to his share of the
plunder. "I really do not know, sir," he replied; "but I hope you do
not think me so mean as to be guilty of stealing yours." "Yes," said
Bligh, "you —— hound, I do think so, or you could have given a
better account of them." It was after this offensive accusation that
Christian determined, in the first instance, to quit the ship, and on the
morning of April 28, 1788, finding the mate of the watch asleep, on
the spur of the moment resolved to lay violent hands on the captain,
and assume the command of the *Bounty.* The language attributed to
Bligh reads like a translation into the vernacular, but if Christian kept
his designs to himself, it is strange that they were immediately understood and acted upon by a body of impromptu conspirators. Testimony, whether written or spoken, with regard to the succession of
events "in moments like to these," is worth very little; but it is pretty
evident that Christian was a gentleman, and that Bligh's violent and
unmannerly ratings were the immediate cause of the mutiny.
    Contradictory accounts are given of Christian's death. It is
generally believed that in the fourth year of the settlement on Pitcairn
Island the Tahitians formed a plot to massacre the Englishmen, and
that Christian was shot when at work in his plantation (*The Mutineers,
etc.,* by Lady Belcher, 1870, p. 163; *The Mutiny, etc.,* by Rosalind
A. Young, 1894, p. 28). On the other hand, Amasa Delano, in his
Narrative of Voyages, etc. (Boston, 1817, cap. v. p. 140), asserts that
Captain Mayhew Folger, who was the first to visit the island in 1808,
"was very explicit in his inquiry at the time, as well as in his account
of it to me, that they lived under Christian's government several years

Silent, and sad, and savage,—with the trace
Of passion reeking from his clouded face;
Till lifting up again his sombre eye,
It glanced on Torquil, who leaned faintly by.
"And is it thus?" he cried, "unhappy boy!
And thee, too, *thee*—my madness must destroy!"
He said, and strode to where young Torquil stood,
Yet dabbled with his lately flowing blood;
Seized his hand wistfully, but did not press,
And shrunk as fearful of his own caress;   150
Enquired into his state: and when he heard
The wound was slighter than he deemed or feared,
A moment's brightness passed along his brow,
As much as such a moment would allow.
"Yes," he exclaimed, "we are taken in the toil,
But not a coward or a common spoil;
Dearly they have bought us—dearly still may buy,—
And I must fall; but have *you* strength to fly?
'Twould be some comfort still, could you survive;
Our dwindled band is now too few to strive.   160
Oh! for a sole canoe! though but a shell,
To bear you hence to where a hope may dwell!
For me, my lot is what I sought; to be,
In life or death, the fearless and the free."

VII.

Even as he spoke, around the promontory,
Which nodded o'er the billows high and hoary,
A dark speck dotted Ocean: on it flew
Like to the shadow of a roused sea-mew;
Onward it came—and, lo! a second followed—
Now seen—now hid—where Ocean's vale was hollowed;
And near, and nearer, till the dusky crew   171
Presented well-known aspects to the view,

after they landed; that during the whole time they enjoyed tolerable
harmony; that Christian became sick, and died a natural death." It
stands to reason that the ex-pirate, Alexander Smith, who had developed into John Adams, the pious founder of a patriarchal colony,
would be anxious to draw a veil over the early years of the settlement,
and would satisfy the curiosity of visitors who were officers of the
Royal Navy, as best he could, and as the spirit moved him.]

Till on the surf their skimming paddles play,
Buoyant as wings, and flitting through the spray ;—
Now perching on the wave's high curl, and now
Dashed downward in the thundering foam below,
Which flings it broad and boiling sheet on sheet,
And slings its high flakes, shivered into sleet :
But floating still through surf and swell, drew nigh
The barks, like small birds through a lowering sky.   180
Their art seemed nature—such the skill to sweep
The wave of these born playmates of the deep.

VIII.

And who the first that, springing on the strand,
Leaped like a Nereid from her shell to land,
With dark but brilliant skin, and dewy eye
Shining with love, and hope, and constancy ?
Neuha—the fond, the faithful, the adored—
Her heart on Torquil's like a torrent poured ;
And smiled, and wept, and near, and nearer clasped,
As if to be assured 'twas *him* she grasped ;   190
Shuddered to see his yet warm wound, and then,
To find it trivial, smiled and wept again.
She was a warrior's daughter, and could bear
Such sights, and feel, and mourn, but not despair.
Her lover lived,—nor foes nor fears could blight
That full-blown moment in its all delight :
Joy trickled in her tears, joy filled the sob
That rocked her heart till almost HEARD to throb ;
And Paradise was breathing in the sigh
Of Nature's child in Nature's ecstasy.   200

IX.

The sterner spirits who beheld that meeting
Were not unmoved ; who are, when hearts are greeting ?
Even Christian gazed upon the maid and boy
With tearless eye, but yet a gloomy joy
Mixed with those bitter thoughts the soul arrays
In hopeless visions of our better days,
When all 's gone—to the rainbow's latest ray.
" And but for me ! " he said, and turned away ;

Then gazed upon the pair, as in his den
A lion looks upon his cubs again ;   210
And then relapsed into his sullen guise,
As heedless of his further destinies.

X.

But brief their time for good or evil thought ;
The billows round the promontory brought
The plash of hostile oars.—Alas ! who made
That sound a dread ?   All around them seemed arrayed
Against them, save the bride of Toobonai :
She, as she caught the first glimpse o'er the bay
Of the armed boats, which hurried to complete
The remnant's ruin with their flying feet,[i.]   220
Beckoned the natives round her to their prows,
Embarked their guests and launched their light canoes ;
In one placed Christian and his comrades twain—
But she and Torquil must not part again.
She fixed him in her own.—Away ! away !
They cleared the breakers, dart along the bay,
And towards a group of islets, such as bear
The sea-bird's nest and seal's surf-hollowed lair,
They skim the blue tops of the billows ; fast
They flew, and fast their fierce pursuers chased.   230
They gain upon them—now they lose again,—
Again make way and menace o'er the main ;
And now the two canoes in chase divide,
And follow different courses o'er the tide,
To baffle the pursuit.—Away ! away !
As Life is on each paddle's flight to-day,
And more than Life or lives to Neuha : Love
Freights the frail bark and urges to the cove ;
And now the refuge and the foe are nigh—
Yet, yet a moment ! Fly, thou light ark, fly !   240

i. *The ruined remnant of the land's defeat.*—[*MS. D. erased.*]

CANTO THE FOURTH.

I.

WHITE as a white sail on a dusky sea,
When half the horizon 's clouded and half free,
Fluttering between the dun wave and the sky,
Is Hope's last gleam in Man's extremity.
Her anchor parts ; but still her snowy sail
Attracts our eye amidst the rudest gale :
Though every wave she climbs divides us more,
The heart still follows from the loneliest shore.

II.

Not distant from the isle of Toobonai,
A black rock rears its bosom o'er the spray,   10
The haunt of birds, a desert to mankind,
Where the rough seal reposes from the wind,
And sleeps unwieldy in his cavern dun,
Or gambols with huge frolic in the sun :
There shrilly to the passing oar is heard
The startled echo of the Ocean bird,
Who rears on its bare breast her callow brood,
The feathered fishers of the solitude.
A narrow segment of the yellow sand
On one side forms the outline of a strand ;[1]   20
Here the young turtle, crawling from his shell,
Steals to the deep wherein his parents dwell ;
Chipped by the beam, a nursling of the day,
But hatched for ocean by the fostering ray ;

---

1. [Compare *The Siege of Corinth,* lines 438, 439, *Poetical Works,* 1900, iii. 467.]

The rest was one bleak precipice, as e'er
Gave mariners a shelter and despair;
A spot to make the saved regret the deck
Which late went down, and envy the lost wreck.
Such was the stern asylum Neuha chose
To shield her lover from his following foes;   30
But all its secret was not told; she knew
In this a treasure hidden from the view.

III.

Ere the canoes divided, near the spot,
The men that manned what held her Torquil's lot,
By her command removed, to strengthen more
The skiff which wafted Christian from the shore.
This he would have opposed; but with a smile
She pointed calmly to the craggy isle,
And bade him "speed and prosper." *She* would take
The rest upon herself for Torquil's sake.   40
They parted with this added aid; afar,
The Proa darted like a shooting star,
And gained on the pursuers, who now steered
Right on the rock which she and Torquil neared.
They pulled; her arm, though delicate, was free
And firm as ever grappled with the sea,
And yielded scarce to Torquil's manlier strength.
The prow now almost lay within its length
Of the crag's steep inexorable face,
With nought but soundless waters for its base;   50
Within a hundred boats' length was the foe,
And now what refuge but their frail canoe?
This Torquil asked with half upbraiding eye,
Which said—"Has Neuha brought me here to die?
Is this a place of safety, or a grave,
And yon huge rock the tombstone of the wave?"

IV.

They rested on their paddles, and uprose
Neuha, and pointing to the approaching foes,
Cried, "Torquil, follow me, and fearless follow!"
Then plunged at once into the Ocean's hollow.   60

There was no time to pause—the foes were near—
Chains in his eye, and menace in his ear;
With vigour they pulled on, and as they came,
Hailed him to yield, and by his forfeit name.
Headlong he leapt—to him the swimmer's skill
Was native, and now all his hope from ill:
But how, or where?   He dived, and rose no more;
The boat's crew looked amazed o'er sea and shore.
There was no landing on that precipice,
Steep, harsh, and slippery as a berg of ice.   70
They watched awhile to see him float again,
But not a trace rebubbled from the main:
The wave rolled on, no ripple on its face,
Since their first plunge recalled a single trace;
The little whirl which eddied, and slight foam,
That whitened o'er what seemed their latest home,
White as a sepulchre above the pair
Who left no marble (mournful as an heir)
The quiet Proa wavering o'er the tide
Was all that told of Torquil and his bride;   80
And but for this alone the whole might seem
The vanished phantom of a seaman's dream.
They paused and searched in vain, then pulled away;
Even Superstition now forbade their stay.
Some said he had not plunged into the wave,
But vanished like a corpse-light from a grave;
Others, that something supernatural
Glared in his figure, more than mortal tall;
While all agreed that in his cheek and eye
There was a dead hue of Eternity.   90
Still as their oars receded from the crag,
Round every weed a moment would they lag,
Expectant of some token of their prey;
But no—he had melted from them like the spray.

v.

And where was he the Pilgrim of the Deep,
Following the Nereid?   Had they ceased to weep
For ever? or, received in coral caves,
Wrung life and pity from the softening waves?

Did they with Ocean's hidden sovereigns dwell,
And sound with Mermen the fantastic shell?   100
Did Neuha with the mermaids comb her hair
Flowing o'er ocean as it streamed in air?
Or had they perished, and in silence slept
Beneath the gulf wherein they boldly leapt?

VI.

Young Neuha plunged into the deep, and he
Followed : her track beneath her native sea
Was as a native's of the element,
So smoothly—bravely—brilliantly she went,
Leaving a streak of light behind her heel,
Which struck and flashed like an amphibious steel. 110
Closely, and scarcely less expert to trace
The depths where divers hold the pearl in chase,
Torquil, the nursling of the northern seas,
Pursued her liquid steps with heart and ease.
Deep—deeper for an instant Neuha led
The way—then upward soared—and as she spread
Her arms, and flung the foam from off her locks,
Laughed, and the sound was answered by the rocks.
They had gained a central realm of earth again,
But looked for tree, and field, and sky, in vain.   120
Around she pointed to a spacious cave,
Whose only portal was the keyless wave,[1]

1. Of this cave (which is no fiction) the original will be found in the ninth chapter of "Mariner's Account of the Tonga Islands" [1817, i. 267-279]. I have taken the poetical liberty to transplant it to Toobonai, the last island where any distinct account is left of Christian and his comrades.
[The following is the account given by Mariner : "On this island [Hoonga] there is a peculiar cavern, which was first discovered by a young chief, whilst diving after a turtle. The nature of this cavern will be better understood if we imagine a hollow rock rising sixty feet or more above the surface of the water, into the cavity of which there is no known entrance but one, and that is on the side of the rock, as low down as six feet under the water, into which it flows ; and, consequently, the base of the cavern may be said to be the sea itself." Mariner seeing some young chiefs diving into the water one after another, and not rise again, he inquired of the last, . . . what they were about? " ' Follow me,' " said he, " ' and I will take you where you have never been before. . . .' " Mariner prepared to follow his companion, and, guided by the light reflected from his heels, entered the

(A hollow archway by the sun unseen,
Save through the billows' glassy veil of green,
In some transparent ocean holiday,
When all the finny people are at play,)
Wiped with her hair the brine from Torquil's eyes,
And clapped her hands with joy at his surprise;
Led him to where the rock appeared to jut,
And form a something like a Triton's hut;   130
For all was darkness for a space, till day,
Through clefts above let in a sobered ray;
As in some old cathedral's glimmering aisle
The dusty monuments from light recoil,
Thus sadly in their refuge submarine
The vault drew half her shadow from the scene.

opening in the rock, and rose into the cavern. The light was sufficient, after remaining about five minutes, to show objects with some little distinctness; . . . Nevertheless, as it was desirable to have a stronger light, Mariner dived out again, and, priming his pistol, tied plenty of gnatoo tight round it, and wrapped the whole up in a plantain-leaf: he directed an attendant to bring a torch in the same way. Thus prepared, he re-entered the cavern, unwrapped the gnatoo, fired it by the flash of the powder, and lighted the torch. "The place was now illuminated tolerably well. . . . It appeared (by guess) to be about forty feet wide in the main part, but it branched off, on one side, in two narrower portions. The medium height seemed also about forty feet. The roof was hung with stalactites in a very curious way, resembling, upon a cursory view, the Gothic arches and ornaments of an old church." According to one of the matabooles present, the entire family of a certain chief had, in former times, been condemned to death for conspiring against a rival tyrant—the chief to be taken out to sea and drowned, the rest of the family to be massacred. One of the chief's daughters was a beautiful girl, to whom the youth who discovered the cave was attached. "He had long been enamoured of this young maiden, but had never dared to make her acquainted with the soft emotions of his heart, knowing that she was betrothed to a chief of higher rank and greater power, but now, . . . no time was to be lost; he flew to her abode . . . declared himself her deliverer if she would trust to his honour. . . . Soon her consenting hand was clasped in his: the shades of evening favoured their escape . . . till her lover had brought a small canoe to a lonely part of the beach. In this they speedily embarked. . . . They soon arrived at the rock, he leaped into the water, and she, instructed by him, followed close after; they rose into the cavern, and rested from their fatigue, partaking of some refreshments which he had brought there for himself. . . ." Here she remained, visited from time to time by her more fortunate Leander, until he was enabled to carry her off to the Fiji islands, where they dwelt till the death of the tyrant, when they returned to Vavaoo, "and lived long in peace and happiness."]

VII.

Forth from her bosom the young savage drew
A pine torch, strongly girded with gnatoo;
A plantain-leaf o'er all, the more to keep
Its latent sparkle from the sapping deep.   140
This mantle kept it dry; then from a nook
Of the same plantain-leaf a flint she took,
A few shrunk withered twigs, and from the blade
Of Torquil's knife struck fire, and thus arrayed
The grot with torchlight.   Wide it was and high,
And showed a self-born Gothic canopy;
The arch upreared by Nature's architect,
The architrave some Earthquake might erect;
The buttress from some mountain's bosom hurled,
When the Poles crashed, and water was the world; 150
Or hardened from some earth-absorbing fire,
While yet the globe reeked from its funeral pyre;
The fretted pinnacle, the aisle, the nave,[1]
Were there, all scooped by Darkness from her cave.
There, with a little tinge of phantasy,
Fantastic faces moped and mowed on high,
And then a mitre or a shrine would fix
The eye upon its seeming crucifix.
Thus Nature played with the stalactites,[2]
And built herself a Chapel of the Seas.   160

1. This may seem too minute for the general outline (in Mariner's Account) from which it is taken.   But few men have travelled without seeing something of the kind—on *land*, that is.   Without adverting to Ellora, in Mungo Park's last journal, he mentions having met with a rock or mountain so exactly resembling a Gothic cathedral, that only minute inspection could convince him that it was a work of nature.

[Ellora, a village in the Nizám's dominions, is thirteen miles north-west of Aurangábád.   "It is famous for its rock-caves and temples. The chief building, called the kailás, . . . is a great monolithic temple, isolated from surrounding rock, and carved outside as well as in. . . . It is said to have been built about the eighth century by Rájá Edu of Ellichpur."—Hunter's *Imperial Gazetteer of India*, 1885, iv. 348–351. The passage in Mungo Park's *Journal of a Mission to the Interior of Africa*, 1815, p. 75, runs thus: "June 24th [1805].—Left Sullo, and travelled through a country beautiful beyond imagination, with all the possible diversities of *rock*, sometimes towering up like ruined castles, spires, pyramids, etc.   We passed one place so like a ruined Gothic abbey, that we halted a little, before we could satisfy ourselves that the niches, windows, etc., were all natural rock."]

2. [Byron's quadrisyllable was, probably, a poetic licence.   There is,

VIII.

And Neuha took her Torquil by the hand,
And waved along the vault her kindled brand,
And led him into each recess, and showed
The secret places of their new abode.
Nor these alone, for all had been prepared
Before, to soothe the lover's lot she shared :
The mat for rest ; for dress the fresh gnatoo,
And sandal oil to fence against the dew ;
For food the cocoa-nut, the yam, the bread
Born of the fruit ; for board the plantain spread 170
With its broad leaf, or turtle-shell which bore
A banquet in the flesh it covered o'er ;
The gourd with water recent from the rill,
The ripe banana from the mellow hill ;
A pine-torch pile to keep undying light,
And she herself, as beautiful as night,
To fling her shadowy spirit o'er the scene,
And make their subterranean world serene.
She had foreseen, since first the stranger's sail
Drew to their isle, that force or flight might fail, 180
And formed a refuge of the rocky den
For Torquil's safety from his countrymen.[L]
Each dawn had wafted there her light canoe,
Laden with all the golden fruits that grew ;
Each eve had seen her gliding through the hour
With all could cheer or deck their sparry bower ;
And now she spread her little store with smiles,
The happiest daughter of the loving isles.

IX.

She, as he gazed with grateful wonder, pressed
Her sheltered love to her impassioned breast ; 190
And suited to her soft caresses, told
An olden tale of Love,—for Love is old,
Old as eternity, but not outworn

---

i. *Where Love and Torquil might be safe from men.*—[*MS. D. erased.*]

however, an obsolete plural, *stalactitæ*, to be found in the works of John
Woodward, M.D., *Fossils of England*, 1729, i. 155.]

With each new being born or to be born :[1]
How a young Chief, a thousand moons ago,
Diving for turtle in the depths below,
Had risen, in tracking fast his ocean prey,
Into the cave which round and o'er them lay ;
How, in some desperate feud of after-time,
He sheltered there a daughter of the clime,   200
A foe beloved, and offspring of a foe,
Saved by his tribe but for a captive's woe ;
How, when the storm of war was stilled, he led
His island clan to where the waters spread
Their deep-green shadow o'er the rocky door,
Then dived—it seemed as if to rise no more :
His wondering mates, amazed within their bark,
Or deemed him mad, or prey to the blue shark ;
Rowed round in sorrow the sea-girded rock,
Then paused upon their paddles from the shock ;   210
When, fresh and springing from the deep, they saw
A Goddess rise—so deemed they in their awe ;
And their companion, glorious by her side,
Proud and exulting in his Mermaid bride ;
And how, when undeceived, the pair they bore
With sounding conchs and joyous shouts to shore ;
How they had gladly lived and calmly died,—
And why not also Torquil and his bride ?
Not mine to tell the rapturous caress
Which followed wildly in that wild recess   220
This tale ; enough that all within that cave
Was love, though buried strong as in the grave,
Where Abelard, through twenty years of death,

1. The reader will recollect the epigram of the Greek anthology, or
its translation into most of the modern languages—

> "Whoe'er thou art, thy master see—
> He was, or is, or is to be."

[Byron is quoting from memory an "Illustration" in the notes to
Collections from the Greek Anthology, by the Rev. Robert Bland, 1813,
p. 402—

> "Whoe'er thou art, thy Lord and master see.
> Thou wast my Slave, thou art, or thou shalt be."

The couplet was written by George Granville, Lord Lansdowne
(1667-1735), as an *Inscription for a Figure representing the God of Love*.
(See *The Genuine Works, etc.*, 1732, I. 129.)]

When Eloïsa's form was lowered beneath
Their nuptial vault, his arms outstretched, and pressed
The kindling ashes to his kindled breast.[1]
The waves without sang round their couch, their roar
As much unheeded as if life were o'er;
Within, their hearts made all their harmony,
Love's broken murmur and more broken sigh.   230

X.

And they, the cause and sharers of the shock
Which left them exiles of the hollow rock,
Where were they? O'er the sea for life they plied,
To seek from Heaven the shelter men denied.
Another course had been their choice—but where?
The wave which bore them still their foes would bear,
Who, disappointed of their former chase,
In search of Christian now renewed their race.
Eager with anger, their strong arms made way,
Like vultures baffled of their previous prey.   240
They gained upon them, all whose safety lay
In some bleak crag or deeply-hidden bay:
No further chance or choice remained; and right
For the first further rock which met their sight
They steered, to take their latest view of land,
And yield as victims, or die sword in hand;
Dismissed the natives and their shallop, who
Would still have battled for that scanty crew;
But Christian bade them seek their shore again,
Nor add a sacrifice which were in vain;   250
For what were simple bow and savage spear
Against the arms which must be wielded here?

1. The tradition is attached to the story of Eloïsa, that when her body was lowered into the grave of Abelard (who had been buried twenty years), he opened his arms to receive her.
[The story is told by Bayle, who quotes from a manuscript chronicle of Tours, preserved in the notes of Andreas Quercetanus, affixed to the *Historia Calamitatum Abælardi*: "Eadem defuncta ad tumulum apertum deportata, maritus ejus qui multis diebus ante eam defunctus fuerat, elevatis brachiis eam recepit, et ita eam amplexatus brachia sua strinxit."—See Petri Abelardi *Opera*, Paris, 1616, ii. 1195.]

XI.

They landed on a wild but narrow scene,
Where few but Nature's footsteps yet had been;
Prepared their arms, and with that gloomy eye,
Stern and sustained, of man's extremity,
When Hope is gone, nor Glory's self remains
To cheer resistance against death or chains,—
They stood, the three, as the three hundred stood
Who dyed Thermopylæ with holy blood.   260
But, ah! how different! 'tis the *cause* makes all,
Degrades or hallows courage in its fall.
O'er them no fame, eternal and intense,
Blazed through the clouds of Death and beckoned hence;
No grateful country, smiling through her tears,
Begun the praises of a thousand years;
No nation's eyes would on their tomb be bent,
No heroes envy them their monument;
However boldly their warm blood was spilt,
Their Life was shame, their Epitaph was guilt.   270
And this they knew and felt, at least the one,
The leader of the band he had undone;
Who, born perchance for better things, had set
His life upon a cast which lingered yet:
But now the die was to be thrown, and all
The chances were in favour of his fall:
And such a fall! But still he faced the shock,
Obdurate as a portion of the rock
Whereon he stood, and fixed his levelled gun,
Dark as a sullen cloud before the sun.   280

XII.

The boat drew nigh, well armed, and firm the crew
To act whatever Duty bade them do;
Careless of danger, as the onward wind
Is of the leaves it strews, nor looks behind.
And, yet, perhaps, they rather wished to go
Against a nation's than a native foe,
And felt that this poor victim of self-will,
Briton no more, had once been Britain's still.

They hailed him to surrender—no reply;
Their arms were poised, and glittered in the sky.   290
They hailed again—no answer; yet once more
They offered quarter louder than before.
The echoes only, from the rock's rebound,
Took their last farewell of the dying sound.
Then flashed the flint, and blazed the volleying flame,
And the smoke rose between them and their aim,
While the rock rattled with the bullets' knell,
Which pealed in vain, and flattened as they fell;
Then flew the only answer to be given
By those who had lost all hope in earth or heaven.   300
After the first fierce peal as they pulled nigher,
They heard the voice of Christian shout, " Now, fire ! "
And ere the word upon the echo died,
Two fell; the rest assailed the rock's rough side,
And, furious at the madness of their foes,
Disdained all further efforts, save to close.
But steep the crag, and all without a path,
Each step opposed a bastion to their wrath,
While, placed 'midst clefts the least accessible,
Which Christian's eye was trained to mark full well,   310
The three maintained a strife which must not yield,
In spots where eagles might have chosen to build.
Their every shot told; while the assailant fell,
Dashed on the shingles like the limpet shell;
But still enough survived, and mounted still,
Scattering their numbers here and there, until
Surrounded and commanded, though not nigh
Enough for seizure, near enough to die,
The desperate trio held aloof their fate
But by a thread, like sharks who have gorged the bait;
Yet to the very last they battled well,   321
And not a groan informed their foes *who* fell.
Christian died last—twice wounded ; and once more
Mercy was offered when they saw his gore ;
Too late for life, but not too late to die,[i]
With, though a hostile hand, to close his eye.
A limb was broken, and he drooped along

i. *Too late it might be still at least to die.*—[*MS. D. erased.*]

The crag, as doth a falcon reft of young.[i.]
The sound revived him, or appeared to wake
Some passion which a weakly gesture spake :   330
He beckoned to the foremost, who drew nigh,
But, as they neared, he reared his weapon high—
His last ball had been aimed, but from his breast
He tore the topmost button from his vest,[1][ii.]
Down the tube dashed it—levelled—fired, and smiled
As his foe fell; then, like a serpent, coiled
His wounded, weary form, to where the steep
Looked desperate as himself along the deep ;
Cast one glance back, and clenched his hand, and shook
His last rage 'gainst the earth which he forsook ;   340
Then plunged : the rock below received like glass
His body crushed into one gory mass,
With scarce a shred to tell of human form,
Or fragment for the sea-bird or the worm ;
A fair-haired scalp, besmeared with blood and weeds,
Yet reeked, the remnant of himself and deeds ;
Some splinters of his weapons (to the last,
As long as hand could hold, he held them fast)
Yet glittered, but at distance—hurled away
To rust beneath the dew and dashing spray.   350
The rest was nothing—save a life mis-spent,
And soul—but who shall answer where it went?
'Tis ours to bear, not judge the dead ; and they
Who doom to Hell, themselves are on the way,
Unless these bullies of eternal pains
Are pardoned their bad hearts for their worse brains.

i. *The crag as droop a bird without her young.*—[*MS. D. erased.*]
ii. *He tore a silver vest* ——.—[*MS. D. erased.*]

1. In Thibault's account of Frederick the Second of Prussia, there
is a singular relation of a young Frenchman, who with his mistress
appeared to be of some rank. He enlisted and deserted at Schweidnitz ;
and after a desperate resistance was retaken, having killed an officer,
who attempted to seize him after he was wounded, by the discharge of
his musket loaded with a *button* of his uniform. Some circumstances
on his court-martial raised a great interest amongst his judges, who
wished to discover his real situation in life, which he offered to disclose,
but to the *king* only, to whom he requested permission to write. This
was refused, and Frederic was filled with the greatest indignation, from
baffled curiosity or some other motive, when he understood that his
request had been denied. [*Mes Souvenirs de vingt ans de séjour à
Berlin, ou Frédéric Le Grand, etc.*, Paris, 1804, iv. 145-150.]

XIII.

The deed was over!   All were gone or ta'en,
The fugitive, the captive, or the slain.
Chained on the deck, where once, a gallant crew,
They stood with honour, were the wretched few   360
Survivors of the skirmish on the isle;
But the last rock left no surviving spoil.
Cold lay they where they fell, and weltering,
While o'er them flapped the sea-birds' dewy wing,
Now wheeling nearer from the neighbouring surge,
And screaming high their harsh and hungry dirge:
But calm and careless heaved the wave below,
Eternal with unsympathetic flow;
Far o'er its face the Dolphins sported on,
And sprung the flying fish against the sun,   370
Till its dried wing relapsed from its brief height,
To gather moisture for another flight.

XIV.

'Twas morn; and Neuha, who by dawn of day
Swam smoothly forth to catch the rising ray,
And watch if aught approached the amphibious lair
Where lay her lover, saw a sail in air:
It flapped, it filled, and to the growing gale
Bent its broad arch: her breath began to fail
With fluttering fear, her heart beat thick and high,
While yet a doubt sprung where its course might lie. 380
But no! it came not; fast and far away
The shadow lessened as it cleared the bay.
She gazed, and flung the sea-foam from her eyes,
To watch as for a rainbow in the skies.
On the horizon verged the distant deck,
Diminished, dwindled to a very speck—
Then vanished.   All was Ocean, all was Joy!
Down plunged she through the cave to rouse her boy;
Told all she had seen, and all she hoped, and all
That happy love could augur or recall;   390
Sprung forth again, with Torquil following free
His bounding Nereid over the broad sea;

Swam round the rock, to where a shallow cleft
Hid the canoe that Neuha there had left
Drifting along the tide, without an oar,
That eve the strangers chased them from the shore;
But when these vanished, she pursued her prow,
Regained, and urged to where they found it now:
Nor ever did more love and joy embark,
Than now were wafted in that slender ark.   400

XV.

Again their own shore rises on the view,
No more polluted with a hostile hue;
No sullen ship lay bristling o'er the foam,
A floating dungeon:—all was Hope and Home!
A thousand Proas darted o'er the bay,
With sounding shells, and heralded their way;
The chiefs came down, around the people poured,
And welcomed Torquil as a son restored;
The women thronged, embracing and embraced
By Neuha, asking where they had been chased,   410
And how escaped?   The tale was told; and then
One acclamation rent the sky again;
And from that hour a new tradition gave
Their sanctuary the name of " Neuha's Cave."
A hundred fires, far flickering from the height,[i.]
Blazed o'er the general revel of the night,
The feast in honour of the guest, returned
To Peace and Pleasure, perilously earned;
A night succeeded by such happy days
As only the yet infant world displays.[ii.]   420

J. 10th
1823.

i. *Their hollow shrine* ——.—[*MS. D. erased.*]
ii. *As only a yet infant* ——.—[*MS. D.*]
{ *As only an infantine World* ——.
{ *As only a yet unweaned World* ——.—
[*Alternative readings.   MS. D.*]

END OF VOL. V.